ONE MORE RIVER TO CROSS

ONE MORE RIVER TO CROSS

The Story of British Military Bridging

by
Colonel J H Joiner

When the Flood come along for an extra monsoon,
'Twas Noah constructed the first pontoon,
To the plans of Her Majesty's Royal Engineer,
With the rank and the pay of a Sapper.
Rudyard Kipling.

LEO COOPER

First published in Great Britain in 2001 by
LEO COOPER
an imprint of
Pen & Sword Books Ltd
47 Church Street, Barnsley
South Yorkshire
S70 2AS

ISBN 0 85052 788 0

A CIP record for this book is available from
the British Library

Printed in the United Kingdom by CPI UK

The author gratefully acknowledges the sponsorship of the undermentioned in supporting the publication of this book, thus providing a permanent record of one important aspect of the history the Corps of Royal Engineers.

*The Institution of
Royal Engineers*

Mabey & Johnson Ltd

WILLIAMS FAIREY
ENGINEERING LIMITED

Contents

Bridges Mark I and II – The Hopkins Bridges – The Battle for Arras – The Emergence of Assault Bridging During the Final Advance – The Victoria Cross – Railway Bridging – Bridging Operations Outside NW Europe – Operations in Italy – Operations in Egypt and Palestine – The Campaign in Mesopotamia.

Briggs Bridge – The Butterley Bridge – The Flambo Bridge – Assault Bridging during the War – The Scissors Bridge 30ft, No 1 – The Tank Bridge 30ft, No 2 – The Tank Bridge, SBG – 79 Armoured Division and the Assault Engineers – The ARKs –The Inglis Assault or Mobile Bridge – The Bailey Mobile Bridge – The Plymouth Bridge – The Brown Bridge – The Dalton Bridge – Skid Bailey – Track Bridges – Floating Equipments – The Class 50/60 Raft – The Close Support Raft – The Indian Mat Bridge – The PN Boat – The Eastern Army Boat – The Infantry Assault Boat – Railway Bridging – The Equipments – RSJ Span Railway Bridges – The Plate Girder Bridges – The Standard Through Truss Railway Bridge – The Unit Construction Railway Bridge – The Everall Sectional Truss Railway Bridge – Callender-Hamilton Railway Bridging – Bridge Trestles and Piers - Expedient Bridging – The Role of the Royal Army Service Corps.

Bridging Crane – Postwar Railway Bridging – The Sectional Plate Girder Railway Bridge – The Improvised Heavy Girder Railway Bridge – The Infantry Assault Boat Raft – The Far East Assault Boat Raft – The 50 Ton Bridging Crib – The 500 Ton Bridge Test Rig – And what of MEXE?

Bridge – The Wadi Kuf Bridges – Sapper Bridge – The Korean War – Queens' Bridge – The Falklands Campaign – The Gulf War – Operations in Bosnia – Bridging in Nepal.

Foreword

by General Sir John Stibbon KCB OBE

Throughout history military commanders have appreciated the essential need for freedom of movement in the furtherance of their operations and they have looked to their engineers to maintain the mobility of their forces. The most obvious constraint to movement is the water obstacle and bridging, in all of its forms, has been the stock in trade of the Sapper.

Colonel Joiner has provided in this book a unique record of the development of British military bridging equipment over the centuries. He traces the evolution of military bridge design as a function of construction time, load carrying capacity, and flexibility of use and identifies the milestones in design achievement, linking them with fascinating examples of bridging operations throughout history. *One More River to Cross* is therefore much more than a simple compendium of bridging. It is meticulously researched and succinct in the telling, and provides a fascinating read for both the military and the civil engineer.

The book also demonstrates how the United Kingdom has been at the forefront of military bridge design, and notably so since the First World War. The universal use of the Bailey Bridge in the Second World War and its outstanding contribution to the successful operations in Italy and NW Europe, and the highly successful world-wide sales of the Medium Girder Bridge to some 36 foreign armies are but two examples of where we have led the world. Both designs emanated from the scientists and engineers of the EBE and later MXEE at Christchurch, and I am grateful to take this opportunity to record the outstanding contribution that the Christchurch Establishment has provided to the Corps of Royal Engineers, and to the Army, over some 75 years. Equipment procurement cycles today can take as long as 10-15 years; the EBE produced the Bailey Bridge into service within a year of the design being initiated.

I am also grateful to the author, for his generous and well-deserved acknowledgement of the role played by the Royal Army Service Corps Bridge Companies in their invaluable support to the Corps' bridging operations.

There is not much that can be said about British military bridging that is not recorded in this book. It is both a work of history and a reference, and I commend it not only to my fellow Sappers but also to all those with an interest in the application of scientific and engineering innovation to the unknowns of war.

John Stibbon

Preface

My aim in writing this history of British Military Bridging, hopefully of interest to the Civil Engineer as well as to the Military Engineer, has been twofold. Firstly I have set out to record, in one volume, brief details of the 170 or so British military bridging equipments that have been developed over many many years. In this, I have endeavoured to keep descriptions of the various equipments reasonably short, to avoid producing no more than a mass of dimensions and minutiae. However to assist the reader, I have included as an Appendix a complete chronological list of the equipments and, as a further Appendix, brief technical notes on equipments and materials. Further details of many of the equipments can be obtained from the many excellent sources held at the Royal Engineer Library, in Brompton Barracks, Chatham.

Although most of the equipments mentioned have been fully developed and have come into service, I have included some that did not progress beyond prototype stage, but nevertheless have been important as a vital link in the development chain. Inevitably however there have been many ideas proposed at the bridging establishment at Christchurch and elsewhere, excellent in their own ways, that have not been developed further, possibly because of financial restraints or the lack of a firm military requirement, and these I have not included.

My second objective has been to collect together details of some of the more important bridging operations undertaken by the Corps of Royal Engineers, and in this, various campaign histories, and in particular the volumes of *The History of the Corps of Royal Engineers*, have proved most useful. I have not of course detailed the great many military campaigns that the British Army has been engaged in over the centuries, particularly at the zenith of the British Empire during the 19th Century, but have restricted my account to those campaigns in which bridging has played an important and often significant part. I have also included a number of bridging operations carried out far from the heat of battle, in the main since the end of the Second World War.

In conclusion I must mention two conventions that I have adopted. Firstly I have used the military ranks of officers current at the time of the events described, ignoring any subsequent promotions and decorations. And secondly, since almost all the equipments included in this book were designed in Imperial units, it has seemed sensible to retain such units in their description. However for the more recent equipments, described in the later chapters, I have used metric units, but have included the Imperial equivalent in brackets for comparison purposes.

Acknowledgements

In writing of military operations carried out in this century I have been able to draw on the many excellent articles published in *The Royal Engineers Journal.* My sincere thanks are due to the authors of such articles, details of which are given in the Bibliography. The eleven volumes of *The History of the Corps of Royal Engineers* have also proved invaluable.

In addition, many fellow officers and friends have kindly read, given advice and then approved those sections of my draft of which they had detailed knowledge; their help and support is very much appreciated. In particular I would mention Mr J M H Barnard, Major J N Barnikel, Lieutenant Colonel M H Briggs, Dr P S Bulson, Mr E Longbottom, Mr M A Napier, Mr T S Parramore, Major R E Ward, Mr D Webber, the late Brigadiers S A Stewart and H A T Jarrett-Kerr, the late Colonel R T Weld, the late Sir Ralph Freeman and the late Mr A W Hamilton.

I am also indebted to those firms, in addition of course to my sponsors, who have provided information and comments on equipments of their manufacture; namely Balfour Beatty Power Networks Ltd, Butterley Engineering Ltd, Eisenwerke Kaiserslautern GmbH, Laird (Anglesey) Ltd, and Thos Storey (Engineers) Ltd.

The photographs and drawings I have collected from many sources, and I have acknowledged sources, where possible, in the illustration captions. The bulk of the earlier photographs included, however, are from the 73,000 or more photographs taken at the Bridging Establishment at Christchurch from 1922 onward, now kept at The Imperial War Museum, London, and reproduced here with kind permission of Mrs Hilary Roberts, Head of Collection Management, Photographic Archives. Some photographs reproduced are Crown Copyright and these have been reproduced by permission of the Ministry of Defence. I am also grateful for permission to reproduce the many photographs included from the Royal Engineer Library at Chatham, and for the assistance given by the Library staff over the years. Assistance provided by Colonel J E Nowers, Director of the Royal Engineer Museum at Chatham, and by Mr D Fletcher, Curator of the Tank Museum at Bovington is also much appreciated.

The five maps were produced to a high standard by Mr D J Cannings and Mrs V T Smith of The Royal School of Military Survey, by kind permission of Lieutenant Colonel J F Prain RE, the Chief Instructor.

I must also acknowledge use of the title for this book, first proposed by the late Colonel John Davies for his book on military bridging which unfortunately did not progress beyond the stage of a first rough draft and notes, kindly made available to me by his son Christopher.

Last but by no means least, I gratefully acknowledge the support and patience of my wife Olive, over what has seemed to her an eternity.

Abbreviations

ABCA	American, British, Canadian, & Australian (Equipment study group)
ABLE	Automotive Bridge Launching Equipment
AGRE	Army Group Royal Engineers
AEV	Armoured Engineer Vehicle
AFB	Axial Folding Bridge
AFV	Armoured Fighting Vehicle
ANZAC	Australian & New Zealand Army Corps
APB	Air Portable Bridge
APC	Armoured Personnel Carrier
ARDE	Armament Research & Development Establishment
ARK	Armoured Ramp Carrier
AVLB	Armoured Vehicle Launched Bridge
AVRE	Armoured Vehicle Royal Engineers
BAOR	British Army of the Rhine
BB	Bailey Bridge
BEF	British Expeditionary Force
BMB	Bailey Mobile Bridge
BPB	Bailey Pontoon Bridge
BRAVE	Bridge Articulated Vehicle Equipment
BR80/90	Bridging for the 1980s/90s
BS	British Standard
BSB	Bailey Suspension Bridge
CCRE	Commander Corps Royal Engineers
CE	Chief Engineer
CET	Combat Engineer Tractor
CF	Carbon Fibre
CFRP	Carbon Fibre Reinforced Plastic
C-H	Callender-Hamilton
CRE	Commander Royal Engineers
CS	Close Support
CSB	Close Support Bridge
CSR	Close Support Raft
DCE	Deputy Chief Engineer
DDSB	Deliberate Dry Support Bridge
DFW	Director of Fortifications and Works
DGFVE	Director General Fighting Vehicles & Engineer Equipment
DRA	Defence Research Agency
DREE	Director Royal Engineer Equipment
DUKW	A General Motors Amphibious Vehicle
DWSB	Deliberate Wet Support Bridge
EBC	Experimental Bridging Company

EBE	Experimental Bridging Establishment
EEF	Egyptian Expeditionary Force
E-in-C	Engineer-in-Chief
ESTRB	Everall Sectional Truss Railway Bridge
EWBB	Extra Widened Bailey Bridge
FBE	Folding Boat Equipment
FCT	Final Concept Team (for BR80)
Fd Coy	Field Company
Fd Sqn	Field Squadron
FV	Fighting Vehicle
FVRDE	Fighting Vehicle Research & Development Establishment
GHQ	General Headquarters
GREF	General Reserve Engineer Force
GS	General Staff or General Support
GSB	General Support Bridge
GSOR	General Staff Operational Requirement
GSR	General Staff Requirement
GST	General Staff Target
HAFB	Heavy Assault Floating Bridge
HFB	Heavy Floating Bridge
HGB	Heavy Girder Bridge
HyF	Heavy Ferry
ICST	International Concept Study Team (for BR80)
IE	Indian Engineers
IFOR	Implementation Force (in Bosnia)
ISD	In Service Date
IWM	Imperial War Museum
IWT	Inland Water Transport
LAFB	Light Assault Floating Bridge
LAR	Light Assault Raft
LBG	Large Box Girder
LFB	Light Floating Bridge
L of C	Line of Communication
LR	Light Raft
LSL	Landing Ship Logistic
LSOR	Land Systems, Operational Requirements
LVT	Landing Vehicle Tracked (the Buffalo)
LWT	Light Wheeled Tractor
MAB	Mobile Assault Bridge
MACH	Mechanically Assisted Construction by Hand
MERADCOM	Military Engineering Research & Development Command
MBT	Main Battle Tank
MEXE	Military Engineering Experimental Establishment
MGB	Medium Girder Bridge

MGO	Master General of the Ordnance
MLC	Military Load Class
MOD	Ministry of Defence
MVEE	Military Vehicle & Engineering Establishment
MWT	Medium Wheeled Tractor
OBM	Outboard Motor
OC	Officer Commanding
OR	Operational Requirement
ORBAT	Order of Battle
PALB	Pre-assembled Landing Bay
PE	Procurement Executive
PMGEE	Project Manager General Engineer Equipment
PROFOR	Protection Force (in Bosnia)
PWD	Public Works Department
RAC	Royal Armoured Corps
RARDE	Royal Armament Research & Development Establishment
RASC	Royal Army Service Corps
RCE	Royal Canadian Engineers
RCT	Royal Corps of Transport
RE	Royal Engineers
REME	Royal Electrical & Mechanical Engineers
RHQ	Regimental Headquarters
ROF	Royal Ordnance Factory
RORO	Roll on Roll off
RSC	Royal Staff Corps
RSME	Royal School of Military Engineering
RTR	Royal Tank Regiment
SAEC	South African Engineer Corps
SBG	Small Box Girder
SC	Steering Committee (for BR80)
SFOR	Stabilisation Force (in Bosnia)
SME	School of Military Engineering
SP	Self-Propelled
SPGRB	Sectional Plate Girder Railway Bridge
SRDE	Signal Research & Development Establishment
SWBB	Standard Widened Bailey Bridge
SWR	Steel Wire Rope
UCB	Unit Construction Bridge
UCRB	Unit Construction Railway Bridge
VAB	Vickers Assault Bridge
WVL	Wheeled Vehicle Launcher

CHAPTER ONE

An Introduction To The Military Bridge

The Military Bridge

During conflict it is often necessary to cross rivers or other obstacles where no bridges exist or where they have been demolished by the enemy. It is then the task of the engineers of an army to provide the means by which such a crossing may be made. For small detachments the use of boats and ferries may be resorted to, but for forces of any size, accompanied by tanks and artillery, bridges must be built to facilitate movement of troops and supplies. Such a bridge may be defined as a Military Bridge, and it differs fundamentally from the Civil Bridge, usually built by a government agency or a local authority as part of the overall infrastructure of a country.

The major difference between the two types of bridge is that of construction time; whereas an important Civil Bridge may be months or even years in construction, the Military Bridge must be in position in the shortest possible time, thinking in terms of hours rather than months. The permanency of the Civil Bridge leads to very detailed location and site investigation and design. On the other hand the siting of the Military Bridge is severely restricted by tactical considerations and its design will usually be completed making use of basic military bridging manuals, either using local materials to build an improvised bridge or, more likely, using an equipment bridge, which relies on the assembly of a number of factory prefabricated components into a complete bridge. The cost of the Civil Bridge is likely to be high, involving considerable financial investment for a project that will be in use for many generations to come. Of course the cost of an equipment bridge is also likely to be high, but although it may only be in place and use for a matter of days, or even hours, the end product is one that can be used time and time again if required, on a wide range of sites in different locations around the world.

There is, however, sometimes an overlap between the two types of bridge as defined above, arising from the occasional building of Military Bridges for long-term usage. An excellent example would be the building of a number of bridges in Britain by the Romans in the First and Second Centuries AD; these bridges were built primarily for military use but became part of the infrastructure of the country, some remaining in use long after the Romans had withdrawn from these shores. More recent examples occurred in great numbers in Europe after the Second World War, when many road and rail equipment bridges were built by the Allies in late 1945 and early 1946 to replace bridges destroyed by bombing or demolition, in order to speed the rehabilitation of the liberated countries and of Germany before permanent bridges could be constructed. Some of these 'temporary' bridges, including a number of substantial bridges built across the River Rhine, remained in constant use for many years.

There is one further type of Military Bridge that was usually of a very permanent nature, and that is the drawbridge, built to provide access to a castle or fortification across a man-made obstacle or moat. Such bridges were usually built as an integral part of the castle's construction and are really outside the scope of this book.

The Importance of Military Bridging

How important then is Military Bridging to the modern army? The main wartime role of a Field Squadron in the British Army's Corps of Royal Engineers is twofold, and can be summed up by the expressions Mobility and Countermobility. First the Sappers must be capable of maintaining the mobility of our own forces by, for example, the construction and maintenance of roads, railways, airfields and of course bridges. Secondly, we must deny mobility to an enemy, by demolishing bridges, laying minefields, destroying roads, and generally producing all manner of obstacles in his path. In the advance the Sappers must be able to replace bridges destroyed by the retreating enemy, or indeed those previously demolished by our own forces whilst retreating; whilst in retreat the Sappers must be able to replace bridges in rear areas that may have been destroyed by enemy aerial or artillery attack or by sabotage. In both cases the keeping open of lines of communications is of prime importance.

Without the pressures of battle such bridges could be built using locally available materials, such as timber and steel beams, and would thus be improvised in time-honoured Sapper fashion. In modern warfare, however, speed of operations is most important and the use of specially designed and purpose manufactured equipment bridging that can be rapidly deployed and constructed affords considerable flexibility of operations to the commander in the field. Indeed equipment bridging, capable of adaptation to any bridging site without extensive preparation of the equipment or the ground, has become indispensable to the military commander, as important to the success of a military operation as the tank, artillery and other specialized military equipment.

Equipment bridging is of particular importance during the advance. A commander will normally build his lines of defence along natural obstacles, such as a major river or canal system or a range of hills, and he will at the same time increase the value of the obstacle by demolishing bridges crossing the rivers and canals or ravines in the hills. Fighting troops and their vital equipment can bypass such obstacles by use of boats or ferries, or possibly helicopters, to enable a bridgehead to be established on the far bank of a river, but, as soon as possible, replacement bridging is essential in order that the vast quantities of fuel, food, ammunition and other stores required by the modern army in battle can be brought forward to maintain the speed of advance. Writing of Bailey Bridging after World War II, Field Marshal Lord Montgomery wrote 'As far as my own operations were concerned, with the Eighth Army in Italy and with the 21 Army Group in NW Europe, I could never have maintained the speed and tempo of forward movement without large supplies of Bailey Bridge.'

The Pedigree of the Bridge Builders

Because of the wide scope of the subject, this book will, in the main, only consider bridging equipments and operations of the British Army, but as a matter of general interest it is worthwhile mentioning briefly the ancestry of the subject. From the earliest of times rudimentary boats have been used to ferry warring tribesman from one side of a water obstacle to the other, and in the late Ninth Century BC portable floats are recorded as being used by the troops of the Assyrian Queen Semiramis to cross the Indus. From the same period an ancient bronze relief shows a rudimentary floating bridge being used by the Assyrian troops of Salmanassar III.

In 513 BC, Darius the Persian was in pursuit of the Scythians, whose country lay to the north of the Danube, and to this end he hired a fleet of ships, which he sent up the Black Sea coast with instructions to sail up the Danube and form a bridge across the river, using the ships as pontoons. Darius' fleet was manned by Ionians, at that time Greek allies of Darius, and they built a bridge across the Danube and provided the bridge guard. However, the attack upon the Scythians proved abortive and, after Darius and his troops had withdrawn, the Ionians broke up the bridge and sailed home.

One of the earliest records of a major obstacle being crossed by a string of boats connected together to form a floating bridge for a military operation is that of the crossing of the Bosphorus, also by Darius, in 493 BC. Darius planned to lead a large army of well-trained men from Asia into Europe, invading Macedonia. First, however, he had to cross the 3,000ft wide Bosphorus, and the size of his army precluded the use of boats to ferry across his many soldiers with their horses and stores. Little is known about the construction of the bridge except that it was made of boats lashed together and was designed and built under the direction of one Mandrocles of Samos, who must therefore rank as one of the earliest bridge engineers of the last two and a half thousand years.

Darius' son Xerxes also staged a foray into Macedonia, in 480 BC, but he bridged the Hellespont (now known as the Dardanelles) at Abidos, where the water gap was recorded by Herodotus as being seven furlongs (about 4,600ft). The bridge was destroyed by a great storm, whereupon Xerxes ordered the execution of the engineers who had built it. He then ordered the Hellespont to be chastised with three hundred lashes of the whip, whilst his

Figure 1.1. *A 19th Century engraving of the Bridge of Xerxes across the Hellespont.* (Illustration of Herodotus).

officers proclaimed, 'You salt and bitter stream, your master lays this punishment on you for injuring him, who never injured you. But Xerxes the King will cross you, with or without your permission. No man sacrifices to you and you deserve the neglect by your acid and muddy waters.' Two further bridges were then built; one was supported by 360 boats and was built by Phoenician engineers, and the second, using 314 boats, was built by Egyptian engineers. (Figure 1.1). The boats were anchored head and stern, with their keels in line with the direction of the current to reduce the load on the anchors, which were formed from large baskets filled with stones. Two cables ran the length of each bridge, and once all the boats were in position these were tightened by wooden capstans placed on each shore. Planks were lashed to these cables and brushwood and soil were then spread to form a wearing surface for the deck. Xerxes was eventually defeated and driven back into Asia, whereupon the ropes from the two bridges were taken by the Greeks and presented to their gods in the temples of Athens.

Tables were turned when Alexander the Great invaded Persia in 334 BC, as he crossed the Hellespont in the other direction; his expedition took him as far east as the Indus. Alexander bridged a number of rivers, including the Euphrates, but crossed the Indus using ferries. His method of building the floating bridges probably differed little from that used by Darius and Xerxes, but Xenophon records that on one occasion the boats from which the bridge was to be built had to be brought to the river from a site some twelve miles away. The boats were carried on chariots and this is probably the first recorded instance of land transport being used to form a bridging train.

The Romans developed the method of constructing floating bridges used by the Persians and Greeks, using fewer boats connected together by

4

Figure 1.2. A detail from Trajan's Column in Rome, showing a Roman bridge of boats.

supporting timbers or girders spanning between them, rather than a continuous line of boats anchored side by side. Thus, the Roman armies in the time of Julius Caesar were provided with bridging equipment in the form of timber platforms that could be supported by boats made of plaited willow branches and covered with animal skins. (Figure 1.2). The usual method of construction, described by Caesar, was to build out from the home bank by floating boats downstream and adding them progressively to the head of bridge. On some occasions a tower would be built on the leading boat and manned by soldiers so that it could command the bridgehead on the far bank; it thus became what might be considered a very early assault bridge. Such equipment was used by Caesar for the crossing of a number of rivers during his Spanish and Gallic campaigns in the First Century BC. Major floating bridges included those across the the River Saône in France and across the River Sewgro in Spain, but one of the more interesting bridges was that built across the Rhine in 55 BC and believed to be sited near Coblenz. Caesar only required the bridge for a short while and a floating bridge would have served his purpose; however, he wished to impress the Gauls and therefore had a much more complex structure built across the river, using obliquely driven twin piles, connected by cross transoms to support the road bearers. Records state that the bridge was completed in ten days from the initial collection of timbers, and that after it had been in use for eighteen days Caesar returned across the bridge and demolished it.

After the Roman Army landed in Kent in 43 AD and began the systematic conquest of Britain, the campaign against the Scots culminated in the building of Hadrian's Wall. This was backed up by a complex system of supporting roads and bridges, including three large bridges across the River Tyne. The main bridge, Pons Aelius, was sited at what is now Newcastle and is estimated to have been 735ft long. The remains of the stone piers of the

Figure 1.3. A possible reconstruction of a Roman Bridge at Chester. It is now known that the bridge passed around rather than through the towers. (Frank Gardiner)

bridge across the Tyne at Corbridge, possibly 500ft long, are visible to this day below the surface of the water. Many other bridges were built to open up the country (Figure 1.3) including those at York, Cirencester, Colchester and Rochester, and of course across the River Thames at London, where the Roman roads of Watling Street and Stane Street crossed the river, somewhere in the vicinity of the present London Bridge.

As the Roman Empire was extended, more and more permanent bridges were built, generally improving the infrastructure of conquered countries and easing the administration of the occupying Roman armies. For these more permanent bridges the Romans used flat segmental timber arches, heavily braced, spanning between masonry piers, and, less frequently, masonry arches. They also used wooden lattice fences as handrails on their bridges to prevent those using the bridges accidentally falling over the side. Major permanent bridges included the famous arch bridge at Avignon in France and the Great Bridge of Trajan, a masonry pier bridge built across the Danube, some 2600ft wide at the bridge site. Trajan was Roman Emperor from 98 to 117 AD and had the bridge built by Apollodorus of Damascus to guarantee the supply line of his legions in conquered Dacia, roughly the equivalent of modern-day Hungary. The timber arches, which spanned between masonry piers, were of 170ft span, a span not exceeded for another 1000 years. The bridge stood for 150 years, until it was demolished by the Romans when they withdrew from Dacia, but details are permanently recorded on Trajan's Column in Rome.

After the collapse of the Roman Empire and the withdrawal of their Armies from Britain in the middle of the Fifth Century, their legacy of fortifications, roads and bridges served the local population for many years to come. Successive centuries saw the continued civilization of the country, the Anglo-Saxon colonization, incursions by the Vikings, and eventually the invasion by the Normans in 1066. Many substantial masonry bridges, often fortified, replaced and supplemented the timber Roman bridges as they fell into disrepair, and as the country developed.

6

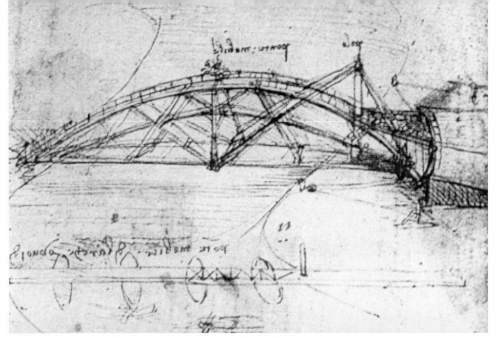

Figure 1.4. Leonardo da Vinci's proposal for a military bridge, circa 1480.

There was, however, little of note in the way of military bridge building until the early Middle Ages. In Italy Leonard da Vinci spoke of his skills in the field of military engineering when he applied for a post in the court of Ludovico il Moro. In 1482 he wrote, 'I know how to build light strong bridges, made to be easily transported, so as to follow, and at times escape from the enemy, as well as others which are safe from damage by fire and from battle wear, easy and convenient to take apart and build.' His proposal for such a bridge incorporated wheels and rollers, and a caisson counterweight, but did not progress beyond his early sketches. (Figure 1.4).

The Sappers as Bridge Builders

At this time in Britain troops were raised as required for a particular campaign, and there was no standing Army in this country before the Restoration of Charles II in 1660. Prior to this pioneers and artificers were raised like other troops and their officers and engineers were employed as such for only as long as their services were required. A few engineers had been employed permanently from earlier times, chiefly for the building of fortifications, and these were known as 'King's Engineers', one of the earliest being Waldivus Ingeniator, mentioned in the Doomsday Book of 1086 and probably the Chief Engineer of William the Conqueror. Bishop Gundolph was another of William's engineers and was responsible for the construction of the White Tower in the Tower of London and the strengthening of Rochester Castle.

However, the invention of gunpowder and the introduction of the cannon eventually lead to the introduction of the Ordnance Train. In the military sense the term 'train' implies a procession of personnel and vehicles, travelling together and carrying equipment in support of a military operation, and the trains eventually included soldiers who would now be known as artillery, engineer and ordnance personnel, the engineers engaged for service being known as 'Train Engineers'. The development of the Ordnance Train is considered in more detail in the next chapter.

In 1716 a regular Corps of Engineers was formed, consisting of twenty-eight engineers. The rank and file for the Corps were still raised as required for each campaign, but in 1772 the formation of the first Company of Soldier Artificers was approved, as a result of unsatisfactory work carried out by civilian artificers during improvement to the fortifications of Gibraltar. The company gradually increased in strength and in 1786 became two companies. The following year, the year in which the Corps of Engineers was granted the title Royal, the formation of a Corps of Royal Military Artificers was authorized. Six companies were originally raised, mainly for work on fortifications at the home ports, but in 1793 a further six companies were recruited, expressly for active service, and four years later the two companies of Soldier Artificers at Gibraltar were incorporated into the Corps; Royal Engineer Officers were normally allocated to the companies for specific tasks. In 1813, as a result of the increasing importance of field engineering and siegecraft in the Peninsular War, and pressure from within the Corps supported by the then Viscount Wellington, the purpose and training of the Corps was changed and a new title granted, 'Royal Sappers and Miners'. The final development took place after the Crimean War, when, in 1856, the Royal Sappers and Miners became one Corps with the existing Corps of Royal Engineers, the Privates of the new combined Corps being redesignated as Sappers.

Six years later, in 1862, when the Government of India was assumed by the Crown, the 300 engineer officers of the Honourable East India Company amalgamated with the 384 officers of the Corps of Royal Engineers. However, the three existing Indian Corps of Sappers and Miners remained as part of the Indian Army, with British officers and Indian personnel. The Indian Corps were eventually known as Queen Victoria's Own Madras Sappers and Miners, King George V's Own Bengal Sappers and Miners, and the Royal Bombay Sappers and Miners.

Over the years the Corps grew from strength to strength. At the time of Waterloo there were ten Companies, officered by sixty Royal Engineer officers. By the time of the Boer War the Corps included Field Companies, Fortress Companies, Bridging Battalions, Railway Battalions and many more specialized sections such as the Balloon Sections, the Searchlight Sections and Survey Sections. During the First World War the Corps expanded from a strength of 25,000 all ranks to one of 330,000 all ranks, and, after the inevitable postwar reduction in size, expanded again to a Second World War peak of about 280,000, with a wide range of specialized units covering all aspects of Sapper work. The basic unit within the Corps remained as the Field Company until after the war, when Companies were renamed Field

Squadrons, although the four mounted troops working with the Cavalry Brigade at Aldershot were formed into a Field Squadron as early as 1909. In the main it has been the Field Company or Squadron responsibility to meet the bridging requirements of the Field Army. The exceptions have been the Armoured and Assault Squadrons set up during the Second World War to man the armoured bridgelayers used extensively during that war, and the Amphibious Squadrons established in the early 1970s to operate amphibious bridging.

Types of Military Bridging

The two fundamental types of bridging used in military operations and already referred to are **Improvised Bridging** and **Equipment Bridging.** The earliest military bridges were always improvised, making use of locally available materials such as stone, timber and flax or papyrus with which to make ropes. The bridging of wide water obstacles would be achieved by using locally available boats to support timbers spanning between them. With a much wider range of local materials available today, however, the design is more likely to consist of steel joist spans supported on timber trestle bents or timber piles, the timber decking possibly protected by a tarmac wearing surface. (Figure 1.5) Improvised bridging is still taught at the Royal School of Military Engineering and has a definite place in the training of the modern Sapper, since circumstances can arise where it is the most practical solution to a bridging problem. Such circumstances might include inaccessibility of a site, non-availability of equipment bridging, or the requirement to produce a more permanent bridge, for example one that might stay in position for a number of years in support of a local community.

The equipment bridge has developed over a long period of time, stemming initially from the introduction of the Ordnance Trains in the Seventeenth Century discussed above. The need arose most probably from a flexibility of operations, and considerably reduced delays resulting from the assembly of the local materials and boats required to build an improvised crossing. Speed of construction has always been the prime advantage of the equipment bridge, becoming much more important with the advent of the lorry and then the tank. As the modern army has become more and more sophisticated, with advanced weapon systems and target location equipment, this need to build bridges rapidly has become even more important; so much so that a recent requirement called for 120m of floating bridge to be constructed, crossed by a battle group of 150 vehicles, dismantled and dispersed to a distance of 4km (2½ miles) in one hour. The speed of construction and the other factors affecting design will be discussed later in the chapter, but first the different types of equipment bridge should be mentioned.

The two basic types of equipment bridging are the **Floating Bridge**, a bridge which crosses a river or canal and is supported by a buoyancy system of boats or pontoons, and the **Fixed Bridge** or **Dry Bridge**, a bridge which spans from bankseat to bankseat across a wet or dry obstacle. The Fixed Bridge may of course have a number of spans, supported by ground-bearing piers founded on land or in water, depending upon the type of obstacle. Another important group, usually referred to as **Assault Bridges**, includes preassembled bridges pushed into position under assault conditions by a battle tank, or, for shorter spans, bridges carried and launched by armoured vehicles. **Line of Communication Bridges**, used to keep open the main supply routes, have very often been improvised if time has permitted. Otherwise, with less emphasis on speed of construction, they might well be built using equipment that would be obsolete for front line operations; for example in present times using Bailey Bridging or Heavy Girder Bridging whilst the more modern Medium Girder Bridge would be used operationally. **Railway Bridging** is of course a specialized form of Line of Communication Bridging and played a very important part in the success of

Figure 1.5. An improvised bridge built by Sappers during training in 1914.

operations in Italy and NW Europe during the Second World War. However, with the envisaged pattern of modern warfare, there is no foreseeable role for the heavy and slowly built bridging equipment used to replace demolished railway bridges during those campaigns, and no stocks of such equipment are now held.

It must be said that the nomenclature used for equipment bridging has been inconsistent over the last eighty years. Floating Bridges have been named as such, as for example in the case of the Inglis Floating Bridge of the First World War, or as Pontoon Bridges, as for example with the Bailey

Pontoon Bridge of the Second World War, whilst after the war the term 'floating bridge' was again used for the Heavy and Light Floating Bridges. The latest equipment, the M3, is based upon an amphibious vehicle and is understandably called the 'M3 Amphibious Bridge'. The offshoot of the Floating Bridge, that is the all-important Ferry, used to cross water obstacles prior to the building of a bridge, has been called such, as for example with the Heavy Ferry, or a Raft, as with the Class 50/60 or the Close Support Rafts.

Fixed Bridges were often named after their inventor, as with the Hopkins and Hamilton Bridges and of course the Bailey Bridge, but since the Bailey descriptive names have been used, as with the Air Portable Bridge or the Medium Girder Bridge. When such bridges have been used in the floating role, they have been described as such, as with the Floating Medium Girder Bridge.

Assault Bridging, dating from the Lock Bridge of the First World War, has been variously named. In general the term has been used to describe bridges such as wheel- or track-mounted Inglis or Bailey Bridging that could be pushed across an obstacle by a tank under assault conditions, or the many bridges that have been carried and launched by an armoured vehicle. However, the latter have often been called Tank Bridges, as for example in the case of the Tank Bridges Nos 1 to 7 and 10 to 12. The bridges were never mounted on battle tanks, however, but always on an armoured chassis based upon a battle tank with the turret and ancillary equipment removed. Hence the No 8 and No 9 Bridges were known officially as Armoured Vehicle Launched Bridges (AVLBs), although in common usage they soon became referred to as the No 8 and No 9 Tank Bridges, whilst the Chieftain Bridgelayer became referred to as an AVLB.

It will be seen later that the trilateral American British and German Bridging for the 1980s project adopted the terms 'wet support bridge' and 'dry support bridge' for the first two groups of bridge mentioned above, and that later still these terms were again modified. However, in order to avoid confusion the generic terms 'floating bridge', 'fixed bridge ' and 'assault bridge' will be used throughout this book, using specific names for equipments as applicable.

The Evolution of Equipment Bridging

The continual development of military bridging equipment is subsequently dealt with in detail, but it is perhaps worthwhile to summarize in this introductory chapter some of the major landmarks in this development. The first equipment pontoons date from the time of the early Ordnance Trains in the late seventeenth century. A variety of pontoons and various forms of trestle were subsequently developed over the next two centuries, improving the performance of floating bridges, but there were no real advances in the realm of dry bridging, other than the development of standard designs for elementary trusses and the introduction of steel joists for use as stock spans.

Probably the first true equipment fixed bridge that could be assembled in the field from a number of standard components was the Inglis Light Pyramid Bridge, designed by Inglis at Cambridge just before the First World War. This bridge was a light footbridge but Inglis developed his ideas and eventually produced a design for a bridge capable of carrying a 35 ton tank; the Mark III version of his bridge was used during the Second World War. The Hopkins Bridge was another fixed bridge developed during the First World War, but in the main, floating bridges used during the War used the already existing Mark II Pontoon Equipment.

The next milestone was the establishment of the Experimental Bridging Company RE at Christchurch in 1919, which is dealt with in detail in Chapter Five, and is perhaps the most important single event affecting the history of British military equipment bridging. The existence of the now sadly defunct establishment at Christchurch, eventually devoted to the development of a wide range of equipment for the Sappers as it expanded over the years, contributed enormously to the success of the Allied Forces during the Second World War and has been the envy of many foreign armies.

Another important landmark in the evolution of military bridging was the introduction of the tank, substantially increasing the load for which new bridges had to be designed. The maximum load to be carried by forward bridging equipment rose from 4 tons in 1914 to 30 tons in 1941, and subsequently very much more. The tank also opened up the possibility of a whole new range of bridging equipments which could be carried and launched from the tank itself. The first assault bridge was the simple Lock Bridge developed at the end of the First World War; it was carried at the front of a Heavy Tank Mark V** and could span up to 20ft. Considerable development of assault bridging took place at Christchurch between the wars, leading to a number of successful designs, at spans up to 30ft, used during the Second World War. Further developments after the War led eventually to the introduction of the No 8 Armoured Vehicle Launched Bridge, with an effective span of 80ft, the longest assault bridge in use in the world in the late 1980s.

Chapter Five considers the innovative work of Martel at Christchurch in the early 1920s and during his subsequent career. Martel did much to advance the science of equipment bridging, his most important contribution being the design of the Small and Large Box Girder Bridges; these were the first bridges to make use of dogs and pins to connect bridging units together in order to form girders, thus simplifying construction and giving flexibility of span. These deck bridges used either two, three or four girders placed side by side, depending upon the load to be carried, a principle, together with that of pin-jointed panels, subsequently adopted by Bailey in the development of his bridge. Another bridge developed prior to the Second World War which used a principle to be adopted by Bailey was the Hamilton Bridge; this was a through type bridge which used either two, three or four trusses either side of the bridge to form the main girders and also used the girders in either one or two storeys, to improve the load capacity and achievable span as required.

This does not, however, detract in any way from the brilliance of the Bailey Bridge design which was developed at Christchurch during the Second World War. The bridge provided the Sappers with an equipment that could be mass-produced and was easily transported and handled in the field. It was extremely versatile, being readily adapted for different load classes and spans and providing a bridge that could be used as a dry bridge, a floating bridge, an assault bridge, a railway bridge and even as a suspension bridge. The full story of Bailey Bridging is told in Chapter Seven.

The next milestone in the evolution of equipment bridging was the introduction of aluminium alloys, considered in Chapter Eleven. Various light alloys had been available during the Second World War, but with inevitable wartime shortages of all materials their use had to be restricted to aircraft production. After the war limited use was made of the new material to produce deck panel and launching nose transoms for the Heavy Girder Bridge, but the first major use of lightweight alloys was with the Heavy Assault Floating Bridge, which came into service in the early 1960s, and used aluminium alloys for the main girders, the landing bay cross girders, the deck panels and the centre pontoons. At the same time work on a light alloy tank bridge was in hand and the No 6 Tank Bridge came into service in 1963. Later in the 1960s, however, a much stronger aluminium alloy was developed for the design and manufacture of the Medium Girder Bridge (MGB).

The MGB was a landmark in its own right. Developed at Christchurch in the 1960s, it came into service with the British Army in 1970 and has proved to be the most successful military bridge developed anywhere in the world since the Second World War Bailey. It has been sold to no less than thirty-six armies, including those of the United States and most of the NATO countries, netting the Ministry of Defence many millions of pounds in design royalties. The bridge was designed as a fixed bridge but, like Bailey, proved to be versatile, lending itself to use as a multi-span bridge with piers and as a floating bridge with a variety of buoyancy units. It is considered in some detail in Chapter Twelve.

The Amphibious Bridge M2 was of German design and manufacture, but it was purchased by the British Army and therefore warrants a place in this story. It came into service at about the same time as the MGB and its introduction presented a major step forward in the realm of floating bridges, using for the first time a vehicle with a good road performance that was fully buoyant in its own right and could drive straight into a river for use as a bay of floating bridge or a self propelled ferry. The bridge is also considered in detail in Chapter Twelve, and the much-improved Amphibious Bridge M3 is described in Chapter Fifteen.

The last stage in this brief review brings the story to the proposals for various concepts for Bridging in the 1980s and 1990s. These concepts stemmed from a trilateral United States, United Kingdom and German collaborative project which started in 1969. The whole subject is covered in detail in Chapter Fifteen and Appendix F, but in brief the original concept envisaged a basic bridge design that could be carried and launched from an wheeled vehicle for use in the fixed and floating roles and from an armoured vehicle in the assault role. Many years of collaborative effort finally came to an end in 1982, for a variety of reasons, but British proposals have been successfully developed further under contract by NEI Thompson (later Thompson Defence Projects Ltd and subsequently integrated into Vickers Defence Systems). The new equipment came into service in the mid-1990s.

The Design of Military Bridges

The parameters that govern the design of a military bridge are laid down by the intended user. The basic requirements will include such factors as the load class, which will be considered in more detail later in the chapter, the proposed span, and of course the type of bridge required. Many other factors must be taken into account, however, by the military bridge designer, factors which may or may not be specified by the user. Some of these factors are mentioned below, but they are not listed in order of importance, because relative importance will change with prevailing circumstances. Even so, in the present day financial climate, the **Cost of the Equipment** must come at the top of the list, since there is a danger that a too sophisticated and complex equipment will simply price itself out of the market. The question of cost is of course equally important in the case of civil bridges.

Military bridges are essentially temporary structures, possibly remaining in place for no more than an hour or so. It follows that, with frequent erection, dismantling and relocation, **Reliability in Use** is of great importance. They must also be reliable under the effects of constant trafficking, particular attention being given to meeting the required fatigue life of the bridge. Again this is a factor that is equally important with civil bridges, as is the case with **Ease of Production**, which is particularly important in times of war and obviously relates to cost.

Other factors are of much greater importance in the design of military bridges than with civil bridges. The speed with which the crossing of an obstacle can be achieved is very often of prime importance to the successful outcome of an operation, and therefore the military bridge must be capable of **Easy and Rapid Construction** in the field, ideally by a minimum of men. It must be **Robust**, to resist mishandling and accidental damage, and it must be **Easily Repairable and Maintained** in the field. It must be **Adaptable**, for use on a wide variety of sites and at a range of spans, and, ideally, for use in varying roles, the supreme example of this adaptability being the Bailey Bridge. It must remain operational in a **Wide Range of Climatic Conditions**, usually ranging from Tropical to Arctic extremes. It must be able to resist the effects of **Nuclear, Biological and Chemical (NBC)** attack. And lastly, it must be **Readily Transportable**, with manageable components, by road and rail, and often by air.

These then are some of the factors that the designer has to balance, one against the other, in producing his final design. All were considered in the latest operational requirement for the current generation of military bridging, and yet it is interesting to note that an *Aide-Memoire to Military Sciences*, dated 1845, lists all of the factors except the last three, as being 'very relevant to Field Bridging'.

Apart from the general considerations outlined above, the designer will also have to take account of many specific factors, such as bank condition requirements, estimated bank bearing pressures, permitted bridge deck and ramp slopes, vehicle crossing speeds, design loadings for wind, mud, snow and ice, permissible bridge deflections, estimated current speeds for floating bridges, required operating speeds and freeboard for rafts, ease of launching and launching loads, protection against corrosion, and so on. The Trilateral Design and Test Code for Military Bridging, which resulted from the Bridging for 1980s project discussed in Chapter Fifteen, has eased the work of the designer considerably, in that many of these requirements have now been clearly specified.

There is, however, one factor in which the military bridge designer had an important advantage over his civil bridge counterpart. This is the predictability of loading; not only can the military bridge be designed to carry a specific Military Load Class, but the speed of crossing can also be controlled to some degree; in addition the spacing between vehicles is specified and can also be controlled. These aspects of loading are much less predictable with the civil bridge, which therefore has to be designed for more extreme loading and with a higher factor of safety, whereas that normally used for military bridge design is 1.5, working with ultimate stresses, or 1.33, working with 0.2% proof or yield stresses. In addition, an impact factor of 15% is applied to live loadings, which are considered as acting at maximum eccentricity. The predictability of loading also means that military bridges can be designed with a finite fatigue life, since vehicle crossing of a bridge can be monitored, a virtual impossibility with civil bridges. If design for fatigue is critical, a fatigue life of 10,000 crossings at maximum vehicle loading is usually considered adequate.

The Load Classification of Bridges

To conclude this chapter of introduction, the load-carrying capacity of bridges must be considered, since the 'Load Class' of bridges will be constantly referred to throughout the book. This Load Class has always been of prime importance for the Sapper, who must ensure that the bridge that he has constructed is not overloaded, resulting in permanent damage or even possible collapse of the bridge which could have far-reaching effects upon the outcome of a military operation, far beyond that of the mere loss of the equipment. It has therefore proved essential to classify the strength of a bridge as built and it is of interest to see how the system currently in use has evolved.

Instructions in Military Engineering, published in 1887, included a comprehensive table of likely loads, their weights, and the estimated immersion depth of the pontoons then in service for each load. It then left it to the RE officer to decide the safe load of the pontoon bridge, depending on the condition of the river. The loads ranged from the extreme of the 'Steam Sapper with coal and water' (weight 13,350lb and immersion depth 28in), through 'Elephants, loaded and Cattle, crowded' (weight 9,275lb and immersion depth 20in), and 'Pack Bullocks and Camels', to 'Cavalry in marching order' (weight 4,000lb and immersion depth 9½in). The table also referred to use of the equipment either as a Heavy Bridge or as an Advanced Bridge.

The Manual of Military Engineering of 1894 specified different combinations of service pontoons to form Light, Medium or Heavy bridges and laid down typical loads that could be carried by each type, ranging from infantry in file to a loaded elephant. *The Manual of Field Engineering* of 1911 made it clear that 'the officer superintending the construction of a bridge is responsible that it is strong enough to carry the weight it is intended to carry', and stated that a signboard should be placed at each end of the bridge specifying, for example 'Bridge to carry Infantry in fours' or 'Bridge for all arms. No road machines.'

Throughout the First World War the classification of bridges as Light, Medium and Heavy continued in use, together with the minor classifications for Footbridges and Pack Bridges. However, the advent of the motor vehicle and the tank meant that the three main classes had to be more clearly defined and a fourth class added - that for the tank. In brief, the load classes were defined as follows:

Light Loads - Infantry in fours, cavalry in single file, pack mules and camels.

Medium Loads - 6in howitzer and limber, all types of motor lorry with axle loads up to 8 tons.

Heavy Loads - Heavy artillery, tractors, lighter varieties of tank up to 16 tons in weight, and axle loads up to 16 tons.

Tank Loading - An unrestricted stream of traffic, with heavy tanks, up to 35 tons in weight, maintaining a spacing of 75ft.

To confuse the issue further, however, Stock Spans, which are discussed in detail in Chapter Four, were defined as Type A Bridges (for 17 ton axle loading) and Type B Bridges (for 13 ton axle loading); vehicles were then classified as A loads, which could only pass over Type A bridges, or B loads, which could pass over Type A and Type B bridges.

The rapid increase in variety and weight of military vehicles during and after the war, and the existing confusion with regard to the subject, caused the Royal Engineer Board to give the matter some attention. In 1928 the Board started to collect data on a wide variety of vehicles, and by 1932 details of some 400 vehicles had been collected with the object of deciding which vehicles could and which could not safely cross existing equipment bridges. A bridge classification system was agreed upon, based upon a Light Class for

Brigade Group transport, a Medium Class for Divisional transport, a Heavy Class for Corps and Army vehicles, including tanks, and a Super-heavy Class for abnormal loads exceeding the Heavy Class. Two minor classes catered for foot troops and pack animals crossing obstacles in the early stages of operations, using for example the Kapok Assault Bridge. From the information collected it was now possible to slot each vehicle accurately into its correct load class, but even so the only way of deciding whether or not a particular vehicle could safely cross a bridge was to stop the vehicle, determine its type, look it up in Staff Tables and define it as Light, Medium or Heavy, before making a decision. With common vehicles there was no real problem, but with more unusual or new types of vehicle difficulties arose from out-of-date Staff Tables, which were in any case far from comprehensive. The marking of bridges as previously mentioned provided no solution, since marking for example a Small Box Girder Bridge as a 'Medium Bridge', meant very little to an infantry driver on a dark and wet winter night.

The work of the RE Board continued, however, and was to solve all the difficulties in a very neat way. Under a new scheme introduced in late 1938 all bridges were given a load class number which indicated approximately the live load in tons that could safely cross; this assumed an 80ft spacing of vehicles and took account of the maximum bending moments and shear force that could be sustained by the bridge. At the same time all vehicles were given a class number, indicating the equivalent live load that they imposed on a bridge. The original load classes used were 3, 5, 9, 12 and 18, with an additional load class of 24 being added shortly afterwards. Obviously a vehicle could not safely cross a bridge with a class number lower than its own, and since all vehicles and all bridges were clearly marked with their load class, using black numbers on a yellow ground, it was apparent to all concerned whether or not a bridge could be safely crossed.

The new scheme was finally adopted in 1939 and proved of outstanding value to Engineer and Army Staffs alike. It was rapidly extended to include the classification of civil bridges, thus enabling major routes to be classified. It was subsequently modified by the introduction of a series of hypothetical vehicles, each specified by a weight in short tons (which roughly equated to the class number), a length of wheel base, an axle loading and so on, and for tracked vehicles a width over tracks and the track length. This gave rise to a series of definitive load classes, so that, once a vehicle had been classified by a standard procedure, it could be allocated a load class nearest to but above its true classification. The system has been adopted by the NATO Armies, the current Military Load Classes, or MLCs, being 4, 8, 12, 16, 20, 24, 30, 40, 50, 60, 70, 80, 90, 100, 120, and 150. Because a tracked vehicle is invariably shorter than a wheeled vehicle of the same class load, the bending moments and shear forces induced in a bridge by the two vehicles will differ; for this reason it is not unusual for a bridge to have different load classifications for the two types of vehicles, for example MLC 100(wheeled) and MLC 70(tracks).

18

CHAPTER TWO

From the Middle Ages to the Nineteenth Century

Edward I Invades Wales

One of the earliest examples of the use of military bridging in the Middle Ages dates back to Edward I's invasion of Wales in 1282. At that time the absence of roads and the densely wooded terrain made the country almost impenetrable to Edward's army, but by making full use of a thousand pioneers and three hundred woodcutters Edward succeeded in driving the remnants of the Welsh Army back to the area of Snowdonia. Edward's next objective was Anglesey and a naval force was dispatched there in August. He then planned to link Anglesey to the mainland with a floating bridge and thus establish a new invasion route to Snowdonia. Some forty pontoon boats for the bridge proved too heavy and large to be carried by the Naval ships, and ships had to be specially purchased at Chester. By November his carpenters had completed the bridge, but a defeat was to follow. One version of this suggests that his forces in Anglesey crossed the bridge and advanced inland, only to find that their return route over the bridge had been cut by a rising tide; the Welsh attacked, driving many of the troops into the sea and causing many casualties. Another version of the defeat suggests that the advancing column was surprised by the Welsh and that during their hasty retreat back over the bridge, it was overloaded, causing many of the pontoons to sink and many of the troops to be drowned.

Edward in Scotland

Some years later Edward turned his attention to fighting the Scots and, after a period of truce in 1302, fighting again broke out in 1303. With the bridge across the Forth at Stirling denied him by the Scottish garrison in the castle, Edward foresaw the need to cross the river elsewhere. He therefore commissioned the construction of three prefabricated bridges at King's Lynn, in Norfolk, under the supervision of Magister (or Master) Richard, his King's Engineer at Chester. Richard brought across a team of carpenters from Chester and they set to work sawing and shaping the timbers from which the bridges were to be constructed. The bridges were of different sizes, the records clearly distinguishing a *maior pons*, a *medius pons* and a *minor pons*, the later probably being no more than a footbridge; each bridge was constructed with a defensive tower (or brattice) and a drawbridge. It is presumed that the bridges were floating bridges, to be supported on boats, because recorded purchases included a large number of anchors and hawsers. Some three months later the work had been completed at a cost of about £938, and the components, the carpenters tools and chests of bolts with which to assemble the bridges were loaded onto a fleet of thirty ships which set sail for Scotland. The exact sites at which the bridges were constructed is not known, but by mid-June Edward was in Clackmannan, two miles north of the river, from whence he advanced into Fife and eventually besieged Brechin.

The Ordnance Trains

The first volume of the *Corps History* records the ever-expanding role of the engineer within the army during this early period, but there is little information on military bridging after Edward's campaigns in Wales and Scotland until the development of the Ordnance Trains is mentioned. One of the earliest mentions of such a train is of that used at the Siege of Boulogne in 1544. This train was commanded by an engineer, John Rogers, who was appointed as Master of the Ordnance. It was predominantly an Artillery Train, with a Master Gunner and seventy-one Gunners, but was the predecessor of the much larger Ordnance Trains that were to follow.

From then on, and until the end of the Seventeenth Century, Ordnance Trains were raised when required for a particular compaign. It was realized, however, that it made administrative sense to combine the artillery and engineer support required by an army into a single train, and the engineer element of a train became increasingly significant, the train being organized in a manner most suitable to the campaign. One of the earliest mentions of equipment bridging being carried by the British Army was for the Campaign in Flanders in 1692. The Ordnance Train included not only forty-two cannons and howitzers with 200 ammunition wagons, but also forty tin boats or pontoons complete with wagons, as well as entrenching and artificers' tools. Another train of the same period, enlisted to accompany the Channel Fleet on a summer expedition, included sixty-eight assorted artillery pieces, twenty-nine pontoons and 100 scaling ladders. Once the Flanders War had ended, the various trains were disbanded, but in 1698 a Warrant was issued for the first train to be maintained in peacetime. This train included six Engineers at a salary of £100 per annum and four Sub-Engineers at £50 per annum, although there were at that time another twelve King's Engineers, nine in England and three in Ireland.

The Eighteenth Century

The Century opened with the War of the Spanish Succession, which was waged from 1702 to 1713 and led to the acquisition by Great Britain of the fortress of Gibraltar. A Warrant authorizing establishment of a train for service with Marlborough's army in the Low Countries had been issued even before war had been declared, and the command was given to an Engineer officer, Colonel Holcroft Blood. It was not, however, this train that Marlborough employed for the bridging of the Rhine, prior to his surprise march to Bavaria and the subsequent Battle of Blenheim. The Rhine crossing was made in late May 1704, south of Coblenz, where the river was narrower and the current slower than further north, above the confluence with the Moselle. The bridges of boats were provided by the Margrave of Wurtemburg, one of Marlborough's allies, and the cavalry were the first to cross, to be followed two days later by the infantry, the guns and wagons. Blood's command of the Low Countries Train placed him in command of the artillery, in which post he so distinguished himself at the Battle of Blenheim, in August 1704, that he was promoted to Brigadier General. Bridging aspects of the train were also in evidence at the battle, bridges being built across the Kessel at an early stage. Later a number of bridges were built across the Nebel, approached by causeways built of brushwood and straw across marshy ground. Over seventy squadrons of cavalry and twenty-eight battalions of infantry advanced across the stream prior to the main attack upon the French forces.

The War finally ended with the Treaty of Utrecht in 1713. The several trains that had been raised for service during the War, including three distinct trains raised for service in the Spanish Peninsula, one for Cadiz, one for Barcelona and one for Portugal, were disbanded. Indeed most of the army was disbanded and only a few officers were retained on the permanent establishment of the Ordnance Board. The Chief Engineer of the time suggested a separate establishment for artillery and engineers, and this was approved by Royal Warrant in 1716, resulting in the establishment of a Corps of Engineers, consisting of twenty-eight engineers, and the Royal Regiment of Artillery.

For a while Europe remained at peace, but the role of the engineers in Scotland in the early Eighteenth Century warrants mention. General Wade, a professional soldier of some note who had distinguished himself in the Netherlands, Spain and elsewhere, was sent to Scotland in 1724 to pacify the country in the wake of the 1715 and 1719 rebellions. Wade was not an engineer, but set about using his engineers to develop a

Figure 2.1. The Wade Bridge at Crubenmore in Scotland.

21

network of simple gravel and hardcore roads to connect highland forts, not only for the easy movement of his soldiers but also to stimulate trade and generally open up the country. The work involved the building of no less than forty masonry arch bridges and over 250 miles of road during the period from 1725 to 1745; twenty-five of the bridges survive to this day, although many are in an advanced state of collapse. (Figure 2.1).

During the remainder of the eighteenth century our main adversary remained France, first in Europe, then in the American Colonies from 1754 until the fall of Quebec in 1759. By 1778 the American War of Independence, which had started in 1776, spread when France and Holland allied with Spain and declared war against the British. Gibraltar was under siege from 1779 until early 1783, and four years later the title 'Royal' was conferred on the Corps of Engineers in recognition of their valiant service during the siege.

Wellesley in India

In the early Nineteenth Century General Sir Arthur Wellesley commanded the British forces in India during the Second Maratha War, from 1803 to 1805, having gone to India with his regiment in 1796. His opponent, the Indian Prince Scindia, was considered an exponent of mobility in his campaigns. Wellesley therefore decided to move against Scindia in the Deccan during the monsoon season, when Scindia's army would be largely immobilized by floods and the numerous swollen rivers. Wellesley planned to use a Bridging Train to overcome these obstacles and bring Scindia to battle at a place of his own choosing. Orders were therefore issued for a Bridging Train to be assembled in Bombay by the Bombay Government and then dispatched to join Wellesley's forces. For a variety of reasons, however, the assembly of the train was delayed and, although it was at last dispatched, it was itself bogged down and never reached Wellesley.

Faced with this delay, Wellesley drew up instructions for the construction of pontoons to form his own train. The pontoons themselves were of basketwork construction, some 10ft in diameter and 2ft 3in deep, and were covered with skins, rather in the nature of a coracle. They were thus very light and portable, being anchored close together with a light superstructure spanning between each, and with provision of ropes, anchors and windlasses. The equipment proved a valuable asset, but for some reason was not present for the crossing of the Kaitra prior to the Battle of Assaye, the crossing being made by making use of a convenient ford. The battle marked the end of the war and soon after Wellesley returned to Europe to become embroiled in the war against Napoleon.

The Napoleonic Wars

Europe was racked by a series of wars as the Eighteenth Century drew to a close, and once again we found ourselves fighting the French, first against Revolutionary France and then against the expansionist empire of Napoleon Bonaparte. It is outside the scope of this book to describe the various well-documented battles and campaigns of the Napoleonic Wars in any detail, campaigns that took place from Cairo to Copenhagen and from Portugal to Moscow. Two bridging operations are worthy of mention, however, as being indicative of the increasing importance of this aspect of the work of the military engineer.

The Bridging of the Tagus at Alcantara. By the spring of 1812 most of the permanent bridges across the River Tagus in Central Spain had been destroyed. Lord Wellington, as Wellesley had now become after his successful campaign in Portugal, was anxious to improve his supply route from Badajoz for the pending attack on the forts of Salamanca, and it was therefore decided to restore one of the principal arches of Trajan's Bridge across the Tagus at Alcantara. This was a formidable task, since, in blowing the bridge during the Talavera campaign, Wellington's forces had left a gap about 100ft wide across a precipitous chasm some 140ft deep. (Figure 2.2).

The officer entrusted with the preparations for the crossing was Lieutenant Colonel Sturgeon of the Royal Staff Corps, rather than an officer of the Corps of Royal Engineers. The Royal Staff Corps had its origins in 1799. The Duke of York, the Commander-in-Chief, was then forming an

Figure 2.2. Repairs to a span of the bridge across the Tagus, carried out in 1812. (Military Bridges by H Douglas - 1816 edition).

expeditionary force for service in the Helder, and the Master General of the Ordnance proposed to supply the usual small detachment from his Engineers Department. The Duke of York did not consider the size of this detachment to be adequate, and in view of the general low standard of the Artificers, he formed a military company of pioneers to supplement the engineer force, to work under the control of his Quartermaster General rather than under the MGO. As a result of the success of this arrangement a corps of pioneers, including both officers and other ranks and known as the Staff Corps, was established the following year, becoming the Royal Staff Corps, on reorganization, in 1803. At one stage of the Napoleonic Wars ten companies of the RSC were deployed, and later two further companies were formed, but from 1827 onward there was a gradual disbandment of the Corps, the disbandment being complete by 1839.

Sturgeon's design for the bridge was in fact very ingenious; it was to be a suspension bridge, fabricated from 6½in ropes and timbers at Elvas, some way away from the site, and was an excellent example of bridging improvisation. The ropes and timbers were formed into a vast net, which was then rolled up and transported to the bridge site on a pontoon wagon, other wagons carrying the remaining stores. Once on site, channels were cut in the masonry on either side of the gap into which straining beams were placed to anchor the tackles. Two strong hawsers were then strung across the gap and hauled tight, to support the unrolled bridge as it was pulled across. The work was finished in good time, opening up a passage across the Tagus for a column of siege artillery, which duly arrived at Salamanca some nine days later.

The Bridging of the River Adour. After the siege of San Sebastian in Northern Spain in 1813 Wellington's army advanced into France and, in the winter months, Wellington left part of the army to invest Bayonne while he advanced eastward to Toulouse. To achieve a complete blockade of Bayonne it was necessary to cross the River Adour, and Wellington decided to do this to the west, between the city and the sea. The bridge site selected was about two and half miles from the town, which gave it some protection from the garrison, but, being nearer the river mouth, resulted in considerable tidal effects and a required bridge length of some 900ft.

Lieutenant Colonel Elphinstone, Wellington's Commanding Royal Engineer, was in overall command of the operation, whilst Lieutentant Colonel John Burgoyne was appointed Commanding Engineer to the force employed in the crossing. Burgoyne had served as a Captain under Lieutenant Colonel Fletcher during the crossing of the Douro in Portugal in 1809, and was to be the first RE officer to reach the highest rank in the British Army, that of Field Marshal. He superintended the difficult plan involved and worked closely with Lieutenant Colonel Sturgeon RSC, who had designed the Alcantara bridge. It was clear that ordinary tin pontoons would be quite useless for this crossing, since the swell from the ocean caused considerable turbulence when meeting the fast-flowing river, fed at this time of the year by numerous mountain torrents. It was decided therefore to build a bridge using local coastal vessels called *chasse-marées*, each forty to fifty feet in length; forty-eight of these boats were hired from local ports and were to be anchored at 30-40ft centres across the river. There were insufficient baulks to carry the superstructure and so it was decided, at the suggestion of Lieutenant Colonel Sturgeon, to use five 13in cables strung from shore to shore and laid over notched sleepers spiked to the deck of each boat. On one shore the cables were to be attached to 18 pounder guns which would be dropped into the morass behind the steep retaining wall at the top of the bank, whilst on the other bank the ends of the cables were to be attached to capstans. Each boat carried a share of the bridge superstructure, including forty-eight 3in planks, 9in wide and 12ft long; the five centre boats also carried the coils of cables that could then be paid out towards each bank to anchor the bridge. Two Sappers were put aboard each boat to supervise the fixing and levelling of the cables. When all was ready the flotilla was split into five divisions, each in command of a Royal Engineer officer, and put to sea on 22 February 1814 under naval escort.

Wellington had ordered that a bridgehead should be established on the far bank to facilitate construction of the bridge, and to this end jolly boats and tin pontoons were brought up to ferry troops across the river. Two rafts, each of three pontoons, were constructed and these, with some difficulty, made a number of crossings on a fixed line; eventually, however, the pontoons were used individually, each with four oarsmen, and carried between twelve and twenty soldiers on each trip. By this means a bridgehead of some 8,000 troops was built up and successfully defeated a sortie from the garrison. As a result of a heavy surf and high winds the flotilla was meanwhile having great difficulty in crossing the sandbar at the mouth of the river. In the event eleven boats turned back, two were sunk and only thirty-four succeeded in reaching the bridge site, largely, according to Admiral Penrose who commanded the naval escort, 'because the zeal and science of the Royal Engineer officers commanding the divisions triumphed over the difficulties of navigation'. Luckily there were enough boats to complete the bridge and as soon as they had been anchored stern and aft, construction of the bridge proceeded at pace throughout the night; by noon next day troops began to cross to the far bank. The bridge remained the principal line of communication for the army in France until the end of the war, and was described by the historian Napier as 'a stupendous undertaking, which must always rank amongst the prodigies of war'.

The Founding of the Royal Engineer Establishment

As the Napoleonic Wars progressed it became apparent that the officers of the Royal Engineers and Military Artificers were lacking in the technical skills of what would now be termed Combat Engineering. This view had been expressed by a number of senior officers, including Wellington himself, who was well aware of the exposed and dangerous nature of the engineers' task, particularly during the siege and subsequent assault stage of the battle. Captain Charles Pasley, who had gained considerable experience during twelve years of active service during the Wars, was a strong advocate of improved engineer training, but his pleas fell upon deaf ears. Completely incapacitated from further active service by wounds received at Flushing, he devoted his energies to improving the standard of training and, whilst in command of a company of Artificers at Plymouth, arranged, at his own expense, a course of practical and theoretical training for young officers of the Corps and his men. This coincided with a report from Wellington advocating the expansion of the Engineers' establishment to include a Corps of Sappers and Miners and, since Pasley's course had proved highly successful, it lead to the appointment of a committee to examine Pasley's plans for future training. The committee eventually approved and accepted the whole of his proposals. On 23 April 1812 a Royal Warrant was issued authorizing the setting up of a Royal Engineer Establishment at Chatham for the instruction of the Corps of Royal Military Artificers (from 1813 the Royal Sappers and Miners), and junior officers of the Royal Engineers 'in the duties of Sapping and Mining and other Military Field Works'. The new Establishment was set up at Chatham and Captain Pasley was appointed its Director, in the rank of Major.

Thus was established this most important seat of military engineer training, one that was to play a prominent part in the development not only of military bridging but also of all aspects of military engineering in years to come. The Corps must be forever indebted to Pasley for his foresighted and energetic work in setting up and developing the Establishment, which went from strength to strength under his Directorship. He remained as Director until 1841, eventually in the rank of Colonel; he then left to become Inspector-General of Railways, in the rank of Major General, and was knighted on his retirement in 1846. The first Chatham-trained Sappers took part in the siege of San Sebastian in 1813, but it was not until the Crimean War in 1854 that the real value of Pasley's work was felt. In August 1869 the Establishment was renamed the School of Military Engineering and in 1962 was granted the Royal prefix, to mark the one hundred and fiftieth anniversary of its founding.

The Bridging or Pontoon Trains

Engineer support for the British Army had obviously developed during the wars of the Eighteenth Century, and bridging equipment was always included in the Ordnance Train when it was foreseen that it would be needed. Too often, however, reliance had been placed upon our allies to provide the necessary mobile engineer force, and it was not until the Peninsular War, when we were allied with Spain and Portugal, as ill-equipped as ourselves, that attention was given to organizing the transport of engineer equipment on a satisfactory basis. Thus, in the winter of 1812, the first regular Bridging Train was set up and formed part of the Army in the Peninsula from April 1813. A report by Lieutenant Colonel Sir R Fletcher RE gives some details of this train. The train included no less than 346 personnel, namely two Royal Engineer officers, nineteen civil Artificers and Sappers and Miners, a Lieutenant and sixty-six men of the Portuguese Navy, and 250 drivers. About 750ft of bridging was carried on forty-eight carriages and wagons, drawn by 520 oxen and 283 draught horses. More will be said later about the thirty-three pontoons, but the very size of the Train made it an unwieldy unit, and a march from Abrantes to Sardura in the spring of 1813 resulted in sixty-eight accidents, although admittedly many were of a minor nature.

Wellington took considerable interest in the Bridging Train and, as a result of lessons learnt during the march referred to above, ordered that all the pontoon wagons should be drawn by horses. To this effect he ordered, as a temporary measure, the withdrawal of the horses used by his Artillery Brigade of 9 pounders and replaced them with the oxen now surrendered by the Bridging Train. In May 1813 he wrote: 'We have been sadly delayed by the movements of our bridge, without which it is obvious that we can do nothing; the equipment is quite new and has marched only from Abrantes, but there has already been much breakage and I understand the carriages are shamefully bad. I shall have sad work with this bridge throughout the campaign, and yet we can do nothing without it.' Thus Wellington acknowledged the importance of bridging equipment in the successful completion of his campaign and it is pleasing to record that gradually the Train was brought to an efficient state of operation.

Lieutenant Colonel Carmichael Smyth was Wellington's CRE at the Battle of Waterloo, and had been given the task of forming the Pontoon Train prior to the battle. After the battle he took the opportunity to produce, from the Headquarters in Paris, a small booklet on *Instructions and Standing Orders for the Royal Engineer Department serving with the Army on the Continent*, and this included interesting comments on the possible organization of a Pontoon Train. Smyth proposed a train commanded by a Major of the Corps and divided into two divisions, each of two bridges; each division would be commanded by a Captain, with a Subaltern in charge of each bridge. Each bridge would consist of twenty pontoons, together with the necessary superstructure and a wide range of engineer stores. Pontoon carriages would be drawn by eight horses, and store wagons, a forge wagon and spare horses would accompany each bridge. The establishment of each bridge would include ninety Sappers and Miners (including three drummers), 116 drivers with their officer and NCOs, and a trumpeter, a petty officer and twelve seamen, with a total of 231 horses. Smyth's Instructions placed great store on the need to avoid constant changes in the personnel of the Train and also the need to maintain a high standard of training of the Sappers in all aspects of bridging. However, with the end of the war, general disarmament took place, economy reigned supreme and in the long period of peace that followed up until the Crimean War in 1854 the Corps sank into the routine of peacetime soldiering, in which bridging did not figure highly.

The Tin Pontoon

The pontoons in use by European Armies at the end of the seventeenth century are discussed later in the chapter. However, in general terms they were invariably of the open type, flat-bottomed with near vertical sides and wedge-shaped at the extremities; construction usually consisted of a framework of wooden scantlings covered with suitable cladding. At that time the French used copper cladding and the Germans leather, whilst the British and Dutch pontoons were clad in tin. The Tin Pontoons (Figure 2.3 and Appendix B) used by the British Army during the Napoleonic Wars were almost certainly little changed from those included in the Ordnance Trains used during the Flemish Wars at the end of the Seventeenth Century. However, the pontoons were unwieldy and easily swamped. It could be said, cynically, that that was why the Sappers employed the Royal Navy to man their pontoons during the Napoleonic Wars, but perhaps the Sappers were being sensible because an Engineering Memoir of the period states that 'the pontoons were only suited to tranquil streams, not subject to sudden floods; for if any sudden rise of the water should occur, or if the river becomes disturbed by

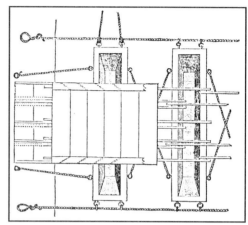

Figure 2.3. The shore bays of a Tin Pontoon bridge.
(Aide Memoire to the Military Sciences, Vol III - 1850).

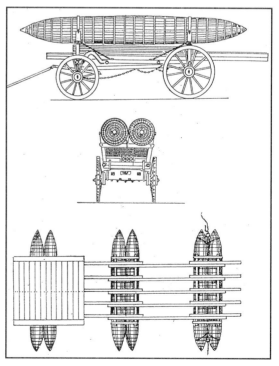

Figure 2.4. James Colleton's design for a bridging buoy, circa 1814.

winds, they filled and sank.' With this drawback in mind, in about 1814 Colonel Sir James Colleton produced his design for the fundamentally new **Colleton Pontoon or Buoy**. The pontoon was cylindrical in shape, with long conical ends, in order to reduce water resistance. (Figure 2.4). The first pontoons were made of wooden staves, put together as for a barrel and held in place by metal hoops, and were thus sometimes referred to as Buoy Pontoons. Difficulties occurred in trying to form bridge with these pontoons, however, and they were not introduced into service.

Congreve's Trough

In the main this chapter has so far dealt with floating bridges, and indeed it will be seen, when considering bridging equipment during the remainder of the Nineteenth Century, that pontoon equipments predominate. Mention should be made, however, of the Congreve Trough, developed during the early part of the century by Sir William Congreve. Sir William, who was born in 1772, was an inventor of some merit and is best known for his invention of the Congreve Rocket, which was used successfully during the Napoleonic Wars, particularly during the crossing of the Adour in 1814 mentioned previously. The Congreve Trough was a logical development of the simplest expedient for crossing a stream, that is the use of a fallen tree or a plank. The Troughs were 14ft long and 1ft 6in wide, with a U-shaped cross-section. Three Troughs were carried in one wagon and were simply laid across a stream, side by side, to form a simple bridge for the passage of field artillery and troops; alternatively the Troughs could be positioned across the gunwales of boats to form a raft. The Congrieve Trough was a direct ancestor of the 12ft and 20ft tracked bridges that were slung on the sides of vehicles and used extensively during the Second World War.

Congreve died in 1828, having achieved an office with the grandiose title of Comptroller of the Royal Laboratory at Woolwich and Superintendent of Military Machines. In this post he had succeeded his father, Lieutenant General Sir William Congreve, who had himself invented a simple but ingenious type of assault bridge. (Figure 2.5). The bridge was constructed from a few timber members lashed together and mounted on a two-wheeled axle; it could be constructed some way away from an obstacle and then wheeled down to a small river or ditch in a few minutes, thus providing support for an assaulting column, although it was never knowingly used in anger.

Figure 2.5. Congreve's simple assault bridge. (Military Bridges by H Douglas - 1853 edition).

The Pasley Pontoon

In 1817, in an attempt to overcome the shortcomings of the open Tin Pontoon, Charles Pasley, Director of the newly formed Engineer Establishment at Chatham and now a Lieutenant Colonel, proposed a new form of pontoon, which was decked in. (Figure 2.6 and Appendix B). Pasley's proposals resulted from a series of experiments carried out on the River Medway at Chatham, dating from the founding of the Establishment in 1812. The new pontoon was eventually adopted by the Army and remained in service for many years, although it was of course introduced too late for use during the Napoleonic Wars. Pasley's Pontoon had a pointed bow and a square-ended stern, and introduced the principle of joining two pontoons together, end to end, to form a bipartite pontoon. Thus two of these, sometimes named demi-pontoons, could be lashed together, stern to stern, to form a single bridge-supporting pier. A two-wheeled cart, drawn by two horses, carried two demi-pontoons with their stores, so that two carts could convey all the materials needed to build a two-pier raft, a number of such rafts being used to form a bridge. On a favourable site a number of rafts could be built at the same time and it was said that the rafts could be built in about fifteen minutes and then connected into bridge in another fifteen minutes, comparable times being taken to dismantle the bridge and reload the stores.

Figure 2.6. *The Pasley Pontoon of 1817.* (Military Bridges by H Douglas - 1853 edition).

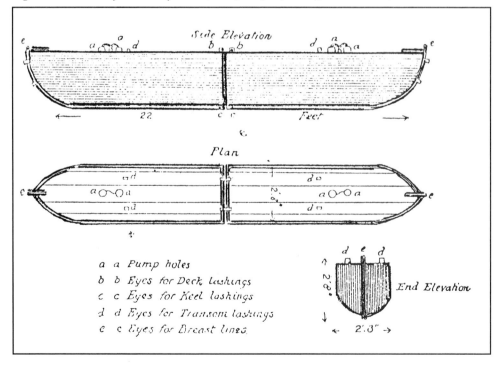

The Blanshard Pontoon

In 1828 Major T Blanshard constructed a completely new type of pontoon, cylindrical in shape, with hemispherical ends and made of tin. (Figure 2.7 and Appendix B). However, the version of the new pontoon adopted for use by the British Army as standard equipment in 1836 had modified paraboloidal ends; this version was 24ft 6in in length. Four rows of sunken handles placed at intervals around the circumference were used not only to carry the pontoon but also to lash down saddles used to support the bridge superstructure. Two pontoons, together with the baulks, chesses and the rest of the superstructure needed to form a raft, were carried on a single carriage, together with anchors, buoys, oars and other watermanship stores. Rafts were coupled together to form a bridge, which could carry a light field gun with pontoons at 24ft spacing, although heavier loads could be carried by progressively closing up the pontoons. A further modified version of the pontoon is described in *Instructions in Military Engineering -Volume I Part III - Military Bridges (1870)*. (Figure 2.8). This version, to a design attributed to Admiral J C Caffin, was basically a Blanshard Pontoon with minor improvements, but was sometimes referred to as the **Caffin Pontoon**. The design reverted to the use of hemispherical ends, resulting in a slight reduction in the overall length, and also in the weight. By this time, however, the Blanshard Pontoon was on the way out, soon to be replaced by the Blood Pontoon, as will be seen later.

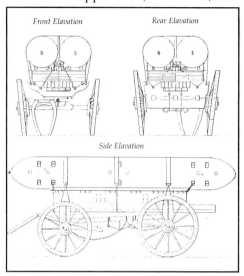

Figure 2.7. The early version of the Blanshard Pontoon, adopted in 1836. (Military Bridges by H Douglas - 1853 edition).

Figure 2.8. A model of the Caffin version of the Blanshard Pontoon. (Royal Engineer Museum).

Figure 2.9. Blanshard's Infantry Pontoons, loaded on a standard bridging wagon.

A smaller version of the Blanshard Pontoon had conical ends and measured only 14ft 10in in length; weighing only 140lb, it could conveniently be carried by two men. (Figure 2.9). The **Small or Infantry Blanshard Pontoon** could be used to build a rapidly placed infantry assault bridge, and could, with care, carry light guns. An interesting bill of the time lists the items involved in the manufacture of a Small or Infantry Blanshard Pontoon; the pontoon was made in Dublin in 1844 and lists:

92 sheets of tin	53s 8d
13lb of tinman's solder	6s 6d
2 bushels of charcoal	2s 6d
3lb of paint	1s 6d
15½ days' work for a Sapper tinman	15s 6d
½ days' work for a Sapper painter	6d
TOTAL COST	£4 0s 2d

The possible origin of the Blanshard Pontoon is mentioned in Major General Sir Louis Jackson's book *One of Wellington's Staff Officers*. Apparently a Colonel William Stavely, who was the staff officer in question and an officer of the Royal Staff Corps, was ordered to Mauritius, with his company, in 1821. He assumed various appointments in the Island, including a year spent as Governor, and remained there for twenty five years. He did not forget his experiences in the Peninsular Campaign, however, and amongst his other activities invented a light infantry bridge consisting of metal cylinders with attachments to which a superstructure could be fitted. He showed his design to Blanshard, whilst he was on duty on the island, and later claimed that Blanshard subsequently took his drawings back to England and got the design adopted under his own name. The full truth of the matter will never be known, but no doubt Stavely's ideas had considerable influence on the final design developed by Blanshard, and the ideas of both men probably owed much to the concept for a cylindrical pontoon experimented with by Colleton. Time and time again in the development of equipment bridging the old adage that 'Every invention has its pedigree' rings true.

Whether or not this story is true, Blanshard was an inventor in his own right and later invented a very ingenious drawbridge. This used the suspension principle and was used in Bermuda for the passage of ditches surrounding fortified places. The roadway consisted of rectangular panels hinged together laterally and supported by two chains, one above the other and connected by vertical iron rods. The ends of the chains were connected to windlasses, by which means the roadway could be raised into position or lowered to the bottom of the ditch.

Equipments of our Allies and Enemies

Although this book tells the story of the British military bridging equipments, it is worthwhile reviewing briefly the equipments of some of our European neighbours before and during what was a time of continual development. The **Dutch** were perhaps the first nation to adopt small boats or pontoons for use in military bridging. During the Thirty Years War (1618 - 1648) the Dutch used flat-bottom pontoons, with near vertical sides and with 45° slightly tapered bows. The pontoons were built with timber frames and were clad with iron plate, either painted or tin-coated. This type of pontoon was adopted by the French, who are said to have had a complete pontoon train of such equipment in 1672. The **French** also used timber-framed pontoons clad in leather or waxed canvas, and later in copper. However, just before the Revolution of 1789 the French adopted a much larger pontoon, named after its proposer as the **Bateau Gribeauval**. This pontoon was some 36ft long and nearly 7ft wide; weighing nearly 2 tons, it could carry fifty to sixty men across a river and was used by Napoleon to cross the Danube in 1809. The **Bateau Militaire** was adopted by the French in 1829 and a version of the pontoon was used by the American Army from 1858 until well into the twentieth century. (Figure 2.10). The pontoon had a

Figure 2.10. *The modified French Bateau Militaire adopted by the United States military service, circa 1865.* (Military Bridges by H Haupt, 1864).

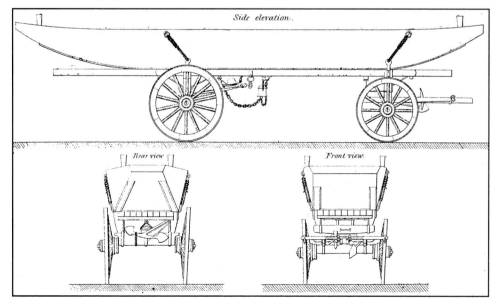

length of 31ft and width of 4ft 7in, rather smaller than the Bateau Gribeauval, and weighed only 1650lb. It was framed in oak with a cladding of fir planks, and the prows were curved, rather like those of a canoe.

The Russians favoured a pontoon covered with canvas. (Figure 2.11). The 1759 design of one Captain Andrei Nemoy of the Imperial Russian Army was for a pontoon constructed in the form of a flat-bottomed punt, about 21ft long, 5ft wide and rectangular in cross-

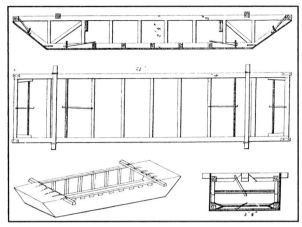

Figure 2.11. The Russian pontoon of 1759, which remained in service for 150 years. (Military Bridges by H Haupt, 1864).

section; the timber framework was so constructed that it could be dismantled and packed into a small wagon. The canvas cover was transported rolled and both sides were treated with a composition concocted from hemp-seed oil, loam, India Rubber, soot, bees-wax and flour; the canvas was brought up over the sides of the timber frame and secured to the top transoms. The equipment was used operationally, notably during the Battle of Eylau in 1807, during Napoleon's advance into Prussia, and remained in service in the Russian Army until 1909.

The Austrian Army made use of flat-bottomed wooden pontoons similar in form to those used by the French. However, in 1827 Captain Baron K Von

Figure 2.12. The bow section of the Austrian Birago Pontoon. (Proceedings of the RE Committee, 1887).

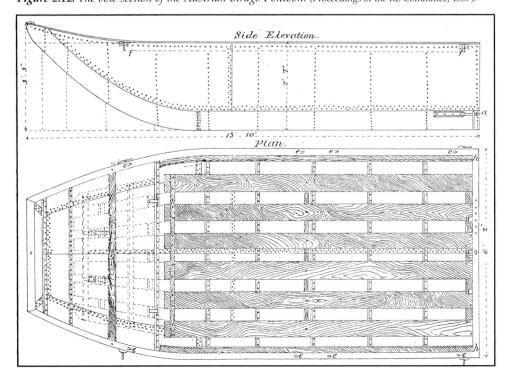

Birago (later to become a Brigadier and Chief Officer of the Royal and Imperial Austrian Army Engineer Corps) put forward his idea for producing a pontoon in parts that could be joined together on the bridge site to produce a pontoon pier. The idea was suggested to solve the problem of transporting the long and bulky pontoons necessary to produce a bridge of reasonable capacity. His pontoons were trapezoidal in section, the centre sections being 11ft 6in long and the bow sections 15ft long. (Figure 2.12)   Pontoon piers could be formed by using two bow sections connected stern to stern, or two bow sections with centre sections connected between them. The idea of joining two pontoons together, stern to stern, was of course first proposed by Pasley some years earlier, but the Birago Pontoon was the true forerunner of the bipartite and tripartite pontoon piers used to this day. The pontoon was adopted by the Austrian Army in 1841; initially clad in timber, the pontoons were subsequently clad in 1mm thick boiler-plate and later still in steel. Birago also designed a trestle for use with the Austrian Army and the Birago Trestle was later adopted by the British Army, remaining in service until the end of the century; the trestle is discussed further in the next chapter.

Two Unsuccessful Proposals

The **Forbes or Equilateral Pontoon** was proposed in about 1840 by Sergeant Major Forbes of the Royal Sappers and Miners. It was a variation on the cylindrical pontoon, the cross-section consisting of three sectors of cylinders arranged as the side of an equilateral triangle; the cylindrical portions of the pontoon thus met in three edges parallel to the pontoon axis and the ends consisted of three curved surfaces corresponding to the sides of the pontoon and meeting at a point. Whichever side of the pontoon was uppermost, a boat-like section was presented to the water, the cross-section meaning that under increased loading the horizontal section at water level also increased; in addition a broad deck was available on which to fix the superstructure. During two years of extensive trials at Chatham the Equilateral Pontoon proved difficult to manage when compared with the cylindrical Blanshard Pontoon, and eventually the idea was abandoned.

A second unsuccessful pontoon was the **Fowke's Pontoon**, worthy of mention more for the importance of the inventor than the invention. Captain Francis Fowke joined the Royal Engineers in 1842 and was a product of Pasley's School of Architecture at Chatham. He demonstrated great inventive powers, his inventions including a portable military fire engine, a collapsible camera and a portable bath. His work in the architectural and engineering field, however, was outstanding, his many achievements including the design of the interior of the Dublin National Gallery, the South Kensington Museum, the Museum of Science and Art in Edinburgh, and the outline design for the Albert Hall in London. Unfortunately he died in 1865, from overwork, before detailed planning of the Albert Hall could be completed. Fowke's design for a pontoon in 1858 was for a 23ft long, 4ft 6in wide collapsible boat, timber-framed and canvas-covered. It was not adopted in the United Kingdom, although it did meet with some success in America, and was undoubtedly the forerunner of the highly successful Folding Boat Equipment of the 1920s, used extensively during the Second World War.

Inflatable Pontoons

Experiments with inflatable boats and pontoons have been carried out from as early as 1830, when a Lieutenant Blaydes, of the 81st Regiment, produced a model of such a pontoon in the form of a canoe. Blaydes was at the time a student at the Royal Military College, Sandhurst, and his model canoe, with airtight compartments, was made from canvas impregnated with India Rubber. Experiments in the United States were very much more advanced, however, and from an article published in 1849, describing a system of military bridging using India Rubber pontoons, it appears that a Captain Lane of the United States Army had built a 350ft long experimental bridge across the deep and rapid River Tallapoosa in Alabama in 1836. A floating pier using inflatable pontoons was presented to a US Army Board of Officers in 1839 by a Mr Armstrong, each pier consisting of three cylindrical pontoons, each 18ft long and 18in in diameter when inflated. The pontoons were made from two layers of strong canvas, impregnated with a solution of India Rubber, strips of the same material being used to attach the three pontoons together to form a pier. Two such piers, with a timber deck some

Figure 2.13. Colonel Cullum's India Rubber Pontoon Bridge. (Military Bridges by H Haupt, 1864).

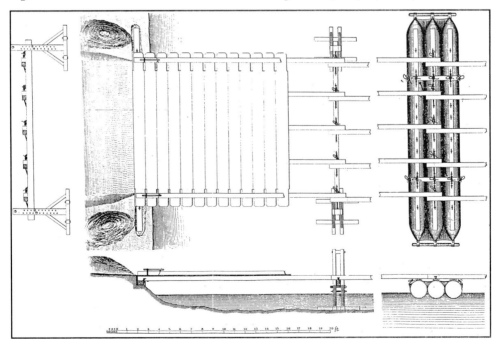

18ft long by 9ft wide, could carry a 6 pounder gun and fifty men with ease, and yet the pontoons could be folded up into a box about 3ft long, by 2ft, by 18in.

A version of the bridge, invented by Colonel George Cullum, US Army, used pontoons formed from three inflated cylinders, 20in in diameter, which were connected side by side to form a single boat 20ft long and 5ft wide. (Figure 2.13). Each cylinder was divided into three airtight compartments and was inflated by bellows. They were manufactured from two layers of strong cotton duck cloth, the outer layer being coated on both sides and the inner on its outer side only, with vulcanized or metallic rubber, a mixture of rubber, white lead and sulphur discovered by Charles Goodyear in 1839. The three cylinder pontoons were anchored at 18ft centres to form bridge or could be formed into rafts, a great advantage being that the pontoons and cordage for a 350ft bridge could be carried in a single wagon. Pontoons of this type were manufactured for use by the US Army during the war against Mexico in 1846-48, although they were not in fact used operationally. The bridging trains formed for the Mexican War remained in service for a dozen years or so, by which time, however, the vulcanizing had begun to degenerate, badly affecting the canvas.

Some Russian equipment was purchased and used by the Union Army in the American Civil War of 1861-65, (Figure 2.14). However, as a result of experience during the war, the version of the French Bateau Militaire previously mentioned was chosen to replace the by now unserviceable inflatable pontoon bridge. The Army Engineers of the Northern States much preferred this new equipment and the wooden pontoons were used to build what proved to be the longest operational floating bridge built since Xerxes' crossing of the Hellespont in 480BC. The bridge, across the River James, was

Figure 2.14. *Russian equipment used during the crossing of the Rapidan by the Army of the Potomac in 1864, under command of General Meade.*

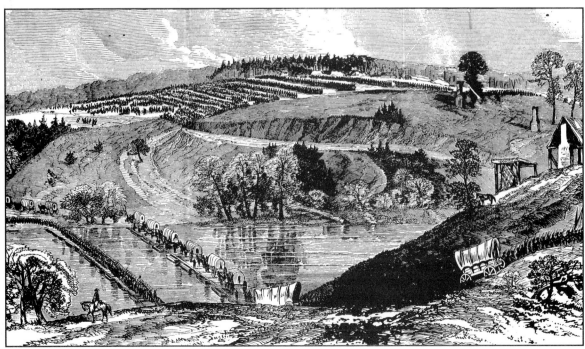

constructed using 101 pontoons and had a total length of 2170ft, a length for an equipment bridge that was not exceeded until 21 Army Group bridged the River Maas in 1945. For forty hours the bridge was crossed by Grant's Union Army of the Potomac in a continuous stream of infantry, artillery and wagons stretching for some fifty miles.

Nearly a hundred years after the experiments with their earlier equipment the American Army once again made use of inflatable pontoons, in their Steel Treadway Bridge - M2 (not to be confused with the German Amphibious Bridge - M2 of the 1970s). The M2 was extensively used during the Second World War and was considered by many to be the best floating assault bridge used by any nation during the war.

As far as Britain was concerned, experiments were carried out at Chatham on India Rubber pontoons in about 1850 and indicated that in certain circumstances they would be of great use. A raft formed from two pontoons, each of three inflated cylinders, successfully carried a 12 pounder gun and twenty soldiers, as well as the rowers, and such a raft was used operationally, with success, to cross rivers in the Cape of Good Hope. During the Crimean War, considered in more detail in the next chapter, the equipment assembled for use by A Troop of the Engineer Train did include ten small India Rubber boats of unknown type, but no great interest was taken in the use of inflatable pontoons until the turn of the century, when the Air Raft Equipment, discussed in Chapter 4, came into service.

The Afghanistan Campaign of 1839

With the end of the Napoleonic Wars in 1815, Europe experienced forty years of comparative peace, a peace disrupted by the outbreak of the Crimean War in 1854. Britain, however, was engaged in a number of minor wars and campaigns in India during this period, of which the Afghanistan Campaign and the Sikh Wars are perhaps typical,

Very little bridging equipment was held by the British in India during the early Nineteenth Century. In the main this was because of the difficulties of transporting such equipment across difficult terrain in sufficient quantities needed to cross the many large rivers encountered, rivers liable to severe flooding in the monsoon season. The usual practice for crossing major water obstacles was by use of small ferries, built with two or more local boats; on occasions the ferries or rafts would be joined together to form a bridge. A good example of this was provided by the bridging of the Indus at Bukkur during the advance of the British Army into Afghanistan in 1839. At Bukkur the river breaks into two channels, forming an island on which the town stands. Two bridges were therefore built, that in the western channel being 570ft long and that in the eastern channel 1050ft long. The former was built using nineteen local boats, or zoraks, whilst the latter used fifty-five zoraks. The building of the bridges was far from easy; the current at one point reached a speed of 5 feet per second, and in places the riverbed proved to be of solid rock, which caused problems with the anchorages for the boats. The operation was a success, however, and within four days of its completion two infantry brigades and a cavalry brigade crossed the bridge, together with a battery of 9 pounders; on the last day 2000 horses and 5500 camels crossed without incident. A full account of the building of the bridges is given in Volume IV of the *Professional Papers of the Royal Engineers.*

The Sikh Wars of 1845 to 1849

During the First Sikh War of 1845-46 the shortage of bridging equipment was sorely felt. The Sikh invasion across the River Sutlej in North-West India rendered a British counter-invasion inevitable, but all the local boats on the river were in the hands of the enemy or had been sunk by them. The Governor-General therefore ordered a fleet of sixty boats to be built in Bombay, some to be armed with light cannon and all to be equipped with the materials necessary for the building of a bridge. The boats were eventually tracked up the Rivers Indus and Sutlej to Ferozepore. A Bridging Train of twenty-eight Pasley Pontoons was available, but the pontoons proved far from satisfactory; much of the woodwork had become badly warped by the tropical sun and there was great difficulty in connecting up the timber decking and baulks to form the fourteen rafts that the Train could produce. In fact it was found that the whole Train, which required some 250 bullocks to pull the wagons, produced the same rafting capacity as a couple of local zoraks or chuppoos, which needed but four local boatmen to operate the rafts, compared with the 100 trained Sappers needed to operate the Pasley rafts. Nevertheless in early 1846 a bridgehead consisting of six regiments of native infantry and a troop of horse artillery was established on the far bank of the river, making use of the fourteen Pasley rafts and seven chuppoos which had been raised and repaired.

Work on the bridge started the following day. A shear line was passed to a pontoon raft anchored in midstream and the boats that had been brought up from Bombay were warped out and anchored into position, one by one. A second line was now passed to the far bank and the remaining boats were passed from stern to stern of those already placed, before being warped into final position. The twenty-one boats forming the bridge were moored at 26ft centres and were progressively connected by heavy baulks, bolted and keyed in place, as each boat was positioned. The decking was also laid progressively and early the next day the bridge was completed, the decking having been covered with brushwood and earth. For the next four days a continual procession of troops, camels, carts, ponies, camp followers and even elephants crossed. A second bridge was built, 70 yards below the first, and both bridges were used for the crossing of the heavy artillery. The first bridge was then dismantled and the boats used to build a bridge nine miles up the river at Nuggar. Both bridges remained in position for some time and played a very important part in the successful conclusion of the war.

During the Second Sikh War of 1848-49 the Bridging Train proved a little more useful. After a defeat at Gujerat in February 1849 the Sikhs retreated across the River Jhelum and burnt all the local boats. Whilst waiting for the Bridging Train to arrive, a strong British force crossed the river by fording five parallel streams of the river some 8 miles above the town of Jhelum. A bridge was needed, however, in order to cross the heavy guns and stores, but the river was in flood and at Jhelum was some 1200ft wide; this was too wide to bridge and crossing by pontoon rafts would have been unacceptably slow. However, the Train Commander, Lieutenant Crommellin, Bengal Engineers, ascertained that only one of the five fords previously used had become impassable by the flooding of the river. He therefore decided to build his bridge at the site of this ford, where the branch of the river was only 300ft wide. In the event fourteen rafts were built near Jhelum and tracked down river to the bridge site. After three of the rafts had been anchored into position on the home bank, the fourth could not be held and was lost downstream. An unsuccessful attempt was then made to build by booming out, adding rafts at the shore end. Rafts were now dropped below the bridge and an effort made, by rowing and hauling, to bring them into bridge against the current. Eventually six rafts had been connected up on the home bank in this way and a further five were placed in position, with difficulty, on the far bank. A large flat-bottomed native boat was then obtained and, securely anchored to two large stone-filled cradles, was dropped downstream into position between the two ends of the bridge. The bridge was completed by hauling two more rafts into position either side of the native boat, which was then decked over. The copper-clad Pasley Pontoons were in poor condition and leaked considerably; indeed, during the passage of heavy ammunition carts, the decking of the bridge was occasionally under water. Nevertheless the bridge fulfilled its purpose and the pursuit of the Sikhs continued apace.

Mrs Fitzherbert and a Brighton Bridge.

This chapter has chronicled many of the wars fought by the British Army up until the mid-Nineteenth Century, and therefore, to restore the balance in some small way, a light-hearted bridging anecdote quoted in Volume II of the *Corps History* is perhaps worth repeating.

Soon after the formation of the new Corps of Military Artificers in 1787, a detachment of a Company of Artificers was employed in a training exercise at Brighton. Whilst they were bridging a small stream, Mrs Fitzherbert, wife of the Prince of Wales happened to pass by, and was intrigued with what she saw. She was so impressed that she noted the name of the NCO in charge, a Sergeant John Johnson, and left with him sufficient money for each man to receive an extra day's pay. Soon afterwards Sergeant Johnson received a commission in the 29th Foot and it was always considered that his promotion was due to Mrs Fitzherbert's interest in the bridging operation.

CHAPTER THREE

The Late Nineteenth Century

The Crimean War

During the second half of the Nineteenth Century Britain became engaged in one war after the other, in what is now known as the Middle East, in China, India and in Africa. Some of the wars and campaigns involving more interesting bridging operations are mentioned in this chapter, but others include the wars in South Africa through from 1847 to 1885, the China War of 1857-60, the war in Egypt of 1882-85, the war in Burma of 1885 and the Sudan Campaigns of 1885-1899.

The Crimean War with Russia broke out in 1854. After so many years of comparative peace in Europe, the lessons of the Peninsular War had been forgotten and the British Army found itself ill-prepared and equipped to go to war. The training of the Corps was of a high standard, thanks to the zeal of Pasley at Chatham, but field engineer equipment was in a poor state indeed, despite the efforts of General Sir John Burgoyne to obtain funds to provide transport and equipment for the Corps. It is outside the scope of this book to examine this situation in any detail, but at an early stage it was felt essential to have a Bridging Train with the Army in the Crimea and soon after the arrival of the first two Companies of Sappers, the 7th and 11th, a third Company, the 10th, under Captain Bent, was earmarked to form the Train. The Company embarked for Varna, the British base on the Black Sea coast, in May. It was equipped with Blanshard Pontoons, although Lord Raglan was very pleased when Burgoyne, then his second in command, agreed that a trial should be made of the 'Emperor's Pontoon, the construction of which would be attended with no great expense', the Emperor's Pontoon being the timber pontoon of the French Army.

In the following July a detachment of the 10th Company was sent to Rustchuk, at the request of Omar Pasha, the Turkish leader, to build a bridge across the Danube. French pontonniers and British sailors accompanied the party, but transport problems resulted in the 130 mile journey from Varna taking no less than five days to complete. On arrival at Rustchuk the party was joined by Captain Bent who took charge of the bridging operations. Two bridges were built; the first was a bridge of boats, built across the main stream of the river and some 2700ft long. It was a very substantial bridge, the boats being anchored at 40ft spacing, centre to centre, and with a very solid decking, the roadway being over 18ft wide. The bridge was thus able to carry the heaviest loads and was obviously meant to remain in place for some time. Construction was completed in eight days and the bridge, the

41

major bridge built during the war, was opened by Omar Pasha in person, who complimented officers and men on their excellent work.

The second bridge was built across a creek to an island in the Danube, and was only 450ft long. This bridge was a trestle bridge, a type of bridge construction not previously mentioned in this book. The simplest bridging trestle consists merely of a transom, which supports the decking of the bridge, and two or more legs, which support the transom. The trestle legs may be vertical or splayed, and may rest upon the ground, upon a groundsill, or may be pile-driven into the ground. The trestle may be guyed to hold it in a vertical position, or it may be built as a twin trestle, the two halves of the trestle being connected so that they support each other. Trestle bridging is particularly suited for use in shallow rivers, where the river bed is sound and firm, but is of course of little use in deep, fast-flowing rivers, liable to sudden flood. Trestles may be improvised, using local timbers, as was undoubtedly the case with this bridge across the Danube. They can, however, form part of a wet-bridging equipment, and are then used to build the landing bays to which rafts could be successively connected to form the bridge. An example of such a trestle is that which formed part of the Modified French Pontoon Equipment used during the American Civil War; this trestle had splayed legs from which the transom was suspended by chains, so that its level and height could easily be adjusted. The trestle used with the American Inflatable Pontoon Bridge, mentioned in the previous chapter, had vertical legs in which pinholes were drilled so that, once again, the level and height of the transom could be adjusted.

The Engineer Train

Mention has already been made of the poor state of equipment in the Army at the beginning of the Crimean War. In particular the detachments of Royal Sappers and Miners serving with the several Infantry Divisions were limited not only in the necessary basic engineer stores but also in the means to carry such stores as they did have. Efforts were made to improve the situation and eventually sanction was given for the raising of a troop, within the Corps, solely for the purpose of caring for and transporting engineer stores. The unit set up for this task was the 23rd, or Driver Company, of the Royal Sappers and Miners, but its name was soon changed to that of A Troop, Royal Engineer Train. In the event peace was proclaimed in the spring of 1856, before the Troop got farther than Constantinople (now Istanbul), and it was recalled with the rest of the army during the summer. The Troop, with its men, horses and wagons, but no proper stores establishment, now languished at Aldershot, employed on general transport duties. A wide range of equipment had been assembled for use by the Troop, under the direction of Major J Stokes RE, CRE for the Turkish Contingent. The stores included entrenching tools, artificers tool kits, two bridges, each consisting of thirty-two Blanshard Pontoons and ten small India Rubber boats. The majority of the stores were absorbed into the vast mass of general stores returned to England after the war and disposed of as rapidly as possible. Most of the Engineer stores ended up at the Royal Engineer Establishment at Chatham and a golden opportunity to set up a permanent Engineer Park was thus lost to the Corps.

Luckily the matter did not rest there and over the next few years various committees and reports considered the whole question of supply and transport of ammunition and stores for an army in the field. General Burgoyne, now Inspector General of Fortifications, took a very active part in these deliberations. His memorandum to the Parliamentary Under-Secretary of State for War, in November 1862, strongly advocated an Engineer Train with two troops, one to hold engineer field equipment and the second to hold pontoon equipment. Matters had dragged on for some time, but a report from America did much to bring matters to a head. General Franklin, in a report to a US Senate Committee considering the disaster at the Battle of Fredericksburg, when 10,000 men of the Federal Army were lost, killed, wounded and missing, said: 'I would like to impress as firmly upon the Committee, as it is impressed upon my mind, the fact that this whole disaster has resulted from the delay in the arrival of the pontoon bridges. Whoever is responsible for that delay, is responsible for all the disasters which have followed.'

The case for readily available and adequate military bridging could hardly have been put more succinctly and shortly afterwards Burgoyne won the day, authority being given for the permanent establishment of a proper Engineer Train. An order was issued in May 1863 for the development of the still-existing A Troop into a Pontoon Troop, and the addition to it of a B Troop which would hold field equipment for the Sappers. In addition a Depot Detachment was set up to maintain both troops. The establishment of the Pontoon Troop was set at four officers and 207 NCOs, Sappers and Drivers, now of course all members of the Corps of Royal Engineers, since the Corps of Royal Sappers and Miners had been incorporated into the Corps of Royal Engineers in October 1856, after the Crimean War. The bridging equipment consisted of twenty-four of the improved Blanshard or Caffin Pontoons, together with the baulks, chesses, anchors, oars and so forth necessary to build a floating bridge, together with twelve heavy pontoon wagons and eight other assorted wagons.

The Indian Mutiny of 1857-1859

No sooner was peace declared in the Crimean War than Britain was faced with the Mutiny in India. There were a number of minor bridging operations during the Indian Mutiny, although none were particularly noteworthy. The bridging of the River Gumti, prior to the recapture of Lucknow, should be mentioned, however, because it was achieved by the building of two cask bridges, another type of bridging not previously mentioned in this book. (Figure 3.1). Bridging by this method was favoured by many foreign armies and is recorded as having been used by the Emperor Maximinus to cross the River Isonzo during his march on Rome as early as 237 AD. A great number of casks or barrels accompanied most armies, being used not only to carry and store water but also meat and victuals. Once the heads had been removed to take out the contents, a great number of these water-tight casks were thrown away or used for fuel. In fact these casks were a very valuable bridging expedient and it was a comparatively easy matter to form them into rafts, arranging them perhaps in three or four rows, each of ten or twelve casks. Such rafts, with suitable timber decking, had a considerable load capacity and could be connected together to form a bridge. In preparation for the attack on Lucknow, 4 and 23 Companies Royal Engineers were joined with a Company of Madras Sappers and Miners and one of Bengal Sappers to form an Engineer Brigade. On the night of 4 March 1858 two cask bridges were built across the Gumti by the Brigade; it was a very difficult and troublesome operation, but the work was completed by the afternoon of the 5th and General Outram's forces crossed the river on the

Figure 3.1. A raft made of casks being floated-in beside an incomplete cask bridge.

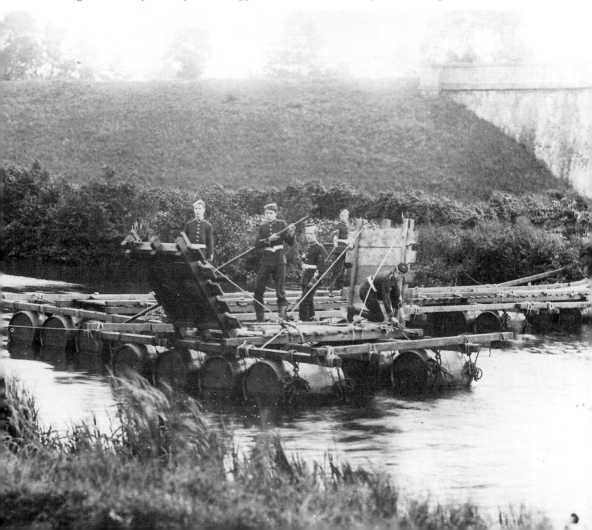

6th, although it was not until the 21st that fighting finally ceased.

The previous July the crossing of the mighty Ganges, into the District of Oude, had proved a most difficult and hazardous undertaking. The river was some 1,600 yards wide at the crossing point and its waters were swollen by monsoon rains. The existing bridge of boats had been broken up by the rebels and the parts scattered, whilst all ferryboats had been destroyed or removed. Fortunately a small steamer, the Berhampooter, manned by Madras Fusiliers under the command of Captain Spurgin, was on hand and managed to round up twenty or so small boats. With these a small force of Highlanders was put across the river in the early hours of 21 July, the bridgehead being slowly built up on successive nights. During the crossing the engines of the steamer proved inadequate to cope with the force of the current and dependence was placed entirely upon the boats, despite the fact that in some cases they took up to eight hours to complete the two mile round trip.

Berthon's Boat

It was about this time that a collapsible boat was invented by the Reverend E L Berthon, of Fareham, Hampshire. The boat consisted of a timber framework, lined within and covered without with strong canvas, which was impregnated with marine glue or vulcanized India Rubber. The framework consisted of six longitudinal timbers and a keel piece, connected together at the ends, which could be folded out and kept in position by diagonal trusses. When collapsed the longitudinal timbers were packed side by side, with the canvas covering folded between them. The boat was large and heavy, being 20ft long, 9ft wide and 4½ft deep, and was capable of carrying fifty to sixty men. Baulks could be fitted to the gunwales to form a bridge, with the boats spaced at 20ft centres. Berthon's model of his boat gained a prize at the Great Exhibition of 1851, but the weight of the full-size boat precluded it from adaptation for military purposes.

However, Berthon patented various others forms of his collapsible boat and a smaller version of the boat was adapted as the **Light Infantry Bridge Equipment**. (Figure 3.2). This new boat, also known

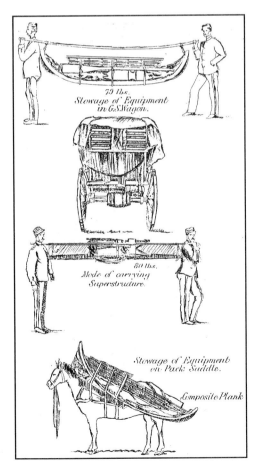

Figure 3.2. The Light Infantry Bridge Equipment, invented by the Reverend E L Berthon.
(Instructions in Military Engineering, Vol I Part 3 - 1887).

as Berthon's Boat and manufactured at the Berthon Boat Works, was a mere 9ft long. A small two-legged trestle fitted into mortise holes cut in the bottom members of the boat, and was guyed to the gunwales; a roadway, consisting of composite planks, 8ft long and 18in wide, could then be laid between adjacent boats to form a light bridge. The folded boat could conveniently be carried by two men, slung between them on a pole, the deck unit, trestle, anchor, etc, forming another similar load; the equipment could also be carried as a pack load, one horse carrying a complete bay. It remained in service until the 1890s.

The Abyssinian War

By 1867 the Emperor Theodore of Abyssinia had for some time been holding prisoner the British Consul and a number of missionaries in his mountain stronghold at Magdala; this was in retaliation for the British refusal to join with him in a campaign against the Turks. In order to secure the release of

Figure 3.3. A sketch by Lieut F W Graham of the iron girder rail bridge built across the Koomaylee Torrent.

46

the prisoners the British Government dispatched an expeditionary force to Abyssinia in late 1867, under the command of the Engineer General, Sir Robert Napier. The war that followed deserves brief mention because it was essentially an engineers' war and involved, for the first time, railway bridging. The problems of the campaign were not military but logistic, in short, how to convey an army, with its guns and stores, nearly 400 miles from the Red Sea coast across a desert to the mountain fortress of Magdala. Eventually the decision was made to build a railway from the base port, set up at Zoolla, to run across the desert to a base camp at the edge of the foothills at Koomaylee, after which a road would be built to Magdala. The expeditionary force was a combined British and Indian Army force; most of the railway construction was carried out by Indian Army troops under the command of Captain Darrah RE, and 10 Company Royal Engineers took an active part in building the roads and supplying engineer support.

The 5½ft gauge railway line ran for 10½ miles, together with another 1½ miles of sidings and loop lines. The work was beset with difficulties; the six engines supplied were already old and worn out, and different sizes of rail had been sent from India. The line rose some 350ft and eight iron-girder bridges had to be built to cross dried river beds at various points, the largest bridge being of three 20ft spans with a clearance above the river bed of 12ft. (Figure 3.3). From the railhead at Koomaylee a 63 mile road was built, rising to a height of 7400ft; another 40 miles of cart track gave way to a track suitable only for elephants and mules. The railway line carried considerable quantities of stores and troops and did much to bring the campaign to a successful conclusion, with the fall of Magdala in April 1868. On his return to England Napier was thanked by Parliament and was granted a peerage as Lord Napier of Magdala; he was promoted to the rank of Field Marshal in 1883.

The Blood Pontoon

By the 1860s many of the original Blanshard Pontoons, which had been adopted in 1836, were in very poor condition and needed replacing. Despite the improvements of the Caffin Pontoons, a lack of buoyancy inherent with the cylindrical design and some unsteadiness when in bridge gave rise to concern. The opportunity was therefore taken to review all the equipment of the Train and in 1867 officers of the Corps were invited to submit ideas for a new pontoon. A young Lieutenant, Bindon Blood, later to become General Sir Bindon Blood, had been posted to A Troop in 1865 and his proposals for a new pontoon were accepted for trials. Blood was posted to Chatham to carry out the manufacture and subsequent trials of his pontoon, which was finally adopted for service in 1870.

Blood's new timber-framed and timber and canvas-covered pontoon in fact completed the design circle of pontoons used by the British Army and

Figure 3.4. A model of the Blood Pontoon, held in the Royal Engineer Museum at Chatham.

returned to the open type of construction of the Tin Pontoons used in the Napoleonic Wars and before, although in this case each end of the pontoon was decked over for about 3ft 6in. (Figure 3.4 and Appendix B). An innovation of the design was the introduction of a central saddle beam; this carried the ends of the baulks spanning between the pontoons, in preference to the gunwale loading used in previous designs. The idea arose after a visit by Engineer officers, arranged by the Royal Engineer Committee, to the leading military nations of Europe to examine the floating bridge equipments used in their armies, when it was noted that the Austrians used such a saddle beam, whilst the French preferred gunwale loading. In Blood's design the saddle beam supported a pontoon saddle to receive the ends of the long baulks which spanned between the pontoons in bridge. This use of the saddle beam, which could be removed when the pontoon was to be used as a boat to ferry troops or stores, introduced a flexibility into the bridge that was lacking when the baulks were fixed directly to the pontoon gunwales.

After completion of the trials on his pontoon at Chatham (Figure 3.5), Blood was posted to India. There he found the Pasley Pontoon, long discarded in England, still in service. However, in 1875 he took part in extensive manoeuvres arranged by Lord Napier of Magdala, the Commander-in-Chief, for the visit of the Prince of Wales to India, and he was

48

***Figure 3.5.** Trials with the new Blood Pontoon in progress at the SME.* (RE Library).

able to demonstrate the new and recently arrived Blood Pontoons to the Prince during this visit.

A Royal Bridge

The prowess of A Troop was royally demonstrated at Windsor in 1872, on the occasion of a Royal Review in honour of a state visit by the Shah of Persia. Their task was to build a 250ft bridge across the Thames at Datchet, and the Troop marched from Chatham to Windsor, taking four days so to do and encamping on route at Woolwich, Wimbledon and Hounslow. A steep bank slope on the Windsor side of the river necessitated the cutting of an approach ramp, whilst on the Datchet bank the river gradually shoaled and a pier of fascines and wooden stakes had to be built.

On 24 June Queen Victoria arrived to watch the construction of the bridge proper, and on arrival of Her Majesty the order was given to 'Boom out Bridge in Double Time'. Unloading of the pontoon wagons and booming out now proceeded simultaneously, and the bridge was completed in just 22 minutes. Eighteen wagons were unloaded, fifteen of the new Blood Pontoons being used in bridge, two pontoons being used as anchor boats, and one being kept in readiness as a spare. Five battalions of Foot Guards crossed the bridge, with officers mounted, and after they had recrossed in the evening a 45ft cut was made in the bridge to reopen the river for river traffic.

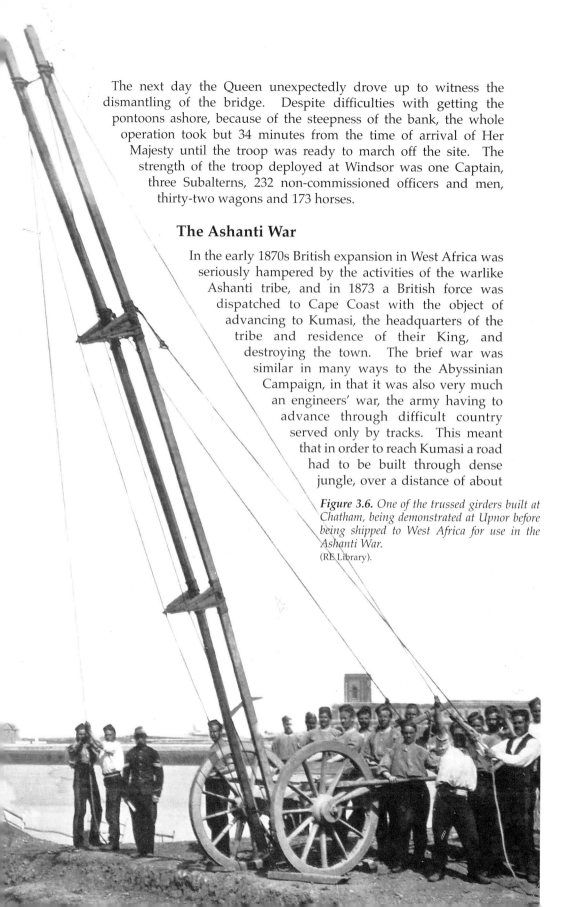

The next day the Queen unexpectedly drove up to witness the dismantling of the bridge. Despite difficulties with getting the pontoons ashore, because of the steepness of the bank, the whole operation took but 34 minutes from the time of arrival of Her Majesty until the troop was ready to march off the site. The strength of the troop deployed at Windsor was one Captain, three Subalterns, 232 non-commissioned officers and men, thirty-two wagons and 173 horses.

The Ashanti War

In the early 1870s British expansion in West Africa was seriously hampered by the activities of the warlike Ashanti tribe, and in 1873 a British force was dispatched to Cape Coast with the object of advancing to Kumasi, the headquarters of the tribe and residence of their King, and destroying the town. The brief war was similar in many ways to the Abyssinian Campaign, in that it was also very much an engineers' war, the army having to advance through difficult country served only by tracks. This meant that in order to reach Kumasi a road had to be built through dense jungle, over a distance of about

Figure 3.6. One of the trussed girders built at Chatham, being demonstrated at Upnor before being shipped to West Africa for use in the Ashanti War.
(RE Library).

160 miles. In addition to the problems of building defended staging posts for the troops along the road and laying a telegraph line along a good length of it, bridges had to be built to cross the many streams and rivers. For the first time the Corps employed the new Steam Sapper, much to the astonishment of the natives. This new toy of the Corps was used to operate a saw bench to cut up the large quantities of timber needed for the bridges and also to haul heavy loads inland from the beachhead.

The major bridge constructed was over the River Prah. At the crossing point the river was some 190ft wide and the outdated Blanshard pontoons that were available were too few in number to produce an adequate crossing. Twelve trussed girders had previously been manufactured at Chatham and these proved most suitable. (Figure 3.6). The metal girders were 30ft long but for ease of transport had been made in three 10ft sections that could be bolted together in the field. Each girder consisted of two beams, connected side by side at about 2ft centres; tension rods and queen posts were fixed underneath to improve the load capacity. Timber chesses were produced locally to give a trackway 2ft 6in wide and two such trackways, side by side with a suitable gap between them, could carry a 9 pounder gun. The girders were supported on timber cribs, which were built on the shore from logs placed lengthways and breadthwise, and had a grated bottom to retain the sandbags with which they were filled after being floated into position. Timber transoms were then added to support the ends of the trussed girders, and any additional girders needed to complete the span were made up on site.

The advance upon Kumasi continued and during the last stages the gallantry of Lieutenant Bell RE of 28th Field Company RE resulted in the award of the Victoria Cross. On 4 February 1874 the town was captured, the King's palace was blown up and the town fired. Withdrawal to the coast followed and the last of the Engineer forces embarked in early March.

The Demise of the Engineer Train

Further expansion of the Engineer Train had taken place in 1870, when a new troop, C Troop or the Telegraph Troop, was added, increasing the total strength of the Train to sixteen officers, 718 NCOs and men, and 362 horses. The unit, still under the command of a Captain, was now larger than a regiment, but further reorganization was to follow. A review of the United Kingdom Army envisaged the formation of Army Corps, each consisting of three Divisions. Four Field Companies of Engineers, each with their own field equipment, were to be attached to each Army Corps, one Company to be allotted to each Division and the fourth, together with a Field Park and a Pontoon Troop, to be attached to Corps Headquarters. The establishment of a Pontoon Troop was eventually fixed at twenty pontoon wagons, each carrying one Blood Pontoon and the superstructure for one bay of bridge, four wagons loaded with trestles and extra superstructure, and six store wagons; the Troop thus carried 300ft of pontoon bridge and 60ft of trestle bridge.

To effect this reorganization B Troop of the Engineer Train was split up into four sections and a Field Park, and one section was attached permanently to each of the Army Corps Field Companies. The changes were effected in 1877 and the title 'Train', which had been adopted at its first formation, was dropped. In 1884 C Troop was amalgamated with two Telegraph Companies to form a new Telegraph Battalion, and only A Troop, the Pontoon Troop, remained, to see service in Tel-el-Kebir, Egypt, later that year. It was here that they experienced considerable difficulties with the lack of buoyancy of the Blanshard Infantry Pontoons, by now obsolete but supplied because none of the new pontoons were available in store. In 1888 a second pontoon troop, a new B Troop, was raised, and a mounted detachment was organized for service with the Cavalry Division. In 1899, just prior to the South African War, the two troops joined to form a Bridging Battalion.

The manning of the Battalion is worthy of comment. The French Army had established a Corps of Pontonniers many years before, members of that Corps taking part in bridging operations across the Danube, with our 10th Company, during the Crimean War. The French example was noted and soon after the formation of the Pontoon Troop in 1856 it was decided that, while it would be officered from the Royal Engineer general list, the men should be specially enlisted, in order to ensure they would be physically capable of handling heavy pontoon equipment. The men of the unit were thus heavier and taller than most Sappers and indeed of soldiers of any Corps in the Army, except perhaps for the Guards. The special class of pontooniers enlisted for the Troop were sent straight to Aldershot for their training, most being enlisted as labourers but nevertheless receiving Engineer pay. Excellent work was done by these specially enlisted men during the South African War, but during the post-war reorganization of the early 1900s the class of pontooniers was abolished. An interesting sidelight concerned a sporting achievement of the Bridging Battalion, who in 1899 won no less than thirteen inter-service Tug of War championships, making full use of their pontooniers to defeat all opponents.

The Clauson or Mark II Pontoon

Meanwhile, experiments were carried out to improve the Blood pontoon and in 1883-4 a number of the pontoons were cut in half with the intention of providing greater flexibility in floating bridge construction, by combining complete and half pontoons in the one bridge. However in 1889 the British Army adopted a new pontoon, the invention of Lieutenant J E Clauson RE of A Troop. (Figure 3.7 and Appendix B). Clauson adopted the two-section principle used many years before in the Pasley Pontoon and then later in the design of the Austrian Birago Pontoon, to which his new pontoon showed considerable similarity. However, whereas Pasley used two identical sections which were connected together by lashings, Clauson used a bow

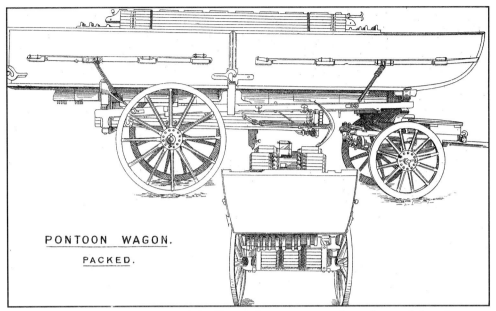

PONTOON WAGON.

PACKED.

Figure 3.7. *Bow and stern sections of the Clauson Pontoon connected together on their pack wagon.*
(Military Engineering (Provisional) Vol III - 1921).

section, with tapered bow and square stern, and a stern section with square ends, so that when the two sections were joined together by easily manipulated phosphor-bronze couplings, the complete pontoon had a tapered bow and square stern. *Military Engineering Part III - Military Bridging and the Use of Spars - 1901* refers to the new pontoon as the Mark II Pontoon; from this it can only be assumed that it had previously been decided to refer to the superseded Blood pontoon as the Mark I, although no record of this can be traced.

The Mark II Pontoon provided great flexibility of design, in that the equipment could be used in various combinations, according to the load to be carried, although in each case the pontoons remained at 15ft centres in bridge. For a Light Bridge, carrying infantry in file, bow and stern sections of pontoons were used separately, the superstructure being so arranged that a total length of bridge double that in normal use could be built. For the more normal Medium Bridge the two pontoon sections were joined together, and five baulks were used per bay, although nine were needed to support the chesses under especially concentrated loads such as gun wheels or elephants. To form a Heavy Bridge a tripartite pontoon was formed, using alternately one stern section between two bow sections, and then two stern sections with one bow section, so that all the pontoons sections were utilized in bridge; the Heavy Bridge also used nine baulks per bay. Both sections of the pontoon were undecked and were very manoeuvrable as a boat, when joined together, or when formed into a raft.

Special pontoon wagons carried either one complete pontoon or a bridging trestle, in both cases with 15ft of superstructure, the baulks and

Figure 3.8. Sappers training with the Clauson or Mark II Pontoon at Wouldham in 1914.

chesses being stowed in racks under the wagon body, so designed that they could be rapidly unloaded. The equipment was highly successful and was the main British pontoon bridge used during the First World War (Figure 3.8) and, with minor modification, was retained in service until 1924.

Bridging Trestles

For some time now bridging trestles had formed part of the equipment carried by the Pontoon Troop. A modified version of the **Birago Trestle** was initially used; this was based upon a trestle developed by Colonel Birago of the Austrian Army, of Birago Pontoon fame. (Figure 3.9 and Appendix B).

The Birago Trestle was replaced by the **Weldon Trestle** in the late 1890s. (Figure 3.10 and Appendix B). This new trestle was the invention of Colonel Weldon and incorporated pressed steel shoes which could be fitted to the bottom of each of the trestle legs. Height adjustment was made by differential tackles fixed to brackets at the top of each leg, and a lever strap was fitted to each end of the transom to keep the two trestle legs at right angles to the transom during height adjustment; in due course an improved

Figure 3.9. The modified Birago Trestle, used until the 1890s, and replaced by the Weldon Trestle. (Instructions in Military Engineering Vol I Part 3 - 1887).

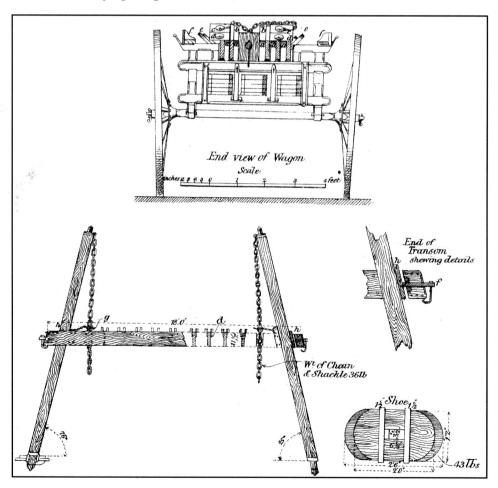

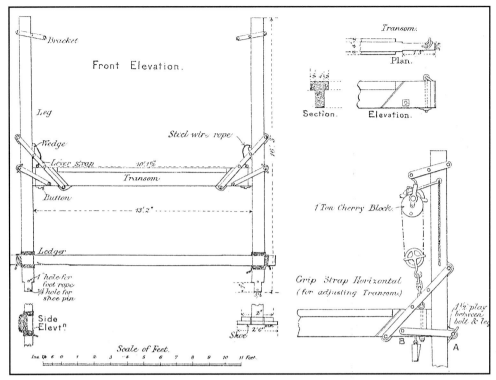

Figure 3.10. The Weldon Trestle, which remained in use until the 1920s. (Military Bridging and the use of Spars - 1894).

version of the strap was introduced, known as the **Marston Lever Strap**. The trestle proved very effective, either to form the landing bays of a pontoon bridge or to make use of the pontoon equipment superstructure to form a trestle bridge across a dry or wet gap. It was widely used during the First World War, known officially as the **Mark IV Trestle**, although still widely referred to as the Weldon Trestle; it is presumed that the Birago Trestle was considered to be the Mark I Trestle, the first version of the Weldon to be the Mark II and the Mark III and Mark IV Trestles slightly modified versions of the original. It remained in service until it was replaced by the Mark V Trestle in the 1920s.

The Light Bridge and Raft Equipment

A version of Berthon's Boat, adopted as the Light Infantry Bridge Equipment, has already been mentioned earlier. In the 1890s another version of the collapsible boat was introduced, designed for transport by mules or small carts and for use by the RE Troop. This version complied with the requirement for mule transportation by ensuring that no part of the equipment exceeded 6ft long, except for the 12ft road bearers and the 9ft sculls. (Figure 3.11). The 4ft 6in long bow and centre section boats were lashed together to form piers, and two 18ft piers were used to form a raft which could carry a 3 ton load such as a Horse Artillery gun, using channel-shaped skids to support the gun wheels. Shorter piers, formed from one bow and one centre section boat, were used to form a Light Infantry Bridge, improvising a roadway between the skids using baulks and planking.

Lock Bridges

Brief mention should be made of Lock Bridges, which were improvised bridges constructed from spars and timbers, and sometimes referred to as Frame Bridges. Bridges of this type could be used to replace demolished bridges where the abutments were still largely intact and could thus be used to support the feet of the timber frames forming the bridge. The form of construction was also suitable for use in mountainous country and was certainly used during the Peninsular Campaign. In the Single Lock Bridge, used for spans up to about 30ft, two such frames would be used, one seated at the foot of each abutment. (Figure 3.12). The frames were

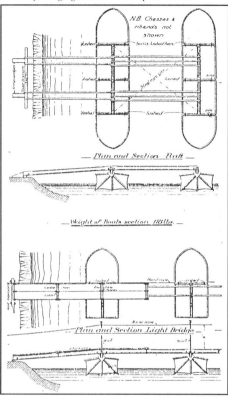

Figure 3.11. *The Light Bridge and Raft Equipment, using 4ft 6in long collapsible boats.* (Military Bridging and the use of Spars - 1901).

Figure 3.12. *The Single and Double Lock Bridge.* (Manual of Military Engineering - 1901.)

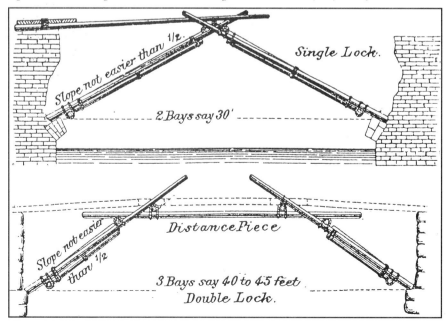

inclined at about 30° so that they interlocked at their tops; baulks would then be laid spanning from the top of each abutment to a single transom at the interlock of the two frames; chesses and ribands completed the bridge. For the Double Lock Bridge, used for spans up to about 45ft, the two inclined frames locked into a horizontal connecting frame, made up of distance pieces and cross transoms. A three span bridge was thus formed, which was again completed with baulks, chesses and ribands.

The South African War of 1899

In South Africa the British fought a war against the Zulus in 1879 and a war against the Boers in 1881, following the annexure of the Transvaal in 1878. A second war against the Boers broke out in October 1899, when the Boers declared war against the Government of South Africa; this was a war on a much larger scale than the First Boer War, with the deployment of a larger force of Engineers than had ever previously been deployed in any British campaign. In November A Pontoon Troop of the newly formed Bridging Battalion was dispatched to South Africa as part of an Army Corps, the strength of the Troop being supplemented in men and equipment. The Troop was equipped with thirty Clauson or Mark II Pontoons and twelve Weldon Trestles, which it had had made in Maritzburg; in addition the Field Companies were each equipped with two Mark II Pontoons and the superstructure to form a raft. In late November the remainder of the Bridging Battalion and all available pontoons were dispatched to the Cape, and in January 1900 authority was given for the raising of new C and D Pontoon Troops for the Battalion.

In October 1899, at an early stage of the war, Mafeking and then Kimberley had been besieged by the Boers. In November Ladysmith, which had become the most important military post in the Colony, was also besieged, but it was during the advance to secure the relief of Kimberley that one of the earliest bridging operations of the war took place. In late November 7 Field Company of the Royal Engineers pushed on toward the River Modder, endeavouring to secure the railway bridge before it could be destroyed by the Boers. Unfortunately they were too late, but the main body of the relief force managed to cross the river to the west of the bridge and the Engineers then devoted themselves to the building of a temporary bridge to replace that destroyed; this proved a difficult task and the bridge was not completed until 10 December.

Many other successful bridging operations were carried out during the war, the name of Major J L Irvine RE figuring prominently in the accounts. Irvine commanded A Troop of the Bridging Battalion, which was operating in the eastern area of South Africa, and typical of the exploits of the Troop is the account of the crossing of the River Tugela in mid-January 1900, during the advance to relieve Ladysmith. The proposed site, near Trichard's Drift, was a difficult one, with high banks and a swift current, but careful planning by Major Irvine ensured that all the required stores were to hand and the bridge was completed within three hours. Construction of a second bridge, for heavy traffic, was at once started, and this bridge was completed by the same evening. On 1 February A Troop built two more bridges over the Tugela, one on a very difficult site with banks between 30ft and 40ft high. A third bridge was built under heavy fire in three-quarters of an hour, eight Sappers being wounded. Later in the month, after the British Forces had withdrawn back across the Tugela, it became necessary once more to cross to the north bank of the river and Major Irvine selected a site about 300ft wide across which A Troop built a Heavy Bridge under constant artillery fire from the Boers. The infantry crossed and attacked the heights held by the enemy, fighting continuing for four days. It was then decided to move the bridge to a site further down the river, and so it was dismantled during the night of 26 February, carried with great difficulty over the hill and rebuilt on the new site in less than three hours on the morning of 27 February. The attack was then renewed and the Boers retreated, leaving the way clear for General Buller's forces to relieve Ladysmith on the following day. The steep banks of many of the South African rivers and streams precluded the use of pontoons and later in the campaign the pontoons of A Troop were withdrawn and replaced by special trestles designed by Major Irvine to suit the local conditions.

Meanwhile, Field Marshal Lord Roberts had arrived as Commander-in-Chief in South Africa and in the western zone of operations made preparation for an advance into the Orange Free State. This advance was to be made with a new Army Corps which included, in its Cavalry Division, the newly arrived C Troop of the Bridging Battalion, under the command of Captain G A Travers RE. Within five days the force had advanced across the Modder and after a rapid march relieved Kimberley on 15 February. (Figure 3.13). During Roberts' subsequent advance, C Troop were involved in a major crossing of the River Orange, at Norval's Pont, the original bridge having been destroyed by the Boers. At first light on 15 March 1000 troops were ferried across the river in pontoons to provide a covering force, extending in a semicircle some 1500 yards in radius from the proposed bridgehead. By 6.45am the first pontoons were in position and three hours later forty pontoons had been placed. At this point, however, the river was over 750ft wide, and C Troop were forced to make use of old Mark I, or Blood, drill pontoons shipped out from the SME because of the shortage of new bridging equipment in the UK. These old pontoons were at the head of the bridge and many leaked badly, to the extent that some had to be replaced, four trestle spans and 72ft of barrel piers being used to complete the 798ft bridge. The bridge was finally completed by 4.45 in the afternoon, with the help of 47 Fortress Company, enabling the British Forces to cross into the Orange Free State. After five days' continuous use it was dismantled and rebuilt at a more convenient point, 200 yards above Norval's Pont.

By now there was little resistance from the Boers, although for two years

Figure 3.13. A bridge across the River Modder, built by C Troop of the Bridging Battalion in February 1900, using Clauson Pontoons. (Boer War Museum).

guerilla warfare continued, during which time large numbers of blockhouses were built in an effort to contain the Boer commando. To facilitate movement of the convoys needed to resupply one of the blockhouse lines, Sapper improvisation was demonstrated in the building of a 120ft span suspension bridge over the River Rhenoster in November 1901. Twisted and doubled 2¾ in cables were use for the main suspension cables, and timber from local gum trees was used to make the transoms, roadbearers and anchorages. The bridge was built in 10ft bays, with eight baulks per bay, the roadway consisting of two layers of corrugated iron covered with 6in of earth. The sides were hedged with brushwood and the whole bridge was stiffened by four timber frames under the bridge and by wire side ties. The bridge could carry a laden ox wagon and proved its worth when the river rose 20ft above its normal winter level.

A peace treaty was finally signed at Pretoria in May 1902. By this time Roberts had returned to England and Lord Kitchener, that most famous of Sappers, had become Commander-in-Chief. But before ending this brief review of bridging effort in the Boer War, mention should be made of the influence of the railway on the progress of the war. By the end of the Nineteenth Century the Transvaal and the Orange Free State railway network extended over 4600 miles of British South Africa. It was realized early on that the South African railways would play a very important part in the conduct of the war and a Department of Railways was set up as part of the Army Corps to take charge of the railway system. 8 and 10 Railway Companies RE were sent out to assist in railway work and they were supported by four Fortress Companies and, later, by a Railway Pioneer Regiment. A very considerable Sapper effort went into repairing and replacing the great number of railway bridges destroyed by the Boers, essential work in maintaining the system that was of the greatest importance for the movement and resupply of our forces, and an important factor in our final victory. (Figure 3.14).

Figure 3.14. A temporary replacement for the demolished railway bridge at Kaapmuiden, built during the advance into the Transvaal in September 1900.

CHAPTER FOUR

The First World War

The Turn of the Century

After the end of the South African or Boer War in 1902 most of the regimental units, including the Pontoon Trains, returned to England, and the next ten years or so saw a number of important changes in the organization of the Army, and of course in the Corps, resulting from the experiences gained during the war. These changes are outside the scope of this book, but those that affected the bridging role of the Corps are obviously of interest. The first such change was the disbandment of D Pontoon Troop of the Bridging Battalion, to be followed, in 1905, by the conversion of A, B and C Pontoon Troops to 1, 2 and 3 Bridging Companies.

In April 1906 the Evelyn Wood Committee submitted their final report on the overall organization of the Royal Engineers; among many recommendations, they agreed that two Field Companies should be allocated to each Division and that both companies should carry out bridging, telegraph and searchlight duties in addition to their normal field engineering duties. For bridging they recommended that a small bridging element should be attached to one of the Divisional Field Companies, carrying equipment to build 150ft of bridging. The majority of the Committee's recommendations were accepted and consequently, in 1907, a number of changes were made to bring Royal Engineer field units into line with the new organization of the Army. The building of bridges for the Army now became the responsibility of the Field Company rather than of a specialist unit, and the special trade of pontoonier, which had served the Corps so well during the South African War, was abolished. The short-lived Bridging Companies were converted into three Bridging Trains, although the third train only survived until 1910, when it was disbanded. The Trains were in cadre form only, to be expanded in case of war, and each was organized as two half-trains, each half-train carrying 300ft of medium bridge. In early 1912 the 1st Bridging Train was stationed in Aldershot Command and the 2nd Bridging Train formed part of the Eastern Coast Defence Forces. Although at this time there were about 275 officers and 8,300 other ranks of the Corps actually serving with units, the total strength of the two Trains stood at a mere twenty Warrant Officers, NCOs and men. This might seem disproportionately low, but it must be remembered that in 1912 the Corps was still manning eleven Telegraph and Signal Companies of various sorts (despite the Evelyn Wood Committee recommendation), as well as an Air Battalion, and over thirty Fortress, Works and Coast Battalion Companies.

By now the Bridging Trains had become no more than equipment holding units.

Meanwhile yet another committee, under the chairmanship of Field Marshal Lord Kitchener, had been considering the organization of the Corps and possible increases in its strength to keep pace with advances in modern science. The committee recommended that the war organization of the Army should include three Field Companies in each Division rather than two, and that the bridging equipment allocated to the Field Companies should be formed into a Divisional Bridging Train, to be in many ways the forerunner of the Field Park Company. However, by the outbreak of war in 1914 this recommendation had not been implemented and the establishment of the Corps still included just the two Bridging Trains set up in 1907; it was not until the end of 1914 that the third Field Company was added to each Division.

During this period the Bridging Sub-Committee of the Royal Engineer Committee carried out a long series of experiments involving pontoon construction. During the South African War it had been found that long immersion of the Mark II Pontoons made the cladding sodden, increasing the weight of the pontoons and decreasing their buoyancy. Experiments were therefore directed towards development of metal-framed and clad pontoons, but it was found that if the skin was made thin enough to keep the weight within reasonable limits it was liable to be easily punctured and that metal frames strong enough to withstand the stresses involved were excessively heavy. The Mark II Pontoon therefore remained as the standard pontoon equipment with which we went to war, although a reduction was made in the number of layers of canvas used in the cladding to marginally

Figure 4.1. The Weldon Trestle loaded on its pack wagon. (Military Engineering (Provisional) Vol III-1921).

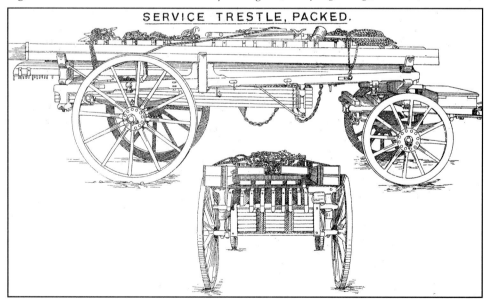

SERVICE TRESTLE, PACKED.

increase the buoyancy and minor modifications were made to increase its load-carrying capacity. At a later stage of the war the **Mark III Pontoon** was introduced; this was identical in size and configuration to the Mark II, but had a different cladding, to eliminate the problems with the canvas cladding previously mentioned; details are given in Appendix B.

At the outset of the war each of the two Bridging Trains was equipped with forty-two of the bipartite Mark II Pontoons, each carried on a Pontoon Wagon with 15ft of superstructure, as shown in Figure 3.7. Each Train also carried sixteen Weldon, or Mark IV, Trestles, loaded two to a Trestle Wagon, together with the additional superstructure required. (Figure 4.1). In addition each Field Company was equipped with two Pontoon Wagons and one Trestle Wagon. A development of the Light Bridging and Rafting Equipment (described in the previous chapter) was also carried by the Field Companies. This was the **Light Raft Equipment**, which used two boats to form each raft, each boat being formed by coupling together a pointed bow section and two stern sections; each section was 6ft 3in long. (Figure 4.2).

Figure 4.2. The Light Raft Equipment, afloat and wagon-packed. (Military Engineering Part IIIB - 1914).

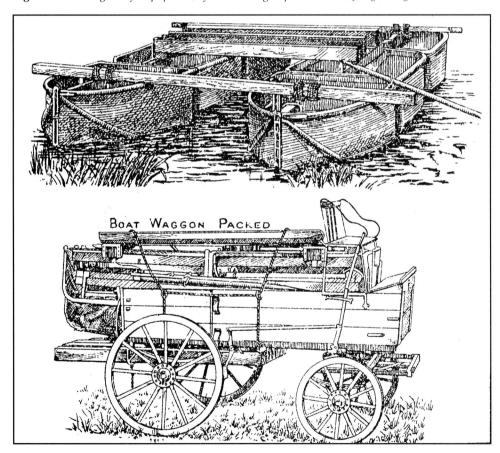

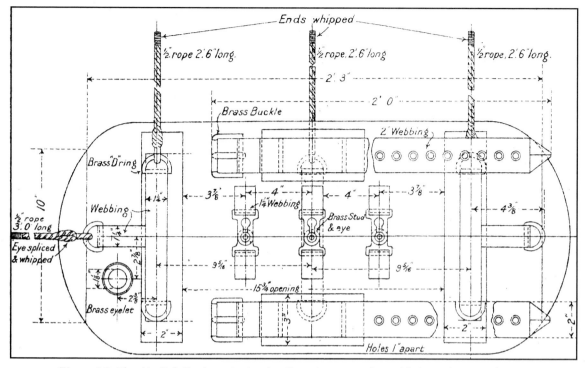

Figure 4.3. *The Air Raft Equipment, showing the outer canvas bag with its various attachments.* (Military Engineering Part IIIB - 1914).

One further equipment that deserves mention, although it was not used by or issued to the Corps, is the **Air Raft Equipment**. (Figure 4.3). Each raft consisted of sixty canvas bags, each about 30in long and 13in in diameter and containing an inflatable rubber inner bag. Webbing straps and buckles were fitted to the outside of each bag so that bags could be strapped together in groups of twelve to make a pontoon; five such pontoons were formed into a raft, using baulk saddles and wheel-ways. The raft was issued to the cavalry and could carry any limbered vehicle in the cavalry division, including the RHA guns and the RE tool carts; it would not carry horses, however, and was not very suitable for carrying men, as it had no decking. A special version of the Air Raft, design for transport by camel, was issued to the Field Company in Egypt.

Wartime Expansion

The events leading up to the outbreak of war in 1914 between the Triple Entente of Britain, France and Russia and their allies on the one side and the Central European powers of Germany, Austria-Hungary and their allies on the other, have been written of at length and need no repetition here. Suffice to say that in 1914 the British Army was probably better prepared for war than ever before, thanks largely to the unceasing efforts of Lord Haldane, Secretary of State for War from 1905 to 1912. As a result of his efforts, which included the creation of a second line of defence, the Territorial Force, the outbreak of war found Britain with an army of six well trained and reasonably equipped expeditionary Divisions, backed up by a further fourteen Territorial Divisions and a Regular Army Reserve of some 130,000 men.

As far as the Corps was concerned, it was undoubtedly handicapped by having no representation at the highest level of the War Office organization. This arose from the major reorganization of the Army and the War Office, recommended by the Esher Committee between 1902 and 1904. The post of Commander-in-Chief of the Army was abolished, together with that of one of his four principal staff officers, the Inspector General of Fortifications and Engineers, a Corps appointment at Lieutenant General level. In 1904 an Army Council was established, headed by a Chief of the General Staff; at a much lower level a new post of Director of Fortifications and Works was created, in the rank of Brigadier General. The new DFW was one of several directors who worked under the Master General of Ordnance, who was now one of the four members of the Army Council. The Esher Committee did not charge anybody with the responsibility for preparation for war from the Engineer point of view, and although the post of DFW was upgraded to Major General level in 1911, it was not until October 1941, during the Second World War, that the post of Engineer-in-Chief was established at the War Office.

The Corps was also handicapped (as indeed were other branches of the Army) by a complete underestimation of the scope and duration of the pending war and a false appreciation of the type of operations likely to be encountered. The Army was eventually to be deployed in many parts of the world, throughout Europe, in the Middle East, in Africa and even, after the Armistice, in northern Russia. The scope of these widespread operations might be judged from the rapid expansion of the Corps during the war, which is admirably covered in Volume V of the *Corps History*, but more important statistics are worth quoting here. The number of different types of RE units rose from twenty-four in 1914 to almost 160, many being highly specialized, such as camouflage, forestry and gas units. The number of Field Companies rose from fifteen to 226; this was in line with the expansion of the British Army element of the Empire Forces deployed overseas, which rose from six Divisions in 1914 to seventy Divisions in 1917. The total strength of the Corps rose from about 25,000 all ranks (including the Special Reserve and the Territorials) to almost 230,000 all ranks, to which could be added another 85,000 Sappers in the Transportation side of the Corps. These figures did of course include a very large element of the Corps engaged on Signal Service duties, since the Royal Corps of Signals was not established until July 1920.

Sapper Re-equipment

Funds available before the war for war munitions and stores were very limited, being based upon the concept of an Expeditionary Force based upon seven Divisions, and the sum allocated specifically for engineer stores and equipment was totally inadequate for the war that was to come. In August 1914 Lord Kitchener became Secretary of State for War and immediately increased our overseas commitment to seventy Divisions, backed up by an expansion of the Indian Army to two million fighting men and substantial support from the Dominions. Once this considerable increase in our commitment was made, it became clear that the organization for supply of Sapper stores and equipment would itself need very considerable expansion. With the outbreak of war the office of the DFW was extensively reorganized to cope with the envisaged expansion of all types of engineer work; the provision of engineer stores, previously the responsibility of sub-branches of FW4, now became the responsibility of two new branches, FW8 under a Chief Mechanical Engineer and FW9 under a Chief Electrical Engineer; the heads of both branches reported direct to the DFW and both branches faced an enormous task in the equipping of the rapidly expanding Corps.

Supply of bridging equipment was organized by FW8, under the control of Captain R Oakes RE, previously the Inspector of Iron Structures with DFW, and later promoted to Brevet Lieutenant Colonel in post. A measure of the task facing FW8 was demonstrated by the need for more pontoon equipment. The Expeditionary Force of 1914 was equipped with only 108 Mark II Pontoons, held in the two Bridging Trains that went to France early in the war and in the Field Companies. This number was eventually increased to nearly 3,000, and considerable detailed redesign was necessary to meet difficulties in quantity production and to increase the load-carrying capacity to cater for recently introduced motor transport.

Whilst this met the demand for floating or pontoon bridges, the Sappers had not previously been equipped with an equipment bridge for use over dry gaps, other than the Weldon Trestle which could only be used in limited circumstances. It soon became clear that the rebuilding of demolished road and rail bridges using locally-acquired materials was far too slow and this need for heavy bridging was confirmed during the crossing of the River Aisne in September 1914, referred to later, when it was realized that in many cases single demolished spans of long bridges could be successfully bridged, given the right equipment, thus avoiding the need to build long floating bridges as replacements. FW8 were therefore instructed to design and procure a series of stock spans that could be used for this purpose, to be held in Engineer Store Depots and not as part of the equipment of field units. Two further bridges, the Inglis Bridge and the Hopkins Bridge, were introduced subsequently and will be considered in more detail later.

The Stock Spans

In early October, GHQ of the British Expeditionary Force (BEF) formally asked the War Office to provide sixteen steel girder bridges, together with a supply of pile drivers. The bridges were to be capable of carrying the Army's heaviest load, which was the 8in howitzer with a 13 ton axle loading. The design was produced in the office of FW8, working to size and weight limits laid down by the Sapper staff at GHQ. In December 1914 first orders were placed, for just over 4100ft run of bridging, in span lengths of 13ft, 30ft and 60ft, but before delivery could be completed the maximum axle load was increased to 17 tons, as a result of the introduction of a new 6in Mark VII gun on a naval carriage. A further order for bridges to carry this increased load was therefore placed in March 1915, the span range being extended to include lengths of 16ft, 21ft 6in, 30ft, 60ft and now 85ft. (Figure 4.4). An order was also placed for a Canal Lifting Bridge, to a design produced at GHQ. Some details of the **Type A and Type B Stock Span Bridges**, of which various marks were produced, are given in Appendix B.

The initial orders for the Type A and Type B Bridges were hastened at all levels but by mid-1915 it became clear from the military situation in France that there was no immediate requirement for the quantities of bridging ordered. Considerable difficulties arose in finding suitable storage space for the bridges in the BEF area, but the War Office made it clear that considerable efforts had been made by all those concerned in production of the bridging and in due course a suitable area was found at Le Havre, where a permanent Heavy Bridging Depot was eventually set up, remaining in operation until the end of the war. Altogether over 27,000ft of Type A Bridging and over 4,000ft of Type B Bridging had been ordered by mid-1917, whilst a further order for 21,250ft of Type A and the increased capacity **Type AA** spans was placed in early 1918.

Figure 4.4. An 85ft Class A Stock Span. (Work of the RE in the European War, 1914-1919, Bridging).

The Canal Bridges

Belgium and Northern France are served by a network of canals, along which considerable quantities of war materials were shipped during the early stages of the war. It was thus important to keep these vital supply routes open and it was decided that, although the canals could have been bridged at high level, the same result could be more easily attained by using lift bridges of various forms. The maximum width of the locks on the canal system was in the order of 20ft, and so a standard span of 21ft 6in was agreed upon for the British lifting bridges. The early bridges were standard 21ft 6in span Type A Bridges, with the necessary lifting gear at either end. **The Davit Bridge** consisted of four lattice davits at the corners of the bridge, with a lifting gear of differential blocks. With no counterweights, uneven lifting at the corners jammed the bridge and since it required four men to raise and lower the bridge and as it was in any case difficult to erect, it was rarely used. **The Portal Bridge** incorporated four columns at the corners of the bridge, braced by shallow girders at the top, both across the canal and across the roadway. There was a counterweight equal to the weight of the bridge and the lifting gear consisted of a worm gear and hand chain. The actual bridge was supplied by four different manufacturers, each working to his own detailed drawings, which meant that spares were not interchangeable. The bridge was easy to erect, however, and was widely used. With the **Pont Levis**, two independent towers were erected on either side of the roadway on the home bank and were braced together at the top. A long arm was pivoted at the top of each tower, and a counterweight fixed being the two arms at the home bank end of bridge. The far end of the bridge was then supported by cables hung from the ends of the arms and the bridge was raised like a drawbridge, using a winch and cable attached to it via a pulley at the top of the towers. The bridge made use of the standard 21ft 6in span Type A Bridge, but subsequently a Mark II version was produced which used special plate girders with cross girders and longitudinal girders to form the bridge proper (Figure 4.5).

Figure 4.5. The Pont Levis Mark II, with a 22ft clear span, used for canal crossings. (Military Engineering Vol III Bridging (Provisional) - 1921).

Early Bridging Operations

During the early stages of the war the withdrawal of the French Fifth Army before the advancing German columns forced the BEF to retreat from its first positions on the Mons Canal. (MAP 1). Many bridges were demolished during this retreat and by the end of August I Corps had withdrawn as far as the River Aisne, where once again bridges were demolished. By 3 September the whole of the BEF had crossed the Marne and had reached the outskirts of the Paris entrenchment camp, but by the 5th the great retreat came to an end and in a few hours was converted into a victorious advance that forced the German Army back to the Aisne.

During their retreat the Germans failed to demolish those Marne bridges on the British front that we had not previously destroyed during our retreat. III Corps were held up, however, whilst a bridge was built at La Ferté; this bridge was the first to be built by the Field Companies during the war and was sited just below the demolished masonry bridge at the south of the town. During the earlier retreat of the BEF, the pontoons of 1 and 2 Bridging Trains on their cumbersome horse transport had been sent back to Le Mans,

MAP 1 ~ NORTH - WEST EUROPE, THE FIRST WORLD WAR
Showing towns and rivers mentioned in the text; roads and railways have been omitted for clarity

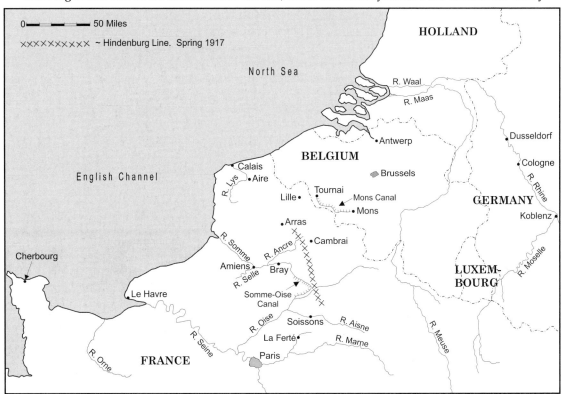

some 120 miles south-west of Paris, and so the 220ft bridge was constructed using the trestles and pontoons of 7 and 9 Field Companies, together with four barrel piers, two boats and one barge. 7 Company constructed the approaches for the bridge whilst 9 Company built the bridge itself. Extra decking and material for the superstructure had to be found locally and barrels were collected from neighbouring wine cellars, their contents having supposedly been run to waste, although a number of dead-drunk German soldiers are reported to have been captured. Work on the bridge continued until the early hours of 10 September, the gap finally being closed by a rowing boat brought in by Lieutenant R G Wright RE of 7 Company. 4 Division started crossing at once and by the following morning the bridge was dismantled; the companies collected their pontoons and rapidly followed up the advancing troops. The two Bridging Trains, each equipped with forty-two pontoons and sixteen trestles and with a complement of about 360 horses, had meanwhile been sent up by train from Le Mans, but were still two days march behind the advancing forces.

The BEF now advanced to the River Aisne, although nearly all of the Field Companies found themselves so far back in the order of march that they had the greatest difficulty in moving up their bridging equipment when it was required. Nevertheless a number of pontoon bridges were built to replace the permanent bridges destroyed by the retreating German Army and a number of footbridges were built across the gunwales of barges moored in the river. With no reserve of engineer effort to hand, the Field Companies were fully stretched to maintain the newly constructed bridges, the combination of heavy rain and German shelling having resulted in a swollen river full of floating debris; the bridges were thus in constant danger of being swept away and had to be dismantled frequently to clear the river.

It was during the crossing of the Aisne that the name of Martel first appears in this story. The old road bridge across the Aisne at Soissons consisted of several stone arches, one of which had been demolished by the retreating Germans, leaving a gap of some 75ft. With no suitable equipment bridge available, Lieutenant G le Q Martel RE, as he was then, commanding a section of 9 Field Company, prepared a design for a wooden lattice girder bridge, to be made of local materials; the heaviest timbers were 9in x 3in and the decking timbers were floorboards from neighbouring houses. Work began on 30 September and the four girders had been made and tested by 5 October. Many hands helped with the launching of the trusses and at one time the Chief Engineer of III Corps and his driver were seen pulling guy ropes. The bridge was completed by 7 October having taken some sixty hours to build; it gave rise to great interest with the French troops who named it the Pont des Anglais.

Supply in the Field

The deployment of bridging equipment within the BEF was of prime importance. By August 1915 the two Bridging Trains with the BEF had been supplemented by a third Train in the United Kingdom, but by August 1916 the Trains existed no more and had been replaced by 12 Pontoon Park Companies, two of which were located in the UK. Two further Pontoon Park Companies were formed within the BEF in the following year, together with a Cavalry Corps Bridging Park, Advanced Park Companies and Base Park Companies. The decentralized distribution of bridging equipment within the BEF was obviously an advantage to the Field Companies, considerably reducing reaction time for the onset of bridging operations.

The Stock Spans were of course held further back, and mention has already been made of the setting up of a Heavy Bridging Depot at Le Havre. However, as the size of the British commitment increased, it became necessary to distribute equipment on a wider front and a second Heavy Bridging Base Depot was set up near Calais early in 1917. Meanwhile each of the Armies operating as part of the British Forces had set up its own Heavy Bridging Depot. These were first designed to be Barge Depots for canal traffic, formed to provide mobile storage for bridging equipment as it was received from England. Each Army was equipped with a fleet of 280 ton barges, including a workshop barge, two store barges (each carrying a number of stock steel spans), two barges carrying pile drivers, derricks and timber, and two turntable barges. By the end of 1915 three of these barge fleets had been completed, with a fourth well on the way to completion. It was intended that the barges themselves could be used to form a bridge if necessary, known as a **Barge Bridge**, and the turntable barges were equipped with a double roadway, a 60ft Type B through bridge erected on a turntable, and a set of shore trestles. When it was required to bridge a gap, the 60ft bridge was rotated on its turntable and the barge filled with water until the bridge came to rest on its end bearings. In addition each of the barges in the depot was fitted with superstructure, trestles and decking able to carry a 16 ton axle load and it was calculated that it would be possible to form a bridge over most of the canals in Belgium and France using three such barges. In practice these bridges were not used because of subsequent widespread destruction of the canal system by the Germans, and in early 1917 it was realized that canal transport of bridging equipment was not really feasible during an advance. The Barge Depots were therefore disbanded and the barges were subsequently passed across to the Inland Water Transport branch of the Corps. The Army Bridging Depots remained, however, acting as central depots where the heavy bridging equipment for all the Divisions in an Army could be parked and maintained.

Charles Inglis

The appointment of an E-in-C for the BEF, in the rank of Major General, was made in July 1915; Brigadier General G H Fowke, who was originally the Brigadier General RE at GHQ, and subsequently Chief Engineer BEF, became the first officer in this post. Initiative for the design of the Type A and Type B Bridges, discussed earlier, had come from the General's staff, and the Royal Engineer Committee was little involved. However, the Committee had been considering various designs for light transportable bridges, the one design that proved worthy of further development being that of Charles Edward Inglis. Inglis was born in 1875 and in 1901 gained a Fellowship at King's College, Cambridge. In connection with his work with the Royal Engineer section of the Cambridge University Officers' Training Corps he produced, in 1913, a design for a lightweight bridge designed to carry infantry in single file; this was to be the first of a number of military bridge designs that Inglis produced over the next twenty-five years or so.

Inglis was commissioned into the Corps in 1914 and from 1916 to 1918 was in charge of the department responsible for the design and supply of military bridging for the Corps. In 1918 he retired with the rank of Major and was appointed an OBE for his services; he returned to Cambridge and the following year was elected to the Chair of Mechanical Sciences, a post which he held until 1943, when he became Vice Provost of King's College. Inglis was a man of great ability and was highly honoured during his lifetime. He was elected a Fellow of the Royal Society in 1930 and President of the Institution of Civil Engineers in 1941. He became Professor Emeritus of Engineering at Cambridge and was knighted for services to the country in war and in peace in 1945. Charles Inglis was a great friend of the Corps, particularly in support of young officers taking Cambridge University degree courses between the wars. He died in 1952, at the age of 76.

The Inglis Triangular Bridges

Inglis' light footbridge, designed in 1913, was known officially as the **Inglis Portable Military Bridge - Light Type** and is of importance because it was the first British equipment bridge of the fixed or dry bridge as opposed to the wet or floating bridge type. (Figure 4.6). It could be rapidly constructed, required little training and was easily transported. It was of unusual design in that it was of triangular cross-section, with a single top compression member and two bottom tension members. The two Warren girders forming the bridge trusses were thus inclined together at the top, with a common top chord, forming in effect a number of pyramids and giving rise to its popular name of the **Inglis Pyramid Bridge**. The girders were formed from 8ft long drawn steel tubes, each fitted with a welded steel tongue, a screw and a nut at both ends. To connect two tubes, adjacent nuts were slackened off and the two tongues inserted into a cast-steel junction box; a pin was then passed through a slot in each tongue and the nuts tightened to lock the joint. Steel transoms connected the lower 8ft panel points of the two girders and supported a narrow wooden gangway; light sway bracing was fitted in each bay.

It was usual to construct the bridge on a small two-wheeled erection

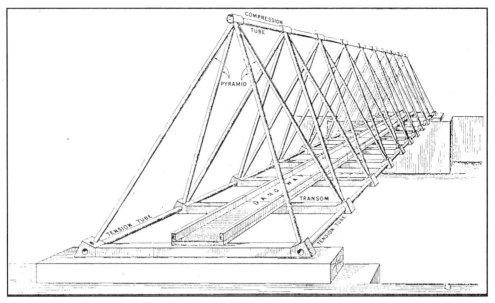

Figure 4.6. The Inglis Portable Military Bridge - Light Type, from Inglis' own 1915 handbook.

trolley, close to and parallel to the gap or river that was to be crossed. The forward end of bridge was built sufficiently long to cross the gap, and the rear end, subsequently dismantled, extending far enough for the erection team to bear down on the home end whilst the completed bridge was rotated like a swing bridge. The heaviest part of the bridge was the transom, weighing about 190lb, but the tubes were light and the simple construction meant that, when first demonstrated in France, a 108ft bridge was built across a canal by an untrained party of Army Service Corps troops in thirteen minutes. The bridge could carry infantry in single file over spans of up to 96ft. A bridge capable of carrying a 3 ton vehicle across a 96ft gap could be improvised by placing two footbridges across the gap at 16ft centres. Crossbeams would then be lashed to corresponding transoms on the two bridges and road bearers and chesses added to complete the bridge.

Figure 4.7. The Inglis Heavy Type Bridge. (Work of the RE in the European War, 1914-1919, Bridging).

The RE Committee referred Inglis' proposals for his foot bridge to GHQ in France who asked that trials be carried out at the SME, as a result of which an initial order for ten sets of 88ft span bridge were placed for use with the BEF. This resulted in a request for a similar type of bridge that could carry first-line transport, and Inglis produced a design for the similar **Inglis Heavy Type Bridge**, using 12ft long tubes and capable of carrying loads of up to 7 tons over spans of up to 96ft. (Figure 4.7).

75

An order for seventeen of the Heavy Type Bridge was placed and the first was received in France in early 1916, but the triangular cross section of the bridge made it unsuitable for passage of transport, and although a twin bridge version, similar to that for the Light Type bridge, could be built, it was in the event overtaken by the design of the Inglis Bridge Mark I, which will be considered later.

Training for Bridging

With the introduction of the new steel bridges in 1915 it was realized that officers, NCOs and Sappers of the Corps would need training in their use and erection. Since the bridges were being shipped into Le Havre it was decided to arrange training courses in the use of the bridges there, under direction of the Depot Stores Officer. Eight courses were arranged, for nearly 100 officers and 300 NCOs, but the administrative burden on the Depot staff was too great and in 1916 it was decided to set up an RE Bridging School. The School was established at Aire, on a by-pass of the River Lys, in October 1916. By early 1918, however, with an ever-increasing range of equipments to be held in order to cover the subject adequately, the School had outgrown the Aire site, and this, coupled with the threat of a probable German advance in the spring of 1918, necessitated a move. A new site was found at Monchy Cayeux on the River Ternoise. The first class was held at the school in October 1918, just prior to the Armistice, after which the School was reorganized to run courses for regular RE officers in bridge engineering and general construction. In all, the Bridging School instructed over 400 officers and 2000 men in bridging subjects, predominantly from the Army Troops and Tunnelling Companies, since these companies, with their heavier equipment and their motor transport, were better suited for the erection of the new girder bridges than the Field Companies.

Floating Equipments

Before the war it had been realized that the continuing introduction of the motor vehicle would considerably increase the loads to be carried by military bridges, and a number of experiments were carried out with Mark II Pontoon equipment to enable it to carry 3 ton lorries. Minor modifications to the pontoons were made and have already been referred to, but in 1914 it was decided that the entire pontoon equipment holding must be scrapped and replaced with a new equipment capable of carrying heavier loads. Unfortunately this decision was overtaken by the onset of the war and, although the Mark III Pontoon was introduced during the war, it was not until 1922 that a completely new pontoon equipment was brought into service; as a result severe restrictions were placed on the loads that could be carried by our floating bridges during the war.

The Sankey Bridge. The prewar experiments just referred to were carried

Figure 4.8. A Sankey Type B Bridge under load, with a Pont Levis Mark I in the background. (Work of the RE in the European War, 1914-1919, Bridging).

out by Field Companies during the period 1912-1914 and a solution proposed by Captain C E P Sankey RE proved the most satisfactory, being adopted in the absence of the development of a new equipment. Sankey used the Mark II Pontoon to form the floating piers of the bridge but used stock-rolled steel joists to carry the roadway instead of the baulks originally used with the equipment. (Figure 4.8). Three variations of the bridge were used, Type B (which would carry all Type B loads and Type A loads in an emergency), Type C (which would carry a heavy commercial lorry), and Type D (which would carry loaded 3 ton lorries). A number of Sankey Bridges were used during the final advance in the autumn of 1918, but the close spacing of the pontoons made it most suitable for use in rivers with sluggish currents.

The Heavy Steel Pontoon. During the early days of the war the War Office considered the possible need for heavy floating bridges during a crossing of the Rhine, should operations extend into Germany. A design was produced for a bridge using a Heavy Steel Pontoon and capable of carrying a 14 ton traction engine across a river some 1500ft wide; each pontoon, 45ft long and with an 8ft beam, would have weighed about 5 tons, with superstructure weighing a further 3½ tons. After discussions with GHQ of the BEF it was decided that a crossing of the Rhine was most unlikely, but the Chief of the General Staff requested that supplies of such bridging should nevertheless be made available for the crossing of other major rivers. This

Figure 4.9 The Inglis Heavy Pontoon Bridge, using Heavy Pontoons and the Mark II Inglis Bridge, at Christchurch after the War (IWM T5)

was contrary to the views of his Chief Engineer, who considered that steel girder bridges resting on fixed foundations, such as existing or piled piers, provided a better solution for the crossing of such rivers. In the event, orders for this additional bridging were not placed, due to priority of other work in the UK, and experiments continued on the use of standard 280 ton French barges to form suitable long-span bridges.

The Heavy Pontoon. A number of Heavy Pontoons were subsequently manufactured, however, just before the Armistice. (Figure 4.9 and Appendix B). The pontoons, which differed from the proposed Heavy Steel Pontoons and were somewhat lighter, were intended for possible use with the Mark II Inglis Bridge in the crossing of major rivers such as the Rhine and Meuse. It was also intended that the pontoons would be used to replace the Mark II/III Pontoons in the heavy version of the Sankey Bridge.

Infantry Foot Bridges were constructed in great numbers and were improvised using whatever materials might be available. The floating piers might be made of cork, oil drums, wine casks or perhaps captured German

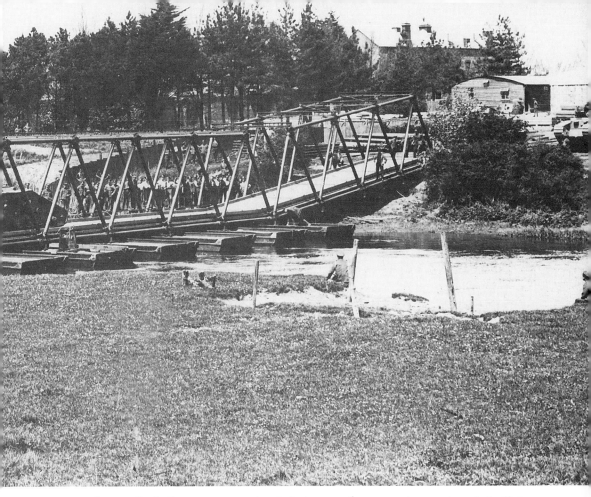

floats. Cork floats were most satisfactory as they were impervious to bullets or shrapnel, and 100 tons of cork was ordered before the final advance in 1918 and made up into floats, although these were all used up within the first few weeks of the advance. Trench boards or planks were placed across the floats to form a light bridge for passage of the infantry in an early stage of an attack, the complete length of bridge having been made up in advance and then carried bodily down to the water's edge.

The Bridging of the Somme in 1917

During the two years or so after the crossing of the Aisne in late 1914, bridging operations were of minor importance and the battle against the enemy remained fairly static. The winter of 1915/16 was spent in reorganizing the BEF for a combined offensive in the following summer, the Battle of the Somme, which was, up to that time, to be the greatest battle in British history. The battle began on 1 July 1916, but for many reasons, well documented elsewhere, it ended in stalemate in November, with a hopeless series of petty attacks by III Corps and the ANZAC Corps.

The initial Sapper effort had been directed to the repair of roads and the opening up of lines of communications, but in February 1917 a partial withdrawal by the Germans and an extension of the British front southward necessitated extensive bridging operations in the area. On 17 March 1917 the Germans commenced a full-scale withdrawal across the Somme in front of the British Fourth Army, falling back to their prepared Hindenburg Line. Reconnaissances showed that all bridges across the Somme had been destroyed and the problem was increased by the need for bridging across the Canal du Nord. The Field Companies of 1 Division started work at once and temporary crossings for the infantry were completed by that evening. Construction of Medium Bridges to carry first line transport started next morning and the first crossing was completed at Brie by the following morning. Six bridges were to be built in this first crossing of the Somme, ranging in span from 24ft to 93ft, and the necessary stores were rapidly dispatched forward to the Army Depot, from which all material had to be transported a further distance of about 10 miles by horse transport, as the roads were not in a fit state to carry motor transport. The entire crossing was ready by 4pm on 28 March, two days ahead of the estimated completion date, and a special message of congratulations to the engineers of the Fourth Army was received from the Commander-in-Chief. This was the first heavy bridging operation of any importance carried out during the war and was highly successful; subsequently a number of other bridges were constructed across the Somme and its tributaries, including four 60ft spans.

Early in the following year a German offensive against the southern British Armies was expected and in anticipation of this a considerable amount of additional bridging was carried out on the Somme during February and March. Some bridges were strengthened to carry tanks, the more important bridges on the main supply routes were doubled and many new bridges were built. Over sixty bridges were constructed during this period, ranging from a 90ft Hopkins Bridge and several AA Type Bridges of various spans to six Pont Levis and one Portal Lifting Bridge. The American Army, having asked for the supply of various spans for instructional purposes, agreed instead to participate in the work and attached a number of their engineer units to assist the Field Companies of the British Fifth Army.

The Advent of the Tank

It is a Sapper officer, Lieutenant Colonel E D Swinton RE, who is credited with first proposing a practical concept for an armoured vehicle, armed and mounted on tracks, to overcome the difficulties of advancing against a defence relying on a network of trenches which was backed up by barbed wire and batteries of heavy machine guns. His proposals, made in late 1914, were taken up by Winston Churchill, then First Lord of the Admiralty, and trials took place in early 1916. The original vehicles were known as **Land Cruisers**, but were re-named **Tanks** by Swinton, in the deceptive pretence that they were to be used for water supply, and it is as such that they have been known ever since. In May 1917 the Heavy Branch of the Machine Gun Corps, which had been formed under Swinton's command to take charge of the trials, became the Tank Corps, under the command of another Sapper officer, Brigadier H J Elles, who went on to lead the tanks to their dramatic initial success at Cambrai in November 1917.

The Corps was thus much involved with the introduction of this new weapon of far-reaching potential, but its effects upon bridging were almost certainly not foreseen, presenting as it did a very substantial increase in load to be carried by our bridges. The increase has continued to this day, the Class 60 requirement for bridging in the early 1980s giving way to the Class 70 requirement of the 1990s. During 1917 considerable effort was expended in the reappraisal of our bridging equipments, now required to carry a maximum load of 30 tons instead of the previous maximum of 17 tons. Some of the stock spans proved incapable of conversion to carry the increased load and were later discarded; others could be adapted by decreasing effective spans, increasing the number of roadbearers (as with the A Type 30ft span bridge, which was reinforced by increasing the number of steel beams from three to four), or by minor modification (that for the 60ft A Type bridge being no more than an increase in bolt size). The new and modified bridges were termed **AA Type Bridges** to differentiate them from the A and B Types still in service.

The Inglis Bridges Mark I and Mark II

Meanwhile Major Inglis, now responsible for design of military bridging for the BEF, was asked by the Engineer-in-Chief to consider the adaptation of his ideas on tubular bridging to carry heavier loads. The result was the **Inglis Bridge Mark I**, which again used tubes rapidly connected together to form Warren trusses, but this time with the more conventional rectangular cross-section for the bridge. (Figure 4.10). The bridge was built in 12ft bays and could carry A loads (that is the 17 ton axle load - about Class 40 using the current Bridge Classification System) over gaps of up to 96ft. The cross-girders, or transoms, and overhead bracing were manufactured from rolled steel joists, lightened by the cutting of holes in the joist webs. Cast steel junction boxes, into which the ends of the tubular members were fitted, were bolted on to the ends of the transoms and to the ends of the lighter overhead bracing members. Supplies of the new bridge began to arrive in France in

Figure 4.10. An 84ft span Inglis Bridge Mark I at La Motte, April 1918. In the foreground is a four-span Mark II Stock Span Bridge. (Work of the RE in the European War, 1914-1919, Bridging).

Figure 4.11. A Mark II Inglis Bridge at Christchurch, with launching tail still in position. (Military Engineering Vol III Bridging (Provisional) - 1921).

early 1917 and, being easily erected and dismantled, the bridge was widely used during the final advance in 1918. It had one disadvantage in that the horizontal tubes were 11ft 10½in long, whereas the diagonal members of the trusses were 12ft 11in long, which could cause some confusion on a dark night.

Unfortunately the transoms of the Mark I bridge were not strong enough to carry the new heavy tanks and at the end of the war the **Inglis Bridge Mark II** was under trial. (Figure 4.11). This bridge was very similar to the Mark I version, but had 15ft bays and all the tubular members were interchangeable. It was capable of carrying the 35 ton Mark V** tank over a 105ft span and was launched using a construction trolley in the same manner as was the Inglis Light Pyramid Bridge, at a rate of about 10 minutes a bay. It was a very good bridge, in Martel's view probably the best military bridge capable of carrying heavy loads, such as tanks, in existence at that time. A penalty, however, was the cost of the bridge, the use of steel tubes resulting in a slower rate of production and a higher production cost than, for example, for the Hopkins Bridge, developed at about the same time and built from standard rolled sections, bolted together. This is a design constraint that applies to this day, since increases in load class and decreases in required construction manpower and building time inevitably increase design sophistication and manufacturing costs.

The Hopkins Bridges

Early in 1917 a general advance in the BEF area of operations was anticipated and orders were placed for the extra bridging that might be needed for an advance of up to 50 miles. The opportunity was therefore taken to replace the cumbersome 85ft span Type A Bridge with a new bridge designed by Captain Hopkins, formerly a Bridge Engineer with the Great Western Railway. (Figure 4.12). **The Hopkins 120ft Span Bridge** was a through-type bridge using Warren trusses connected by overhead bracing; the trusses were 16ft 3in in depth and were formed from standard steel sections bolted together. Although the bridge was appreciably cheaper to manufacture than

82

Figure 4.12. The launching of a 120ft Hopkins Bridge, showing temporary cross-bracing. (Work of the RE in the European War, 1914-1919, Bridging).

the Inglis Bridge, with its heavy steel tubes, the bolted construction considerably increased the building time, which was quoted as about 4,000 man-hours for a 120ft bridge. Because of this it became common practice towards the end of the war to build an Inglis Bridge where speed of construction was important and subsequently replace it with a Hopkins Bridge when the pressures of battle permitted, thus enabling the Inglis Bridge to be redeployed elsewhere.

The specification for the bridge required that it should be able to carry tanks, that the heaviest single section should weigh no more than 1½ tons and that it should weigh less than the 85ft Type A Bridge; all of these conditions were easily met, the weight of the heaviest section, for example, being only just over half a ton. The bridge could be constructed with spans in multiples of 15ft and could carry tanks at spans up to 150ft and a 17 ton axle load at spans up to 195ft.

The bridge proved very successful and at the beginning of 1918 a similar bridge, the **Hopkins 75ft Span Bridge**, was ordered. This bridge, also with 15ft bays, was of a lighter design and was intended as a replacement for the 60ft span Type A Bridge. It did not show the reduction in weight that had been hoped for, however, and by the end of the war, later that year, only a few had been manufactured. The bridge could carry tanks at spans up to 90ft and a 17 ton axle load at spans up to 105ft. In the autumn of 1918 Hopkins produced a design for the **Hopkins Lorry Bridge**, a light lattice girder bridge designed to carry lorries up to 5 tons in weight over a 75ft span. (Figure 4.13). The bridge was still in the experimental stage when the war came to an end and only one bridge was sent to France, where it was used at the Bridging School at Monchy Cayeux.

Figure 4.13. A 60ft span Hopkins Lorry Bridge. (Work of the RE in the European War, 1914-1919, Bridging).

Figure 4.14. Typical use of Steel Bridging Cubes to form bridge piers, for a steel girder bridge at Vieux Conde. (Work of the RE in the European War, 1914-1919, Bridging).

The Battle for Arras

Comparatively little bridging was carried out during the Battle for Arras in April 1917, but operations in Arras itself warrant mention to illustrate the difficulties under which the Sappers at times operated. The bridge carrying the main Arras-Cambrai road over the railway line just north of the station had been completely destroyed by the explosion of the ammunition stored under it for use by the howitzers in the railway sidings. 557 (Glamorgan) Army Troops Company spent nearly a week clearing debris and completed the replacement crossing in the next fortnight. Two three-span bridges were built, side by side, each consisting of a 60ft span Heavy Bridge, a 21ft 6in span and a 14ft span; the piers were built using Steel Bridging Cubes, resting on concrete foundations. (Figure 4.14 and Appendix B). Shelling was almost continuous and during the three weeks of construction some thirty casualties included Major General E R Kenyon, Chief Engineer of the Third Army.

Another important road bridge over a railway cutting near Arras was repaired under heavy fire by 289 Army Troops Company. Holes in the arches were filled with reinforced concrete, which involved the erection of falsework to a height of nearly 40ft. During the period of the repairs fourteen Royal Engineers and eighty-three others engaged in the work were killed or wounded.

The Emergence of Assault Bridging

As the war on the Western Front became more static, the trench system was extended considerably, leading to a requirement for a means to cross the trenches and other small obstacles easily. Early in the war, at War Office request, William Foster & Company of Lincoln produced a petrol tractor capable of towing the Army's 15in Howitzers. This was through the offices of Admiral Bacon, Manager of the Coventry Ordnance Works, who later suggested to Mr William Tritton, Managing Director of William Foster, that if each tractor could be modified to carry a small portable bridge it would then be able to cross trenches in its path. Tritton produced a design for such a bridge and one of the tractors was modified to carry the bridgelaying device. At the subsequent trials the tractor was able to cross an eight foot trench in about three minutes. The proposal was not developed further because of the vulnerability of the tractor and its crew without the protection of heavy armour plating and because of its limitations when used against a multi-trench system. The seeds for a bridgelaying vehicle had been sown, however.

Later in the war the newly introduced tanks were able to cross minor obstacles without difficulty, but it was soon realized that engineer assistance would be needed to enable them to cross many of the larger natural obstacles that might hold them up and that this assistance would be needed in the forefront of the battle. The first specialist units to carry out this task were not set up until 1918, right at the end of the war, but much of the preparatory work was carried out beforehand, in part by the Royal Engineers and in part by the newly formed Tank Corps, with its high complement of ex-Sapper officers.

The first equipment to appear was a simple sledge bridge, towed behind a heavy tank and simply dragged across a ditch or trench that was too wide for the medium tanks to cross. The bridge consisted of two steel joists, 20ft long and cross-braced together, on to which was bolted a timber deck. Once the bridge had been dragged across the obstacle the towing attachment could be released from inside the tank, leaving the bridge in place for the medium tanks to follow through. A number of these bridges were manufactured but they were little used in action.

Another bridging device that was developed at an early stage was a simple obstacle crossing expedient for the infantry operating in support of the tanks and consisted of a trench board carried at the rear of the tank in the form of a drawbridge. Once the tank had crossed a deep obstacle, or perhaps a trench filled with barbed wire, the bridge could be lowered into position from inside the tank, enabling the infantry to cross with ease.

By now, however, it had become clear that the advent of the tank was to have a profound affect on military bridge design. Not only was it to affect the load-carrying capacity of our existing and future bridging, but it was realized that it provided a potential source of power that could be used in a variety of engineer tasks; it also became clear that special mechanized Sapper units would eventually be needed to carry out these tasks. Inglis, in his official capacity as bridge designer, now visited the headquarters of the Tank Corps in France to discuss these implications, one result being the redesign of his Mark I Bridge to enable it, in the Mark II version, to carry the heavy tanks. A further result of Inglis' visit was a decision to start work on a tank mounted bridge, requested by the Tank Corps to enable it to cross short gaps under fire. A span of 30ft would have been ideal to enable the tanks to cross the many small streams and the canals that criss-crossed the French countryside, but it was eventually decided to develop a 21ft span bridge which could be used to cross the canals at the locks. The resulting bridge was the **Lock Bridge**, not to be confused with the improvised Lock Bridges of the previous century, in which timber frames interlocked to form a support for the road bearers and bridge decking. The bridge consisted of two girders, spaced at 6ft 6in centres and 21ft long, and connected by four crossbeams. It was mounted on the front of the Heavy Mark V** Tank in the

Figure 4.15. Mark IV Tanks loaded with fascines prior to the Battle of Cambrai in 1917. (Tank Museum, 867/E6)

manner of a drawbridge and was supported by a system of chains passing up over an A frame hinged to the tank and thence to the rear of the tank. It was placed by lowering the leading edge of the bridge onto the far bank and then dropping the rear end onto the home bank. The bridge, considered in more detail in the next chapter, was never used in action and although 25 of the Mark V** Tanks were completed before the Armistice, none of them went to France.

To enable tanks to cross wider obstacles under fire a mobile bridge, known as the **Inglis Assault Bridge**, was made and tested. The bridge consisted of a standard Inglis Bridge mounted on twin idle tracks; the idea was developed too late for use in France but was a sound one and trials continued at Christchurch after the war, as described in the next chapter.

Parallel with Inglis' work was the development of the simple fascine, used for many centuries to bridge small ditches, into a mammoth **Tank Mounted Fascine**, weighing a ton and a half. (Figure 4.15). One particular saw mill, near Bermicourt, was charged with the preparation of the vast quantities of brushwood needed, and in all some 21,000 bundles of brushwood were prepared, sixty or seventy being bundled together to form each fascine; chains were used to hold the bundles tightly in place, the ends of the chains being tensioned between two tanks. In preparation for the Battle of Cambrai in 1917 over 350 fascines were prepared at Central Workshops, together with 110 sledges on which fascines could be towed.

Bridging During the Final Advance

The success of the German offensive in early 1918 resulted in the destruction of many bridges and the loss of a quantity of bridging equipment; a number of replacement bridges were now built, and much use was made of the Inglis bridges, which could be rapidly built and then dismantled and moved to a new site once a permanent bridge had been constructed, since only a limited number of the new bridges were available. The major bridging effort of the war came in the final advance against the Germans, however, from August until 11 November 1918, when the armistice was signed. Prior to this some 180 standard span heavy bridges had been erected during the four years of the war, and of these only those built across the Somme by the Fourth Army in 1917 had been built under conditions now to be experienced during this final advance. In contrast, during the three months that elapsed between the beginning of the Fourth Army advance and the Armistice, 326 standard steel bridges were built, almost twice the number built during the previous four years of war. In addition over 200 bridges were built using timber or salvaged materials. This was in addition to the many hundreds and possibly thousands of light bridges built during this three month period, including footbridges of various types for use by the infantry, and pontoon bridges used for the passage of first line transport and field guns; indeed on one river line no less than thirty pontoon bridges were in position at the same time on a single Army front.

No attempt could be made to describe in any detail the mammoth effort involved in these bridging operations. The excellent use to which the Inglis Bridges was put, already mentioned, is worth typifying, however. One 85ft Inglis Bridge was erected at Vaire on 11 August; it was then dismantled and re-erected at Bray on 30 August; it was then replaced by a steel joist bridge supported on piled piers so that it could be used yet again, for the crossing of the Selle River in October.

One further bridge is considered worthy of mention in some detail as it was the longest single span bridge built during the advance, and its erection was not without its problems. This bridge, a 180ft span Hopkins Bridge, was built on the Third Army front on the Hermiest-Havrincourt road. The approach road to the original brick arch bridge crossed a dry cutting for the new Canal du Nord, which had been under construction at the outbreak of war, and was some 100ft above bed level. To avoid observation from the enemy a new bridge site was selected, further south, and at this point the gap was 180ft wide and 85ft deep. Setting out and the assembly of stores started on 27 September and on the 28th a start was made on the bridge construction; excavations for the abutments, anchorages and launching gear were also completed on that day. A delay of several hours was caused by the breakdown of stores lorries, but construction of the bridge had been completed by midday on 1 October. The standard method of construction for this type of bridge was to build the complete bridge, less its decking, lower it by means of jacks onto rollers and then to haul it across the gap by means of derricks and winches placed on the far bank. In this particular case the bridge girders had been extended backward, so that the total length of bridge was now 240ft, and a 20 ton weight had been placed at the end of the extension in order to reduce the load on the tackles; this increased the total launching weight to about 120 tons. Launching commenced after dark on 1 October and continued the next day, but when the roller overhang had increased to 112ft, still short of the abutment rollers, some failure of bottom chord members over the centre rollers occurred. The failure was caused by a very slight variation in roller spacing relative to the bottom chord spacing, which threw the whole load onto one of the chord webs. The replacement of the damaged members and the placing of a second set of rollers caused a further delay of some seven hours, but by 5pm on 2 October the head of bridge was some 120ft beyond the abutment rollers. Troubles were not yet over, however, and when the head of bridge was 8ft from the far abutment rollers, one of the winches jammed; a crib pier had to be built under the end of the span so that it could be jacked up and the weight taken off of the tackle. Shortly afterwards the other winch jammed; the end of bridge had again to be jacked up, and it was not until 4pm on 4 October that the bridge was finally jacked down into position. Placing of the transoms, deck beams and decking followed and extra horizontal bracing was installed in view of the length of the bridge; this bracing took the form of wire ropes tied back from the bridge at third span points to anchorages placed on the banks 60ft each side of the bridge centre line. The bridge, which was built by fourteen officers and 310 men of the New Zealand Tunnelling Company and 565 and 577 Army Troops Companies RE, was finally opened to traffic at first light on 6 October.

The Victoria Cross

Mention has been made of the hundreds of infantry footbridges built during the last three months of the war as part of the final assault. Extreme bravery during the placing of such bridges resulted in the award of no less than three Victoria Crosses to members of the Corps, literally within days of the Armistice. A posthumous Victoria Cross was awarded to Corporal James McPhie for conspicuous bravery on 14 October 1918, and Victoria Crosses to Major A H S Waters DSO MC RE and Sapper A Archibald for their bravery on 4 November 1918. (Figure 4.16). The official citations for these awards are included in Appendix F, together with those for Captain T Wright RE and Captain W H Johnston RE, who won their awards in 1914, and for Major G de C E Findlay MC* RE, who also won his award on 4 November 1918.

Figure 4.16. Major Waters and Sapper Archibald were both awarded the VC for their bravery during the crossing of the Oise-Sambre Canal. (Painting by Peter Archer).

Figure 4.17. *A timber rail bridge across the Canal du Nord.* (Work of the RE in the European War, 1914-1919, Bridging).

Railway Bridging

Although the rivers and canals in Belgium and France played a vital part in the resupply of the BEF, the railway system was of prime importance. In 1917 it was estimated that to maintain simultaneous attacks on three Army fronts, while merely holding the rest of the frontline, it would require 200 trains per day to the railheads. In fact the average number of trains actually run was rather less, being 150-160 per day, of which up to forty might be ammunition trains; the limiting factor was the transport forward of the railheads, as the area of country only passable by horse transport rapidly widened. There was an initial reluctance by the French to our participation in railway operations, as they had undertaken to maintain and repair their rail network in support of the BEF, but by late September 1914 8 Railway Company RE was involved in the repair of the demolished railway bridge Pont de Metz, near Saleux. This was the first task in a vast programme of new construction, reconstruction and repair carried out by Sapper railway units over the next four years. Considerable new construction work was carried out in conjunction with the French to improve and double the existing rail network and by the middle of 1915 there were eleven British railway construction companies working in France. No attempt will be made to describe in detail any of the bridges built during this period, suffice to say that 306 demolished or weak rail bridges were rebuilt and a further 230 new bridges built. (Figure 4.17). In all over 7 miles of bridging were constructed as part of a railway construction programme involving over 2,600 miles of track, either for new lines and sidings or for reconstruction of damaged lines.

Bridging Operations Outside NW Europe

Bridging operations so far described in this chapter have been confined to NW Europe, by far the most important area of operations during The First World War. Fighting during the war took place in many parts of the world, however, notably in Italy (1917-18), Gallipoli (1915), the Balkans (1915-18), in Egypt and Palestine (1914-18), in East Africa (1914-18) and in Mesopotamia (1914-1924). Within the confines of this book it would be quite impossible to describe the many bridging operations in which the Sappers were involved during these campaigns, but some of the more notable operations will be briefly described.

89

Operations in Italy.

Italy entered the war in 1915 but it was not until the end of 1917 that British troops were involved, after the withdrawal of the Italian army to the River Piave, north of Venice, in the face of a fierce Austrian and German offensive. After a summer of intermittent fighting the Italians planned a major offensive for the autumn of 1918; this was to involve an opposed crossing of the Piave, engaging the British in their major bridging operation of the campaign. The river, with a bed about a mile wide, ran in many channels of varying depth, and in the dry season was fordable in many places; just before the battle, however, it was in full flood, after heavy rains.

On the front of the attack almost the whole of the British XIV Corps sector lay opposite a large island, the Grave di Papadopoli, held by the Austrians. The island was some three miles long and a mile wide, and its distance from the home bank varied from 300 to 700 yards. The attack on the island was launched by using footbridges to cross to a small island, which was then used as a stepping stone to ferry the infantry across the fast stream in small flat-bottomed boats manned by men of 18 Company of Italian Pontieri. Additional footbridges were constructed to the main island by the remainder of the Italian company and the Sappers of 101 Field Company RE; these bridges were made from boats similar to those used for the ferrying, spaced 20ft apart and connected by special strong duckboards. The site of the footbridges was exposed to machine-gun fire and the bridges had therefore to be dismantled at first light and re-erected each night. Once the island had been taken, on 25 October, construction of a pontoon bridge from the home bank to the island was put in hand, making use of detachments of a Bridging Train that had been sent down from France. This proved a difficult task, as the Sappers, having been continuously engaged in trench warfare for some long time, were ill-trained in pontoon work. In addition the Mark II Pontoons were not really adequate for use in the 8 knot current experienced in the deeper channels of the river, which was about 1600ft wide at the site selected. The bridge was finally completed at midday on 27 October, making use of some of the pontoons of the Italian company where the current was faster, as these pontoons were larger and had a greater freeboard than the Mark II Pontoons. Three Weldon Trestles were then used to complete the last fifty yards of bridge.

The final attack against the far bank of the river was then launched, the infantry wading between the many small intermediary islands which were in due course connected by bridges. Meanwhile, however, news was received that a number of bridges being used by the Italian 56 Division had been swept away before their troops could cross. Units of that Division were therefore diverted to cross the British bridge to Papadopoli and in the resulting congestion disaster struck. The current scoured under the leg of one of the Weldon Trestles, the flood waters swept over the bridge deck and all three trestles and two Italian pontoons were swept away. Attempts to repair the bridge by letting down Mark II Pontoons on long cables were unsuccessful, as the pontoons were uncontrollable in the fast current, to the end that one finally capsized, drowning some of the crew. The bridge was finally repaired using more Italian pontoons, and remained in use until after the Armistice in November.

Operations in Egypt and Palestine.

After the British declaration of war against the Turks in November 1914 the defence of the Suez Canal became of prime importance, with large Turkish forces stationed in Syria and Palestine, some 120 miles away. The Suez Canal was about 100 miles long, varying in width from 400ft in flat ground to just under 300ft in the shallow cuttings, and at that time some 34ft deep. The Sweet Water Canal, some 30ft wide, parallel to the main canal and on its western side, had been built at the same time to provide a water supply. Following the withdrawal from Gallipoli at the end of 1915 many of the British troops were brought back to Egypt, which was built up as a strong base from which an offensive against the Turks could eventually be mounted across Sinai and up into Palestine. The canals were crossed by a number of bridges and those across the main canal had, of course, to include cuts to enable shipping to pass. Many of the light bridges and ferries were now supplemented by bridges to carry lorries and heavy artillery, these new bridges having to cope with a rise and fall of water level of up to 5ft in places and to include an opening span of 170ft. The heavy bridges built at El Kubri, Shallufa and Qantara consisted of timber-piled piers on each bank which were connected by gangways to floating landing bays, each consisting of two flat bottomed steel pontoons secured together. The outer pontoon of each landing bay had a bascule arrangement to operate a short lifting span to connect with the opening span; this span consisted of two large flat-bottomed coal barges connected by heavy timber trusses and capable of being opened by a trained crew in five minutes. A number of medium bridges, additional light pontoon bridges and five large fixed ferries were also constructed and in December 1915 it was decided that the Sweet Water Canal should be bridged using the pontoon equipment of the 42nd, the Australian and the New Zealand Divisions.

This very considerable bridging effort, carried out with the full cooperation and help of the Suez Canal Company, enabled the Egyptian Expeditionary Force (EEF), which had been formed in March 1916, to advance up into the Sinai Desert and led to the three battles for Gaza in 1917 and to the capture of Jerusalem in December 1917. North of Jerusalem the EEF embarked on its first opposed river crossing. The Nahr el Auja reaches the sea three miles north of Jaffa and was a considerable obstacle, about 45ft wide and 10ft deep, with the depth and the four knot current increasing constantly with the heavy rains. The banks were soft and muddy and the Turks held the high ground to the north. The bridging equipment of four field companies, comprising twelve Mark II Pontoons and six Weldon Trestles, was supplemented by wine casks formed into barrel-piers, and rafts for the first assault were made from orange trees and canvas water tanks. Heavy rains hampered operations, but by making use of the ford at the mouth of the river and after extensive use of the improvised ferries, a number of crossings were made and the Turks forced to withdraw to the north by 22 December. With the assistance of the Royal Navy, who supplied a diving party to help in the piling, four semi-permanent piled trestle bridges were eventually built across the Auja by 14 Army Troops Company RE; this company had earlier been responsible for building six timber trestle bridges across the Wadi Ghazzee, south of Gaza, the longest being some 530ft long.

The crossing of the Jordan in March 1918, on the road from Jericho to Amman, was fraught with difficulties arising from bad weather and heavy flooding. An Army Bridging Train had by now been formed by XXI Corps to take charge of all the EEF pontoon equipment and this was joined by 13 Pontoon Park, which had been formed at Qantara on 1 March, and an Australian bridging detachment equipped with non-standard light steel pontoons found in Alexandria. The original plan was to build a standard pontoon bridge, a barrel-pier bridge and a sheet raft footbridge on the site of the original bridge that had been destroyed by the Turks. A second bridge, using the light steel pontoons, was to be built on the site of a ford, some three miles to the south. This bridge was successfully completed by the Australians on 22 March, but strong currents and heavy enemy opposition prevented the raft crossing on the northern bridge site, and building there was delayed until troops who had crossed the river further south had cleared the enemy bank. It was now decided to build the second pontoon bridge further south, near to the Australian bridge, and its construction was

Figure 4.18. General H R L G Alexander, C-in-C Middle East Forces, at the Allenby Bridge in December 1942. (IWM E20459).

completed later that day. The footbridge and the barrel-pier bridge were eventually finished and a further pontoon bridge was built on this site using pontoons unused on the ford site. The advance on Amman began early on 24 March, but meanwhile maintenance of the Jordan bridge became difficult following a rapid rise in the river after heavy rains. The pontoon bridge was moved to a new position where pontoon bays could be substituted for the trestles, and the barrel-pier bridge had to be lengthened as the river widened. It was eventually threatened by driftwood and debris, which could not be shifted even by explosives, and in the end the bridge had to be swung to release the debris; this was no easy task as the anchorages were submerged and the cables had to be cut by explosives. In three days the river had risen by over ten feet, but now it started to subside and eventually the bridge was rebuilt, the span now being over 200ft. Problems also occurred with the pontoon bridges, which had to be lengthened, and on 28 March the southern bridge was dismantled. At one stage two GS wagons went over the side of the bridge during the night, damaging two bays of the bridge, which was, however, rapidly repaired.

In April a new pontoon bridge and a permanent steel cable suspension bridge was built across the Jordan and plans were drawn up for a three span steel girder bridge. This bridge was completed after the Armistice and was named the Allenby Bridge after General Sir Edmund Allenby, C-in-C of the EEF; it remained in use for many years, until it was destroyed during the Arab-Israeli Six Day War of 1967. (Figure 4.18).

The Campaign in Mesopotamia

In anticipation of Turkish involvement in the war, which came at the end of October 1914, Britain had already dispatched a force to Bahrein on the Persian Gulf, charged with carrying out operations against Turkish Mesopotamia and safeguarding the Anglo-Persian Oil supplies. Once war broke out the British force moved up to the mouth of the Shatt-el-Arab and in due course the Military Engineer Services built a substantial base at Basra, with considerable support from Indian Army units. The terrain in Mesopotamia (which lies between the Rivers Tigris and Euphrates, and is now part of modern Iraq) presented many problems to the military engineer; the population was founded close to the Tigris and Euphrates, the rest of the country being sparsely populated and with little development of road or rail communications. This meant that the campaign followed the line of these major rivers, crossing and recrossing them continuously, the crossings often being opposed. In addition there were no local materials or timber available and shade temperatures of 120° and even 130° were not unusual.

Many bridges were built during the campaign, some over 750ft long. Indeed, up until the capture of and advance beyond Kut in September 1915 and the subsequent withdrawal of our forces to the town prior to its siege by the Turks, the Bridging Train of King George V's Own Bengal Sappers and

Miners, under the command of Captain E W C Sandes RE, bridged the Tigris seventeen times, using pontoons and the local boats known as danacs. The Bridging Train had a perilous voyage during the subsequent withdrawal to Kut; it was without escort or pilots and was outdistanced by the troops on land. In a final brush with Turkish cavalry it lost the last of its eighteen pontoons and reached Kut with twelve rafts of leaking Arab boats. Luckily it was able to obtain more boats to enable it to bridge the Tigris on 5 December, thus enabling 6 Cavalry Brigade to cross the river and withdraw safely, although immediately after the crossing a number of the boats foundered. After a long siege the garrison at Kut finally surrendered to the Turks on 29 April 1916 and the remnants of the Bridging Train were marched into captivity with the remaining survivors of the garrison.

Meanwhile No 2 Bridging Train of the Bengal Sappers and Miners had arrived from Roorkee and, with the importance of bridging in this campaign, became the most important engineer unit in Mesopotamia. Royal Engineer units arrived in early 1916, soon after the Imperial General Staff relieved Army Headquarters India of operational command in the theatre. In due course Kut was retaken, Baghdad was captured on 11 March 1917 and preparations were made for a final offensive up both sides of the Tigris towards Mosul, just south of the Turkish border. On 1 November 1918 the Turkish Sixth Army surrendered at Mosul, having heard that an armistice had been signed the previous day.

Mesopotamia remained a theatre of war, however, until the peace treaty was ratified in 1924, and one bridge built during this post-armistice period certainly warrants mention. This bridge was that built across the Tigris at Mosul to the design of Lieutenant Colonel J F Turner RE, CRE of 18 Division. The existing Arab bridge was totally inadequate for heavy motor transport and a pontoon bridge was needed to enable the Division to carry out its routine tasks. At the crossing point selected the river was about 500ft wide at low level and 700ft wide at high level, with a rise and fall of 30ft and a maximum flood current speed estimated to be 25 knots. To bridge this very difficult site Turner proposed a crossing in the form of a suspension bridge laid on its side, the load on the cables being the force of current. Three horizontal catenary cables, each consisting of seven 3in wire ropes, were supported on twenty-four fully decked floats and anchored to massive concrete anchorages on either bank. Further cables were taken downstream from the decked floats to hold the wooden bridge pontoons in position; these pontoons were formed, in pairs, into rafts and connected by timber Warren truss girders which carried the roadway. Work started on the bridge in early 1920 and construction proper started in September; the 815ft long bridge, capable of carrying loaded armoured cars, was known as Turner's Folly because few believed that it could withstand the force of the river. It was opened in September 1921 and, although poorly maintained by the Mosul Municipality, remained in use until a severe flood washed it away in 1928.

CHAPTER FIVE

The Early Years at Christchurch

The Barracks, Christchurch

The end of the First World War saw the setting up of a permanent home for the innovation and development of bridging equipment for the British Army at The Barracks, Christchurch. The Barracks were built in the last decade of the Eighteenth Century to house cavalry and horse artillery units deployed to defend the South Coast against possible invasion by the French. Later duties of the troops included assistance to the excisemen in pursuit of gangs of local smugglers who plied their trade between France and the local coastline between Poole and Christchurch harbours. The Barracks were enlarged a number of times, but remained predominantly an artillery barracks, with occasional attachments of cavalry units and then, in 1918, with the incursion of the Sappers.

During the later stages of the War the continual development of the tank made it clear to the General Staff that the rapid bridging of tank obstacles would be of great importance during an advance; it was therefore decided, in 1918, to form three special Royal Engineer Tank Bridging Battalions. These units were to be the first mechanized Royal Engineer units and their formation was instituted at Christchurch in October 1918. Each battalion was to be equipped with twelve of the new Mark II Inglis Bridges, together with the Heavy Pontoons necessary to enable long floating bridges to be constructed for a possible crossing of the River Rhine. In addition each battalion was to be equipped with forty-eight tanks fitted with the new 21ft Canal Lock Bridge, also designed by Major Inglis. Major G le Q Martel DSO MC RE, later to become Lieutenant-General Sir Gifford Martel, had been closely connected with the development of these equipments while with the headquarters of the Tank Corps in France and he was now sent home to command one of the new battalions. However, the formation of the battalions was overtaken by events and Martel arrived home a few days before the Armistice was signed on 11 November 1918 to find that two of the battalions had already been disbanded. His battalion was thus the sole survivor of these first Assault Engineer units and that was not to survive for long, as it was reformed into the Experimental Bridging Company, Royal Engineers, on 28 February 1919, remaining under Martel's command.

Thus was established this most important home of military bridging, situated in an ideal location, with good trial sites both in and outside the Barracks, and with the River Stour flowing alongside the Barracks to provide the necessary water obstacle for the development of floating bridges and equipments. The Experimental Bridging Company was disbanded in August 1925, to be replaced by the Experimental Bridging Establishment, or EBE. The new unit was predominantly a civilian establishment, although Sapper officers continued to be posted to the unit and military command was not relinquished until Sir Donald Bailey became the first civilian Director in January 1957.

Policy direction of the work at Christchurch was vested in A Committee of the Royal Engineer Board; this more executive body had replaced the old Royal Engineer Committee, which had not been revived after the Armistice in 1918. The Board had three committees, A Committee responsible for Field Engineer Equipment, B Committee responsible for Air Defence, and C Committee responsible for Signal Matters; at a later stage D and E Committees were set up to deal with Radar and Camouflage respectively. In the early 1930s the Board's name was changed to the Royal Engineer and Signal Board, although in fact the Corps of Signals had been established from the Signal units and the Signal Service of the Royal Engineers as long ago as 1920.

Martel Takes Command

Martel's initial task at Christchurch was to continue trials on the Inglis Rectangular Bridge Mark II and the Canal Lock Bridge. He had first to contend with the effects of demobilization on his unit, however, since many of his best men wished to return to civilian life, re-enlistment threatening the possibility of a posting to the north or south of Russia, where we were still fighting. Martel overcame this problem to some extent by using a loophole in the regulations to re-enlist some 600 of his men for a three or four-year tour of duty, on the understanding that they would not be posted away from Christchurch. This action invoked the strong displeasure of the Army Council, when he was able successfully to resist a War Office order to send a draft of 400 of his Sappers to Northern Russia. Nevertheless unit strength dwindled to between 300 and 400 men, but many excellent artisans were retained and Martel was then able to give his full attention to the subject of bridging.

The Lock Bridge and the Royal Engineer Tank

As a result of his experiences with the Tank Corps, Martel was determined that full use should be made of the valuable source of power available in the engine of the tank, foreseeing that it could be used to assist the Sapper in a variety of engineering tasks in the field. The initial design of the Canal Lock Bridge, as proposed by Inglis, had worked satisfactorily during trials, but Martel reasoned that use of the tank engine to enable the bridge to be placed hydraulically would be an obvious advantage. The only tanks that were available in any number for modification were the Heavy Tanks and Martel suggested that all Royal Engineer Field Companies should have one section of these tanks to assist in their work. Work was therefore put in hand to design and test the necessary modifications to the standard Heavy Tank Mark V** that would enable it not only to carry and lay the Canal Lock Bridge, but also to assist the Sapper in a number of ways. (Figure 5.1) The modified tank became known as the Royal Engineer Tank and was basically the Mark V** adapted to carry a jib hinged at the front; the jib could be raised or lowered by a hydraulic ram mounted on top of the tank and operated by a pump driven off the main engine. This modification gave the tank the ability to pick up the 21ft Lock Bridge, carry it cross-country to an obstacle, and lay it under fire in less than a minute and without exposure of the crew.

The tank jib could also be used to suspend a two ton, two-piece roller, which was then towed cross-country in front of the tank to explode contact mines and to clear a mine-free path. During trials, mines containing up to 9lb of explosive were successfully exploded in this way without proving too unpleasant for the tank crew. The jib could also be used as a crane, able to lift loads up to 15 tons, and could place demolition charges accurately, the charges being fixed to the end of a long pole and then positioned against the obstacle. Towing trials were completed, using a Fowler Plough to cut communication trenches and a Mole Drainage Plough to bury as many as twenty or more signal cables at depths down to 2ft 6in. Although the Tank Corps had employed specialist tanks for some of these tasks during the War, such tasks were normally the responsibility of the Royal Engineers and the development of a Royal Engineer Tank, operated by Sapper units, was considered highly desirable, in order to eliminate organizational difficulties and to simplify training. Many policy changes were taking place within the Army, however, and, after the static warfare of the First World War, training and re-equipment favoured mobile operations. In such operations the heavy wartime tanks, designed for trench warfare, had no part and the Mark V** Tank soon became obsolete. The prototype Heavy RE Tank was destined to survive only in the humble role of a heavy mobile load that could be used to test new bridges at Christchurch. The principle lived on, however, and was revived in the Second World War, when it was used with great success in the

Figure 5.1. The Royal Engineer Tank launching a 21ft Canal Lock Bridge, capable of carrying a 35 ton tank. (IWM T18).

guise of the Armoured Vehicle Royal Engineers, or AVRE, which performed such sterling work during the Allied Campaign in Italy, in the invasion of Europe in 1944 and during subsequent operations.

The Inglis Assault Bridge

Major Inglis had completed his design of the Mark II Bridge, described in the previous chapter, in the minimum of time, but no major faults had come to light during trials and the bridge was easy to transport and erect. Hence further trials at Christchurch were mainly concerned with floating versions of the bridge and with Inglis' proposals for its use in the assault role. (Figure 5.2). A 135ft length of the bridge was mounted on a pair of idler tracks, instead of on the normal construction and launching trolley, so that the complete bridge could be pushed across country by the jib at the front of the RE Tank. When a river obstacle was reached the tank would continue pushing the bridge forward until the idler tracks dropped over the near bank and the nose of the bridge grounded on the far bank. Under suitable conditions the bridge could be placed in position across a 70ft obstacle in about a minute from the time of arrival on site, ready to take a heavy tank and with no exposure to fire of the tank crew. This version of the Inglis Bridge was not introduced into service, mainly because of the demise of the RE Tank; however, it does serve to illustrate the on-going nature of development, since various forms of mobile bridge, using the same principles but applied to the Mark III Inglis and the Bailey Bridge, were tested and used in the Second World War.

Figure 5.2. A 135ft Inglis Assault Bridge, pushed into position on idler tracks by an RE Tank. (Tank Museum 410/G4).

The Large Box Girder Bridge

Whilst the trials of the Inglis and Lock Bridge continued at Christchurch, Martel started work on what was probably his most important contribution to military bridging. He had thought for some time that the girder bridges currently in use, that is the Hopkins Bridge, the Stock Spans and the various types of Inglis Bridge, had basic shortcomings. Thus, a high percentage of the total weight was taken up in providing the roadway between the main girders; the bridges lacked adaptability, the same form of construction often being used for both short and long spans, which was obviously uneconomical; the bridges were slow to construct and, particularly in the case of the Inglis bridge with its tubular members, were expensive to manufacture. Martel therefore proposed an entirely new form of military bridge construction, one that would use prefabricated bridge components in the form of boxes that could be rapidly fitted together, using pins or dogs, to form the bridge girders. Furthermore the number of girders that would be used could be varied according to the span or the required load capacity of the bridge. (Figure 5.3 and Appendix B). Without doubt one can see here the emergence of some of the principles that were to be so successfully exploited

Figure 5.3. The superstructure for the Large Box Girder Bridge. (Military Engineering Vol III Part II, Pam 1, 1932).

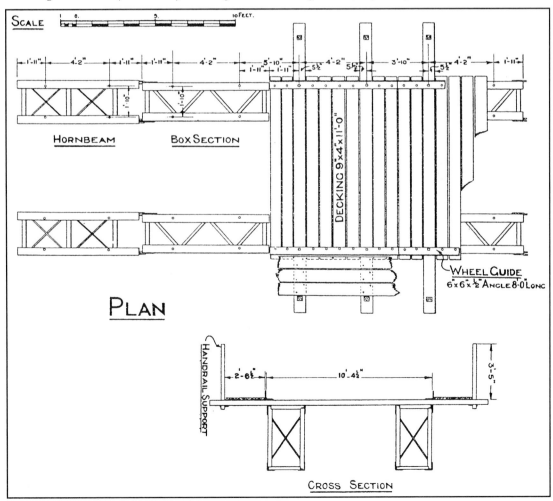

in the development of the Bailey Bridge some 20 years later.

The normal method used for launching the girders was by means of a derrick and preventer tackle, but other methods included the cantilevering of the girders across the gap, either with or without centre support, or the floating of the girders into position using pontoons to support the leading end. Once in position the girders were adjusted laterally to the correct

Figure 5.4. A prototype Large Box Girder Bridge under trial; an Inglis Bridge Mark II can be seen in the background. (IWM BG14).

spacing; the decking was then laid directly on to the girders, thus eliminating the need for cross girders. A longer decking plank was used in every fifth position, in order to support footwalks on either side of the bridge. The decking was held in place by angle iron curbs to give a finished roadway width of almost 10ft 6in.

Martel submitted his proposals for the bridge to the Royal Engineer Board in 1920. It was immediately seen that, with only three essential parts to the bridge, that is the boxes, the hornbeams and the decking planks, the bridge would be economical to manufacture and to transport, and also simple, although perhaps rather slow, to build in the field. Further, it could be easily widened to take two-way traffic, by adding further girders and adjusting the decking. After extensive trials the bridge was adopted by the Army in 1925 and was officially called the Large Box Girder Bridge, although at the time most Sappers referred to it as Martel's Girder Bridge. (Figure 5.4).

The Inglis Heavy Floating Bridge

Soon after the Armistice Major Inglis, who had by now returned to Cambridge, produced a design for a Heavy Floating Bridge, utilizing the few Heavy Pontoons that had been produced at the end of the War for use with the Inglis Mark II to form a long floating bridge. This bridge, which was to have been used by the now defunct RE Tank Bridging Battalions, was the first in which a continuous girder was to be used to spread a heavy vehicle load over a number of pontoons, thus reducing the size of the required pontoons considerably. Inglis' new proposal, however, was the first for a floating bridge specifically designed with a continuous stiffening girder. He reasoned that the use of long landing bays at either end of the bridge would eliminate the need for troublesome trestles and that the continuous girder would result in economy in the use of pontoons, which could be spaced according to the bridge load capacity required and could be replaced easily if damaged. On the other hand it was accepted that continuous construction made it difficult to form cut, that is to break bridge in order that river traffic may pass, and meant that a method of articulation had to be incorporated in the girder to cope with rises and falls in river level.

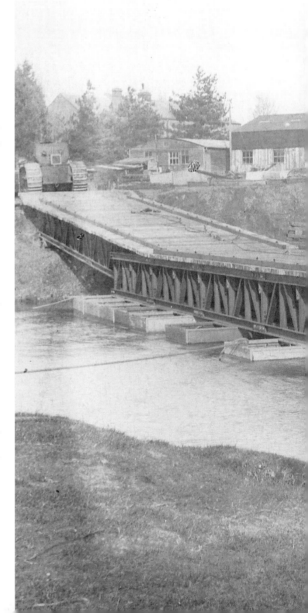

A prototype bridge was built and tested at Christchurch; this used twin lattice girders, about 3ft 6in high, supported by the old Mark II pontoons and with the decking laid directly on top of the girders. (Figure 5.5). The trials were not a great success, mainly because of the excessive weight of the girders, and the Royal Engineer Board decided that this form of construction was best suited for long bridges such as for the Rhine crossing, for which use of course the Heavy Pontoon/Inglis Mark II combination had been intended. With this in mind the Board decided that replacement of the shorter span and outdated Mark II/Mark III Pontoon Bridge was more urgent and development of the Inglis Heavy Pontoon Bridge did not proceed further.

Figure 5.5. The experimental Inglis Heavy Floating Bridge, on trial using Mark II Pontoons. (IWM P3).

Martel Leaves Christchurch

In December 1920 Martel received a nomination for the Staff College at Camberley and handed over command to Major A V T Wakely MC RE the following month. Martel's enthusiasm and interest in bridging were to continue, however, particularly during his command of 17 Field Company RE, as will be seen later. He left behind a first-class, well-knit unit, one to which he devoted all of his working and leisure time, except, as he quotes in his autobiography, 'on hunting days and when shooting'. He was in all ways an excellent officer, very highly thought of by his men, even some 70 years later by such as Percy Button, who served under him in the Experimental Bridging Company as a Lance Corporal Fitter and Turner. Button returned to Christchurch after demobilization, to become, as a fitter, one of the half-dozen or so civilians forming the staff of the new EBE; he served for another 39 years before retiring in 1964 as Workshops Foreman at MEXE, an excellent example of the extensive experience in military bridge design and development built up at Christchurch over the years.

Martel's keen interest in all sporting activities is exemplified by his efforts to win the UK Army Rugby Cup. He persuaded his men that they should all play rugby, as being much more of a man's game than mere football, and built up a strong unit team. Then, expecting the arrival of four new subalterns from the 'Shop' at Woolwich, he suggested that he should personally select his new officers, on the grounds that the work at Christchurch necessitated having officers with a strong mechanical bent. After much argument he went up to Woolwich and selected two good three-quarters, a fly half and a forward for his team. In fact all of the officers did well and rose to high rank; 2nd Lieutenant G R McMeekan RE, who led the scrum, returned to Christchurch as a Brigadier in 1946, as the first Chief Superintendent of the Military Engineering Experimental Establishment, or MEXE as EBE then became. The rugby team reached the semi-final of the UK unit team championship, only to be narrowly defeated by the eventual winners.

A New Pontoon Bridge

Meanwhile, at the end of 1920, the Royal Engineer Board initiated its first major new development - the replacement for the outdated Mark II / Mark III Pontoon Equipment, used with the timber-legged Mark IV or Weldon Trestle. The small open pontoons, formed from a bow and stern section to produce a 21ft long unit, had many shortcomings, not least of which was an unsuitability for use in fast currents; this had been demonstrated during the War in Northern Italy, when flood conditions had caused pontoons to swamp and sink.

First proposals for the new pontoon envisaged steel construction throughout, to reduce maintenance problems and to ensure rapid

Figure 5.6. The Mark IV or Consuta Pontoon on its wagon. (IWM P80).

manufacture during an emergency. Eventually a type of plywood called Consuta was used, however, as this gave a saving in weight of some 500lb per pontoon. (Figure 5.6 and Appendix B). The pontoon, subsequently named the **Mark IV Pontoon**, was completely decked in, to increase its safe buoyancy to about 6½ tons. (Figure 5.7 and Appendix B). A new **Mark V Trestle** was designed for use with the pontoon and this had mild steel legs,

Figure 5.7. The Consuta Pontoon Bridge Trestle Mark V. (Military Engineering Vol III, Part II, Pam 3, 1934).

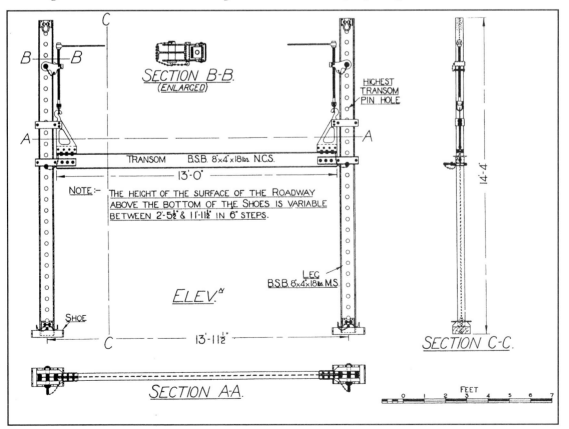

Figure 5.8. *A 30 cwt lorry crossing a Light Bridge, formed from Mark IV Pontoons and Mark V Trestles.* (IWM P120).

14ft 3in long and made from 8in x 4in British Standard Beams. 22ft long road bearers spanned from the shore to the trestle and thence to the first and subsequent mild steel pontoon saddles, centrally placed on the pontoon piers; ribands and Oregon pine chesses completed the decking.

Various forms of bridge construction could be used. Bipartite piers spaced about 21ft apart and used with single trestles at either end of bridge formed the Medium Pontoon Bridge, capable of carrying an 8 ton tank. The Heavy Pontoon Bridge, able to take an 18 ton tank, used rafts formed from two bipartite piers linked together, the rafts also being spaced about 21ft apart; this bridge needed a double trestle pier at either end because of the increased

Figure 5.9. *The Consuta Pontoon Bridge Trestle Mark VI.* (Military Engineering Vol III, Part II, Pam 3, 1934).

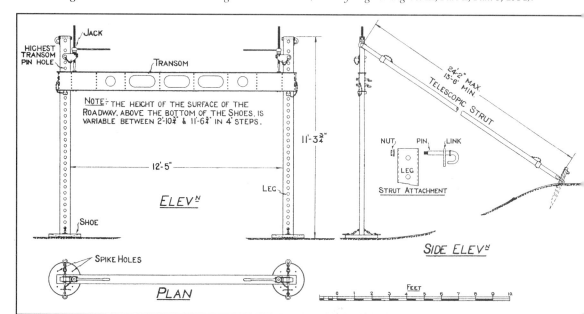

load capacity. (Figure 5.8). A Light Pontoon Bridge could also be constructed, using single 21ft pontoons, and the equipment could additionally be used to form rafts for ferrying troops and equipment over wide rivers. The new bridge had successfully completed all of its trials by 1924 and came into service in 1927, but a few years later a much stronger trestle was introduced. (Figure 5.9 and Appendix B). This was the **Mark VI Trestle**, which could be used singly at each end of the Heavy Bridge, in place of the double trestle pier needed with the **Mark V Trestles**.

Four methods were commonly used for building the bridges. The **Forming Up Method** connected up pontoon piers and superstructure in succession at the head of bridge; the **Rafting Method** constructed two or more pontoons into rafts and then joined them up to form bridge; in the **Swinging Method** the complete bridge was constructed alongside the home bank and then swung into position; in the **Booming Out Method** the connection of pontoons and superstructure was completed in succession from the home bank, pushing out the growing string of pontoons until it reached the far bank.

The Rawlinson Committee, set up in 1919 to consider the future organization of the Royal Engineers, had decided that the various bridging equipments used by the Sappers should be held and transported by Bridging Parks of the Royal Army Service Corps. In accordance with this recommendation the new pontoon equipment was issued to Pontoon Bridging Parks RASC (later to become the familiar Bridging Companies RASC of the Second World War). It was carried on specially modified 3 ton six wheeled lorries, a far cry from the horse drawn Pontoon and Trestle Wagons of the First World War. Despite the Rawlinson Committee decision, the Folding Boat Equipment and the Small Box Girder Bridge, both developed later, were retained by the Sappers within the Divisional Field Park Companies.

The Infantry Assault Bridge

The last chapter mentioned the extensive use made of light improvised foot bridges during the campaign in France; such bridges consisted of light floats made from petrol tins, cork, sheet metal or any convenient material, with a simple footwalk spanning between the floats, enabling infantry to cross a river obstacle in single file. These light float bridges proved of such importance during the last stages of the War that Christchurch was charged with the task of developing a standard equipment to meet the need. Trials to produce a satisfactory float started in 1920 and a number of designs were tested, using, for example, cork, kapok and even hydrogen-filled floats. Although the design was continually evolving, by 1923 a kapok-filled canvas float had proved to be most satisfactory and was finally adopted for the equipment, which thus became known as the **Kapok Assault Bridge**. The final version of the bridge used timber footwalks, clipped on at each end to

Figure 5.10. Launching a Kapok Assault Bridge at Christchurch, with Heavy Pontoons in the background. (IWM ex EBE).

the central metal bar forming part of the saddle strapped to each float. Floats were spaced at 6ft 6in centres, rope handrails were fitted and light guys held the bridge in place against the effects of current. (Figure 5.10).

The bridge was easily built and launched, both float and decking panel being easy one man loads. Trials followed on kapok float rafts and on a light pack bridge for horses, which used either two or three lines of decking panels. Once again the bridge was held by the RASC Pontoon Bridging Park, twenty-seven bays of bridge being carried on a 30cwt lorry and a 15cwt trailer.

Folding Boat Equipment

One more important floating equipment was developed during this period; this was the Folding Boat Equipment or FBE, subsequently much used during the Second World War and playing, with the Bailey Bridge, an important part in the Rhine crossings in 1945. The equipment was developed as a means of getting light vehicles across a river in immediate support of an attack, thus overcoming the inevitable delays that occurred before a Medium Pontoon Bridge could be deployed and completed.

At an early stage a folding boat, made of the new aluminium alloy Duralumin, had been inspected in Germany; trials with various folding dinghies followed before the final version evolved. (Figure 5.11 and Appendix B). As it was finally developed, the basic unit of the new equipment was a folding boat made from three pieces of ½ in plywood, comprising the bottom and two sides of the boat, the sides being attached to the bottom by continuous fabric hinges. The ply was so shaped that, when folded, the sides of the boat lay flat against the bottom, but when the sides were raised the bottom panel was raised up at the ends. The boat could ferry

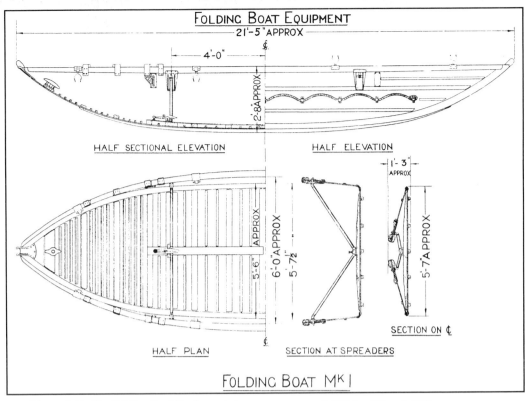

FOLDING BOAT EQUIPMENT
21'-5" APPROX

4'-0"

2'-8" APPROX

HALF SECTIONAL ELEVATION   HALF ELEVATION

1'-3" APPROX

APPROX
6'-0" APPROX
5'-6" APPROX
5'-7½"
5'-7" APPROX

SECTION ON ₵

HALF PLAN   SECTION AT SPREADERS

FOLDING BOAT Mᴷ I

Figure 5.11. The Folding Boat Equipment. (Military Engineering Vol III, Part II Pam 2, 1934).

sixteen armed men rapidly across a river, using a crew of commander and four to row the boat, or fitted with a Coventry 7½hp outboard motor; in still water a maximum of thirty armed men could be carried, including the crew. Three distinct types of superstructure were developed, enabling the building of either a tracked raft, a decked raft or a landing stage for use as such or as part of a bridge.

The FBE Tracked Raft, with a 3 ton capacity, consisted of two boats connected by two long transoms laid across the four gunwales. (Figure 5.12).

Figure 5.12. The Folding Boat Equipment end loading or tracked raft. (IWM P219)

Two 14ft long trackways, running in the fore and aft direction of the boats, were fixed to the transoms to form the raft deck, with short 9ft trackways at either end to form the ramps. The raft was independent of any particular landing site and was thus known as a free-ranging raft or ferry, being propelled either by oar or, more satisfactorily, by outboard motor, giving it a speed of about 3 to 4 knots in still water.

The FBE Decked Raft, with a 4½ ton capacity, also used two boats, but with 20ft of decking, comprising nine road-bearers with 10ft long chesses and ribands, built directly across the four gunwales; the deck was thus at right angles to that in the tracked raft. (Figure 5.13.) With no ramps, the raft had to be operated between landing stages built on both river banks; the landing stage normally consisted of an anchored decked raft, with the inshore boat replaced by an FBE Trestle, connected in turn to the shore by a bay of decking.

The FBE Bridge could be constructed rapidly by connecting up a series of decked rafts, or floating bays, between landing stages constructed on opposite banks of the river. The trestle used for the landing stages was the

Figure 5.13. The Folding Boat Equipment decked raft, using a third boat and ramps to act as a shore loading raft. (IWM P214).

FBE Trestle Mark I, which was very similar to the Trestle Mark V developed for the Pontoon bridge, but was of course smaller and capable of taking only Light loads. It was fitted with telescopic tubular struts to anchor the tops of the trestle legs back to the bank.

The FBE was adopted by the Army in 1928 and included a small three man **Folding Dinghy**, 10ft 3in long and with a beam of 4ft 3in. Although robustness and long life-expectancy had been sacrificed to some extent to produce a light, easily handled and constructed equipment, its flexibility in use was a great advantage. Thus it provided Field Companies with a useful boat to ferry stores and men, a free ranging ferry, and a fixed ferry capable of being rapidly converted into a Light bridge; the equipment was highly thought of by the troops.

D C Bailey

It was towards the end of the FBE development period that Bailey first became involved with military bridging. Donald Coleman Bailey was born in Yorkshire on 15 September 1901. He was educated at The Leys School, Cambridge, and then at Sheffield University, where he was awarded a Bachelor of Engineering degree in 1923. He first took up employment with Rowntrees of York and, after subsequent spells with the LMS Railway and the City Engineer's Department at Sheffield, during which he was involved with civil bridge design, he applied and was accepted for the post of Civilian Staff Engineer at the EBE. He came south to Christchurch in August 1928, met his first wife, Phyllis, and continued to live locally until he died in 1985, apart from a short spell spent at Shrivenham, where he was Dean from 1962 to 1966.

In 1928 the EBE had a very small and close-knit staff, under the command of Captain R D Davies RE. The major effort was being directed towards the completion of the FBE and Bailey soon found himself involved in this and in the design of the new Mark VI Trestle, as an active and respected member of the small team.

The Work of 17 Field Company RE

Meanwhile Martel was still very much involved in the military bridging field. Since the end of the War there had been little or no advance in the mechanization of the Royal Engineer Field Companies; indeed the Field Company of the mid-1920s differed little in personnel, equipment and transport from that of the late Nineteenth Century. The advent of the six wheeled 3 ton lorry in the early 1920s completely changed outlooks in the Army, however, and in April 1926 it was decided to set up an Experimental Mechanized Force to carry out tactical and operational trials on Salisbury Plain. It was also decided that 17 Field Company, under the command of Major Martel from June 1926, would become the first mechanized field company in the Corps of Royal Engineers and would operate with this new force.

The choice of Martel to command the Field Company was a case of poetic justice, since as long ago as November 1916, when he was a Brigade Major with the Tank Corps, he had written a paper entitled 'A Tank Army', in which he had put forward ideas for an independent tank force, to be used operationally and not merely in support of the infantry. The setting up of the new Mechanized Force, based upon the 7th Infantry Brigade at Tidworth but containing two Tank Corps battalions, was thus very much a step in the direction suggested by Martel.

Martel and 17 Company worked very closely with the EBE and the RE Board during the next two years or so and carried out extensive trials of new Sapper equipments, as well as trials on field unit establishments and equipment tables. There was much interest in the work of the Mechanized Force and many demonstrations and inspections resulted. These included a demonstration to the Dominion Prime Ministers in November 1926, when 17 Company demonstrated Stepping Stones, the Bateman Assault Bridge and elements of the Small Box Girder Bridge. An inspection by the Secretary of State for War followed in August 1927 and by the King of Afghanistan in March 1928. There was a demonstration for Members of Parliament later in the summer, but the highlight of the year was undoubtedly the inspection by HM King George V in July 1928. Many new ideas evolved during this period and some of the trial work relating to bridging is worthy of mention.

Bateman's Assault Bridge

Further development of the Tank Lock Bridge had been curtailed by the demise of the heavy and cumbersome tanks of the First World War. By now the much lighter Vickers Medium Tank Mark I was in quantity production, together with the Dragon Artillery Tractor, based upon a similar chassis. The considerable reduction in weight, from around 30 tons to about 12 tons, meant that it was no longer viable to carry a bridge supported at the front of a tank, as with the Lock Bridge. Major H H Bateman RE, who had commanded the Bridging Company since January 1923 and had now become the first Superintendent of the EBE after the reorganization of 1925, produced a clever alternative design for a tank-mounted assault bridge. (Figure 5.14). The prototype 30ft bridge was carried on the Dragon Artillery Tractor and was launched horizontally by winching it forward, whilst at the same time holding down the rear of the bridge. The tractor provided enough counterweight to enable spans of up to 20ft to be bridged in this manner, but for longer spans a light launching way was first pushed across the gap to support the front end of the bridge proper as it was subsequently launched. The bridge consisted of a framework made from steel joists and had no decking, so that it could only be used by tracked vehicles. Successful trials were carried out by 17 Company, but the bridge was not developed further,

Figure 5.14. Bateman's Assault Bridge, mounted on a Dragon Artillery Tractor. The 30ft bridge is being launched across a 20ft gap. (IWM T40).

mainly on the grounds of cost and a reluctance on the part of the authorities to commit specialist vehicles, still in short supply, solely for a bridging role.

During this period a simple trackway bridge was also tested. This was in effect a development of the Congreve Trough of the early 19th century and it interesting to note that the idea that such a bridge should be widely used was first suggested by Winston Churchill during the First World War. As First Lord of the Admiralty Churchill had an interest in the operations of the Royal Naval Air Service Armoured Car Division operating in France and, in a memorandum dated 23 September 1914, he wrote 'It is important that motor transport and armoured motor cars should be provided to a certain extent with the means of bridging small cuts in the road, and an arrangement of planks capable of bridging a ten or twelve foot span quickly and easily should be carried with every ten or twelve machines.' The proposal now considered consisted of two 18ft long metal tracks or channels, very similar to those used with the Bateman Bridge. The trackways were carried attached to the sides of the Vickers Medium Tank Mark II. The intention was for the tank crew to assemble the two channels into a simple bridge, using spacing bars, near to the site at which the crossing was required, and then to place it in position. No satisfactory method of launching was devised, other than to manhandle the bridge, and the idea was not considered further until the mid-1930s, when various forms of trackway bridge were developed.

Stepping Stones

Another assault device developed jointly by EBE and 17 Company consisted of timber frameworks known as Stepping Stones, which could be placed in line across a small stream or river to enable a tank to cross. Each framework was made from two timber trestles, joined by timber bracing to form a

113

Figure 5.15. *Martel's Stepping Stones expedient for crossing shallow streams. Martel can be seen on the extreme left.* (Tank Museum 880/01).

skeleton box, about 4ft square in cross-section and 12ft long. The Stepping Stones were strung together by short ropes, four ropes connecting each pair, and with longer ropes attached to the leading and trailing units. The line of Stepping Stones was set out at right angles to the river bank; then, as the far bank party of four Sappers pulled on the long leading ropes, the six Sappers detailed off to each unit carried them down to the river bank and successively pushed them into the water. Once the line of Stepping Stones had been floated across the river, the leading and trailing ropes were made fast to pickets, and guy ropes were fitted up and down stream. (Figure 5.15.) Stepping Stones could cope with streams up to 4 or 5ft deep and up to 100ft wide; they could be placed in position quite quickly and enabled a Vickers Tank to cross a water obstacle in a few minutes. However, tank drivers were loath to linger on the structure and crossings at speeds of up to 15mph could be quite spectacular and hair-raising. The equipment did not progress beyond the trial stage, although some work was done on a larger Stepping Stones for use in water up to 8ft deep and for spans up to 200ft.

The Mat Bridge

This was another device tried out in 1926 and was an attempt to reduce the eight to ten-hour delay that occurred after the infantry had crossed a river obstacle, using their Kapok Assault Bridges and before completion of a Medium Pontoon Bridge enabled support vehicles to be brought up. The bridge consisted of a continuous mat of 11ft long deal planks, 1½in thick and made up into 7ft long panels which were connected together by fishplates. Short planks, raised at 45°, were fixed at both ends of the deck planks to improve the flow of water beneath the mat and to prevent the water flowing over the deck. The bridge thus floated on the water and operated on the principle that provided a vehicle crossed at reasonable speed, it would always be climbing on to a part of the mat that had yet to become submerged. Various forms of longitudinal stiffening were used to bring the flexibility of the mat within reasonable limits. The need for this became apparent after the first trial; as a six-wheeled Morris was being driven over the bridge at about 10mph, the mat developed an excessive bow wave in front of it; this had the effect of slowing the vehicle down to such an extent that it eventually stopped and slowly sank. The problem was easily overcome, but the final version of the equipment proved to be rather heavy and cumbersome, and the design did not proceed further. The principle was revived during the Second World War, however, initially as the Indian Mat Bridge, then as the Clover Floating Airstrip, and finally as the Swiss Roll, a device developed by a Mr R M Hamilton for running lorries ashore on the Normandy beaches.

The Kapok Assault Bridge Raft

The raft was another of Martel's innovations, again aimed at rapid deployment of support vehicles across a river obstacle in support of the Infantry. In particular Martel had in mind the passage of the small two-man tankettes deployed with the Mechanized Force for evaluation. The Force included, as part of the 3rd Tank Battalion, eight Carden-Loyd and eight Morris-Martel tankettes, the latter having been developed from the one-man tankette that Martel had designed and constructed with his own hands in 1925. The raft was formed from twenty-eight Kapok Assault Bridge floats, preassembled in three layers, to form a 12ft by 13ft timber-decked unit; this was then folded in half so that it could be more easily transported by lorry. The raft was unfolded, in the upside down position, once the lorry reached the river bank; the vehicle then backed down to the water's edge and the raft was tipped over into the water. The raft was often used on exercises, but its disadvantage was that good firm access for the transporting vehicle was required right down to the water's edge.

The Small Box Girder Bridge

By far the most important equipment with which 17 Company became involved was the Small Box Girder Bridge, or SBG. Development of the Large Box Girder Bridge, or LBG, had gone well and the bridge was now in service; however, the bridge had been designed to take what were, in those days, heavy military loads, tanks up to 18 tons in weight over spans up to

80ft, and was thus necessarily heavy and slow to build. With the introduction of the lighter Medium Tanks, and with a maximum Army vehicle loading, apart from the tanks, of about 8 or 9 tons, it became clear that a Medium Class bridge, much easier to transport and build, would be a very useful item of equipment. A span of about 60ft was selected, since this was thought to be the maximum span likely to be needed to replace the majority of civil bridges demolished in war, and it was decided to use, once again, the box girder principle, so successful with the LBG, but using this time a much lighter girder to match the reduced loading and span requirements.

Martel produced some initial proposals, although the detailed design was carried out at the EBE by Captain R D Davies RE, who had taken over from Bateman as Superintendent in November 1926. (Figure 5.16.) Some of the first girder units were made in the EBE and the first set of equipment was available for trials by 1928, although trials involving this set and two further modified sets carried on into the early 1930s. From the beginning 17 Company had been involved in launching trials and eventually a method using a 22ft 9in light launching nose, with a 2ft diameter detachable wheel fitted at the end, was adopted; one launching nose was attached to the front of the 66ft 6in girder and one at the rear. The girder and launching noses were mounted on rollers and pushed across the gap by hand, with Sappers acting as counterweight; on the point of balance a dozen or more men

Figure 5.16. Trafficking trials for the prototype Small Box Girder Bridge in 1929. (IWM M167).

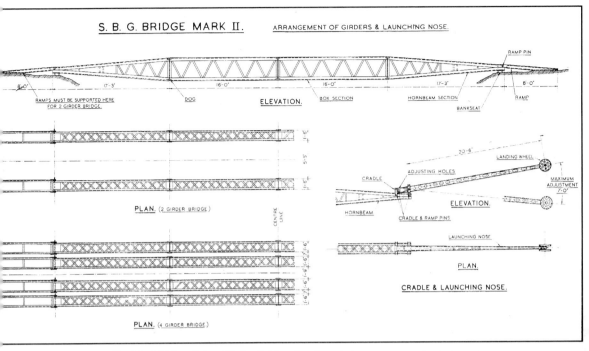

Figure 5.17. The Mark II Small Box Girder Bridge showing girder arrangements. (Military Engineering Vol III, Part II, Pam 5, 1939).

doubled across the girder to lift on the nose and complete the launch. Using this method of construction at one of the demonstrations in 1929, 17 Company was able to bridge a 60ft gap in just under 20 minutes from time of arrival at site to first vehicle crossing.

As finally adopted in 1933, the bridge consisted of an 8ft 6in timber-decked roadway supported on two or four girders, able to bridge clear spans of 32, 48 or 64ft; the two-girder version could take Medium loads at a 64ft span. The layout of girders and the method of launching is shown in Figure 5.17, which shows the Mark II version of the bridge, incorporating minor modifications and introduced in 1936. The decision to use high-tensile structural steel and welded construction for the box sections (recommended by Donald Bailey) resulted from considerable research into welding techniques and joint design, research that paid valuable dividends later in the design of the Bailey Bridge. (See Appendix B). A bridge set was carried in five vehicles, three carrying loads of girder and ancillary equipment and the other two the decking. Two bridge sets were allocated to each Divisional Field Park Company and one further set to the RASC Pontoon Bridge Park for each Division; each set could produce one 64ft or two 32ft two girder bridges, or one 48ft four girder bridge.

Although 17 Company was initially involved with the development of the

117

SBG, its useful work was soon to cease. In 1928 the mechanized force operating on Salisbury Plain was renamed the Experimental Armoured Force and shortly after was disbanded. Martel handed over command of his Company and left for India, and although the Armoured Force was resurrected in 1931, in a new form as the 1st Brigade, Royal Armoured Corps, no steps were taken to include an armoured Royal Engineer unit. It was not until the Second World War that increased tank production made possible the formation of the first armoured engineer units.

The End of a Decade

Thus came to an end a very eventful decade in the history of military bridging at Christchurch. The ten years or so to 1930 had seen the setting up of the establishment from scratch, very considerable contributions from Martel and the arrival of Bailey on the scene. The Large Box Girder Bridge was in production, the Small Box Girder design had been virtually finalized and the Sappers now had the FBE, the Consuta Pontoon Equipment and the Kapok Assault Bridge. In addition valuable experience had been gained in the techniques of military bridge design and fabrication, experience that was to pay handsome dividends in the period up to and including the start of the Second World War. And all this from an establishment with a minimum of staff and a shoe-string budget.

CHAPTER SIX

Rearmament in the 1930s

Lean Times at Christchurch

Between 1929 and 1936 the Army experienced what was perhaps one of its leanest periods. With the economic situation in the early 1930s and the swing towards disarmament in the aftermath of the First World War, all things military were out of favour and very little development work took place. In late 1932 the total strength of the EBE consisted of one Royal Engineer officer (Captain S G Galpin RE, who had just taken over from Major J B H Doyle OBE RE as Superintendent), one qualified civil engineer (Mr D C Bailey) as design officer, one draughtsman, and twenty or so workshop and labouring hands - the grand total of personnel directly employed in the design, manufacture and testing of bridging equipment for the Corps of Royal Engineers. Numbers shrank still further later and at one time there was considerable correspondence with the War Office arguing the case for the retention of the single professional civilian - Mr Bailey. Luckily good sense prevailed and Bailey remained in post, building up the experience that led to the development of the bridge named after him in the early stages of the war that was to come. As we shall see, the course of the war would have been very different without the vast quantities of mass-producible Bailey Bridge that was to be made available to the Allied Forces.

The Large Box Girder Mark II

One equipment that did receive attention during this period was the Large Box Girder Bridge, the introduction of heavier tanks then looking a distinct possibility. A General Staff Specification for the re-design of the bridge was drawn up and in 1931 tenders were invited from a number of leading engineering firms. None of the designs submitted could approach that of the EBE, however, which proposed the use of high-tensile steel members together with welding to replace the previously used riveting of joints.

With the slow pace of rearmament the Mark II Large Box Girder Bridge was not actually adopted by the Army until 1938. The main changes from the earlier version are listed below.

1. An increase in the size of the Box Unit from 8ft x 4ft to 10½ft x 5½ft, which had the effect of increasing the weight to 1500lb. This was considered to be a sixteen man load, although the manual did suggest the use of an NCO and a carrying party of twenty-four to speed up construction. (Figure 6.1).

Figure 6.1. *A recruit party training with the LBG Mark II in 1940.* (IWM).

2. Replacement of the 8ft Hornbeam Unit of the Mark I version by a new two-part end of bridge girder, comprising an intermediate section and a shore section, each 10ft long; this was necessary because of the increased depth of the main box units.

3. The use of Chrome Molybdenum Steel Dogs to connect the sections of the girders; these replaced the previously used steel pins which had necessitated projecting and easily damaged lugs at the box corners.

4. Alignment of the sections by dowels while the dogs were positioned. Later, a better fixing was provided by welding pins at the corners of the boxes; steel links then fitted over the pins and were held in position by split pins.

As a result of these improvements and the use of higher-strength materials, the capacity of the four girder version of the bridge was increased from about Class 18 at a span of 80ft to Class 24 at a span of 130ft.

The Tide Begins to Turn

The events leading up to the outbreak of the Second World War have been written of at length elsewhere and need not be repeated here. Suffice it to say that after Hitler became Chancellor of Germany early in 1933 and the Nazi party came to power at the subsequent elections, the tide gradually began to turn. In March 1936 Germany reoccupied the Rhineland and war clouds really began to form. It became clear that we had a small, ill-equipped, out-of-date army, and soon financial restrictions began to ease and equipment development became more urgent. As far as the EBE was concerned, there was a slight improvement in the staffing situation and a considerable impetus to re-examine the capacity and capabilities of our bridging equipments.

British Tanks Between the Wars

Part of this re-examination was concerned with changes in existing and projected tank loading. Since the introduction of the tank on the battlefield, the task of the Sappers involved with bridging had increased considerably, bridges now being required for much heavier loads and often on sites well away from main thoroughfares. It is therefore worthwhile at this point to digress slightly and consider the changes in the development of tanks that took place between the wars.

Tank Nomenclature during this period was complex and muddled, and a brief resume of the salient points, up to the present time, may help. During the First World War British tanks were classified as Heavy Tanks, Mark I, II etc and Medium Tanks Mark A, B etc. The Heavy Tanks, weighing in the region of 30 tons, were either Male, armed with a 6pdr gun in each side sponson, or Female, armed with two machine guns in each sponson; the Medium Tanks weighed in the region of 15 - 20 tons.

After the First World War the letter system of distinguishing marks for Medium Tanks was replaced by Roman numerals and in the mid-1920s each new type of tank was given the prefix 'A'. Additionally, experimental models of a new tank would be given an 'E' number, for example A6-E2, but mark numbers were still used for distinct variations of a basic type. In the mid-1930s the General Staff decided that the 'A' prefix should be retained, but that tanks should be classified as Heavy, Cruiser or Light. This new classification used the name Cruiser instead of Medium for the much faster and more lightly armoured tanks in the middleweight bracket. Subsequently the category of Heavy Tank was dropped and that of Infantry Tank was introduced for the slower, more heavily armoured tank, intended to be used in close support of the infantry. This new classification had little relevance to all-up weight; for example the A11-Infantry Tank Mark I, (named the Matilda I, when all tanks were given names in late 1941) weighed about 11 tons, whereas the A22-Infantry Mark IV (named the Churchill I) weighed closer to 40 tons.

After the Second World War the 'A' prefix was dropped and all military vehicles were given an FV, or Fighting Vehicle, number during development. On entering service all tanks were given a name beginning with the letter 'C', following the pattern of the Churchill and the Centurion, the latest additions being the Chieftain and the Challenger.

The Tanks in Question. A series of **Light Tanks**, weighing between 5 and

7 tons, was introduced in the late 1920s with the A4-Vickers Light Tank Mark I; the Mark VI version of this tank saw service in the Western Desert in 1939. However, the backbone of the Royal Tank Corps from the early 1920s to the war was the A2-Vickers Medium Tank Marks I and II, the Mark I coming into service in 1923 at a weight of about 12 tons. The first of the **Cruiser Tank** series, that is the A9 and A10, and then the A13 (which as the A13 Mark III was known as the Cruiser Mark V or Covenanter, subsequently used to carry and launch the No l Tank Bridge) weighed in between 12 and 18 tons in the late 1930s. Finally the **Infantry Tanks** ranged from the Matilda I, previously mentioned, at 11 tons, through the 17 ton Valentine I (which was the Infantry Tank Mark III, a Vickers developed tank with no A number) to the A12-Infantry Tank Mark II, or Matilda II, weighing 26½ tons.

A New Pontoon Bridge for the 30s

It was against the background of the gradually increasing weight of the Army's tanks that bridging development at Christchurch proceeded in the years just prior to the Second World War. Work on the Matilda II started in November 1936 and the design of a new pontoon bridge, ordered in early 1936 by the Royal Engineer and Signal Board (as the RE Board had now become), was the first equipment to be affected by the advent of the new tank. The new bridge was originally intended to have a 14 ton capacity, but with a capability of being strengthened to take a 20 ton load if required. The bridge, comprising the **Pontoon Mark V** (Appendix B) and the **Trestle Mark VII**, was needed to replace the Consuta or Mark IV Pontoon and the Trestles Mark V and VI developed in the 1920s. Alternative designs were considered and model tests were carried out at the National Physical Laboratory. It was then decided to accelerate the programme so that full-scale trials could be held in the summer of 1937 and orders for trial equipment were placed so that the first six pontoons were delivered to EBE in January. By this time, however, the General Staff had decided to increase the load capacity to 18 tons with a possible strengthened capacity of 24 tons, in order to accommodate the new Matilda II. The change in requirement caused frantic recalculation and redesign, the pontoon having to be lengthened by about 3ft. It was decided to carry the 18 ton load on two-pier rafts and the 24 ton load on three-pier rafts, each pontoon pier comprising two pontoons coupled stern to stern. Full-scale trials took place during 1937 at the Wyke Regis Bridging Camp in Dorset, the troop trial equipment having been ordered straight off the drawing board; acceptance of the equipment took place soon after. The design was finalized and contracts placed during the next few months, the hastening of the whole procedure for development, trials and subsequent manufacture clearly illustrating the widely held concern for rearmament.

The normal method of bridge construction started with the building of a trestle bay, using the new Mark VII Trestle, which differed only in detail from

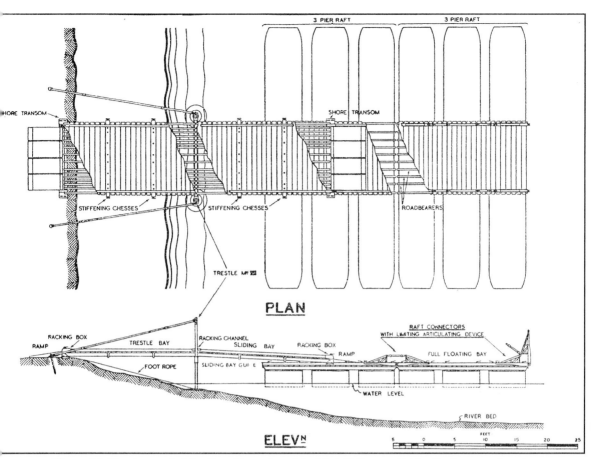

Figure 6.2. The shore end of the Class 24 version of the Mark V Pontoon Bridge Equipment, adopted in 1939. (Military Engineering Vol III, Part II, Pam 3, 1940).

the previous Mark VI. The required number of rafts, each about 21ft long, were then built on the home bank and were warped out one at a time to be connected up at head of bridge. (Figure 6.2). The rafts, built with two pontoon piers for Class 18 construction and three piers for Class 24, were coupled together using special raft connectors; these incorporated tubular steel struts designed to limit articulation as the load passed over the junction between adjacent rafts. The equipment could be used to construct a Class 30 shore-loading raft (which became known as the Bat Wing Raft) by connecting together two three-pier rafts and then removing the two outer piers; the four remaining piers formed the raft, with the overhang of decking at each end of the raft acting as the ramps. A 66½ ft long 40 ton raft also evolved, using six Mark V Pontoons and a four girder Mark III SBG Bridge as the superstructure.

The bridge was adopted and was available with the Field Force in 1939; it was a reasonable equipment as first conceived, but suffered by being stretched in the design stage, and without doubt the third pontoon pier necessary in each raft for the Class 24 bridge, which soon became the norm with increases in vehicle weights, was an uneconomical and cumbersome

123

method of construction. The bridge was never used operationally and really came into its own by providing a ready source of Mark V Pontoons for use with the Bailey Pontoon Bridge.

A big drawback with the new equipment was its reliance on the use of the inshore trestle and hence on the unpredictable condition of the riverbed on which the trestle rested. (Figure 6.3). Captain S A Stewart RE (later Brigadier Stewart CBE) became Superintendent of EBE in November 1936 and remained in this most important post until September 1941; he was thus Superintendent during the vital period before war broke out and right through the early stages of the development of the Bailey Bridge. He recalled that during the late 1936 trials of the prototype Mark V Pontoon at Christchurch there was some difficulty in obtaining a suitable test load. An experimental 17 ton tank with sprung suspension was located at Bulford; the tank did not go to production because of its high cost, but this one example was the pride and joy of the Tank Corps Brigadier, who only agreed to its loan after much argument. To everyone's dismay, a trestle foot rope failed just as the tank was passing over the trestle and on to the floating bridge proper; the foot of the trestle leg slowly slid down the bank but luckily stopped just as the tank was on the point of balance. Fortunately all 35 tons

Figure 6.3. The Class 18 version of the new pontoon bridge, with an extended landing bay. (WO photograph).

Figure 6.4. The long landing bay developed for the Mark V Pontoon Bridge Equipment. (IWM 1108).

of Christchurch's old faithful, the RE Heavy Tank Mark V**, was on hand and once shackled to the rear of the trial tank managed to pull it back to safety. The Brigadier was not at all amused when he finally heard of the incident.

An improvised version of the bridge overcame problems arising from the use of trestles by using a 48ft four girder Mark III SBG Bridge as a landing bay. However, at a later stage a special long-landing bay was designed for the bridge, and this new bay, which spanned from the shore on to the first floating bay of bridge proper, eliminated the need for the trestle, the trestle bay and the end-floating or sliding bay. (Figure 6.4). It consisted of a four-girder box girder type bridge almost 42ft long; the girders were formed from a centre section and two hornbeam sections, very similar to SBG sections but slightly shorter in length. Sections were coupled together by mating chrome molybdenum steel dowels with corresponding holes in the end of the adjacent section; each dowel had a machined neck into which was slid a stainless steel locking plate, thus locking sections firmly together. An alternative version of the Class 30 shore-loading raft made use of this special long-landing bay as its superstructure.

The Small Box Girder Bridge, Mark III

The Small Box Girder Bridge was similarly affected by the advent of the Matilda II. The Mark I Bridge, adopted in 1933, had been modified in a minor way in 1936. Thus the SBG Mark II incorporated minor strengthening of the box unit diagonals, introduced a strengthened deck panel and abandoned the link pin connectors in favour of connecting dogs, similar to those introduced with the LBG Mark II.

Redesign of the bridge as the SBG Mark III, to take the increased loading of the Matilda II, was undertaken by the EBE during a slack period; the

Establishment was thus in the happy position of being able to respond to a subsequent official request for upgrading by dispatching the new drawings by return of post. The bridge was in production within a few weeks and replaced the SBG Mark II in 1939. In general the basic design remained unchanged, the increased strength being obtained by use of heavier steel sections for the box and hornbeam units, which raised their weights by about 200lb; heavier connecting dogs were also used. The superstructure was largely unchanged, although slight changes in girder width meant locating channels were repositioned and thus the Mark II and the Mark III deck systems were not interchangeable. In fact, although the Mark II and Mark III SBG Bridges were not clearly distinguishable one from the other, they were not interchangeable at all and, to avoid confusion, the lightening holes in the girder diaphragms were made circular in the Mark III, whereas they had been peardrop-shaped in the Mark II. The net result of the improvements was to increase the capacity of the two-girder bridge from Class 9 to Class 12 at a span of 64ft, and that of the four-girder bridge, at the same span, from Class 18 to Class 24.

Foreign Exploitation

Without doubt the Large and Small Box Girder Bridge designs presented a major advance in the evolution of military equipment bridging, a fact that was not lost on foreign armies. The Japanese KTT military bridge, which was designed and fabricated by the Yokogawa Bridge Works in 1929, was very similar in many respects to Martel's LBG design of 1920, the first British bridge to use pins to connect boxes or panels together. The KTT Bridge used box sections of similar size and configuration to the LBG, which were pinned together at the corners to form girders that were then laid side by side to form a deck bridge. Admittedly the KTT Bridge was of welded rather than riveted construction, but the similarity was striking; at a later date the Mark II version of the LBG was itself of welded construction.

In the mid-1930s the German Army copied the design of the SBG almost exactly, calling their bridge the Kastenträger-Gerät, literally the box girder equipment. The K-Gerät used the same panel length as the SBG, but slightly amended the bracing details. A 1943 article in the German magazine Military Engineer describes the bridge being used on the Russian front in conjunction with pontoons and goes on to say that 'the bridge has given good service and is similar to bridges used in enemy armies'. Its use prompted an instruction in a Royal Engineers Training Memorandum of the same year to the effect that, although the SBG Mark III was by then obsolete in the British Army, training with SBG should occasionally continue to enable units to utilize captured enemy equipment

In the US Army of the 1930s the Engineer Corps had for years relied on the use of trestle or piled bridges for communication bridging. The Engineer Board then decided that the time constraints on construction of such bridges were not acceptable and commissioned the design of new girder bridges. The new designs, produced by Sverdrup and Partners of St Louis in the mid-1930s, were for the H-10 and H-20 bridges, modelled very closely on the British SBG and the LBG Bridges respectively. Subsequently the Americans faced the same problem as the British - a constantly increasing weight of the new battle tanks necessitating a heavier load class for their bridges. Thus by 1941 the Americans were actively evaluating the new Bailey Bridge, prior to its adoption for their Corps of Engineers.

Folding Boat Equipment Mark III

The original Folding Boat Equipment, which had been adopted in 1928, also came in for some re-design, resulting in the FBE Mark II of the mid-1930s. (Figure 6.5). In fact the changes were minimal; the boats of the two Marks were almost identical, the roadbearers were made wider so that only seven were used per raft or half landing bay instead of nine, and steel ribands were used to replace the timber ribands of the Mark I. The total effect of these and other minor changes was to raise the decked raft capacity from 4.5 tons to 5.2 tons, which thus still remained at Class 5.

By 1938 however, the newly formed Mobile Division, later to become the famous 1st Armoured Division, stated a requirement for a floating bridge

Figure 6.5. The Mark II version of the FBE Raft, inspected by the 'Men from the Ministry'. The lorry is loaded with the latest version of the Kapok Raft equipment. (IWM V6555).

that would carry all of their divisional transport other than the tanks - that is with a Class 9 capacity. It was decided that the quickest way to meet this new requirement was to re-design the Folding Boat Equipment Mark II, and this EBE set about with alacrity. The basic design of the boats was again little changed, although additional fittings meant that the Mark II and Mark III boats were not interchangeable. The superstructure of the new bridge was completely changed, however. (Figure 6.6). The previously used timber roadbearers and chesses were discarded in favour of a new system comprising four metal road bearers per bay of bridge; the bearers, about 20ft long and each weighing 380lb, supported rectangular deck panels, about 3ft x 3ft 4in, which were dropped into position to rest on the bottom flanges of the road bearers. Floating bays were connected together using special bay connectors, which limited articulation and thus helped to spread the effects of a load over a greater length of bridge; this enabled full use to be made of the available buoyancy of the boats. A newly designed **FBE Mark III Trestle** was also introduced, very similar to that used with the Mark I and Mark II bridges, but strengthened to cope with the Class 9 loads.

The new equipment proved very successful and various forms of Class 5 and Class 9 raft evolved, both shore loading (with balancing gear) and for use with properly constructed landing bays, although there was no decked raft version as with the previous FBEs. Its speed of erection was such that

Figure 6.6. *An eccentric loading test on the Mark III version of the FBE, designed to carry Class 9 loads.* (IWM 761).

the Sapper unit which came down to Christchurch to carry out trials was able to build 120ft of bridge across the Stour in 40 minutes, in the dark and having seen the equipment for the first time that same afternoon. FBE Mark III was adopted by the Army in 1939 and became the standard Class 9 divisional floating bridge; it was extensively used throughout the War, not least in the Rhine crossings of 1945.

The Callender-Hamilton or Unit Construction Bridge

During this period of increased activity at EBE, an important bridge had been developed well away from the Establishment at Christchurch. Mr A W Hamilton was a civil engineer employed, in the late 1920s, by the Iraqi PWD on the Asiatic motorway through the Zagros Mountains. A considerable number of bridges were involved in the road construction and, with no standard civil design available, various types of British surplus military equipment were used, mainly the 120ft Hopkins Bridge and the 60ft Mark II Stock Span, together with a number of purpose-designed bridges. Hamilton conceived the idea of producing a range of components that could be fitted together in variable multi-tier and multi-truss construction to produce bridges suitable for a wide range of span and load requirements. This multi-tier multi-truss form of construction was of course to be used later to give the Bailey Bridge its versatility. In addition he proposed that the strength of individual members of the bridge should be varied as required by bolting together between one and four angle sections to form each member. This gave rise to the name by which the bridge was adopted by the British Army, that is the Unit Construction Bridge, although throughout the War it was still widely referred to as the Hamilton Bridge. (Figure 6.7).

Figure 6.7. A 90ft span Hamilton Unit Construction Bridge, with single trusses and undecked. (IWM 359).

Figure 6.8. *Test-loading the Hamilton Bridge, using traction engines provided by Hampshire County Council.* (IWM 636).

Hamilton patented his ideas in 1933 and 1934, and offered his proposals to the War Office. Interest was immediately aroused and the Royal Engineer and Signal Board ordered a full-scale trial at EBE, using a 140ft double truss bridge. After various static test loadings a live-load trial was decreed, to ensure that the bolted joints would stand up to vibration. The problem was to find enough heavy vehicles with which to load the bridge, as no tanks of sufficient weight then existed. Stair Stewart recalled that it was decided to use steam traction engines - it was before the days of the diesel - and it was found that it was just possible to get six of these, weighing some 80 tons, on to the 140ft span at one time. (Figure 6.8). Hampshire County Council produced them and they arrived from all parts of the county, towing their caravans behind them, at a maximum speed of about 5mph. The rollers had no brakes other than a hand wheel which took about ten seconds to apply, an emergency stop being effected by slamming the regulator into reverse; there were a number of accidents until the drivers learned to do this gently. During three days about a hundred crossings were made by these cumbersome vehicles, snorting fire and smoke and with whirling flywheels and frequent minor collisions. The bridge passed the test without difficulty, but the experiment was not repeated with the Bailey Bridge four years later.

As the bridge was obviously suitable for civilian as well as military use, Hamilton was encouraged to find a firm that would adopt and manufacture the bridge for the civilian market and thus reduce the cost of development and manufacturing overheads for the War Office. This he eventually did, in the form of Messrs Callender Cable and Construction Co Ltd, and as a result the equipment became known as the Callender-Hamilton (or C-H) Bridge. A subsidiary, Messrs Painter Bros of Hereford, were also involved, adding the important improvement, unique at that time for bridging, of being able to galvanize the proposed bridge components to improve durability in service and in storage. Two sizes of bridge were tested for commercial exploitation; the Type A Bridge used 5ft bays and 5ft high trusses, and was intended for footbridges and short spans, and the Type B Bridge, which used 10ft bays and 10ft high trusses. There was provision for steel trough, timber or reinforced concrete decking. Large quantities of the bridging were manufactured just before the War, by far the greater part of the 9,000 ton production being for the Ministry of Transport and local authorities, for use as emergency bridging in case of wartime damage to civil bridges.

The Army adopted the Type B Bridge as the Unit Construction Bridge, which used two single trusses for spans up to 80ft and two double trusses for spans up to 140ft. In both cases single storey construction was used to produce a Warren-type girder and, with some restriction on vehicle spacing, the bridges could carry tracked vehicles up to 30 tons in weight. The individual strength of the members was varied according to the load and span selected, by bolting together up to four basic 10ft long 6 x 6 x ⅜ in mild steel angles. Steel cross-girders were used between the trusses to support wooden roadbearers and timber decking, giving a roadway width of about 10ft between ribands. Sappers usually used a derrick and preventer tackle to launch the bridge girders (Figure 6.9), although Hamilton devised various

Figure 6.9. Launching a double truss Hamilton girder using a derrick and preventer tackle. (IWM H8216).

alternative methods, including the cantilever launching of a light bridge structure which could then be reinforced in situ as required. With its multitude of gusset plates and bolts, the bridge was fairly slow to build, large spans easily taking some days to complete. For this reason it was adopted as the Army's permanent or semi-permanent bridge, whereas the rapidly built and launched SBG Bridge remained as the tactical bridge for the Sappers.

Hamilton was commissioned into the Corps just before the Second World War and was posted to India in 1940 to organize mass production of the Callender-Hamilton aircraft hanger. On arrival he also became involved with the manufacture of the C-H Bridge for use by the Indian Army, and well over 100 spans were fabricated for use in South-East Asia Command, over forty spans being erected on the Tamu-Kalewa Road for the advance into Burma across the River Chindwin in 1944.

It is interesting to note that subsequently Archie Hamilton and Donald Bailey were given identical monetary awards by the special commission set up after the war to consider matters of 'Contribution to the War Effort'. The work of General Martel was similarly rewarded.

W T Everall

Whilst Hamilton was developing his ideas for the Unit Construction Bridge, W T Everall was working on his proposals for a lightweight bridge of similar nature, also using a minimum of standard parts and also using a Warren girder as the main truss. In 1910 Everall had been appointed as bridge engineer on the North-Western State Railways in the Punjab. During the course of his duties he acted as advisor to the Military Engineer Service with regard to bridgework in the Indian Northern Command and in the North-West Frontier Province, for which services he was awarded the OBE and was twice mentioned in despatches. Everall's design for his **North Western Railway Portable Type Steel Road Bridge** was developed as a result of a request for a light bridge that could carry motor transport and could be carried by camels.

The bridge consisted of two Warren girders, arranged either as a through bridge or as a deck bridge. Top and bottom members, diagonals and cross-members were all interchangeable and were accurately jig drilled for assembly by rivets or bolts; the heaviest was 8ft long and weighed no more than 167lb, deemed to be a suitable load for a camel. The bridge members could also be used to build trestles up to 16ft high. The bridge could carry a single load (comprising two 7 ton axle loads at 8ft 6in spacing), at clear spans of up to 120ft in 8ft increments.

Whilst Hamilton's bridge was adopted for general use by the Army, the Everall bridge was adopted for use in India. The first two bridges were built on the Chitral Road to replace bridges over the Usherai and Panjkora Rivers, washed away by the floods of 1929. That at Usherai was a 72ft span deck-

Figure 6.10. *Everall's bridge across the River Usherai in North West India.* (RE Journal - Dec 1931).

type bridge built across an 80ft deep gorge, and replaced an unstiffened suspension bridge, which, although 20ft above normal water level, was nevertheless topped and half washed away by the flood. (Figure 6.10). The bridge over the Panjkora was also a deck-type bridge, of 112ft span, and was built some 70ft above water level. It is interesting to note the cost of these bridges in 1930. The cost at railhead worked out at £8 per foot run; the cost of transporting the bridges to site was another £8 per foot run and the erection cost was £3 per foot run. Additionally, the abutments for the Usherai bridge cost £450 and those for the Panjkora bridge £900, giving at total cost for the two bridges as approximately £1800 and £3000 respectively.

In the late 1930s Everall returned to the UK and acted as a consultant to the War Office on the development of railway bridging. He was then commissioned into the Corps and subsequently played a leading part in this development, his work including the design of the Everall Sectional Truss Railway Bridge, described in a later chapter.

The Christchurch Crib

A very simple but useful bridging accessory developed during this period was the skeleton steel bridging crib. The idea for the crib originated with the 3ft Steel Bridging Cube used in the First World War, as shown in Figure 4.14 and described in Appendix B. Martel had left 17 Field Company RE in 1928, on departing for India, and there he gave some thought to the problem of providing an alternative to the trestle for heavy loads. What evolved was the **Roorkee Pattern Steel Crib**, which was basically a steel skeleton box, 18in square in section and either 3ft or 6 ft long. The cribs could be joined together in any direction by using four ⅜ in bolts, enabling piers or trestles to be built to any height in 18in increments. Although a number of the cribs were made in Roorkee and proved to be most satisfactory after many trials, Martel's descriptive article in the RE Journal did not appear to raise much interest at home. In Martel's words 'Perhaps the idea is too deeply embedded that India can produce no new ideas'. The idea was not lost, however, and the design for a steel crib was further

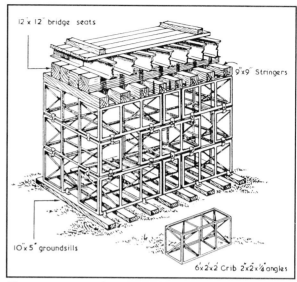

Figure 6.11. *A simple pier built using Christchurch Cribs.* (Military Engineering Vol 3, Bridging Pt 1 - 1957).

developed at Christchurch. (Figure 6.11) The new crib weighed about 200lb and was widely known as the **Christchurch Crib**, although the official title later adopted was the **Bridging Crib 20 Ton**, used to differentiate it from the heavier **Bridging Crib 50 Ton** of the 1950s, described in a later chapter. Christchurch Cribs could be used to form piers of considerable height, making use of crib clamps and load-spreaders, and each crib could support a load of 20 tons when loaded vertically on end or 40 tons when loaded on its side. The cribs were widely used in bridging operations in the Second World War and for a variety of other purposes.

Assault Bridging before the War

Soon after Bailey's arrival at the EBE in 1928, the decision had been made not to proceed further with a tank-launched bridge. However, continued developments in the realm of tank design in the 1930s rekindled experimental work at the EBE on tank-launched or assault bridges. In this connection the term Assault Bridge is usually used to denote a bridge carried or launched by an armoured vehicle; exceptions to the rule were the very light Infantry (or Kapok) Assault Bridge developed in the 1920s from the First World War equipment (used by the Infantry to cross water obstacles during an assault and described in the previous chapter) and the postwar Light and Heavy Assault Floating Bridges (subsequently renamed the Light and Heavy Floating Bridges respectively). Three different prototype assault bridges were produced during the late 1930s and, although none of them went beyond the single prototype stage, all are worthy of mention because each employed a different launch method, subsequently developed for use in later equipments.

The Dragon Assault Bridge

Preliminary designs and studies for this bridge were produced by Martel, by now a Brevet Lieutenant Colonel. Work at EBE, which started in September 1936, was the responsibility of Lieutenant H A T Jarrett-Kerr RE, the only Sapper officer in the 1930s to obtain a First with two Distinctions in the Cambridge Mechanical Sciences Tripos. Jarrett-Kerr was later responsible for much of the detailed design work of the Bailey Bridge; as a Brigadier he went on to become, in 1962, the last military Director of the Military Engineering Experimental Establishment, or MEXE, as EBE became after the War.

As with the earlier Bateman Assault Bridge the Dragon Artillery Tractor was again used as the launch vehicle for the bridge. Although the tractor was only superficially armoured, it was at least tracked and had similar manoeuvrability to that of a light tank. (Figure 6.12). The bridge itself was made up of SBG ramp sections, to give a total length of 34ft 6in, and was transported fully decked and upside down, on top of the tractor. The leading end of the bridge was carried in a steel cradle, hinged to the front of the tractor. To launch the bridge two hydraulic rams were extended to raise the cradle and bridge into the vertical position, at the same time raising into position a light derrick which was also hinged to the tractor. The bridge could then be lowered to the ground, using a winch cable reeved over the derrick and back to a hydraulic motor located inside the tractor. When the bridge had been fully launched, the cable was automatically disconnected, thus disengaging the bridge from the vehicle.

Figure 6.12. The experimental SBG assault bridge, mounted on a Dragon Artillery Tractor and launched by the 'up and over' method. (IWM 653).

Jarrett-Kerr recalled that during the first test on the prototype bridge a weld on the frame gave way and the SBG collapsed on top of him, luckily without harm. Apparently this was because he had trusted in Martel's design, although no backup calculations had been provided for him to check; this was a genuine case of 'back to the drawing board'.

Work on the Dragon Assault Bridge ceased towards the end of 1938, because of promising progress made on the Scissor Bridge project, and also because the Dragon Tractor was by then obsolete. The 'up and over' method of launching an assault bridge was revived later, however, and was very successfully used in the 1960s with the Centurion launched 52ft Tank Bridge No 6, in the 1970s with the Chieftain launched 44ft Tank Bridge No 9, and later, with the Vickers designed 44ft bridge launched from their Mark III Main Battle Tank.

The Scissor Assault Bridge

The principle of the Scissor Bridge was first suggested by Captain S G Galpin RE, the then Superintendent of EBE, in 1935, but was not pursued. It was not until 1938 that the idea was taken further, when a practical application of the principle was devised by Captain S A Stewart RE, who had taken over from Galpin in November 1936; the detailed design was carried out by Mr D M Delaney, a Scientific Civil Servant at Christchurch. A prototype Light Tank Mark V with its turret removed was selected as the launch vehicle; this small tank had a three-man crew and weighed about 5 tons. The bridge itself was purpose built, designed to carry tracked vehicles weighing up to about 7 tons over clear spans of 26ft; it was 30ft long overall and comprised two

Figure 6.13. The experimental Scissors Assault Bridge, mounted on a prototype Mark V Light Tank. (IWM 861).

welded trackways connected together by suitable bracing. The trackways were made in halves, hinged together at bottom chord level at mid-span, so that the bridge could be carried folded in half on top of the tank. (Figure 6.13).

The problem now was to devise a satisfactory method of unfolding and launching the bridge and then disengaging the tank. This was overcome by devising a clever system of support frame and launching frame which were both rotated about a common hinge at the front of the tank by means of a long 2in diameter screw; the screw was operated by an engine-driven screw-feed gearbox mounted on top of the tank. As the launch proceeded, large rollers at the front of the frames came to rest on the ground; this prevented any further rotation of the support frame and by this stage the bridge had been raised almost to the vertical position, still folded. (Figure 6.14). Continued operation of the drive screw rotated the launching frame and the bridge about the rollers now resting on the ground; as this happened the bridge was automatically unfolded by two steel cables running from the support frame to large cam wheels located at the bridge

Figure 6.14. The bridge half-way through the launch process. (IWM 863).

hinge position and on the inside of each trackway. The bridge was finally lowered into position fully extended, a cable-release mechanism was operated and disengagement of simple couplings on the launching frame enabled the tank to withdraw.

Stewart was a brilliant innovator, who later developed and patented a lawn edge trimmer and the hazard warning light used for road repairs, both commercially produced ideas. He made a magnificent model of the proposed bridge, in his own workshop, to demonstrate its viability, and approval was then given for the manufacture of a prototype, although the launching mechanism was subsequently modified to enable it to be fitted to the Light Tank Mark VIB chassis. By now, however, the light tanks were becoming obsolete and work on the project was discontinued in July 1940, in favour of the more substantial 34ft Tank Bridge No 1. This bridge, described in detail in a later chapter, was launched in a similar manner and was mounted first on the heavier Covenanter Tank and then on the Valentine. The scissor principle of launching was to be used again later, in 1946, with the experimental 34ft Tank Bridge No 4, and again in 1970 with the highly successful 80ft Tank Bridge No 8, mounted on a Chieftain Tank chassis. The original Scissor Bridge, mounted on the Light Tank Mark VIB, is believed to have been shipped to the Middle East in 1941 for combat trials, but was apparently lost en route and no further evidence of its history exists.

The Wild Assault Bridge

The Wild Assault Bridge was the third assault bridge prototype produced in the late 1930s and work on the project started in August 1938, just before that on the Scissor Assault Bridge. The design and construction of the prototype was carried out entirely by Messrs M B Wild & Co Ltd of Birmingham and, as with the Scissors Bridge, the requirement was to produce a bridge that would take a 7¼ ton tracked vehicle over a clear span of 26ft, using the Light Tank Mark VIB as the launch vehicle.

The 30ft bridge was carried within a skeleton framework carried on top of the tank; each of the two trackways were divided at mid-span and were carried with the rear half of each immediately above the front half. During the launch sequence the front half of the bridge, carried next to the tank, was pushed forward to the correct position for being coupled up to the rear half; the rear half of bridge was then lowered, to be automatically coupled up and locked to the front half. The complete bridge was then picked up by the hook of a travelling jib attached to the skeleton framework, moved forward clear of the tank and over the gap, and then lowered into position by tilting the jib forward. (Figure 6.15). To reduce the travelling width of the load, the two tracks were positioned close together within the skeleton framework and were then opened out to the correct spacing by a linkage, which operated just before the bridge was seated on the ground.

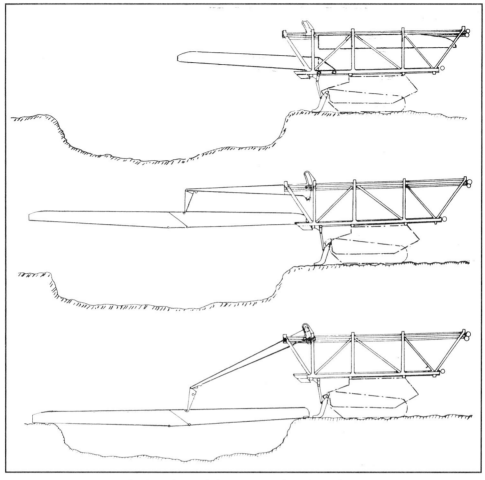

Figure 6.15. *Stages in the launching of the M B Wild Tank Bridge.* (Bridging Monograph 8.008 - Development of Armoured Bridge Laying Vehicles).

The mechanism was ingenious, operated by a system of steel wire ropes from a specially designed winch driven by the tank engine. It was intended that the whole sequence of launching and recovery would be carried out automatically, but in practice considerable difficulty was experienced in making the system work satisfactorily, and in fact a fully successful launch was never achieved. In view of the excellent progress being made with the Scissors Tank Bridge, work on the Wild project was abandoned in late 1939. Although the principle was not taken beyond the prototype stage in the UK, it was successfully used later in Germany. Thus the German Biber Tank Bridge of the 1970s, mounted on the Leopard Tank, carries the rear half of the bridge on top of the front half, which is then slid forward so that the two halves can be coupled up prior to the horizontal launching of the bridge.

The Germans again used this principle in their version of launcher for the trilateral US-UK-FRG Bridging for the 80s project, which will be considered later.

Trackway Bridges

A range of trackway bridges, which can possibly be classed as rudimentary assault bridges, was produced during the pre-war period. (Figure 6.16). All used the same principle of carrying two simple trackways or channels, usually on the side of a vehicle, which could then be placed in position across small obstacles as they were encountered; various methods were used to maintain the correct distance between the two trackways. After crossing the obstacle the vehicle could then either leave the trackways in position for following vehicles or retrieve them for reuse later. An 18ft version, carried on the sides of a Vickers Medium Tank Mark II, was described in the previous chapter, but did not progress beyond the prototype stage. Versions produced during the mid 1930s included the following:

1. The **Lanchester Armoured Car Bridge.** (Figure 6.17). This was 27ft

Figure 6.16. One of the experimental track bridges produced before the War. This 20ft version was launched by the drawbridge method. (IWM 885).

Figure 6.17. The Lancaster 27ft Armoured Car Bridge, launched from the front of the vehicle. (IWM 95).

long and designed to be launched from the front of a vehicle or the armoured car rather like a drawbridge, using a simple timber A-frame and cables.

2. A **12ft Lorry Bridge** carried on the side of the lorry for placement by hand when required.

3. A more robust **12ft Tank Bridge** version of the lorry bridge which used chains between the trackways to maintain the correct spacing.

4. The **16ft Rolls Royce Armoured Car Bridge**.

These 'variations on a theme' gave rise in due course to the 12ft and 20ft Track Bridges used during the War and described later.

Prepared for War?

As the war approached, the Sappers had made considerable efforts to update their bridging equipments, and by the mid-1930s any remaining Inglis Mark II and Hopkins Bridges, together with the First World War Stock Spans, had been discarded. Thus despite some shortcomings they were now well served, at least in quality if not in quantity. To summarize the situation at the outbreak of war, the equipments available to the Corps were as follows:

For personnel:	The Kapok Assault Bridge.
For 5 ton loads such as light tanks:	Folding Boat Equipment Mark II.
For 9 ton loads such as a laden 3 ton lorry:	SBG Mark II, and a few sets of FBE Mark III.
For loads up to 24 tons:	SBG Mark II (4 girder version), SBG Mark III (2 and 4 Girder versions), and the Mark V Pontoon Bridge.
For loads up to 30 tons:	LBG Mark II and the Hamilton Unit Construction Bridge, and various Stock Spans (26ft, 32ft and 37ft) introduced in late 1939. All were slow to construct and were thus only really suitable for use in rear areas.

In addition the Army had recently adopted the Bridge and Vehicle Classification System evolved over a considerable period by the EBE and described in detail in Chapter One; the new system was to prove of outstanding value to Engineer and Army Staffs alike.

And thus the Sappers came to War.

CHAPTER SEVEN

The Outbreak of War and the Bailey Story

September 1939

It was seen in the last chapter how a gradual swing towards rearmament started in Britain after the reoccupation of the Rhineland by Germany in 1936. In March 1938 German troops occupied Austria and set up a Nazi government. A few months later the Munich crisis resulted in a postponement of the inevitable conflict that was to follow, but on 12 March 1939 Hitler invaded Czechoslavakia and it became clear that war could not be avoided. The Territorial Army was doubled in size and in May compulsory service with the Militia was introduced. With the signing of a non-aggression pact with Russia on 23 August 1939, Hitler felt safe to act against Poland, but his invasion of Poland on 1 September led to the mobilization of the British Armed Forces, since Britain and also France had mutual support treaties with that country. A final ultimatum from the British Government went unanswered and at 11.15am on 3 September 1939 Britain and France declared war on Germany.

One result for the Corps, and indeed for the Army as a whole, was the vast expansion of our Armed Forces that was to take place over the next few years. At the outbreak of the War, Regular Army strength of the Corps was about 1300 Sapper officers and 11,800 other ranks; by May-June 1945 the total strength of the Corps, including of course mobilized Territorial units, had risen to 21,700 officers and 259,000 other ranks. Even this peak figure of about 280,000 all ranks was less than the Corps strength in the First World War, but the total number of Engineers in the closely integrated British, Empire and Commonwealth Forces was well in excess of the First World War figure. This massive twenty-one fold increase in the size of the Corps was obviously accompanied by a correspondingly vast increase in the requirement for Sapper equipment; and this at a time of rapid advances in technology and the sophistication of other equipments in the Armed Forces, brought about by pressures of war and the ready availability of finance for defence spending. In particular, advances in tank design and armament, and the consequent increases in the all up weight of the new tanks, were of prime importance to the military bridge designer.

Procurement of RE Equipment

Before considering the problem facing the Sappers and how it was met, it is worth looking briefly at the method of procurement that evolved during the

War. Before the War, 'A' Committee of the Royal Engineer and Signal Board controlled experimentation, research, development and design connected with engineering in its application to the needs of the Royal Engineers and of course the The Royal Corps of Signals. In 1934 the Board had come under the control of the Director of Mechanization, who was in turn on the staff of the Master General of the Ordnance, or MGO, and it was the MGO who was ultimately responsible for ensuring that the Corps was supplied with the equipment that it needed. On 1 August 1939 a new Ministry of Supply, or MOS, was set up to take control of all weapons production, and the MGO and his staff were transferred to this Ministry. The Royal Engineer and Signals Board continued to exist, but a new Director of Engineer and Signal Equipment, later to become the Director of Royal Engineer Equipment, or DREE, working within the new ministry, assumed responsibility for design and production of Royal Engineer equipment. This had the distinct advantage of improving liaison between the equipment design, production and inspection staffs, and also made easier the allocation and procurement of materials in short supply because of the War.

Responsibility for overseeing the Experimental Bridging Establishment and, from 1942, the new Experimental Tunnelling Establishment at Christchurch, and also the Experimental Demolition Establishment at Bovington, was transferred from the War Office to DREE, but work at the EBE was virtually unaffected. In 1938 new workshops and huts to accommodate extra staff had been built at Christchurch, but in 1939 the staff still consisted of the Superintendent (now Major S A Stewart RE, the post having been upgraded on the day war broke out), Mr D C Bailey (the civilian designer), Mr D M Delany (a second civil engineer who had joined EBE in February 1937), and a small nucleus of military and civilian staff. By 1940, although still not large, the staff had been increased by a further three civilian engineers and another Sapper officer, Captain H A T Jarrett-Kerr RE, who had previously served at the EBE in the mid-1930s and had been specifically recalled to work on a new **Heavy Pontoon Bridge**; in addition there were about ten draughtsmen and fifty or so workshop and outside staff. A period of intense activity was to follow, as will be seen later, with workshops working 24 hours a day, in two shifts, to keep pace with the work load, particularly for the new Bailey Bridge. The Establishment was thus poised for the very considerable effort that went into the design and development of new bridging equipments for the Sappers, not only the Bailey Bridge considered in this chapter, but a wide range of floating and assault equipments that will be discussed in the following chapter. This effort was to continue unabated, the Establishment reaching a peak wartime strength of about 500. Major G H Hunt MC RE took over from Major Stewart on 25 September 1941, and was promoted in post to Lieut Colonel in May 1943 and then, as Chief Superintendent, to Colonel on 15 January 1944.

An early result of the setting up of the new Ministry of Supply was the appointment of a Director of Scientific Research, and one of his first tasks was to establish an advisory committee of eminent scientists, known as the Advisory Council on Scientific Research and Technical Development, or more briefly as the Scientific Advisory Council. One of the Council's sub-committees was the Structural Engineering Committee or SEC, which met for the first time in March 1940, with Professor R V Southwell as its Chairman; members included Professors R S Hutton, A J Sutton Pippard, and C E Inglis, and of course Mr D C Bailey. The committee was able to provide valuable assistance and advice to the EBE on such matters as safety factors, design and construction practice and test procedures.

The Sapper Armoury

As detailed in the last chapter, by the outbreak of War the Corps had updated its bridging equipment as far as possible and despite some shortcomings the Sappers were well served with equipment of a high quality. A certain amount of bridging equipment was sent to France but little was used and all was destroyed or captured before Dunkirk. It soon became clear that with the rapid expansion of the Corps, there was going to be a considerable shortage of equipment, pending a massive rearmament programme. The equipments available were summarized at the end of the previous chapter, and the list shows that there were no less than seven equipments all capable of carrying loads of 9 tons or more. Although each had been developed for a specific purpose, with some overlap of capabilities, such a wide range of bridging equipment, particularly spread rather thinly, gave rise to all sorts of problems of manufacture, storage, repair and training and, not of least importance, the availability of a specific type of bridge where and when actually needed in the field.

The overriding shortcoming of the equipments however, in view of developments in the tank world, was their load carrying capacity. Both the SBG and the Mark V Pontoon Bridge had been designed to take a 24 ton load, and even the more slowly constructed LBG Mark II and Unit Construction Bridge took only a 30 ton tank. Methods were devised to increase the capacity of the Pontoon bridge to 26 tons, to take the Matilda II, and that of the other bridges to 40 tons, but at best such solutions were makeshift, involving in some cases a considerable reduction in span capability. The problem was brought to a head by progress in the development of a new Infantry Tank.

The Churchill Tank

With the construction of the Siegfried and Maginot Lines in Europe, there remained in many military minds a vision of a future war fought across a network of trenches, requiring close support for advancing infantry. This would need the development of bigger and better armoured tanks, which could advance in the face of heavy fire for a final assault against strongly defended fortifications. A specification drawn up in September 1939 led to the development of the A20-Infantry Tank, and the two prototypes manufactured weighed in at about 43 tons in mid-1940. Trials were disappointing and the project was abandoned; however one of the two vehicles provided the basis for the A22-Infantry Tank Mark IV, or the Churchill Tank. The first production models of the Churchill appeared in mid-1941 at an all up weight of about 39 tons, thus firmly setting the load capacity for a new Sapper bridge at Class 40, although of course the requirement for a Class 40 bridge had been foreseen and acted upon for some time.

It is interesting to note that while the A22 Churchill was being developed from the A20 prototype, an alternative, known as TOG, was also under development. The design was very similar to that of the First World War Heavy Tanks, and indeed the two TOG prototypes were designed by the First World War design team of William Foster & Co of Lincoln, and subsequently manufactured by them; hence the name TOG used for these tanks, being the acronym of 'The Old Gang', although the acronym has also been ascribed to the committee of the First World War experts who drew up the specification for the tank. Valuable experience was gained from the production of the two prototypes, but by the time they had been produced the Churchill had been accepted as the new Infantry Tank, and the project was abandoned. This was very lucky for the Sappers, because TOG 2, fitted with a 17pdr gun, weighed close on 80 tons; although the Bailey Bridge could be built at Class 70 and upward, normal construction was at Class 40, and without doubt a standard of Class 80 for our wartime bridging would have had very far reaching effects.

A New Inglis Bridge

The first contender for a new bridge for the Sappers was proposed by Professor Charles Inglis, of Cambridge University. In 1939 Inglis proposed a redesigned version of the Mark I and Mark II Inglis Bridges developed during World War I. In 1939 the new Infantry Tank was at a very early stage of development and the new bridge was intended to take no more than Class 24 loads. This new version of the Inglis Bridge again used tubular members made up into Warren type trusses, but this time Inglis proposed the use of one, two or three trusses to form each main bridge girder; this feature, which provided considerable flexibility for the Sappers building the bridge in the field, had of course been used in the Hamilton Unit Construction Bridge, and was to be used again later with the Bailey Bridge. In addition Inglis reverted to the 12ft bay length used with the Mark I Bridge, the Mark II having had 15ft bays. This had a very important consequence; whereas the Mark II Bridge used light castellated beams and diagonal sway bracing in each bay of bridge to provide lateral stability to the top chords of the bridge girders, the reduced headroom in the Mark III Bridge, resulting from the reduction of tube length and hence girder depth, meant that overhead bracing of any form was not viable.

Early trials of the prototype of the new bridge were carried out by Inglis at Cambridge and were attended by DREE and staff from the EBE, who expressed concern that the test loading did not comply with the guidelines laid down by the new Structural Engineering Committee. These guidelines required that a military bridge should be tested by eleven applications of a test load equal to the maximum live load to be carried by the bridge multiplied by an impact factor of 1.15 and by an overload or safety factor of 1.5. The test load was to be applied at maximum eccentricity and there was to be no increase of permanent set between the tenth and eleventh application of the load. An alternative test loading, more suitable for long and fairly heavy bridges required to carry only low load classes, specified application of a load equal to 1.25 times the maximum dead load plus the live load including impact. However, EBE comments fell on deaf ears, and when the Controller of Mechanization Development advised in April 1940 that the new bridge must be capable of carrying the new Infantry Tank Mark IV (ie the Churchill), the War Office short circuited the normal channels and placed a £2M order for a hundred 120ft sets of the new Inglis Bridge. Admittedly the need for a new bridge was urgent, but this action caused some argument between the War Office and the Ministry of Supply, who insisted upon retention of final approval for the bridge design, and that to be given only after EBE had fully tested the first-off production.

On 23 January 1941 a 9 bay or 108ft span double tube version of the production Inglis was tested at the EBE, and to the consternation of those present the top chord of one of the girders buckled under the test load (Figure 7.1).

Figure 7.1. A test loading on a Mark III Inglis Bridge at Christchurch, showing the development of a top chord buckle. (IWM 912).

Figure 7.2. The bridge with footwalk brackets and top chord bracing fitted at the near end. (RE Corps Library).

The Structural Engineering Committee came down to Christchurch to inspect the damaged bridge a few days later, as some controversy had arisen between the EBE and Professor Inglis about the method of test loading. Discussions went on until midnight, and it was finally agreed that since much of the new bridgework was already in production, modification of the design to prevent instability of the top chord would have to be accepted and was of prime importance. It was realized that any modification had to take account of the specified headroom and therefore could not include overhead bracing. It was finally agreed to add a footwalk bracket to both ends of each transom; two inclined tubes, adjustable in length, would then connect the end of each bracket to the two adjacent junction boxes in the top chord of each girder. (Figure 7.2). Further stability was provided by connecting the end of each footwalk bracket to the two adjacent brackets by horizontal tubes. During subsequent building of production models of the bridge care had to be taken to ensure that the top chords of the bridge were finally straightened by sighting along them, from end to end, and adjusting the bracing tubes as necessary.

148

The Birth of the Bailey Bridge

The meeting of the SEC held at Christchurch on 29 January 1941 brought to a head a number of the criticisms of the new Inglis Bridge that had previously been expressed by the Committee, not least of which was its unsuitability for the wartime mass production now essential. The Committee realised the seriousness of contemplating a fundamental revision of design in the existing emergency and considered that, having recommended methods of solving the existing problems with the Inglis Bridge, it was appropriate to consider further an alternative design. This design was of course that of Bailey, some work on which had already been done and outline details of which had been given to the Committee at a meeting earlier that month.

The work had started late in 1940, following a visit to Cambridge by Major Stewart, who was still Superintendent of EBE, and Donald Bailey, together with Colonel F E Fowle MC, of the Royal Engineer and Signal Board, to see a loading trial on an Inglis Bridge prototype. It was on the return journey, during discussions on complications of the Inglis design, that Bailey produced the legendary envelope from his pocket, using it to sketch out his ideas for a new bridge made from panels. He had had the basic idea of combining the advantages of the through type bridge, such as the Inglis, with those of the Box Girder Bridges at the back of his mind for some years and it had been briefly discussed at EBE, but no detailed work on the idea had been undertaken. Further investigation was authorized immediately by Colonel Fowle and next morning possible configurations for the panels were discussed, consideration being given to M, N and K type bracing. Jarrett-Kerr then started work immediately on calculations for the K braced panel finally selected.

Over the years EBE had built up considerable experience of the short comings that could arise during equipment design and with this in mind guidelines were drawn up for the new design. These included the following:

1. Maximum flexibility to be aimed at, enabling the bridge to be used as a fixed bridge with a deck and girder system that could be strengthened at will, preferably in situ, to cope with a wide range of spans and bridge loads. Later, it was decided that a pontoon bridge version of the equipment would also be desirable.

2. All parts to be made from readily available materials, avoiding the use of aluminium alloys, for which aircraft production had priority, and making the maximum use of welding.

3. Parts to be capable of manufacture by almost any engineering firm; this meant that tolerances should be reasonable, to make manufacture straightforward, but adequate enough to ensure the complete interchangeability of parts.

4. All parts to fit into a standard 3 ton GS lorry, and with no part to exceed a six man load (say 600lb).

5. Attention to be paid to the system of bridge erection, in particular to the launching and jacking down of the bridge, keeping the underside of the girders free from projections, and providing adequate bankseats and bearings.

Since the design of the new Churchill Tank was now well advanced, the load class for the new bridge was fixed at Class 40.

Design Begins

The actual design work was supervised by Bailey, who was now Chief Designer at the EBE with a largely increased staff, but Captain Jarrett-Kerr, did much of the detailed design work, although of course EBE staff at all levels played a considerable part in making the bridge the success it became. Mr Ralph Freeman (Senior), designer of the Sydney Harbour Bridge, who had joined the Structural Engineering Committee in October 1940 upon the resignation of Professor Inglis and subsequently became its Chairman, took a great interest in the project from the beginning; he was often consulted in the early stages and frequently gave valuable advice.

Early calculations showed that a panel of suitable size to fit into a 3 ton lorry and capable of being carried by six men, could be made up into a 120ft bridge with a load capacity of about 45 tons. As soon as the design had made some progress, a sample panel was made up in the EBE workshops, using mild steel sections, and the SEC and others interested were invited to inspect it; formal approval for work to start on the design proper followed. The concept was for a through type bridge, the main girders being made up from the panels and supporting the roadway between them. The final version of the panel used rolled steel joists for the vertical web and diamond bracing members, in the now familiar pattern. Two additional vertical members, forming diagonals to the diamond bracing, were eliminated at an early stage, once testing had proved that the stiffness of the panel with its welded joints was adequate without them. (Figure 7.3). The first prototype panels were fabricated with 3 x 1½in channels in the top chord and 4 x 2in channels in the

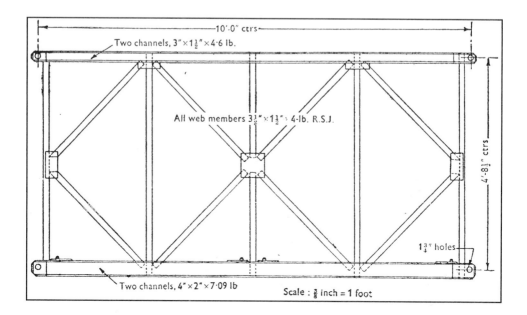

-10'-0" ctrs-

Two channels, 3"×1½"×4·6 lb.

All web members 3½"×1¾"× 4·lb. R.S.J.

4'-8½" ctrs

1¾" holes

Two channels, 4"×2"×7·09 lb

Scale : ⅜ inch = 1 foot

bottom chord; this was because the original optimum design envisaged two storey construction in which the upper panels would be inverted and bolted to the lower panels. After early tests however it was decided to utilize the full strength of the panels in single storey construction, particularly useful for short span or lightly loaded bridges, by using 4 x 2in channels for both top and bottom chords. One of the first prototype panels, with the redundant vertical members referred to above cut out, can be seen at the Royal Engineer Museum at Chatham, and a footbridge made of these panels remained in use at the Christchurch Establishment until its closure in 1994.

EBE staff worked flat out on the project and for some time drawing office staff were putting in a 90 hour week; at the peak Jarrett-Kerr had a team of eight draughtsmen to be kept supplied with design sketches for detailing. Preliminary design work was finished within two months and the first bridge was manufactured and ready for trials by May 1941. The manufacture of this pilot model was outside the capacity of the EBE workshops and Braithwaite & Co, of West Bromwich, were selected to make the 120ft of double truss double storey bridge that was needed for the testing. The firm took a great interest in the design and made many useful suggestions to ease manufacture; they also supplied full details of their jigs and welding procedures which were then available for the benefit of other manufacturers. Minor items of the equipment needed for the initial trials were designed one by one and made in EBE workshops.

Testing the Bridge

Because of the indeterminate nature of the structure, it was decided to subject the pilot model of the bridge to an extensive test programme. The static test load was of course applied in accordance with the SEC recommended procedure, but application of impact and overload factors necessitated a load in excess of 90 tons, applied over a deck length of about 12ft, a far greater load than had ever been applied at EBE before. (Figure 7.4). This test load was eventually achieved by positioning a 1917 Mark V tank at mid-span, and then using an early No 1 Tank Bridge as a ramp to drive two smaller tanks up on to a platform built on top of the Mark V tank. The heavy tank was then filled with pig iron and some tons of steel beams were added to the load wherever possible. Jacks and safety packing had previously been placed at mid-span, and the load was applied by lowering the jacks at the centre of the bridge, the tanks and steel beams remaining in position during eleven applications of the load.

On one occasion such a test caused considerable concern. The Structural Engineering Committee had come down to Christchurch to see the progressive loading of a bridge with gradually increasing overloads, until a point would be reached, just before failure, at which acceptance would be agreed. By 6.0pm, with most of the Committee retired for a short break after a long day of testing, the last load application was under way. As the centre jacks were being slackened off to measure the deflection, one of the workmen reported that his jack remained under slight load and would not slacken. Inspection showed that the top chord on one side of the bridge had failed by buckling, but so slowly that no one had noticed it. The Committee was hastily reassembled and close examination of the failed panel showed that one side of the chord was badly scarred, presumably having been struck by a tank during an earlier test. This damage had obviously caused the failure under severe overload, and all concerned were very relieved. Rooms were booked for the Committee in a local hotel, the men worked well into the night to replace the faulty panel, and the test was repeated successfully next morning.

A number of intentional tests to destruction were also carried out, failure in bending always occurring by local lateral buckling of a top chord in a panel, whilst shear failure always occurred by buckling of the upper diagonals in an end panel of the bridge. As a result of these and further tests involving variation of test loads for different spans, a provisional table of safe loads for a range of spans was drawn up for use by the Sappers. At a later stage wind loading tests were carried out at the National Physical Laboratory, using 1/13 scale models of the bridge.

The bridge passed the test programme with very few modifications and in two months was formally accepted for production. In anticipation of this, a number of firms had been forewarned and orders for materials had been placed. Thus within five months of production being put in hand, the first bridges were with the troops. During the early stages of production, vehicle

Figure 7.4. A 60ft double/single Bailey Bridge under a static overload test. Donald Bailey can be seen in the foreground. (IWM 943).

loading trials, launching trials and troop trials were held, so that construction drills could be finalized for issue of a provisional user handbook.

The Design is Finalized

The bridge as it went into production had two main girders formed from the basic panels, arranged in either one, two or three trusses either side of the bridge and additionally arranged one, two or three storeys high; the clearance between the inner trusses of the girders was 12ft 4in. (Figure 7.5). Each panel was approximately 10ft x 5ft in size and weighed about 570

Figure 7.5. Typical Bailey Bridge cross sections. (The Civil Engineer at War).

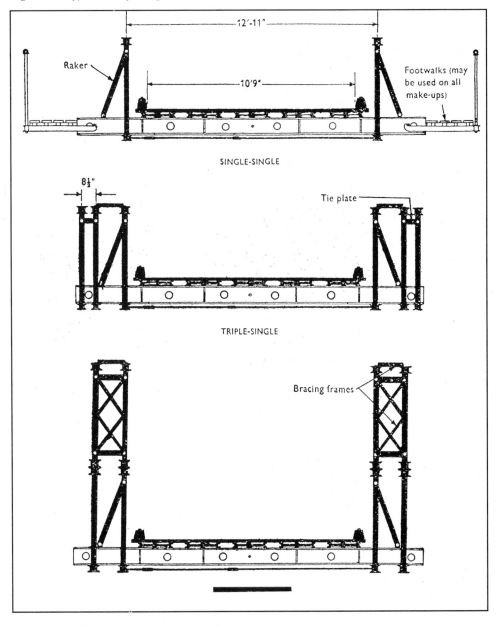

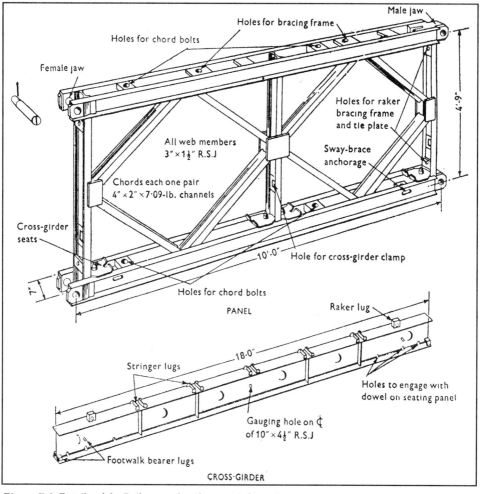

Figures in image: Male jaw, Holes for bracing frame, Holes for chord bolts, Female jaw, Holes for raker bracing frame and tie plate, All web members 3″×1½″ R.S.J, Sway-brace anchorage, Chords each one pair 4″×2″×7·09-lb. channels, Cross-girder seats, 10′·0″, Hole for cross-girder clamp, Holes for chord bolts, PANEL, Raker lug, Stringer lugs, 18·0″, Holes to engage with dowel on seating panel, Gauging hole on ₵ of 10″×4½″ R.S.J, Footwalk bearer lugs, CROSS-GIRDER

Figure 7.6. Details of the Bailey panel and cross-girder or transom. (The Civil Engineer at War).

pounds, a convenient six man load. Male and female jaws were fitted at the corners so that panels could be assembled into trusses, using steel panel pins. (Figure 7.6). Extra storeys were added using chord bolts to bolt on the additional tiers of panels. The timber chess decking was supported on light steel stringers, in turn supported by 18ft long steel transoms. Either two or four transoms could be fitted in each 10ft bay of bridge, depending upon the load to be carried; the transoms were fixed to the bottom chords of the panels using transom clamps, to produce a through bridge with a roadway width of 10ft 9in between the ribands (kerbs), which were bolted down to the outer stringers. The same transoms were also used to provide overhead bracing for the three storey bridge, and the stability of all bridges was ensured by using turn-buckle adjusted lateral (sway) bracing in each bay of bridge. Specially strengthened ramp stringers were provided to build either a 10ft or a 20ft ramp at either end of the completed bridge as required. (Figure 7.7).

Variation of the numbers of trusses, storeys and transoms used per bay gave great flexibility of construction, ranging from the 90ft single/single Class 9 bridge up to the 240ft triple/triple Class 9 or the 150ft triple/triple

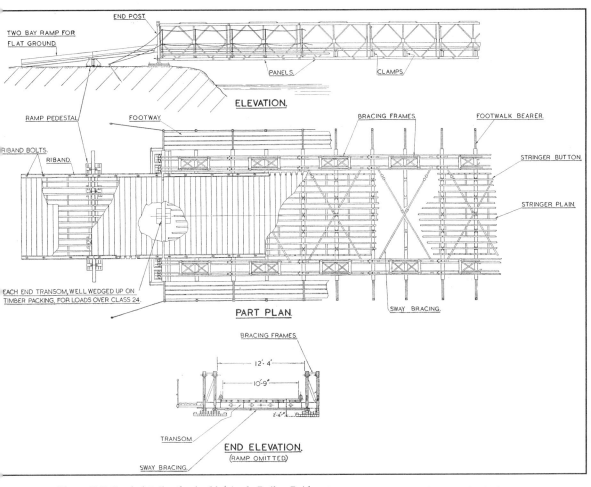

Figure 7.7. Bank details of a double/single Bailey Bridge. (Military Engineering Vol III Part III - 1944).

Class 70 bridge, Class 70 being the design load of the Churchill Tank on its transporter. In this connection it is noted that single/single means that each bridge girder is single truss and single storey, and so on, whilst Class 9, for example, implies a live load capacity of approximately 9 tons. The bridge, with a skeleton launching nose, was normally constructed on rollers, pointing across the river; it was then rolled forward as building continued at the rear end until the launching nose landed on rollers positioned on the far bank. Construction progressed as the bridge was boomed out further and the nose was dismantled; when the span was in its final position the rollers were removed, the bridge jacked down on to bridge bearings and base plates, and the decking completed.

Manufacture

A high strength structural steel developed from BS 968 weldable quality steel was used for the chord and web members of the panels and the transoms. The BS 968 specification was modified to improve weldability, by adjusting the carbon content, and this had the effect of raising the yield point from 21 to 23 tons/sq in (see Appendix B). Once initial problems of welding jig design had been overcome, the welding of the high tensile steel did not present any great difficulties; problems that did arise were usually caused by variation in the alloy content of the steel, since once the upper limits of carbon and manganese were approached, there was little margin between weldability and the point at which welding could be guaranteed. A manganese-molybdenum alloy steel was used for the panel pins, with a yield of about 65 tons/sq in, whilst all other components, such as the stringers and sway-braces, gussets, jaw blocks and small components of the panels, were made from normal BS 15 mild steel.

An interesting problem arose from the need to distinguish easily and in a foolproof manner the high tensile steel sections destined for Bailey from normal rolled sections. The solution was to paint a green line down the centre of the Bailey sections. However this was followed by an outbreak of weld cracking, and it was only after very careful investigation that the cause was traced to sulphur absorption from the paint; the trouble was completely cured by the specification of a sulphur free oil bound distemper for marking the sections.

Jigging and gauging of components during manufacture was of particular importance, in view of the necessity for all similar parts of the bridge to be absolutely interchangeable. Achievement of this was no mean feat considering the vast production runs, the great number of small firms engaged in production, and the extensive use of black rolled sections which could vary within commercially specified tolerances of dimension and trueness. Jigs used were of two types; the welding jigs held together all loose components in their correct relative positions prior to and during welding; and the drilling jigs held complete components prior to drilling, to ensure the correct relationship between holes and other features, the very close tolerances specified over the 10ft pin hole spacing being previously unheard of in structural engineering. During manufacture of the panels, the chords were first welded up complete, with jaw blocks in position; a second welding jig was then used to weld in the verticals and diagonals between the two chords of the panel. The main pin holes were not drilled for at least 48 hours, in order to ensure cessation of any shrinkage and adjustment of residual stresses resulting from the welding.

Mass Production

Without doubt the story behind the early development and manufacture of Bailey is one of great success. To summarize the initial programme, design work started in December 1940, the pilot model was ready for testing in May 1941, production started in July 1941, and the first bridge was with the troops in December 1941. Braithwaite & Co were the first firm to undertake full scale mass production of the panels, but eventually some 650 UK firms became involved in the manufacture of Bailey, firms of all types from the conventional engineering firm to the small garage, and even including, for example, confectioners and football pool proprietors brought in to help with the war effort.

With so many firms involved in the manufacture, and with no choice in wartime but to make use of inexperienced labour, it was initially decided to proof load all panels to ensure that they were to the required standard. This was done by setting up panel testing centres at which all panels were in turn built into a continuous girder; the girder was slowly moved forward, tested panels being uncoupled at the front as new panels were added at the back. The shear test load applied was 55% above working load, whilst that for bending was 17% above. Each centre was capable of testing up to 500 panels a week, working flat out at 16 hours a day. However, once production had peaked at over 25,000 panels a month, the task of testing became such that only a 10% sample could be dealt with, pending the design and installation of more compact testing machines which enabled 100% testing to be resumed. Total production ran into hundreds of thousands of panels, over 70% of which were proof loaded, and yet only 140 panels were rejected for welding defects and a further 131 because of substandard specification in the steel.

The total production figures are staggering. In the last three years of the war over 490,000 tons of Bailey Bridge was manufactured, representing over 200 miles of fixed bridge and 40 miles of floating bridge, for use in all theatres of war. Manufacture included almost 700,000 Bailey panels, almost enough to build a single bridge girder from Christchurch to St Petersburg! The Americans manufactured a further 20 miles of bridge for their own use, but this will be referred to later.

The Bailey Pontoon Bridge

As has been seen, towards the end of 1941 the Sappers had coming into service an excellent fixed bridge, capable of use at a wide range of spans and load classes up to Class 70. Over the next few years this basic design of bridge proved to be versatile perhaps beyond the wildest dreams of the designers. Undoubtedly, however, its major development was for use in the floating role, as the Bailey Pontoon Bridge.

With no projections below the bottom chord of the Bailey panel, it was soon realised that the girders, complete with their decking, could easily be positioned on suitable pontoons to fulfil a much needed requirement for a new floating bridge. Design work was therefore put in hand for a Bailey Pontoon Bridge. The important design aspect to be resolved was the degree of rigidity that would be acceptable in the bridge girders; some rigidity was obviously necessary to enable a load to be spread across a number of floating bays of bridge, but complete rigidity would have resulted in excessive bending moments, even from the action of waves or swell alone. After the use of Professor Southwell's relaxation method of analysis, a system of limited articulation was adopted in which floating bays were connected together by use of special connecting end posts, with a conventional pin connection at bottom chord level and a butting joint at the top. This enabled the connecting posts to transfer the shear forces between bays and to resist sagging moments, but prevented the transfer of hogging moments between adjacent bays.

The standard form of construction finally adopted for the Class 40 bridge linked together the requisite number of floating bays, each of which comprised 30ft of single/single Bailey supported on two pontoon piers. (Figure 7.8). Each bay (32ft long with its connecting posts) was handled in the water as a separate unit before being floated into position for coupling up. The bridge was completed by a landing bay at each end, which spanned from the bank down on to a special four-pier landing bay raft. As with dry span Bailey, construction of the rafts and landing bays could be varied at will, according to the site encountered or the load class required. For example a Class 70 version could be built using double/single construction and three pontoon piers for each floating bay, together with six pier landing bay rafts; the landing bay construction would of course depend upon the span from bank to landing bay raft.

The major new component needed for the bridge was the pontoon. Luckily the Mark V Pontoon was in service, but since this did not provide the necessary buoyancy on its own, a design for a new centre pontoon was produced; this was based upon an early 1940 design for a pontoon to be used with a new **Heavy Pontoon Bridge**, a shallow box girder bridge which did not progress beyond the prototype stage. The new **Bailey Centre Pontoon**

Figure 7.8. Shore details for the Class 40 Bailey Pontoon Bridge. (Military Engineering Vol III, Part III, 1944).

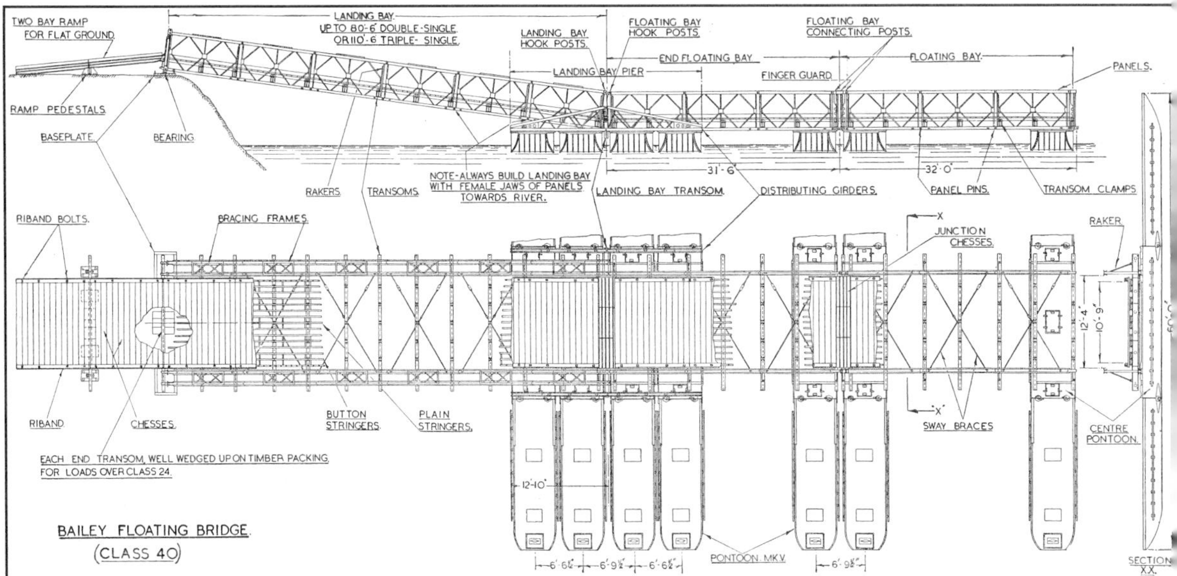

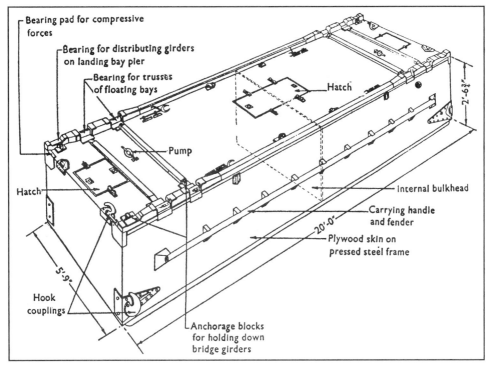

Figure 7.9. The Bailey Centre Pontoon, used with two Mark V pontoons to make a 60ft pier. (The Civil Engineer at War).

was steel reinforced, 20ft long and weighed about a ton. (Figure 7.9). It was fitted with Mark V Pontoon couplings, so that it could be connected between two Mark V Bow Pontoons to form a 60ft long Bailey Pontoon Pier; at its normal minimum freeboard of about 8in, the tripartite pier had a net useful buoyancy of 14½ tons. Other new components for the Pontoon Bridge included Class 40 and Class 70 Distributing Girders, needed to spread the end load of the landing bay over the four or six piers of the landing bay raft, via new Class 40 or Class 70 Landing Bay Transoms which spanned between these girders. By the end of November 1941, 320ft of floating Bailey was ready for a troop trial by the Home Forces, and soon after, a full scale trial of the BPB took place at Wallingford, on the River Thames, using a tank as a live load. During the trial one of the new hook posts, used at the end of the landing bay to transfer its load on to the landing bay transom, failed; rapid redesign and manufacture of a replacement in EBE workshops, within the space of a few days, enabled the trial to be completed while the trial tank was still available. Another variant of the Bailey was thus made available to the Allied Forces, whilst at the same time solving a problem that had dogged the Sappers for years - by providing, with the long landing bay, a means of transferring a vehicle load from the shore to the floating bridge proper, without having to resort to the cumbersome and unsatisfactory trestle equipment.

At a later stage a **Mark VI Pontoon** was introduced. This new pontoon had the same shape and dimensions as the Mark V and similar fittings, so that either could be coupled up to the Bailey Centre Pontoon. It was timber

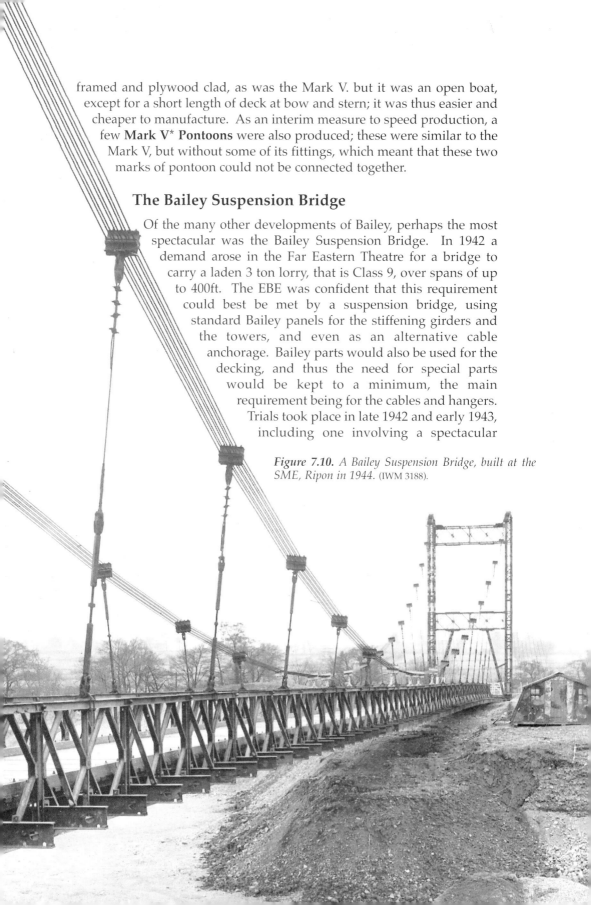

framed and plywood clad, as was the Mark V. but it was an open boat, except for a short length of deck at bow and stern; it was thus easier and cheaper to manufacture. As an interim measure to speed production, a few **Mark V* Pontoons** were also produced; these were similar to the Mark V, but without some of its fittings, which meant that these two marks of pontoon could not be connected together.

The Bailey Suspension Bridge

Of the many other developments of Bailey, perhaps the most spectacular was the Bailey Suspension Bridge. In 1942 a demand arose in the Far Eastern Theatre for a bridge to carry a laden 3 ton lorry, that is Class 9, over spans of up to 400ft. The EBE was confident that this requirement could best be met by a suspension bridge, using standard Bailey panels for the stiffening girders and the towers, and even as an alternative cable anchorage. Bailey parts would also be used for the decking, and thus the need for special parts would be kept to a minimum, the main requirement being for the cables and hangers. Trials took place in late 1942 and early 1943, including one involving a spectacular

Figure 7.10. A Bailey Suspension Bridge, built at the SME, Ripon in 1944. (IWM 3188).

buckling and collapse of one of the towers, and eventually the design for the Bailey Suspension Bridge No 1 was finalized. The design officer for the project was Otto Bondy, assisted by Captain W M D Carey RE and, from late 1943, by Captain R Freeman RE, the son of the Chairman of the Structural Engineering Committee. Freeman, with considerable prewar experience in the construction of long span steel bridges, had been posted to the Establishment soon after obtaining a direct commission into the Corps earlier that year; he and his father were subsequently Knighted, Ralph Freeman (Senior) in 1947 and Ralph Freeman (Junior) in 1970.

The BSB could carry unrestricted Class 9 traffic at a 400ft span, that is with up to five vehicles on the bridge at one time, not closer than 80ft nose to tail. A few sets of the equipment were manufactured, but a production model, known as the Bailey Suspension Bridge No 2, was eventually introduced, of very similar design but with revision and improvement of some minor components. The BSB No 2 could carry unrestricted Class 12 traffic or a single Class 18 vehicle over a 400ft span, but subsequent trials showed that the 400ft bridge would take a single Class 40 load, provided that the top and bottom chords of the stiffening girders were strengthened by the bolting on of chord reinforcements; these reinforcements were similar to the top and bottom chords of the standard panel and effectively doubled its strength. At the School of Military Engineering in Ripon a Field Squadron demonstrated in 1944 that a 400ft BSB could be built in about five days. (Figure 7.10 and Appendix B).

Multi-Span Bailey Bridges

The need for multi-span bridges became apparent once the Allies began their advance up Italy and had to contend with the extensive demolition programme facing them. In many cases viaducts and long bridges had been destroyed by demolition of every span, often leaving partially demolished piers. In such cases it was sometimes possible to level the tops of the piers, position launching rollers, and build a long continuous Bailey right across the gap. The design of adequate support at the piers, invariably not placed to match the Bailey 10ft multiples of span, required careful attention, making full use of distributing beams. Ideally spans were made as near equal in length as possible, and in any case the shortest span needed to be no less than 60% the length of the longest, to counteract any tendency for the end spans to lift from the bankseats when centre spans were heavily loaded. Where the bridge piers had also been blown, full use was made of piers built from Bailey panels and transoms and special components such as crib capsills. Designs were produced for such piers at heights up to 80ft and more, demonstrating the ability of Bailey to produce a solution not readily achievable with any other bridging equipment before or since.

Bailey continuous bridges, built on Bailey cribs, were widely used during the advance into Europe, and extensive use was also made of the

161

Figure 7.11. Dempsey Bridge, a 4000ft timber piled pier continuous Bailey, built across the Rhine in 1945. (HQ 2nd Army Photo Recce Unit).

Christchurch Crib to produce piers for such bridges, particularly during the Allied advance up Italy. Timber piled piers were also used and an excellent example was the Dempsey Bridge, built across the Rhine in 1945 and over 4000ft long. (Figure 7.11). More details of the bridge are given in Chapter Fourteen.

An alternative to continuous construction was provided by the broken-span bridge. Two or more spans of normal Bailey were launched as a single unit over one or more intermediate piers, and once in position the spans were separated at the span junction posts joining them together, so that each acted independently at the full load class for its type of construction. Intermediate supports took any convenient form, although when Bailey cribs were used, the pivot was built at the top of the crib, rather than at the bottom as was the case with continuous construction.

The Canal Lock Bailey

This form of bridge evolved to cope with the canal system of the Low Countries, by providing a bridge capable of spanning a small wet gap, such as a canal lock, that was at the same time capable of being raised to allow passage of barges and other craft. A number of improvised designs based upon Bailey Bridging were employed, any special parts needed being manufactured locally. One design used a short span that was raised about

162

Figure 7.12. *A 30ft span single/single Bailey Canal Lock Bridge.* (Military Engineering Vol III, Part IV Chap II - 1949).

hinges fitted at one end, rather like a draw bridge. Another design used a 30ft single/single Bailey Bridge suspended between 30ft high double/single Bailey towers; the bridge was raised and lowered using the four 3in steel wire ropes located at the corners and connected through pulleys and winches to pre-cast concrete counterweights. (Figure 7.12).

The Bailey Retractable Bridge

This bridge was also designed to meet the requirement for a bridge that could be withdrawn to allow unrestricted passage for shipping, but in this case for use across rivers or canals, rather than across a narrow lock. The bridge was designed to carry Class 40 loads over clear spans of up to 132ft, and was capable of being launched across or withdrawn from a gap in about 15 minutes. Double/double construction was used when the clear span exceeded 80ft, otherwise double/single was adequate. The forward span was of course just greater than the wet gap to be crossed, and a rear span was built 10ft longer; the total length of bridge to cross a 132ft gap would thus be 290ft. The two spans were of continuous construction, and were supported at their junction on two special six wheeled railway bogies, one under each girder, running on two sets of railway track. For forward spans in excess of 100ft a further pair of trolleys supported the rear ends of the girders. For forward spans over 120ft, a four panel high Bailey tower was built on top of the girders at the bogie position, to act as a king post for steel wire ropes supporting both ends of the structure, whilst for 100 and 110ft forward spans double/triple construction was used 30ft either side of the bogie position instead. The bridge was launched and withdrawn by attaching a tracked towing vehicle to one side of the rear bridge, using tow ropes and shackles.

Two other movable Baileys, the Skid Bailey and the track mounted Mobile Bailey, were both used in the assault bridge role, and will be considered in the next chapter, together with the other assault variants such as the Plymouth, the Brown and the Dalton Bridges.

Dual Carriageway Bailey

When a two way bridge was required but width was restricted at the abutment or on a pier, a dual carriageway Bailey was often used. The centre girder had of course to carry twice the load of the two outer girders, and a typical design used double/double for the common centre girder and double/single construction for the two outer girders, the bridge being capable of taking Class 40 loads over an 80ft span. (Figure 7.13). Transoms from each of the two separate carriageways overlapped at the central girder,

Figure 7.13. A dual carriageway Bailey built at the SME, Ripon. (RE Corps Library).

Figure 7.14. A railway viaduct built across the River Biferno in Italy in 1943. The deck type continuous Bailey comprised four 60ft and two 50ft spans. (Railway Construction in Italy).

and this reduced the overall width of the two bridges by about 3½ft, sometimes a useful benefit. Because of this overlap of transoms in the common girder, all four transom positions were used in each bay, and this meant that Class 70 construction, which needed four transoms per bay, was not possible.

Bailey Railway Bridging

Bailey could also be used for rail traffic, when bridges specifically designed for this purpose were not available, and standard designs were produced, in some cases taking advantage of quadruple construction introduced late in the War for Class 100 road traffic. Typical examples of construction used to take the 20 Unit Loading specified in British Standard 153 of 1937, for which all British military railway bridging was designed, were triple/single at 50ft span, quadruple/single at 60ft span and quadruple/double at 90ft span. All these spans were capable of sustaining a 20mph crossing speed, although spans could be increased with a 5mph speed restriction. A standard design

Figure 7.15. The trial launching of a 160ft Class 100 Deck Bailey, using quadruple/triple construction, with launching nose touching down. (IWM 3318).

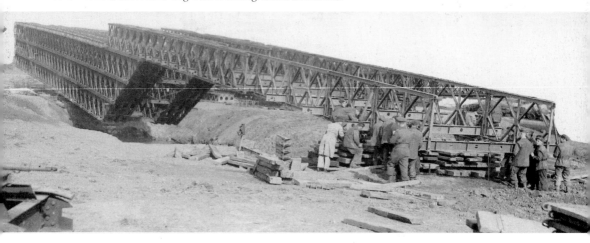

was also produced for a 60ft span Deck Bailey Railbridge, using two quadruple/single girders spaced at rail distance and 10 x 5in sleepers at 2½ ft centres for the decking. (Figure 7.14).

Deck Baileys were also used occasionally for road traffic, either by spacing all the girders at 18in centres or by using normal spacing for the girders and then supporting cross girders at top chord level with improvised yokes. (Figure 7.15).

The American Panel Bridge - Bailey Type

In 1938 the American Army Corps of Engineers faced similar problems to its British counterpart with regard to bridging equipment. It was equipped with a 7½ ton capacity pontoon bridge, a modified version of a Civil War model, and the H-10 and H-20 box girder bridges, based upon the British Large and Small Box Girder designs and mentioned in the previous chapter. They were now faced with the prospect of heavier tanks being developed, at this stage up to 20 tons in weight. The pontoon bridge was modified to take 10 ton loads by extending the length of the pontoons, but by May 1940 plans were in hand for heavier tanks, possibly weighing 50 tons, and a major rethink was necessary. Detailed consideration of the development of American equipment is obviously outside the scope of this book, but suffice it to say that for use on wide river obstacles the Americans eventually developed the M1 Steel Treadway Bridge, based very loosely on a German Army concept of the mid-1930s. This was later developed into the very successful M2 Bridge, with the wider treadways needed to take the latest tanks. The bridge consisted of 12ft long twin steel treadways, resting on steel saddles fixed to 33ft long pneumatic floats; it could take Class 40 loads at current speeds of 7 feet per second and was considered by many to be the best bridge for an assault crossing available to any army during the Second World War.

For fixed or dry support bridging the Americans soon realized that they had nothing that could remotely match the Class 70 capacity of the Bailey being developed in the UK, let alone a bridge that could be used in such a wide range of situations. It was also realized that there would be many advantages to be gained if the British and the American Armies were to standardize on the same equipment bridge. In the summer of 1941 a full set of working drawings of the Bailey Bridge was sent across to America, and three weeks after Pearl Harbor $50,000 was made available for the manufacture of a 200ft triple/double pilot model. Unfortunately production difficulties followed and in the words of their official history, *The United States Army in World War II*, '- early procurement of Bailey was to all practical purposes almost a complete failure'. The case is of course overstated because once initial problems of tolerancing had been overcome, the Americans manufactured 20 miles of Bailey Bridge, or **Panel Bridge - Bailey Type** as they preferred to call it, hardly a 'complete failure'!

These early production difficulties were disappointing because excellent co-operation between EBE and the American authorities had been maintained during the design and testing phases; indeed, at the request of the US a British Liaison Officer was appointed to Fort Belvoir, near Washington, and Major Stewart (recently Superintendent at EBE) was the first incumbent in this post, taking up his duties in May 1942. The duties of the Liaison Officer at Fort Belvoir was later extended to cover all other engineer co-operative projects, and Stewart was the first of a long line of Sapper officers to have held the post.

From the British working drawings already supplied, the US Engineer Board modified the design to take account of differences between British and American standard rolled steel sections and nut and bolt sizes; one result was that the American panel weighed 587lb compared with the 570lb British panel, and the weight of the stringers increased from 190lb to 271lb. At least in theory then the two designs should have been fully interchangeable. In fact however the interpretation of tolerances was not identical and problems with regard to the gauging and inspection of bridge parts meant that not only would some American parts not couple with British parts, but often American parts would not couple with each other. These problems were eventually sorted out, but because of early uncertainty it was decided to earmark initial US production for training in that country and eventually for use in the Far East theatre, and to satisfy the American demand for Bailey in Europe from British sources. This contingency had been foreseen by the Engineer-in-Chief (Major General C J S King, later Lieut General Sir Charles King, KBE, CB) thus ensuring that enough Bailey was available in Italy to cover the advance of both British and American armies. However care had to be taken to avoid mismatching the two equipments and where this could possibly occur, the American panels and end posts were for a time paint marked accordingly.

As part of their Lease/Lend co-operation the Americans later manufactured 25 sets of Bailey Bridge gauges for use in both countries, and also an elaborate 12ft long master gauge, to check and control the accuracy of all other gauges.

Widened Bailey Bridges

In early 1945 the introduction of the American M26 Pershing Tank into the European Theatre of operations and the anticipated introduction of the British Cruiser Tank, Centurion, (A41), necessitated modification of some Bailey Bridges to take these wider tanks. The 41 ton Pershing was 11ft 8in wide and the 50 ton Centurion was 11ft 1in wide, whereas the width between ribands of normal Bailey was only 10ft 9in.

To meet the requirements of 21 Army Group, the modifications were introduced in three stages, namely:

1. The issue of designs for an **Improvised Deck Bridge.**

2. The introduction of the **Improvised Widened Bailey Bridge (IWBB)**, with modification of the normal transom, extension of the sway brace and repositioning of the inner bridge trusses so that the clearance between the inner trusses went up from 12ft 4in to 13ft 9in; this increased the roadway width between ribands to 12ft 6in.

3. Finally **Standard Widened Bailey Bridge (SWBB)** was introduced, with longer and deeper transoms, and longer chesses and swaybraces. The roadway width between ribands was still 12ft 6in but the clearance between inner trusses went up to 14ft 3½in. The girders of SWBB were either double, triple or quadruple truss and the basic load class of the bridge was raised from Class 40/70 to Class 50/80, Class 80 representing a Class 50 tank on its transporter.

It will be seen in a later chapter that the bridge was to be widened yet again, after the war, as the **Extra Widened Bailey Bridge (EWBB)**, with a clear roadway width of 13ft 9¹/₂ins between ribands.

A Success Story

The devotion of a complete chapter of this history to just one equipment may at first seem disproportionate. It must be remembered however that the 'Meccano' like quality of Bailey Bridge meant that it was in fact many bridges in one; and also that the circumstances of the Second World War resulted in truly vast quantities of the equipment being manufactured. In later chapters the wartime use of the bridge will be considered in more detail, but as a measure of its value to the Allies one should bear in mind that almost 2500 Bailey Bridges were built during the Italian Campaign between 1943 and 1945, and over 1500

Figure 7.16. Page's light-hearted view of a Bailey panel party in 1942.

during the advance into Europe from 1944 onward. It had also been used earlier in North Africa and was used extensively in the Far East. The bridge was certainly one of the major inventions of the War, ranking alongside, for example, the jet engine and radar, and without doubt it did much to shorten the course of the War, a view expressed by Field Marshal Montgomery in 1947 and quoted in Chapter One.

However to end this chapter on a lighter note, Page's cartoon of 1942 may well bring back memories to many wartime Sappers. (Figure 7.16).

168

CHAPTER EIGHT

The Equipments of the Second World War

The Scope of Sapper Bridging

After reading the previous chapter, one might be excused for imagining that the Bailey Bridge was the be all and end all of military bridging for the Sappers. Such was the expansion of the Corps and the increased pace of modern warfare however, that a whole range of other bridging equipments was developed during the war, embracing not only alternatives to Bailey but also tank and assault bridges, ferries and rafts, and railway bridges. Considerable use was also made of the prewar equipments described in Chapter 6, notably the SBG and the FBE.

The Inglis Bridge Mark III

The Mark III Inglis, its shortcomings and its eclipse by Bailey Bridging have been considered in the preceding chapter; however the contract for one hundred 120ft bridge sets that was placed in early 1940 ran to completion and the bridge will therefore be considered in more detail. For the Mark III version of his bridge, Inglis reverted to the 12ft bay length used for the Mark I Bridge. (Figure 8.1). The 4½in diameter steel tubes used for the members

Figure 8.1. A 120ft span Class 24 Mark III Inglis Bridge. (Military Engineering Vol III Part II Pam 11 - 1942).

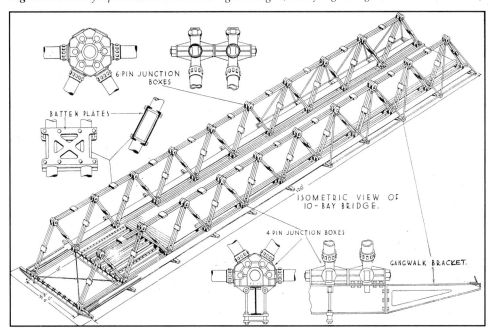

were connected up into equilateral triangles to form the main girders as a Warren truss. The 18ft long steel joist transoms, at 12ft spacing, connected the trusses to give a roadway width of 11ft between ribands, an increase of a foot over the Mark II version. Footwalk brackets were bolted to each end of the transoms, not only to carry the timber slated footwalk but also to connect the system of knee bracing found necessary after the top chord buckling which occurred during the test loading of the first-off production bridge at Christchurch. The bridge could take a Class 40 load at a 60ft span using single truss girders, or at a 120ft span using triple truss girders. It was constructed by cantilevering out across the gap, using a travelling gantry to carry forward and build additional bays at the front end of the bridge; a tail counterweight balanced the overhanging front section of bridge during construction. Alternatively, and much more quickly, the bridge could be erected on a special trolley alongside the gap, again using a tail and counterweight. It was then either swung or rolled forward into its final position; limitations of the trolley restricted the span that could be built by this method to 84ft. Various floating versions of the Inglis Mark III were considered; one version used pontoons each constructed from eight Braithwaite water tanks and located at transom positions.

Inglis put considerable effort into the up-dating of his First World War bridge and an immense amount of work, to this end, was carried out at the Cambridge University Engineering Laboratories. Understandably he was very disappointed that greater use was not made of his bridge during World War II, although this was of course inevitable with the adoption of Bailey Bridging.

The Briggs Bridge

A year or so later Captain M H Briggs RE, serving at the time with the Royal Bombay Sappers and Miners at Kirkee in India, developed his ideas for a light equipment bridge. Having trained in UK with the fairly heavy and slowly built Large and Small Box Girder Bridges, and briefly with the Mark III Inglis, Briggs conceived the idea of a much lighter operational bridge, capable of carrying all Divisional transport up to Class 12 over a 64ft span. The design that evolved, similar in many ways to Martel's box girder bridges, consisted of two light welded box girders, each formed from hornbeam sections, approximately 16ft long, and either one or two 16ft long and 3ft deep centre sections. (Figure 8.2 and Appendix B). Briggs also produced a design for an intermediate pier, to be used for spans in excess of 64ft.

The concept of the bridge was approved and after Briggs had produced working drawings, an order was placed on a firm in Calcutta, in early December 1941, for one prototype bridge set. Tests on the prototype had been completed by the end of March 1942 when GHQ India received news of the successful development of the Bailey Bridge. The decision was

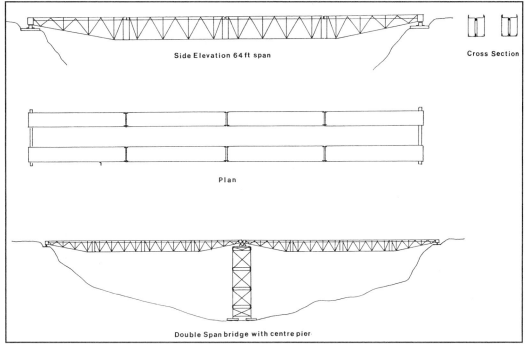

Figure 8.2. The prototype Briggs Bridge, produced in India in 1942. (Martin Briggs).

therefore made not to proceed further with Briggs' design, in anticipation of early delivery of Bailey Bridges, although in fact it was nearly two years before Bailey was received in the theatre.

The Butterley Bridge

By 1943 production of Bailey Bridging was well advanced, and indeed the bridge had by now been used operationally. Nevertheless it was thought prudent to consider possible alternatives, which might of course have proved superior. One such bridge was the Butterley Standard Unit Bridge, developed by the Butterley Company of Ripley in Derbyshire. The bridge comprised five standard units, which sufficed for the construction of all types of bridge from light footbridges to heavy road or rail bridges. The essential feature of the design was the use of 8in x 6in box section chord and diagonal members, jig bored at each end with holes to receive 2in diameter connecting pins. Members were then joined together to form Warren trusses in 10ft modules, using mild steel circular bobbins into which the members were pinned. (Figure 8.3 and Appendix B). The other members comprised

Figure 8.3. A three span Butterley Bridge, erected by nine men and two boys in 120 hours. (Butterley Engineering).

the cross girders and their suspension plates, and floor plates.

After careful consideration the War Office decided not to pursue procurement of the bridge. It did not offer the versatility of Bailey, and although of simple construction, the components could not be so easily manhandled and fitted together; furthermore, although showing a potential lower production cost per ton than Bailey, its excessive weight resulted in a probable greater cost per foot run of bridge. Nevertheless the bridge was further developed by Butterley Engineering Ltd, and was still in production in the late 1950s. It was produced in through and deck bridge versions, with double and treble truss girders as with the Inglis; heavy bridges of over 120ft span required double tier construction

The Flambo Bridge

The Flambo bridge, a product of the Italian Campaign, was certainly one of the more interesting alternatives to Bailey, since it was in fact a locally produced version of that bridge. As the advance upon Rome continued in early 1944, the work of the Sappers behind the lines was on a very grand scale. Many factories and workshops were taken over, including iron foundries, rolling mills, welding and machine shops, saw mills and woodworking shops, and even cement and brick works. Production included steel ingots, rolled sections, nuts and bolts, special Bailey parts needed for specific projects, and a whole host of engineer stores. The work was carried out largely by civilians, working under the control of personnel of the South African Engineer Corps' 80 Engineer Base Workshop.

During the advance in the summer of 1944 over 850 Bailey Bridges were built, including major bridges over 300ft long, and the 8th Army alone was being supplied with three sets of Bailey a day. To ease the problems of shipping, and since in any case stockpiling of Bailey for the forthcoming invasion of Europe meant that very little of the equipment was now available for the Italian theatre, it was decided that there was a need for a replacement bridge that could be built in rear areas, and thus release Bailey Bridges for reuse in the field. Major John Lander RE had recently arrived in Italy from Malta, and was set the task of designing such a bridge. Although restricted by a limited range of steel sections and poor welding facilities, he eventually decided on a copy of the Bailey, using such mild steel sections as were available. The new bridge was known as the Flambo Bridge, the name being derived from Flambeau or the Torch, the code name for the Administrative Echelon of HQ Allied Forces. The Flambo Bridge was designed on the lines of Bailey, with similar parts having the same general shape and dimensions, but the use of mild steel instead of high tensile steel meant not only a reduction in strength when compared with the original, but also an increase in component weight; thus the weight of the Flambo panel was 900lb, compared with a weight of 570lb for the Bailey panel. With no suitable size of RSJ available, the transom was fabricated from angles and flats (Figure 8.4).

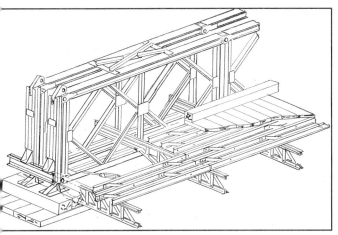

Figure 8.4. *Components of the Flambo Bridge, made by 80 Engineer Base Workshop.*

Production rate of the bridge eventually reached one 60ft Class 40 bridge a day, which was no mean feat considering that the Sappers had to set up production lines, organize the re-establishment of the steel works and rolling mills, and even set up a welding school to train Italian welders. The high rate of production was assisted by the fact that a much slower speed of erection of the bridge was acceptable than with Bailey; hence it was possible to use fishplates and bolts in place of the neater lugs and clamps used with the Bailey Bridge; this obviated the use of a number of specially rolled sections and simplified fabrication. The bridge was designed to use either concrete or timber decking, separate calculations being made in either case for the load carrying capacity.

Without doubt the success of the project was in no small way due to the efforts of Major Lander and Lieutenant Colonel L T Campbell-Pitt SAEC, who commanded 80 Engineer Base Workshop. Almost 290 of the bridges were manufactured, and Major Lander went on to produce a design for a 300ft Flambo Suspension Bridge. The stiffening girders of the bridge were of double/single construction, and the 30ft towers were of square cross-section, using four panels for each 10ft lift. As part of the forward planning for the eventual crossing of the River Po, ten sets of the suspension bridge equipment were produced. However the end of hostilities precluded their use, and only one bridge was actually built; this was Westminster Bridge, built across the River Arno at Incisa, a little south of Florence, and on the main road to Arrezzo.

Assault Bridging During the War

The interest in tank launched assault bridging had been resurrected in the mid-1930s, with trials at Christchurch on the various prototype bridges described in an earlier chapter. However with rapid advances in the techniques of tank warfare it was soon apparent that there was a firm requirement for a bridge that could be carried on a tank and then launched in the minimum of time, without exposure of the tank crew. The problems involved proved difficult to solve, but our work between the wars paid dividends, since the British designs, limited in scope as they were, were at the forefront of assault bridge design during the war. The Russians

173

produced the horizontally launched T-34 MTU assault bridge, the Americans developed various versions of the Sherman Ark and also a Sherman front mounted assault bridge, whilst the Germans decided that assault bridgelaying units were unnecessary. The three tank-chassis launched assault bridges adopted for service by the British Army during the war were the Scissors Bridge 30ft, No 1, the Tank Bridge 30ft, No 2, and the Tank Bridge, Small Box Girder, but various other types of assault bridge were developed, including the ARKs, which will be described later.

The Scissors Bridge 30ft, No 1.

This bridge, known also as the Tank Bridge 30ft, No 1, was a direct descendant of the earlier Scissors Assault Bridge. Both bridges were carried folded in half on top of a bridgelaying tank with its turret removed. They were both launched by unfolding the bridge, scissor fashion, using a launching frame operated by a long steel screw, in turn driven through a screw feed gearbox mounted on top of the tank chassis. The No 1 Tank Bridge was designed however with heavier tank loads in mind, that is to take a Class 24 tracked load over a clear span of 30ft, whereas the earlier bridge could only carry a Class 5 load over a 26ft span.

Work on the new bridge started at the EBE in March 1940, under the direction of Mr D M Delany. (Figure 8.5 and Appendix B). The heavier and more robust bridge necessitated a heavier tank to act as the bridgelayer, and for the first prototype the Cruiser Tank Mark II (A10) was substituted for the much smaller Light Tank Mark V used with the earlier bridge. The A10 tank

Figure 8.5. The prototype 30ft span No 1 Tank Bridge, mounted on the chassis of an A10 Cruiser Tank Mark II. (IWM 909).

174

Figure 8.6. *The prototype bridge mounted on a Covenanter Tank chassis.* (IWM 955).

soon became obsolete however, and it was decided to go to production of the tank bridge with a bridgelayer based on the new Cruiser Tank Mark V, the Covenanter. (Figure 8.6). Minor modifications had to be made to the launching mechanism, and although no alterations to the actual bridge design were necessary, subsequent trials showed that the bridge could safely be upgraded to Class 30 (tracked). To complete the saga of the bridgelayer, one should add that although the Covenanter was a fast tank, it was not a great success; its complicated steering mechanism led to unreliability, with a tendency for the tank to move to the right when the driver pulled the left hand control stick, and vice versa. Although over 1000 of the tanks were built, it was never used in combat and was mainly used for training. Consequently the No 1 Tank Bridge was finally mounted on the chassis of the highly successful Infantry Tank Mark III, or Valentine, using an almost identical launching mechanism to that used with the Covenanter. The Valentine mounted tank bridge was issued at an establishment of six per armoured brigade equipped with the lighter cruiser or medium tanks, both in Italy and in NW Europe; some were also used operationally in Burma.

The Tank Bridge 30ft, No 2.

The advent of the Infantry Tank Mark IV or Churchill, at a weight approaching 40 tons, immediately posed problems regarding the capacity of the No 1 Tank Bridge, as had been the case with our support bridging. In no way could the load class be stretched beyond Class 30, and therefore, in January 1942, work was started on a new and heavier tank bridge. This was to be the No 2 Tank Bridge, also designed to span a clear gap of 30ft but now at a load class of Class 60 for tracked vehicles and Class 40 for wheeled vehicles; again much of the design work on the bridge and its launching

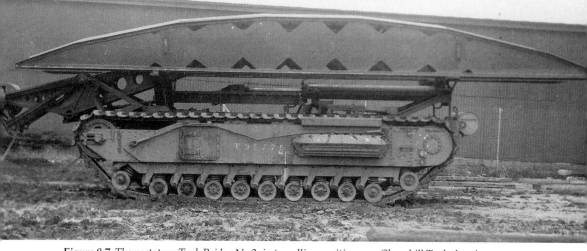

Figure 8.7. The prototype Tank Bridge No 2, in travelling position on a Churchill Tank chassis. (IWM 1468).

mechanism was carried out by Mr D M Delany. A new concept for launching an assault bridge was adopted. The two steel trackways, each in one piece without a central hinge, were connected together by cross diaphragms and carried the right way up on top of the launcher. (Figure 8.7 and Appendix B). The bridge remained horizontal as it was launched, raised and lowered by the rotation through 180° of a launching arm, pivoted at the front of the tank and at the centre of the bridge, rather as in the throwing of a javelin. (Figure 8.8). Once the bridge had been positioned across the gap in front of the bridgelayer, the arm was disengaged and the layer backed away from the site. The launching mechanism, which could also be used to recover the bridge, was operated by the tank driver, the only other crew member being the tank commander.

The bridgelayer used for the No 2 Tank Bridge was either the Mark III or the Mark IV Churchill tank, with of course the turret removed. The

Figure 8.8. The prototype of the later Tank Bridge No 3, demonstrating the launch method used for the No 2 and No 3 Bridges. (IWM 3984).

launching arm fitted to the layer was operated hydraulically and could achieve a launch time of just over 1½ minutes, at the optimum engine speed of 1800 rpm.

The Tank Bridge, Small Box Girder.

The Mark I version of this bridge (known also as the SBG Assault Bridge) was developed by 79 Armoured Division soon after the Division assumed its specialist role in early 1943; the bridge was developed to meet a requirement for a Class 40 assault bridge capable of crossing craters and ditches up to 30ft across and surmounting obstacles such as sea walls up to 12ft high. The requirement was met by using four slightly modified SBG Mark III hornbeam sections to form two girders, spaced apart by special bankseat beams bolted to each end of the bridge. The rear bankseat beam carried a forked bracket which engaged on a nose attachment on the front of an Armoured Vehicle Royal Engineers, or AVRE, the attachment acting as a pivot for the bridge, which was carried drawbridge fashion in front of the AVRE. A system of cables connected to the rear towing eye of the AVRE held the bridge raised at an angle of about 40° to the horizontal, and a quick release mechanism enabled the bridge to be dropped rapidly into position.

A Mark II version of the bridge was developed at EBE by Mr G E Moore. This version used exactly the same SBG layout for the bridge, but modified the launching mechanism by passing the launch cables from the front of the bridge up over an A frame mounted on the rear bankseat beam, and then down to the AVRE winch. (Figure 8.9). This obviously provided a degree of

Figure 8.9. The SBG Tank Bridge Mark II, mounted on a modified Churchill Tank. (IWM 3722).

control over the launch, enabling the bridge to be lowered slowly into position or recovered and returned to the travelling position by use of the winch. Both versions of the bridge carried a small fascine, about 15in in diameter, on the front of the AVRE, to be launched at the rear of the bridge and used as an improvised ramp.

To avoid undue wear and strain on the suspension and tracks of the launcher AVRE, 79 Armoured Division devised a simple method of mounting the complete bridge on a twin rubber tyred bogie. The bridge could then be towed behind the AVRE or another suitable vehicle, and transferred to the front of the AVRE when required. Carriage of the bridge in this way had the added advantages of increasing the road speed of the AVRE and decreasing its effective height for passage under low bridges or similar obstacles.

Another modification introduced by 79 Division folded the bridge in two lengthwise, by means of hinges welded to the SBG hornbeam sections; this produced a more compact travelling position and also improved cross country performance. The bridge was then launched in the manner of a scissors assault bridge.

79 Armoured Division and the Assault Engineers

In addition to the three tank launched bridges dealt with above, there were a number of other assault bridges developed during the war that warrant mention. First however the role of 79 Armoured Division, touched upon in the preceding paragraphs, deserves consideration in a little more detail. The division was formed as a normal armoured division in October 1942, with 18 and 19 Field Squadrons and 508 Field Park Squadron as the Sapper element, but as a result of experience in North Africa and in the Canadian operation at Dieppe in August 1942, it was decided that an armoured formation composed of specialist armoured vehicles would be needed for the final assault on Europe. 79 Armoured Division was selected as the most suitable unit on which to form such a formation, and the division adapted to its new role in April 1943, under the command of Major General P C S Hobart, who had served in the First World War as a Sapper officer, but had transferred to the Tank Corps in 1923. During the summer of 1943 the six companies of 5 and 6 Chemical Warfare Groups joined the division and became 5 and 6 Assault Regiments RE, but by the end of October six other units had been converted to Assault Squadrons, to form 1 Assault Brigade RE. The Brigade comprised three assault regiments (42 Assault Regiment RE being the third) each of four squadrons, and 149 Assault Park Squadron. It should be noted that during the campaign in NW Europe, the term 'Armoured' was substituted for 'Assault' in the titles of the squadrons and regiments, although after the war the title 'Assault 'was again introduced before finally being changed, yet again, to 'Armoured' in 1957.

It was soon realized that if the Sappers were to operate in the forefront of

Figure 8.10. The Armoured Vehicle Royal Engineers, or AVRE, based upon the Churchill Tank, loaded with a fascine. (Tank Museum 504/E2).

an armoured assault, an engineer tank was a necessity, the first proposal for such a vehicle being made by Lieutenant J J Donovan RCE, again as a result of lessons learnt during the Dieppe raid. The Churchill tank was considered the most suitable base vehicle for development. Existing Mark III and IV Churchills, with some minor modifications, were therefore converted by removing the 6pdr gun and substituting a specially designed 290mm calibre Petard spigot mortar, which fired a demolition charge nicknamed the Flying Dustbin. (Figure 8.10). The **Armoured Vehicle Royal Engineer**, or AVRE, became the basic equipment of the assault engineers, mounted with various additional equipments such as the Plough Mine-Lifter, the Snake Mine Exploder, the Fascine, the SBG Assault Bridge and, at a later date, Skid and Mobile Bailey. Additional equipment used by the Assault Engineers included the Churchill mounted ARKs and Landing Vehicles Tracked, or LVTs, which were tracked amphibious vehicles known as 'Buffaloes', whilst for the crossing of the Rhine some of the squadrons were equipped with the new Class 50/60 Raft.

The No 1 and No 2 Tank Bridges were not of course AVRE mounted and were the responsibility of the RAC, six of the No 1 Bridges being allotted to each armoured brigade during the campaign in NW Europe. The division of responsibility between the Sappers and the Tank Corps with regard to specialist armoured equipments was always a little obscure; the mine clearing flail tanks for example, known variously as 'Scorpions' and 'Crabs', were originally operated by the Royal Tank Regiment, with Sappers operating the flail mechanisms; then they were taken over entirely by the

179

Sappers, and finally became once again the responsibility of the RTR.

The sterling work done by the assault engineers during the campaign in NW Europe was matched in no small way in the Italian campaign. High casualties suffered by engineer units during the early stages of the campaign, arising from the assault of prepared enemy positions, and the success of assault engineer units in Normandy, lead to the formation of 1 Armoured Regiment RAC/RE in 1944 and to its expansion into 25 Armoured Engineer Brigade, a combined RAC and RE formation, early in 1945. The new brigade comprised an RAC regiment, operating specialist armoured vehicles such as flame throwers and flails, 1 and 2 Armoured Engineer Regiments, each of three squadrons and armed with ARKs, AVREs and tank dozers, and an Armoured Engineer Park Squadron.

The ARKs

The ARKs were a valued addition to the tank launched assault bridges already described. An ARK was a tank from which the gun turret had been removed and replaced with trackways on top of the hull; ramps were then fitted at either end of the chassis. The vehicle could thus be driven into a gap or up against an obstacle, and its ramps lowered so that other tanks or vehicles could drive over it. It was in effect an Armoured Ramp Carrier and hence became known as an ARK.

The **ARK Mark I** used either the Churchill Mark II or Mark IV gun tank chassis and was the first of the series, with 2ft wide timber trackways fitted immediately above the tracks. On the early models short ramps at the rear ends of each trackway hung vertically during travel, but in a later version the rear ramps were extended to about 12½ft in length and held raised by steel wire ropes whilst in the travelling position, in the manner of a draw bridge. Short ramps at the front of the ARK were raised horizontally when travelling and then lowered into position when the ARK was in use. The ARK Mark I was developed initially by 79 Armoured Division in late 1943 and about 50 were manufactured for use by the Division during the Normandy landings in 1944.

The **ARK Mark II**. After the successful invasion of France, the need to surmount vertical obstacles on the beach head gave way to that for crossing small streams or ditches; most of the ARKs Mark I were therefore converted to ARKs Mark II, by the addition of long hinged ramps at the front of the tank, similar to those at the rear. (Figure 8.11). The rear ramps were still supported by cables direct to the tank hull, but the forward ramps were used in conjunction with a 12ft long king post, to allow more precise control during their positioning. As a further modification, the gap between the two trackways was reduced by widening the left hand trackway and ramps from 2ft to 4ft, thus enabling smaller vehicles to cross.

The **Italian ARK** was developed and manufactured in Italy during that campaign. It was also based on the Churchill Mark II or IV chassis, but,

Figure 8.11. *The Churchill ARK Mark II, with the forward ramp being raised by a Valentine Tank.*
(IWM 3423).

unlike the ARKs Mark I and Mark II, separate trackways were not fitted to the chassis and the tank tracks formed part of the bridge roadway. (Figure 8.12). The front and rear ramps were manufactured from 15ft 3in long American Treadway Bridge ramps, although sometimes a later version of the Treadway ramps, which were wider and shorter, were used. Both front and rear ramps were pivoted about brackets welded to the tank hull and were held in position during travel by 2in steel wire ropes and king posts. The Italian ARK was used extensively during the campaign, either singly, to span

Figure 8.12. The Italian ARK, based upon a Churchill chassis and using American treadway ramp units.

181

Figure 8.13. The BURMARK, based upon the Valentine Tank chassis. (Tank Museum 370/A6)

gaps up to 50ft wide and 10ft deep and coping with a water depth of up to 5ft, or in combination with other ARKS, in tandem or mounted one on top of the other.

The **BURMARK** was a light ramped tank based upon the Valentine chassis, and was intended for use in the Far East theatre, as the name implies. (Figure 8.13). As with the Churchill ARKs Mark I and II, it had trackways built on the tank hull, but the ramps were hinged halfway along their length. It was not developed beyond prototype stage because of the end of the war.

The **Great Eastern Tank Ramp** was really a Super ARK, designed in early

Figure 8.14. The Great Eastern Tank Ramp, based upon a Churchill chassis.

1944 at an establishment known as MD1, at Whitchurch. MD1 was set up in 1939 to develop unusual weapons and the Establishment designed the Great Eastern for the invasion of Europe, to bridge obstacles that were too high or wide for the normal ARK to deal with. (Figure 8.14). The 27ft long sloping ramps were mounted on top of a Churchill chassis, which was again used as the base vehicle; a 13ft length of ramp was hinged at the rear of the main section, and was held in an elevated travelling position by cables. A further 25ft length of ramp section completed the Great Eastern; this was hinged to the front of the main section and was folded back on top of it for travelling. When an obstacle was reached the forward ramp section was propelled into position using a group of 3in rockets and the rear ramp was lowered into position, extending the total length of ramp to 65ft. Only twelve Great Easterns were produced in all and although a few of these reached 79 Armoured Division, this was not until early 1945, too late for the Normandy invasion.

The Inglis Assault or Mobile Bridge

The idea of building a standard equipment bridge some way away from the scene of battle and mounting it on wheels or tracks so that it could be subsequently pushed or towed into position had been explored in the early 1920s, when Inglis' design for a 135ft track mounted version of his Mark II Bridge was built and tested at Christchurch. (see Figure 5.2). This type of assault bridge had one serious disadvantage over the tank bridges and the ARKs, in that some exposure of troops during the launch was usually necessary, to operate any hydraulic mechanism, finally position the ramps, and so on. There was however a need for a rapidly installed bridge for spans in excess of the rather limited capability of the 30ft tank bridges, and this could be met by these mobile bridges. Early wartime work on such a bridge included production of a prototype Small Box Girder Bridge mounted on tracked bogies; the bridge was 95ft in length overall and could span a 50ft gap with vertical banks, but was not proceeded with because of its low load class.

Meanwhile, using the experience gained from the work of the early 1920s, Professor Inglis produced a new design for a mobile bridge, using the Mark III version of his bridge; only minor modifications and additions were made at the EBE. In its final form the bridge consisted of 13 bays of single truss Mark III Inglis, hinged at bottom chord level and fitted with articulating junction boxes and hydraulic articulators at top chord level, so that it consisted of an eight bay forward span and a five bay approach span; it could thus be used to cross an 80ft gap. Transoms and swaybrace were fitted at top chord level for added stability and, to keep the weight down, twin trackways were used instead of the normal decking. The Class 24 bridge was mounted on two tracked bogies, one under each truss, and with ramps fitted at each end was pushed forward by a Matilda tank coupled to the rear of bridge, using a special nose attachment and pusher bar. Before the bridge was launched across the gap, its geometry was adjusted by the hydraulic articulators to suit the gap profile; once the bridge was in position, the load on the articulators was released to lower the nose of the main span to the ground on the far bank.

Extensive trials of the bridge were carried out and it was intended that it would be made available in the field as an Engineer store. However, development work ceased in February 1943, in favour of the Bailey Mobile Bridge, which itself had been under development for twelve months and could carry a Class 40 load.

The Bailey Mobile Bridge

The Bailey Mobile Bridge, which evolved directly from the Inglis Mobile Bridge, was designed at the EBE by Major A H Naylor RE, later Professor of Civil Engineering at Belfast University, and subsequently by Major E Longbottom RE, who went on to design the Medium Girder Bridge in the 1960s. The bridge was of double/single construction, with an 80ft river span coupled to a 70ft approach span, together with 10ft ramps at either end. (Figure 8.15). The two spans were linked using span junction posts and a hand operated hydraulic mechanism, used to raise the forward section of the bridge clear of the ground whilst the bridge was being moved forward, and then lower this river span on to the far bank after launch. The complete bridge was some 170ft long with its ramps, and was supported at its centre on two three-bogie caterpillar tracks, one under each bridge girder. It was pushed forward by either a Sherman tank or a Churchill AVRE, using a special pusher frame mounted on the end of bridge. The BMB was used operationally in Italy in April 1945 in the successful crossing of the River Senio, and remained the current equipment mobile assault bridge, although various improvisations were developed in the field when equipment for the BMB was not available.

The **Plymouth Bridge** was a variation devised and constructed by 1 Canadian Armoured Brigade and 8 Indian Division Engineers, and consisted of 100ft of double/single Bailey mounted on rocking rollers on top of a

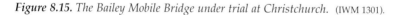

Figure 8.15. The Bailey Mobile Bridge under trial at Christchurch. (IWM 1301).

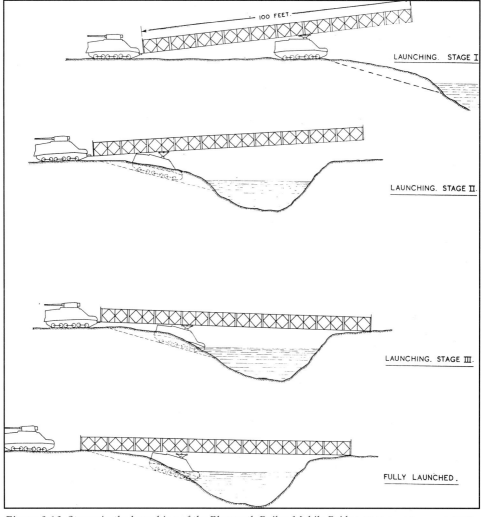

Figure 8.16. *Stages in the launching of the Plymouth Bailey Mobile Bridge.* (Bridging Monograph 8.008 - Development of Armoured Bridge Laying Vehicles).

Sherman tank with its turret removed. A second Sherman supported and pushed the rear of the bridge. (Figure 8.16). The lead tank was driven down a ramp cut into the river bank and, at a convenient point, was stopped whilst the bridge was boomed out over it, until there was sufficient overhang to bridge the gap. Both tanks then moved forward, allowing the nose of the bridge to drop on to the far bank as the lead tank descended the home bank ramp; the rear tank then disconnected from the bridge, using a small explosive charge in its pusher attachment. On the one occasion that the bridge was used operationally, in the assault crossing of the River Rapido in Italy on 12 May 1944, the front tank toppled into the river and was

185

completely submerged, just as the launch was completed by 9.30am. In an effort to place the landing ramp the tank officer and one of the crew were injured, three Sappers were killed and five were wounded. Nevertheless an improvised ramp was soon made and tanks were able to cross the bridge at 10.30am.

The **Brown Bridge** was developed by Captain B S Brown RCE from the Plymouth Bridge and comprised 140ft of double/single Bailey Bridge, with a 30ft double/single tail built without transoms. The 10ft ramps fitted at either end were held up by cordage during the transit and launching of the bridge, which used two Churchill gun tanks (the carrier tank with its turret removed) in place of the Shermans used in the Plymouth Bridge.

The **Dalton Bridge**, developed by Major T R Dalton RE, was an improvement on the Brown Bridge. The bridge again consisted of 140ft of double/single Bailey with a 30ft launching tail, but was mounted on a Churchill ARK and pushed forward by a Churchill AVRE, both vehicles being modified by bolting on the special attachments necessary; this avoided the need to permanently modify the two base tanks by welding on attachments as with the Brown Bridge. Neither the Dalton Bridge nor the Brown Bridge were used operationally.

Skid Bailey, another variation on the Mobile Bailey theme, was developed by 79 Armoured Division as a rapid means of bridging large craters and similar obstacles during the advance into Europe. The bridge was assembled from normal Bailey parts but was fitted with special skids, about 8ft long, bolted to the bottom of each panel. The bridge was built to the required length some way away from the site and was then pushed to its final position using a modified Churchill AVRE; a standard launching nose was sometimes used to assist correct positioning of the bridge.

Track Bridges

Track Bridges, sometimes referred to as **Trackway Bridges**, can possibly be considered as simple assault bridges. Various prototype versions were produced in the 1930s, some of which were considered in Chapter 6. The first such bridges to come into service during the early stages of the war were the **Track Bridges 12ft No 1 and No 2**, both of which were Class 5 although the No 1 Bridge was for wheeled traffic only. In the No 1 Bridge the 12in wide curved deck plate was carried on the centre line of the girders and each track weighed about 150lb. The No 2 Bridge carried the perforated flat deck plate, 17in wide, above the girders and therefore needed wooden kerbs; each track weighed about 220lb.

The **Track Bridge 12ft No 3** was a much heavier version, weighing about 475lb per track, and with a Class 9 capacity for wheeled and tracked vehicles soon replaced the earlier versions, production of which stopped in mid-1942. The flat perforated deck plate was carried on the centre line of the girders which were made from either rolled sections or tubular members, and kerbs

Figure 8.17. *The Track Bridge 20ft, with its transport.*

were formed from flat plate welded to the girders.

The **Track Bridge 20ft** could span a clear gap of 21ft 6in and was the last member of the trackway bridge family, although in fact it became obsolescent before the 12ft No 3 Bridge, probably because its weight (about 1,450lb) and size (2ft 3in wide clear track and 2ft deep girders) made it rather unwieldy. (Figure 8.17). Of similar construction to the previous track bridges, it would take a Class 24 tracked load, a Class 18 six wheeled load or a Class 12 four wheeled load. Two bridges, each consisting of two trackways, were carried on a special 3ton lorry, which was then used to launch them. All the trackway bridges were Engineer stores, not normally held by field units or by the Bridge Company RASC, and their use was an RE responsibility.

Floating Equipments

The floating equipments developed during World War II formed another very important group and within this group the Bailey Pontoon Bridge, dealt with in the previous chapter, was in the fore. However Bailey did not lend itself readily to the rapid production of rafting equipment, essential during the early stages of a river assault to ferry across vehicles, and particularly the tanks, necessary to establish a bridgehead prior to the construction of a floating bridge proper. Within this group the Class 50/60 Raft and the Close Support Raft are the most important, and will be considered in some detail. Many minor equipments and ancillaries have however been purposely excluded from this bridging story, in order to keep within reasonable limits; such exclusions include the various marks of motor boats or tugs used by the Sappers to build their bridges; outboard motors used to propel rafts and ferries, such as the 3½-4hp Seagull, the 22hp Johnson and the 50hp Evinrude; and Storm Boats and inflatable Reconnaissance Boats.

The Class 50/60 Raft

Development of the Class 48/60 Raft, as it was originally known, was started at the EBE in early 1943, with a mind to the future crossing of the River Rhine under assault conditions, before the long span floating Bailey Bridges which would ultimately be required could be built. The requirement was to provide a heavy raft, capable of carrying the Churchill tank; the raft was required to be easily and compactly transported, rapidly launched and constructed, and simple to operate. As finally developed the raft could be constructed with either four or five pontoons, providing a Class 50 or 60 capacity. (Figure 8.18 and Appendix B). For simplicity each pontoon unit was identical and each carried its own superstructure of two hinged panels, folded down on to the deck and raised into position after the pontoon had been launched. Each pontoon was towed on a special trailer, one quarter of the additional equipment required for ramps and so forth being carried by each of the towing vehicles; thus a Class 50 Raft would require four complete

Figure 8.18. The four pontoon Class 50 version of the Class 50/60 Raft, under trial on the Thames. (RSME).

units, whilst a Class 60 Raft would require five, but would then have a 25% surplus of ancillary equipment.

The raft was normally operated as a free ranging ferry, using two DUKWs or four motor tugs to propel it. If used as a captive ferry it was propelled by four 22hp Johnson outboard motors, fitted to special brackets and transoms. Alternatively it could be winched across wide tidal rivers by using two 'Wild Kite' balloon winches located on the river banks. Class 5 roadways were provided, running parallel to the main roadway and outside the panel girders, and located on the bow and stern decks of each pontoon. Access to these roadways was provided by FBE Class 5 Raft ramps but the roadways were not often used, since the ferrying rope guides were mounted on the outer edge of the roadways, which prevented their use when the guides were themselves in use.

After the war the 50/60 Raft was modified by repositioning the panels to give a clearance of 13ft 1in, so that it could accommodate the Centurion Tank. At the same time it was renamed the Class 55/65 Raft, to take account of the 2000lb short ton, adopted to achieve international agreement on the bridge load classification system.

In 1950 23 Field Engineer Regiment in BAOR successfully built an improvised assault bridge using raft equipment, and later that year completed a 320ft bridge, during an exercise, which stood up to the passage of the majority of the armour and all the soft vehicles of an armoured division. The bridge was built with much less effort and in about half the time required for an SWBB pontoon bridge of similar load class across the same gap. The Centurion tanks crossed at two-minute intervals and all vehicles, other than the tanks, dozers and transporters, crossed nose to tail.

The Close Support Raft

This raft was also developed at the EBE in 1943, again specifically with assault crossing of rivers in mind. Although the Folding Boat Equipment Mark III, which had been introduced just before the war, could be used to form a Class 9 shore loading raft, it was a cumbersome affair involving six folding boats. The FBE had of course been designed primarily as a bridge, and the more usual form of FBE raft consisted of two coupled floating bays of bridge operating between two trestle landing bays. The CSR on the other hand was rapidly built and easily operated and was intended to be brought into action at an early stage of a river assault. The pontoons were carried on steel clad timber sledges, which could be removed from their vehicles and then towed down to the ferry site by any suitable armoured vehicle or half-track. Little work on the approaches was necessary, which meant that vehicles could be landed directly on to the enemy shore in a very short space of time. Although it was basically a Class 9 equipment, the raft had adequate buoyancy to carry selected vehicles above Class 9; this enabled assaulting troops to be fully supported by their armoured cars and scout cars, their carriers and even by field artillery tractors with towed 17pdr antitank guns.

The shore loading raft was built with two Mark V, V* or Mark VI bipartite pontoon piers, fitted with special saddles to support the simple superstructure, which consisted of deck and ramp roadbearers and FBE Mark III deck panels. The two ramps, each about 19ft long, were connected by a simple balancing gear, adjusted with a Pul-lift jack, so that one ramp could be raised by a crew member walking on to the other. (Figure 8.19). The equipment was operated as a free ranging raft, using either two or four propulsion units; it could also be operated as a captive ferry with two cross-stream ferry cables, propelled either by onboard propulsion units or by being towed across by winch or vehicle cable.

As with all equipments, modifications and improvements rapidly followed. A three pier raft enabled two extra propulsion units to be fitted and also provided extra freeboard and a reserve of buoyancy, although the three pier raft was still Class 9. A Class 12 version was introduced, using tripartite instead of bipartite piers, and a Class 9 bridge was considered, although the bridge would have been rather restricted in use by the necessary 45ft increments of span. Finally, towards the end of the war, a Mark II CSR was produced, with welded aluminium alloy joist road bearers and cast alloy deck panels. This was the first time that an aluminium alloy was used to any extent in a British equipment bridge (see Appendix B), but

Figure 8.19. *The Close Support Raft, using Mark V Pontoons, being loaded with a 11 ton lorry.* (IWM 2609).

190

within a few years such usage, with all of the advantages that it brought, was to be commonplace. As far as the CSR was concerned, it considerably reduced the weight of the transport units; the weight of the female roadbearer for example, was reduced from 350lb in the Mark I version to 206lb in the Mark II. In addition, building times were decreased, as was the size of the erection party, and the freeboard was increased, although the raft remained at Class 9 in the bipartite pier version.

The Indian Mat Bridge

Martel's work on the 1926 version of a Mat Bridge has been described in Chapter 5. Further experiments using the same principle were carried out by 4 Field Company of the Bengal Sappers and Miners at Roorkee in September 1939; a raft was formed using a bamboo trellis and a large tarpaulin, the edges of which were turned up over a straw filling to form a watertight lip to the mat. Steel channels were placed on the bamboo trellis to act as supports for the wheels of a 30cwt lorry, which was successfully floated on the raft. A bridge version of the mat raft was then successfully built and test loaded.

About a year later, the shortage of all types of bridging equipment in India resulted in Army HQ placing an order for an experimental Mat Bridge to be manufactured in Lahore. A number of problems had to be overcome in developing the Class 5 bridge, including the joining together of the tarpaulins to produce a bridge that would cross a 200ft gap, the difficulty of providing longitudinal strength, and the provision of a satisfactory replacement for the straw edging, which easily became water-logged. Eventually the problems were solved, and a bridge built across the River Jumna at Delhi, early in 1941, used Kapok filled bags to replace the straw edging. After subsequent development the bridge did actually go into production, although the rotting of a number of tarpaulins whilst in storage in the factory caused some problems. By the time the equipment became available to units however a number of other bridging equipments had also became available, and as far as is known the Indian Mat Bridge was never used operationally.

Development work was also undertaken in UK, at the EBE, and in 1943 a 30ft raft constructed from chesses, kapok floats and tarpaulins was successfully tested; subsequently 150ft of bridge constructed in the same way was built across the River Stour, successfully carrying Class 9 loads. (Figure 8.20). Further trials of the bridge were held in which the kapok floats were removed and alternate chesses were displaced first to one side and then to the other, to extend the area of canvas supported by the chesses. The replacement of the steel spreaders, used in the Indian version, by chesses greatly increased the bulk and weight of the EBE version.

An interesting outcome of the early work in India on the Mat Bridge was the eventual design and production of the Clover floating airstrip, built on

Figure 8.20. One version of the Class 9 Indian Mat Bridge. Note the Class 50/60 Raft to the left. (IWM 2021).

the same principles and using, in the first version, canvas sheeting with a decking made from tubes and timber. Discussion of the design is outside the scope of this book, but many details, including those of the successful landing of a Swordfish aircraft on the strip, are given in an article by Lt Col D W R Walker RE in the June 1948 edition of the *Royal Engineer Journal*.

The PN Boat

Mention has been made earlier of the Briggs Bridge, which was designed in India in 1941 in an attempt to overcome a shortage of bridging equipment in the theatre. The PN Boat was similarly designed, initially to meet a need for additional water transport by 23 Indian Division on the India-Burma border, and subsequently for possible use as a floating bridge equipment. The boat was designed by Lt W G Prow RE, who was in fact Captain Briggs' second in command. It was 16ft long, 4ft wide and 2ft deep, with a square stern and inclined bow; it was made with one inch planks from trees felled and sawn by local labour, and the joints were caulked with resin obtained in the hills. The metal fastenings and fittings were made by 305 Field Park Company IE who carried out the boat building. The boat was successfully tested in mid 1942, carrying a payload of about two tons with a freeboard of 6in.

After these successful trials it was suggested that the boats could be formed into bipartite piers to provide, with suitable superstructure, a floating bridge equipment. 1800ft of PN Boat Bridge was therefore fabricated ready for a possible advance into Burma involving the crossing of the

Figure 8.21. A PN Boat Raft being floated into a bridge across the River Manipur in Burma. (Martin Briggs).

Chindwin, a crossing of about 1200ft having been reconnoitred and a 50% allowance made for spares. The 500 PN Boats needed for the 1800ft of bridging were all made locally in the Imphal area, but the superstructure of transoms, spreader beams and decking was manufactured in Assam. The PN Boat Bridge was used for the Tiddim Road crossing of the River Manipur before a Bailey Bridge was built in 1944, (Figure 8.21), but when the advance into Burma finally took place in 1945, Bailey Pontoon Bridging was available and the PN Boat Bridge was thus never used on the Chindwin.

The Eastern Army Boat

The Eastern Army Boat, or the EA Boat, was another timber boat, designed in late 1944 at the Headquarters of the Eastern Army in India, and intended for ferrying and bridging in the theatre. The heavy punt shaped wooden pontoons were 40ft long, 6ft wide, and weighed three tons, although they were constructed in prefabricated sections capable of being transported by Jeep. In January 1945 a special construction camp was set up by 536 Artisan Works Company IE at Kalewa, on the Chindwin, to manufacture the boats, the timber being felled and sawn locally by two Forestry Companies of the Indian Army. In all 540 EA Boats were manufactured, some being used for the construction of the Falls Bridge across the Chindwin, but the majority being used for transport of stores up and down the river.

The Infantry Assault Boat

One final floating equipment that deserves mention is the Infantry Assault Boat; although not a bridging equipment, the boat was used to form an antitank gun raft, widely used by the infantry during the early stages of assault crossings. In the late 1930s various types of boat that could be used to ferry infantry across an obstacle were investigated at the EBE and, as a result of a regatta held there, during which seventeen boats were put through their paces, the two man pneumatic Reconnaissance Boat and the collapsible canvas Assault Boat were selected for production.

The 174lb Mark I Assault Boat, which carried a nine man infantry section and two rowers, soon gave way to the Mark II, about 12ft long and 4ft 8in wide. The boat, with tapered bow and square end, was made with a stiff plywood floor, canvas sides, and a stiff timber gunwale; it folded down to a height of only 4in. In many ways the Mark II Boat was found to be

Figure 8.22. Mark III Assault Boats, with tapered bow and stern, used to form a simple bridge.

194

insufficiently robust however, and eventually a naval type assault boat was adopted as the assault Boat Mark III. This boat was very similar in construction to the Mark II, but the length was increased to nearly 17ft and the width to 5ft 5in, so that it could carry the new increased size infantry section of 18 fully armed men; the weight of the boat increased to 350lb. A simple method of ferrying a 2pdr antitank gun was devised using one Mark III Assault Boat, timber baulks and planks, and a 12ft Track Bridge; various combinations of Mark II or Mark III boats were used to ferry similar light loads, including for example the Bren Gun Carrier which could be ferried suspended between two boats. (Figure 8.22).

Railway Bridging

Prior to the war, with the limited budget available for military equipment, development of railway bridging equipment had a fairly low priority. Indeed in the 1929 edition of the official handbook, *Military Engineering - Volume VIII - Railways*, there is no mention of standard bridging equipment and the clear indication is that design of replacement railway bridges should be on an ad hoc basis, left to the 'specialist bridge engineer'. It was soon realized however that to ensure the rapid resupply of the stores and equipment necessary to maintain the mobility of our advancing troops, the opening up of permanent lines of communication would be essential. These lines of communication were to prove of prime importance to our successful conclusion of the war, particularly so during the advance up Italy and after the invasion of North West Europe, where the sheer bulk and weight of equipment needing to be moved forward made the rapid reinstatement of the railway network absolutely essential. This rapid advance was only made possible by having readily available a supply of equipment bridging, capable of fairly rapid erection, to replace the vast number of rail bridges destroyed by the retreating enemy or by our own aerial or artillery attacks.

Military road bridging equipment was quite unsuitable for rail use, although some work was done in the early 1920s on adapting the Inglis Bridge for rail use, and the Hopkins Bridge was used experimentally as Number 6 Rail Bridge on the Longmoor Transportation Centre Railway between the wars. Bailey was also used occasionally during the war for rail traffic, as mentioned in the previous chapter. In general however far greater loads are sustained by rail bridging, as can clearly be seen from Table 1, and this made the provision of special railway bridging equipment absolutely essential. The table compares the Equivalent Uniformly Distributed Load, or the EUDL, for road and rail bridges of the same span The design loading usually adopted for military railway bridging was as specified in British Standard Specification 153-1937, and was sometimes 16 BS Unit loading, but more often 20 BS Unit loading.

TABLE 1 - COMPARISON OF ROAD AND RAIL EUDL

Span in feet	30	60	100	140	340
Road Class 70 – EUDL in tons	123	139	145	183	374
16 BS Unit Rail Loading – EUDL in tons	136	192	304	388	705
20 BS Unit Rail Loading – EUDL in tons	137	240	371	485	882

At shorter spans the differences in EUDL, all of which include an allowance for impact, are not great, but at spans of 60ft and over it is clear that the railway loading is greatly in excess of the military transport loading.

During the war railway bridging was very much a specialized Sapper task, coming under the aegis of the Transportation Directorate, which embraced such units as Railway Construction Companies, Railway Bridging Companies and Railway Operating Companies. Development and production of the required railway bridging and related equipment was centred on the Railway Bridging Wing of No 2 Railway Training Centre, set up at Derby in November 1939. Lieutenant Colonel W T Everall RE became the Chief Bridging Instructor of the Wing and was the driving force behind development of the new equipments. As mentioned in a previous chapter, Everall was a qualified civil engineer with considerable practical experience in England and in India, where for many years he had been responsible for all new and maintenance bridging work on both the largest railway network, the North Western State Railways, and the network of roads spread over the North West Frontier area. Just prior to the war he acted as a consultant to the War Office on the development of various railway bridging equipments and he was therefore very much the right man in the right job at this time.

The Equipments

In 1939 and 1940 a number of equipments were designed and manufactured to carry loads up to 20 BS Units at maximum speeds of 60mph for passenger trains and 40mph for goods trains, using a standard track gauge width of 4ft 8½in. These equipments included **Steel Joist Spans** for spans from 10 to 30ft, **Standard Plate Girder Railway Bridges** for spans from 30 to 80ft, and the **Standard Through Truss Railway Bridge** for spans in excess of 90ft. In addition the **Light Standard Unit Trestle** and the **Standard Unit Trestle** were developed, together with **6/10ton and 15/20ton Derricks** to aid construction. The trestles are described later in the chapter, together with the **Tubular and Heavy Trestles**.

In the early 1940s the range of equipment was rationalized to provide adaptability to different loadings and gauge widths and to give greater flexibility of spans. The new range included additional **Steel Joist Spans**, and two new equipments, the **Sectional Welded Plate Girder Bridge**, and the **Unit Construction Railway Bridge**. The span range for the new equipments is summarized in Table 2, together with the UK wartime production figures. When the Americans came into the war they were only too pleased to adopt the British designs, and Everall went across to the States to discuss production plans with the Engineer Board and advise on the very close tolerancing required. In due course a further 21,500 tons of these bridging equipments were manufactured in the United States, in addition to tonnages shown in the Table 2

TABLE 2 - WARTIME PRODUCTION FIGURES FOR RAILWAY EQUIPMENT

EQUIPMENT	SPAN RANGE	PRODUCTION (tons)	PRODUCTION (feet)
Rolled Steel Joist Spans	9-39	13,400	67,000
Sectional Welded Plate Girder Bridge	34-40	7,000	23,000
Unit Construction Railway Bridge	55-110	15,100	26,000
Standard Through Truss Railway Bridge	90-150	7,500	7,800
Everall Sectional Truss Railway Bridge	80-400	40,000	38,000
Light Standard Unit Trestle	--	33,000	--
Standard Unit Trestle	--	10,000	--

All the new designs made considerable use of welded construction, particularly so in the case of the UCRB and the Sectional Welded Plate Girder Bridge, in both of which welding took the place of riveting for all the main members. Although welding had previously been used in the UK to repair railway bridging, its extensive use in railway bridge fabrication, as demonstrated in these military bridges, was an innovation that was to be used more and more.

Rolled Steel Joist Span Railway Bridges

Initially, use of Steel Joist Spans implied use of such standard beams that might be available; design curves listed the required section modulus for various spans up to 30ft and different BS Unit loadings, and then suggested the required size and number of beams to provide the bridge. The rationalization of early 1940 settled on five standard span lengths; the 17 and 21ft bridges used 18in x 6in beams and the 27, 31 and 35ft bridges used 24in x 7½in beams. Either two or three beams were grouped as a cluster under each rail position and timber sleepers were fixed directly on top of the beams

Figure 8.23. RSJ spans used in conjunction with 40ft SWPG spans, UCRB, and LSUT piers to form a 250ft railbridge at Tilberg, Holland. (Bridging Normandy to Berlin).

in the usual way. (Figure 8.23). Beams were prefabricated and stockpiled, with bolt holes pre-drilled at one foot increments so that intermediate spans could be formed rapidly by flame cutting the joists to the required length. Pre-assembled cross bracing and spacers were placed at 4ft centres, which enabled bridges to be built at a skew of up to 4ft. To make transport and erection of the bridge easier in difficult country, a sectional joist version was developed; this used 9, 12 and 15ft lengths of the larger size joists, pre-drilled for rapid splicing together on site. The maximum span that could be built with the sectional equipment was 39ft, using one 15ft and two 12ft lengths of joist.

The Plate Girder Bridges

The original **Standard Plate Girder Bridges** were designed and manufactured for 30, 40, 60 and 80ft spans. The 30ft span was a deck bridge consisting of two welded plate girders, whilst the 40 and 60ft spans, of welded construction, were designed to be used either as a deck bridge or as a through bridge. The 80ft span bridge, also of welded construction, was a through bridge, the 6ft deep girders each weighing about 17½ tons; the girders were made in three sections, the heaviest being about 30ft long and weighing 5½ tons. Further details of the bridges are given in Appendix B.

Figure 8.24. Ten 40ft Sectional Welded Plate Girder spans used with LSUT piers to form a railbridge at Hertogenbosch, Holland. (Bridging Normandy to Berlin).

The newer **Sectional Welded Plate Girder Bridge** was a four girder standard 40ft span bridge, that could be shortened by flame cutting to a 37 or 34ft span. The 14ft long plate girder units each comprised a pair of plate girders, 2ft 11in deep, with diaphragms welded between them; one centre unit and two end units, which incorporated stiffened end posts, were spliced together by site bolting to form half the bridge. The two halves of bridge were either launched side by side, using rollers and a light launching nose, or were placed directly, using the 15/20ton Steel Derrick. The two units were then joined together with steel channel spacers, to form either a deck bridge or a half through bridge. (Figure 8.24). As with the new Rolled Steel Joist Bridges, the Sectional Welded Plate Girder Bridge was designed to cater for 1m, 3ft 6in and 4ft 8½in gauge tracks.

The Standard Through Truss Railway Bridge

This bridge was a very substantial bridge, using a Howe type truss of 13ft 8in overall depth. It was designed to be used for spans from 90ft to 150ft in 10ft increments, the two main trusses being spaced at 18ft 2¼in centres to provide

Figure 8.25. Three 120ft spans of Standard Through Truss Railway Bridge, built across the River Volturno in Italy. (A W McMurdo).

the clearance required by the Berne International Gauge for gauges up to 5ft 6in. (Figure 8.25 and Appendix B). Only simple joints had to be made in the field, using rivets or, in some cases, bolts and drift pins. Nevertheless field construction was not easy, the centre top boom section weighing 3.8tons with its gussets and was over 30ft long; other sections were nearly 38ft long, making the use of a crane almost essential. It is not possible to give construction times because of variation in site conditions, but a typical work table for a 150ft span bridge with a Standard Unit Trestle Pier at each end suggests about twelve 12 hour working days for a work force at times as strong as 130 men; this timing included laying the permanent way. The bridge was normally constructed on special erection trolleys at the erection site and was then moved to the bridge site using the existing rails. Launching was achieved using a special launching nose, with counterbalance weights on trolleys at the rear of the bridge.

The Unit Construction Railway Bridge

The Unit Construction Railway Bridge, to a great extent the design of Everall, was introduced to provide a rail bridge in the 50ft to 85ft range that would replace the cumbersome 60ft and 80ft Plate Girder Bridges. The UCRB used N type bracing in a Howe truss configuration, the trusses being 6ft 10in in depth. The trough shaped chords were formed from three plates welded together and were manufactured in 15 and 20ft lengths to give a possible 5ft variation of span when spliced together on site. Vertical and diagonal members were added with cross bracing, end posts and bearings to form a two, three or four girder deck bridge. (Figure 8.26 and Appendix B).

Figure 8.26. Typical cross-sections of UCRB for an 85ft span. (The Civil Engineer at War).

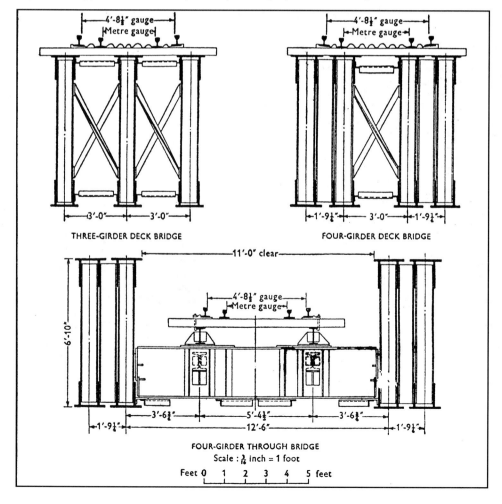

All site connections were made using a prescribed combination of black bolts, drift pins and turned bolts. The bridge was built on rollers and boomed forward, making use of a cantilever launching nose or counterbalancing rear spans.

For the 16 BS Unit loading half-through bridge version, two girders were used at 16ft 2in centres; later however the 20 BS Unit loading half-through bridge became standard, using either two or four girders and with the inner girders at 12ft 6in centres. The heaviest component of the bridge (the 20ft chord member) weighed just over a ton, compared with 3.8 tons for the Standard Through Truss Bridge and 5½ tons for the 80ft Plate Girder Railway Bridge. It therefore became the most widely used of the railway bridges and was certainly the most adaptable. Various methods of construction were possible and considerable ingenuity was shown in its use, skew spans, with a 5 or 10ft lead of one girder over the other, being an obvious possibility. Continuous bridges were developed, mainly as a result of experiences in Italy, where such bridges were used to overbridge collapsed viaducts.

Figure 8.27. Five 75ft spans of UCRB, used with Standard Unit Trestle piers to overbridge a collapsed viaduct near Grizzana in Italy. (A W McMurdo).

(Figure 8.27). Through and deck type lift bridges and a retractable bridge were also designed and built during the advance into Europe. Perhaps the most adventurous development however was that of a floating railway bridge, capable of carrying loaded 30 ton wagons, though not unfortunately locomotives; for this bridge a 100ft length of two girder through bridge was supported at each end by three Mark V Pontoon piers.

The span range of the bridge was later increased to 110ft at a standard 20 BS Unit loading, using alternative and heavier chord members. To distinguish between the old and the new equipments, the 16 BS Unit bridge components were painted battleship grey whilst those of the 20 BS Unit bridge were painted brown. This increase in span range enabled the UCRB to be used in place of the Standard Through Truss Bridge at the bottom end of its span range; it could also be used with track gauges of 5ft and 5ft 6in, which was not possible with the Plate Girder Bridges.

The Everall Sectional Truss Railway Bridge

This railway bridge was developed by Everall late in the war and was therefore only available during the final stages of the advance into Europe. The design bore a general resemblance to the German Roth-Waagner Rail Bridge, quantities of which were captured during the Allied advance, but details were very different and the scope was considerably widened. It was in essence a 'Meccano' type truss bridge, built up of many components, using black bolts and drift pins for the main load carrying connections and black bolts for subsidiary connections. Although it could be used for spans as short as 80ft, it was really intended for major spans, as illustrated

Figure 8.28. Three 230ft spans of ESTB, built across the River Ijssel at Deventer in Holland. (IWM BU11429).

succinctly by the bridge built over the River Ijssel, at Deventer, Holland, in which three 230ft spans of ESTB were built across the water gap together with one 65ft span and seven 125ft spans of UCRB for the approaches. (Figure 8.28 and Appendix B).

The bridges were used for extensive repairs to bridges on the Greek railway network that had been damaged or destroyed during the Second World War, and a number are still in use to this day.

Callender-Hamilton Railway Bridging

The Types A and B versions of Hamilton's bridging concept of the mid-1930s have already been considered in Chapter 6. The bridge was developed commercially as the Callender-Hamilton Bridge before the war and Type B was adopted as the Unit Construction Bridge by the British Army. Hamilton commenced work on rail versions of his bridge in 1938, using heavier truss and deck construction than with the road bridge and ensuring appropriate main line rail clearances between trusses. It has been mentioned earlier that Hamilton, now commissioned into the Corps, was sent to India early in the War to supervise the manufacture of Callender-Hamilton bridging and the Callender-Hamilton aircraft hanger, which he had also designed. At the

Figure 8.29. A 206ft span Callender-Hamilton Type C railway bridge under test at Mogul Serai in 1942. (A M Hamilton)

request of the Indian Central Railway Board in New Delhi the design of the Type C (Light) Railway Bridge was modified to meet their requirements, and in double/double construction could carry Indian main line loading at spans up to 200ft. (Figure 8.29). The Type D (Heavy) Railway Bridge was also manufactured in high tensile steel, and could carry main line loading at spans up to 300ft. The Type C and Type D Railway Bridges were not adopted by the British Army, but warrant mention because they played an important role in keeping the rail network in India fully operational during the war, over 2,000 tons of bridging being built in Calcutta workshops for the Central Railway Board. Subsequently the Engineer-in-Chief's department of the Indian Army decided to standardize on the Type C bridge for projected metric gauge operational work in South-East Asia Command; 4,750 tons of the equipment were ordered, and many bridges were built throughout the Command.

Bridge Trestles and Piers

Simple trestles, such as the Mark VII Trestle used with the Mark V Pontoon Bridge, have been described in previous chapters. Such trestles consisted basically of two legs and a cross transom; they were used as the junction between the shore or landing bay and the end floating bay of a pontoon

Figure 8.30. A Light Standard Unit Trestle pier, used to support UCRB spans across the River Melfa, north of Cassino in Italy. (IWM NA16418).

bridge, but their use ceased once longer and stronger landing bays became viable, as for example in the case of the BPB. The advent of multi-span and continuous span equipment bridges brought with it the need for new trestle equipment however, to be used to build the bridge piers to support such bridges. Two such trestle equipments, the **Tubular Trestle** and the **Heavy Trestle** were developed early in the war, to carry multi-span Bailey Bridges up to Class 70 over dry and wet gaps. The equipments enabled wider gaps to be spanned than could be bridged with a single span and could also result in economy of equipment, since a number of short spans built with trestles often weighed less than the single long span. However later in the war it became common practice to build cribs or piers for Bailey using on site available Bailey panels and the special Bailey parts designed for such cribs, as mentioned in the previous chapter. Cribs of a considerable height were also built using the 6ft x 2ft x 2ft Christchurch Crib, developed in the mid-1930s and described in Chapter 6.

Two further trestle equipments had been developed just before the war, for use with multi-span railway bridges; these were the **Light Standard Unit Trestle** and the **Standard Unit Trestle** (Figure 8.30), the former incorporating a self adjusting camel's foot for the trestle legs, developed from that used with the Trestle Mark VII. Both of the new trestles were developed by Everall in 1939, acting, as was the case with the RSJ Span Railway Bridges, as a consultant to the War Office. The trestles were extremely versatile, and the LSUT in particular was used not only for railway bridging but also for tunnel repairs, stabilization of arches, support of falsework, and so on. They were also used in conjunction with Bailey Bridging, notable for some of the larger bridges built during the advance into Europe. Some details of the trestles are given in Appendix B.

Expedient Bridging

Many ideas for expedient bridging were suggested and tested during the war; such bridges used materials that would be generally available to the Sappers in the field and differed from improvised bridges, which used materials actually to hand on a specific site. A good example of an expedient bridge is the **Indian Mat Bridge**, built from readily available tarpaulins and chesses and considered, in its various forms, earlier in this chapter. A light version of the bridge, known as the **Jeep Mat Bridge** was developed in the Far East Theatre, together with a Floating Barrel Jeep Bridge. Many designs for lightweight bridges making use of vines and bamboos were also produced in that theatre.

Another example of an expedient bridge was the **Light Suspension Bridge**, developed and tested at the EBE towards the end of the war. (See Appendix B). The bridge was intended to provide a means of crossing wet or dry gaps up to 225ft wide, without intermediate support and with use of a minimum weight of stores. The 10ft wide bridge, which was capable of carrying a laden jeep towing a 6pdr antitank gun (a load of about 2½tons), was built from the wire mesh usually used for tracks. The bridge could be built with cribs at one or both ends, to increase the headroom under the bridge, making use of any standard form of crib, made, for example, from timber, tubular scaffolding, Bailey panels or even wire mesh cylinders.

A **Steel Wire Ropeway** was also developed as an expedient method of carrying a jeep and a 6pdr anti-tank gun across an obstacle, using Bailey cribs and SWR. The method was successfully tested at EBE, with a view to its use in the Far East Theatre. (Figure 8.31).

In Italy the 10th Indian Division developed what became known as the **Houdini Bridge**, based upon an extremely simple idea. A steel cable was taken across the river, through two snatch blocks, and then back to a tackle on the home bank. Timber decking was then lashed to the two cables to form a light footbridge. During daylight hours the bridge remained submerged, with the inshore planks removed so that only the ends of the cables were visible, whilst at night the tackles were tightened to provide a bridge suitable for light loads. During the later stages of the campaign these bridges were used frequently, when spans and current speeds were suitable.

However perhaps the most unusual form of expedient bridge considered

Figure 8.31. A brave soldier assists at the test-loading of a steel wire ropeway at Christchurch. (EBE).

was the **Ice Bridge**. Royal Engineer Training Manual No 3 suggests that, in very cold climates, crossing of a river or swamp using existing ice was feasible. 4in of ice was deemed strong enough to support horses and men in single file and 8in of ice strong enough for medium artillery and cruiser tanks. It suggested that the ice could be reinforced by first collecting and trampling any snow on the ice to form a watertight barrier; straw or sacking should then be placed on top of the cleared ice, and the area enclosed by the compacted snow then flooded, to increase the depth of ice. Without doubt such crossings of rivers were made many times on the Russian front.

The Role of the Royal Army Service Corps

So far nothing has been said about the vital role played by the Royal Army Service Corps in the building of literally thousands of bridges during the war. The equipment carried by the Field Company RE has always been of diverse character, covering the whole range of tasks that the Sapper might be called upon to carry out. Much of this equipment consisted of toolkits and similar stores necessary for every day work in the field, whilst the Field Park Companies, established at a level of one Field Park unit to three or four Field Companies, carried the more specialist engineer stores needed by the Field Companies. In the main however bridging equipment involved such a volume and weight of stores that special units of the Royal Army Service Corps, or RASC, were set up in the 1930s simply to carry the equipment and deliver it on site where and when needed by the Sappers - in many ways a modern version of the old Bridging Train.

In 1936 the Field Park Company RE carried a small quantity of FBE, whilst the Pontoon Bridge Park RASC carried more FBE, and also SBG, Pontoon and Trestle Equipment, and Kapok Assault Bridging for the infantry. Engineer Stores Depots were established according to the theatre of operations, and might carry LBG and Stock Spans as well as the large stocks of non-bridging equipment necessary for the field units to operate.

By 1939 the position was little changed, the Field Park Company now carrying some SBG, and both it and the Bridge Company RASC, as it now was, carrying, additionally, the new Infantry Recce Boats and Assault Boats.

With the proliferation of bridging equipments during the war however, the RASC units grew out of all recognition, and by the end of the war the Bridge Company RASC had been expanded to include a number of self contained platoons, each carrying a specific type of equipment, as can be seen from the details given below. The platoons were then used in various combinations, depending upon the operational requirement and the anticipated need.

a. **The Bailey Platoon** (30 bridging vehicles) had four sections each carrying 40ft of Class 40 bridge.

b. **The Pontoon Platoon** (26 bridging vehicles) also had four sections and when combined with the Bailey Platoon could provide 306ft of

Class 40 BPB, with one third floating spares.

c. **The Heavy Bridge Platoon** (22 bridging vehicles) contained the extra Bailey and pontoon equipment necessary to produce Class 70 bridges.

d. **The FBE Platoon** (26 bridging vehicles) had four sections, each with eight boats and able to produce 120ft of Class 9 bridge or various rafts.

e. **The Raft Platoon Type A** (20 tractors and 20 trailers) had four sections and could produce five Class 50 or four Class 60 Rafts.

f. **The Raft Platoon Type B** (24 bridging vehicles) comprised six sections each providing one Close Support Raft.

g. **The Assault Platoon** (19 bridging vehicles and 5 trailers) included an FBE section, an Assault Boat section and a Kapok Equipment section.

Some equipment was still held in the Field Park Company, which included in its Divisional Bridging Platoon RE an 80ft Class 40 Bailey Bridge. However, specialist assault bridging was held by the Assault Engineer units and the tank bridges were held by the RAC, normally at a figure of six bridgelayers to each armoured brigade.

CHAPTER NINE

The Second World War - North Africa and Italy

The Scope of Operations

It would be quite impossible to do full justice to the prodigious bridge building task of the Sappers during the Second World War in a lengthy volume, let alone in a chapter of this brief history. British forces built nearly 2,500 Bailey Bridges during the Italian Campaign between 1943 and 1945, and over 1,500 during the advance into Europe from 1944 onward, quite apart from those built in the Far East and in many other theatres of war. To these totals must be added the hundreds upon hundreds of railway bridges built, mainly in Europe, bridges built using the many other equipments available to the Corps, such as the Folding Boat Equipment, and of course bridges built by our allies. Every bridge will have had its own problems, perhaps the site, the enemy opposition, the availability of men and equipment, or the weather conditions, and each was, in its own way, vital to the successful furtherance of a campaign. Each will be remembered by the Sappers who laboured to build it, often working under enemy fire in conditions of extreme hardship. In selecting just a few of these bridges and briefly describing some of the aspects of their construction, one must therefore remember the many thousands of bridges whose story has remained untold, perhaps apart from a line or two in the official histories.

France and Belgium, 1939-40

The bridging equipment available to the Sappers at the outbreak of war was summarized at the end of Chapter Six. A considerable quantity of this equipment was taken to France with the two British Corps forming the British Expeditionary Force in 1939, but bridging operations before the evacuation from Dunkirk were in the main concerned with the demolition of bridges before the advancing German Army, and all of our bridging equipment was destroyed or abandoned before the evacuation. A planned counter-offensive by the British III Corps, which had arrived in France in April 1940, would have required the building of pontoon bridges across the River Senne to replace those previously demolished, but in the event the counter-attack never took place.

Once the decision to withdraw to the Dunkirk perimeter had been made on 26 May, Sapper units of the withdrawing divisions were involved not only in preparing bridges for demolition but also in providing bridges to relieve bottlenecks for the retreating troops. On 27 May for example 253 Field Company of 3 Division were ordered to build three bridges over the River Yser at Elsendamme, in case the enemy should bomb and destroy the existing bridges. On the way to the site the bridging column was attacked by enemy aircraft, leaving only two vehicles roadworthy, and even in these the boats were found to be riddled with bullet holes. Without an adequate supply of repair patches the boats were finally repaired with clay and pieces of wood. Not withstanding a further air attack as the boats were launched, one bridge was completed before midnight.

Despite the wholesale destruction of vehicles and equipment during the withdrawal to Dunkirk, orders were given that vehicles carrying Folding Boat Equipment should be directed to the beaches. These Folding Boats of the Field Park Companies and the Bridging Company RASC were manned by Sappers of various units and played an important role in the early stages of the evacuation, prior to the arrival of the armada of small boats from England. Many were sunk, thanks to the attention of German dive bombers, and it was an extremely hazardous task for the Sapper crews. As history relates the evacuation was in the end little short of a miracle, almost 340,000 Allied troops being successfully withdrawn by 4 June 1940.

The Mansion House Bridge

The bombing of the UK mainland started soon afterwards, and led, in 1941, to a bridging operation in the heart of the City of London. In early January a large German bomb fell in the open space bounded by the Mansion House, the Bank of England and the Royal Exchange. The space was in fact immediately above the massive concrete and steel trough roof of the Bank Underground Station, and the bomb penetrated this roof before exploding in the ticket hall below. The roof lifted and then fell back into the cavity, leaving a very large crater between 10 and 30 feet deep. Within 90 minutes Sappers and Pioneers started the task of clearing the debris, using plant provided from civilian sources, and within thirteen days had removed nearly 3,000 tons of concrete, steel troughing and girders. The site was the junction of six important roads and it was decided that to restore the east-west flow of traffic as quickly as possible a bridge should be built to join Cornhill and Queen Victoria Street. A roadway could then be cleared around the edge of the crater to form an improvised roundabout, after which the bridge could be removed to enable a new roof for the ticket hall to be constructed.

A Large Box Girder Bridge Mark II was selected as being most suitable, and two spans, 50ft 6in and 113ft 6in, were used, each using four girder construction; calculations showed these as being capable of carrying 12½ ton London Transport buses, nose to tail. The imbalance of the two spans was due to the positioning of lift and escalator shafts, which restricted the positioning of the Light Standard Unit Trestle pier. The building of the two

210

Figure 9.1. *Officers and men of 691 Construction Company RE, ready for the opening of the Mansion House Bridge.*

span bridge was completed in four and a half days by 691 General Construction Company RE; most of the officers, NCOs and Sappers of this unit were volunteers from John Mowlem & Company and the the unit was affectionately remembered by many as Mowlem's Army. (Figure 9.1). The bridge was opened to traffic by the Lord Mayor of London, who crossed in the mayoral car, followed by a No 12 London Transport double decker bus and the whole Company in their lorries.

Bridging in North Africa

Operations in North Africa were precipitated by the declaration of war by Italy on 10 June 1940, followed in a few days by the collapse of France, although fighting did not break out until the Italians advanced on Sidi Barrani in September of that year. Early in 1941 a number of bridges were built following the start of the British offensive in Abyssinia; these included SBG Bridges that had been manufactured in South Africa, the equipment

211

proving ideal for bridging the many deep clefts encountered. Bridges were also built using captured Italian equipment, and a causeway built by South African Engineers used over 2,000 forty gallon oil drums.

Two bridges of note were built across the River Nile, south of Cairo in mid-1942, as part of the plan for the defence of Egypt. The bridges were intended to enable the Eighth Army to cross the river with its tanks and thus engage the enemy, should this become necessary. The spans were considerable, being 2,688ft and 2,760ft respectively, and pontoon equipment could not be spared on this scale. It was therefore decided to construct the bridges using Egyptian cargo sailing boats, known as feluccas, each some 48ft long and with a 17½ ft beam. With changes in fortune however the requirement for the bridges lapsed and they were dismantled in November.

By this time the British advance after the Battle of Alamein, fought in late October 1942, was under way. During their initial withdrawal the Axis forces had concentrated on the demolition of water supply installations, although the single road from the Egyptian frontier into Cyrenaica had been extensively cratered. Once the advance continued into Tripolitania however, the changing terrain made movement off the road more difficult and almost every one of the bridges and culverts crossing the many wadis were destroyed by the retreating enemy. Forward engineer units were thus heavily involved in opening up this important supply route, and a number of bridges were built.

At about this time, on 8 November 1942, combined American and British assault landings were made on the Algerian coast. These were followed by further sea and air landings, leading to an Allied advance on Tunis, the order

Figure 9.2. The first Bailey Bridge built in contact with the enemy, crossing the River Medjerda, at Medjez el Bab in Tunis. (MOD).

of battle now including two Bailey Bridge Platoons of 105 Corps Bridge Company, RASC. The new equipment was put to good use by 237 Field Company of 78 Division, who put a 100ft Bailey across the River Medjerda at Medjez el Bab in Tunis in late November. The bridging convoy was unfortunately set on fire as a result of an enemy air attack during its approach to the site, and with limitations on transport there was barely enough equipment to build the bridge, with no spares. However all the equipment was luckily saved and the bridge was built within twelve hours, the first Bailey Bridge to be built in contact with the enemy. (Figure 9.2).

One of the main tasks of the Sappers during operations in Tunisia was the repair and maintenance of roads, and this included the building of a number of other bridges over wadis and rivers, the most important of which was a 160ft triple-double Bailey at Souk el Khemis, which involved 700 yards of approach road. The official *Corps History* relates that this bridge was on the main forward route, and that after it had been officially opened, the stream of traffic crossing at speed was suddenly brought to a halt by a small Arab donkey cart; the donkey would proceed no further than the ramp, where he sat down, obviously having no confidence in the Class 30 bridge loading sign at the end of bridge. The combined efforts of the Military Police and a number of senior Sapper officers eventually persuaded the donkey to proceed, and the flow of traffic resumed. The bridge was eventually named 'Balaam'.

The building of the first operational triple/triple Bailey, near Teboursouk across the River Tessa, caused some concern. The span of 130ft was too great to take the required Class 70 loading according to the tables issued with the bridge, although calculations on site showed the construction to be adequate. In reply to an urgent telegram, the EBE at Christchurch confirmed that all was well, and it was then decided to build the third storey below the deck, to avoid any possible problems with headroom caused by overhead bracing. After work on the 600 yard approach road, a double/double bridge was built and launched by 8 Field Squadron on 7 and 8 January 1943; a week later the bridge was converted to triple/triple, the third storey being lifted into position, below the decking, from the river bed, using tackles fixed to the existing girders.

The success of the Bailey Bridge was one of the features of the North African campaign. It proved its worth both as a bridge that could be rapidly built by night, once a bridgehead had been established by the infantry, and also as a semi-permanent bridge that could be relied upon to carry continuous heavy traffic with little maintenance. During the campaign some 28 Baileys were built, of which eight were Class 70, and one spanned 170ft at Class 40. The SBG Bridge also proved itself operationally, and even in the final stages of the advance, culminating in the surrender of the German forces on 12 May, a 48ft SBG Bridge was built by 751 Field Company, alongside a 90ft Class 70 Bailey.

The Italian Campaign

The invasion of Sicily followed on 9 July, and although some thirty eight Bailey and twenty Small Box Girder bridges were built during the thirty eight days that it took to conquer the island, none merit comment in any detail. The campaign in Italy presented a very different picture. The first

MAP 2 ~ THE ITALIAN CAMPAIGN, 1943 - 45
Showing towns, rivers etc mentioned in the text

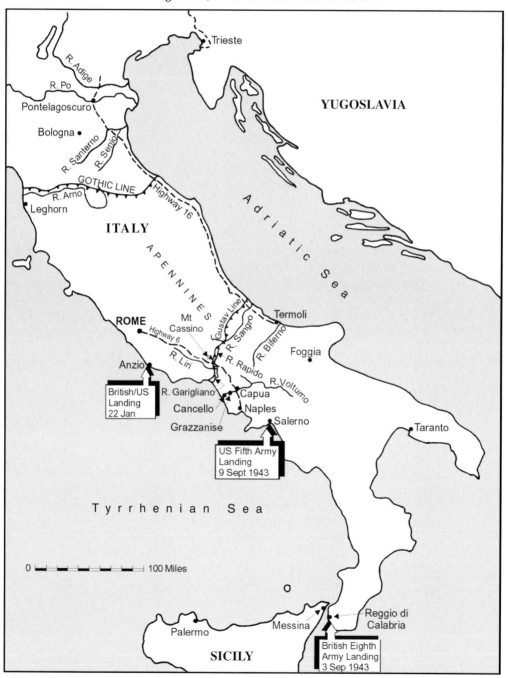

landings, at Reggio in the 'toe' of Italy on 3 September 1943, were almost unopposed, but once inland the British and Canadian troops were faced with the considerable demolition of road and rail bridges by the Germans; within the first few days no less than twenty four Bailey Bridges had been built, and repairs carried out to ten large steel-girder railway bridges. As the front moved northward the extent of demolition increased and eventually reached a vast scale, in a terrain perfectly adapted to it. In the mountainous country north of the Naples-Foggia line, intersected by many rivers, the Germans demolished almost every bridge and culvert, on both road and railway, resulting in an enormous bridge building programme for the Engineers of all the Allied nations involved, a programme already touched upon in the opening paragraph of this chapter. The efforts of the Engineer units of the combined British/American 15th Army Group during the Italian campaign, from 1943 to 1945 is summarized below:

Bailey Fixed Span Bridges built	2,832
Total length (miles)	45
Bailey Floating Bridges built	19
American Treadway Bridges built	101
Folding Boat Equipment built	6,945ft
Permanent bridges constructed	430
Railway bridges and viaducts reconstructed	490

Singling out just five bridging operations from this vast programme is contentious but perhaps the crossings of the Rivers Volturno and Sangro, the Rapido operation, the crossing of the Po and the little known ASAMFU Bridge warrant mention.

The Volturno Operation

The landing of the Fifth Army at Salerno on 9 September was followed by the capture of Naples on 1 October. Before their advance to the north could continue, the Allies were faced with the crossing of the Volturno, the first major opposed river crossing of the war. The Germans had destroyed all the bridges over the river, which had, in the British sector, steep banks some 20 to 30ft high and bridging gaps of two to three hundred feet; in addition the river was subject to flash floods, as were so many of the rivers in Italy. With the British X Corps on the left, between Capua and the sea, and the American VI Corps on the right flank, the X Corps plan envisaged a Class 9 FBE Bridge near Capua (with 56 Division on the right), a Bailey Bridge at Grazzanise (with 7 Armoured Division in the centre), and a Class 30 Bailey Pontoon Bridge at Cancello (with 46 Division on the left).

The assault across the river was launched on the night of 12 October and 7 Armoured Division managed to get part of two Battalions across the river against heavy opposition. The Divisional Engineers established an FBE Class 9 ferry, before starting work on the Grazzanise Bailey Bridge, and despite heavy enemy fire the bridge was completed by 4pm on the 16th; it was the first bridge across and made use of the one remaining span of the destroyed German timber trestle bridge. (Figure 9.3). Work on the floating bridges did not start until the 15th however, because of the shallow depth of the bridge head that had been established. Subsequently the advance on the 46 Division front was very slow, and after a few bays of the Cancello Bailey Bridge had been built, the Corps Commander decided to switch the FBE and Bailey bridge sites, and to build the Bailey at Capua.

Figure 9.3. Construction of a bridge across the River Volturno at Grazzanise, making use of the remains of a German trestle bridge. (Engineers in the Italian Campaign, 1943-1945).

46 and 56 Divisional Engineers therefore exchanged their Bailey and FBE, and 46 Division RE completed their Class 9 FBE Bridge at Cancello late on the 17th.

56 Division RE started work on the Capua Bridge at midnight on 16 / 17 October, assisted by the one squadron from 46 Division RE which had had experience in building floating Bailey. The bridge was the first Bailey Pontoon Bridge to be built in action, and consisted of two 120ft double single landing bays, necessary to cope with the very high river banks and constant changes in water level, and three 42ft floating bays. (Figure 9.4). It was opened to traffic just after midnight on the 19th, having taken just over forty eight hours to build, including considerable work on the approaches; at the peak four hundred and ninety vehicles an hour were crossing the bridge. The bridge was later replaced by a fixed span Bailey and also a

Figure 9.4. The first operational Bailey Pontoon Bridge, built across the River Volturno at Capua, in October 1943. (Engineers in the Italian Campaign, 1943-1945).

Figure 9.5. *A 400ft Bailey Suspension Bridge over the River Volturno at Ponte Annibale, near Capua.* (IWM 3188).

timber piled bridge built by the Americans.

The Allied advance north of the river continued apace, but the river was by no means tamed. The Bailey at Grazzanise was swept away by a sudden river spate and was replaced by a pontoon bridge; this in turn was destroyed by another spate on 11 February 1944, with a 17ft rise in river level. The debris was washed down river and in turn swept away a piled timber bridge at Cancello which had been built after the battle to replace the FBE Bridge on that site. The Grazzanise pontoon bridge was not replaced but US Army Engineers subsequently built another Bailey on the site.

The Volturno was deep enough for wet bridging training to take place all year round, and once the Allied advance had continued northward it was decided to set up an Engineer Training Establishment on the river, with its headquarters at Capua. The first course at the School of Military Engineering, one of the units of the new establishment, began in late January 1944, and this was followed by an extensive programme of courses in the various units of the new Establishment. In addition the ETE became a centre for experiment and trials, including for example the construction of a Bailey Suspension Bridge across the river at Ponte Annibale, the site of the Divisional Engineers Bridging Camp. (Figure 9.5).

Crossing the Sangro

Meanwhile the Eighth Army, on the east coast, faced the Germans across the Sangro. The river was some 1000ft wide between the sea and the first bridge inland, which carried Highway 16, the Army's main supply route from Termoli. Low river banks were edged with flood banks, although the river narrowed towards Paglieta, the site of the second bridge, and the banks there steepened, with no further need for the protective flood banks. The river

217

flow was normally slow, although heavy rains could increase the depth to 6ft across the whole river bed and the current speed up to 12 knots.

The river was reached on 11th November 1943, and a week later 78 Division were able to ford the river whilst the Divisional Engineers prepared the approaches at the sites of five previously selected crossing points. However heavy rain ruled out the further use of fords and it was decided to postpone the second phase of the assault until bridges could be built. Four bridge sites were selected and on the night of 21st/22nd a 100ft Bailey was built by Sappers and Miners of 8 Indian Division. Another, of 140ft span, was built by 78 Divisional Engineers, who also established two ferries that night. Equipment for the third bridge, another 140ft span Bailey, did not arrive in time to enable it to be completed by first light; it was completed the following night but much work remained to be done on the far approaches. On the 23rd the river flooded and nothing could be seen of the bridges except the tops of the girders in the middle of a sheet of water some 1000ft wide. The bridgehead was thus cut off and had to be supplied by amphibians for the next two days. When the water level dropped it was found that only one bridge had been damaged, although all the ferries had been washed away. Accurate German artillery fire and a further flood caused more damage, and then on the 27th the bridge built by the Indian Sappers and Miners, upstream of Highway 16, was hit by shell fire and collapsed. It was decided not to replace the bridge but concentrate on completion of the still unfinished fourth bridge, near to the original Sangro Bridge. The same night the main assault by 8 Indian Division was launched and the battle for the Sangro was virtually over, four further bridges having been built on the front, together with two bridges built upstream by Canadian and Australian Engineers.

The Sangro was not beaten however and on 4 December it rose again. (Figure 9.6). By evening it was up to 6ft deep and running at over 10 knots. It damaged every single bridge that had been built; one collapsed, two were swept away, two had piers destroyed and one suffered minor damage. The water level remained high until the 7th when it was possible to repair two of the bridges and replace a third with a pontoon bridge utilizing FBE and Bailey equipment.

Meanwhile the Squadrons of 8 Army Troops Engineers, under command of their CRE, Lt Col L E A Gwynne RE, had started work

Figure 9.6. Damage caused by a spate of the River Sangro, 4 December 1943. (Engineers in the Italian Campaign, 1943-1945).

Figure 9.7. Launching of the 1,126ft Class 30 Sangro Bridge, carrying the main supply route on Highway 16. (Engineers in the Italian Campaign, 1943-1945).

on what was to be the longest bridge built during the Italian Campaign. This was the high level 1,126ft, Class 30 Sangro Bridge, built on Highway 16 to carry the main supply route north. The bridge was built alongside an existing FBE Bridge, which remained in use and proved very useful during the construction. All nineteen brick arches of the original bridge had been destroyed by the Germans, together with four of the eighteen brick piers. The tops of the piers still standing were levelled and topped with steel cribs and timber bank seats. The debris of the first pair of demolished piers was cleared using a D7 and a D8 bulldozer, and pipe piles were then driven to support the reinforced concrete foundations required for the new piers constructed from Bailey panels. The second pair of demolished piers, adjacent to the north bank, were covered with consolidated spoil from the new approaches, and grillages positioned to support the bankseats. The Bailey was launched in skeleton construction, the second truss and the decking being added once the bridge had been jacked down onto its seatings. (Figure 9.7). Work started on 4 December, and proceeded continuously, making use of floodlights by night. Despite further flooding of the river, the bridge was completed by the 14th, the preparation of the approaches and the piers having proved the determining time factor.

The Rapido Crossings of May 1944

During the winter of 1943/44 the Allied advance to liberate Rome was held up by the German strongly defended Gustav Line. (See MAP 2). The line centred on Cassino, which straddled Highway 6, the inland road from Naples to Rome. At this point the road emerged from the hills, crossed the Rapido, and entered the wide Liri Valley. The village of Cassino was at the junction of the two river valleys, at the foot of a steep hill crowned by the Cassino Monastery, a German stronghold which dominated Highway 6, the river valleys and all the hills to the south. It was here that the Germans made their greatest stand.

Following the successful crossing of the Garigliano to the south and the virtually unopposed landing at Anzio south of Rome in January 1944, three attempts to capture Cassino proved unsuccessful. In early 1944, German resistance stiffened and Allied progress slowed until their Spring Offensive of that year. The plan for this offensive envisaged the advance of the Fifth Army between the Liri Valley and the sea to join up with the forces in the Anzio bridgehead, before pushing on to capture Rome. Meanwhile the Eighth Army, the bulk of which had been moved across to the west of the Apennines to join in the advance on Rome, were to break through the German defences in the Liri Valley and advance roughly parallel to Highway 6 to the east of Rome. The Eighth Army plan entailed an advance on both sides of Cassino to breach the Gustav Line, following an assault crossing of the River Rapido, which although only some 80 to 120ft wide, was deep and swift with current speeds from five to eight knots.

On 11 May both Armies attacked. On the XIII Corps front of the Eighth Army the 8th Indian Division made good progress. By 2am two rafts were in operation, and by the following morning a class 30 bridge had been opened nearby. By 10.30am on the 12th a tank launched Bailey was in use a little to the south. This bridge was the first Bailey Assault Bridge built in the field. It was the Plymouth Bridge, comprising a 100ft double/single Bailey carried forward on two Sherman tanks, and its construction and deployment was described in detail in the previous chapter.

The 4 British Divisional plan included the construction of three Bailey Bridges over the Rapido, the operational order having been written by the Adjutant, Captain J N Barnikel RE, mentioned in later chapters in connection with his work at MEXE on amphibious and future bridging. Congo Bridge was to be built on the left by 7 Field Company RE, commanded by Major M Lowe RE, Blackwater in the centre by 59 Field Company RE, commanded by Major A P de T Daniell RE, and Amazon on the right by 225 Field Company RE, commanded by Major R E Gabbett RE. On the 11th the Division was able to gain only a narrow bridgehead across the Rapido, and the building of all three bridges met with intense enemy opposition and such heavy casualties that operations were called off at first light. It was thus essential to reinforce the bridgehead at the earliest opportunity and the Divisional Commander ordered that a crossing on the Amazon site must be completed during the following night.

Working parties from all three Field Companies started work on the home bank approaches at 5.45pm, as soon as dusk fell, despite continual harassment from enemy artillery and machine gun fire. Assembly of the bridge continued throughout the night and was completed by 4am. A small D4 bulldozer was then used to push the bridge forward during the launch, but when this was put out of action by enemy fire, the final push to the far bank was provided by one of the tanks of the 17th/21st Lancers who were waiting to cross, and the bridge was finally opened to traffic at 5.20. During the construction of the 80ft Class 30 Bailey fifteen Sappers were killed and fifty seven, including three officers, were wounded. (Figure 9.8).

Further bridges were subsequently built, and by the 16th there were five Class 40 and four Class 30 bridges across the river on the Army front. By the

Figure 9.8. *Launching of Amazon Bridge across the River Rapido at Cassino.* (From the original painting by T Cuneo).

18th, resistance at Cassino had been completely neutralized and by the 23rd the Hitler Line, just north of Cassino had been attacked and broken. On the left hand front the Fifth Army reached the Anzio beachhead on the 25th and on 4th June Rome was liberated.

The ASAMFU Bridge

The Allied advance continued during the summer and by the beginning of August was approaching the Gothic Line, the main German defensive line between central Italy and the valley of the Po. It had been decided that for this attack the 8th Army should be moved back to the east coast and by 25 August 1994 the move was complete. The country to the north remained mountainous and difficult to traverse, the Northern Apennines rising to 7,905ft, and all bridges and culverts had been systematically demolished by the retreating Germans. Once the Gothic Line had been breached in early September, reconstruction of supply routes through the Apennines became imperative. On one of these, Ace Route, taken over by the British from the Americans, XIII Corps transport had great difficulty in negotiating the steep diversions. It was decided to build a 480ft Bailey at San Andrea as a matter of urgency in order to eliminate a particularly difficult diversion and 56 Field Company of XIII Corps Engineers started work on 6 October, supported by 500 British and Italian pioneers. The diversion had been made because of the destruction by the enemy of a six span brick arch bridge, over 500ft long and 100ft above the river bed. Two spans were still standing but were damaged beyond use and the demolished piers were in very poor shape; using ladders from the river bed, work on clearing debris from two of the piers started at once and steel cribbing was then built up to carry the bridge seats. The site was very restricted; the river bed was inaccessible to transport, and at the assembly site it proved impossible to unload more than two bridging vehicles at one time. Because of this it was decided to build the bridge from both banks, cantilevered out to meet over the third pier from the north bank, and making use of Sherman tanks as counterbalance. (Figure 9.9). The third pier still stood some 80ft high, with the top inaccessible by ladders, and anti-tank guns were used to blast away the top of the pier; further clearance of the debris was possible once the cantilevered ends of the bridge allowed access from above.

When the two ends of bridge came to be joined up it was realized that the male ends of panel were leading from both banks. A modified link was therefore used to join the bottom chords and the top chords were joined by steel wire rope lashings. According to Bernard Poole, serving with XIII Corps Engineers, this gave rise to the name of the bridge, which the Sappers christened ASAMFU. Other units took this to be a tribal name from the company of Bechuanian Pioneers working on the bridge approaches, but the Sappers were quite clear that it was an acronym for Another Systematic and Military F*** Up!. The bridge was completed in nine and a half days, a very good time considering the difficulties of the site, the continual use of the diversion by heavy traffic, and the distance of the bridge site from the company camp site and bridging store.

Figure 9.9. The 480ft Bailey built on Ace Route at San Andrea, constructed from both banks simultaneously. (J Coldwell).

Further Operations in Italy and the crossing of the Po

The campaign in Italy continued for another seven months, until the final German surrender on 2 May 1945. Progress during the last months of 1944 had been very slow, due mainly to the atrocious weather conditions, which greatly increased the road maintenance task of the Sappers. No attempt will be made to describe bridging operations during these closing stages of the campaign in detail, but these operations were on a considerable scale and warrant mention at least. The assault crossing of the Senio took place on 9 April 1945 and involved a number of bridges of all types. The crossing of the Santerno followed on the 11th, making use of the ARKs of the Assault Engineers as well as Bailey, and by the 23rd, units of the Eighth Army had reached the River Po. By the evening of the 25th the whole of the south bank of the Po within the Eighth Army front had been secured, with Fifth Army holding the river line further to the west. During the 16 days of their final advance, engineers of Eighth Army had built no less than 140 bridges and other crossings, besides the repair and maintenance of many miles of tracks and roads, whilst bridging operations on the Fifth Army front, although less extensive, were equally impressive.

The Po was not a fast river but it was wide - between 400ft and 1,500ft on the front of the assault, and the flood banks were up to 30ft high. The river crossing started on the night of 24th/25th, with V Corps on the right and XIII Corps on the left. All rafting equipment available was allotted to the assaulting troops, including Class 5 Rafts, Class 9 Close Support Rafts, Class 40 Bailey Rafts, and Class 50/60 Rafts, which were operated by the Assault Engineers. (Figure 9.10). By 4pm on the 25th a 470ft Class 9 FBE Bridge was in place, built by the Divisional Engineers of 2 New Zealand Division south of Ficarola, and another, 620ft long, was opened to traffic the following day. The completion of the former bridge enabled Bailey equipment to be moved

Figure 9.10. A Class 40 Bailey Raft ferrying a Churchill Tank across the River Po. (Engineers in the Italian Campaign, 1943-1945).

Figure 9.11. The double landing bay used for the Bailey Bridge across the River Po at Pontelagoscuro. (Engineers in the Italian Campaign, 1943-1945).

to the enemy bank, speeding up construction of a Bailey Pontoon Bridge by building from both banks. The 1,110ft long bridge was built by 13 Corps Troops and was completed by 5pm on the 27th, but an hour later an underwater explosion sank part of one raft and damaged two adjacent rafts. It was never ascertained whether the damage was caused by a mine or by enemy frogmen, but repairs were completed by 2am on the 28th of April. Another Bailey, 1,096ft long and sited at Pontelagoscuro, was completed by 8th Army Troops Engineers by midnight on the 27th. (Figure 9.11).

The advance now proceeded apace and the leading Divisions of both Corps reached the Adige to find, as usual, that all the bridges had been blown, with the exception of one railway bridge; but by the 29th a number of pontoon bridges and a 170ft high level Bailey had been built and were open to traffic. The pursuit of the enemy continued, and on 2 May 1945 the final surrender of all German forces in Italy brought an end to operations.

Mention should be made of Springbok Bridge, built across the Po by the South African Engineer Corps as a semi-permanent bridge to support the continued Allied advance northward. The chosen site was that of a former road bridge situated at Pontelagoscuro, near the site of the Bailey Pontoon bridge built by 8th Army Troops. All four spans of the original road bridge had been destroyed by Allied bombing. A number of proposals for a high level crossing of the Po had been under consideration for some time, including a suspension bridge, a Flambo bridge, four triple/triple simply supported spans, and two designs for a continuous bridge. There were in some quarters serious misgivings regarding the use of Bailey to build long span continuous bridges, but eventually a very detailed and painstakingly calculated design produced by CRE SA Corps Troops was approved. However this was only after CE 8th Army had ruled that final design approval must be given by Donald Bailey himself and that an exact replica of the bridge should first be built over a suitable dry gap and subjected to exhaustive loading tests.

Figure 9.12. Construction of the Springbok Bridge, a high-level continuous Bailey built across the River Po at the close of the Italian Campaign. (RE Journal, Sept 1946).

After the successful completion of the trial, work on the bridge proper commenced. On 26 April delivery of stores commenced, and work began on clearing debris and capping the partially demolished piers with reinforced concrete, using a floating landing stage on the south bank to serve three Bailey pontoon rafts to ferry material. Bailey piers were then erected above the capped piers to support rocking rollers, permanently installed to allow for expansion and contraction of the bridge. The gaps between the piers were 222ft, 270ft, 270ft, and 222ft, all spans beyond the normal range on Bailey, and so the bridge design proposed the use of triple/double Bailey with the bridge trusses reinforced top and bottom with chords cut from Bailey panels. The 990ft long bridge, weighing some 600tons with its launching nose, was hauled across the river by a D8 tractor, using a 1in steel wire rope, after which the decking was laid from both ends. The bridge was designed to take Class 40 loads, although restricted to one such load per span, and was completed in just nine and a half days, work proceeding by day and by night. (Figure 9.12).

Bailey during the Italian Campaign

The impact of the Bailey Bridge upon the successful conclusion of the Italian Campaign was immense and it is difficult to imagine how the Allied advance could ever have been maintained without the ready availability of this excellent bridge. Earlier in the chapter figures were given for the total Bailey build during the campaign, and as the pace of the advance increased so did the need for yet more bridges. During the last twenty four days of the campaign a total of 252 Bailey Bridges, averaging 102ft in length, were constructed, whilst the average expenditure of bridging equipment throughout the battle amounted to some 700 tons per day, or over seven bridge sets. The difficulties of keeping forward units supplied with the equipment were enormous, not only because of the state of and congestion on the roads, but also because of the constant shortage of transport. Indeed the requirement for bridging equipment for the crossing of the River Po caused the Q Staff of the Eighth Army to allot six extra general transport platoons for this purpose, at the expense of moving forward 400 tons of ammunition a day. It was of course the constant need for more bridging that led to the design and the manufacture of the Flambo Bailey, described in the previous chapter, and also gave rise to the need to maintain a continuous programme of bridge reconstruction, thus releasing Bailey for further use forward. (Figure 9.13).

Figure 9.13. A typical example of bridge reconstruction. (RE Journal, Sept 1946).

Railway Bridging during the Campaign

The part played by the Railway Construction Companies of the Corps during the campaign was no less important than that of the Field Companies. It was essential from the outset to re-establish a reliable railway network behind the advancing Allied Armies, thus ensuring the continual replenishment of the vast quantities of equipment, ammunition, and supplies needed by our troops. To this end the Engineers of 15th Army Group reconstructed 490 railway bridges and viaducts, repaired 83 tunnels, and rehabilitated 2,450 miles of track during the campaign.

One of the earliest tasks was the re-opening of the east coast line following the occupation of Tarranto. With very little railway bridging equipment yet available in Italy, a design using double/triple Bailey Bridging was evolved and used to rebuild two important rail bridges on this line, one across the Ofanto, with three spans of 60ft, (Figure 9.14) and the other across the Cervaro, with two spans of 50ft and one of 80ft. The bridge decks had to be reinforced, extra lateral sway bracing provided, and the rail sleepers individually packed; even so severe speed restrictions were applied. The bridges were built by Eighth Army Troops RE, working closely with 160 Railway Construction Company RE, who built the Unit Trestle piers and relaid considerable lengths of track. A further bridge, across the River Biferno, comprised four 60ft spans and two 50ft spans of Deck Bailey. All three bridges carried heavy traffic for some eighteen months until they were

Figure 9.14. The first railway bridge built during the Italian Campaign, across the River Ofanto at Barletta. (A W McMurdo).

Figure 9.15 *A 236ft span bridge across the River Garigliano, built using captured German Roth-Waagner equipment.* (A W McMurdo).

replaced by permanent bridges, but as the advance continued, supplies of railway equipment bridging became available and no further need arose to use Bailey Bridging in this role. A number of Standard Through Truss Railway Bridges were used, but the majority of bridges were reconstructed using the new Unit Construction Railway Bridge (UCRB), and to a lesser extent, the 40ft Sectional Welded Plate Girder Bridge. For long spans, use was made of captured German Roth-Waagner railway bridging, capable of spanning up to 260ft for 16 BSU loading. (Figure 9.15).

The move of the Eighth Army to the west coast in the Spring of 1944, prior to the advance on Rome with the Fifth Army, saw the need to open up a second railway line from Naples, thus giving each Army its own L of C. Transportation units were thus faced with providing rail crossings across the major obstacles previously crossed by the advancing forward troops with their assault and road bridges. Typical of this task was the replacement of the rail bridge across the Volturno at Cancello. All three 125ft spans of the bridge had been destroyed beyond repair or salvage, and the two piers demolished down to about 25ft below rail level. The piers were brought up to level with masonry walls containing a concrete core, and the three spans were then built using Standard Through Truss equipment. The work was carried out by 150 Railway Construction Company RE and since nobody in Italy had erected this type of bridge under operational conditions, its construction aroused considerable interest. The bridge was opened on 20

May 1944, some two months after commencement, and is shown in the earlier Figure 8.25.

A more typical routine construction task that faced the Allied Transportation units was the replacement of a bridge across the Sangro, which consisted of 24 spans, each of approximately 40ft. To conserve equipment always in short supply, 14 of the original spans were filled with an earth embankment; six of the remaining gaps were then spanned using 90ft UCRB spans and the remaining four gaps were spanned with 40ft Sectional Plate Girder spans. However at a later stage it was decided that the restriction of the waterway might be too severe and a number of 10ft rail and concrete box culverts were constructed through the embankments whilst the track remained in use.

Reconstruction of the Italian railway system went on well after military operations had ceased, and included two major rail bridges over the River Po. The first, at Ostiglia, was built by 175 Engineer General Service Battalion of the US Army, supported by US Railway Operating units. The 1,512ft bridge was built using four 75ft spans and four 80ft spans of UCRB for the

Figure 9.16. The American-built rail bridge across the River Po at Ostiglia. (Railway Construction in Italy, 1943-46).

228

main river spans, with eight 40ft Sectional Plate Girder spans and thirteen German 100cm deep steel joist spans for the approaches. (Figure 9.16). The piers were built using Light Steel Trestles founded on timber piling. Work on the bridge took about two months and was finished by early July. During severe flooding in early November, which caused widespread havoc in Northern Italy, the river rose to within seven feet of the underside of the main girders, but slight lateral deflection of the bridge on some of the piers was effectively rectified. The second bridge was built at Pontelagoscuro; the bridge was almost 1,400ft long and replaced the rail bridge almost completely destroyed by Allied bombing. Sixteen timber piled bents were built to support Light Steel Trestle piers carrying the 17 spans of bridge, each an 80ft deck span of UCRB. Work by No 1 Railway Construction and Maintenance Group RE started in August 1945, and took some eight months to complete.

Armoured Engineers in Italy

Little mention has yet been made of the work of the Armoured Engineers in Italy, although the formation of 1 Armoured Regiment RAC/RE in early 1944 and its expansion into 25 Armoured Engineer Brigade early in 1945 has been mentioned in the previous chapter. The Italian ARKs of the Armoured Engineers were first put to use during the advance beyond the Gothic Line in the autumn of 1944, and a good example of such use was seen during the crossing of the River Savio at Cesena in late October. The plan was to form a bridge of three ARKs positioned in line across the river, which was running at a depth of about 4ft. The ARKs were successfully positioned and the bridge taken into use when the middle ARK began to list under load; at the same time the pin securing one of its rear ramps worked loose. The ramp dropped into the water, and with some difficulty the other rear ramp was removed, enabling an AVRE to place a Fascine between the first and second ARKs. Unfortunately the middle ARK then received a direct hit and the damage had to be made good with sandbags and rubble. That night the river rose 3ft, submerging the ARKs, and when the level had dropped next morning, it was found that the Fascine had been washed away and that the river gap had increased. The following day a new Fascine was positioned and a fourth ARK was placed at the near bank to fill the gap in the crossing. This ARK was also fated, as its left hand ramp collapsed, but luckily the river level had by now dropped further and it was possible to dispense with it altogether. That evening the crossing was improved with sandbags and carriers were able to cross.

The ARKs proved invaluable and were put to good use on a continual basis, another crossing worthy of mention being that across the Senio in the Spring of 1945. Early reconnaissance before the assault had not been possible, and the site chosen for the crossing, to be built by F (Cheshire) Assault Squadron RE, proved unsuitable. The new site necessitated the

Figure 9.17. The crossing of the River Senio using the ARKs of The Cheshire Assault Squadron RE. (RE Library).

blowing of a gap in the floodbank to allow access, and the use of an ARK to provide a ramp. A fascine was then dropped into the river bed, and an ARK with its ramps removed was driven on top. Another ARK was then driven on top of the bottom ARK and its ramps positioned to form the crossing. (Figure 9.17). The approaches were improved by an armoured bulldozer and the crossing was completed by 5am, enabling three squadrons of tanks to cross before first light.

CHAPTER TEN

The Second World War - NW Europe and the Far East

The Campaign in North West Europe

Operations in North-West Europe were on a greater scale than those in Italy, and the Allies were faced with having to cross many of the great rivers of France and Germany. The campaign was of course shorter, lasting some eleven months compared with the twenty-three months of the Italian Campaign, but although fewer bridges were built by the Sappers, they tended to be of greater span, partly due to the differences of terrain but also because 21st Army Group fought on the left flank of the Allied Armies and thus had to cross the major rivers nearest to their mouths, where of course they were wider. In all 1509 Bailey Bridges were built, totalling 29 miles of fixed bridge and 3 miles of floating bridge. In addition, 80 Class 9 FBE Bridges were built, innumerable assault bridges were laid and many major railway crossings restored. Again it is quite impossible to do justice to this aspect of the Sappers' work in the campaign, but some of the major river crossings will be briefly described as an indication of this most important task undertaken by the Corps.

Operation Overlord

The literature on the Normandy landings made on the northern coast of France between the Cherbourg Peninsula and Caen on 6 June 1944 is exhaustive. Suffice then to remind the reader that the British Second Army, comprising I Corps and XXX Corps, made their landings on Gold, Juno and Sword Beaches, whilst further west the US First Army landed on Utah and Omaha Beaches. (MAP 3). By midday 6 Airborne Division had established a bridgehead east of the River Orne, to the north of Caen, having secured two bridges over the Orne and the Caen Canal intact; the two bridges were near Benouville and were named Pegasus, captured in a particularly daring glider attack, and Ranville respectively. Good progress had also been made by the other Divisions of the British Second Army.

During the landings the 1 Assault Brigade RE, the formation of which was considered in a previous chapter, played a vital role. During the assault on the beaches their new equipments proved invaluable and subsequently they made full use of their fascines and SBG Assault Bridges to cross the many ditches, craters and minor obstacles encountered during the capture of the

MAP 3 ~ NORTH - WEST EUROPE, 1944-45

Showing towns and rivers mentioned in the text; roads and railways have been omitted for clarity

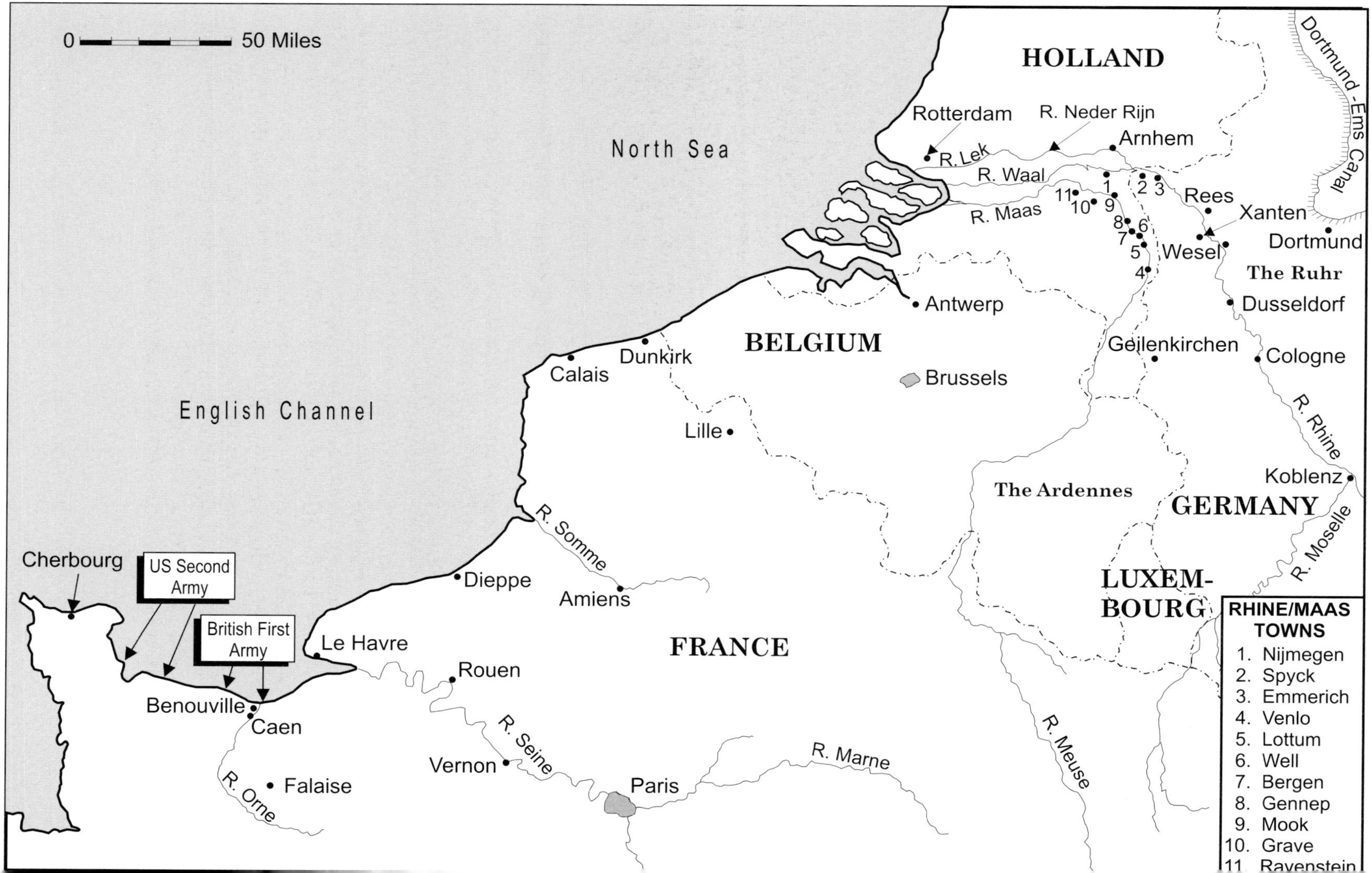

RHINE/MAAS TOWNS	
1.	Nijmegen
2.	Spyck
3.	Emmerich
4.	Venlo
5.	Lottum
6.	Well
7.	Bergen
8.	Gennep
9.	Mook
10.	Grave
11.	Ravenstein

HOLLAND

Dortmund -Ems Canal

Dortmund

Xanten

The Ruhr

Dusseldorf

Cologne

R. Rhine

Rees

Wesel

Arnhem

R. Neder Rijn

R. Lek

R. Waal

R. Maas

Rotterdam

Koblenz

R. Moselle

GERMANY

LUXEM-BOURG

The Ardennes

R. Meuse

Antwerp

BELGIUM

Brussels

Geilenkirchen

North Sea

Lille

Dunkirk

Calais

FRANCE

R. Marne

Paris

R. Somme

Amiens

R. Seine

Dieppe

Rouen

Vernon

English Channel

Le Havre

Falaise

Caen

R. Orne

Benouville

British First Army

US Second Army

Cherbourg

0   50 Miles

Figure 10.1. *London Bridge I, crossing the Caen Canal; the first Bailey built after the invasion of NW Europe.* (Bridging, Normandy to Berlin).

Channel ports and the advance into France, Belgium and Holland, and indeed into Germany itself.

Once the Allied bridgehead had been established, bridging operations began in earnest and the first Bailey Bridge to be built in France, a pontoon bridge subsequently named London Bridge I, was built by 17 Field Company RE across the Caen Canal, which is parallel to and just west of the River Orne. (Figure 10.1). Building of the bridge was marred by ill fortune; stores were disembarked late and some were damaged by enemy fire; there were a number of casualties, some fatal, and Lieutenant Colonel R W Urquhart RE, CRE 3 Division had his jeep blown from under him by a mine. Nevertheless the bridge was completed just after midnight on 8/9 June, and a second bridge, London II across the River Orne, was completed on the 11th with the help of 246 and 263 Field Companies. By mid-July a number of further bridges had been built across the Orne and the canal, opening up five Class 40 routes to improve access to the bridgehead east of the river. These bridges included a 375ft Class 40 Bailey Pontoon Bridge, named York I,

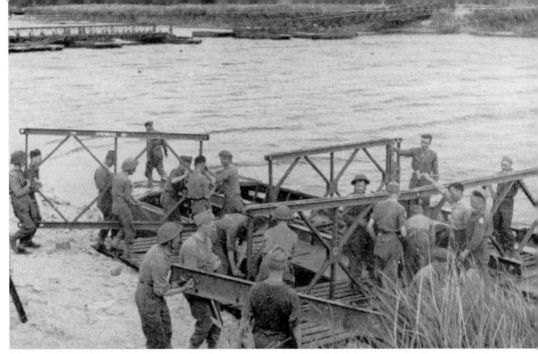

Figure 10.2. Building a floating bay for the nearly completed York I Bridge over the Caen Canal at Ouistreham. (Bridging, Normandy to Berlin).

(Figure 10.2) across the canal at Ouistreham near the coast, and its continuation across the Orne, also a Bailey Pontoon Bridge and named York II. I Corps captured those areas of Caen north of the river between 8 and 10 July, and the opening up of the routes across the Orne enabled the British forces to launch an attack into the bridgehead in mid-July. Meanwhile II Canadian Corps were able to clear the southern suburbs of Caen, enabling its RCE companies to repair the damaged bridges over the river in the town; two of the Class 40 Baileys built across the river at Caen by the RCE were named Churchill Bridge and Winston Bridge. (Figure 10.3).

Figure 10.3. Winston Churchill, C-in-C 21 Army Group and GOC 2nd British Army crossing the Churchill Bridge over the Orne at Caen. (Bridging, Normandy to Berlin).

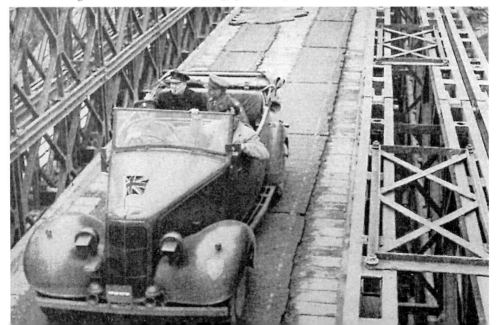

Figure 10.4. *Completing the launch of the UCRB girders for the main-line rail bridge over the River Orne at Caen.* (IWM B 8996).

As in the Italian Campaign, railway bridging was very much in evidence and one major bridge that required reconstruction was that carrying the main Cherbourg-Paris line across the Orne at Caen. The work was carried out by 5 Railway Construction and Maintenance Group RE and commenced on 23 July 1944. The original lattice girder two span bridge, carrying two tracks, had been demolished beyond repair and the first task was to cut and remove all of the steelwork supported on the centre masonry pier. (Figure 10.4). Two 75ft span, twin girder, deck type Unit Construction Railway Bridges were then launched to carry each track, using the existing pier and abutments. The double track was open for traffic on 26 August.

The Crossing of the Seine

Meanwhile American forces in the Cherbourg Peninsula had steadily improved their position and by the end of July the Allies made their breakout towards the Seine. The Seine is a broad river and with the majority of its bridges destroyed or badly damaged, it presented a major obstacle to the Allied advance forward to the French border and thence into the Low Countries. Speed in crossing the river was of the utmost importance, in order to maintain the momentum of the Allied advance and thus deny the enemy time to reorganize his forces for the defence of the river line. However, the task had long been anticipated; units had been specially trained for this major crossing and two bridging columns had been formed, each with over 360 vehicles and carrying sufficient storm boats, rafting and bridging equipment to support an assault crossing by one corps on a divisional front.

The 21st Army Group plan for the crossing was that Second Army would attack on the right flank, with XXX Corps on the right, about Vernon, and XII Corps on the left; at the same time First Canadian Army would attack on the left flank, between XII Corps and the sea. 43 Division was to lead the XXX Corps assault and started the 90 mile approach to the river on 24 August. Next morning the leading battalion reached Vernon, to find that the enemy had withdrawn from the town but were concentrating on the far bank of the river. The road and rail bridges in the town had both been demolished and, since these were on the main supply routes necessary for the Allied advance forward, their rapid replacement was of prime importance. The leading troops arrived at the river bank on the morning of 25 August and the assault began at 7pm that evening, the storm boats being manned by detachments from 583 Field Company RE.

By 10.15pm approval was given for 43 Divisional Engineers to start work on a Class 9 FBE Bridge near to the site of the demolished bridge. By dawn bridgeheads had been established by the lead battalions, despite heavy enemy opposition and many setbacks. Meanwhile all of the rafts required for the bridge had been completed during the night, but enemy machine-gun fire along the line of bridge made it quite impossible to complete the bridge in daylight; indeed early attempts to bring the rafts into bridge resulted in about two-thirds of the crew of each raft becoming casualties. By midday about half of the rafts had been coupled into bridge but enemy fire became so intense that the CRE, Lieutenant Colonel T H Evill RE, was forced to halt operations. By late afternoon progress in the bridgehead eased the situation somewhat and the bridge was finally completed by 5.20pm on 26 August. (Figure 10.5).

Traffic began to flow, but although the passage of infantry support weapons was most welcome, the completion of a Class 40 Bailey Pontoon Bridge, to enable the armour to cross the river in pursuit of the enemy, was still a matter of priority. Construction of the bridge, being built by 7 Army Troops RE, had started earlier that day, but enemy interference delayed its completion until late the following day, when the tanks and vehicles of 11 Armoured Division poured across the 694ft long bridge. During that day a number of tanks had been ferried over the river by 584 Field Company RE, of 15 (Kent) GHQ Troops RE, using Bailey rafts, but once the Bailey Pontoon Bridge had been completed 15 GHQ Troops were able to concentrate on the building of a second Class 40 Bailey at Vernon, which was completed by noon on 29 August. This bridge was 736ft long, excluding its ramps, and was named Saul Bridge, the Class 9 FBE Bridge and the other Bailey having been named David and Golliath Bridges respectively.

The river crossings made by XII Corps on the left flank were of a similar nature, whilst on their front the First Canadian Army met little opposition on the river line and were able to cross almost unheeded. To the south the American troops swept on and by 25 August the First US Army had entered Paris, already taken over by the French Resistance Movement. By now there were few significant enemy forces between the allied Armies and the German border, but as always the need for the opening up of main supply routes was of prime importance and the construction of a rail bridge over the Seine to extend the Allied L of C into northern France was essential. An extensive reconnaissance was carried out by 2 Railway Construction and Maintenance Group RE to select a route that could be repaired in the minimum of time and could be operated without great difficulty. The line selected involved the building of a new bridge across the river at Le Manoir, near Rouen. The bridge consisted of six deck type spans of Unit Construction Railway Bridge, each 75ft long, and two 40ft spans of Sectional Welded Plate Girder Bridge.

Figure 10.5. The David and Golliath Bridges over the River Seine at Vernon. The Class 40 Bailey was 694ft long. (IWM BU206).

Figure 10.6. *The new rail bridge built across the River Seine at Le Manoir.* (Bridging, Normandy to Berlin).

Piers were constructed using Light Standard Unit Trestles, those in the river being founded on adjustable camels feet. Reconnaissance started on 31 August and initial supplies of bridging material arrived on site on 6 September. (Figure 10.6). By 21 September the bridge was ready for test loading, but after it had been opened for traffic it was found necessary to modify the design to cope with barge traffic on the river. This was done by removing one of the deck spans and replacing it with a half-through span, which was later provided with lifting gantries at either end so that the span could be lifted to allow passage of tugs and barges at high water. The river floods in late 1944 were the worst since 1910, with the water level almost up to rail level. The bridge survived, however, and was prevented from being swept away by being loaded with ballast wagons; it remained in operation as trains of wagons were pushed and hauled across by locomotives operating from the bridge approaches.

The Advance to the Rhine

With the Seine bridgehead secured, the immediate objectives of 21st Army Group were to destroy the enemy in north-east France, to secure the Channel ports, particularly the port of Antwerp and to clear the Pas de Calais V Bomb sites. The advance of the Second Army from their bridgehead started at the end of August, and within six days the Army had advanced some 250 miles. Indeed the advance was so rapid at this time that many bridges were captured before they could be demolished by the enemy; for example when Amiens was liberated by 11 Armoured Division on 31 August, three of the four bridges across the Somme were captured intact, with the help of the French Resistance Movement. The advance continued, with many examples of bridging carried out in exceptional circumstances, and by 4 September 11 Armoured Division entered Antwerp.

238

Many natural obstacles still lay ahead, in particular the major rivers, the Maas, the Waal and the Neder Rijn. Confusion sometimes occurs regarding the naming of these three rivers in north-west Europe; the River Rhine splits into two tributaries as it leaves German and enters The Netherlands, namely the Neder Rijn (or Lower Rhine) and the Waal, whilst the River Meuse flows through France and then Belgium, but is renamed the Maas on entering The Netherlands. There was a considerable network of canals to be crossed, including the Maas-Waal Canal just west of Nijmegen. The plan for Operation Market Garden was to use airborne forces to seize crossings over the three major rivers and then to push forward armoured columns to link up with the airborne troops. The engineer commitment for the operation was enormous. Over 9000 Sappers and Pioneer Corps personnel were made available for the special taskforce, under the command of the CE XXX Corps, Brigadier B C Davey, with the object of bridging these major obstacles should the bridges not be captured intact. The detailed plan envisaged the possible building of a Class 9 FBE Bridge, a Class 40 Bailey Pontoon Bridge and a Bailey Barge Bridge over the 800ft wide Maas, with similar Baileys over the 850ft wide Waal and over the 300ft wide Neder Rijn, in addition to a Class 9 FBE Bridge over the latter. Two Class 40 Bailey Pontoon Bridges were to be built over the Maas-Waal Canal, and a dozen Class 40 Bailey Rafts built for use on the two major rivers. The operation and the reasons for its failure have been written of at length and will not be considered here, other than to say that the bridge at Grave, on the Maas, was successfully captured and held, as were both the road and railbridges at Nijmegen, on the Waal, some three days later. Both the bridges at Nijmegen were subsequently attacked by the enemy, first from the air and then by enemy frogmen who managed to demolish a pier of the rail bridge and blow a hole in the deck of the road bridge, which was rapidly repaired by insertion of two Bailey spans. The bridges across the Neder Rijn at Arnhem were not captured and the bridgehead north of the river had finally to be evacuated.

After the failure of the Arnhem operation in late September the Allied

Figure 10.7. Tower Bridge, a Class 30 high-level Bailey subsequently built across the Maas-Vaal Canal by 30 Corps Troops Engrs. (Bridging, Normandy to Berlin).

Figure 10.8. Building the last approach span of Kent Bridge under difficult conditions. (Bridging, Normandy to Berlin).

plan was for 21st Army Group to attack from the Nijmegen bridgehead to meet up with the US Ninth Army, and then force a crossing over the Rhine north of the Ruhr, advancing into the heart of Germany. The US First and Third Armies would attack further to the south. First, however, the German bridgehead west of the Maas had to be eliminated. A major Class 40 Bailey Pontoon Bridge, 626ft long, had already been built at Berg, north of Venlo. The bridge was completed on 9 November, in four days, by 15 (Kent) GHQ Troops Engineers, and was appropriately named the Kent Bridge. (Figure 10.8). An attack by XII Corps in the general direction of Venlo was launched on 14 November and on the first day 81 Assault Squadron RE laid three SBG Assault Bridges to establish bridgeheads over the Wessem and Noorer Canals. Despite atrocious weather, extensive minefields and very difficult ground conditions, the advance continued and by the end of the month virtually the whole of the area west of the Maas had been cleared of the enemy.

The US advance further south also continued but in mid-December the Germans launched their massive counter offensive in the Ardennes, the German force comprising eight panzer divisions and seventeen infantry and parachute divisions. The offensive has been well documented elsewhere and suffice to say here that by 8 January Hitler acknowledged defeat and ordered the withdrawal of his troops. It was not until the 16th, however, that the gap was closed, the majority of the enemy forces having escaped to the east.

Plans for Operation Veritable, the Allied offensive into Germany to clear

240

the west bank of the Rhine, were now put in hand. The attack was launched on 8 February as planned, despite the fact that a thaw had set in at the end of January, resulting in a rapid deterioration of the roads. The capture of Gennep on the 11th enabled 7 Army Troops Engineers to start work on the planned crossing of the Maas. Plans for a new Class 40 maintenance route had been completed sometime previously and approximately 120 lorry loads of bridging equipment had already been earmarked for the project; work was therefore able to start at once, building the bridge at the town ferry site. With the thaw that had set in, the river was running fast, some 800ft wide; it had soon spread extensively on either bank. With the tide still rising, the 816ft of bridge proper was completed just before the site became totally inaccessible, other than by boat. Approach viaducts were then constructed at either end. That at the western end was 2,231ft long and was constructed from fifty floating bays; these were positioned with difficulty between hedges and fences on the flood bank, many of which had to be cleared by use of Bangalore Torpedoes. The eastern viaduct was 961ft long and was built using Bailey spans supported on bridging cribs positioned on the submerged ferry approach road. (Figure 10.9). Altogether the bridge was 4,008ft long, easily the longest bridge so far built during the campaign, but soon after it was opened for urgent traffic on 19 February the water level began to fall, dropping over 14ft in 14 days. This enabled the ferry road to be used as an alternative approach on the west bank and the pontoons were then recovered from this viaduct and replaced with crib piers.

At the same time 6 Army Troop Engineers built a five-span high level Bailey at Gennep, on the line of a demolished railway bridge. The Class 30 bridge consisted of two 200ft end spans, of triple/triple construction, and three 190ft inner spans, of double/triple construction. Since only one of the

Figure 10.9. The Bailey Pontoon Bridge across the Maas at Gennep, showing the grounded pontoons in the right foreground. (Bridging, Normandy to Berlin).

Figure 10.10. The high-level Bailey across the Maas at Gennep, showing piling under way for the parallel rail bridge. (Bridging, Normandy to Berlin).

piers had been partially demolished, it was possible to build the new bridge on the upstream halves of the original rail bridge piers, building up the damaged pier with a Light Standard Unit Trestle. (Figure 10.10).

A rail-bridge was subsequently built alongside this Bailey. Over the river channel four four-girder UCRB spans were used, two of 100ft and two of 150ft span, making use of the downstream halves of the existing piers and new timber-piled piers positioned halfway between them. RSJ approach spans were used at either end of bridge. This rail bridge was not opened for traffic until the end of March, however, too late for the build-up for the Rhine crossing. It was therefore decided that 2 Railway Construction and Maintenance Group RE should reconstruct the bridge across the Maas on the main line between Antwerp and NW Germany. The line crossed the Maas at Ravenstein and the original bridge had been built for a single line on piers wide enough for possible widening at a later stage. This eased the problems of reconstruction, since the two undamaged bowstring spans and two continuous plate girder spans could be jacked sideways almost 20ft, on the piers still standing, to be incorporated into the new bridge. Once the demolished pier had been rebuilt and four piled bents (each of sixteen 14in x 14in piles 60ft long) had been built, six deck type UCRB spans were used to replace the two demolished bowstring spans. The bridge was decked for road use as well as rail, and after its opening on 4 February 1945 opened up the rail L of C into the area between the Maas and the Rhine. This greatly

Figure 10.11. Constructing the UCRB spans to repair the rail bridge at Ravenstein, over the River Maas. (Bridging, Normandy to Berlin).

assisted the build-up for the pending assault across the Rhine, to take place the following month. (Figure 10.11).

The advance continued successfully on all fronts, despite strong enemy opposition, and by the end of the third week in March the whole of the west bank of the Rhine was in Allied hands. During this last phase of operations, and indeed during every phase of the battle since the Normandy invasion, the units of 1 Assault Brigade RE had proved their worth time and time again, making full use of their AVREs and fascines, and their AVRE-mounted SBG Assault Bridges. The No 1 Tank Bridge, mounted on the Valentine chassis, and the No 2 Tank Bridge, mounted on Churchill chassis, both operated by the RAC, were also extensively used, in many cases having been placed under command of the Assault Squadrons by the Armoured Brigades. To quote just one of many many examples of the work of the Sapper Assault Squadrons, 16 and 222 Squadrons were in support of 7 and 11 Armoured Divisions during the last push to the Rhine in late January 1945. North of Geilenkirchen, in Germany, the brunt of the fighting fell on the infantry, and in support 222 Squadron laid two SBG Bridges near Susteren and 16 Squadron laid another across a stream outside Hongen. As the advance continued 16 Squadron then constructed an 80ft skid-mounted Bailey Bridge and pushed it four and a half miles along an icebound road with one of their AVREs, before positioning it across a large crater in the road.

Preparations for the Rhine Crossing

As early as 1942 consideration had been given to the eventual need to force a crossing of the Rhine, mainly with a view to ensuring that sufficient equipment of the right type would be available. The final plan was approved in December 1944 and envisaged a drive by Field Marshal Montgomery's 21 Army Group, reinforced by the Ninth US Army, across the lower Rhine north of the Ruhr. This crossing would be made in conjunction with a crossing by General Bradley's 12th Army Group in the area of Mainz, not shown on Map 3, but some 50 miles south of Koblenz. 12th Army Group would then drive to the north-east to envelop the Ruhr from the south, and both Army Groups would advance side by side to meet the Russian Armies advancing through Poland and East Germany.

The actual timing of the operation depended not only on the clearing of enemy forces from the west bank of the river, but also to a large extent upon river conditions, since both the Rhine and the Maas were liable to serious flooding and possible icing between December and March. Taking account of the many factors involved and also of the need to avoid highly populated and industrialized areas, the most suitable crossing sites selected for 21st Army Group were Rheinberg, Wesel, Xanten and Rees. Improvement of communications west of the Rhine was of prime importance prior to the actual assault and, since most routes involved the crossing of the Maas, a

Figure 10.12. The 880ft high-level Bailey Pontoon Bridge built across the Maas at Lottum, by 6 Army Troop Engineers. (EBE - 3605).

number of bridges were built across the river during the run-up period. (Figure 10.12). The magnitude of the task is illustrated in the table below which lists the major bridges built across the Maas in the Second Army area of operations, in addition to the rail bridge at Ravenstein and the three Bailey Bridges mentioned in the preceding paragraphs. Parallel with this bridge-building programme, considerable effort was expended in repairing and improving the road and rail network feeding the forward area.

TABLE 3 – BRIDGES BUILT ACROSS THE RIVER MAAS IN PREPARATION FOR THE RHINE CROSSING

LOCATION	BRIDGE	BUILT BY	LENGTH	IN USE
MOOK	Class 24 high level Bailey	1 Can Army Engrs	1,286ft	26 Feb
VENLO	Class 9 FBE bridge	8 Corps Tps Engrs	400ft	2 Mar
WELL	Class 40 all weather BPB	7 Army Tps Engrs	751ft	6 Mar
VENLO	As above	15 GHQ Tps Engrs	1,220ft	7 Mar
LOTTUM	As above	6 Army Tps Engrs	880ft	10 Mar
BERGEN	Class 9 FBE bridge	8 Corps Tps Engrs	540ft	11 Mar
VENLO	Class 70 all weather BPB	7 Army Tps Engrs	1,014ft	18 Mar
VENLO	Class 70 one way, class 40 two way, high level RSJ/timber pile bridge	1146 Engr Combat Group, US Ninth Army	925ft	23 Mar

In preparation for the assault crossing, an experimental unit known as 'H Wing' was set up at Nijmegen, on the Waal. Under the command of Major W S Tyzach RE, the task of the unit was to carry out trials of the specialist equipments of the Assault Engineers under conditions akin to those likely to be encountered on the Rhine. In particular, trials were carried out with the new 50/60 Rafts, not previously used in action but most necessary to ferry the British Churchill tanks across the Rhine. The trials included use of RAF Wild Kite balloon winches to pull the rafts across the river, using the method developed at the SME at Chatham, and this involved the manufacture of some specialist equipment by two Dutch engineering firms in Nijmegen.

The Rhine Crossing

The plan for the British Second Army crossing of the Rhine envisaged an assault on a two-corps front, with XXX Corps on the left, in the area of Rees, and XII Corps on the right, in the area of Xanten. In addition 1 Commando Brigade was to launch an attack on Wesel and seize the bridges over the Lippe, south of the town. The engineer task was considerable, the construction and operation of ferries and bridges involving not only the movement forward of the necessary equipment but also the maintenance and improvement of the routes up to the river, the entry and exit points, and also the forward routes on the far bank. In addition all the routine engineer work, such as mine clearance and water point construction, had still to be attended to, and there was also a commitment to build airfields east of the Rhine once our forces had established an adequate bridgehead. In all no less than twenty-eight major Sapper units were allocated to the two Corps for the task, comprising eight Divisional Engineers, four Armoured Divisional Engineers, two Assault Engineer Regiments, and four Corps, two Army and eight GHQ Troops Engineers. These units were supported by two Bridge Companies RASC, a Tipper Platoon RASC, a General Transport Platoon RASC, nine Pioneer Companies, four Mechanical Equipment Platoons RE, and a Naval attachment in charge of heavy tugs, which were to be used to assist in the movement of rafts. All in all a formidable force! Indeed, to quote from Volume IX of the *Corps History*, on the morning after the assault crossing 'One could hardly move a yard without meeting a party of Sappers busy doing some job, small or great, to speed up the movement of the countless hosts of men and vehicles across one of the mightiest and most historic rivers in Europe.'

On the XII Corps front 15 Division was selected as the assault division and all troops concerned in the assault were placed under command. The bridging plan was to establish a tactical Class 40 Bailey across the river at the Xanten ferry site and another all-weather Class 40 Bailey nearby, on the main supply route; a Class 12 Bailey was also required at Vynen, together with a Class 9 FBE Bridge near Wardt. In addition eleven ferries of various types were required, including two Class 50/60 ferries, each of two rafts, and two

LVT Buffalo ferries, operated by the Assault Engineers. Equipment brought forward during the three nights prior to the assault included eighty storm boats and sixty loads of FBE required for Class 9 rafts. XII Corps launched its assault under a clear full moon at 2am on 24 March, five hours after that of XXX Corps. The Commando Brigade had been ferried across by twenty-five Buffalos manned by 77 Assault Squadron some three hours earlier, and the town of Wesel was rapidly captured. On the right brigade front the crossing went according to plan and by 4am the whole of the assault brigade was across. By 6.30am two rafts were in operation, two further rafts having been destroyed by enemy shell fire, although subsequently replaced by reserve equipment. The rafts were in operation for almost three days, moving across many loads of equipment and over 600 vehicles. The assaulting brigade on the left front met stiffer opposition but was soon able to establish a bridgehead. Construction and operation of the Class 50/60 rafts for XII Corps was undertaken by 42 Assault Regiment and although the move forward to the ferry site was delayed by shell fire, two rafts were in operation by the early evening of 24 March. The rafts crossed over 190 tanks during the first thirty hours of their operation, and before their operation ceased on the evening of the 26th, some 250 tanks and fifty other vehicles had been ferried across the river.

The general operational plan and the engineering organization employed by XXX Corps were similar to that of XII Corps. The Corps had launched its assault at 9pm on 23 March, also on a two-brigade front. The ferrying operation did not go as well as with XII Corps, mainly due to stiff opposition from the German defenders of Rees, but, despite many casualties, both of men and rafting equipment, ferrying continued successfully until the 26th when the first bridges were completed. By the evening of the 24th the whole of the east bank of the Rhine on the 21 Army Group front had been cleared of the enemy, with the exception of the continuing resistance at Rees and, to a lesser extent, at Wesel.

But now the requirement was for bridging on a large scale, to speed up the flow of men, tanks and equipment needed for the final push into Germany. (Figure 10.13). Indeed preliminary work on the first bridges had started as early as 7am on the morning of the 24th. The extent of the bridging programme is shown in Table 4.

The semi-permanent Dempsey, Tyne and Tees Bridges, and the Spyck

Figure 10.13. Bridging the Rhine below Rees, from the original by David Cobbs. (Royal Engineers HQ Mess, Chatham).

TABLE 4 – BRIDGES BUILT ON THE 21ST ARMY FRONT FOR THE RHINE CROSSING

LOCATION	BRIDGE NAME	TYPE	BUILT BY	LENGTH	START TIME	ERECTION TIME AND COMMENT
XANTEN	Digger Bridge	Class 40 tactical BPB	7 Army Tps Engrs	1,091ft	0930hr 24 Mar	31 hours. The first Bailey Bridge across the Rhine. In six days almost 30,000 vehicles crossed.
WARDT	Draghunt or Twist Bridge	Class 9 FBE bridge	8 Corps Tps Engrs	1,440ft	1300hr 24 Mar	10 hours, after delays due to enemy action. The first British bridge across the Rhine. Twice broken, once by vehicle damage and then by swamping.
XANTEN	Sussex Bridge	Class 12 tactical BPB	12 Corps Tps Engrs	1,940ft	0800hr 24 Mar	26 hours. This was two bridges joined by a causeway; the smaller bridge was 360ft long.
REES	Lambeth Bridge	Class 15 tactical BPB	30 Corps Tps Engrs	1,206ft	early 25 Mar	24 hours. Work was delayed by enemy action and smoke was used.
HONNEPEL	Waterloo Bridge	Class 9 FBE bridge	18 GHQ Tps Engrs	1,300ft	0800hr 25 Mar	18 hours. Constructed using smoke to avoid enemy artillery fire.
REES	London Bridge	Class 40 low-level BPB	8 GHQ Tps Engrs	1,174ft	1700hr 25 Mar	30 hours. Assistance given by Pioneer Corps troops.
REES	Blackfriars Bridge	Class 40 low-level BPB	2 Canadian Corps Engrs	1,764ft	1000hr 26 Mar	50 hours. Built near Lambeth Bridge but rather longer.
REES	Westminster Bridge	Class 40 all-weather BPB	6 Army Tps Engrs	1,402ft	1100hr 26 Mar	79 hours. Catered for a 20ft range of river level. Low priority for equipment.
XANTEN	Sparrow Bridge	Class 40 all-weather BPB	15 (Kent) GHQ Tps Engrs	1,713ft	am 27 Mar	145 hours. Later extended by an approach bridge to a length of 2,085ft, plus a 645ft RC approach road.
EMMERICH	Maclean Bridge	Class 40 all-weather BPB	1 Canadian Army Engrs	1,656ft	1000hr 2 Apr	85 hours. A change of site was made late on 30 March. A second, low-level, BPB was built nearby.

Note that some timings and bridge lengths vary in different accounts, and cannot at this time be verified.

Figure 10.14. *Digger Bridge, built by 7 Army Troops Engrs at Xanten; nearly 1200ft long,it was the first Bailey to be built across the Rhine.* (Bridging, Normandy to Berlin).

Railway Bridge, all built at the end of the war in Europe, are considered in Chapter 14 and have not been included in the table. A number of bridges built by Engineers of the Ninth US Army and the two semi-permanent Roosevelt Bridges have also been excluded; these two bridges were built across the Rhine and the Lippe at Wesel by 1146 US Engineer Combat Group between 1 and 18 April 1945. Both were timber-piled bridges, with rolled steel joist road-bearers, the Rhine bridge being 1,813ft long and the smaller bridge 411ft long; both were designed to carry Class 40 loads two way and Class 70 loads one way.

Although Digger Bridge was the first Bailey Bridge to be built across the Rhine (Figure 10.14), the honours for the first bridging of the Rhine on 21 Army Group front went to the American Engineers of the Ninth US Army, using their M2 Treadway Bridge, with its pneumatic floats, an excellent Class 40 assault bridge capable of rapid construction times. The bridge was built at Wallach, just south of Wesel, by companies of 17 Armored Engineer Battalion and 202 Engineer Combat Battalion. For two days the American troops were engaged in inflating the floats and assembling the saddles and saddle beams in woods nearby, and in completing a 2,400ft approach road, using Sommerfield Track and timber covered with gravel and crushed rock. Construction proper started at 6.30am on 24 March and by 10.45 US Engineers crossed the river to start work on the 600ft far bank exit road. By 3.30pm, after just nine hours, the 1,150ft bridge was completed and was opened for traffic half-an-hour later, some 24 hours ahead of Digger Bridge.

Westminster Bridge was opened by Lieutenant General Sir Miles Dempsey, GOC Second Army, in a ceremony to mark the completion of all bridging operations for the assault across the Rhine, and detachments of all

Figure 10.15. *General Dempsey, GOC Second Army, opening Westminster Bridge.* (Bridging, Normandy to Berlin).

the engineer units that had taken part in the crossing attended. (Figure 10.15). The General later accompanied Mr Churchill and Field Marshal Montgomery on an inspection tour which gave rise to the newspaper report that "The Prime Minister, after inspecting bridges built by the Sappers across the Rhine, crossed in a DUKW".

Advance from the Rhine

Once the eastern bank of the Rhine had been cleared of the enemy the advance into the heart of Germany continued apace. Bridging remained a major task for the Sappers as the Germans fought fanatically in defence of their homeland, destroying almost every bridge in the path of the advancing Allied forces. By 1 April a bridgehead had been established over the Dortmund-Ems Canal and by 5 April our leading troops had reached the Weser, some 75 miles to the east. On the VIII Corps front a Class 40 Bailey Bridge and a Class 9 FBE Bridge were built by 6 Airborne Divisional Engineers without serious opposition, but further north the attempted crossing by 11 Armoured Division RE was fiercely opposed. Close-range cross fire and air attacks continually interrupted the building of a Class 40 Bailey and on the afternoon of the 6th two air attacks caused forty casualties amongst the Sappers, damaged much of the bridging equipment and badly cratered the bridge approaches. Further efforts to complete the bridge during the following night were eventually abandoned and an alternative site was chosen further to the south, eventually bridged by 15 Divisional RE on the 9th.

Further north XXX Corps reached the Weser in the vicinity of Bremen and bridged the river there without serious problems. The attack on the strongly defended city, which had been heavily bombed by the RAF, was ably supported by units of the Assault Engineers, making full use of their AVREs to reduce enemy strongpoints and demolish road blocks, and skid mounted Baileys to cross partially demolished bridges. By the 27th both halves of the city were in our hands and 15 (Kent) GHQ Tps started work on a 456ft Class 40 Bailey to link the two halves. The bridge was supported on three barges, one about 130ft by nearly 30ft, and two smaller ones, 108ft x 19ft. The bridge was known as Bristol Bridge and was completed on 2 May. (Figure 10.16).

Meanwhile the rapid advance of VIII Corps and XII Corps continued to the south and by 21 April leading troops of VIII Corps had reached the Elbe. As ever, bridging was of the utmost importance and in the two weeks of this 100 mile advance from the Weser to the Elbe Sapper units of VIII Corps alone built no less than thirty major bridges and widened or strengthened another dozen. By the 25th American and Russian troops met near Leipzig, and by the 26th the three Corps of the Second British Army were firmly in position on the south bank of the Elbe. Opposition was now negligible, but the task facing the Sappers was still considerable, the river being some 900ft wide. It

Figure 10.16. Bristol Bridge across the River Weser at Bremen, supported on three barges. (Bridging, Normandy to Berlin).

Figure 10.17. The Bailey Pontoon Bridge across the Elbe at Artlenburg, one of the last bridges to be built before the German surrender. (Bridging, Normandy to Berlin).

was therefore decided to concentrate the bridging effort at one location, near to Artlenburg, within the VIII Corps area. The RE plan envisaged the use of fifteen Field Companies and six Platoons under 11 AGRE, commanded by Colonel R N Foster. In addition 77 Assault Squadron was to use its Buffalos to ferry the Commando Brigade across the river. Much of the engineer task involved the maintenance of main routes and tracks, mine clearance and work on exits on the north bank of the river. The bridging programme included the building of a Class 40 Bailey Pontoon Bridge and a Class 9 FBE Bridge, and the construction and operation of two Storm Boat ferries, a Class 40 ferry and a Class 9 ferry. Despite enemy shelling and frequent air attacks, during one of which VIII Corps Troops Engineers, building the FBE Bridge, lost eight Sappers killed and twenty-two wounded, work proceeded as scheduled. The FBE Bridge was opened only fifteen minutes later than intended and the Class 40 bridge at Artlenburg was completed at noon on the 30th, as planned. (Figure 10.17).

Once across the river, the advance continued, despite stiff opposition in some areas. By 3 May Hamburg had fallen and at 6.30pm on 4 May the surrender of all German forces in north-west Germany was accepted by Field Marshal Montgomery on Lüneburg Heath.

The War in the Far East

Tension in the Far East had increased following the overrunning of large areas of China by the Japanese in the late 1930s and was heightened by the Japanese signing of a tripartite treaty with Germany and Italy in September 1940. The following year, on 8 December, the Japanese air attacks on the

American fleet at Pearl Harbor and on Singapore, Hong Kong and US bases in the Philippines, resulted in a declaration of war by the United States and the United Kingdom. A few days later the United States declared war on Germany and Italy and the die was cast for the expansion of the conflict in Europe to the world-wide arena.

Since this is an account of British bridging operations, little mention has been made of the gallant efforts of our many allies, in particular the Americans and the Chinese. However, details of operations by troops of the Indian Army have been included, since at that time their officers were largely drawn from the British Army, and British and Indian forces were closely integrated during the campaign in Burma. For the same reason the account concentrates on operations in Burma, the scene of the major British effort in the Far East, whilst acknowledging that the war in that theatre spread far beyond Burma, into China, Malaya, Indo-China, Siam (Thailand) and the many islands of South-East Asia. (Figure 10.18).

The war that the Allies now faced was of a very different nature from that to be fought in Europe. The hot and humid climate of the Far East was far removed from the temperate climate of Europe, due in part to the heavy south-west monsoon from mid-May to mid-October. In parts of Burma the annual rainfall exceeded 200 inches, with falls of over 3 inches within 24 hours at times; temperatures in excess of 100°F were commonplace. In addition the infrastructure in many cases was non-existent, particularly in Burma, with its limited railway system and roads that were, in many cases, no more than jungle tracks which disintegrated during the monsoon season. This reflected on the bridging task facing the Sappers of the Royal Engineers and the Sappers and Miners of the Indian Engineers, much of the task being involved with building and replacing timber bridges, improvising crossings and providing ferries over larger rivers. There was thus very much less

Figure 10.18. Australian Sappers watch a Matilda Tank crossing a Small Box Girder Bridge in Papua, New Guinea.

emphasis on the equipment bridging that would be used so extensively during the advance into North-West Europe. Engineer stores, of any sort that might be found in the towns of Europe, did not exist or were in very short supply. And lastly the troops were largely untrained in jungle warfare, with all that that entailed. Without doubt it was a war fought courageously, under conditions of great hardship, almost as much against the severe conditions, the terrain and the climate as against the Japanese.

The Initial Retreat

The surrender of Hong Kong on Christmas Day 1941, the fall of Singapore in February 1942 and the continued withdrawal of Allied troops in the months following, have been extensively written of elsewhere. Needless to say our interest with bridging during this period lay in the field of demolition rather than in the building of new bridges, and during the retreat through Malaya alone over 600 bridges were destroyed in the face of the advancing enemy.

The retreat through Burma took place in early 1942. Road and river communications in the country ran roughly north and south, and passage in an east-west direction was very difficult. (MAP 4). The approach to India in the north-west swept up to the Naga Hills in Assam. The country between the Chindwin and India was particularly inhospitable, with passes as high as 10,000ft. Further south the Chin Hills reached heights of 7,000ft, and parallel with the coastal plane, the Arakan Yomas extended southward at some 2,000ft. There was very little stone for use for road construction other than in the north of the Chin Hills, and the surface soil in much of the lower regions of the Arakan was of poor quality with little stability. The low-lying coastal plain, during the monsoon season muddy and flooded, was cultivated with paddy fields, with very few tracks. The central plain, in the valleys of the great Irrawaddy and its tributaries and the Sittang, was well cultivated and reasonably developed, with a road and rail system serving the major ports, such as Rangoon, to the south. Engineer units, often with little transport, worked unceasingly with whatever tools they could carry, to improve such tracks as there were through the jungle and up through the Chin Hills for our retreating troops. Arrival of the monsoon slowed progress, but at least the monsoon washed away the tracks behind our troops, delaying the pursuing enemy. Again demolitions formed a very important part of our operations and without doubt greatly delayed the Japanese advance towards India; every major bridge on the Japanese line of advance was destroyed, and many, including the Ava Bridge across the Irrawaddy, one of the largest in Asia, were not replaced until after the war.

As our retreating troops approached the Naga Hills, General Sir Harold Alexander's army had been reduced to barely 12,000 men, most of whom were far from fit. However, Indian Army Engineer units had been tasked to improve those tracks in the Imphal Plain leading down to the border with Burma. With the limited time and equipment available the troops worked

MAP 4 ~ THE FAR - EAST CAMPAIGN IN BURMA, 1942-45
Showing towns, rivers etc mentioned in the text

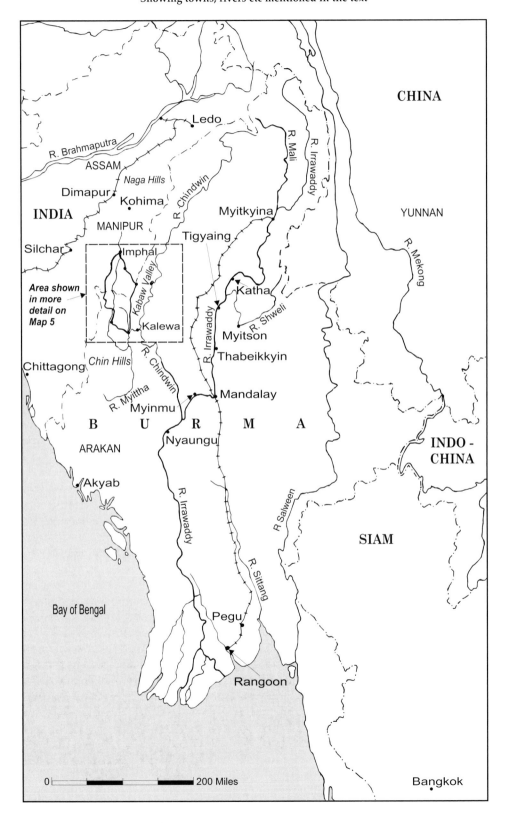

CHINA

Ledo

R. Brahmaputra

ASSAM

Naga Hills

R. Chindwin

R. Mai

R. Irrawaddy

Dimapur

Kohima

Myitkyina

YUNNAN

INDIA

MANIPUR

R. Mekong

Silchar

Tigyaing

Imphal

Area shown
in more
detail on
Map 5

Kabaw Valley

Katha

R. Shweli

R. Irrawaddy

Myitson

Kalewa

Thabeikkyin

Chittagong

Chin Hills

R. Myittha

R. Chindwin

Mandalay

Myinmu

B   U   R   M   A

Nyaungu

ARAKAN

INDO -
CHINA

Akyab

R. Irrawaddy

R. Salween

SIAM

R. Sittang

Bay of Bengal

Pegu

Rangoon

0 |_____| 200 Miles

Bangkok

flat out, their work including the building of a six bay Inglis Bridge across the River Lokchao. Once Alexander's tired troops had crossed the bridge and had reached the safety of the Imphal Plain, the bridge, built by 414 Bridge Construction Section IE, was dismantled and returned to Palel for further use. The initial retreat had come to an end.

Operations in 1943

An advance from Assam into northern Burma was planned to take place after the monsoon of 1942. Unfortunately this operation by the American-Chinese Army under command of General J W Stilwell (US Army), had to be postponed for a number of reasons, but General Sir Archibald Wavell, Commander-in-Chief in India, decided that an attack southward through the Arakan should go ahead. Tracks were extended forward from Chittagong, and many bridges were built using local timbers, including a 400ft span bridge built across the Pruma Chaung by 73 Field Company IE. The campaign finally opened in December 1942, but when the monsoon broke the following May it became necessary to withdraw to our original position and we had achieved little other than to delay the Japanese advance towards India.

Meanwhile, pending a planned advance to the Chindwin by IV Corps, work started on opening up a route forward from Imphal, through Bishenpur to Tiddim, a distance of some 110 miles. The first twenty miles or so to beyond Bishenpur were by local standards reasonably good, but beyond that the track, improved slightly during the retreat from Burma, was little more than a fair-weather Jeep track. In places the track rose to cross hills at 7,000ft, dropping down again to run along sides of valleys with cross slopes of up to 70°. Eventually the track dropped down to the Manipur Valley, some 90 miles from Imphal, and then climbed again, some 2,000ft, to Tiddim, 20 miles further on. (See Map 5, p.263).

A major obstacle on this route proved to be the Manipur River, some 350ft wide at the likely crossing point. The first crossing was achieved using light ferries capable of carrying Jeeps, and, indeed, after enormous efforts, a Jeep track to Tiddim was opened up. In an effort to improve the standard of the route, a 16 ton raft was now built, but rising monsoon waters made all rafts unmanageable and therefore locally made PN Boats were brought up to form a bridge with the original rafts.

By June 1943 the river had risen further and the bridge was swept away. In anticipation of this, plans were already in hand to build a Class 18 Bailey Bridge on the site, as the equipment was just beginning to reach the theatre. Once the water level had dropped sufficiently, work started on the construction of piers for the bridge, using local stone and cement brought forward by mule. Movement forward of the Bailey equipment entailed even more improvements to the route from Imphal, however, and it was therefore decided to build a temporary suspension bridge capable of carrying Jeeps across the river. (Figure 10.19). The heavy cables for the bridge each had to be carried on three Jeeps in tandem over the rough road from Imphal, but the bridge was successfully built by 60 Field Company IE and was opened in August. By December the monsoon was over and the river level had dropped, enabling the PN Boat Bridge to be rebuilt. Further improvements to the road enabled lorries to get through to the site, and stores for the Bailey were brought up so that the Class 18 bridge was completed in January 1944.

The other main route forward from Imphal was that through Palel to Tamu, the route earlier used by General Alexander's retreating Army, and in the spring of 1943 the road was much improved and many timber bridges replaced. The Inglis Bridge originally used to cross the Lokchao had, as already mentioned,

Figure 10.19. A temporary Jeep suspension bridge across the River Manipur, with a PN Boat raft being floated into bridge. (Martin Briggs).

been dismantled. After some difficulty all the parts were reassembled and brought forward from Imphal, and the bridge was finally launched using one bulldozer as a counterweight and another to push the bridge into position. This forward route was vital for the future advance of the Fourteenth Army, and during October 1943, once the monsoons had finished, a vast work force of some 26,000 men, under the command of the General Reserve Engineer Force (GREF), was assembled at Imphal for the task. GREF had originally been set up in the Spring of 1943 to control Engineer work on communications and airfields in Assam, under command of Brigadier S A Westrop. Its new task, to be completed by 1 May 1944, entailed the building of a two-way all-weather road from Imphal to Tamu, some 74 miles long and rising at one point to over 6,000ft.

The force was additionally tasked to carry out bridging and earthworks forward from Tamu and along the Kabaw Valley towards Kalewa, as far as the tactical situation might permit. Many bridges had to be constructed; for the major spans Hamilton Bridging (the Unit Construction Bridge) was used, but many timber bridges were constructed in order to reduce the quantity of equipment to be moved forward. (Figure 10.20). Using a local tree known as the Ind, the bridges were constructed by building timber crib piers and then spanning the gaps with tree trunks, up to 24ft long and 30in

Figure 10.20. *A Hamilton Bridge across the River Lokchao on the Tamu Road.* (Martin Briggs).

in diameter; these were placed side by side before being covered with gravel to form a roadway. Moving the very heavy tree trunks was no easy task, but it was made possible by the use of two Elephant Companies, commanded by Lieutenant Colonel W H Williams, or 'Elephant Bill' as he was known throughout the Fourteenth Army, using a large force of trained elephants that had been employed before the war in the Burma timber industry.

In the Kabaw Valley many **Elephant Bridges** were constructed. Large tree trunks were placed in the stream, parallel to the banks and at 10 to 12ft spacing; further trunks were then laid side by side to span the stream and these were then covered with earth and gravel.

Meanwhile XV Corps had launched a winter offensive down through the Arakan, maintained in due course down the 'Arakan Axis', built in the low-lying country of paddy fields, jungle and forest, intersected by numerous narrow tidal inlets. With a complete lack of road-building materials, the road was built under extreme hardship, surfaced eventually with locally fired bricks from fifty kilns built at intervals alongside the road. A great number of bridges and culverts had to be constructed at the many inlets or chaungs, and over four miles was constructed on timber piles driven by hand-operated piling monkeys.

The Japanese Offensive in Spring 1944

In March 1944 the Japanese launched their spring offensive. They first attacked XV Corps in the Arakan and, although initially they were successful, cutting the 'Arakan Axis', they had not counted on the Allies' use of aircraft to resupply our troops with stores and ammunition. In the end it was the Japanese who had to withdraw, for lack of supplies. At last the British and Indian troops had gained a major success against the Japanese, producing an enormous boost to morale.

Figure 10.21. A temporary Assault Boat cable ferry, replacing the destroyed Bailey Pontoon Bridge crossing the River Manipur.

At the same time the Japanese launched a heavy attack on the central front towards Imphal. This stopped work on the Tamu Road, although by now the road was almost complete and over thirty miles of the Tiddim Road had also been completed. The withdrawal of 17 Division had already been ordered, in order to prevent it being overrun, and the Indian Engineers of the Division had the unenviable task of blowing up many of the bridges and culverts that they had so recently completed, including the Class 18 Bailey Bridge recently built across the River Manipur. (Figure 10.21). By the end of March the Japanese had isolated IV Corps in the Plain of Imphal and a small garrison at Kohima. Units of GREF were therefore tasked to improve the track running west from Imphal to Silchar. Work on the track is worthy of mention because it illustrates the type of task facing the engineers in this inhospitable country. The track, through the densest jungle, was little more than a mule track, extending for some 110 miles and kept open for Jeeps only with constant maintenance. It crossed five ranges of hills at heights up to 6,000ft and included five river crossings, four with suspension bridges, over 300ft long and 150ft above river level. One of the bridges, badly damaged by a Japanese patrol, was repaired by using parts from an old dismantled bridge, straightening damaged slings and splicing broken cables.

Meanwhile XXXIII Corps, at Dimapur, north of Imphal, had been reinforced and by 18 April 1944 had broken through to relieve Kohima, although the area around the town was not finally cleared of enemy troops until late May. The onset of the monsoon delayed the relief of IV Corps at Imphal, but by 22 June advance elements of the two Corps met and the siege was broken. The Japanese offensive had been beaten, with 50,000 of the enemy dead in the hills around Imphal and Kohima. The Allies had won the first of the two decisive battles of the campaign in South-East Asia.

The Allied Offensive of 1944

In July 1944, despite the onset of the monsoon, Vice-Admiral Lord Louis Mountbatten, who had been appointed Supreme Commander of the newly formed South-East Asia Command in August 1943, decided that the advance back into Burma should proceed as rapidly as possible. The plan involved the southerly advance of General Stilwell's forces east of the Irrawaddy, and to the engineers of 36 British Division fell the task of repairing the railway running south to Mandalay. On the first 150 miles of the line they replaced thirty bridges, up to 200ft in length and capable of taking 12 ton axle loads. Eventually a daily lift of some 8,000 ton-miles was achieved on this stretch of line, using Jeeps fitted with rail wheels as locomotives to pull captured enemy rail wagons. The jungle tracks were almost impenetrable during the monsoon and corduroy and brushwood surfacing had to be used for considerable lengths; some 6,000ft of teak-trestle bridging was also built to cross the innumerable streams and gullies. The two major river crossings, across the Shweli, south of Katha, and the Irrawaddy at Tigyaing, were achieved using a variety of equipments, in the later case even sections of captured Japanese pontoons.

On the central front, centred on Imphal, the plan envisaged a two-pronged drive south towards Kalewa (situated at the junction of the Chindwin with the River Myittha), the crossing of the Chindwin at that point and then a drive to the east. 5 Indian Division was to advance down the Tiddim Road and then eastward through Kalemyo to Kalewa. The road, built at great effort the previous winter, by now scarcely existed, having been extensively destroyed during our retreat in the face of the Japanese offensive of March 1944 and then further damaged when the Japanese retreated. The task of opening up the route again and maintaining it for the passage of supply vehicles was prodigious, and gullies and streams were crossed using whatever means were to hand - culverts, elephant bridges, timber trestle bridges and Bailey equipment, now becoming more readily available. In many cases completed bridges were swept away, as further flash floods, brought about by the monsoon, changed watercourses and washed out abutments.

Steadily the advance continued. In September the Manipur, previously crossed in early 1943, was re-crossed, initially with two Class 5 FBE Ferries built in competition by 2 and 21 Field Companies IE, and then later by a Class 24 and subsequently by a Class 40 Mark V Pontoon Raft, all operated as flying ferries, using double 3in SWR as ferry cables. The crossing was achieved in the face of very difficult conditions; current speeds averaged eight knots, at one time reaching twelve knots, to the extent that at one stage the current speed was such that the bollards securing the FBE traveller leads were pulled out, leaving gaping holes in the boat. The Class 24 Bailey raft could carry twelve loaded artillery mules or up to twenty-eight unladen mules; mule screens were found to be unnecessary, but it is said that the General's elephant could not be persuaded to step onto the raft. On a more sombre note, on the last trip of the ferry using a single folding boat, the boat capsized and five men were drowned.

The main route to be developed, however, was that from Tamu, down the Kabaw Valley to join the road from Tiddim at Kalemyo. As recorded previously, the road as far as Tamu had already been completed to two-way Class 30 standard the previous spring, before the Japanese offensive, but the road had been reduced to a morass by the monsoon and by the retreating Japanese. A fair-weather road was therefore cut on a new alignment, bulldozed through the thick jungle at a rate of 3 to 4 miles a day, providing the sole Line of Communication for the Fourteenth Army and carrying a traffic density that built up to 3,000 vehicles a day. Dust now took the place of mud, and the road had to be constantly watered to lay the dust and maintain a hard running surface.

The advance down the Kabaw Valley was lead by 11 East African Division, supplied by air, and on 12 November 1944 their forward troops made contact with units of 5 Indian Division near Kalemyo.

The Crossing of the Chindwin

By 19 November a Brigade from 19 Indian Division crossed the Chindwin at Tonhe, north of Sittaung, using an FBE ferry built by IV Corps Troop Engineers, and by the end of the month the rest of the Division had been ferried across into the bridgehead. By 2 December 11 East African Division reached the Chindwin at Kalewa and the Fourteenth Army was now poised for the major crossing of the river.

Plans for a bridge had been made some weeks before, including those for an alternative Class 12 version, to be used if equipment for the proposed Class 30 bridge should be destroyed or damaged. The equipment had to be transported from the railhead at Dimapur, over 300 miles away, to Imphal, and thence down the Tamu road through the Kabaw Valley to a bridge dump some 26 miles from the bridge site. This in itself was no mean feat, as the hilly roads were without doubt some of the worst in the world. The final approach though the Myittha Gorge to Kalewa was little better and twenty-two timber bridges and nine Baileys had to be built on this 26 mile stretch alone before the bridging lorries could get through to the bridge site, and even then the passage of the lorries was, to say the least, precarious.

By 1 December all stores and personnel had been assembled at the bridge dump, the Bailey equipment comprising four sets of 130ft double/double Bailey Bridge, four Class 40 shore loading Bailey Rafts and three sets of tripartite pontoon equipment. On 3 December units of the East African Division crossed the river using boats and light rafts to set up a bridgehead.

Work started on the bridge on 6 December, under the command of Colonel F Seymour-Williams, Commander of 474 Army Group Engineers, which comprised 67, 76, and 361 Field Companies IE, 332 Field Park Company IE, a company of the Pathan Engineer Battalion IE, and 852 and part of 854

Figure 10.22. Grub Bridge, crossing the Chindwin at Kalewa and built in December 1944.

Bridge Companies IE. The final site chosen for the bridge was moved downstream from that originally intended, because of the attention of Japanese artillery and to avoid any risks during construction. Because of the limited amount of equipment available, it was decided to build the Bailey rafts upstream on the Myittha River, where there was more shore space and also better cover for the bridging vehicles. It was also decided that construction should only take place during daylight hours and at a measured pace. In spite of this the bridge, named Grub Bridge after Colonel Seymour-Williams' small son, was completed by 10 December and, with work on the approaches also completed, the first vehicle crossed at 3pm. (Figure 10.22).

The length of the bridge as actually built has been variously recorded as 1,082ft, 1,095ft and 1,153ft, but even at the shortest recorded length the bridge was certainly, at that time, the longest Bailey Pontoon Bridge built in any theatre during the war, although longer span bridges were to be built subsequently over the Rhine.

Although the moving of the bridge site entailed the construction of a 500 yard causeway across soft sand, built of alternate layers of Sommerfield track and coir matting, the move paid dividends, as the bridge was built without enemy interference. However, on 11 December the BBC announced that a Bailey bridge had been built across the Chindwin, and early on the 12th it was attacked by five Japanese Zero planes. Three of the planes were shot down and one small bomb hit the bridge. Luckily damage was superficial and the bridge was closed for only twenty minutes or so for repairs, but casualties included one dead and two wounded. No further attacks took place.

The bridge was used continuously for over ten weeks, but was then replaced by the Class 18 Falls Bridge, located two miles upstream; it was then dismantled and floated downstream for use on the Irrawaddy and other rivers. Bailey superstructure was used for the Falls Bridge, which took one field company of Indian Engineers, under command of Lieutenant Colonel R St C Davidson RE, five weeks to build. However, it was intended as a more permanent structure than the Grub Bridge, able to withstand a flood tide of 40ft and a flash-flood current speed of 12 knots, and to this end Bailey Tripartite Pontoon piers were replaced by more substantial Eastern Army Boat piers, used to form 80ft single/single Bailey rafts. The centre span of the new bridge had a river clearance of 15ft, to allow free movement of IWT craft on the river.

The Tamu-Kalewa Road

Work on the Tamu-Kalewa Road, which had been abandoned at the time of the Japanese 1944 Spring offensive, had been resumed in October (see Map 5). The road was now to be developed from the fair-weather road used during the advance to the Chindwin to a Class 70 two way all-weather road, south from Tamu, through the Kabaw Valley and the Myittha River gorge to Kalewa, anticipating that this road would take the whole of the maintenance traffic for the forces advancing into Central Burma across the Chindwin. The work was carried out by a special force, working under command of Colonel P O G Wakeham, 145 DCE Works, and involved the maintenance of the existing fair-weather road (to enable forward movement of supplies to continue), the construction of a service road for construction traffic, and the building of the Class 70 road itself. A 100ft trace was cleared through the heavy teak forest, with its dense undergrowth of thorn bush and creepers, and the 22ft 6in wide road was then built 10ft above the flood plain to avoid flooding in the monsoon. Because of the limitations of manpower, machinery and plant, a method of surfacing that was at that time unique for a road project was employed, although it had been used with success on airfields in India. This consisted of grading and compacting the soil at its optimum moisture content and then sealing it with two thicknesses of Prefabricated Bituminous Surfacing. This method of construction proved to be highly successful and the 76 mile road as far as Kyigon was completed by mid-April 1945.

Work then started on the final 18 mile stretch to Kalewa, but because of the topography of the gorge and the lack of plant it was not possible to cut a new trace for the road and consequently construction traffic and L of C traffic had to run over the existing track as it was virtually rebuilt. By now the monsoon had broken and heavy rains ruled out the method of construction used earlier. The road was therefore built using a conventional method of 6in of soling topped by 3in of waterbound limestone; this required approximately 75,000 tons of stone, 45,000 tons of which had to taken from the river bed, broken by hand and hauled to the road site. Work on this final section of road was not completed until 1 August 1945. At one time no less than fifteen engineer units were employed on the project, assisted by thirty-one Indian Pioneer Companies and five General Transport Companies.

MAP 5 ~ THE ROUTES BACK INTO BURMA

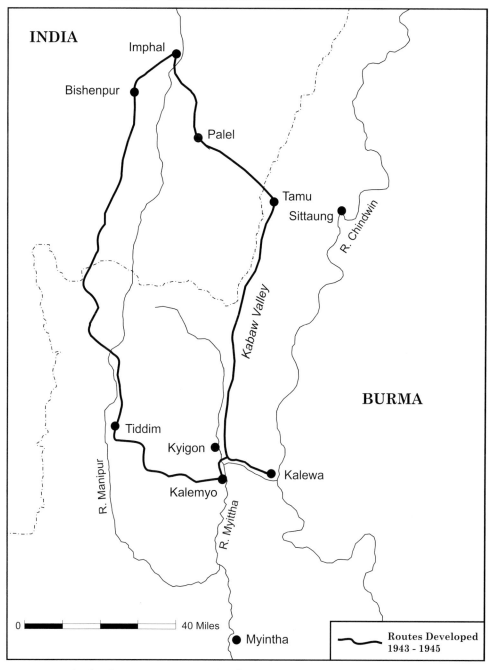

The bridging programme for this project was extensive. In all 145 bridges were built between Tamu and Kalewa, totalling 8,500ft of bridging, although apart from a three span bridge of 240ft length, the spans in general did not exceed 140ft and seventy-two of the bridges were Stock Spans of 40ft and less. The remainder of the bridges were Hamilton Bridges (forty-one in number)

263

and Bailey Bridges (thirty-two in number), the latter being used to the exclusion of the Hamilton Bridge for the last stretch of road from Kyigon because the rapid construction time for the Bailey avoided lengthy road closures.

The Crossing of the Irrawaddy

By the end of December 1944 the Fourteenth Army, under command of Lieutenant General W J Slim, had three firm bridgeheads over the Chindwin and the advance continued apace as the Japanese forces withdrew to defensive positions east of the Irrawaddy. The XV Corps offensive in the Arakan continued, with the ultimate objective of the liberation of Rangoon, whilst, to the east, Slim's plan envisaged a two-prong attack across the Irrawaddy to the north and to the south of the main Japanese forces; the southerly attack had the objective of cutting the Japanese supply lines from Rangoon.

The planned assault crossing of the Irrawaddy, one of the great rivers of the world, was in itself a major operation. The river runs through Burma for over thirteen hundred miles, providing a major highway for trade and communication in the country. The water level and the river width vary considerably according to the timing of the monsoon, but in the post-monsoon period of early 1945 the current was slow and the water level low.

By 14 January 1945 units of XXXIII Corps' 19 Indian Division had established a bridgehead over the river in the region of Thabeikkyin, north of Mandalay, and, despite fierce counterattacks, which went on for almost a month, they managed to hold on to the bridgehead and even extend it. (Figure 10.23). The first major assault was planned to take place in the area of Myinmu, however, where the river width varied from 1,000 to 1,500 yards, with a current speed of 2-3 knots and bank heights as much as 30ft above water level. The crossing by 20 Indian Division, also of XXXIII Corps, was launched near Allagappa, west of Mandalay on the night of 12/13 February. Some of the lighter equipment was flown in by air, but most of the assault equipment had had to be transported from Dimapur, over the long and arduous road system. The equipment assembled included four Class 18 Bailey Rafts, three Class 9 FBE Rafts, some 140 assorted assault boats and thirty-five outboard motors, remarkably little for an assault at Divisional level. However, by 16 February the Division was firmly established on the east bank of the river and was ready to commence further operations.

The assault by IV Corps was launched some one hundred and thirty miles to the south, near Nyaungu, west of Mandalay and just below the junction of the river with the Chindwin. Again most of the ferrying equipment had to be brought forward from Dimapur and much was lost or damaged on the way; in all some 250 lorry loads of stores were assembled in the concentration area. The river was very wide at the three sites selected, with water gaps of 1,200, 1,800, and 3,700 yards respectively, and it was decided to use the upstream site first so that the returning boats could drift downstream to the remaining two sites. On the night of 13/14 February the first wave of infantry successfully crossed in silently paddled assault boats. The second wave was to be ferried over in folding and assault boats fitted with outboard motors, but for various reasons the assault was not launched until dawn was breaking. After their journey forward from the concentration area, several of the outboard motors, dusty, damp with condensation and in some cases damaged, failed to start. Many of the Sapper operators became casualties as the boats were raked by enemy machine-gun fire and the small armada drifted downstream under constant attack. Luckily the majority of the boats were eventually retrieved to the west bank of the river, thanks to many acts of great heroism, and rapid reorganization enabled a further assault to be launched at 10am. This proved to be a complete success. Rafts and ferries, including three Class 40 Bailey Rafts, were now rapidly put into operation and by nightfall the leading Brigade had established a firm bridgehead. By the 15th the majority of 7 Indian Division was safely across the river.

The next phase of the operation involved the crossing of the two mechanized brigades of 17 Indian Division and an armoured brigade. Obviously additional and heavier equipment had to be brought forward and eventually six Class 40 Bailey Rafts, six Class 24 Bailey Rafts, thirteen Class

Figure 10.23. A Bailey raft used to cross the Irrawaddy south of Thabeikkyin. (IWM SE 2004).

9 FBE Rafts and several assorted crafts were working from four landing stages on each bank. An air of competitiveness now developed and a large blackboard appeared, showing the crossing completion rate of the various ferries. Many of the rafts sported coloured pennants as the beaches mushroomed with large notices, such as "Blue Line - Quickest and Safest" or "Red Line - Best Timings". Tanks, armoured cars and every sort of vehicle were rushed across, achieving a crossing rate of up to 100 vehicles an hour, and by the 22nd the whole of 17 Division and the armoured brigade were across the river and ready to advance. Most Corps troops were also safely over the Irrawaddy.

The crossing by the British 2 Division, 25 miles west of Mandalay, did not go so well. The Division had reached the bank of the river opposite Ngazun by late January, but was not ordered to cross until 24 February. The intervening period gave the troops ample time to train and prepare for the crossing and also made available the assault equipment recently used by 19 and 20 Divisions. Unfortunately the pause had given the enemy time to reorganize and, in particular, to cover the most suitable sites that might be used for the crossing. Three initial crossing sites were chosen, with 208 Field Company RE detailed to man the assault and FBE boats. Many of these craft were damaged whilst being brought forward to the river and the bright moonlight ensured that enemy fire disabled many others, resulting in the abandonment of the right-hand crossing. The first wave of troops at the central crossing landed successfully, but enemy fire prevented the return of the boats to the home bank. Luckily the crossing at the third site was more successful and the infantry were ferried across in DUKWs, manned by 5 Field Company RE, until mid-morning of the 25th. (Figure 10.24). By now the building of FBE Rafts was under way and a Bailey Raft was put into action to enable a bulldozer to cross and improve exits from the river. All manner of craft were now brought into action at the central crossing site and by the evening of the 27th most units of the Division had successfully crossed the river.

Figure 10.24. *Crossing the Irrawaddy at Ngazun at first light on 26 February 1945, from the original by David Cobbs.* (Royal Engineers HQ Mess, Chatham).

Crossing the River Shweli

The concentration of forces for the next phase of the advance against the Japanese now required a crossing of the River Shweli by the British 36 Division. The Division had been operating in the north with the Allied Force under command of Lieutenant General D I Sultan (US Army), who had replaced General Stilwell in October 1944. In January the Division had made contact with patrols of 19 Indian Division and soon after had forced a crossing of the river by ferrying at Myitson. To maintain the pace of their advance, however, it was decided that a bridge across the river was needed and the site chosen involved an initial crossing to an island with a 540ft bridge, and construction of a further 243ft bridge to the far bank. The bridges were an extreme example of improvisation, since the Division was being maintained by air from Ledo, some 300 miles to the north, and no equipment or materials could be made available. The task was given to 15 Engineer Battalion IE, armed only with its unit tools and equipment, one compressor saw, and a supply of steel rods with which to make spikes. Teak was felled locally and used to make no less than forty-five single-bent trestles, all to be placed without the help of any mechanical equipment. Working flat out the troops completed the bridge, named Mountbatten Bridge, in eight working days.

Another bridge of note built across the Shweli was a Bailey Suspension Bridge built by American troops in March 1945. (Figure 10.25). In late 1942 General Stilwell, with the mission of supporting China but now without a land supply route to that country, had drawn up plans for a road to run from Ledo, in the Assam Province of India, south and east across North Burma to join up with the old Burma Road east of Bhamo, and thence into China. Work on the Ledo Road started in December 1942, but the proposed route went through some of the most hostile terrain in the world. (Figure 10.26).

Figure 10.25. The longest Bailey Suspension Bridge built during the war, crossing the River Shweli. (IWM 3690).

Figure 10.26. Working on the Ledo Road; typical conditions encountered during road building operations in Burma. (IWM 4409).

Resulting difficulties, compounded by an initial lack of equipment, atrocious monsoon weather conditions, and of course Japanese opposition, particularly around Myitkyina (the enemy main supply base in northern Burma, which sat astride the proposed route of the road) meant that the final link up with the old Burma Road was not made until after the monsoon of 1944. Many bridges were built during the construction of the road, including a number of American H-20 bridges, favoured by Brigadier General L A Pick, in charge of construction from October 1943, because the bridge required less cargo space than the Bailey, which had by then replaced the H-20 as standard US Army equipment. Bailey was used, however, for some of the bridges built towards the end of the campaign, including a 560ft bridge built across the River Mogaung in October 1944 by 1304 Engineer Aviation Battalion.

The Bailey Suspension Bridge, already mentioned, was built by B Company of 209 Engineer Combat Battalion in March 1945 and was dedicated to US Army Engineers lost in the fight for Myitkyina. The bridge is variously reported as being 440ft and 450ft long and was the longest BSB built during the war.

Formal completion of the Ledo Road was announced by newly promoted Major General Pick in May 1945, when he described the task as the toughest job ever given to US Army Engineers in wartime. The road was subsequently renamed the Stilwell Road, at the suggestion of Chiang Kai-shek.

Figure 10.27. An improvised timber bridge, subsequently swept away by a sudden flood. (IWM 287670).

Bridging Improvisation

This is probably a good point to pay tribute to the role of improvised bridging during the whole of the campaign in the Far East. With shortages of equipment of all types, due to supply problems caused by the most difficult terrain and by a high rate of equipment attrition caused by extreme climatic conditions, a much greater reliance had to be placed upon the use of whatever was to hand to provide the bridges required by our advancing troops. (Figure 10.27). Many straightforward timber trestle bridges were built, but other examples of improvisation include:

> a. Construction of tarpaulin and bamboo mat rafts capable of carrying all divisional loads except Class 12.
> b. Construction of larger decked rafts using American Ranger or British Reconnaissance Boats built into a bamboo framework and wholly wrapped in a 40ft square tarpaulin.
> c. Use of two layers of square -mesh track and FBE boats (without FBE superstructure) to provide a Class 5 bridge.
> d. The building of a 200ft Jeep bridge using barrels lashed on top of a timber superstructure.
> e. Use of jungle vines to construct aerial ropeways and suspension bridges.
> f. Design and construction of a range of suspension bridges, including, for example, a 200ft span Class 9 bridge built in New Guinea, which had a timber stiffening truss.
> g. Construction of light footbridges made entirely of bamboo, the bindings being of bamboo strip.
> h. Many variations of the Indian Mat Bridge design mentioned in an earlier chapter.

Certainly without such extensive improvisation the rate of advance of the Allied troops would have been seriously affected.

The Advance to Rangoon

With the Fourteenth Army across the two major river lines the advance continued and despite fierce opposition from the Japanese, Mandalay fell on 21 March. However, with seven divisions to be maintained and the very poor state of road communications from Manipur, the bulk of supplies, including engineer stores, had to be brought in by air. Thus if the campaign in Burma was to be brought to a rapid conclusion it was essential to capture Rangoon and establish a seaborne line of communications before the onset of the monsoon. The advance on Rangoon, some 350 miles to the south, began.

Prior to the monsoon most of the rivers were low and caused few bridging problems, although as our forces progressed southward they were confronted with wider gaps and major demolitions. Thus for the advance of IV Corps alone, from Meiktila to Rangoon, the estimated requirement of 1,900 tons of Bailey equipment proved to be almost correct. As the leading troops reached the outskirts of Pegu it was found that all three bridges across the river had been prepared for demolition. A battalion of the lead brigade managed to ford the river just before the bridges were blown and, although a Bailey was put across the remains of one of the demolished bridges, its approaches became unusable as the monsoon broke in earnest. A Bailey Pontoon Bridge was also put across, but this was washed away the next night by a sudden river spate. Finally, on 2 May, a Bailey was built over the demolished centre span of the main railway bridge, and once it had been decked and the remaining rails removed, the whole of 17 Division was able to cross. The Bailey equipment had been flown into the forward airfield by C47 Dakota transport aircraft. However, by 3 May the monsoon had put the airfield out of action and 48 Brigade were held up by a demolished bridge 32 miles from Rangoon until a site could be found that could be crossed with the limited equipment still available.

Meanwhile, operations in the Arakan had continued successfully, freeing 26 Indian Division for an airborne and seaborne assault on Rangoon. The assault was planned for 2 May, but the day before, a reconnaissance plane spotted the news, written on a roof by released prisoners of war, that the enemy had left. The assault nevertheless went ahead, hampered only by the torrential rains of the monsoon that had just broken, and occupation of the town was completed by the 5th, just as news came that the war in Europe had ended.

The End of the War

Units of 26 Division met up with those of the advancing XXXIII Corps on 18 May and at the end of the month a major reorganization took place in preparation for the liberation of Malaya. In Burma the advance continued on all fronts, containing and mopping up the enemy forces who, in their retreat, carried out large numbers of demolitions. In the remaining three months of the war 19 Indian Division alone had to build thirty-six Bailey Bridges, nineteen timber bridges and a 220ft span suspension bridge for mules and infantry. They also built the first example of a 200ft suspension bridge that had been designed locally so that all parts could be carried by man-pack; the bridge took four hours to erect.

On 6 and 7 August the Allies dropped atomic bombs on Hiroshima and Nagasaki, and on the 14th the Japanese Government unconditionally surrendered. After nearly four years the War in the Far East was finally over.

CHAPTER ELEVEN

The Postwar Era

Postwar Expansion at Christchurch

The end of World War II relieved the pressure of work at Christchurch to some extent, enabling a major reorganization to be put in hand. This culminated in March 1946, when the three wartime establishments at Christchurch, that is the Experimental Bridging Establishment, the Experimental Demolition Establishment, and the Experimental Tunnelling Establishment, were merged to form the Military Engineering Experimental Establishment, or MEXE. Brigadier G R Meekan DSO OBE became the first Chief Superintendent of the new Establishment on 22 March 1946, taking over from Colonel G H Hunt MC, who had been Superintendent of the EBE, successively as Major, Lieutenant Colonel and then Colonel, since September 1941. The new Establishment became responsible for research and development of all engineer equipment for the Sappers, expanding its traditional role of bridging to include equipments necessary for the building of military roads and airfields, for the supply of fuel, water and power in the field, for minewarfare and demolitions, and to meet the ever increasing interest in mechanical handling and earth moving plant. To enable the Establishment to fulfil this requirement, it was reorganized in the late 1940s into four groups, the Bridging Group, the Roads and Airfields Group, the Electrical and Mechanical Group, and the Explosives Group, which worked closely with the Armament Research Establishment at Fort Halstead, Kent.

In 1946 Bailey was knighted for his valuable contribution to the Allied victory, and as Sir Donald became the Assistant Director of MEXE; in 1957 he was to become the first civilian Director of the Establishment. He was further honoured in 1946 by the award of the Honorary Degree of Doctor of Engineering by the University of Sheffield, his old University, an honour of which he was justifiably proud.

The Postwar Programme

Bridging equipment developed during the war had been designed primarily to carry vehicles at a maximum of Class 40 and of width between 8 and 9ft. The flexibility of Bailey enabled greater loads to be carried without much sacrifice of efficiency and improvised methods had been evolved to increase the roadway width of this and some other equipments. However continual increases in vehicle weights and dimensions, coupled with lessons learnt during the war, emphasised the need for new and more efficient equipments, and to this end a series of War Office Specifications (or Military Characteristics) were issued soon after the war, centred on Class 15/24 and 50/70 equipments. Major items in the new equipment programme included Class 15/24 and Class 70 floating assault bridges, Class 24 and Class 70 fixed or dry support bridges, and a Class 50/70 raft, together with ancillary items such as a bridging crane and a high speed tug. The new requirements for tank bridges are dealt with in Chapter Thirteen.

Work on the new equipments was slowed down initially by the reorganization at Christchurch mentioned above and also by the general postwar reorganization of the civilian technical staff of the Ministry of Supply. Nevertheless a start was made on the design of the Class 15/24 floating bridge and the Class 70 fixed bridge in 1946, and during this period valuable work was completed on a number of projects that had been in hand at the end of the war, such as modification of SWBB for the floating role and finalization of the design for the airportable Mark 5 Motor Tug.

New Structural Materials

Before considering the new equipments in more detail, mention must be made of the impact of new materials on bridge design. Towards the end of the war the supply position with regard to aluminium alloys had improved considerably, and consideration was given to their use for those bridging components in which a worthwhile saving of weight might be expected. For example the Mark 2 version of the Close Support Raft used light alloy in a minor way by introducing cast alloy deck panels and welded light alloy roadbearers. The main advantage in using light alloys is that whilst the density is roughly one third that of steel, even in the late 1940s alloys were available with strengths 60% higher than that of mild steel. On the other hand, the lower modulus of elasticity of light alloys is a disadvantage, which means for example that to prevent excessive deflection, an alloy girder requires a greater depth of section than would a steel girder similarly loaded. To illustrate possible savings in weight, experimental light alloy transoms for SWBB were fabricated just after the war; the transom weights were as follows:

High Tensile Steel Transom............650lb
Riveted Light Alloy Transom.........420lb
Welded Light Alloy Transom.........308lb.

The use of light alloy for the transoms and also for the stringers in SWBB, together with the possible reduction in thickness of decking resulting from increased stringer strength, showed a weight saving of 1.14 tons per 10ft bay of bridge. This reduction in dead weight enabled most permissible spans to be extended by 10ft.

Another disadvantage of using aluminium alloys is that they are, in general, softer than steel, and thus light alloy components are more easily damaged. They are also much more expensive, pound for pound, than components made in alloy steels. A whole range of new techniques had to be developed for fabricating the alloys; some are more suitable for argon-arc welding than for metallic-arc welding and trials using both methods were conducted. Some are not weldable at all because of a high copper content, and various methods of cold riveting had to be developed. Cold forming is very much more difficult with light alloys than with steel because of a much reduced plastic range. On the other hand light alloys can easily be extruded, enabling complicated sections to be produced for specific uses.

War time development of alloy steels had not been neglected. In the manufacture of the Bailey Bridge during the war, use was made of a high tensile steel having a working strength some 50% higher than mild steel and with good weldability. Developments in manufacturing techniques now made available even stronger steels for use in the new bridges, with strengths up to 85% higher than mild steel. The possibility of using other materials such as plastics and resin-impregnated timber was also considered, and a series of minor trials investigated their potential usage.

An Experimental Class 18 Raft

Taking advantage of more readily available supplies, the use of aluminium alloys in bridging was taken one stage further in late 1945, with the design of an experimental Class 18 Raft, very similar in concept to the Close Support Raft (CSR), but using, for the first time, light alloy for the main girders of a bridge or raft. The girder panels were of trussed form and of riveted construction, pinned together at top and bottom of each panel to form four continuous girders for the raft superstructure; the ramps included tapered panels and were linked together using normal CSR balancing gear; cast alloy deck panels were used, similar to those of the CSR Mark 2. (Figure 11.1). The Class 18 Raft used four bi-partite Mark 5 Pontoon piers and although it was

Figure 11.1. An experimental Class 18 Raft, similar to the Class 9 Close Support Raft, but with trussed and riveted light alloy girders. (IWM 3979).

not developed beyond the prototype stage because of the end of the war, it provided valuable experience in the use of light alloys for military bridge construction.

An Experimental Light Alloy Pontoon

Another experimental equipment making full use of the new materials was the Light Alloy Pontoon. This was developed towards the end of the war for use with standard bridging equipments, such as Bailey and the CSR, in the Far Eastern Theatre. The intention was to provide a pontoon that could not only be carried on normal road transport, but also in the transport aircraft and gliders likely to be used in that theatre. The complete pontoon was formed from three distinct sections, the bow sections, the intermediate sections, and the centre sections. The short bow section nested into the intermediate section during transport, the two sections weighing about 600lb and being about 10ft long when coupled. The centre sections had folding sides to reduce the overall depth of the section for transport, using rubber seals to maintain water-tightness; the 11ft long centre sections weighed about 800lb. The connecting bolts were of steel, suitably plated, but otherwise aluminium alloy was used throughout; the framework was made from extruded or rolled sections, using light alloy castings where necessary, and the pontoon was covered with 16g aluminium sheeting. (Figure 11.2 and Appendix B).

Floating bay piers for Class 40 BPB comprised two centre sections, with intermediate and bow sections at either end, three such piers being used for each 42ft bay of bridge. Landing bay piers used an extra centre section, six such piers being used to support a Class 40 landing bay. Over 150 centre sections were manufactured. together with about 130 intermediate and bow sections, but introduction of the pontoon on a large scale was pre-empted by development of the new Assault Floating Bridges.

Figure 11.2. *An experimental light alloy folding pontoon pier; the 50ft long pier is rigged to take the Close Support Raft superstructure.* (IWM 4246).

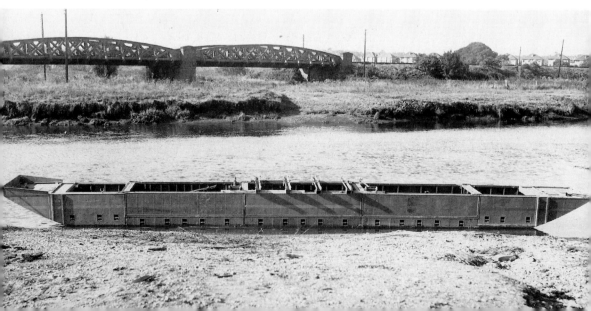

The New Floating Equipments

The Bailey Pontoon Bridge was an excellent bridge in many ways, and indeed a Class 80 floating version of Standard Widened Bailey was produced in 1947. However it was, for example, much slower to construct than the American Treadway Bridge and could not really be considered an assault bridge. The Class 50/60 raft developed for the Rhine crossings had the distinct advantage that the bridge girder panels were carried folded down on the pontoon deck, and merely had to be raised on hinges into the vertical position before being coupled up to the panels on the next pontoon. This principle could obviously be applied to the construction of a whole bridge as well as to that of a raft, as demonstrated in 1950 by an Engineer Regiment in BAOR and described in Chapter 8. It was to be the construction principle used for the new Class 15/24 and Class 70 floating assault bridges.

The Light Assault Floating Bridge

In early 1947 preliminary designs for a new Class 24 floating bridge were submitted to the Engineer-in-Chief for his consideration. The requirement called for a rapidly built bridge capable of carrying the transport of an Infantry Division and light SP anti-tank artillery. In November the basic concept for a through bridge with panel girders supported on bipartite piers was accepted and this early concept was eventually developed into the Class 30 Light Assault Floating Bridge, or LAFB, with Mr B T Boswell as the Project Officer; Bruce Boswell was a wartime Sapper officer and later became Head of the Establishment at Christchurch.

The concept was remarkably simple; a 3 ton GS vehicle carried two pontoons, 17ft 6in long and 5ft 9in wide, which could be coupled up to form a bipartite pier, incorporating the roadway as part of the deck of the pontoons. Two further pontoons, producing a second pier, were carried on a special single axle trailer towed by the 3 tonner. (Figure 11.3). In bridge the

Figure 11.3. The Light Assault Floating Bridge transport load. (IWM 8098).

piers were spaced at 12ft 6in centres, so that each complete lorry and trailer load provided 25ft of floating bridge. A pontoon panel was hinged to each pontoon deck and once raised into position formed part of the main distribution girder, the pontoon panels being alternated with plain panels, which positioned the piers at their correct spacing. Deck sections were then positioned to span between the gunwales of adjacent pontoons, and 2ft 6in wide footwalks were also provided. The distributing girders were at 13ft 6in centres when raised into position, which gave a roadway width of 11ft between kerbs. At each end of bridge four close coupled pontoon piers formed a landing bay raft, which supported the offshore end of a 27ft landing bay, constructed from plain and pontoon panels, transoms, deck sections and various minor special parts. (Figure 11.4).

LAFB was the first military bridge to use hydraulic articulators to adjust the height of its landing bays, the articulators enabling the landing bays to articulate freely under slow changes of water level, but to lock automatically whenever a vehicle crossed the bridge. The articulators could be manually operated and were inserted into the top chord of the distributing girders at each end of bridge, between the bridge proper and the landing bay. The bridge made full use of the new materials, the pontoon being made of light alloy throughout, whilst the landing bay transoms were formed from light

Figure 11.4. The Light Assault Floating Bridge at the RSME, Chatham. (IWM 9978).

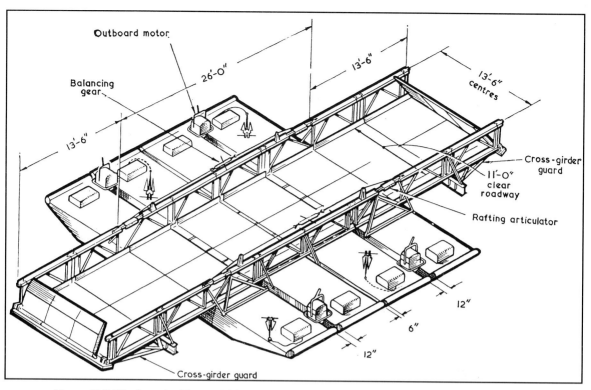

Figure labels: Outboard motor, Balancing gear, 26'-0", 13'-6", 13'-6" centres, 13'-6", Cross-girder guard, 11'-0" clear roadway, Rafting articulator, 12", 6", 12", Cross-girder guard

Figure 11.5. *The four pier Class 12 Light Assault Raft. (Military Engineering Vol III Part VII - 1964).*

alloy extrusions (see Appendix B); the chords and diagonals of the 6ft 3in x 3ft panels were manufactured from high tensile steel.

A **Light Assault Raft** (LAR) could also be formed with the equipment, using four close coupled piers for a Class 12 raft (Figure 11.5) or seven for the Class 30 raft. The hydraulic articulators were not used to raise and lower the raft ramps, since they were comparatively slow to operate. A balancing gear was used instead, together with simple rafting articulators through which panel pins were inserted to take the load once ramps were in the correct position. Rafts were propelled by standard outboard motors.

Mock-up trials were held at MEXE in 1948, but it was not until 1954 that full scale troop trials were held, in BAOR and in Canada. Further inevitable delays followed and the first nine sets of equipment were not delivered until March 1958. During a demonstration at the SME, a 350ft bridge was built in 65 minutes, but a reasonable construction time for a normally trained squadron, working under similar conditions, was considered to be about 1¾ hours. The equipment was carried by the Light Platoon of the RASC Bridge Company, which comprised twenty 3 ton truck and trailer loads, capable of building a 460ft bridge, four Class 30 rafts or five Class 12 rafts.

The equipment was designed for erection in successive stages in separate and well dispersed areas, relying upon the use of at least two 7 ton bridging cranes, dozers to prepare erection sites and approaches, and motor tugs to handle the two pier rafts once in the water. The relationship between the various areas is shown diagrammatically in Figure 11.6. In the Bridge Marshalling Harbour the RE unit took over responsibility for the equipment and vehicles from the RASC Bridge Company, and assembled the bridging cranes and other plant. In the Preassembly Area the pontoons were assembled into piers, using the bridging cranes; the truck-borne pontoons were grounded for subsequent assembly, whilst the trailer-borne pontoons were coupled up, centred on their trailers, and towed away to be out rigged. In the Outrigging Area the superstructure was erected on the pontoons, the two pontoon girder panels being raised into the vertical position and two plain girder panels being added, diametrically opposite and one on each side of the pontoon pier. The Bridge Site was of course the length of river and river bank within which the bridge or ferry was to be built and used. The pontoon piers were launched directly into the water from their trailers and coupled up into two pier rafts, prior to being coupled into bridge.

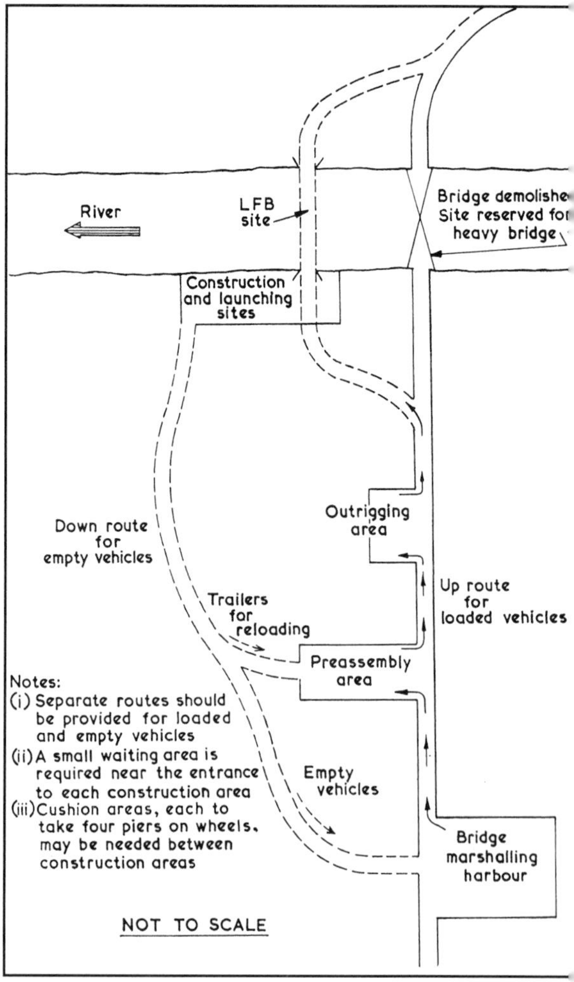

The Outrigging Area was kept well away from the river to minimize the concentration of vehicles on the river bank, and in suitable circumstances the three assembly areas could be totally or partially co-located. A monorail system for transportation of outrigged pontoon

Figure 11.6. *Diagrammatical layout of the LAFB construction areas.* (Military Engineering Vol III Part VII - 1964).

piers to the river bank launching site was developed for use in cases of difficult terrain.

Although LAFB was designed primarily for the assault role, it was superseded in this role by the advent of the amphibious bridging equipments in the 1960s. It then became known as the Light Floating Bridge or LFB, and the raft as the Light Raft or LR. During the early 1960s eight glass reinforced plastic versions of the pontoon were manufactured, mainly to assess the vulnerability to damage and ease of repair of this comparatively new material; most of these pontoons were sent to the Far East for assessment in a tropical climate.

The Heavy Ferry

Work on the Class 50/70 Heavy Ferry, or HFy, started in early 1947, with Major W A Vinycomb MC as Project officer. Preliminary work had already been carried out during the previous year on a timber decked steel pontoon incorporating an in-built propulsion unit in the form of a Hotchkiss Cone Propeller Unit. It was decided that a bow loading raft had many advantages over a side loading raft such as the Class 50/60 Raft, and by 1950 a pilot model of such a raft was under construction at MEXE. By this time however the design of the heavy gunned Conqueror Tank (FV 214) was well advanced, and the required load capacity of the raft was increased to Class 80.

In its final form, as the Class 80 Heavy Ferry, the raft comprised three distinct pontoon units. (Figure 11.7 and Appendix B). The light alloy **Main Pontoon** was designed to carry any load up to Class 80, and had a hydraulically operated 20ft ramp permanently hinged at the bow end of the pontoon. The pontoon had a square stern and four such pontoons could thus be coupled together to provide the main body of the ferry, 64ft long by 15ft wide, with a 20ft ramp at both ends. The **Buoyancy Pontoons** were 16ft long and were merely needed to provide additional buoyancy for the ferry, and their flush decks could only carry light stores. The **Propulsion Pontoons** provided the means of propelling the ferry at speeds of 6 knots laden or 7½ knots when unladen. The water jet propulsion system finally chosen was the Gill system, driven by a Rolls Royce B80 Mark 5L engine. An axial flow pump drew water through an inlet grating in the bottom of the pontoon into a U-tube, and then forced it out again through guide vanes as a jet, 15° to the horizontal. The system had the overriding advantages of a

Figure 11.7. Components of the Heavy Ferry. (Military Engineering Vol III Part IX - 1964).

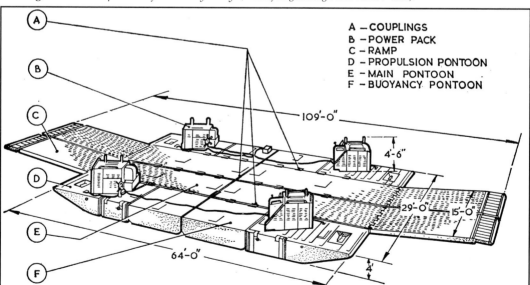

A — COUPLINGS
B — POWER PACK
C — RAMP
D — PROPULSION PONTOON
E — MAIN PONTOON
F — BUOYANCY PONTOON

considerable saving in draught and 360° steering.

The various pontoons were connected together in the water, using spring loaded self actuating linkages, to form a free ranging ferry with a 15ft wide roadway, 109ft long from ramp end to ramp end. The strength of the ramps and their hydraulics was such that a ferry could operate with a laden 3 ton GS cargo truck positioned on each pair of ramps, cantilevered out, leaving room on the deck for a further four such vehicles.

Four 10 ton GS trucks were used to transport the main pontoon units, each carrying one of the propulsion pontoons and towing a main pontoon with its ramp folded over, on a special four wheel, 5 ton trailer, FV 2861A, from which the pontoon could be launched directly into the water; two 3 ton GS trucks were used to carry the four buoyancy pontoons. The propulsion and buoyancy pontoons could be unloaded by bridging crane, or towed off of the trucks using special unloading ramps; the pontoons could then be lifted into the water or towed or sledged across country by dozer and pushed into the water, since all were provided with thick bottom skins and towing lugs.

The Heavy Ferry went a long way towards solving the problems of getting heavy support weapons across a water obstacle in time to enable assaulting infantry to repulse an enemy counterattack. (Figure 11.8). The ferry could be built in an hour with good conditions, if necessary well away from the main axis of the attack, and could then be brought into operation exactly where and when required. It was capable of carrying six 3 ton GS trucks, three 10 ton GS trucks, or of course the main battle tank, and could, with good traffic control and vehicle discipline, achieve ten round trips an hour across a 400ft water gap carrying a single tank, or eight round trips with a mixed load of vehicles. Despite the start made on the design of the equipment in 1947, troop trials were not completed until 1955, and the first off production raft was not available until the end of 1957.

Figure 11.8. Heavy Ferry trials on Southampton Waters, using a Centurion Tank as the test load. (IWM 12876).

Figure 11.9*. Heavy Assault Floating Bridge trials at Class 100, using a Conqueror Tank on its transporter.* (IWM 18252).

The Heavy Assault Floating Bridge

The third major wet support equipment developed in the immediate postwar period was the Heavy Assault Floating Bridge, or HAFB, although design work did not start until the early 1950s, some time after that on LAFB and HFy. The small design team responsible for development of the bridge was led by Dr Philip Bulson, a wartime Sapper officer who eventually became Head of the Establishment at Christchurch from 1974 to 1985. HAFB was intended to supplement the other two equipments, with a requirement, at Class 80, to carry all divisional transport and, additionally, to carry Class 100 loads with some restriction on vehicle spacing and at reduced current speeds. In fact the production equipment was rated as Class 80(tracked) or Class 100(wheeled), without speed restrictions. (Figure 11.9).

The basic concept of the bridge was that of a scaled up LAFB, the main difference from LAFB being the introduction of a much larger pontoon pier to take the far greater loads. (Figure 11.10). The piers were spaced at 17ft centres compared with 12ft 6in for LAFB, and a tripartite pier was used; the centre pier was of aluminium alloy construction, whilst the two bow pontoons were made of mild steel, although in early prototypes plywood construction was used for these bow pontoons. The bridge was again of the

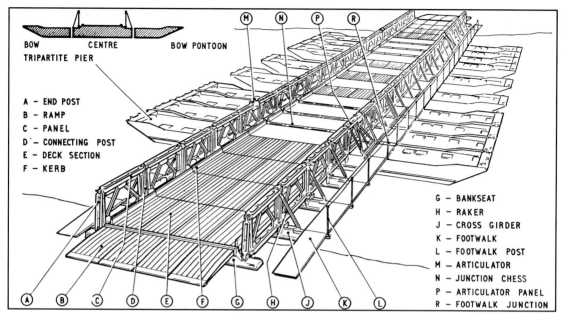

BOW   CENTRE   BOW PONTOON

TRIPARTITE PIER

A – END POST
B – RAMP
C – PANEL
D – CONNECTING POST
E – DECK SECTION
F – KERB

G – BANKSEAT
H – RAKER
J – CROSS GIRDER
K – FOOTWALK
L – FOOTWALK POST
M – ARTICULATOR
N – JUNCTION CHESS
P – ARTICULATOR PANEL
R – FOOTWALK JUNCTION

Figure 11.10. Heavy Assault Floating Bridge components. (HAFB Handbook - 1961).

through type, with the distributing girders now spaced at 18ft centres, to give a 15ft roadway width between kerbs. The landing bay was increased in length to 37ft 9in, its offshore end supported by four of the tripartite pontoons; as with LAFB, hydraulic articulators were used, accommodating a rise and fall of river level from 6ft 6in below to 2ft 6in above bank seat level.

The other main difference between LAFB and HAFB was that HAFB used aluminium alloy for the girder panels, the first British bridge so to do. (See Appendix B). Previously, girder panels had been manufactured in steel, because welding was the most effective way of transmitting the heavy loads from the jaw blocks to the main members of the pin-connected panels, and welding of the aluminium alloys then available was not practical. In the case of HAFB however, considerable deflection of the main girders was essential if adequate buoyancy was to be obtained from the pontoon supports within the 100ft vehicle centres of convoy loading. To obtain this deflection with a steel girder would have meant excessive pin hole clearances or very shallow, and therefore heavier, panels. The problem was avoided by using aluminium alloy panels, the alloy having a much lower Young's Modulus than steel and thus allowing the girder to deflect to a greater extent.

The HAFB centre pontoon was carried on a truck GS, 10 ton, bridging, 6 x 6. The same vehicle towed a four wheeled, 5 ton trailer, FV 2861A, previously used with the Heavy Ferry, on which were loaded the two bow pontoons. (Figure 11.11). A bridge set comprised eighteen of these floating bay units, together with two additional 10 ton trucks and trailers carrying the stores for

282

Figure 11.11. *An outrigged pier of the Heavy Assault Floating Bridge, on its four-wheeled trailer.* (IWM 31864).

the landing bays. The complete bridge set could provide a bridge 322ft long between the bank seats.

In general the method of construction followed that used for LAFB, much of the work being completed in an preassembly area, using bridging cranes, and then in an outrigging area, well before H hour. This avoided troop and vehicle concentrations at the actual bridge site, although of course the landing bays had to be constructed on site. Construction was rapid and on operational training exercises 200ft river bridges were constructed in about 1 hour 20 minutes, by day and by night.

The Certificate of Approval of Design was issued in early 1959 and the bridge was in service with our troops in Germany in 1962. By 1960 however the writing was on the wall for Britain's immediate post war tank, the FV 200 series Conqueror, which, at 68 tons, had come into service in 1955 as the heaviest and biggest gun-tank ever produced in the UK. Comparatively few of the tanks built and design of the 54 ton Chieftain was well under way by 1960, the new tank coming into service in 1966. Thus even before the steel bow pontoons for HAFB were in full scale production, a Class 60 version of the bridge was being considered. This version proposed a shortened tripartite pontoon pier, using the normal centre pontoon and two shortened bow pontoons. The pontoon pier was to be preassembled well away from the bridge site and towed to the river as a complete unit, using the standard trailer to form an articulated load on the tractor and semi-trailer principle. A Preassembled Landing Bay, or PALB, was also proposed, using flip over sides to reduce the width for road travel; this was to be towed in a similar fashion, using the same 'fifth wheel' principle.

This modified version of HAFB would have reduced the need for bridging cranes and eliminated that for a preassembly area; it would also have speeded up construction times considerably. However, although a prototype PALB was indeed manufactured at the ROF Woolwich and preliminary trials were carried out at MEXE, the advent of amphibious bridging in the early 1960s put paid to the idea. Although only a prototype, the fabrication of PALB was treated with considerable interest at MEXE, because it was the first bridging equipment to make extensive use of the new aluminium-zinc-magnesium alloys currently under investigation. The equipment was manufactured from extrusions and plate in the French alloy Superalumag T35, welded throughout and relying on the excellent recovery properties of the heat affected zone after welding. Further details of this group of alloys are given in the next chapter. Very soon after the development of a Class 60 version of HAFB ceased, 'Assault' was dropped from the equipment's name, as had been the case with LAFB, and it became simply the Heavy Floating Bridge, or HFB.

The Heavy Girder Bridge

As has already been mentioned, the main thrust of equipment development at Christchurch during the immediate post war period was directed towards providing new floating bridges for the Sappers, to overcome the shortcomings of Bailey used in that role. The Bailey Bridge was to be used for many years to come as the standard fixed bridge, albeit in an improved version, but its big brother, the Heavy Girder Bridge, developed in the late 1940s, was to prove an important addition to the range of bridging equipments available.

Following the decision to develop the new range of FV 200 armoured vehicles, a General Staff Specification for a Class 100 fixed bridge was issued in May 1946. Many different design alternatives were considered before the prototype design, upon which the present version of the Heavy Girder Bridge was based, was selected in early 1948. Trials at MEXE on two 150ft prototypes commenced in mid 1950 and by 1955 the first 40 production sets of bridge had been issued, with 60 more sets on order. Thus once again the re-equipment cycle was about ten years.

Major Eric Longbottom, who had served at Christchurch during the war, was offered a post at MEXE on demobilization from the Army in 1946, and was largely responsible for the design of the new bridge, taking over from Mr Pitt H Jones. As finally developed the bridge was a multi-truss panel girder bridge, using Bailey type panels 12ft 6in long and 6ft deep, and each weighing 1,445lb. It was designed to carry the FV 200 series vehicles on their transporters, using single storey construction with single, double, or triple trusses, according to the span (Figure 11.12). Trusses could also be chord reinforced if required, increasing the maximum possible single storey span to 187ft. Double storey girders were not used, to avoid the possibility of top

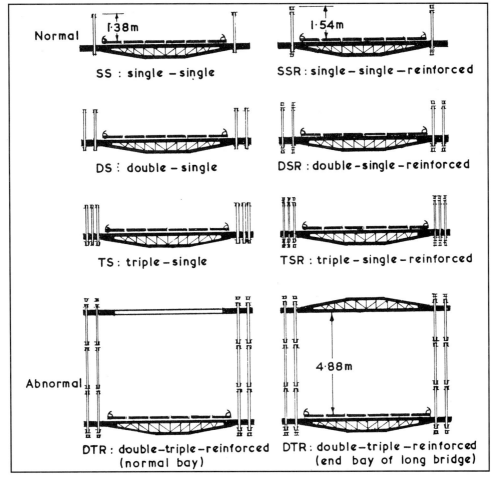

Figure 11.12. *Construction configurations for the Heavy Girder Bridge.* (Military Engineering Vol III Part IV - 1979).

chord buckling. However such buckling was avoided with triple storey construction by the use of overhead bracing, and a 300ft span at Class 100(wheels)/80(tracks) was achievable using double/triple (reinforced) construction. (Figure 11.13). The excessive weights involved introduced

Figure 11.13. *A double/triple reinforced Heavy Girder Bridge under the new test rig at Christchurch.* (IWM 25976).

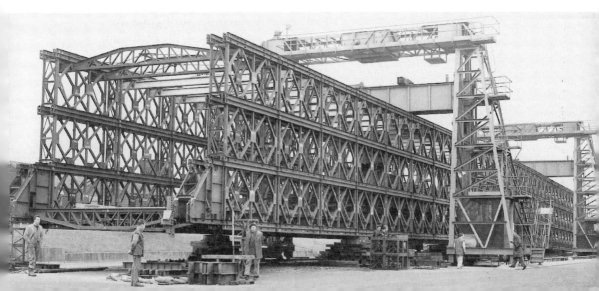

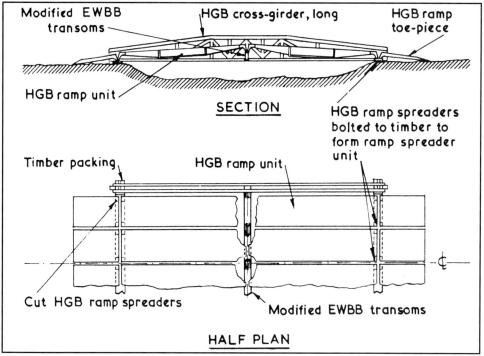

Inside the figure:

Modified EWBB transoms

HGB cross-girder, long

HGB ramp toe-piece

HGB ramp unit

SECTION

HGB ramp spreaders bolted to timber to form ramp spreader unit

Timber packing

HGB ramp unit

Cut HGB ramp spreaders

Modified EWBB transoms

HALF PLAN

Figure 11.14. Components of the 25ft HGB overbridge. (Military Engineering Vol III Part IV - 1979).

problems in construction and launching however, and it was usually quicker to build two shorter spans with an intermediate pier.

All bridge components could be carried in the standard 3 ton GS lorry (later to become, in the 1960s, the 4 tonne truck), and the bridge was designed to be constructed using mechanical aids or the specially designed Coles bridging crane. Construction by hand was just possible, given the time and enough men, eighteen men being needed to carry the panel, and sixteen the transom. The bridge was launched in a similar manner to the Bailey, by cantilevering out with a launching nose and erection rollers, and in daylight, on a reasonable site, a party of 30 men with a crane could have a 100ft bridge built and open for traffic in 4 hours, although demonstration builds were achieved in 2 hours or less.

The **25ft HGB Overbridge** evolved as a very useful adjunct to the main equipment, using two inverted HGB transoms or cross girders as the trusses for the bridge and a modified EWBB transom attached to the centre of each cross girder as a single transom at the centre of the bridge. HGB ramp sections were used as the bridge decking, one end of each resting on the EWBB transom and the other on HGB ramp spreaders at each end of bridge; HGB toe pieces completed the bridge. (Figure 11.14). The overbridge could take Class 70 wheeled vehicles and Class 40 tracked vehicles, but its ability to take the Chieftain tank was limited by the changes of ramp slope, since the bridge was packed up at the ends to ensure a minimum 3 inch clearance under the centre transom.

The **HGB Pier Set** was designed to provide an intermediate support for multi-span HGB. It used double truss HGB panels on end for the main pier supports and specially developed horizontal and diagonal bracing members. Other special parts developed included a pier capsill, to support the span junction cross beam, and a half panel to allow the pier height to be increased by increments of 6ft 3in up to a maximum height of 100ft.

Floating HGB evolved in the mid 1950s, using 62ft 6in floating bays of standard single/single HGB construction supported on quadripartite pontoon piers, of welded steel construction and 82ft long overall. The form of construction used was similar to that for the Bailey Pontoon Bridge, that is with a landing or shore bay at each end of bridge (supported by a landing bay raft, connected to an end floating bay), and with the required number of floating bays completing the bridge. Distributing girders connected the piers for the landing bay raft, the number of piers needed depending upon the length of the landing bay required, which could be up to 187ft 6in long in triple single reinforced construction. After production and proving of pilot model pontoon piers and some other parts, it was decided that commercially available **Storey Uniflote Pontoons**, each 17ft 4in long, would be used to form the quadripartite piers; the pier length was thus reduced to 70ft overall, and the reduced buoyancy meant cutting the floating bay length back to 50ft. By this time however evaluation of amphibious bridging equipments was already in hand, and the floating version of HGB did not really advance very far, although of course it had the considerable advantage of offering a Class 100 floating bridge with an 18ft 10in wide roadway.

An **HGB Model** was developed in 1958. A full size bridge was included in the atomic weapon response trials held in Australia in 1956, but following the moratorium on such trials, it was decided to carry out further tests on structurally accurate models of the bridge. A number of 1/10 scale models of the bridge were therefore manufactured at Christchurch (Figure 11.15) and

Figure 11.15. The structurally accurate model of the Heavy Girder Bridge used to predict the effect of nuclear attack. (IWM 22894).

these were subsequently subjected to simulated nuclear attack at the Atomic Weapons Establishment at Shoeburyness and in Canada.

The Extra Widened Bailey Bridge

Towards the end of the war the Bailey Bridge had been progressively widened, first as the Improvised Widened Bailey Bridge and then as the Standard Widened Bailey Bridge (SWBB), as described in Chapter Seven. Early in 1949 it was appreciated that the date of introduction of the new FV 200 series tank might precede that of the Heavy Girder Bridge, development of which had started in 1946. The War Office therefore decided to proceed with the introduction of a new and wider version of Bailey, a paper scheme for which had already been produced, as an interim solution to supplant the SWBB. The bridge was known as the Extra Widened Bailey Bridge or EWBB, and forty five years later it was still held in Engineer Stores Depots for emergency use.

The bridge was designed for Class 30 and Class 80 loading, with a roadway width between ribands of 13ft 9½in and a width between girders of 15ft 8in ; this compared with widths of 12ft 6in and 14ft 3½in respectively for the SWBB. The SWBB transom was retained but the inner truss position used with the double, triple or quadruple truss SWBB was eliminated, to allow widening of the roadway. EWBB thus reverted to the single, double and triple truss construction originally used with Bailey Bridging, a 150ft span Class 80 bridge being achievable with triple/triple construction. The increased roadway width necessitated the addition of an extra line of stringers, with new longer chesses and lengthened swaybraces, and of course the stringer cleat position on the SWBB transoms had to be adjusted. Various other minor modifications included the staggering of the stringers to increase the strength of the deck. A Class 80 floating version of the bridge, the Extra Widened Bailey Pontoon Bridge, was developed, using EWBB as the superstructure on Mark 5 and Mark 6 Pontoons, and in due course the various special constructions used with normal Bailey, such as continuous bridges and broken span bridges were introduced; a reinforced version, capable of carrying the Centurion Tank on its transporter and known as the Class 80(Cen) Bridge was also introduced.

The Coles Bridging Crane

Although the use of a bridging crane was not absolutely essential for the construction of single storey HGB, the bridge was designed with the use of a crane in mind. It was however essential to have a crane to handle HFy units, and the use of a crane enabled considerable pre-assembly of LAFB and HAFB to be carried out away from the actual bridging site.

The crane developed in the early 1950s for use in the bridging role was the Coles Crane, mounted on an AEC 10 ton 6 x 6 HGS chassis. (Figure 11.16).

The 30ft crane jib could be slewed through the full 360° and had a capacity of 7 tons whilst operating at a 9½ ft radius or 1¼ tons at the full 30ft radius. The crane was powered by a diesel engine coupled to a variable speed generator mounted on the crane superstructure. The vehicle was unusual in that it could be driven and steered forward and backward at slow speed by the crane operator, from his

Figure 11.16. The Coles Bridging Crane, mounted on an AEC 10 ton chassis.

operating cab in the revolving superstructure. This could cause much amusement at demonstrations, when the vehicle driver was seen to climb down from the the driving cab and walk away, to all intents and purposes leaving the vehicle moving forward out of control, whereas it was in fact being driven by the crane operator from his cab.

Postwar Railway Bridging

During the war, the repair and operation of the badly damaged railway network of Western Europe had been of prime importance in maintaining the advance of the Allies into Europe and in achieving the subsequent victory; it was also important in furthering the postwar economic recovery of the liberated countries. The onset of the Cold War, and the possibility of a short nuclear battle being fought in Europe, produced a very different scenario for the Army however, one in which railway operation had a very much reduced role. In particular, the prospect of replacing damaged railway bridges and reinstating damaged railway lines, which had proved a very time consuming procedure during the war, became very unlikely in a possible nuclear conflict. Since in any case the Sappers still held a more than adequate stock of equipment railway bridging developed during the war, development of new equipment was, in the main, restricted to experimental work on new plate girder railway bridges and on the use of the HGB for railway traffic. It would be appropriate to mention here that as a result of the report of the McLeod Committee (Chaired by General Sir Roderick McLeod), the Royal Corps of Transport came into existence on 15 July 1965. The new Corps took over the former RASC role of providing road transport support for the Army, and also the Sapper responsibilities for operation of military railways, maritime transport and military ports, as well as that for movement control. Responsibility for railway construction and maintenance involving civil engineering tasks remained with the Sappers, although the newly formed Ministry of Public Building and Works assumed responsibility for railway maintenance from 1 April 1967.

The Sectional Plate Girder Railway Bridge

The wartime 40ft span Sectional Welded Plate Girder Bridge suffered the drawback of all railway bridging in that considerable on-site bolting was necessary, in this case to connect up the three 14ft lengths of plate girder. This drawback was also present in a new design for a plate girder railway bridge produced after the war which was to use 10ft and 14ft lengths of girder to produce a bridge with a span range from 38ft to 56ft in 2ft increments. A new bridge, considered in the 1950s and confusingly called the Sectional Plate Girder Railway Bridge (Welded having been dropped and Railway added to the name used for the wartime plate girder railway bridge) proposed to avoid the problem by pinning the sections of plate girder together at top and bottom flange level. The welded mild steel plate girders, 4ft 8in deep compared with a depth of 2ft 11in for the wartime bridge, were to be provided in 12ft and 16ft lengths which could be pinned together with or without end posts; this would enable a wide range of spans to be achieved, from 35ft up to 70ft, capable of carrying the heaviest rail loads at speeds of up to 40mph. The bridge was intended to be used as a deck type bridge, using two girders, with diaphragms, for spans up to 48ft, and four girders bolted side by side for longer spans. It could also be used as a through type bridge, with either one or two main girders on each side of the rail track. (Figure 11.17). Development of the bridge did not get much beyond the production of accurate working models and manufacture of some prototype components, largely because of the general trend away from military railway operations mentioned above.

Figure 11.17. *A model of the Sectional Plate Girder Railway Bridge through span, with end posts fitted* (MEXE).

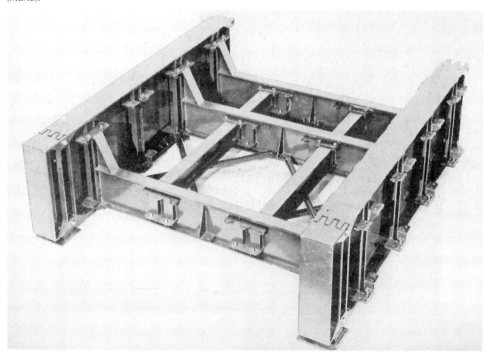

The Improvised Heavy Girder Railway Bridge

The Transportation Training Centre at Longmoor still thrived after the war, and indeed until its final closure in October 1969. As a Sapper training centre, until of course it was taken over by the newly formed RCT in 1965, it was the scene of such practical experimental railway bridging work as there was after the war. Full use was made of the Longmoor Military Railway, which served the dual purpose of providing an operational railway for training purposes and connecting the various rail linked military store depots in the area. Apart from innumerable builds (and dismantling) of standard railway bridges by Young Officer courses over the years, many trials were held to improve construction drills of equipment bridges. Experiments were also carried out on the use of HGB for railway use, an example of which was an 81ft span quadruple single reinforced deck bridge, trafficked successfully by coupled locomotives in 1957. (Figure 11.18). This

Figure 11.18. An 81ft improvised Heavy Girder Rail Bridge, using quadruple/single construction, at the Transportation Centre, Longmoor. (MEXE).

and similar trials established the feasibility of HGB used in this role, but with the continued demise of interest in the use of military railways, no practical use was made of this use of HGB.

The Infantry Assault Boat Raft

An equipment that deserves mention in this chapter is the Infantry Assault Boat Raft, although the equipment did not in fact go to production. It did however involve a considerable design effort one way and another over a number of years. Various adaptations of the Mark III Assault Boat to carry infantry equipment during a river assault were discussed in Chapter Eight. With the advent of the Mark IV Assault Boat after the war, use of the boat for rafting was again the subject of considerable experiment, the aim, as stated in 1956, being to produce a rapidly constructed Class 6 raft. The Mark IV Boat had a length of 17ft 6in and a beam of 6ft, compared with dimensions of 16ft 8in and 5ft 5in for the Mark III, but it had a slightly reduced payload. In the mid and late 1950s a series of tests were held to find a suitable raft combination, despite the fact that in late 1957 the Infantry decided that the requirement for an Assault Boat Raft no longer existed. One such test in 1958 used four different superstructures, each mounted on two piers formed by coupling two Mark IV Assault Boats stern to stern. The superstructures tested included improvised timber versions (with both fixed and hinged ramps) and that of a modified FBE Mark III Tracked Raft. In addition different methods of mounting the superstructures were considered, namely, directly on to the gunwales, on trestles placed in the bottom of the piers, and on a saddle fixed across the gunwales. A design for a four boat end-loading raft, also based upon the FBE Tracked Raft superstructure, was at the same time produced by the RSME at Chatham, and was widely taught and used there. After considerable correspondence the project was reinstated in 1961 and a Military Characteristic was drawn up; the raft was to be Class 6, using four Mark IV Assault Boats and was to have a 28ft clear deck.

Early tests at MEXE established that an end loading raft would be difficult to operate at current speeds in excess of 2½ knots, and design proceeded on the basis of a side loading raft with a purpose designed superstructure. The design officer for the project was Colonel R T Weld, an ex-Sapper officer who had previously served at MEXE and had now returned to the Establishment as a scientific civil servant. The superstructure consisted of two trussed trackways mounted directly on to the boat gunwales. Each trackway was formed from two parallel sided inner sections and two tapered ramp sections, all sections being pinned together at top and bottom chord level, so that the ramps were not freely hinged. (Figure 11.19). A newly developed high strength and weldable aluminium alloy was used to fabricate the trackways (see Appendix B), an alloy that was to play an important role in subsequent development of the Airportable Bridge and the Medium Girder Bridge. Despite satisfactory trials with the prototype raft, the infantry once

Figure 11.19. *The prototype Class 6 Infantry Assault Raft, using Mark IV Assault Boats.* (IWM 33977).

again decided that there was no firm requirement for such a raft, probably making this decision in the light of more pressing requirement for other equipments and a limited available budget.

The Far East Assault Boat Raft

Thus it was that, with the outbreak of the Borneo Emergency in the early 1960s, the Commonwealth Brigade operating in support of the Sultan's forces found themselves without a suitable raft with which to ferry light equipment across the many water obstacles encountered in the Borneo jungle. Major J P Fitzgerald-Smith RE, an innovative Sapper who was at the time Workshops Officer at Engineer Base Workshops, Singapore, had produced a design for a simple trackway, fabricated from aluminium alloy plate. The trackway could be carried slung on the side of Army Landrovers and used to enable the vehicles to cross the deep monsoon drains alongside the main roads and thus easily gain access to the jungle. To overcome the rafting problem Fitzgerald-Smith adopted the trackways for use with the Mark IV Assault Boat to form a Class 3 Raft. (Figure 11.20). Two boats were connected end to end to form a single pier and two further boats were used, one either side of the centre pier. Twin lengths of trackway were then laid across the gunwales of the two single and the double boats, and firmly bolted to the handrails of the boats by long hook bolts. Short lengths of

Figure 11.20. *The Class 3 version of the Far East Assault Boat Raft, using Mark IV Assault Boats.* (MEXE).

trackway were hinged at each end of the tracks forming the deck, to form the ramps of the side loading raft, the ramps being raised and lowered by hand and locked in position with a simple articulator.

Propulsion of the rafts caused a problem. The Seagull Outboard Motor (OBM) was not powerful enough for use with the Mark IV Assault Boat and the 410 OBM developed for use with the Light Assault Floating Bridge was not widely available in the Far East. Other OBMs available in Engineer stores were not in good condition, many being of World War II vintage, and the eventual solution was to purchase new Johnson OBMs from the local bazaar. These Johnsons were of standard design, and not of course the military specials normally used by the Sappers, which had extended shafts to enable them to be used on pontoons with relatively large freeboards. To overcome the difficulty of the shorter shafts, Fitzgerald-Smith designed a special bracket, known as the Bracket Universal Raft Operating, or BURO, consisting of a wooden transom to which the OBM could be fixed, the transom being raised or lowered within a framework by means of a small pul-lift jack. The raft proved very successful but was very much a local expedient and was not in fact used other than in the Far East. A Class 6 version employed two double Mark IV Assault Boats and four trackways.

294

The 50 Ton Bridging Crib

One further minor but important piece of equipment developed during this period was the 50 Ton Bridging Crib. The crib was very similar to the 20 Ton Bridging Crib of the 1930s, which proved so useful during the war, but was designed to cater for the heavier bridging loads now being encountered. (Figure 11.21). The crib was made from 2½in x 2½in x ¼ in high tensile steel angles, internally braced with 1in x ½in mild steel flats; this compared with the 2in mild steel angles and 1½in x ¼ in flats used for the 20 Ton Crib. The new crib measured 4ft x 2ft x 2ft and weighed 230lb, whereas the older crib measured 6ft x 2ft x 2ft and weighed

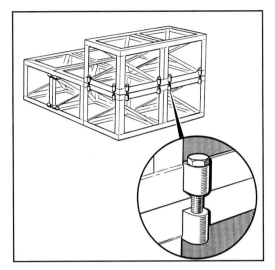

Figure 11.21. The 50 Ton Bridging Crib, showing the use of the Bridging Crib Clamp.
(User Handbook).

200lb; it was supplied hot dipped galvanized, whereas the 20 Ton Crib was merely corrosion protected by paint.

The 500 Ton Bridge Test Rig

The development of the Bridge Test Rig, which played a very important part in the development and testing programme of so many of the postwar bridges, also took place during this period and is worthy of mention. The rig was designed and manufactured at MEXE in the late 1950s, to provide an accurate and rapid means of applying proof loads to military bridges and their components, but it was also made available for use by other R and D establishments, and subsequently became increasingly used for testing containers and other engineering structures in the civil field. The rig consisted of two independent rail mounted gantries, 40ft high, which could be spaced at any distance between 19ft and 150ft. During a loading cycle the legs of each gantry were locked to the rails on which they travelled, the 170ft long rails themselves being mounted on a massive buried concrete foundation reinforced with four 170ft long Bailey panel girders. Each gantry carried a loading beam which could apply a vertical load of up to 250 tons to a structure up to 35ft wide, 29ft high and 600ft long; thus the very largest of bridges could be test loaded using the rig, as illustrated in Figure 11.13. Each gantry could also be used to apply a tensile load of up to 150 tons if required. During a test the loading beam could be lowered at a rate of 1¼ in per minute as the loaded structure deflected, with a possible maximum deflection of 40in. The use of the new test rig represented a quantum leap forward

295

compared with the method of testing the Bailey Bridge prototypes in 1942, described in detail in Chapter Seven..

And what of MEXE?

And what meanwhile had happened at Christchurch during the 1950s? Brigadier Sir Millis R Jefferies had taken over as Chief Superintendent from Brigadier G R McMeekan in April 1950, to be replaced himself by Brigadier L R E Fayle in July 1953. In April 1956 the title of the senior post at MEXE was changed to Director and at the end of the year Sir Donald Bailey took over from Brigadier Fayle, to become the first civilian Director of the Establishment. The two wings of the mid 50s, that is the Bridging Wing and the Mechanical Wing, were enlarged as the decade proceeded, and by 1958 MEXE had been reorganized into four wings, the Bridging Wing, the Structures Wing, the Mechanical Equipment Wing, and the Pavement Construction Wing, together with a Research Group which supported the technical branches. The small Explosives Group of the early 50s still survived as the Mines and Explosives Group, only to be transferred to the ARDE at Fort Halstead in 1959. Other facilities included a well equipped workshops, a central drawing office, a library, a photographic section, a strong administrative section, and of course the Bridge Test Rig of the late 1950s. All in all a far cry from the EBE of the 1930s.

CHAPTER TWELVE

Bridging For The 1970s and 80s

Into the Next Decade

The fifteen years after the war had seen the development of a number of excellent new bridges. However, at the beginning of the 1960s requirements were finalized for new and more sophisticated equipments, notably the Medium Girder Bridge, the Airportable Bridge and Amphibious Bridges, with the realization that these new equipments would most probably not come into service until 1970 or beyond.

The reasons for these new requirements were various. National Service, which had been introduced after the war to replace conscription, was finally phased out in 1962. This considerably reduced the size of what was, for this country, a large peacetime army of over 260,000 to a much smaller and all Regular Army of just over 155,000, and this in turn reduced the quantities of equipment of all types needed by the Army. This much smaller Regular Army, which was, in the next decade, to be withdrawn from most of our overseas bases, was to become very much more professional and highly trained, capable of handling the continually more complex and technically advanced equipments being developed for all arms. Further, the decision to withdraw the bulk of our troops to UK and rely on a Strategic Reserve that could, if necessary, be rapidly deployed worldwide, produced a requirement for airportability of equipments, including of course bridging equipment for the Sappers. In addition the Sappers were calling for bridging that could be built with fewer men, in faster times, and to carry greater loads.

All in all this was a considerable challenge to MEXE, but once again Christchurch was able to meet the challenge and the excellent range of new equipments considered in this chapter was, in due course, brought into service. During this period, in the early and mid-1960s, MEXE was perhaps at the zenith of its history. The establishment employed a staff of almost 1000, extensive test sites had been established at Hurn and Barnsfield Heath, and facilities were improved to include a hydrodynamic test tank, extended engine and materials testing laboratories, and further office accommodation. A certain amount of adjustment was made to the roles of the four design wings. Thus the Bridging Wing, which dealt with fixed bridges, became the Bridging and POL Wing, the Mechanical Wing became the Electrical and Mechanical Wing, and the Pavement Construction Wing became the Plant, Roads and Airfields Wing. Structures Wing, which dealt with tank bridges and floating bridges, was unchanged, but the Research Group was enlarged to a Wing and now included a Plastics Laboratory, a Corrosion Laboratory,

Fatigue Laboratories, and Metallurgical Laboratories. By now MEXE had become widely accepted internationally in both military and civilian engineering circles, as a centre of expertise in military bridge design, plant and equipment testing and evaluation, and in many other areas of military engineering equipment design.

In September 1962, after thirty-four years spent at EBE/MEXE, Sir Donald Bailey went on to become Dean of the Royal Military College of Science at Shrivenham, where his reputation and prestige did much to enhance the status of the college. In 1966 he retired from the Civil Service and returned to live in Christchurch, where he had first settled in 1928. He was replaced at MEXE by his Deputy Director, Brigadier H A T Jarrett-Kerr, who had served at the EBE as a young officer before the war, and again during the war, working on the design of the Bailey Bridge.

The Class 16 Airportable Bridge

The requirement for the Class 16 Airportable Bridge, developed in the early 1960s, resulted directly from the decision to set up the UK based Strategic Reserve referred to above. The requirement was to produce a bridge for the Sappers that was compact, light and, above all, easily airportable, for use in the initial air-transported phase of Limited or Cold War operations. The equipment was to be adaptable either as a ferry (the primary function), a floating bridge or a 50ft span dry gap bridge, the 100ft span dry gap bridge originally called for having been deemed to be not feasible. The design team that worked on the bridge was lead by Colonel Weld, previously mentioned in connection with the Infantry Assault Raft, and the author, at that time serving at MEXE as a Project Officer in the rank of Major. In May 1962 MEXE put forward a proposal at a Design Presentation Meeting for a bridge constructed from light alloy boxes. The boxes and the ramps were to be internally stiffened, so that when joined together, by dovetail or interlocking joints along the bottom faces and by tension and shear connectors at the top faces, they provided the main girders and the transoms of the bridge. The top of the boxes would then provide the bridge deck.

For the floating versions of the bridge the boxes themselves were to contribute much of the necessary buoyancy, additional buoyancy being provided by pneumatic floats coupled on to the short ends of each box. There were a number of untried aspects to this design, not least the behaviour in a fast current of a floating bridge that was in effect one continuous pontoon; it was felt that the elimination of the more normal spaces between individual pontoons could cause problems with floating debris and might also cause stability problems in shallow rivers. A further unknown was the use of the stressed-skin type of construction proposed for the boxes, not previously used in military bridge construction. In view of these uncertainties, DREE decided that, although work should proceed on the new design, a more conventional design should be produced at the same

298

time, to provide a fall back position if required, and also to provide a yardstick with which to compare costs and anticipated performance.

A firm of consulting engineers, Posford, Pavry and Partners, was chosen to produce the more orthodox design for the APB. In brief, their design consisted of 14ft long panels with male joints at each end, connected together with female jointed connecting posts; transoms were to be spaced at 7ft intervals, supporting 14ft long deck panels. The floating and raft versions of the bridge were to be supported on 42ft long piers formed from fairly conventional 21ft long pontoons. The pontoons were to be only partially decked, to allow stowage of the bridge and decking panels inside the pontoons for road and air transport. In the event, the development and production cost estimates for the MEXE version of the new bridge were lower than those for the Posford Pavry version, and this swayed the final decision towards acceptance of the outline MEXE proposals.

As finally developed, the Air Portable Bridge did not differ to any great degree from MEXE's original proposals. It consisted of a series of light alloy boxes, each 12ft x 4ft x 15in and weighing about 600lb, seven of which could be joined together along the long sides to form, with 12ft tapered ramp sections at each end, a 50ft span dry gap bridge. (Figure 12.1) The top of the boxes formed the deck of the bridge, to give an 11ft wide roadway. Prototype boxes were made from aluminium sheet welded together rather like a large egg box, but this form of construction proved too heavy and the welded sheet had a tendency to exfoliation corrosion; the design was therefore modified to use a welded lattice framework on which the outer skins were riveted and bolted. Various forms of construction were considered for the 1½ in deep deck of the boxes, which had to resist local bending loads as well as the total compressive bending load on the bridge. A light alloy sandwich with an alloy honeycomb infill, similar to that used for the wings of the latest RAF V Bombers was considered, with polystyrene

Figure 12.1. The 50ft dry gap version of the Air Portable Bridge. (IWM 57294).

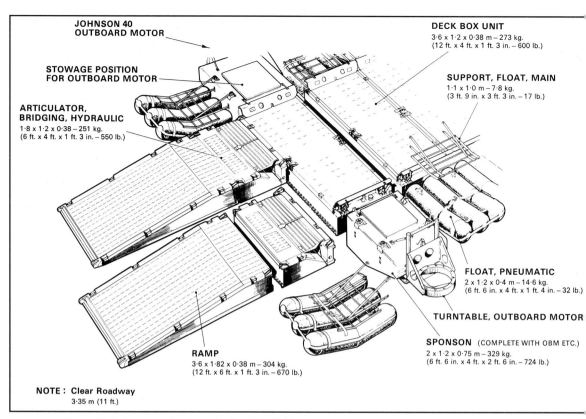

JOHNSON 40
OUTBOARD MOTOR

STOWAGE POSITION
FOR OUTBOARD MOTOR

ARTICULATOR,
BRIDGING, HYDRAULIC
1·8 x 1·2 x 0·38 – 251 kg.
(6 ft. x 4 ft. x 1 ft. 3 in. – 550 lb.)

DECK BOX UNIT
3·6 x 1·2 x 0·38 m – 273 kg.
(12 ft. x 4 ft. x 1 ft. 3 in. – 600 lb.)

SUPPORT, FLOAT, MAIN
1·1 x 1·0 m – 7·8 kg.
(3 ft. 9 in. x 3 ft. 3 in. – 17 lb.)

FLOAT, PNEUMATIC
2 x 1·2 x 0·4 m – 14·6 kg.
(6 ft. 6 in. x 4 ft. x 1 ft. 4 in. – 32 lb.)

TURNTABLE, OUTBOARD MOTOR

RAMP
3·6 x 1·82 x 0·38 m – 304 kg.
(12 ft. x 6 ft. x 1 ft. 3 in. – 670 lb.)

SPONSON (COMPLETE WITH OBM ETC.)
2 x 1·2 x 0·75 m – 329 kg.
(6 ft. 6 in. x 4 ft. x 2 ft. 6 in. – 724 lb.)

NOTE : Clear Roadway
3·35 m (11 ft.)

Figure 12.2. Components of the Air Portable Bridge. (Laird Anglesey Ltd).

considered as an alternative infill material. However, the final version used aluminium alloy extrusions, welded together along the axis of the bridge. The ramps were of similar construction to the boxes, extensive use being made of a recently developed Aluminium-Zinc-Magnesium weldable alloy (see Appendix B).

For the floating versions of the bridge, pneumatic floats were added at each end of the boxes, to provide additional buoyancy and also to improve the water profile. (Figure 12.2) The floats were made from a neoprene-nylon fabric made up into three tubes, which were bonded together but were not separately airtight. Thus each float had a single inflation point and could be inflated by connection to a Land Rover exhaust, by use of Aqualung air bottles or a compressor, or, for topping up the working pressure of 2.4psi, by a small manual inflation pump. To resist upward thrust on the float, a support framework was fitted above each float and coupled to the ends of the main boxes. At each corner of the raft the pneumatic float was replaced by a small light alloy pontoon, or sponson, which provided the mounting for a 40HP Johnson outboard motor, and also served as a carrying case for the OBM during road or air transport. Articulator units were installed at each end of the floating bridge or raft between the end box and the ramp sections,

300

to provide a means of raising and lowering the ramps and adjusting for river water levels; the articulator units were 6ft wide so that each could raise or lower one 6ft wide ramp section.

The bridge was an unrestricted Class 16 bridge, but in the floating version it could, with speed restrictions and provision of extra raft buoyancy (achieved by the addition of two extra boxes and floats), carry the Class 20 Medium Wheeled Tractor and other specified Class 17/19 loads. The equipment was carried on special trailers, towed by Land Rovers, the dry gap bridge requiring three trailer loads, and the raft five loads. Various combinations of equipment could be carried in the Argosy and Hercules medium range aircraft and all components could be airlifted by the Wessex helicopter, either as bundled loads or loaded trailers.

Technical trials of the new equipment were followed by troop trials held during 1967, in UK, FARELF and Australia. An interesting trial involved the carriage and placing of a complete dry gap bridge by helicopter. In an early trial the slings were attached to the end boxes of the bridge, rather than at the ends of the ramps. Consequent vibration induced greatly accelerated fatigue in the top ramp connectors, and as a result one of the ramps fell off over Sussex. Some years later, during the Falklands Campaign, a 42ft bridge was successfully placed by this method, using a Chinook helicopter.

The first production bridge sets, manufactured by Laird (Anglesey) Ltd, were issued to the British and Australian Armies in 1970. A bridge set consisted of enough equipment to form either four rafts, each with a clear deck length of 40ft, (Figure 12.3) 192ft of floating bridge, or four 50ft clear span dry bridges. The equipment proved simple and quick to build, the 50ft dry gap bridge taking about 20 minutes to construct with a party of

Figure 12.3. The production version of the APB Raft showing the protective canvas float covers in use. (IWM 719987-1).

sixteen men, and the self-propelled raft about 40 minutes with twenty-four men.

The 20ft Inflated Bridge

Whilst the Airportable Bridge was being developed, the idea of an inflated bridge for similar use in airborne operations and by expeditions was seriously considered. Structures produced by inflation of tubes or slabs of flexible fabric have obvious advantages when low bulk and light weight are more important considerations than long life or robustness, good examples being the recce boats used by the Sappers and inflatable lifeboats. A clear span bridge, however, is a more complex structure and in the mid-1960s it was decided to examine the practical difficulties by designing and building an experimental bridge, which was manufactured at Cowes by British Hovercraft.

To save time, and since the project was no more than a feasibility study, existing rather than purpose-developed fabrics were used, and the bridge decking was merely timber planked. The bridge was therefore made from three-ply dinghy-floor fabric, with the upper load bearing surface comprising wooden slats capable of taking the compressive loads in the bridge; flexible steel wires were bonded to the lower surface to take longitudinal tension. The bridge was 20ft long overall, without its 8ft long inflated ramps, and 9ft wide, giving an 8ft wide roadway. Longitudinal and transverse internal diaphragms kept the depth to 2ft at mid-span at the inflation pressure of 2psi. In trials the bridge, which could be stowed as an 8ft long pack, 2ft in diameter and weighing about 700lb, successfully carried a long-wheeled-base Landrover, both as a dry bridge and also as a raft. (Figure 12.4). However, for a number of reasons the idea was not pursued, although, in fact, what might have been thought a drawback, that is possible rapid deflation by small arms fire, did not prove so, since the bullets left only tiny pinholes in the structure, resulting in a very slow escape of air.

Figure 12.4. The 20ft clear-span experimental inflatable bridge. (IWM 42168)

Amphibious Bridging

Some experiments with a modified tracked vehicle, which incorporated flip-over floats to provide buoyancy and a deck to carry light vehicles, had taken place during the war at the EBE. The idea had not been developed beyond the simple prototype stage, however, and had remained dormant. In the early 1960s the idea was considered further and a requirement for an amphibious bridging equipment was specified, the construction, recovery and dispersal times to be compatible with the conditions imposed by modern weapons and surveillance systems. The target was to build a Class 60 bridge at the rate of about 400ft per hour, under operational conditions and with a minimum of men; in addition there was a requirement to build Class 60 rafts, from the same equipment, in under 30 minutes; the requested in-service date was 1965.

The idea of an amphibious bridge was an attractive one. It would have the advantage that the bridging units would be mobile in their own right, with a considerable cross-country capability, would be self-propelled once in the water and capable of being rapidly joined together to form bridge, and could each carry its own complement of Sappers, acting as driver and crewmen to join up the units in the water. A concentration of men and logistic vehicles at the bridge site would thus be avoided. On the other hand, the equipment units would be completely dedicated to wet bridging, would require a specialist unit to operate, and would obviously be fairly sophisticated, and thus expensive to buy and maintain.

The EWK-Gillois

No equipment existed in the British Army that could match the requirements for the new bridge and no preliminary work had been carried out at MEXE. Attention was therefore focused on the Amphibious Bridge Equipment EWK-Gillois, the invention of a French Army Officer, Colonel Jean F Gillois, which had been developed and manufactured by Eisenwerke, Kaiserslautern, in West Germany. By the summer of 1960 sufficient units were available to enable the US Army Engineer Research and Development Laboratories (ERDL) to undertake technical trials in Germany, and arrangements were made for a British officer to attend these trials. The American Army provided valuable assistance in training a UK Trials Team, recruited in BAOR, and the team was subsequently moved to UK to carry out further trials with the three bridge and two ramp units that had been ordered by the War Office. (Figure 12.5)

Delivery of the UK units was taken in January and March 1961, and the extensive trials that followed involved the Fighting Vehicles Research and Development Establishment (FVRDE), the Signals Research and Development Establishment (SRDE), and No 8 Maintenance and Advisory Group REME; the amphibious trials included trials in the Solent Estuary and

Figure 12.5. *Trials with the Gillois Equipment on the River Thames.* (IWM 26726).

on the River Thames. The trials were coordinated by MEXE under the control of Mr J N Barnikel, a Regular Sapper officer who had served at MEXE and then retired from the Army as a Major, to become a Scientific Civil Servant. Bill Barnikel later became project officer for the M2 and a decade later was to lead the International Concept Study Team working on the Bridging for the 80s project. It was possible to curtail the UK trials to a

Figure 12.6. *The Gillois Amphibious Bridge Unit, with its pneumatic floats inflated.* (MEXE 'At Home' Publication).

considerable extent by taking account of the ERDL Report on the equipment, which had readily been made available to MEXE, and also of the West German Federal Army Test Establishment Report on two amphibian ferries that had been carried out in 1959.

The Gillois Bridge Unit was in effect an amphibious, four-wheeled, Class 36 road vehicle, equipped with an engine and suspension system to make it suitable for both road and water travel. (Figure 12.6 and Appendix B) Buoyancy and stability in the water were enhanced by the fitting of pneumatic floats to each side of the vehicle, the floats being strapped to saddles which first had to be attached to mounting brackets on each side of the hull; the floats were then inflated using the vehicle air compressor. Each unit carried a crew of four, who needed about 30-40 minutes to rig the unit for water entry. Rigging was normally carried out well away from the river, the degree of preparation depending upon the access to the bridge site, since the unit width with its floats fully inflated was 19ft. Once in the water, the road wheels were completely retracted into the hull of the vehicle and the unit superstructure, which had an effective length of 26ft 3in, was rotated hydraulically through 90° and then widened to give a 13ft 2in wide roadway. Propulsion in the water was provided by a rudder propeller, which was mounted on top of the unit for road travel and then swung through an arc of approximately 270° and lowered hydraulically for water travel.

The Gillois Ramp Unit or Carrier was a similar amphibious vehicle, but carried the bridge ramp, consisting of two 26ft 3in long treadway sections. Once the Ramp Carrier had been rigged and entered the water, the ramp was rotated and widened in a similar manner to the bridge superstructure, but once the Carrier had delivered its hydraulically operated ramp to the bridge or ferry, it disengaged and did not form part of the floating system. The non-utilization of this amphibious vehicle in the bridge proper was considered a major limitation of the equipment.

There was a third Gillois unit known as the Ferry Unit, which was similar to the Bridge Unit, but did not utilize a superstructure; a 16ft 5in ramp was permanently mounted at the rear of the vehicle, which permitted vehicles to load and unload along the axis of the unit straight on to the unit deck. Pneumatic tubes were used either side of the unit to provide the additional buoyancy necessary to support a Class 20 load. Three Ferry Units were purchased by the US Army for trials but procurement was not considered in UK.

The US trials reported excellent construction times for the equipment, between 525ft and 780ft of bridge being built in an hour, depending upon the current speed and site conditions. Construction times of 17min by day and 24min by night for a Class 60 raft built from three Bridge Units were also achieved during the trials in Germany. Early trials indicated a permissible Class 50 loading for the bridge, although a Class 60 loading was deemed safe with current speed not in excess of 4 knots and with a minimum vehicle spacing of 100ft. Apart from a number of specific and detailed deficiencies, the US report concluded that the equipment met most of the US Military Characteristics approved for a new amphibious bridge, and an order was placed for a further fourteen units for use with the US Forces in Europe.

23 Amphibious Engineer Squadron

The UK reaction to the various trials was also favourable and the Gillois was accepted for service in October 1961, subject to modification of the equipment to overcome the shortcomings highlighted in the US and UK trials. In May 1962 1 Troop of 50 Field Squadron was therefore reformed as 23 Amphibious River Crossing Cadre, equipped with seven Gillois Amphibious Units (with a capacity to provide about 184ft of floating bridge), and a small REME workshop. The Cadre was reformed as 23 Amphibious Engineer Squadron in 1963, under the command of Major J L Booth RE, with one Gillois Troop, one Field Troop, a workshops, and a large headquarters. The number of Gillois units was not increased, however, for reasons that will become evident, and by 1964 the Squadron was beginning to train with a new equipment, borrowed rigs of the German Amphibious Bridging and Ferrying Equipment - M2.

The Amphibious Bridging and Ferrying Equipment - M2

Soon after the Gillois equipment had been accepted for service a possible German alternative, the M2, was discussed at an Anglo-German Bridging Group meeting. At the request of the UK the Germans carried out comprehensive Centurion Tank loading trials with the bridge at the Federal German Testing Establishment, Koblenz, and these were followed by further marine trials in Germany in early 1962, using the three prototype vehicles that had been delivered a year earlier. By June 1962 sufficient information was available to prove conclusively that the M2 was markedly superior to the EWK/Gillois in nearly every respect and, further, that the two equipments could be in service at about the same time. As a result, War Office acceptance of the Gillois equipment was withdrawn in July 1962. One rig of the M2 equipment, on loan from the Federal German Army, arrived in UK in August 1962 and after limited marine and ferrying trials at MEXE, which were mainly concerned with comparing its performance with that of the Gillois, the rig was sent to FVRDE for automotive trials. The culmination of these and further trials was a firm decision to proceed with the procurement of the M2 equipment for the British Army. (Figure 12.7 and Appendix B)

The M2 equipment was developed, under contract to the Federal German authorities, by the Klockner-Humboldt-Deutz (KHD)/Eisenwerke, Kaiserslautern (EWK) consortium, EWK being the same firm that had manufactured the Gillois. The M2 unit was a Class 24 amphibious vehicle,

Figure 12.7. Bogging trials for an M2 unit at Hurn, near Christchurch. Note the Gillois unit in the background. (IWM 32685).

with the buoyancy, decking and ramps needed to construct a bridge or a ferry. Side pontoons were stowed inverted above the hull for road travel and these were then rotated into the outrigged position hydraulically, before the vehicle entered the water. Four bridge/ramp stringers were housed upside down for road travel, two under each stowed side pontoon; they were pinned to the side pontoons and were thus rotated with them as the pontoons were outrigged. The stringers were then swung into position, using an assembly gantry crane at the forward end of the vehicle, either to span between adjacent units or as hydraulically operated landing ramps at the end of the bridge or ferry.

Various forms of construction were possible with the equipment; a single rig could be used as a Class 10 ferry, using two bridge/ramp stringers on either side; two rigs could be used to form a Class 30 ferry, either open or close coupled, and three rigs could be formed into a close coupled Class 60 ferry with full width, 18ft 4in wide ramps. For Class 60 bridge construction the centre section of the wet gap was spanned by open coupled rigs at approximately 28ft centres, but close coupled rigs were used at either end to form landing bay rafts.

The trials in UK and in Germany highlighted many advantages of the M2 equipment over the Gillois, including greater mobility over soft ground, negligible time needed to outrig the side pontoons, immediate steered propulsion after water entry, higher water speeds, the shielding of the propellers to prevent damage, a wider roadway, greater versatility for ferry production, improved safety due to greater compartmentation of the hull and the need for fewer units to produce a similar length of bridge. On the negative side, the ramp reach and height range was not so good as with the Gillois. As a result of the trials a decision was made to proceed with procurement of the M2 for the British Army, subject to various modifications suggested by the trials, modifications in many cases already in hand for the production equipments ordered for the German Army. It is interesting to note that the American Army also decided not to proceed further with Gillois procurement and went on to produce their own version of an amphibious bridge, the Mobile Assault Bridge or MAB. The MAB was similar in many respects to the other equipments, but adopted an increased road travel width of the main hull (i.e. 12ft compared with 10ft for the Gillois and 9ft 10in for the M2) to make it possible to dispense with supplementary buoyancy.

28 Amphibious Engineer Regiment

With the firm decision to proceed with procurement of the M2, it became apparent that, with such a specialized equipment, intended for use within a comparatively small area of Western Germany, the formation of a new regiment to handle the equipment would be necessary. Initial training with the new equipment was begun in 1964, using M2A rigs on loan to 23 Squadron, the M2A being the trial version of the equipment. However, with the inevitable production delays, bearing in mind that both British and German armies were buying the equipment, it was not until 1969 that the original Gillois units were replaced by new M2B rigs, the improved version of the M2 incorporating the many modifications requested by the British and German Armies. (Figure 12.8) The Squadron then reorganized on the basis of three troops, each holding eight rigs. By early 1970 enough rigs were becoming available to begin formation of the new Regiment, and by August Lieutenant Colonel H J Goodson RE took command of the new 28 Amphibious Engineer Regiment. (The original 28 Field Engineer Regiment was formed in 1951 and saw service in Benghazi (1951), Korea (1951-1955) and Christmas Island (1956-1957), before being disbanded in 1957.)

23 Amphibious Engineer Squadron now lost one troop to a newly formed 64 Amphibious Engineer Squadron, and in September its Support Troop re-formed into 28 Amphibious Engineer Workshop. In the following January 23 Squadron lost its independence and was absorbed into the new Regiment

Figure 12.8. *Training on the River Weser in BAOR, using the production M2B rigs.* (IWM 71219-2).

and a third squadron, 73 Amphibious Engineer Squadron, began forming up. Formation of the Regiment was soon complete and on 7 April 1971 the Corps Commander, Lieutenant General Sir John Sharp KCB MC, took the salute at the Formation Parade. Initially each of the three amphibious squadrons had an establishment of three troops, each troop holding eight rigs; the rigs were manned by a four man crew consisting of a driver, a pilot, a crane operator, and a deckhand. In 1976 73 Squadron moved to Osnabruck and lost its amphibious role. A Headquarters Squadron was formed, which later became 71 Amphibious Engineer Squadron (Headquarters and Training) and then, later still, 71 Amphibious Engineer Support Squadron. The Regimental establishment thus included 23 and 64 Amphibious Engineer Squadrons, each with thirty rigs divided between two troops, and 71 Amphibious Engineer Support Squadron, with fifteen rigs.

When the Regiment began to form up in 1970, it occupied Bindon Barracks in Hameln, which was at that time housing 26 Regiment RCT, whose main role was to carry the wet bridging equipment of 1(British) Corps, BAOR. An unfortunate result of the purchase of M2 was that the role of the RCT Regiment ceased to exist, and the Regiment, which had had strong links with the Sappers over many years, was disbanded. Much of their manpower cover was used to provide cover for the formation of the new Sapper regiment.

After the rigs had been in service for a number of years each required a complete base overhaul. At the same time the opportunity was taken to convert the rigs to M2D standard, incorporating engine-inflated buoyancy bags to upgrade the equipment to Class 70, necessary to carry the latest Challenger battle tank. The planning time for the construction of 328ft

309

(100m) of Class 70 bridge was then between an hour and an hour and a half, whilst that for a Class 70 ferry, using three close coupled rigs, was 30 minutes. On a good site the bridge could traffic up to 150 vehicles or fifty tanks in an hour. In the mid-1990s a new version of the equipment, the M3, was introduced, and this is described in Chapter 15.

The Mexeflote

One further floating equipment developed during the 1960s was the Landing Ship Logistic (LSL) and Harbour Pontoon Equipment, also known as the Mexeflote Equipment, the concept of Mr E Longbottom, previously mentioned for his work at the EBE as a Sapper Major during the war, and later for his work on the Heavy Girder Bridge. The equipment was designed for use by the Royal Corps of Transport, who took over the transportation work of the Corps in 1965. Mexeflote was designed to form either self-propelled rafts or causeways, or to be transported preassembled on the side of an LSL and then free-dropped into the water on arrival at a beach for lighterage use or as a causeway. (Figure 12.9 and Appendix B) The equipment consisted of three types of steel framed and steel clad pontoon, a bow pontoon which had a wedge shaped forward section, hinged at the bottom, which could be raised or lowered hydraulically and centre and stern pontoons, both divided into two watertight compartments.

The equipment was Class 60 and could be used in a number of ways. A basic raft consisted of three strings of pontoons, each comprising a bow, a centre and a stern pontoon, to give an overall deck size of 66ft x 24ft; such a raft could carry a Class 60 tank or three 3 ton trucks. The type of raft normally carried by an LSL was 126ft x 24ft, formed by the addition of

Figure 12.9. *A Class 60 powered lighterage raft formed from Mexeflotes.* (Mexeflote PUH - July 1966).

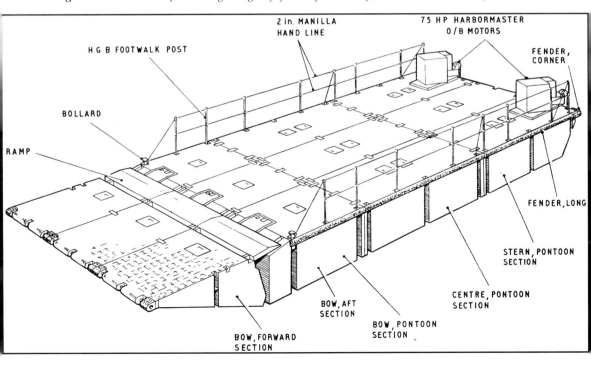

another nine centre pontoons; two such rafts would normally be carried on the sides of the LSL for causeway operation. Various other combinations could be formed into causeways or floating platforms of any desired shape or size to meet a particular requirement; the 66ft x 24ft raft could even act as a single span Class 60 bridge, if, for example, under-scoured in a dried up causeway. Rafts could be propelled at about 5 knots by two Harbourmaster 75hp outboard motors and for use in sheltered waters a Mexeflote tug could be formed from two bow and two stern pontoons, two outboard motors providing ample power and a high degree of manoeuvrability. The required operating conditions for the equipment were severe; pontoons had to be capable of connection into rafts or causeways in 2ft waves, for operation in 4 to 5ft waves; in addition the equipment was required to survive unladen at moorings in 9 to 10ft waves and, whilst in tow, in 12ft waves.

A New Alloy

Brief mention has already been made of the weldable aluminium-zinc-magnesium alloy used for manufacture of the Airportable Bridge. Such is the importance of this alloy to the bridge designer, however, that it warrants further consideration before the Medium Girder Bridge, in which it was used extensively, is considered in detail. There had been an increasing interest in lighter-weight equipments since the war, arising not only from an interest in possible airportability of equipments, but also from the obvious possible economies in transport and manpower. As a result extensive use of low and medium strength aluminium alloys was made in the design of the Light and Heavy Assault Floating Bridges, and to a lesser extent in other equipments. However, such use had been restricted to the use of aluminium alloy castings, for example for decking panels, and to forgings and extrusions that could be riveted together, since the H15 and H30 alloys used could not be welded without serious loss of strength. In the early 1960s, however, a range of aluminium-zinc-magnesium alloys was developed with medium strength and excellent recovery properties of the heat-affected zone after welding and natural ageing. A number of proprietary alloys were used in the early development stages of the APB and MGB, such as High Duty Alloys Hiduminium 48 with 4.5% zinc and 2.5% magnesium, Imperial Aluminium Company's Impalco 720 using 5% zinc, 1.25% magnesium and 0.4% copper, and the French Superalumag T35. All of these alloys had attractive properties in terms of strength and weldability, and also featured high toughness and good formability.

During the experimental use of these and similar alloys at MEXE some problems were found with stress corrosion, although this problem was largely overcome by better control of the heat-treatment process and by limiting the zinc/magnesium content to no more than 6%. Consequently MEXE developed the aluminium alloy defined in DGFVE Specification 232, containing 4% zinc, 2% magnesium and 0.35% manganese. Achievable strengths of the alloy in the solution treated and artificially aged condition are given in Appendix B; suffice to say here that within 30 days of welding, the strength of the heat-affected zone recovers to approximately 80% of the parent metal strength. The latest version of the alloy, that is DGFVE Specification 232B, includes the addition of 0.15% copper to further enhance resistance to stress corrosion.

MEXE pioneered the welding of the relatively thick sections of the new alloy used in the manufacture of bridging equipments, making use of the Metal-Inert-Gas (MIG) and the Tungsten-Inert-Gas (TIG) welding processes. These processes employ an electric arc as the heat source, the arc being shrouded by a shield of argon gas to prevent atmospheric contamination, and to allow a clean sound homogeneous weld to be made without the use of chemical fluxes.

The Medium Girder Bridge

Development of the Medium Girder Bridge (MGB) began in the early 1960s, with a requirement to provide a hand-built bridge able to carry Class 60 loads over spans of up to 100ft. The bridge was intended for use on battle group re-supply routes and also, when it could be built out of contact with an enemy, as an alternative to the armoured vehicle launched bridges. It was to make full use of the latest aluminium alloys available and would therefore replace, except on lines of communication, Extra Wide Bailey Bridge and the Heavy Girder Bridge, being lighter, easier to handle, quicker to build and requiring less transport. The project engineer for the development was Mr E Longbottom, already referred to in this chapter, and the bridge as developed proved to be an outstanding success. With many innovative features, it was widely acclaimed within military engineering circles throughout the world. Indeed MGB was, in the 1970s and 1980s, what Bailey Bridging had been in the 1940s and 1950s, an excellent bridging equipment, versatile and highly thought of by the Sappers.

The Medium Girder Bridge as originally proposed was to be a single storey through bridge. However, to provide maximum flexibility in use, it was decided to proceed with a design based upon two storey construction, which would also, in a single storey version, meet the BAOR requirement for a rapidly constructed shorter span bridge. It was thus developed as a twin girder deck bridge, capable of carrying Class 60 loads in single storey construction at a span of 30ft and in two storey construction at a span of 100ft (Figure 12.10), although with the advent of the heavier Challenger Battle Tank in the 1980s, the maximum load at a 100ft span was raised to MLC 70 by some reduction in the permissible fatigue life. The 9ft 1in long deck units fit between the longitudinal girders, which themselves form part of the deck, to give a roadway width of 13ft 2in, to which can be added a 2ft 3in wide footwalk in the double storey version. Bankseat beams connect the two girders at either end of bridge and ramp units hook onto these beams to

Figure 12.10. *A 100ft span double storey and a 30ft span single storey Medium Girder Bridge.* (IWM 50202).

provide access. In single storey construction the girders are formed from box shaped top girder sections, each 6ft long and 1ft 9in deep, which are pinned together; thus the single storey bridge, generally the most economical for crossing short gaps, is constructed from just four major components - the top panels, the deck units, bankseat beams and the ramp sections. In double storey construction three extra major components are needed; triangular bottom panels are fitted below the top panels, increasing the overall depth of the girders to 5ft, whilst the sloping ends of the bridge are formed using junction and end taper panels together with the top panels and bankseat beams. (Figure 12.11) Of the seven major components, all of which are made in Aluminium Alloy to DGFVE Specification 232B, the majority weigh less than 400lb and are easily handled by four men, with only the bankseat beam (570lb) and the end taper panel (600lb) as six-man loads.

The equipment is brought to the bridge site strapped onto special MGB pallets, which are carried on bridging

Figure 12.11. *Components of the Medium Girder Bridge.* (Military Engineering Vol III Part III, 1980).

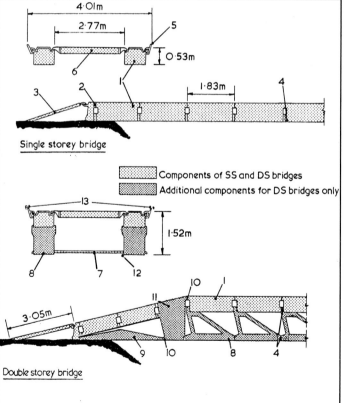

Part No.	Part	Part No.	Part
1	Top panel	7	Sway brace
2	Bankseat beam	8	Bottom panel
3	Ramp unit	9	End taper panel
4	Panel pin	10	Headless panel pins
5	Kerb	11	Junction panel
6	Deck Unit	12	Bracing pin
		13	Luminary

313

Figure 12.12. Launching a 100ft span double storey Medium Girder Bridge.

trucks, on special MGB trailers or by helicopter. On site the pallets are then pulled from the trucks or trailers on to the ground for easy accessibility. The bridge is constructed on roller beams, one beam being used for single storey bridges and two, 15ft apart and built into a building frame, for double storey construction. This rapidly assembled building frame incorporates jacks at the ends of the roller beams, which enable them to be set level on uneven ground and maintain the level should the frame baseplates settle unevenly; the jacks also enable the launch level of the bridge to be adjusted as it nears a high far bank. The frame thus ensures that the bridge can be built on unprepared and uneven ground and with banks at different heights, providing that the longitudinal or cross slope does not exceed 1 in 10.

All bridges are launched undecked and without a footwalk or kerbs, using a centrally mounted launching nose. (Figure 12.12) For single storey bridges up to 50ft in length, only a light launching nose connected to the forward bankseat beam is needed, but for longer single storey and double storey bridges heavy launching nose units are used to extend the light launching nose; these are connected to the bridge by a launching nose roller and cross girder, which enables launching nose units to be added and pushed forward as the bridge is being built.

Rapid construction is facilitated by an ingenious method of joining units together. (Figure 12.13) The two ends of the top panel are identical, so that the panel can be brought into bridge

Figure 12.13. Details of the Medium Girder Bridge top panel.
(Military Engineering Vol III Part III, 1980).

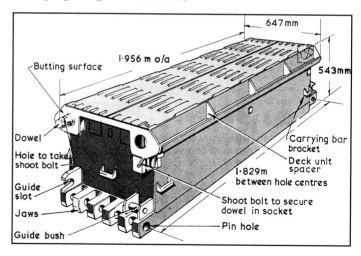

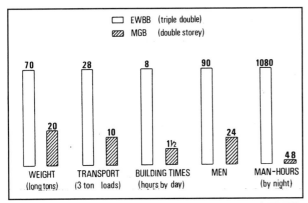

Figure 12.14. A comparison between MGB and EWBB, both bridges built at 100ft span, Class 60.

either way round. When in bridge the compressive loads in the top chord are taken by butting surfaces between panels, and tensile loads during launching of the bridge are taken by shoot bolts passing through vertical holes in top chord dowels. At bottom chord level, panels are connected by 28½ in long high tensile steel pins which pass through multiple jaws. The pins are very easily inserted because the jaws are located in respect to each other by a guide bush and slot system directly above them; under the weight of the completed bridge or traffic the bush deflects to allow the full load to be taken by the panel pin and the jaws. A similar multiple jaw system is used for the bankseat beam and the other MGB panels. The six lug multiple jaw system has one further function; the MGB has been designed so that any failure due to fatigue will occur in the panel jaw lugs, and since the outer lug, which is easily inspected, has been designed to fail first, any apparent failure can be detected well in advance, at least 1000 full load crossings before failure of a second lug.

This rapid construction is demonstrated by the planning times, that for a 30ft span Class 60 single storey bridge being 30 minutes, by day, and that for a 100ft span Class 60 double storey bridge, 90 minutes, although actual timings little more than half of these planning figures have been achieved with well-trained troops and good conditions. Compared with EWBB, which would have to be built as a triple/double bridge to carry Class 60 loads at a span of 100ft, the MGB shows a reduction of planned building time of about 80%; other comparable savings are illustrated in Figure 12.14.

Development of the bridge proceeded rapidly during the 1960s, culminating in successful user/troop trials in the UK and in BAOR in 1967. Later in that year the United States Army, which had expressed considerable interest in the bridge and later carried out their own evaluation trials, purchased large quantities for their forces. The bridge was manufactured in quantity by Fairey Engineering Ltd of Stockport (which became Williams Fairey Engineering Ltd in 1986), and entered service with the British Army in 1971.

Multi-Span MGB

Multi-span double storey bridges of any length can be built without crane assistance by making use of the **MGB Span Junction Set** and either the **MGB Portable Pier Set** or some other form of pier. However, the launching

315

Figure 12.15. The MGB Portable Pier Set, used to build a two span bridge. (IWM 72782-109).

sequence for more than three spans is complicated and launching stresses restrict the length of individual spans to 84ft; for these reasons the use of the floating version, if possible, is preferable for long bridges.

The Portable Pier Set provides the MGB with a two-legged pier, which can be assembled during the building of the bridge. (Figure 12.15) The legs are built up in 10ft lengths, and up to four sections can be used in wet gaps, and six sections, giving a total pier height of 60ft, in dry gaps. The pier can be erected independently in a river or ravine before the bridge is launched, but more usually is assembled on the bank in front of the bridge-building rollers and then raised and connected to the span junction bay as the bridge is boomed forward. Once the bridge is in its final position, articulators are used to adjust the pier legs into the vertical (or any other) position.

Floating MGB

The versatility of MGB is shown by the adaptation of a bridge designed for use as a dry gap bridge to the floating role. A Class 70 floating bridge can readily be constructed using either single or double storey MGB, the single storey version being quicker to build and requiring fewer bridge components, but more pontoons, than the double storey version. On the other hand double storey construction is most suitable for use when a considerable rise and fall of water level is expected, because the use of Span Junction Sets enables long landing bays, up to 87ft in length, to be constructed. Any type of floating support can be used, provided that adequate buoyancy and stability is available, and Heavy Floating Bridge pontoons, Heavy Ferry pontoons, Uniflote pontoons, M2 Amphibious Bridge rigs and the specially designed MGB Pontoons, considered later in this chapter, have all been used successfully. Single storey MGB can also be used to form ferries for load classes up to Class 90.

One of the first major trials of Floating MGB was conducted in Germany in 1974. The bridge was constructed by 4 Field Squadron across the River Weser, near Nienburg. HFB tripartite piers were used with specially manufactured saddles to locate the MGB on the pontoons. Three pier landing bays were used at either end of bridge whilst single piers were used for the intermediate supports spaced at seven-bay intervals. Double storey construction was used for the 331ft long Class 60 bridge and after a number of trial builds a demonstration was held at which the bridge was built in 1 hour 20 minutes; this time did not include the time to off-load pallets to the ground and erect the MGB building frames, but did include the launching of the pontoons from their trailers.

Reinforced MGB

The **MGB Reinforcement Set** was developed to increase the single span capability of MGB up to 162ft at Class 60 and to 138ft at Class 70. (Figure 12.16) The kit consists of 12ft long reinforcing links which are pinned together as the bridge is launched to form a pair of solid chains, one under each of the bridge girders. The links are connected to the bottom panels at each end of the bridge by a reinforcing anchorage and are positioned about 8ft below the bottom of the girders by reinforcing posts. The chains are then tensioned by pulling the posts towards the vertical position by means of TIRFOR cable jacks, the amount of tensioning being kept to the minimum necessary to remove any slack in the Reinforcing Set. The Reinforcing Set is manufactured from the same alloy as the bridge and the links employ the same 'fail safe' design for the six-lug connections that is used in the bridge girders.

Figure 12.16. A 118ft double storey MGB used with the Reinforcement Set to increase the load class to 100. (IWM 78133-1).

The Success of MGB

The Medium Girder Bridge must rate as the most successful military bridge developed since the war, a tribute not only to the designers at MEXE but also to Fairey Engineering Ltd, who were granted the sole manufacturing rights; the company was awarded The Queen's Award to Industry for Resourcefulness in Exports in 1976, 1977 and 1991. Sales throughout the world have exceeded £M450, and the equipment has been sold to thirty-six countries, including most of our NATO allies, notably the United States (for use by their Corps of Engineers and the Marine Corps), Germany and Italy and also to Switzerland. Sales have of course resulted in considerable payments of royalties to the Ministry of Defence.

For his outstanding work on the bridge, Eric Longbottom was awarded an Individual Merit Promotion to Assistant Director (Engineering) in 1972, the Merit Promotion of an Engineer Grade as opposed to a Scientific Grade Civil Servant being a very rare event.

The Bailey Cable Reinforcement Kit

Although by 1971 MGB had just entered service with the British Army, the Sappers still had large stocks of Bailey Bridging. It was therefore thought prudent to examine a Cable Reinforcement Kit for Bailey that had recently been developed in the United States. The equipment sought to reduce the quantity of stores required for long span Bailey Bridges by using underslung cable reinforcement to redistribute the stresses in a bridge. A similar concept had been examined at MEXE in the 1950s but had been abandoned because of the excessive clearance needed under the bridge to accommodate the reinforcement.

A Reinforcement Kit was obtained from the US under a Standardization Agreement and trials were held at the RSME, Chatham, in 1971. The kit was designed for installation after construction of the bridge, prestressing cables being passed from one end of bridge to the other and then anchored to cable-connecting beams. Queen posts were connected to the lower chords of the bridge, at approximately one-third span positions, so that at mid-span the cables were held in position about 8ft below bottom chord level. Hydraulic rams were used to tighten the cables and produce a slight hogging in the bridge. It was found that the use of the kit achieved major savings in the quantity of equipment needed for a particular span and also savings in building man-hours. However, the extensive use of bolts and threaded nuts to take up slack in the cables was not thought compatible with the simplicity of Bailey, and the inability to install the kit during construction of the bridge was also thought to be a disadvantage. The RSME concluded that a system using quickly connected solid links or rods for the reinforcement would have many advantages, and indeed this was the system subsequently adopted for Reinforced MGB. After trials in the States, during which the reinforced

318

bridge was described by one observer as looking like a giant banjo, the US Army seriously considered developing a cable reinforcement kit for use with the MGB; in the end, however, the US Army settled for the solid-link kit developed at Christchurch.

The End of an Era

As the 1960s drew to a close, a fundamental change was to take place at MEXE. But, first, a singular honour was bestowed on the Establishment. At a special meeting of Christchurch Borough Council held on 28 January 1969 it was unanimously resolved -

> THAT in appreciation of the close association of the Military Engineering Experimental Establishment (MEXE) with the Borough of Christchurch since 28th February 1919, when the Experimental Bridging Company, Royal Engineers, was first formed and established on the site of the Barracks which had existed since 1793, and in recognition of the highly important role of the Establishment in support of the Armed Forces of the Crown, particularly during the World War of 1939-45, THE COUNCIL OF THE BOROUGH OF CHRISTCHURCH do hereby grant to THE MILITARY ENGINEERING EXPERIMENTAL ESTABLISHMENT (MEXE) at CHRISTCHURCH the HONORARY FREEDOM of the BOROUGH OF CHRISTCHURCH with the right, privilege and honour of marching through the streets and highways of the said Borough on ceremonial occasions with bayonets fixed, bands playing, drums beating and colours flying.

The Freedom Ceremony took place on 6 May 1969. (Figure 12.17). An

Figure 12.17. *A No 8 AVLB passes the saluting base at the Freedom Parade.* (MVEE slide).

illuminated scroll declaring the Freedom was placed in a casket made from old oak from the Christchurch Priory Church and was presented to Mr R A Foulkes, who had taken over as Director from Brigadier Jarrett-Kerr in October 1965, on behalf of the Establishment. At the same time the Establishment presented the Borough with a new mace, designed by Dr P S Bulson and made in the workshops at MEXE. The troops on parade, including contingents from the Sappers, RCT, RAOC and REME, then marched through the town, headed by the Corps Band and leading a cavalcade of MEXE-produced equipments of all types. At the town hall the salute was taken by the Mayor, Alderman Mrs Dorothy Baker JP, accompanied by the Director of MEXE and General Sir Charles Richardson, the Master General of the Ordnance, together with other senior officers.

Meanwhile, high-level discussions on the future of MEXE were already under way at the Ministry of Defence, as part of a rationalization programme for the Ministry Research and Development Establishments. It was clear that there was some overlap of responsibilities between MEXE and the Fighting Vehicles Research and Development Establishment (FVRDE) at Chobham, chiefly in the engine-testing and the material research fields, and it was therefore decided to bring the two establishments together, as the Military Vehicles and Engineering Establishment, or MVEE. The headquarters of the new establishment was based at Chertsey, in Surrey, although MEXE remained at Christchurch, renamed the Military Vehicles and Engineering Establishment (Christchurch), or MVEE(C). MVEE came into being on 1 April 1970, and Mr Foulkes then retired as the last Director of MEXE; he was replaced by Brigadier R A Lindsell MC, who became a Deputy Director of MVEE. MVEE (Chertsey) assumed responsibility for overall management of the workshops, drawing office and other support facilities at Christchurch, and there was considerable rationalization of the work carried out by the Materials Research Wing at Christchurch and that at Chertsey. The other four wings of the mid-1960s were reduced to two in number, the Bridging Wing and the Mechanical Wing, with a considerable reduction in functions and staff at Christchurch. In 1972 Brigadier Lindsell retired and Mr B T Boswell, a wartime Sapper officer, became Head of the Engineer Equipment Division of MVEE, answerable directly to the Director of MVEE at Chertsey. It will be seen later that the process of run-down of the Research and Development Establishments was to continue and that further rationalization was on the horizon.

The Westminster Abbey Bridge

It was at this time that MEXE was involved in a minor bridge, certainly not of the military genre. The bridge was presented to Westminster Abbey by the Institution of Civil Engineers to mark the 150th Anniversary of the Institution and to honour eminent engineers buried in the Abbey. The assistance of MEXE was requested and the aluminium alloy bridge was

Figure 12.18. The Westminster Abbey Bridge.

made in their workshops, to a design by Dr P S Bulson. The bridge girders were coated with a stone coloured plastic, better to blend in with its surroundings in the Abbey. (Figure 12.18)

The bridge was erected by Sappers of 24 Field Squadron and was formally opened at a simple ceremony on 8 April 1970. It improved access for the public into the Sanctuary where the High Altar stands, but was removed in 1998 when public access to the area it served had to be restricted in order to conserve the intricately decorated marble pavement in the area.

Commercial Exploitation of Military Bridging

Since the war the potential for use of Bailey Bridging and the Callender-Hamilton Bridge (the original version of the Unit Construction Bridge) for temporary and permanent civilian bridging has been exploited worldwide

Figure 12.19. *Extensive use of Bailey in the late 1940s, for temporary works on a dam for the Electric Company of Canada.*

by the civil engineer. (Figure 12.19) It therefore seems appropriate to conclude this chapter by considering how such exploitation stands today and, very briefly, other bridges that the firms involved have developed.

Mabey and Johnson Ltd

The firm at the forefront of the current manufacture and supply of Bailey, and indeed of its continued development, is Mabey and Johnson Ltd. The firm was founded in 1923 and since then has expanded considerably, now being one of the Mabey Group of Companies. The firm has been awarded the Queen's Award for Export Achievement no less than five times, in 1973, 1978, 1982, 1987 and 1998, as well as receiving the European Award for Steel Structures in 1972 and 1998.

The firm has pioneered the development of the Bailey Bridge since it was granted manufacturing rights in 1967. Initially they simplified the design of the panel and decking, eliminating the worst fatigue details in the panel. They then improved the lateral bracing of the bridge and introduced an all-steel deck for more permanent applications. The biggest improvement to date, however, has been the design of the 7ft high Compact 200 super panel, which has more than doubled the strength in both shear and bending of the original 5ft high Bailey panel. This effectively reduced the cost of bridges performing similar functions by some 30%, at the same time substantially extending the range of spans available. This system, the Mabey Compact 200, of which details are included later, has proved highly successful and is manufactured in Mabey and Johnson's highly automated factory using robot technology and sophisticated machinery.

The Mabey Super Bailey

Super Bailey was first produced by Mabey and Johnson in 1967, as a first-stage improvement on the wartime military equipment, with which it was completely interchangeable. Use of an improved grade of steel, together with modified web members and weldments, resulted in substantial increases in shear and fatigue strengths of the bridge. New swaybraces and transom clamps were introduced and an alternative steel decking was developed. These improvements, together with the major step of galvanizing all components, rendered the equipment more suitable for use in permanent civilian applications.

The Mabey Compact Bridge System

In 1983, however, Mabey and Johnson produced their greatly improved Compact Bailey, after extensive static and fatigue testing at Christchurch and elsewhere, and as a result Super Bailey became no longer competitive, structurally or economically. The basic size and configuration of the Bailey panel was retained, but channel sections were now used for the verticals and diamond bracing, and Grade 55C steel was used for the structural members. However, the main innovation in the basic design was the introduction of a single high-strength steel transom in each bay of bridge, used with vertical bracing frames to develop full 'U' frame stability with the trusses, which, with a factor of safety of 1.7, realized the full potential of the high-strength steel. Roadway widths of either 10ft 10in or 13ft 6in were available, with either steel or timber decking. Construction up to triple truss reinforced double storey was possible; a 200ft span bridge of this construction sustained the American Highway HS25 loading without distress, with 100% overload and full impact allowance whilst under test at Christchurch. (Figure 12.20).

Figure 12.20. The testing of the Mabey Compact 100 Bridge at Christchurch. Note the positioning of the single transom in each bay. (IWM 80906-7).

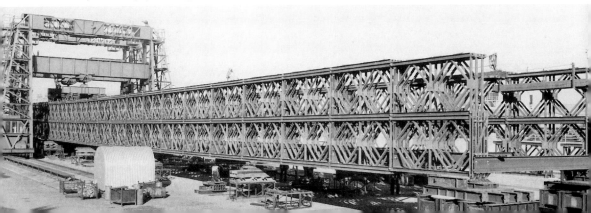

Figure 12.21. *A Mabey Compact 200 Bridge in Sweden, during evaluation by the Swedish Army.* (Mabey & Johnson).

The success of Compact Bailey, now known as **Compact 100**, with slightly amended roadway widths, was further enhanced by the introduction in 1986 of the **Compact 200 Bridge System**. Compact 200 is essentially similar in design to Compact 100 and most of the bridge components are common to both systems. Although the panel length of 10ft has been retained, the panel depth has been increased to 7ft, compared with the 4ft 9in depth of the Compact 100 panel. (Figure 12.21). This, together with the use of thick-web channel sections especially rolled for Mabey and Johnson by British Steel, results in an increase in panel strength over Compact 100 of some 80%, and over the original Bailey panel of some 110% - more than double. On longer spans this ensures a more economical design, using fewer components for increased loading. Compact 200 is usually built in single storey construction, but can be built in up to quadruple panel truss construction where necessary. It can also be built to produce a two-lane bridge with a roadway width of 24ft (7.35m). The bridge has now been adopted as the **Logistic Support Bridge** for the Army.

324

The Mabey Universal Bridge

The Universal Bridge, introduced in 1976, is the heavy-duty member of the Mabey bridging family and has been used worldwide, particularly in the more demanding areas of the USA and Europe. (Figure 12.22). The basic panel has been increased from the 10ft x 5ft 1in of Bailey to 14ft 9in x 7ft 9in, that is even larger than the scaled-up size of 12ft 6in x 6ft 6in used in the Heavy Girder Bridge; the panel uses 5in chord members instead of the 4in members used with the Bailey panel, and the diagonal size has been increased from 3in to 4in. Transoms are positioned equidistant, over the pin joint and at the central vertical of the panel. Partial chord reinforcements and special end shear panels were introduced to allow greater truss efficiency. A wide range of construction forms are possible, enabling for example a three lane bridge at 265ft span to be built. Either timber, steel or

Figure 12.22. A two span, two lane Mabey Universal Bridge in America, with a footwalk on one side. (Mabey & Johnson).

325

concrete decking may be used, with roadway widths varying from 10ft 9in to 35ft 9in, according to the transom size and construction strength selected.

The Universal Bridge broke new ground in Bailey concept terms by removing many of the features associated with the temporary use of Bailey, whilst enhancing low maintenance and high performance. It was with this equipment and the many full-scale tests performed on it that Mabey engineers gained their unique experience and understanding of the behaviour of panel bridges. The bridge, like all new developments, including the Compact 100 and 200 and now the Super Universal, was full-scale tested to prove its capacity, and this in turn has added to the firm's store of knowledge. A minimum factor of safety of 1.7 for all Mabey and Johnson bridges followed the test series. The year 2000 brought the latest development of the Universal Bridge, with stronger and more efficient trusses and longer deck units.

Mabey Compact Pontoons

The Mabey Compact Pontoon has side and end panels, bulkheads and frames which are manufactured under factory conditions and can then be shipped worldwide as a flat-pack for assembly on site. The pontoon panels and frames are quickly bolted together using a Mabey jig to ensure accurate assembly, and top and bottom skin plates are then welded in position to complete the construction. The basic centre pontoon is 19ft 1¾ in long, 8ft wide and 4ft 3in deep, and the bow pontoon is slightly longer. The pontoons can be assembled into pontoon piers, using between two and five units, for use in floating bridge work, or can be assembled into a range of ferries, with a load capacity of up to 107tons.

The Mabey Uniflote, formerly the Thos Storey Uniflote

The Uniflote is similar in many respects to the Mexeflote considered earlier, and limited purchases of the equipment were made for Army use prior to production of the Mexeflote. Indeed, after its introduction in 1956, Uniflotes were used in the Floating HGB trials of the late 1950s. The equipment is a unit-construction flotation system, consisting of identical floating units which can be assembled into rafts of various capacities. The rafts can then be used for a variety of uses, for example to transport heavy loads by water, to act as a floating bridge support system (see Figure 12.23), as a ferry or as a landing stage, and even as a floating helicopter pad. The standard unit are a steel-framed, square-ended pontoon, 8ft wide, 4ft deep and 17ft 4in long; this compares with dimensions of 8ft x 4ft 9in x 20ft for the Mexeflote. 12ft and 18ft ramp and 6ft scow end units are also available, as well as a 6ft deep version of the Uniflote, and a 'knock-down' version is available to minimize shipping costs. All units are fitted with connectors on the sides and ends so that the Uniflotes can be joined together in the water from deck level, the

Figure 12.23. *The launching of a Mabey Compact 200 Bridge to form a floating bridge with Uniflote Pontoons, at Xai Xai in Mozambique.* (Mabey & Johnson).

connectors allowing full transmission of shear and bending loads between the units in a raft. Various accessories are available, such as connectors to allow Uniflotes to be spaced apart, and saddles to support bridge girders or winches.

Thos Storey (Engineers) Ltd

The second firm that has been heavily involved with the development of Bailey over the years is Thos Storey (Engineers) Ltd, the firm founded by Thomas Storey in Stockport in 1939. After the war and as a direct result of its involvement in wartime production, the firm was granted a sole licence until expiry to manufacture Bailey Bridging by the National Research Development Corporation. The firm joined the Acrow Group in 1960 and continued to expand successfully, winning the Queen's Award to Industry for Resourcefulness in Exports in 1969 and again in 1977. Following the receivership of the Acrow Group in 1984, Thos Storey (Engineers) Ltd, still a viable and profitable member of the Group, arranged a management buy-out and once again became independent. A decision was made in 1994 to close its bridging manufacturing business, selling its bridging and flotation business to Mabey and Johnson, and also the intellectual property rights to all Acrow equipment. Sir Donald Bailey had become a technical consultant to the firm when he retired from the Civil Service in 1966 and retained close contact with the firm until he suffered an incapacitating stroke in the early 1970s.

Storey Bailey Bridging

After initial production of the Bailey Bridge as used by the Army during the war, Storey first modified the panel to include a built-in transom clamp; soon, however, the sizes of rolled steel beam used for vertical and diagonal members in the panels ceased to be available and a new panel was introduced using rectangular hollow sections for these members. At the same time the opportunity was taken to make use of the more readily available Grade 55C steel (see Appendix B) and the built-in transom clamp was dropped, being no longer advantageous with use of the hollow sections; a new steel decking system was also introduced. The equipment was known as Storey Bailey Bridging.

The Acrow Panel Bridge

In 1971 Thos Storey (Engineers) Ltd produced the Acrow Panel Bridge. This took full advantage of latest materials and manufacturing techniques, with the intention of eliminating some of the limitations that had become apparent in Bailey, bearing in mind that it had been introduced nearly 30 years earlier as a bridge for temporary use under wartime conditions. Many types of unit construction were studied, but none were found to offer advantages over the Bailey principles when the prime factors of cost, simplicity, speed of erection, carrying capacity and versatility were considered. The basic configuration of the Bailey panel was therefore retained, improved performance resulting from the continued use of rectangular hollow sections and Grade 55C steel as with the Storey Bailey Bridge. The main change to the panel was the moving of the transom position from its original position adjacent to the panel verticals to a new position in the bottom of the panel diamond, a configuration used with success in the Heavy Girder Bridge. (Figure 12.24). The resulting stronger transom seat meant that heavier and stronger transoms could be used, only two being used, at 5ft spacing, in each 10ft bay of bridge, as opposed to the two or four used with Bailey; this enabled rakers to be fitted at 5ft intervals, thus improving the stiffness of the top chord. The overall result of the various structural improvements was that the shear capacity of the new panel was some 67% greater than for Bailey, the bending capacity was increased by about 25% and the fatigue life was about four times that of the standard Bailey panel. Other improvements included the introduction of a

Figure 12.24. *Triple/single spans of Acrow Panel Bridging, used for a Ro Ro ferry terminal. The Uniflote support for the span link is grounded twice a day at low tide.* (Thos Storey plc).

range of decking systems, offering four different roadway widths, from 11ft 3in to 23ft 8½ in wide, and three different decking strengths, together with a choice of timber or steel decking. Additionally, panels and other components were provided either painted or hot-dipped galvanised. A wide range of construction forms was possible and the bridge was also adaptable as a floating bridge, or as a railway bridge, making use of special railway transoms, stringers and swaybrace.

In 1987 the earlier Acrow Panel Bridge was improved, as the **Acrow Panel 500 Series Bridge**. Among other improvements the new bridge introduced a stronger transom, fabricated from Universal Beam sections in BS 4360 Grade 55C steel. The transom was manufactured in four lengths, to give varying deck widths, and each length was available in two weights, for different load specifications. The basic panel configuration was retained but a single transom was now used in each 10ft bay of bridge and instead of being positioned at the bottom of the bracing diamond, it was placed between the vertical members of adjacent panels, making the configuration

329

Figure 12.25. A 100ft span Acrow 700 Series Panel Bridge, used as a Bascule Bridge. Note the revised transom positions. (Thos Storey plc).

the same as with the Mabey Compact Bridge.   A new range of transversely stiff deck units was also introduced.

A yet further development, the **Acrow Panel 700 Series Bridge**, was introduced in 1988 in response to Mabey and Johnson's Compact 200. In this version the 10ft panel length used in the previous bridge was retained, but the vertical depth between panel pinhole centres was increased from 4ft 9in to 7ft 2in, to produce a deeper truss, which proved more economical in many circumstances. (Figure 12.25). The transom and decking system was common between the 500 and 700 Series bridges.

The Acrow Heavy Bridge

The Acrow Heavy (or AH) Bridge was developed for temporary or permanent use over long spans subjected to heavy loading. The bridge was of the Warren Truss type, using 30ft bays, and components are bolted together on site. (Figure 12.26). Unit construction, making use of jig-controlled manufacture of components, ensured trouble free-assembly, rapid construction, interchangeability of parts and easy maintenance typified in the manufacture of Bailey. Components were of welded fabrication, using BS 4360 steels, either Grade 43A for the mild steel components or Grade 50B

Figure 12.26. *Launching a 210ft Acrow Heavy Bridge in Turkey, using a Bailey launching nose.* (Thos Storey plc).

for the high tensile structural steel components (see Appendix B). The bridge was designed with an unimpaired bottom chord to facilitate its launching over rollers, using a cantilevered launching nose as with the Bailey. Its 20ft or 24ft wide carriageway, for which a variety of decking systems could be used, could carry two-way highway loading in single spans of up to 330ft, whereas the Acrow Panel Bridge was normally limited to a span of 200ft; single track railways could also be carried over similar spans using shorter cross girders to reduce the truss spacing. The bridge was first produced in 1968.

The Callender-Hamilton Bridge

The commercial production and development of Hamilton's pre-war bridge, adopted by the Army as the Unit Construction Bridge, has been dealt with in Chapter Six. The bridge was then manufactured in considerable quantities, for use by the Ministry of Transport as wartime emergency bridging, by Messrs Callender Cables and Construction Co Ltd, as the Callender-Hamilton Bridge. Manufacture of the bridge has continued since the war and is now undertaken by Balfour Beatty Power Networks Ltd, one of the Balfour Beatty plc group of companies, to the extent that C-H bridges have been used in over 46 countries world wide, for both road and rail use. (Figure 12.27)

Over the years many variations of the bridge have been introduced, using increased girder depth and heavier angle sections or channels to accommodate longer spans and heavier loadings. In all cases, however, the original format and design concept has been maintained, retaining the original Warren truss configuration, although additional bracing within the truss is sometimes used to improve span or load carrying capacity. The current range runs from the CH3, for spans of 12m up to 42m, through the CH6, for spans from 55m to 72m, to the CH8D for spans from 90m to 128m, both CH6 and CH8D with overhead bracing. A long span bridge of the 8D type has been supplied to Ethiopia producing a multi-lane through bridge

331

Figure 12.27. The Goria Bridge in Bangladesh, with seven 88m spans of Callender-Hamilton Type B8 Bridge. (Callender-Hamilton Bridges).

with a clear span of 128m (420ft). However, the CH10 bridge is at present under development and will have an effective span of 140m (460ft).

A wide and varied range of bridges is thus available, from small footbridges up to large multi-lane road and rail bridges, many using basic components common between types. A particular advantage of the C-H deck type bridge is that extra trusses can be added to increase the width of roadway and accommodate extra lanes of traffic. All components of C-H bridges are galvanized to BS EN 1S0 1461 and are constructed from BS EN 10025 weldable structural steel with bolted connections.

Williams Fairey Engineering Ltd

The considerable production of the Medium Girder Bridge by Fairey Engineering was detailed earlier in this chapter. In 1986 Fairey Engineering was taken over by Williams Holdings and became Williams Fairey Engineering Ltd, still operating from the Stockport factory. Production of the MGB continued, albeit at a reduced scale, but the firm is still active in the development of military bridging, its latest development being the **Axial Folding Bridge**, the brain child of Mr Stuart Parramore, whose work at MVEE on the ABLE/BRAVE concept for BR80 is considered in Chapter Fifteen.

The Axial Folding Bridge (AFB) was originally designed to meet a US

Navy requirement for a light weight bridge that could be used in conjunction with their USN causeway system and for the RORO offloading of shipping. (Figure 12.28). The bridge is formed from 5.83m x 4.04m (19ft 1½ in x 13ft 3in) light weight, high strength aluminium sections of bridge that fold up into compact modules, two of which can be palletized and handled as a standard ISO container load. Tapered ramp sections, of similar length, are hinged so that they can be articulated upward to form a flat deck bridge. A reinforcement set is also available to increase the span range of the bridge, which is capable of spanning gaps from 17m (56ft) at MLC 70 (using three modules), up to 47m (154ft) at MLC60 (using eight modules). Construction times of less than an hour have been achieved for a 41m (135ft) bridge, using a team of eight men, and during a recent exercise the bridge crossed 6,500 vehicles, including battle tanks. A modified version of this bridge has now been formally accepted by the US as the MLC 100 **Heavy Dry Support Bridge**.

Production of the **Medium Girder Bridge Pontoon**, a concept of MVEE

Figure 12.28. Unfolding a module of the Williams Fairey Axial Folding Bridge. (Williams Fairey Engineering Ltd).

that was subsequently developed by Fairey Engineering, has also continued. (Figure 12.29). Although not purchased by the British Army, because of adequate stocks of M2 and M3 equipments, the pontoon has proved highly successful and has been purchased by a number of overseas armies. The pontoon is open topped and can be nested for easy storage and transport, four of the pontoons being carried on an Ampliroll truck or a special trailer, both of which can be tipped up to allow each pontoon to be launched individually. The pontoon is constructed from the marine grade aluminium alloy NS8. It is 26ft long, 8ft 7in wide and 3ft 10in deep, and weighs 2400lb, with a buoyancy of about 12 tons; two pontoons are connected end to end to form a bridge pier.

Figure 12.29. Loading nested Williams Fairey Engineering MGB Pontoons onto a Ampliroll truck. (Williams Fairey Engineering Ltd).

The latest contribution to military bridging by Williams Fairey Engineering is the development of the new **Air Portable Ferry Bridge** for the Sappers, which will replace the Air Portable Bridge of the 1970s. The new bridge will be an MLC 35 system based upon an upgraded version of the MGB and will be transportable in the C130 aircraft. The system will provide a light bridge up to 28 span, a fly-forward bridge up to 14m span, and a powered RORO ferry.

CHAPTER THIRTEEN

Assault/Armoured Bridging Since the War

The Origins of 32 Assault Engineer Regiment

The formation of the Assault Engineers, as part of 79 Armoured Division in NW Europe and the combined RE/RAC Assault Brigade in Italy, was considered in Chapter Eight. With the end of the war in Europe the strength of the assault engineers declined continuously for almost twenty years. This was of course partially due to the run down in the size of the armed forces after the war, but it was also brought about by the realization that the prospect of such specialized units being used in a massive breaching operation, as in the Normandy invasion, was no longer a possibility. Considerable effort was directed towards the development of assault bridging equipment during the postwar period however, and eventually there was a realization that Assault Engineers could play a very useful part in engineer operations in support of the Armoured Division, and to some extent the Infantry Division.

The swing of the pendulum is reflected by the history of the Assault Engineers, whose pedigree is included at Appendix D. After the end of the war in Europe, during which the regiment had most recently been actively engaged in the Rhine Crossing, 42 Assault Regiment RE was moved back to UK, to prepare for a move to the Far East. However, the war against Japan came to a sudden end in August 1945, and after demobilization of many of its personnel, elements of the regiment returned to Hameln in Germany as part of the occupational forces. Elements from the other two assault regiments of 1 Assault Brigade RE joined them in Hameln, to consolidate as 42 Assault Regiment RE. In early 1948 the Regiment was redesignated 32 Assault Engineer Regiment and soon afterwards came home to UK, to reform at full strength at Perham Down. In 1951 the Regiment took over responsibility for Flail Tanks from the RAC, but by 1954 had lost two of its squadrons and on 1 July 1957 was disbanded, only 26 Assault Squadron remaining.

Meanwhile an experimental armoured force had been created in the mid 1950s, within 6 Armoured Division in BAOR. The aim was to put everything on tracks within this force, and 28 Field Squadron, which was part of 27 Field Engineer Regiment, the divisional engineer regiment, was reorganized into two Field Troops, mounted on half tracks, and two Armoured Troops, equipped mainly with Churchill Bridgelayers which had been hastily shipped over from 26 Assault Squadron in UK. The Sappers were given a six week tank training course by the local tank regiment in Minden and the force, which was about brigade strength, took part in a major autumn exercise.

26 Assault Squadron moved from Perham Down to Hohne in BAOR in August and September 1957, and became part of 1 British Corps Troops. The squadron was redesignated 26 Armoured Engineer Squadron, and once again the Sappers had an Assault Squadron, or an Armoured Engineer Squadron (as it was now known) as part of BAOR, but the full swing of the pendulum will be seen later. This change of name from 'assault' to 'armoured' was to be the last of a number of such changes, backward and forward since the assault regiments were formed in 1943, 'armoured engineers' now being considered the more appropriate title.

The Equipment Situation in 1945

Apart from the Churchill Flail Tanks and AVREs, the main assault equipments available at the end of the War comprised the No 1 Tank Bridge, mounted on the Valentine Tank chassis, the No 2 Tank Bridge, mounted on the Churchill Tank chassis, and the Small Box Girder Tank Bridge, mounted on the Churchill AVRE, all capable of spanning a clear gap of 30ft. Also available were the ARKs Mark I and II and the Italian ARK. Within a space of twenty five years or so the Sappers were to be equipped with the No 8 Armoured Vehicle Launched Bridge (AVLB), or Tank Bridge, able to carry the very latest battle tank, at Class 70, across a 75ft gap. The evolution of this bridge, through the Centurion mounted equipments of the 1960s to the Chieftain mounted equipments of the 1980s, makes interesting reading.

The No 3 Tank Bridge

Work on the No 3 Tank Bridge started in early 1945, with the original object of producing a bridge capable of carrying tanks with wider tracks than could the No 2 Tank Bridge (9ft 6in overall width) and the SBG Tank Bridge (10ft 3in overall width). Specifically the bridge was intended to carry the American T26 tank (which became the M26 General Pershing, 11ft 2in over tracks) although an order for 500 of the tanks was subsequently cancelled after half a dozen or so had been delivered, because of the end of the war.

Nevertheless development and production of the bridge went ahead, the effective length and load class being the same as for the No 2 Bridge, that is 30ft and Class 60(Tracks) respectively. The bridge consisted of two 34ft long, 4ft wide trackways, each made up of steel plate girders, with light alloy deck panels; the end sections of decking were of welded steel construction. The trackways or girders were spaced 2ft 8in apart and were connected at each end of the bridge by a rigid bankseat beam. This spacing enabled a Jeep to cross the bridge without the need for central decking, and gave an overall width of 10ft 8in, sufficient to accommodate the Centurion Tank.

For travel over long distances the bridge could be mounted on a single

Figure 13.1. *The Tank Bridge No 3 carried in the assault position by the Churchill AVRE.* (IWM 4296).

axle trailer and towed by a Churchill AVRE fitted with a towing frame. When the bridge was required for operational use, it was transferred to the front of an AVRE which had been modified by the fitting of a rear mounted winch, and pivots at the front which could accept the home end of the bridge. (Figure 13.1). The forward end of the bridge was supported, raised at an angle of about 40° to the horizontal, by a tackle passing over a forward tackle pole and thence to the rear winch. The bridge was thus raised or lowered in the manner of a drawbridge by means of the winch, which had a remote control operated from within the AVRE. Once in its final position the bridge was disconnected by operating release toggles at the front pivots and firing a blow-out pin in the lifting tackle. This method of launching the bridge was similar to that previously used for the SBG Tank Bridge.

A slightly different version of the bridge used cross diaphragms and tubular diagonal bracing instead of the end bankseat beams. The girders were moved further apart to give an overall width of 11ft, and the bridge was launched by the javelin method of launch, as used with the No 2 Tank Bridge. This version of the bridge, which was carried and then launched by a Churchill Bridgelayer, was used operationally during the Korean War in 1951 and is shown in Figure 8.8.

The ARK Mark III

The Mark III ARK was also developed in 1945 with the intention of carrying the American General Pershing, but in this case development did not go

Figure 13.2. The Churchill ARK Mark III with its ramps lowered. (IWM 3891).

beyond the pilot model stage. (Figure 13.2). The length of the ramps was increased to 19ft, compared with the 12½ft ramps of the ARK Mark II, and this made the ramp slope much easier for the crossing of heavier tanks. The total operational length of the equipment was thus about 60ft, and the width of the trackways was also increased, to about 4ft, permitting passage of tanks up to 11ft 2in over tracks. With the cancellation of the Pershing tank order and the projected development of the FV 200 series of armoured vehicles, which included the FV 203 ARK, work on the Mark III Ark was abandoned in early 1946.

The No 4 Tank Bridge

The No 4 Tank Bridge was also designed in 1945 and was intended as a light alloy replacement for the No 1 Tank Bridge. (Figure 13.3). Thus it was a 34ft long scissor launched bridge, with an effective span of 30ft. It was carried folded in half on top of the Valentine Bridgelayer and used exactly the same launching mechanism as the No 1 Tank Bridge. The bridge was fabricated in aluminium alloy throughout (see Appendix B) and was of riveted plate girder construction, using, in the main, ½in diameter alloy rivets. 'Top hat' extrusions spanned between the two plate girders of each main girder to

Figure 13.3. The experimental Tank Bridge No 4 carried on the Valentine Bridgelayer. (IWM 5701).

form the decking, and timber inserts were then bolted into the troughs so formed, to provide a wearing surface and prevent damage to the extrusions. Only one prototype of the bridge was built and details of its load class are uncertain.

A New Postwar Tank

In 1946 a new AFV development was to have a considerable impact on Sapper bridging equipment for some years to come. The story started in 1944, when the development of an Infantry Support Tank, designated the A45, was put in hand. The new tank was to have worked alongside the A41 Heavy Cruiser Tank, also under development and later to be known as the Centurion. However by 1946 a concept for a new unified Cruiser/Infantry tank was formalized in the requirement for a Universal Tank, to be based on the A45. This initiated work on a range of armoured vehicles known as the FV 200 series.

A prototype FV 201 tank was completed in 1947, but by late 1948, after considerable delays in the development programme, it was realized that when FV 201 finally entered service it would be incapable of meeting the potential Soviet threat. It was decided that the Centurion, which had entered service in late 1946, could undertake many of the roles envisaged for the FV 200 series, and in 1949 the project was cancelled. Nevertheless the FV 200 chassis was further developed, to produce the FV 214 Conqueror Tank, a heavy gun (120mm) version intended to engage an enemy at ranges beyond the Centurion capability. The first prototype of the new tank was completed in 1950, and 180 Conqueror Tanks were subsequently manufactured between 1956 and 1959. One other variant of the series survived, the FV 219 Armoured Recovery Vehicle.

The Conqueror was not a successful tank, difficult to maintain, limited in range, and not very reliable. However it was the biggest and heaviest gun tank ever to go into production in the UK, weighing 65 tons, and although it was phased out of service in 1966, its size and weight directly influenced British military bridge design for a decade or more. Thus the advent of the FV 200 series in 1946 resulted in the upgrading of the SWBPB to Class 80, whilst the Heavy Ferry, Heavy Girder Bridge and Heavy Assault Floating Bridge were all designed for Class 80 loading during the next decade.

Sapper Variants in the FV200 Series

A number of Sapper variants in the new series of armoured vehicles were considered but non progressed beyond the design study and model stage. These included:

the FV 202 - a turreted AVRE, known also as the A45 AVRE(T);

the FV 203 - a load carrying AVRE, known also as the A45 AVRE(L);

and the FV 208 - a bridgelayer.

The FV 202 - A45 AVRE(T) was to be the turreted version of the Engineer Tank in the FV 200 series, fitted with a demolition charge projector in place of the normal tank gun. A proposal for a dozer blade that would be carried at the back of the tank and then rotated vertically through 180° to the front when required for use was considered, and proposed front loaded devices included an assault bridge, a lifting derrick, mine laying attachments and mine clearing rollers. A crew of five was envisaged.

The FV 203 - A45 AVRE(L) was to be a load carrying version of the Engineer Tank, without a turret but with twin trackways mounted on top of the chassis, which could be used either to form the basis of an ARK or as a flat bed to carry engineer stores. It was intended that the crew compartment would accommodate the crew of three and nine assault engineers; ancillary equipments envisaged for the AVRE(L) included an ARK, a mobile bridge and an assault bridge (possibly the No 3 Tank Bridge laid by the drawbridge method), a fascine cradle, anti-mine and mine laying equipment, and a 10 ton swing crane.

The FV 203 ARK. Proposals for the ARK version of the FV 200 series of armoured vehicles were based upon the A45 AVRE(L). One proposal for the ARK included a 24ft front ramp, folded back on to the trackways on top of the vehicle, and a 34ft rear ramp towed behind the vehicle on a collapsible axle, with the idea that if necessary the front ramp could have been jettisoned and the rear ramp moved to the front of the vehicle and used as a drawbridge launched 34ft assault bridge. Yet another proposal suggested double jointed front and rear ramps, folded over on to the top of the vehicle and both launched by the scissor method; this would have provided a deployed span of about 75ft. (Figure 13.4). In all cases the ramps were to be of aluminium alloy welded construction, with riveted and pinned cross girders and diaphragms.

Development of the FV 202, 203 and the ARK was a joint responsibility of MEXE (who were responsible for developing the ARK ramps, the Assault Bridge adaptation and mine laying equipment), and the Fighting Vehicle Development Establishment, or FVDE, at Chertsey (who were responsible

Figure 13.4. *A model of the double-jointed ramp version of the proposed FV 203 ARK, based on the A45 AVRE(L).* (IWM 10054 - 12).

for work on the vehicle hulls, winches, the dozer, the trailer, and anti-mine equipment). Work progressed to the stage where manufacture of full size mock-ups was in hand, and at a later stage some work was carried out on a proposal for a Heavy AVRE, FV 215, which would have replaced both FV 202 and FV 203, but all work was eventually cancelled in favour of the Centurion AVRE FV 4003.

The Gas ARK

As part of the MEXE development programme on the FV 203 ARK, experiments were carried out on the possibility of launching the ramps by using high pressure gas instead of by the more conventional hydraulic operation. A Gas ARK test rig was built, and the proposal was that cordite would be burnt within a cylinder to produce gas at a pressure of up to 3,000psi; the gas would expand against a piston within the cylinder, which could be suitably harnessed to launch the ramps. A simple adjustment to the linkage would enable the same system to be used to recover the ramps. A number of trials proved the feasibility of the scheme, which had some advantages over hydraulic operation of the ramps, but there were also disadvantages and it was decided that the first prototype FV 203 ARK, which was not of course completed before the project was cancelled, would have hydraulically operated ramps.

The FV 208 Bridgelayer and the No 5 Tank Bridge

With the very ambitious FV 200 series development programme, work on the FV 208 Bridgelayer did not progress very far before this project was also cancelled, most of the bridging input to the programme concentrating on the FV 202/203 variants. There is no firm evidence that the bridge that would have been developed for use with the FV 208 was known as the No 5 Tank Bridge, however this seems logical as it was the only projected tank bridge between the experimental No 4 of 1945 and the Centurion mounted No 6 Tank Bridge, work on which started in 1950. In 1946 a steel lattice framework representing the probable shape and size of a new tank bridge was mounted on an early model of the A41 Centurion Tank for manoeuvrability trials. The bridge mock-up was mounted as a complete structure, upside down, on the tank, obviously intended for launching by the up and over method. It thus presented a large and bulky structure during its trials in the country lanes around Chobham, where the trials were carried out by the Fighting Vehicle Proving Establishment (FVPE). At this stage the trials were obviously carried out with the design of the FV 208 in mind, but the trials showed that carriage of a tank bridge longer than 52ft and wider than 14ft as a single unit on top of a tank was not feasible, and these restricting parameters were later adopted during development of the No 6 Tank Bridge. It also became clear that the FV 208 Bridgelayer with its bridge in position would be too high to disembark from the tank landing craft LCT Type 8 then in use.

The Churchill Mark VII AVRE

With the cancellation of the FV 200 project and associated development work on the FV 202/203 AVREs, work started on an improved version of the Churchill AVRE, based upon the Mark VII version of the tank. The wartime AVREs had been based upon the Mark III and Mark IV versions of the tank and had been armed with a 290mm calibre Petard mortar, firing a 40lb demolition projectile at an effective accurate range of about 80 yards. The Mark VII Churchill had substantially increased armour, and the new AVRE had a modified turret mounting an OBL 6.5in (165mm) low velocity AVRE gun. This new gun had been under development since 1948 and had an accurate range of 1,000 yards, firing 61lb HESH (High Explosive Squash Head) rounds at a rate of four per minute. The AVRE could be fitted with a dozer blade, which increased its load class from Class 50 to Class 60, and was fitted with a fascine cradle enabling it to carry a 6/7 ton fascine. (see Figure 13.15 later in this chapter). The AVRE (FV 3903) underwent troop trials in 1950, was in production in 1952, and came into service in 1954.

The Churchill Linked ARK

A further result of the cancellation of work on the FV 202/203 AVREs was the development of the Churchill Linked, or Twin ARK, intended as a replacement for the wartime ARKs, in lieu of the aborted FV 203 ARK. This equipment introduced a new concept for the ARK system, in that two ARKs were used to form a bridge, locking themselves together, side by side, as they approached the gap. When the vehicles reached the centre of the gap, the ramps on each were unfolded independently to form the twin track bridge. The front and rear ramps on each ARK were carried on the fixed section of trackway mounted on top of the tank chassis, folded in two, and were then

Figure 13.5. A Churchill Linked ARK, with its 7ft wide single trackway. (MEXE Handbook - June 1958).

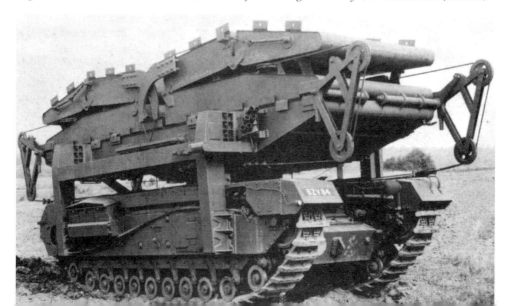

launched by a system of cables and pulleys using the scissor method. The ramps were 7ft wide, which enabled wheeled vehicles to cross a single ARK. (Figure 13.5). When two ARKs were locked together, the space between adjacent trackways was 4ft 6in, and an improvised deck of timber sleepers could be laid between the trackways if required. The wide roadway of the linked ARKs enabled both Centurion and Conqueror tanks to cross, the 71ft total length of bridge effectively spanning a 65ft gap. Technical trials of the Linked ARK (FV 3901) took place in 1954 with acceptance trials the following year, and the equipment remained in service until 1965, when it was replaced by the Centurion ARK.

The No 3 Tank Bridge Mark II

With the demise of the FV 208 Bridgelayer and the No 5 Tank Bridge, and pending development of the No 6 Tank Bridge on the Centurion Bridgelayer, a Mark II version of the No 3 Tank Bridge was introduced in 1953. The Mark II bridge used the same basic girders as the earlier bridge but with some strengthening to upgrade the bridge to Class 80, thus enabling it to carry the Conqueror Tank. The new bridge was designed to be launched by the Churchill Bridgelayer and not the AVRE, and thus used cross diaphragms and tubular bracing to space the girders and act as the pivot for the launching of the bridge by the javelin method. (Figure 13.6). The

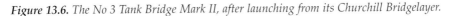

Figure 13.6. The No 3 Tank Bridge Mark II, after launching from its Churchill Bridgelayer.

diaphragms and bracing were modified to increase the overall width to 12ft 1in, again to accommodate the Conqueror Tank. To cater for any unevenness of bankseats, the diaphragms were pinned to the bridge girders at the tops only, and were deliberately designed so that at excessive loading they would fail before damage could be caused to the bridge girders; they were thus treated as semi-expendable, and four spare diaphragms were supplied with each Bridgelayer.

The Centurion Tank

The A41 Centurion Tank had been under development since 1944, as a Heavy Cruiser tank, but although six prototypes were completed before the end of the war, they arrived in Germany too late for operational use. Limited production in 1946 and 1947 coincided with the initiation of the project for the new Universal Tank, as part of the FV 200 series of armoured vehicles, and it was not until the FV 200 project had been abandoned in 1949 that the Centurion was firmly accepted as the standard battle tank for the British Army. Over 2,600 of the tanks were manufactured from 1951 to 1956, and the total production exceeded 4,400 tanks. The Centurion was a very successful tank, exported for use in a number of foreign armies and used in combat from Korea through to Vietnam. It was also an important tank for the Sappers, since it was used as a bridgelayer for the No 6 Tank Bridge, as the Centurion ARK, and as the Centurion AVRE, still in use in the late 1980s.

The No 6 Tank Bridge

Work on the No 6 Tank Bridge started at MEXE in 1950 under the supervision of Mr Delany, who had been responsible for much of the prewar development work on tank bridges. But in the mid 1950s Mr T S Parramore, who had earlier joined the staff at MEXE from the aircraft industry and was responsible for the design of the Bridge Test Rig mentioned in Chapter Eleven, took over the project soon after the first prototype had been produced. Full account was taken of the FVPE trials with the steel framed mock-up bridge referred to earlier. These trials had indicated 52ft x 14ft as the maximum practical size of a bridge that could be carried on top of a tank, without resorting either to folding the bridge in half, as for a scissor launch, or to bringing the two tracks together for road travel. As finally developed, the 52ft long and 5ft 8½in wide twin tracks were spaced 2ft 6in apart, and thus the bridge fitted exactly into the FVPE parameters.

The bridge was designed to be carried and launched by the Centurion Tank, and the first mock-up bridge was carried on a modified Centurion Mark 1 chassis in 1952. The first working prototype bridgelayer, produced in 1956, was based on a Centurion Mark 7 chassis, but the production version of the bridge used the Centurion Mark 5 as the base tank; the layer thus became known as the Bridgelayer, Centurion Mark 5 (FV 4002). It should be noted that, as was the case, for example, with the Churchill Mark VII AVRE, the designation of many of the Centurion variants used the mark number of the base vehicle rather than of the variant, noting also that vehicle mark numbers were changed from Roman to Arabic numerals in 1948. The Mark 5 tanks had the turrets removed of course, and were further modified by removal of the fire control equipment and ammunition bins, and the fitting of a roof plate with an access hatch over the turret ring.

The bridge was carried upside down on the bridgelayer, and was the first British production tank bridge to use the up-and-over method of launch, although the Russians had used this method for launching light bridges from their BT-2 and T-26 battle tanks as early as 1937. (Figure 13.7 and Appendix B). The 52ft length of the bridge, enabling it to carry Class 80 loads over a clear span of 45ft, was a considerable improvement on previous British tank launched bridges, most of which had been only 34ft long, with a clear span capability of 30ft. The penalty of using such a length of tank bridge in a single span was one of mobility, the sheer size of the bridge making it very difficult to manoeuvre the bridgelayer through the narrow streets in some German towns and villages and through heavily wooded areas. Another drawback was the high profile presented during the launching of the bridge, making it visible, during daylight hours, from a considerable distance, although this disadvantage was minimized to some extent by the fact that the bridge could be launched and placed in about a minute and a half and recovered in about two minutes. There was a considerable flexibility in permissible site conditions, the bridge coping with a cross slope of 1 in 10, a fore and aft slope of up to 1 in 4, and a difference in bank heights of up to 8ft.

Although development work on

Figure 13.7. A Centurion Bridgelayer launching a pre-production version of the Tank Bridge No 6. (IWM 21403).

345

the bridge started in the early 1950s, acceptance trials of a pre-production model of the equipment did not take place until 1960. Full scale production of the bridge began in 1961, and the Centurion Mark 5 Bridgelayer and the No 6 Tank Bridge finally came into service in 1963, both with 26 Armoured Engineer Squadron and also with the RAC, initially on a scale of three to each regiment. However the problem of mobility caused by the size of the equipment meant that the bridgelayers often lagged behind the RAC gun tanks, and special routing was often necessary. Because of this the bridgelayers were eventually all transferred to 26 Armoured Engineer Squadron, where central control of deployment and maintenance proved a much more efficient way to use this excellent equipment.

The Centurion Mark 5 AVRE

The Centurion AVRE, FV 4003, was developed by FVRDE in the mid 1950s as a replacement for the ageing World War II Churchill AVREs. The first prototype was produced in 1957 and after user trials in 1962, the new AVRE came into service in 1963. The FV 4003 was based upon the standard Mark 5 Centurion Tank, with its welded hull and cast turret with welded roof plate. It was powered by a Rolls Royce Meteor Mk IVB 12 cylinder petrol engine and its main armament was the 6.5in (165mm) demolition gun, firing a 61lb HESH projectile at an effective range of up to 1,000yd. It was fitted with a hydraulically powered dozer blade and had a fascine cradle mounted on the front of the chassis which could carry either a fascine or a roll of Class 60 Trackway. (see Figure 13.17 later) Its rotatable towing hook could be used to tow the two wheeled trailer (FV 3705) which carries the Giant Viper mine clearing system or the 7½ ton four wheeled AVRE Trailer (FV 2721) carrying, for example, a second Pipe Fascine. The AVRE had a crew of five, the driver and the co-driver seated in the front of the hull, and the commander, gunner and loader in the turret.

During the mid 1980s a number of Centurion Main Battle Tanks that had previously been used by the Royal Artillery as forward observation posts were converted to AVREs. These vehicles retained their 105mm L7 guns and are thus known as Centurion AVRE 105s, the former AVREs being known as Centurion AVRE 165s. The AVRE 105 could be fitted with a mine plough as an an alternative to the dozer blade of the AVRE 165.

The Centurion ARK

Development of an ARK based upon the Centurion chassis started in 1958, at FVRDE Chobham. Once again the Centurion Mark 5 was used as the base vehicle, the turret being removed and the turret ring covered with an armoured plate, as with the Centurion Mark 5 Bridgelayer. Wading screens were fitted to the chassis and the main and auxiliary engine exhaust pipes were extended to allow wading to a depth of about 8ft. A superstructure on

Figure 13.8. *A Centurion ARK with ramps in the folded position.* (British Military Vehicles - 1966).

the top of the chassis supported two longitudinal trackways with ramps fitted at either end; with the ramps extended an 80ft long bridge was formed, effectively spanning a gap of 75ft. Each ramp was formed from three sections; the main section was folded over on top of the chassis trackways, and the centre and tail sections, pinned together as one unit, were then folded over on top of the main section. (Figure 13.8). The ramps were thus launched in the scissor fashion, in a similar manner to those of the Churchill Linked ARK, using a hydraulic pump driven by the main engine. An innovation in the design was the ability to vary the spacing of the trackways and ramps. This was done by means of a screw mechanism located at either end of the superstructure and enabled the width of the ARK to be reduced during road travel or during transportation by rail, whilst at the same time permitting the trackways to be opened out for passage of large vehicles, up to the maximum of Class 80. Centre decking panels were provided for use at the maximum spacing of the trackways. Recovery of the ramps was a slow and tedious task, as it was with the Churchill Linked ARK.

The Centurion ARK was designated FV 4016 and entered service with the Sappers in 1965, forming the basic equipment, with the Centurion Bridgelayer (FV 4002) and the Centurion AVRE (FV 4003), of the Armoured Engineer Squadrons in BAOR. The equipment was subsequently withdrawn from service in 1977.

CAMP

An interesting use of the Centurion ARK was as a mobile pier, known as the Centurion ARK Mobile Pier or CAMP. Under certain river conditions it was found that a deployed ARK could cause damming of the river, creating scour and turbulence. To overcome this problem some ARKs had their ramps removed and became CAMPs. A CAMP could be driven into the river parallel with the banks, and would then be used as a pier to support the off-

Figure 13.9. *CAMP deployed with two No 6 Tank Bridges, alongside a Centurion ARK, across the River Leine in BAOR.* (Tank Museum 2136/E3).

shore ends of two No 6 Tank Bridges. (Figure 13.9). On one exercise an even longer bridge was formed, using two CAMPs and three No 6 Tank Bridges. This was in fact an early form of Combination Bridging, of which more will be said later.

The Fortunes of 32 Regiment

It was seen earlier that 32 Assault Engineer Regiment was disbanded in 1957, its last remaining squadron returning to BAOR as 26 Armoured Engineer Squadron. In 1965 2 Field Squadron RE was reformed as 2 Armoured Engineer Squadron and moved to Hohne to join 26 Squadron as part of a newly formed 32 Armoured Engineer Regiment. The Regiment was equipped with all of the Centurion based engineer equipments; at one stage each squadron had three troops, each holding three AVREs and two No 6 Tank Bridges, and a fourth troop holding four Centurion ARKs, but establishments were often varied to suit current tactical policy in BAOR.

In early 1969 a reorganization of the Royal Engineer units of 1 British Corps was put in hand, eventually leading to a Sapper establishment of two smaller Engineer Regiments (each of two Field Squadrons), an Armoured Engineer Squadron and a Field Support Squadron in each Division, all under command of a Divisional CRE at full Colonel level. As part of this reorganization the role of 32 Armoured Engineer Regiment was changed and it became 32 Engineer Regiment. The regiment remained at Hohne, eventually consisting of 7 and 30 Field Squadrons. For a time 26 Armoured

Engineer Squadron remained as part of the regiment, although not under operational command, but 2 Armoured Engineer Squadron moved to Iserlohn, provisionally as part of 26 Engineer Regiment. In September 1969 31 Armoured Engineer Squadron was formed at Hohne, and moved to Osnabruck in March 1971.

In April 1971 the three Armoured Engineer Squadrons became fully independent, each being placed under command of one of the BAOR Divisions. 2 Squadron was at Iserlohn, under command of 4 Armoured Division, 26 Squadron remained at Hohne, under command of 1 Armoured Division, and 31 Squadron was at Osnabruck, under command of 2 Division. Although the Sappers now had three Armoured Engineer Squadrons, once again they were without an Armoured Engineer Regiment.

The Chieftain Tank

Meanwhile, as a result of the demise of the FV 200 series project, and the consequent decision to retain the Centurion as the main battle tank for the British Army, it was realized that a replacement for the Centurion would eventually be needed, and a requirement for such a tank was drawn up by the War Office in the 1950s. Work on one surviving variant of the FV 200 series, the FV 214 Conqueror had continued, but this was the heavy gun version, intended for long range anti-tank support, as opposed to the FV 201 version, which would have been the main battle tank. The new tank, to be known as the Chieftain, was developed at FVRDE and the first prototype was completed in 1959. After production of six more prototypes, the tank was accepted for service in 1963, although it did not enter service until 1967, because of problems with the multi-fuel engine, the transmission and the suspension. As with the FV 200 series, once development work on the new tank, the FV 4201, was under way, serious consideration was given to alternative uses for the basic chassis. These included the FV 4203 - a Royal Engineer support vehicle, FV 4204 - an Armoured Recovery Vehicle (ARV) and the FV 4205 - a Bridgelayer. Development of the ARV is outside the scope of this book, but that of the other two was of considerable importance to the Sappers.

FV 4203 and the No 7 Tank Bridge

In anticipation of the acceptance for service of the new Chieftain Tank, a General Staff Target, GST 24, was issued in the early 1960s for a general support vehicle, based upon the Chieftain chassis. At an early stage it was decided that all the requirements of GST 24 could not be met by a single vehicle, and that an ARV would be required in addition to two versions of an Armoured Engineer Vehicle (AEV), that is an AEV(Gun) and an AEV(Winch). The AEV(Winch) was to carry a short span bridge (up to 20ft clear span), to be used as a replacement for the fascines that had been used for many years to cross narrow rivers and streams. The vehicle was also to have a dozing capability and was to be able to cross water gaps unaided, if necessary by snorkeling; its bridge and winch would then be used to assist the vehicle to climb steep banks and thus exit from a river under its own power. In due course a General Staff Requirement was issued for the two AEVs, but in 1967 the GSR was amended, eliminating the gun version of the AEV, and renaming the AEV(Winch) the **Chieftain AVRE**.

Two main proposals had been considered for the twin track bridge to be carried by the AVRE. The first made use of folded tracks to be launched by the scissor method, either to be carried on a trailer towed by the AVRE until required or to be permanently mounted on the vehicle. The second scheme proposed a single piece bridge carried upside down on top of the vehicle and launched by the up-and-over method. This second scheme was that finally adopted, and development work on the bridge continued under the project leadership of Mr J M H Barnard. It is assumed that this bridge was in fact the No 7 Tank Bridge; although no firm evidence for this assumption can be found, it would seem logical, since the No 6 Tank Bridge came into production in 1961 and development work on the No 8 AVLB also started in the early 1960s.

An early prototype of the bridge was tested in mid 1965, using a prototype AEV, (Figure 13.10) and by 1970 the design had been finalized and two Chieftain AVREs, complete with their bridges, were ready for full troop trials. The bridge was of welded construction, fabricated from the new aluminium-zinc-magnesium alloy (see Appendix B). It was a Class 60 bridge

Figure 13.10. A prototype No 7 Tank Bridge, being launched from a prototype Armoured Engineer Vehicle (Winch) in 1965. (IWM 46941).

Figure 13.11. *The troop trial version of the No 7 Tank Bridge mounted on the 1970 version of the Chieftain AVRE fitted with fording snorkel.* (IWM 76573-78).

with a clear span of 20ft, formed from two trackways each 25ft long and 2ft 9in wide, with a 5ft 9in gap between them. The trackways were connected by two beams, which could be folded to reduced the width of the bridge for road transport. Box section alloy deck panels were provided to fill the gap between the trackways when the snorkel tube was not fitted, although the User Handbook for Troop Trials, issued in early 1971, makes no mention of deep wading and the requirement for the snorkel had presumably been dropped by then. (Figure 13.11). The AVRE itself was fitted with a 30 ton winch and a dozer blade with a bucket capability; apart from its normal use, the dozer blade acted as an earth anchor during winching operations and as a pivot for the launching of the bridge. Several successful launch cycles for the bridge were carried out at MEXE. Bank exiting trials of the prototype

351

AVRE, using the bridge as a ladder, were not carried out, but limited trials were completed at Christchurch using the bridge and a Centurion ARV. On one such trial the tide overtook events and the ARV, not being fitted with a snorkel tube, was drowned, amid many red faces.

Whilst this work was in progress at MEXE and FVRDE at Chertsey, development of the **Combat Engineer Tractor**, or CET, was also in hand. A General Staff Requirement (GST 26) for an armoured engineer equipment with a good earth moving capability had been issued in 1962, and in 1968 two prototypes were manufactured by the Royal Ordnance Factory at Leeds. After trials and a major redesign, with the object of making the vehicle amphibious, a further seven prototypes were delivered in the early 1970s. With the realization that full scale production of both the CET and the Chieftain AVRE would almost certainly never be authorized, all work on the AVRE and the No 7 Bridge was then halted, and the CET was formerly accepted for service in 1975, as FV180, finally coming into service in 1978.

The No 8 Armoured Vehicle Launched Bridge

Preliminary studies for a tank bridge to be mounted on the Chieftain tank chassis were put in hand in 1961, at a stage when prototypes of the new tank were still being manufactured. The 1946 trials with a No 5 Tank Bridge mock-up, referred to earlier in the chapter, had shown that 52ft was the maximum load length that could be carried on top of a tank chassis if reasonable mobility and manoeuvrability were to be maintained. The new bridge design therefore envisaged a 100ft long bridge, to be folded in half on top of the tank and launched by the scissor method. The bridge was to be Class 60, with a clear span of 95ft; it was to be of riveted plate girder construction, using aluminium alloy, with twin tracks and an overall width of 13ft 2in. The bridge was to be raised hydraulically and then lowered into position by winch and cable.

Development proper started in 1964 and the bridge that finally evolved varied fundamentally from that originally envisaged, in that the material was changed, the span was reduced, and a fully hydraulic launch was used. Initially the project officer for the new bridge was Mr Parramore, who had worked on the No 6 Tank Bridge, but after an internal reorganization Mr M A Napier, yet another wartime Sapper officer to join the civilian staff at MEXE after the war, took over the project. When he left on promotion in 1970 Stuart Parramore once again became the project officer.

Work on the bridgelayer, which was designated FV 4205, also started in 1962, based upon the standard Chieftain Battle Tank, fitted with the Leyland L60 12 cylinder multi-fuel engine. Modifications to the tank chassis included removal of the gun and turret, the hull top being closed by an armoured plate housing the commander's hatch and periscope. The front glacis casting was replaced by a special casting to which was fixed the hydraulically operated launching mechanism. A bridge support structure was attached to the rear of the vehicle, and the internal layout of the hull was also modified, to provide accommodation for the three man crew (commander, driver and radio operator), NBC filtration equipment, and the hydraulic and electrical controls for launching the bridge.

The move away from aluminium alloy, by now accepted in its weldable medium strength form as the most suitable material in most circumstances for military bridge construction, was perhaps the most important change from the early concept for the new tank bridge. It was decided to reduce the overall length of the bridge to 80ft and restrict the folded height of the scissor launched bridge to 6ft, to improve mobility of the launch vehicle. There was also a limit placed on the weight of the bridge; between 25 and 30% of the weight of a battle tank is taken up by the turret, the main armament and its ammunition, and when these are removed in a bridgelayer version of a modern tank, the balance available for the bridge plus its launching mechanism is in the region of 12 to 14 tons (The final production weight of the bridge was just 12 tons). With these factors in mind a material with a high strength/weight ratio was needed for the new bridge, one with a high modulus (to avoid excessive deflection), adequate ductility, good weldability and low distortion. The material chosen was 18% nickel-cobalt-molybdenum maraging steel, developed by the International Nickel Company. Details of the alloy (and the equipment) are given in Appendix B and it can be seen that the proof stress for the steel is fairly close to the ultimate stress. The criteria for design however was the permissible stress under working load for the required fatigue life of 10,000 full-load crossings at maximum span, and with this in mind the required fatigue life was confirmed, in due course, by full-scale laboratory tests on a prototype bridge girder. The bridge decking and bracing frames and struts were manufactured from DGFVE Specification 232 aluminium alloy.

The bridge is launched in three stages, each controlled by hydraulic cylinders operated by a hydraulic pump driven by a power take-off from the main engine. The sequence is clearly shown in Figure 13.12. The bridge can be launched in about three minutes, (Figures 13.13 and 13.14) and recovery of the bridge, which can be from either end, takes about ten minutes.

The bridge as eventually manufactured for use with the Chieftain Bridgelayer, FV 4205, was officially designated the No 8 Armoured Vehicle Launched Bridge, or No 8 AVLB. This was a more logical name than the No 8 Tank Bridge, since very few tank bridges have ever been launched from true battle tanks, rather than from armoured vehicles based upon a tank chassis, but nevertheless the bridge is commonly known as the No 8 Tank Bridge, whilst the Bridgelayer has become known as the AVLB. After completion of prototype trials with 26 Armoured Engineer Squadron in Germany in 1969, an Acceptance Meeting for the new bridge was held later that year. At the meeting the DGFVE congratulated MEXE on the excellence of the design of the bridge and the launching system, and the formal

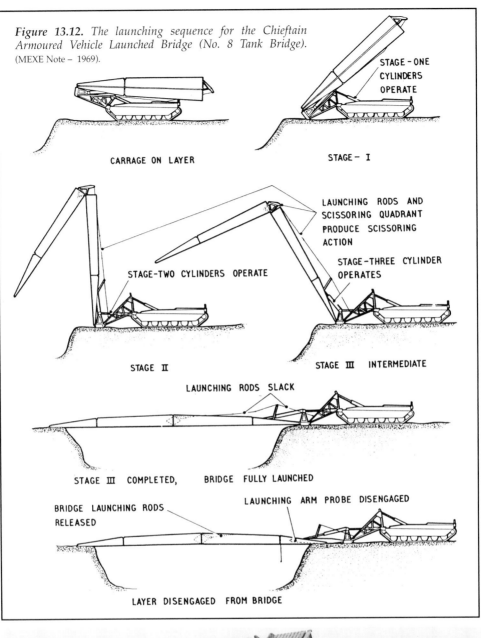

Figure 13.12. *The launching sequence for the Chieftain Armoured Vehicle Launched Bridge (No. 8 Tank Bridge).* (MEXE Note – 1969).

CARRAGE ON LAYER

STAGE-ONE CYLINDERS OPERATE

STAGE – I

STAGE-TWO CYLINDERS OPERATE

STAGE II

LAUNCHING RODS AND SCISSORING QUADRANT PRODUCE SCISSORING ACTION

STAGE-THREE CYLINDER OPERATES

STAGE III INTERMEDIATE

LAUNCHING RODS SLACK

STAGE III COMPLETED, BRIDGE FULLY LAUNCHED

BRIDGE LAUNCHING RODS RELEASED

LAUNCHING ARM PROBE DISENGAGED

LAYER DISENGAGED FROM BRIDGE

Figure 13.13. *Completion of Stage One of the No 8 Tank Bridge launch from the Chieftain Bridgelayer* (IWM 59112).

Figure 13.14. Stage Three of the Tank Bridge launch in progress. (IWM 59115).

Certificate of Approved Design for the No 8 AVLB was issued in the following year. The bridge itself was manufactured by Vickers at their Elswick Works and the bridgelayer was jointly manufactured at ROF Leeds and ROF Nottingham.

Deployment of the system to BAOR began in 1974. With an effective span of 75ft, that is 30ft greater than that of the No 6 Tank Bridge that it replaced, the bridge has remained the longest span Class 60 AVLB in service world wide. However with the advent of the Class 70 Challenger Tank another full scale fatigue test was carried out, this time using a production girder, and as a result of the test the rating of the bridge was increased to Class 70.

Fascines

So far only passing reference has been made of the fascine, literally a bundle of long sticks, as a means of crossing streams and small rivers. Small fascines have been used by the Sappers for many years, for example to improve tracks and reinforce earth works; indeed the 1914 edition of *Military Engineering - Volume III, Bridging,* even suggests a design for a simple 'Bird's Nest' raft made from tarpaulins and small fascines. The first use of fascines by a tank force was at Cambrai in 1917, when the British tanks used them to enable the tanks to cross the German trenches. The vast expansion of the Army's tank force in the Second World War led to the development of a much larger fascine however, and the standard wartime fascine was made up of a number of rolls of chestnut paling and brushwood, tied up with wire rope to form a cylindrical bundle about 6 to 8ft in diameter and 12 to 16ft long. Lengths of tubular steel scaffolding pole were used to strengthen the fascine and sometimes two or three long sections of 12in diameter Armco culverting would be included, to lighten the weight and prevent the fascine acting as a dam when dropped into a stream; the Armco culverting can be seen in Figure 8.10.

The fascine, weighing between 6 and 10 tons depending upon its length,

355

Figure 13.15. A chestnut paling fascine mounted on a Churchill Mark VII AVRE. (MEXE Handbook - June 1958).

was usually mounted on the front of an AVRE, supported on a wooden or steel cradle. (Figure 13.15) The cradle was hinged to the AVRE chassis and sloped forward; the fascine was then held in position by a steel wire rope, passing around it and then through a length of chain and a quick release mechanism to the rear of the AVRE. On release of the cable, the cradle tipped forward under the weight of the fascine, which would then roll forward into position, breaching an obstacle up to 15ft wide and 8ft deep. The mounting of a fascine on the front of an AVRE caused visibility problems for the commander, who would often ride in an exposed position on top of the fascine in order to direct the driver; a folding periscope was made available, which could be pushed up through the cupola of the AVRE, but it did not prove popular.

The Inflatable Fascine

During the mid 1960s, Dr P S Bulson, one time project leader for the Heavy Floating Bridge and later Head of the Engineer Equipment Division of MVEE, completed a number of research projects on inflatable structures, including work on the inflatable bridge discussed in Chapter Twelve. One project was for an inflatable fascine, cylindrical and with hemispherical ends. The cylindrical section was about 16ft long and the fascine was some 10ft in diameter. It was made from neoprene-nylon fabric, and was initially inflated to a pressure of 0.25psi, although under a test load of 30 tons the pressure increased to nearly 3psi. A 17 ton tracked APC was used for

356

Figure 13.16. *A trafficking trial on an inflatable fascine using a 17ton tracked APC.* (IWM 44450).

trafficking trials; passage of the tracks directly on to the fabric punctured the fascine, but, as with the bridge, deflation was very slow and the vehicle crossed safely. A ¼in thick rubber pad was then placed over the repaired fascine, and twelve successful crossings of the APC were made. (Figure 13.16). A Mark 2 version of the fascine was made later, incorporating a self aspirating system, a double external wall, and flat as opposed to hemispherical ends. The idea was not developed further at the time, although some thought was given to the use of an inflatable core for the current Pipe Fascine.

The Pipe Fascine

The Pipe Fascine, an updated version of the chespale fascine, was the brainchild of Major J M Allen RE, and evolved during a tour he spent at MVEE in the mid 1970s. The fascine is constructed from a number of pipes manufactured from black high density polythene, and consists of an outer band of 30 pipes, fastened together in a continuous loop, which wrap around an inner core of 45 pipes. The outer pipes are held together by lengths of chain located in holes drilled through the pipe walls at four positions along their length. These outer pipes are strengthened at the points at which tracked vehicles would cross the fascine by the insertion of short lengths of reinforcing pipe of a thinner wall thickness. The 45 inner pipes are loose within the outer ring but are restrained from lateral movement by a net secured over each end of the fascine.

The fascine as described is known as the **Maxi Pipe Fascine** (Figure 13.17 and Appendix B) and has an overall diameter of about 7ft (2.2m). It is 15ft (4.75m) long and weighs approximately 2½ tons, very much lighter than the 6 to 10 tons of the chespale fascine. It can be launched and recovered from either the AVRE or the CET, without exposure of the crew, by operation of a

Figure 13.17. A Maxi Pipe Fascine being carried on a Centurion Mark 5 AVRE. (IWM X79664-2).

quick release mechanism, and once in position provides a Class 70 crossing for tracked vehicles, either being used individually or, for larger gaps, in combination.

The **Mini Pipe Fascine** is an adaptation of the equipment and consists of a bundle of six of the outer pipes used in the Maxi Pipe Fascine, joined together by chain in the same way as with the larger fascine. The overall diameter of the smaller version is about 22in (550mm) and it weighs about 460lb. The fascine can be carried on the sides of the AFV 103 (Spartan) or the AFV 432 Armoured Personnel Carrier, and is launched by the release of two quick release mechanisms with minimum exposure of the vehicle crew. It is used either singly or in small numbers, depending upon the size of gap, and provides a crossing for light or medium tracked or wheeled vehicles.

The No 9 Armoured Vehicle Launched Bridge

With work on the No 8 AVLB well in hand, it was decided that there was a case for having a shorter span bridge that could also be launched from the Chieftain Bridgelayer and would thus replace the No 6 Tank Bridge and the Centurion Bridgelayer. Design studies at MEXE started in 1968, under the project leadership of Mr Barnard, who had worked on the No 7 Tank Bridge, and these were followed by the issue of a GSR for the new bridge in mid 1969. The length chosen for the new No 9 AVLB (or No 9 Tank Bridge) was 44ft, giving it an effective span of 40ft, which compared with the 45ft effective span of the No 6. (Figure 13.18). After a study of the relative costs,

358

Figure 13.18. A Chieftain Bridgelayer crossing the No 9 Tank Bridge it has just launched. (MVEE slide).

weights and strengths of various steels and aluminium alloys, the material finally selected for the main structure of the bridge was a Grade 55E steel to BS 4360 (see Appendix B).

The cross section of the two trackways forming the bridge are basically similar to that used in the No 8 AVLB, and the bridge is launched by the up-and-over method, using the same launching mechanism on the Chieftain Bridgelayer that is used to launch the No 8, Stage One raising the bridge from the horizontal to about 45°, Stage Two raising it to the vertical position, and Stage Three lowering the bridge to the ground.

Proof loading of the first prototype caused a large permanent set, which indicated that some yielding had occurred in the tension flange. Subsequent investigations of the parent metal revealed that the steel used, known as Thirty Oak, was not up to the Grade 55E specification. Mr Parramore had now taken over project leadership and a second prototype was designed which included a number of modifications suggested after field and user trials of the earlier version. These included modification to the bridge profile to increase the depth of the girders towards the toe by introducing a second kink in the top chord; additionally the four 22ft sections forming a complete bridge, instead of being left and right handed, were modified to be interchangeable, by having one male and one female jaw at bottom chord level of each. For this second prototype a weight constraint, originally placed on the bridge to enable two bridges to be carried on a transporter, was removed and it was manufactured using a new steel, Hyplus 29, which appeared to meet the full requirements of Grade 55E steel.

To illustrate the type of testing to which a modern bridging equipment might be subjected, it is worth quoting the test programme used for the second prototype of the No 9 AVLB. One trackway was first subjected to **Proof Loading Tests**, in which the test load applied took account of full eccentricity of the required Class 60 loading of the bridge, impact, and the safety factor. Eleven applications of the test load were applied, at positions producing maximum bending stresses and then maximum shear stresses. This test cycle was then repeated with one corner support of the trackway progressively lowered to 8½in below the other three, and the bending test was repeated with one corner jacked up 6in above the other three. Finally a full proof load was applied at the centre of the trackway at full eccentricity. During these tests stresses were continuously monitored using 67 strain gauges fixed at various parts of the structure.

Field Trials were then carried out, using the second prototype trackway and a suitably modified first prototype trackway to form a complete bridge. These trials involved 45 launches and recoveries, 60 vehicle crossings, and 40 launch probe engagements under the various site conditions specified in the GSR. The trials also included 38 miles of cross country running with the bridge mounted on the launcher and a further 200 miles of cross country travel using a revised rear support system for the bridge, during which the bridge was launched and recovered at 10 mile intervals.

Radio Trials were carried out by the Signals Research and Development Establishment, Christchurch, to confirm that the optimum position for the three aerials on the bridgelayer, which had already been selected during the No 8 AVLB trials, were satisfactory with the No 9 Bridge in position.

Fatigue Tests were carried out using one of the two first prototype trackways, failure occurring in one of the male tension lugs at just over 210,000 load cycles, the desired in-service minimum life being a mere 10,000 load cycles. Nevertheless the design of the production jaw block was modified, substituting a forging for the original machined jaw block; the grade of steel used for the block was also improved.

Finally, **Interface Trials** were carried out to ensure that the prototype bridge was fully compatible with the Chieftain Bridgelayer, which was of course then in service.

The total cost of development of the No 9 AVLB was in the region of £240,000; this was against a sum of £200,000 approved in 1969, which had been increased to £260,000 in 1972. An Acceptance Meeting for the new bridge was held in December 1973 and the Certificate of Approval of Design was issued in February 1974, although the bridge was not available to the Armoured Engineers in BAOR until 1978, because of manufacturing delays. Each Chieftain Bridgelayer was then normally equipped with one No 8 and one No 9 AVLB, one bridge being carried on the bridgelayer and the other on a specially adapted Scammell Crusader prime mover which towed a semi - trailer. Original plans to include two No 9 AVLBs with each bridge set were abandoned because of financial restrictions.

The Rebirth of 32 Armoured Engineer Regiment

It was seen earlier that in 1971 the three Armoured Engineer Squadrons had come under command of the CREs of their affiliated Divisions. In the late 1970s however a Restructuring Plan was implemented in BAOR, with the objective of reducing the manpower level of the troops in Germany without impairing their effectiveness unduly. The plan originally envisaged the disbandment of the armoured engineer squadrons and the reallocation of the bridgelayers to the four proposed engineer regiments. The introduction of the new Combat Engineer Tractor was to compensate for the loss of the AVREs that would result. Trials proved this to be a mistake, as a result of which the bridgelayers and a number of AVREs were centrally held in a new 26 Corps Armoured Engineer Squadron, which was based at Munsterlager at the end of 1978. The squadron comprised an HQ Troop and six Armoured Troops, each of two sections; the sections were identically equipped with two Chieftain Bridgelayers, each with a No 8 AVLB and a newly introduced No 9 AVLB, and a Centurion AVRE.

26 Squadron had inherited most of the equipment previously held by 32 Regiment, and its size was almost unmanageable. It was therefore decided, in 1980, to reform 31 Armoured Engineer Squadron, at Munsterlager. The new squadron joined with 26 Squadron, a REME Workshops and a Regimental HQ to form a resurrected 32 Armoured Engineer Regiment, which proudly used the bull's head emblem of the famous wartime 79 Armoured Division as its regimental crest. In April 1983 77 Armoured Engineer Squadron was formed to complete the establishment of the Regiment, but a move in 1986 to form a fourth armoured engineer squadron was aborted.

At Last, a Chieftain AVRE

It was seen earlier that the project for a Chieftain AVRE was abandoned in the early 1970s, once the development of the CET had proved successful. Although the Armoured Engineers were delighted with their new CETs, their introduction meant that the Centurion AVREs, which came into service in 1963 and were based upon the Mark 5 Centurion chassis, manufactured between 1955 and 1958, had been in service for over 25 years as the main weapon system of the Regiment. Indeed, by the mid 1980s, the AVREs were, in many cases, older than their young drivers! A solution, although perhaps not a complete one, was provided by the advent of the newest main battle tank for the British Army, the latest in the series of tanks in the FV 4030 series which evolved from the Chieftain. The new tank was originally designed to meet a requirement for the Iranian Army in the mid 1970s; it was based upon the Chieftain but had improved mobility and power, and incorporated the new and highly effective 'Chobham' armour. After the fall of the Shah of Iran the order for the FV 4030/2, called the Shir 2, was cancelled and a further improved version of the new tank was purchased by Jordan as the Khalid. The FV 4030/3 was subsequently further developed into the heavily armoured **Challenger**, its battle weight of 62 tons making it a Class 70(T) load.

The Challenger came into service with the British Army in 1983, and whilst highlighting the ageing limitations of the Centurion AVRE, provided at the same time a means of overcoming some of these limitations. The RE Wing at the Armoured Corps Centre at Bovington investigated the feasibility of converting a number of Chieftains made surplus by the introduction of the new tank into AVREs. The idea was taken up with enthusiasm by 32 Armoured Engineer Regiment and in due course a concept demonstrator was produced. This proved so successful that an initial requirement for 13 Chieftain AVREs was agreed, although this was later increased to 17. To maintain a power to weight ratio for the new AVRE that was compatible with the Challenger that it would support, the 12 ton turret of the Chieftain battle tank was removed and this has meant that the AVRE had no armament, or specifically no demolition gun. It had however a mounting for either a mine plough or a dozer blade, and it could tow a Giant Viper or an AVRE trailer. It also had a top hamper on which it could carry three Pipe Fascines or six rolls of Class 60 Trackway, which could be launched without exposure of the crew (Figure 13.19). A No 9 Tank Bridge could also be carried on this top hamper, enabling the AVRE to accompany the Chieftain Bridgelayer with a spare bridge.

Production in industry would have delayed introduction of the new AVREs until the early 1990s and so it was agreed that the conversion should be carried out by 21 Engineer Base Workshops at Willich in Germany. The project was extremely successful and demonstrates the versatility of the Corps when called upon to meet a challenge. The first Chieftain MBT, minus its turret, was delivered to Willich in February 1986 and work on the

Figure 13.19. A Chieftain 'Willich AVRE' being loaded with a second pipe fascine. (Tank Museum 3056/B2).

seventeenth vehicle had been completed by the end of 1987. The work at Willich was carried out under the supervision of Lt Col J F Johnson RE, who acted as project manager and has written a full account of the project in the September 1987 issue of the *Royal Engineer Journal*. The unit cost was in the order of £70-80,000, compared with a probable cost approaching £400,000 had the work been completed by industry - a considerable saving to the MOD.

The majority of the newly converted Chieftain AVREs were issued to the two squadrons of 23 Engineer Regiment, in support of 3 Armoured division. Only four were allocated to 32 Armoured Engineer Regiment, whose armoured equipment holding in early 1989 was as follows:

TABLE 5 - EQUIPMENT HOLDINGS OF 32 ARMOURED ENGINEER REGIMENT IN 1989

EQUIPMENT	26 SQN	31 SQN	77 SQN	32 REGT TOTAL
Chieftain Bridgelayer	9	9	9	27
No 8 AVLB	6	6	4	16
No 9 AVLB	5	5	6	16
Scamell Crusader/semi trailer	5	5	5	18*
Centurion AVRE 165	6	6	6	18
Centurion AVRE 105	3	3	-	6
Chieftain AVRE	-	-	4	4
Combat Engineer Tractor	4	4	4	12

(*Three transporter trains were held by 65 Corps Support Squadron at that time)

The reliability of the new AVREs was not as good as it might have been. This was in no way due to the efforts of the Workshops at Willich, who did an excellent job, but was caused, in the main, by the state of the chassis. Most of the Chieftain hulls used were those of the older tanks in the tank fleet, and ideally the chassis should have been given a base overhaul before the conversion, many having motored well in excess of the target mileage between overhaul. This was borne out during the Gulf War when one Regimental Commander considered them underpowered, unpredictable in use, and inadequate to the task, in numbers and quality. However, the intention was that the Willich AVREs would be a short term solution only, and in the early 1990s, as production of the new Challenger proceeded, Vickers Defence Systems undertook the conversion of a further 48 Chieftain MBTs into Chieftain AVREs. All of these were in service by 1994, and the 'Willich AVREs' went out of service, other, for example, than for use at the RE Wing Bovington, as of course did the old Centurion AVREs.

Combination Bridging

Combination Bridging, that is the use of two or more different equipment bridges in combination, has seemed a logical development since the early days of such bridges. The 1921 edition of *Military Engineering - Volume III, Bridging*, gives details of combining the Mark II Inglis bridge with Heavy Pontoons to form a floating bridge, and in 1942 the new Bailey Bridge was combined with existing Mark V Pontoons to form the Bailey Pontoon Bridge. In 1980 bridges using MGB spans supported on M2 landing bay rafts were built during BAOR exercises. In recent times however the expression has tended to be used in connection with multi-span bridges involving assault equipments, examples of which exist from the 1960s onward. In the mid 1960s the Armoured Engineers bridged wide rivers on exercises in Germany by using two or three No 6 Tank Bridges in series, with Centurion ARK Mobile Piers or CAMPs as intermediate piers, as described earlier. At bridge camps in 1968 and 1969 32 Armoured Engineer Regiment carried out trials with combined No 6 Tank Bridges, with a No 6 Bridge and an ARK, and with tandem ARKs.

The use of two or more tank bridges in tandem to form multi-span bridges needs very careful reconnaissance of the river bed, to ensure that it will support adequately the submerged end of a bridge and will not scour unevenly. The launching of the second and subsequent bridges must then be carried out with some precision to ensure a fully stable structure. However,

Figure 13.20. A good example of combination bridging using No 8 and No 9 Tank Bridges. (IWM X78832-82).

provided that conditions are suitable, the technique provides a means of crossing very wide river obstacles, and has become accepted as a standard procedure. (Figure 13.20). To this end 1in thick pads of polyvinyl material have been bonded underneath the ends of the ramp sections on both the No 8 and the No 9 Tank Bridges, to give a non-slip contact between the bridges when used for combination bridging and also to prevent excessive deck damage. The use of an assault bridge pier or trestle to replace the forward ramp sections of the No 8 AVLB also enables assault bridges to be used in tandem. Experiments on this concept were carried out at Christchurch in the late 1970s, and are considered in more detail in Chapter Fifteen.

The Close Support Squadron

In the mid 1980s, the concept for close support for the BAOR Armoured Divisions began to develop. This was reflected to some degree in the decision to change the name of Assault Bridging to Close Support Bridging, as discussed later in Chapter 15. With a move towards improving mobility of battle groups and armoured brigades the idea developed of deploying a Close Support (CS) Engineer Regiment, a General Support (GS) Engineer Regiment and a Field Support Squadron with each Division. The organization of the squadrons involved was radically changed, bringing together a mixture of armoured and field engineer Sappers and involving a considerable increase in the equipment holding of the squadrons. Various groupings of command and control procedures and equipment were examined during the trials, resulting in a suggested Close Support Squadron organization shown in outline below, but excluding the Squadron HQ.

TABLE 6 - SUGGESTED OUTLINE CLOSE SUPPORT SQUADRON ORGANIZATION (PEACE)

UNIT	PERSONNEL	AVRE	CET	AVLB	Fd Section	Miscellaneous
1 CS Troop	1 + 34	2	2	2	1	-
2 CS Troop	1 + 34	2	2	2	1	-
3 CS Troop	1 + 36	2	2	-	2	-
Echelon	1 + 40	-	-	-	-	4 Br Tptr & 3 LWT
Fitters	0 + 20	-	-	-	-	1 ARRV & 3 AFV 434*

(* The REME variant of the AFV 432 Armoured Personnel Carrier)

A number of articles on this new concept have appeared in the *Royal Engineer Journal*, culminating in Colonel P J Russell Jones' article in December 1990. This article resulted from his experiences as CO 23 Engineer Regiment, the regiment chosen to carry out the highly successful trials held in BAOR and at the British Army Training Unit Suffield in Canada during 1988 and 1989.

During the Gulf War of 1991, 21 and 23 Engineer Regiments were organized on the CS Squadron basis, a subject considered in more detail in the next chapter, as is the deployment of 32 Armoured Engineer Regiment during that war.

Options for Change

In July 1991 the Secretary for State for War announced changes in the organization of the Regular Army, known as Options for Change, to take account of the changing international scene, with particular regard to the demise of the Soviet threat. Changes involved the intended disbandment of a number of Sapper Regiments and took account of lessons learnt during Operation Granby, the Gulf War. It was decided that the future War ORBAT for the Corps would include Close Support Regiments, rather than Close Support Squadrons. In BAOR, Divisional Engineers would include three CS Regiments, together with a General Support Regiment, whilst in UK, Divisional Engineers would include two such regiments, together with a General Support Regiment and a Parachute Squadron. The five Close Support Regiments would each consist of an RHQ, a Headquarter Squadron, an Armoured Engineer Squadron and a Mechanized Field Squadron.

Although this spelt the end of 32 Armoured Engineer Regiment as such, it was realized that for ease of training, equipment maintenance and repair, and provision of support facilities, it would be sensible to co-locate the Armoured Squadrons together in peacetime. Thus 26, 31 and 77 Armoured Engineer Squadrons remained with the Regiment, located at Hohne and, from 13 April 1993, known simply as 32 Engineer Regiment.

The reorganization under Options for Change necessitated the setting up of two new Armoured Engineer Squadrons in the UK, and in January 1993 8 Field Squadron RE, originally formed as a Company of the Guernsey and Jersey Military Artificers in 1778, re-roled as 8 Armoured Engineer Squadron. 3 Field Squadron RE, originally formed at Dover as the 3rd Company Royal Military Artificers in 1787, was similarly re-roled in August 1993. Both of the new Armoured Squadrons form part of 22 Engineer Regiment in peacetime, and were based at Perham Down, on the Wiltshire-Hampshire border.

After the reorganization the basic Armoured Troop for all five Armoured Squadrons included three command vehicles, three AVLBs and three Chieftain AVREs, by now all Centurion AVREs having been retired. Each Squadron also had a Support Troop, holding three CETs and three Tank Bridge Transporters (Tptr) for each of its Armoured Troops, plus a Fitters Section and general support vehicles. There was a basic difference between the BAOR and UK Armoured Squadrons however in that the former had four Armoured Troops each, whilst the UK Squadrons had only two, supported by a Field Troop mounted in AFV 432 APCs. All squadrons held one No 8 and one No 9 Tank Bridge for each AVLB system, carrying the bridges either on the Chieftain Bridgelayer or on the Tank Bridge Transporter.

New Equipments

In the mid 1990s new Close Support Bridges, considered in more detail in Chapter 15, came into service. The Chieftain Bridgelayers were converted by Vickers to launch the new No 10 and No 12 Tank Bridges, and Vickers also won a contract to develop a new bridging trestle to be launched with the tank bridges. In 2000 work started on the development of Challenger based Engineer tanks, namely the Titan and the Trojan, to replace, respectively, the Chieftain Bridgelayers and AVREs. This gave the promise of the Sappers having Engineer tanks of the same generation as the MBTs currently in service, for the first time for many years

The Strategic Defence Review

The results of a very comprehensive Strategic Defence Review (SDR) were announced in July 1998, and included developments of considerable significance to the Corps in general. With regard to the Armoured Engineers, the cornerstone of the SDR was to deliver formations at a high state of operational readiness, and this required the formation of two new dedicated Close Support (CS) Regiments in UK, 26 Engineer Regiment (in support of 1 Mechanized Brigade), and in due course 23 Engineer Regiment (in support of 16 Air Assault Brigade). The proposed organization for the reorganized CS Squadrons of 1 (UK) Armoured Division is shown in Table 7, excluding the Squadron HQ and fitters section.

TABLE 7 – PROPOSED ORGANIZATION FOR THE POST SDR UK ARMOURED ENGINEER SQUADRON

ARMOURED TROOP	FIELD TROOP	SUPPORT TROOP	ECHELON
3 x AVRE	4 x Field Sections in	4 x CET	3 x TBT
3 x AVLB	AFV432 APCs	3 x LWT	
3 x No 10 Tk Br		2 x MWT	
6 x No 12 Tk Br		1 x Crane	

The Vickers Armoured Bridgelayer

Although the Vickers Armoured Bridgelayer or VAB has not been procured for the British Army, it is nevertheless of British design and manufacture and warrants a place in this history. (Figure 13.21) Preliminary work on the VAB was started by Vickers Defence Systems, manufacturers of the No 8 Tank Bridge, in the late 1970s. The VAB forms part of a family of supporting vehicles for the Vickers Main Battle Tank Mark 3, a family that now includes

Figure 13.21. The Vickers Armoured Bridgelayer launching its 44ft bridge. (Vickers Defence Systems).

the Howitzer SP155 and an ARV. The tank itself mounts a British L7 105mm tank gun and is powered either by a Perkins CV12 800E V12 diesel engine developing 800bhp, or by a General Motors alternative. The hull, automotive and running gear components of the VAB are based upon those of the Mark 3 Tank, with accommodation for a crew of three consisting of commander, driver and radio operator. The standard bridge fitted to the VAB, in service with the armies of Nigeria and Kenya, is launched hydraulically by the up-and-over method used with the No 6 and No 9 Tank Bridges. It is a Class 60/70 twin track bridge, each track being 13.41m (44ft) long; the width of the bridge is 4.16m (13ft 7¾ in).

An alternative launching method for the VAB was proposed, but not fully developed, to enable it to launch the German Biber Tank Bridge. This bridge is Class 50/60 and has an overall length of 21.9m (72ft). The bridge is in two identical halves which are carried one on top of the other, on top of the Biber Tank; the sections are coupled up during the launch, making use of a cantilever launching jib mounted on top of the tank chassis, and the bridge is finally placed by lowering the launching boom.

Vickers also developed a 22.5m (74ft) AVLB and launch system for the Korean K1 Tank and manufactured the first few systems at Newcastle. Subsequently more than 50 systems were produced under licence in South Korea.

368

Chapter Fourteen

Postwar Bridging Operations

The Cessation of Hostilities

In the years immediately following cessation of hostilities the Corps was engaged in a number of bridging operations in many parts of the world, in many cases aimed, as for example with the Rhine bridges, in restoring normal communications in areas suffering the aftermath of war.

In the Far East many bridges on the Singapore to Penang road in Malaya had to be rebuilt, largely using Bailey equipment; the largest of these was at Jura where a 490ft long three span bridge was built by 470 Army Troop Engineers and opened in March 1946.

In Burma a major pontoon bridge was built across the Irrawaddy at Myitkyina to replace a previously built US pontoon bridge. The dual carriageway Class 30 deck bridge was built with as much standard equipment as possible. American H-20 girders were used for the seven 112ft 6in approach spans, five spans being used for the eastern approach and two for the western approach. At both ends of bridge the offshore approach span was connected to the floating section of bridge through a special steel trestle which allowed adjustment for the tide. The 850ft long floating section of the bridge was continuous over its whole length and was supported by seven 100ft long steel pontoons, equally spaced and each anchored upstream and downstream to the river banks by 3in SWR. The total length of the bridge was 1638ft.

The building of Springbok Bridge and a Bailey Pontoon bridge across the River Po in Italy has been described in Chapter Nine. After the campaign a more permanent floating bridge was built across the river in July 1945 and was named **Swansong Bridge**. (Figure 14.1). Eight spans of Bailey, of varied

Figure 14.1. The Swansong Barge Bridge across the River Po, in Italy; construction nearly completed. (RETM No 20).

construction, were supported on wooden flat bottomed barges, found in the lower reaches of the river, and each about 100ft long and 20ft wide. Bailey piers were constructed within the barges to raise the level of the bridge and thus allow passage of barge traffic on the river. The landing bays had to allow for a rise and fall of some 25ft and were therefore constructed as double landing bays, the two articulated spans of each being supported at their junction by a twin barge pier. A 30ft bascule bay with two 10ft cantilever spans was inserted to facilitate joining the two halves of the bridge during construction and to allow for changes in bridge length due to fluctuation of water level. The bridge was built in about six weeks by units of 10 Corps Troops RE, formerly 16 GHQ Troops RE.

The Rhine Bridges

Nearer home the bridges built across the Rhine in Germany just after the end of the war must rank amongst the major Sapper bridge building operations of all times and merit more detailed consideration. As the war drew to a close the need to restore communications in Europe on a more permanent basis had been anticipated, essentially to ensure adequate maintenance of the Allied Armies. Work on four semi-permanent bridges across the Rhine and Neder Rijn therefore started even before the final German surrender on Lüneburg Heath on 4 May 1945. The **Dempsey Bridge** was built at Xanten by 18 GHQ Troops Engineers in April and May 1945 and was a Class 40 Bailey Bridge built on timber piles, and was thus known as a Timber Piled Bailey, or TPB; the piles, some almost 100ft long, were driven using a Bailey piling rig mounted at the head of the advancing, continuously launched bridge. (Figure 14.2). The bridge was over 4,000ft long and included a short

Figure 14.2. Building the Dempsey Bridge across the Rhine in 1945. (2nd Army Photo Recce Unit).

75ft navigation span, quite inadequate for the large barges in use on the Rhine. Indeed nemesis came a year or so later in the form of a Belgian barge Captain; ignoring all rules he tried to take his string of five barges through the navigation gap in one go. He succeeded, but carried away 400ft of the bridge; it was never rebuilt.

Even longer bridges were the twin **Tyne and Tees Bridges**, respectively Class 70 and Class 40 Bailey Bridges built alongside each other across the Rhine at Rees. These two bridges were built by 50 (Northumberland) GHQ Troops Engineers, also in May and June 1945. With an overall length of 4,980ft, they were the longest military bridges built in the world. They were built with timber piled piers on the approach spans and steel box piled piers for the main river spans. (Figure 14.3). These main spans were constructed by prefabricating sections of bridge which were then transported to the head of bridge and swung into position using a 10 ton derrick, to form what was

Figure 14.3. *Installing a Bailey cross girder between the Tyne and Tees Bridges across the Rhine in 1945.* (2nd Army Photo Recce Unit).

Figure 14.4. The Spyck Railway Bridge across the River Rhine. (Bridging - Normandy to Berlin).

in fact a continuous jetty; the construction was therefore known as BPJ or Bailey Piled Jetty construction. In addition two steel piled bridges were built across the Neder Rijn at Arnhem and two timber piled bridges across the Ijssel at Zutphen.

Yet another major bridge built during this period was the 2,340ft long **Spyck Railway Bridge** built across the Rhine between Spyck and Emmerich. (Figure 14.4). Construction of the bridge was carried out from both banks simultaneously and included six 35ft RSJ approach spans, twenty-seven 75ft two girder deck type Unit Construction Railway Bridge spans, and one 105ft four girder through type Unit Construction Railway Bridge span; this latter span was later converted to a lift span to allow passage of river traffic. Construction by 2 Railway Construction and Maintenance Group RE started on 7 April 1945 and was completed by 10 May. Work included the driving of over 450 60ft piles to form the piers and the laying of 2,750 yards of single-line railway track to enable the first train to cross on completion day.

The eventual surrender of the German Armed Forces left the British Army and its allies in Germany with the prospect of the occupation of the country for some years to come, a country whose vital river, canal, rail and road network had been under constant attack and was by then all but destroyed. During the first year of occupation alone 6,000 miles of railway and 2,000 miles of roads were repaired by the Corps and by the Royal Canadian Engineers, making full use of a considerable and willing German labour force. Over 500 temporary road and rail bridges were built, totalling some 16 miles of bridge-work, the most important of the bridges being those across the Rhine and the Elbe. In the British-Canadian Occupation Zone alone, which stretched from the North Sea and the Baltic down to Cologne, the wreckage of seven rail bridges and ten road bridges blocked the Rhine, ensuring that nothing could move on the river and not very much could cross it. Additionally many of the large towns on the Rhine are located on

372

both sides of the river and the lack of bridges caused many administrative problems during a difficult period of restoration. Replacements for the temporary assault bridges built across this major water obstacle during the last stages of the war were thus urgently necessary. The semi-permanent road bridges so recently built at Xanten and Rees, with their inadequate navigation spans, were situated far from major population areas and therefore were not really suitable for perhaps years of use until new and permanent Rhine bridges could be built. The building of true semi-permanent bridges across the Rhine to open up the main road and river communications of the country was therefore a matter of some urgency, not only for the benefit of the occupying troops but also as a necessary stage in the restoration of normal life in the country. The Royal Engineers of 1st British Corps were therefore given the task of building major temporary bridges across the Rhine at three vital points.

Freeman Bridge, the first of these bridges to be completed, was at Düsseldorf, although the planning of fixed ice-proof bridges at Wesel and Cologne was well advanced. Major Ralph Freeman, the son of Mr Ralph Freeman, then Chairman of the Ministry of Supply's Structural Engineering Committee, had been involved in various trials of Bailey Bridging and had been posted to the staff of the Chief Engineer 21 Army Group soon after the invasion of Europe as a bridging advisor with the grandiose title of Deputy Assistant Director, Royal Engineer Equipment (Technical), or DADREE(Tech) for short. Freeman was heavily involved with the initial design and procurement for the Wesel and Cologne bridges, and the concept and planning for the Düsseldorf bridge were also his responsibility. The finally agreed concept, which was essentially his, was for a high-level floating Bailey, using Bailey piers built on pontoons, similar to those used for Tower Bridge in Holland. (Figure 14.5). The design could thus be likened to

Figure 14.5. The Freeman Bridge built across the Rhine at Düsseldorf, looking west towards Neuss. (R Freeman).

a number of portal-frame spans, with the portal legs based upon floating piers made up from US NL (Naval Lighterage) Pontoons, of which large stocks were available; the portal spans were linked to one another by short hinged spans. The bridge could not be made ice-proof, but was designed so that the large floating bays could be rapidly disconnected and floated into a nearby dock in the event of the usual two- or three-day ice warning. The urgently needed bridge had to meet the minimum 8m height and 25m width clearance requirements for river traffic, and this was achieved by using a long double storey navigation span.

Work started on the piling and superstructure for the approach spans across the dry flood plain in early August 1945, using German labour. A few weeks later Sappers of 18 GHQ Troops Engineers, under command of Lieutenant Colonel T Burrowes RE, started to build the main floating bridge. Work progressed rapidly and the Class 24 bridge, 2,391ft in overall length, was opened on 4 October 1945. The ceremony was performed by the Corps Commander and, when the Union Jack was removed from the bridge plaque, it was a complete surprise for Freeman to see that the bridge had been named after him. A London daily newspaper reported next day that the opening ceremony had been carried out by a (non-existent) Lieutenant General Freeman, the reporter no doubt assuming that the bridge could not possibly have been named after a mere temporary Major, war-substantive Captain!

Montgomery Bridge was built across the Rhine at Wesel and was so named because Wesel was the site of the first crossing of the Rhine by the 21st Army Group some five months earlier, a crossing made by Engineers of the 9th US Army, using Treadway M2 equipment. A timber trestle bridge, constructed by 1146 US Engineer Combat Battalion Group and named the **Roosevelt Bridge**, already existed at the site and it was decided as a temporary measure to cut a 70m gap in it to open up the Rhine for river traffic and then use the deck of the single lane bridge as false work from which to build a new bridge. For the first six weeks the American bridge was occupied by German contractors driving 70ft long cylindrical steel Franki piles, 22in in diameter. These piles were filled with concrete and topped with massive concrete caps, with pier heads wide enough to take two single lane Bailey Bridges side by side. The piers were designed to resist impact from the large ice floes that were common on the Rhine during harsh winter months.

It was not until mid-October that the Sappers of 12 Corps Troops RE, under the command of Lieutenant Colonel L F Heard RE, were able to start work on the superstructure. In all a number of Sapper units were involved and overall control of the project was vested in Colonel K H Osborne DSO MC, of 14 Army Group Royal Engineers, a command unit with no troops of its own.

Once the Bailey for the southern span had been completed on top of the American bridge, it was jacked up in three sections, onto trolleys made from

374

Figure 14.6. *The twin carriageway Montgomery Bridge crossing the Rhine at Wesel, showing the southern span in its final position.*

Bailey launching rollers and special parts. Suitable rails had already been fixed to the pier tops and the three sections of the bridge were then moved sideways simultaneously, before being jacked down onto the final bearings, leaving the falsework in position for the building of the northern bridge. (Figure 14.6).

The double carriageway bridge, with cycle track between, was over 2,030ft long and took about six months to complete from conception to its opening on 5 February 1946. The 240ft navigation spans allowed 30ft (9.15m) of headroom over the maximum recorded water level and thus met all navigational requirements. The Bailey superstructure took the Sappers some four months to complete, working usually in two shifts and using searchlights to floodlight the work when daylight failed; the weather was bitterly cold during that winter and the men had often to work in tank suits to keep warm.

The plaque at the end of the bridge stated plainly 'Montgomery Bridge. This bridge is 2,032 feet long. 2,400 tons of Bailey Bridge and 6,720 tons of reinforced concrete were used in its construction. Built under command of 14 Army Group Royal Engineers by 12 Corps Troops Royal Engineers.' The plaque then went on to list the many units that were involved in the construction.

The **Patton Bridge** was the third major Rhine bridge built by the Sappers.

375

Figure 14.7. Construction of the Patton Bridge across the Rhine at Cologne.

It was built at Cologne and was similar in many ways to Montgomery Bridge, being built at about the same time. It was also to be a high level Bailey Bridge, built on Franki pile piers. However, the build up of traffic on an adjacent single way American timber-piled bridge, not this time used to support falsework, meant that in December some redesign took place to enable the new bridge to carry a maximum loading of heavy lorries nose to tail. (Figure 14.7). Bailey bridging could easily be built to take the greater load for the normal spans, but the navigation span presented a problem. In the end German Army heavy railway bridging equipment was used for the two navigation spans, built side by side. These were assembled downstream from the bridge on a framework made from Bailey equipment and trestles. Supported on 1,000 ton Rhine barges, they were towed into position; the barges were then partially flooded until the spans settled onto their bearings. This and the other two major Rhine bridges were expected to remain in use for no more than five years. In fact Montgomery Bridge remained in service until the late 1950s and Patton Bridge was not replaced until the 1960s. Dr Ludwig Erhart, Adenauer's Finance Minister and briefly his successor as Chancellor of the Bundesrepublik, has been quoted as saying, 'Without these bridges the economic miracle of Germany's recovery would have been long delayed'.

Artlenburg Bridge.

The building of this bridge across the River Elbe is of interest because it was carried out mainly as a military exercise. It had been noticeable during the closing stages of the war that Canadian and American Engineer units were more proficient than the Sappers in the rapid construction of temporary bridges, using the steel 'metre beams' commonly used in Europe, supported

376

on heavy timber trestles or timber piles. This was probably because of their training and the normal methods of semi-permanent bridge construction often used in their home countries. The Chief Engineer of BAOR therefore decided that every formation of Sappers should build such a bridge as part of its training programme during the summer of 1946. The largest of these bridges was that at Artlenburg, the site of Montgomery's assault crossing of the Elbe at the end of April 1945, just before the final German surrender on 4 May, and was built by units of 7 Armoured Division and 5 Division Royal Engineers. Preparatory work started on 1 August 1946 and the main build on the 12th. The finished bridge was 1,530ft long, with a 140ft Bailey navigation span and thirty shorter spans, supported on timber triple bent piers, topped in some cases by timber trestles. The bridge was completed and opened on 16 September 1946.

Some 46 years later 28 Amphibious Engineer Regiment marked almost 21 years of amphibious bridging history by building a Class 70 bridge across the Elbe at Artlenburg with their M2 Rigs in just two hours, at night.

The Wadi Kuf Bridges

Since the immediate postwar period the Corps has built many more bridges worthy of detailed examination. The list is extensive, including for example that built in Austria by 11 Independent Field Squadron RE, the **Radkersberg International Bridge**, built across the River Mur to open up the road between Austria and Yugoslavia. The bridge was formally opened by Dr Figl, the Austrian Federal Chancellor, on 6 September 1952, in the presence of the CIGS, Field Marshal Sir William Slim. However, the building of the bridges across the Wadi Kuf in Cyrenaica will be described in a little more detail as being typical of the many bridging projects undertaken.

After 1943 the former Italian colonies of Tripolitania and Cyrenaica were administered by the British, the unified state of Libya coming into being in 1951. In 1948 1 Infantry Division was moved from Palestine to North Africa and one of the early tasks given to the Sappers of 1 Division Royal Engineers, then stationed in Benghazi, was the replacement of bridges on the coast road between Barce and Derna. The road had originally been built by the Italians, and to cross the Wadi Kuf near Beida, or Al Bayda, the Italians had built two large concrete bridges and a long sloping viaduct clinging to the edge of the cliff. During the last retreat of the German and Italian Armies before Montgomery's 8th Army in 1942, the enemy blew both bridges and a gap, some 200ft long, in the viaduct. The Sappers of the 8th Army had created a temporary crossing across the wadi by dozing a six-leg zigzag road down the eastern side of the wadi and then along the bottom of the gorge. This road was passable to 3 ton lorries but little else, and a replacement for the original crossing was obviously required.

1 Division Engineers built four bridges in all. The main one, or No 1 Bridge, was a 280ft triple/single Continuous Bailey, with the three spans

supported on 40ft high Bailey crib piers; this replaced one of the original concrete bridges. (Figure 14.8). The wadi was a dry watercourse, subject to occasional heavy flooding caused by rare rainfall in the winter months; because of this the piers were based upon mass concrete foundations extending 5ft up the bottom panels of the piers. The bridge was launched up a slope of about 1 in 34 to conform to the existing road levels and had to be built on the skew to accommodate an S-bend in the road. This necessitated considerable blasting of the cliff face at the rear to make room for the tail of the bridge as it was built; because of this the tail was kept short and full use made of kentledge, which included a D4 dozer. The launching nose was kept as light as possible as the bridge was pushed out over the site of the first

Figure 14.8. The 280ft span No 1 Wadi Kuf Bridge in Libya, built by 23 Field Squadron in 1948. (J H Joiner).

pier, enabling the pier panels to be hoisted up into place from the wadi floor. The bridge was built by 23 Field Squadron, under the command of Major R E Ward RE, who, with Major RE Young DSO DFC RE, was responsible for the bridge design.

No 2 Bridge was built further up the wadi side to span the gap in the reinforced concrete viaduct. It was a 210ft Continuous Bailey with one central 20ft pier and was built by 12 Field Squadron RE, commanded by Major L Scott Bowden DSO MC* RE. The 1 in 14½ gradient of the viaduct caused some problems, since the bridge had to be built at the same slope, and special arrangements had to be made to counteract the effects of expansion caused by high midday temperatures. This problem was overcome by embedding the downhill end posts in concrete and ensuring that the baseplates at the pierhead and the top end of the bridge were well greased to allow movement during any expansion of the bridge. No 3 and No 4 Bridges were non-equipment bridges, the former built by cutting into the limestone cliffs and then building an embankment and large culvert round the head of a deep ravine entering the wadi, and the latter consisting of a reinforced concrete slab carried on large RSJs, with rebuilt masonry abutments and wing walls.

In the main all of the work was carried out by young National Service Sappers assisted by a large detachment from a Mauritian Pioneer Company, all pleased to tackle a task of which they were justifiably proud. Typical of the problems faced in working in a fairly remote and not very hospitable site was that of procuring the large quantities of sand required for the concreting - it had to be hauled up more than 1,000ft from the beaches near Appollonia, 25 miles away down a twisting track past the ruins of the ancient Greek city of Cyrene. The bridges were formally opened by Emir Idris el Senussi, later to become King Idris of Libya, on 18 April 1949, and were still in place in the early 1990s, although no longer in use. Their replacement, completed in 1972 on an adjacent site, was designed by the Italian engineer Morandi, and is listed in the 1976 Guinness Book of Structures as being, at that time, one of the longest cable-stayed concrete bridges in the world, with a centre span of 925ft (282m) and two side spans of 322ft (98m).

Sapper Bridge

Sapper Bridge warrants mention as probably the longest equipment continuous bridge ever built in the UK by the Corps. It was built in 1949 to carry foot traffic from the north bank of the River Thames to the south bank site selected for the 1950 Festival of Britain, and was built by 36 Engineer Regiment, under the command of Lieutenant Colonel P A Easton OBE RE. For almost a year before construction started, work on the design of the bridge had been in the hands of the staff of the Chief Engineer, London District, supported by continual expert advice from the staff at MEXE, and it was decided that the 1060ft long bridge would be a triple/triple Standard Widened Bailey Bridge. In order to prevent interference with river traffic, the roadway of the bridge was to be built at the same level as the Charing Cross railway bridge, some 30ft above ground level at the building site and 60ft above the river at low tide. A further problem was caused by the need to link up with a concourse in the north bank, which meant that the last span of 170ft would have to be detached from the main continuous spans and swivelled through 7½° in order to rest on a steel portal frame adjacent to the railway bridge. The bridge was designed to carry a loading of 8,000 foot passengers an hour, with a possible side-wind loading of 90mph, and for this reason the lower sway bracing was doubled, and single bracing and underslung transoms added at top chord level. The calculated expansion of 5in was to be catered for by welding the bridge to the top hamper of No 3 pier, thus ensuring two-way expansion.

The six river piers and the north bank portal frame were built by the London County Council engineering department, and steel caps were fitted to the pier tops, on which balancing beams and rocker rollers were positioned, ready for construction of the bridge proper to begin. After a period of training at the Regiment's Maidstone Barracks and at Wouldham Bridge Site, Chatham, 57 and 58 Field Squadrons RE deployed to an old TA campsite reasonably adjacent to the bridge site.

Because of the height above water level requirement, the bridge had to be built and boomed out some 30ft above ground level at the south bank building site. To this end a launching platform was first built, consisting of 100ft of triple/single Bailey supported on four Bailey piers. Launching rollers were then bolted to the top chords of each of the triple panel girders. Triple/single girders for the bridge proper, varying from 60ft to 80ft in length, were then constructed on decauville trolleys on the ground before being swung up into position on top of the launching rollers, using a Henderson steam crane with a 120ft jib. The additional storeys were built in the same way and then swung up onto the previously positioned lower storeys. Rails had been fixed to the deck of the launching platform and on these a special launching trolley was built; this was fitted with forward and rear tackles and was connected to the rear end of bridge, which was then boomed out, once transoms, sway brace and so on had been added. The trolley was then disconnected and withdrawn for the next boom.

Construction went according to plan, but mention should be made of a much-publicized mishap that occurred during the booming-out of the first span. When the front end of the bridge reached a point just 2ft from the first pier the bridge tipped up and the nose dropped slowly into the water. At a late stage in the design it had been decided to add chord reinforcement, and the effects of this additional weight had not been taken into account when calculating the stability of the bridge on the launching rollers. The bridge could easily have been retrieved by hauling it back under cover of night, but a new river wall of expensive granite had just been completed beneath the bridge, and the fear of damage to the wall meant that the bridge had to be dismantled piece by piece in full public view. However, once the span had been extricated, building went on smoothly and according to the planned programme, being finally used and admired by many thousands of visitors to the Festival the following year. (Figure 14.9).

Figure 14.9. *Sapper Bridge built by 36 Engineer Regiment for the Festival of Britain; the launching nose approaches the north bank of the Thames.* (RE Journal).

The initial minor disaster was soon forgotten and the completion of the bridge proved a terrific fillip to the morale of the regiment, demonstrating the bridging capability of an Engineer Regiment consisting largely of National Servicemen with little or no previous experience of Bailey Bridging.

The Korean War

During the early stages of the Korean War, which started with the invasion of South Korea by North Korea on 25 June 1950, the Corps was represented by 55 Independent Field Squadron RE, commanded by Major A E Younger RE, which formed part of 29 British Infantry Brigade. American forces were present in far greater numbers and one of the first bridging operations carried out by the Sappers made use of their equipment. This was the bridging of the River Han by 55 Squadron as part of the engineer support for the withdrawal of 1 Republic of Korea Division in the winter of 1950, soon after Chinese forces intervened on the side of the North Koreans. The Class 30 floating bridge was built using American M2 equipment which the Sappers had never seen before; nevertheless the bridge was built in the time stipulated in the US manuals, a fact which did much to improve relationships between the two Engineer Corps. The following April, 55 Squadron had again to rely on US equipment to build an infantry footbridge and a Class 12 assault bridge for an assault crossing of the Hantan Gang and Imjin Rivers.

At this stage bridgelayers were available to the squadron, but for logistic reasons were held on the establishment of the 8th Hussars. Major Younger relates that when the Commonwealth Brigade was held up by a demolished culvert in February 1951 1 Troop guided a Churchill Bridgelayer to the site to place its No 3 Tank Bridge. The operation was witnessed by General M B Ridgway, UN Commander, and C Squadron 8th Hussars then crossed the bridge together with some carriers from the Glosters. After dark, when the tanks had returned, the bridge was retrieved and 1 Troop built a timber baulk replacement bridge before dawn. The work was supervised by Lieutenant Keith Eastgate RE, the HQ subaltern, who was tragically killed later in the campaign.

In July 1951 the various units of Commonwealth forces were combined into 1 Commonwealth Division. Sapper representation was expanded to include 12 Field Squadron RE, 64 Field Park Squadron RE, and 57 Independent Field Squadron RCE, who joined 55 Squadron to form 28 Field Engineer Regiment, under the command of Lieutenant Colonel P N M Moore DSO**, MC, RE. The engineer problems in Korea were considerable, embracing all aspects of Sapper work but by now the fluid nature of the campaign considerably diminished, with the UN forces holding the south bank of the Imjin River and the Chinese forces deployed some 7km north of the river. Patrolling across the river was important and for ease of movement across the river 55 Squadron built and operated a Class 12 ferry,

Figure 14.10. Vehicles of 1 Commonwealth Division crossing the Imjin River, using an American M2 Pontoon Bridge built by the 58th Engineer Company, 8th US Army. (IWM MH31576).

known as Teal, on the division left flank, whilst 12 Squadron established another ferry, known as Pintail, on the divisional main axis. As well as these two ferries 57 Squadron RCE operated a Class 50/60 ferry at the Pintail site. These crossing points remained in use until the end of the war and were considerably developed.

After consolidation of the UN line south of the Imjin it was decided to push the 1 US Corps defensive line further forward to include dominating ground some 25-30 miles north of the river. (Figure 14.10). By October 1951 all objectives had been achieved and the line was to remain virtually unchanged until hostilities ceased with the announcement of a truce on 27 July 1953. Maintenance of the crossings across the Imjin at Teal and Pintail was of prime importance; frequent flooding was a constant problem, rainfall of as much as 6in being recorded in seventeen hours at one time. Indeed on one occasion the river rose by 37ft at the Pintail site, with an estimated current speed close to 15 feet per second. These conditions caused constant troubles with ferry cables, with frequent breakages due to floating debris or overstrain. At one time a cable fixed well above the water level was broken when a complete house, swept down river on the flood, floated into it.

In preparation for the 1952 rains US Army Engineers built a single way timber trestle bridge over the Imjin at Teal and completed a two way steel and concrete bridge at Pintail just four days before the first major flood. The special arrangements made to keep the bridges open included deployment of a troop of tanks to shoot at and break up large items of debris, and use of a motor tug team to guide debris through the gaps in the bridges, using pole charges to demolish obstacles. Even so, on 29 July 1952 the river rose 30ft and the first major flood tore a 280ft gap in the timber bridge at Teal, despite heroic efforts by Sappers to clear the debris with explosives. Luckily additional cable-ways had been constructed at both sites and Class 50/60 and American M2 rafts were operating at Pintail and Teal respectively.

The maintenance of the approach roads to the ferry sites was also a constant problem, particularly during the wet season, and involved considerable engineer effort. However, the war had now become almost completely static; 1 Commonwealth Division moved into reserve in February 1953 and after returning to its position in the line in April the Sappers were engaged in routine tasks such as tunnelling, road maintenance and fieldworks, with little involvement in bridging of interest. No major damage was caused during the floods that year, the bridge that had been swept away at Teal having been replaced with a Class 50 two way semi-permanent low level bridge in January, so designed that it would be submerged by flood water, allowing debris to pass over the top of the deck during severe flooding. Meanwhile peace negotiations continued and on 27 July 1953, just over three years after the initial invasion by the North Koreans, a truce was agreed.

To close this brief account of bridging operations during the Korean War, I relate an episode told me by Sapper John Morley, who served with 55 Field Squadron during the War. It concerns the naming of a short double/single Bailey Bridge of no great significance, built to replace a culvert previously demolished, rebuilt, and demolished yet again as the battle was fought to and fro across the Imjin. The bridge was built by 1 Troop of the Squadron in mid 1951. The Park Troop Commander, Lieutenant Brian Swinbanks RE, was temporarily acting as 1 Troop Subaltern prior to the building of the bridge when he was unfortunately killed by enemy action. Swinbanks had had a girl friend who was a Windmill Girl at the Whitehall Theatre in London and as a result some of the Windmill Girls had been sending welfare parcels of chocolates and cigarettes out to Korea for the Sappers. What could have been more appropriate therefore than the naming of the bridge as Windmill Bridge, in honour of Lieutenant Swinbanks and the generosity of the Windmill Girls. A small plaque naming the bridge was placed on the hillside nearby.

Queens' Bridge

Queens' Bridge, built in Holland in 1954, deserves mention as it was built as a combined operation between British and Dutch Army Engineers. The bridge was built across the River Maas at Well, roughly half way between Nijmegen and Venlo. The British Army of the Rhine were anxious that a bridge capable of carrying loaded tank transporters should be built across the Maas in that area, in order to improve their lines of communications, and the Dutch had plans to build a permanent bridge, but not in the foreseeable future. It was therefore decided that a semi-permanent bridge should be built by the two nations as a joint venture. Negotiations, particularly with regard to funding, took many months before an agreement was reached on the split of work between the two countries. The Dutch agreed that the approach roads and embankments should be built by the State PWD, known as the Rijkswaterstaat, and that they would let contracts for and pay for the concrete abutments, foundation work and piling. Transportation and supply of the Bailey equipment was to be a British responsibility, whilst the building of the bridge would be undertaken by 37 Corps Engineer Regiment (which had just changed its title from 37 Army Engineer Regiment) and A Company, 112 Pontoneer Battalion of the Royal Netherlands Army.

The site finally selected for the bridge was just upstream of the site to be used at a later date for the permanent bridge, so that the same approach roads could be used for both. It was in fact the site on which a Bailey Pontoon Bridge was built by 7 Army Troop Engineers in March 1945, although that bridge was removed soon after the end of the war. At this point the river was some 400ft wide but the need to cross flood plains and a minor road meant that the total length of bridge would be 1,385ft, with a subsidiary span of 140ft across an adjacent flood channel.

Design of the Bailey superstructure was carried out by the Engineer staff at HQ BAOR. The load class was to be Class 80 (Centurion), and this gave rise to considerable discussion on the type of construction to be used. Ideally Heavy Girder Bridge would have been most suitable but it was not available at that time in sufficient quantities. Bailey was therefore selected and in the end Standard Widened Bailey was used rather than Extra Widened Bailey, because it allowed longer spans to be built over the navigation channels. The two 160ft navigation spans were to be of quadruple/triple construction, and it was decided to undersling the bottom storey, thus raising the level of the roadway within the bridge and eliminating the need for restrictive overhead bracing. The 80ft approach spans, six on one bank and seven on the other, were to be of quadruple/single construction, whilst the standard quadruple truss Bailey piers were supported on concrete piled foundations or concrete grillages where ground conditions were suitable.

After the lengthy negotiation and planning stages had been completed, work on the abutments and foundations started in February 1954 and in early April joint training of the British and Dutch troops started in earnest. In May 37 Corps Engineer Regiment, commanded by Lieutenant Colonel A C Lewis, moved to Well and the next day the first panel was placed; by the end of the week six piers had been constructed. An excellent detailed account of the building of the bridge, written by Major K M Robertson RE, who was OC 40 Field Squadron RE and acted as OC Bridge, has appeared in the *Royal Engineer Journal* (September 1955) and so details will not be repeated here. Suffice to say that the bridge was completed by 31 July, the approach spans on each bank having been built as continuous spans and launched up a 1 in 30 gradient towards the centre of the bridge, prior to the

Figure 14.11. *The Queens' Bridge built across the River Maas in Holland by British and Dutch Army Engineers.*

positioning of the two navigation spans. (Figure 14.11).

The bridge was named Queens' Bridge as a tribute to Their Majesties, Queen Elizabeth II of Britain and Queen Juliana of the Netherlands. It was formally opened on 3 September 1954 by General Sir Richard Gale, Commander in Chief Northern Army Group and British Army of the Rhine.

The bridge remained in use until 1980, and impressive as that might seem, it did bring to light certain limitations which caused headaches for the bridge keepers, the Rijkwaterstaat. The bridge rusted badly, the quadruple construction making it almost impossible to paint, and eventually severe rust caused the authorities to reduce its load classification; this problem does not arise of course with modern adaptations of the Bailey Bridge, which are galvanized to prevent rust. In icy weather the 1 in 30 approaches proved treacherous, and liberal use of salt may have helped the traffic but also aggravated the rusting. The long bridge could of course only be used for one way traffic and this necessitated the installation of traffic lights, manually operated by day and automatically at night; traffic delays were considerable and the cost of operating the system was heavy. It was eventually replaced by a new 3,100ft long concrete bridge, the spans of which were designed as double cell box girders. Shortly after the opening ceremony of the new bridge a very large floating crane was used to lift out the two Bailey navigation spans, one by one and each weighing some 150 tons; the rest of the Bailey was dismantled soon afterwards.

The Falklands Campaign

After many years of argument with Britain over the sovereignty of the Islands, Argentinian Forces invaded the Falkland Islands on 2 April 1982.

The events leading up to the invasion, the considerable logistic problems facing the UK, and the pursuance of Operation Corporate (the military operation by the UK to re-possess the Islands) have been written of in considerable detail elsewhere and need not be reiterated here. Bridging operations were of a minor nature but warrant comment, however, because one involved the first operational use by the Sappers of a helicopter for bridge emplacement.

The first Engineer unit to embark for the Falklands, on 9 April 1982, was 59 Independent Commando Squadron RE, forming part of 3 Commando Brigade. The initial landing of the task force took place on 21 May, and included a Troop of 9 Parachute Squadron RE, attached to 2 Battalion Parachute Regiment, and 11 Field Squadron RE, deployed to give Harrier support to the force. Also included in the force were three Mexeflote detachments of 17 Port Regiment RCT, supporting Landing Ship detachments of that regiment. The build up of forces continued and eventually included 5 Infantry Brigade, the main body of which arrived in San Carlos Water on 2 June. The Sapper element of the Brigade included 36 Engineer Regiment (commanded by Lieutenant Colonel G W Field MBE RE, who was appointed Force CRE and Engineer Advisor to the Land Forces Commander), the remainder of 9 Parachute Squadron, and 61 Field Support Squadron.

During the advance of the British Forces south and then east towards Port Stanley the bridge between Fitzroy and Bluff Cove was found to have been blown by the enemy. One pier had been destroyed and a 60ft gap blown at the eastern end. The area was heavily mined and 9 Squadron had to clear the mines before work on repairing the bridge could commence. Materials that would have been used to repair the bridge had been aboard the the the *Sir Tristram*, which, with the *Sir Galahad*, was attacked by Argentinian aircraft and badly damaged on 8 June whilst unloading in Fitzroy Creek. The Squadron therefore had to make use of locally salvaged materials, and welded together scrap RSJs to replace the demolished spans. (Figure 14.12). the *Sir Galahad* was eventually towed out to sea and sunk, but the *Sir Tristram* survived the war and the tank deck was used for troop accommodation in

Figure 14.12. *The repaired bridge between Fitzroy and Bluff Cove in the Falklands.* (Martin Cleaver).

Port Stanley for a time.

Later on the bridge across the Murrel River, on the other 'main route' to Port Stanley, collapsed when a Samson recovery vehicle was being driven over it. An Airportable Bridge (APB) was available with 9 Squadron at Fitzroy although several parts, including the launching nose, were missing, having been lost during the attack on the *Sir Tristram*. Colonel Field therefore ordered the Squadron to build the bridge on the ground at Fitzroy so that it could be flown in by Chinook helicopter. By keeping the speed of the helicopter down to about 40 knots and hovering when the bridge started to oscillate, the pilot successfully transported the bridge to the new site, despite high winds and turbulence in the mountains. A new timber abutment had to be built for the bridge since only 42ft of bridge was available, and once the original bridge had been completely removed and the Samson lifted out of the gap (using the Chinook once more - the proverbial 'Sky Hook'), the APB was successfully placed in position.

Meanwhile the advance on Port Stanley continued, supported by a massive bombardment by artillery and naval guns, and on the evening of 14 June the Argentine Commander in the Falklands agreed to the surrender of all his forces in the Islands.

The Gulf War

The Sapper contribution to the successful conclusion of the Gulf War against Iraq, and indeed to the rehabilitation of Kuwait after the war, was very considerable, with upward of 4,500 Sappers deployed at one time, about a third of the total strength of the Corps. The Engineer ORBAT is of interest because for the first time Engineer Regiments deployed operationally in the new close support formation outlined in Chapter Thirteen. Thus when 21 Engineer Regiment, commanded by Lieutenant Colonel J D Moore-Bick OBE RE, deployed with 7 Brigade in the early Autumn of 1990, it consisted of a General Support Squadron (1 Field Squadron), a Close Support Squadron (4 Field Squadron), 45 Field Support Squadron, and additional armoured engineer support provided by 26 Armoured Engineer Squadron from 32 Armoured Engineer Regiment. The Close Support Squadron had two Field Troops and two Armoured Troops. For Operation Granby, the name given to British participation in the Gulf War, the Regiment was supported by 49 EOD Squadron, 14 Topographic Squadron, and elements of the Military Works Force. 39 Engineer Regiment was also deployed to provide engineer support in the Force Maintenance Area behind the Brigade rear boundary.

In November 1990 it became clear that the land campaign would require a larger force, and soon afterwards 7 Brigade was joined by 4 Brigade to form 1 (BR) Armoured Division. Engineer support for 4 Brigade was provided by 23 Engineer Regiment (commanded by Lieutenant Colonel D J Beaton RE), the Regiment that had previously carried out the close support squadron trials in Germany, but now reorganized on lines similar to those of 21

Regiment for operations in the Gulf. In early January 1991, 32 Armoured Engineer Regiment, commanded by Lieutenant Colonel A R E Hutchinson RE, joined the other Sapper Regiments in the Gulf, deploying with its two remaining squadrons, that is 31 and 77 Armoured Engineer Squadrons. The Regiment was supported by 37 Field Squadron from 35 Engineer Regiment, to give an improved combat engineer capability, and by two Flail Troops, equipped with the Aardvark Flail, manned by personnel from 25 Engineer Regiment. By now 1 (BR) Armoured Division was at full strength.

It was anticipated that the tank bridges would be needed for the crossing of oil pipelines that crisscross large areas of Kuwait. Some of these were of large diameter, and it was considered that our forces might have to cross these rapidly without fracturing them. The use of the No 8 Tank Bridge with rapidly placed trestles, mentioned in the previous chapter in connection with combination bridging, was considered but discarded, because of the trestle height and because a second bridge would have been required for exiting. RARDE(Christchurch) therefore suggested the use of steel wedges with the Tank Bridges, to be placed at the central joint between the main deck sections to arch the bridge over the pipelines, and to be bolted to the bridge to avoid permanent modification. Subsequent trials with the 44ft span No 9 Tank Bridge showed that achievement of a worthwhile mid-span height increase resulted in unacceptable ramp slopes. Indeed CO 23 Regiment decided to leave his No 9 Tank Bridges with 45 Field Support Squadron, now part of Divisional troops, and only carry the No 8 Tank Bridges with his AVLBs, considering them more versatile for gap and pipeline crossing. With this longer tank bridge the wedges produced a mid-span height increase of about 7½ ft, but this could be further increased by the use of additional wedges at the junction between the forward ramps and the main sections of the deck. In the event very little use was made of the No 8 Tank Bridge in this role. (Figure 14.13).

By 17 January 1991 the UN deadline for Iraqi withdrawal from Kuwait passed and the air bombardment started. Such was the ferocity of this bombardment that the the land war, which started in the early hours of 24 February, lasted but 100 hours. The role of 32 Regiment had by now changed from that of a major assault and breaching unit to that of route development and protection. The Regiment became known as the Route Development Battle Group, and the task of

Figure 14.13. A Challenger Tank crossing a No 8 Tank Bridge fitted with wedges, during Operation Granby in the Gulf. (RE Journal August 1991).

breaching the Iraqi obstacle belt extending along the whole of the Kuwait/Iraqi border was undertaken by US 1 Infantry Division. 1 (BR) Armoured Division then attacked through the breaches into Southern Iraq and swung eastward. The Sapper role during this phase of the war and indeed during the whole operation has been written up in detail in the RE Journal, giving full acknowledgment to the sterling work of all branches of the Corps. The very briefness of the landwar precluded any major bridging operations, but integrated engineer support proved indispensable.

A factor that caused some concern with regard to use of the tank bridges was the general upgrading of armour on armoured vehicles. The Centurion AVREs of 32 Regiment were equipped with add-on armour and toe pieces, with extra glacis and skirt plates. The Chieftain AVREs and Bridgelayers deployed with 21 and 23 Regiments were fitted with front chain mail, to defeat HEAT missiles, and Warrior side armour, and some were modified to accept the Pearsons Mid-Life Improved Mine Plough or the Universal Dozer Kit. All the Chieftain AVREs carried Pipe Fascines to cross antitank ditches, and a number carried Class 60 Trackway. Lieutenant Colonel D J Beaton RE, CO of 23 Engineer Regiment, writes that 'All uparmouring was gratefully received by the tank crews, but the combination of chain mail and the front mounted Magnetic Induction Mine Clearing Coil made vision from the vehicles even more difficult than usual, particularly at night, and the vehicles came more and more to resemble ungainly research prototypes'. The main battle tanks were of course similarly uparmoured, and the Challenger, already a Class 70 load, ended up nearer Class 80, causing some anxiety regarding possible crossing of our assault bridges by these heavy loads.

The land war itself was of brief duration, but during the period of intensive training under operational conditions that took place beforehand, CO 21 Regiment, supporting two Armoured Battle Groups, decided it better to reorganize into two equal squadrons, each with two Field Troops, an Armoured Troop and five CETs. Obviously the concentration of armoured engineer assets is desirable if, for example, a major breaching operation is predicted, and such concentration considerably eases maintenance and logistic problems. On the other hand, in fast moving modern warfare there is a good argument for ensuring that all Battle Groups have the improved mobility asset provided by spreading armoured engineer equipment more widely, although one must accept that the support provided may well be eroded by any unserviceability within the small number of equipments then available to each Battle Group. The matter is without doubt contentious, but the Engineer-in-Chief's paper on Options for Change, dated July 1991 and discussed in more detail in Chapter Thirteen, outlined a War ORBAT for Divisional Engineers which included a Close Support Regiment, consisting of an RHQ, a Headquarters Squadron, an Armoured Engineer Squadron and a Mechanized Field Squadron, thus retaining full flexibility as required.

Operations in Bosnia

The final withdrawal of Sapper units from the Gulf on completion of Operation Granby was not long over before long term involvement in support of United Nations operations in the former Yugoslavia was under way. After minor Sapper support for a Field Ambulance in early 1992, 35 Engineer Regiment, supported by 519 Specialist Team Royal Engineers (STRE), deployed to Bosnia for a six-month tour in October 1992. Initial reconnaissance identified many tasks including the need to repair or replace twelve bridges on the main supply routes; two of the main road bridges had been partially demolished with explosives. In the event 1000 kilometres of roads were constructed, upgraded and maintained during a very difficult winter, and 23 minor bridges and one major bridge were repaired during the regimental tour, known as Operation Grapple 1.

So began a continuing commitment for the Corps that ran for five years and more. In that time most of the Engineer Regiments of the Corps spent a six month tour in Bosnia, some returning for a second tour, in what were known as Operations Grapple 1 to 7. The Sapper work covered the normal range of work associated with the Corps, including road building and maintenance, water and electricity supply, the building of accommodation for UN forces, EOD clearance, and survey work. In addition a great many bridges were built to replace those destroyed during the fighting between the Bosnia Muslims, the Serbians and the Croatians. The new bridges included Extra Wide Bailey Bridges, Heavy Girder Bridges, Medium Girders Bridges, Mabey and Johnson Compact 200 Bridges and improvised bridges.

Operation Grapple ceased at the time of the Dayton Peace Accord in November 1995, and the United Nations Protection Force (PROFOR) gave way to the NATO led Implementation Force (IFOR). Meanwhile Corps support had continued, if anything at an increased pace, with the need to restore the devastated infrastructure of the country, and when 38 Engineer Regiment, on Operation Resolute 1, handed over to 36 Engineer Regiment, on Operation Resolute 2, in April 1996, Colonel J S Field, Commander of Royal Engineers in Bosnia, had identified no less than 28 sites on main roads in the UK area of operations that still needed bridging, in addition to many smaller sites requiring some attention. In December 1996 IFOR in turn gave way to the Stabilization Force (SFOR), supported by the UK Operation Lodestar, with the Corps still heavily committed.

Of the large number of bridges built by the Corps in Bosnia, brief descriptions of two will serve to illustrate some of the problems involved. The first operation took place during Operation Grapple 4, and involved the bridging of the River Neretva at Mostar; it was unusual in that the Sappers were first engaged in a demolition. The original bridge on the site, known as the **Tito Bridge**, had been demolished early in the conflict, along with four other bridges across the river in the town, effectively isolating a Muslim enclave on the east bank of the river. The American International Rescue

Committee therefore funded the building of an EWBB on the site by Muslim engineers, in 1993. The new bridge had scarcely been opened for a month when it was badly damaged by fire from a Croat tank, making it impassable to vehicles. In early 1994 a local cease fire was agreed and plans to rebridge the Neretva on the Tito site were under way. The plan envisaged the building of a broken span EWBB, comprising 14 bay and 9 bay double/double reinforced spans supported on a 30ft Bailey pier. Delaunching of the existing badly damaged spans was not deemed feasible and so is was decided to demolish the bridge and remove the pieces from the site. (Figure 14.14).

The operation was to be a joint British/Spanish project, with a troop of Sappers from 61 Field Support Squadron and engineers from the Spanish Battalion (SPABAT). After decking and non-structural members had been removed from the bridge, 140Kg of the explosive PE4 were placed to cut the bridge into 3 bay sections, which could then be cut into manageable sections for removal by the SPABAT's 25 ton crane. On 27 August preparations were complete and with almost half of the population of Mostar being moved away from the possible danger zone, the demolition was fired, with complete success.

Once the debris had been cleared from the site construction of the pier was soon completed. However, water seepage behind the home abutment caused a slight problem and the length of bridge was increased to prevent possible future undermining of the abutment. As finally built the two bridge spans were increased to 15 and 10 bays respectively, which with a cantilever span bay and span junction bay required for the longer span resulted in a total bridge length of 270ft. The bridge was declared open for vehicle traffic on 12 September, the third bridge to occupy the site in as many years, and a vital step in restoring the quality of life for the people of Mostar.

Figure 14.14. *The damaged Tito Bridge across the R Neretva in Mostar, Bosnia, prior to its demolition to make way for an EWBB built on the site by British and Spanish Engineers in 1994.* (Major T O Dunn RE)

The **Kulen Vakuf Bridge** was built by Sappers of 26 Armoured Engineer Squadron during Operation Resolute 1. Kulen Vakuf is a small town on the River Una whose valley forms the boundary between Croatia and Bosnia, and as such was a possible site for strained relations between the previously warring factions. By April 1996 relations were improving but it was decided that a bridge was required for light armoured vehicles in case further unrest should develop. The bridge site selected was across a deep gorge with a gap of some 25m, and it was decided that a Medium Girder Bridge would be most suitable. The site was a difficult one, with a derelict house and a narrow curved approach road on the home bank, and a difficult vertical rock face on the far bank restricting the slewing distance of vehicles once off the bridge ramp. The later problem, on what became known as 'the site from hell', was solved by laying trackway at right angles to the far bank ramp and using hardcore as a base on the ramps to prevent excess damage.

The build of the 11 bay double storey MGB went ahead as planned but with considerable difficulty, most certainly not under conditions ever experienced during normal training and with considerable credit to those involved. Unfortunately the house causing obstruction to the booming out of the bridge had to be demolished, a small price to pay, however, for the establishment of this important crossing. (Figure 14.15).

Engineers of other nations were also actively engaged in bridge building in Bosnia and the increasing demands of IFOR and the involved Partners for Peace saw an increase in the involvement of Mabey and Johnson in the area. Following reconnaissance in January 1996 more than 20 bridges were constructed by engineers of many countries, not least of which were Hungary and Romania. The use of the Mabey Compact 200 bridge system

Figure 14.15. A Medium Girder Bridge built at Kulen Vakuf, Bosnia, in 1996. (The Sapper - July 1996).

became necessary when load and clear span requirements exceeded the capabilities of other in-service bridges. The performance of the Mabey bridges under such demanding circumstances gained them a very high reputation and may have influenced a later decision by the British Ministry of Defence to adopt it as their Logistic Support Bridge (LSB) to replace EWBB and HGB. The Bailey type bridge lives on!

Bridges built during this period include two built by Romanian Engineers in the area of Doboj during the period May to July 1996. The first was the **Doboj North Bridge**, a 30m span Compact 200 bridge, later the target of a terrorist attack which led to minor repairs which closed the bridge for a few days. The larger bridge was the **Doboj South Bridge**, with a span of 98m, which was constructed in late June and early July 1996. The old bridge had been destroyed and still lay in the Usora River; this led to the need for much preparatory work including repair and strengthening of a pier. The Doboj South Bridge was officially opened on 5 July 1996 and was an extremely important construction due to its location in the middle of the Inter Entity Boundary Line, on the site of the old confrontation line between the Serb and Federation populations.

Later that year extensive repairs to the **Slavonski Brod Bridge** were carried out. Several spans of the bridge had been damaged or destroyed during the conflict; some spans could be repaired but, after reconnaissance, design and planning by the Royal Engineer Military Works Force a Hungarian Engineer contingent erected a three span Mabey and Johnson Universal Bridge across four of the original damaged spans. Preparatory work included removal of the damaged spans of the old bridge and the placing of a fabricated steel support structure, using a Blackhawk helicopter, on one of the piers to transmit large dead loads during the launching of the bridge. The MLC 80 bridge was 162m long and weighed over 300 tonnes; it is the longest panel bridge in Europe constructed in a single launch. The Slavonski Brod Bridge was officially opened by Admiral Lopez, Commander IFOR on 7 September 1966, some six weeks after work commenced. (Figure 14.16).

Figure 14.16. The 162m long Slavonski Brod Bridge, a three span Mabey Universal Bridge. (HQ ACE Rapid Reaction Corps).

Bridging in Nepal

Meanwhile the Corps was engaged in other bridging operations, in the ancient Kingdom of Nepal, many thousands of miles away. At the height of the 1993 monsoon season the rainfall in Nepal was the highest recorded for over 100 years. The devastating floods that followed killed hundreds of people and made thousands homeless; they also caused many landslides and the destruction of three bridges on the Prithvi Rajpath, a vital route from India into Kathmandu, the capital of Nepal. The reopening of this road, normally bringing in some 1,500 lorry loads of supplies a day to support the large population of the Kathmandu valley, was vital, and the assistance of the Queen's Gurkha Engineers (QGE) in Hong Kong was requested through our Ambassador and Defence Attaché in Kathmandu on 21 July. The UK Government and the MOD subsequently agreed to the deployment of a QGE Squadron to assist with the construction of temporary bridging along the Prithvi Rajpath, under the codewords Operation Rivers.

Meanwhile a small reconnaissance party, headed by Major J R White RE, OC of 68 Gurkha Field Squadron, arrived in Kathmandu on 23 July. After reconnaissance of the route using a Royal Nepalese Army (RNA) helicopter, he reported that work on repairs to landslip lengths of the road were already under way by the Nepalese Department of Roads. However, it was clear that temporary replacement of the three bridges would require some 170m of Class 30 bridging equipment. A more detailed reconnaissance followed on mountain bikes! 100ft of Bailey Bridging had already been earmarked in Hong Kong, and the UK Overseas Development Administration had already received quotations for the supply of two 70m bridges from both Mabey & Johnson and Thos Storey (Engineers) in UK. Troops in Hong Kong had been placed on standby and with the final approval of the MOD on the evening of 27 July, one troop of 68 Gurkha Field Squadron and one troop from 67 Gurkha Field Squadron were flown into Kathmandu.

During the next few days the water levels at the sites for which the two 70m bridges were required, that is at Mahadev Besi and Belkhu, subsided a little and it was decided to concentrate on building the bridge at Malekhu. On the morning of 4 August a chartered Russian Antonov 124, the largest aircraft in the world, flew 130 tons of Bailey Bridge and other stores from Hong Kong into Tribhuwan, Kathmandu's airport. As a result of careful pre-planning, the aircraft was unloaded in four hours, and after initial delays, caused by demands for more pay by the lorry drivers, the first bridging convoy set out on the 90km journey to Malekhu the next morning. With only fifteen trucks available, each had to make the journey three or four times, an operation not made easier by the state of the Prithvi Rajpath. The bridge site was not an easy one; the original bridge had been on a bend in the road and had narrow approaches, and many lorries and buses had been abandoned on either side of the demolished bridge. Nevertheless within 90 hours of the arrival of the Antonov in Kathmandu, the Bailey stores had been offloaded, sorted, and moved to Malekhu, and the bridge built and opened for traffic, partially opening this important route. Fifty soldiers from the RNA assisted in the construction of the bridge, working alongside their compatriots of 2 Troop, under the command of Lieutenant I K Stewart RE. (Figure 14.17).

The more demanding tasks of replacing the bridges at Belkhu and Mahadev Besi remained. At Belkhu, a causeway provided temporary passage across the river, and work was already proceeding on the excavation, through silt and mud, of the foundations of the original piers, under command of Lieutenant E W Judge RE. The plan was to build two equipment piers on top of these foundations, to support the new 70m bridge. However, on 10 August Judge reported that more rain had caused the river to rise 2m overnight, sweeping away all of the preliminary work and once again cutting of the road to Kathmandu. In the light of this further flood, the possible vulnerability of new equipment piers caused Major White to reconsider the design of these two remaining bridges. Alternative 70m single spans were considered, but engineers with Mabey & Johnson, with whom the ODA had now placed contracts for the supply of two of their Compact 200 Bridges, advised that double storey construction would be necessary, and even then its use would be restricted. It was therefore decided to opt for two span double/single bridges, each supported by just one pier, built on the foundations of one of the destroyed piers.

Since the floods of 10 August had also caused further landslips on the

Figure 14.17. *Launching the 25m triple/single Bailey at Malekhu, Nepal in August 1993.* (British Forces Hong Kong).

Prithvi Rajpath, it was decided to concentrate first on the replacement bridge at Mahadev Besi, being the nearer to Kathmandu of the two remaining sites. In the event the plan to build both bridges to the same design went ahead, although the pier at Mahadev Besi was improvised using spare Bailey components, whilst that at Belkhu used Christchurch Cribs; the foundations of both piers were protected by concrete filled gabions. Work now proceeded according to plan, the Compact 200 Bridges having been flown into Kathmandu from RAF Mildenhall by five US Air Force C5 Galaxy aircraft. On 27 August the bridge at Mahadev Besi was pushed forward on its rollers and shortly afterwards the 23 bay bridge touched down on the far bank. On 1 September the bridge at Belkhu was also completed and was immediately proved by a backlog of well over a thousand laden lorries.

68 Squadron returned to Hong Kong on 11 September, justly proud of the valuable assistance that they rendered to the home country of their Gurkha Sappers in a time of extreme need. Not only had they built the three bridges on the Prithvi Rajpath, but their Military Plant Foreman, WOII P C Mansfield, and their Clerk of Works Construction, Staff Sergeant Blaha Rai, supervised Sappers of the RNA in the building of a fourth bridge, a 32m Bailey at Bhainsa on the Tribhuwan Rajpath, a mountainous road running directly down into India from Kathmandu. It is sad to note that the days of the Squadron were numbered, and some three months later it was disbanded under the Options for Change policy.

A much fuller account of this disaster relief work in Nepal, written by Major White, appears in the August 1994 issue of the RE Journal, and has formed the basis of the limited account given here.

CHAPTER FIFTEEN

Bridging into the Future

The Development Cycle

Before considering the equipments now coming into service, it is worthwhile examining how the development procedure for Engineer equipment has evolved. It became evident in Chapters Eleven and Twelve that since the War it has often taken something like ten years from the initial statement of a requirement for a new equipment until the equipment was actually with the troops in the field. This was in marked contrast to the wartime record of the Bailey Bridge, which was with the troops one year after the design was initiated, and obviously requires some explanation. The reason, of course, was that during the War vastly increased resources were made available for the development of equipments, coupled with an almost complete lack of financial restraint. A positive will to reduce administrative delays to a minimum flowed from the vital urgency to equip our troops with the best and most up-to-date equipment possible during the War, the result of which was to dictate the whole future of our country and indeed the world. This ensured that wartime equipment production on the scale of that of the Bailey Bridge was possible. Under all the financial restraints, checks and balances of peacetime, and with a much more bureaucratic approach, the situation since the war has become very different.

At the beginning of the 1960s the Engineer-in-Chief retained responsibility not only for the provision and distribution of engineer equipment, through his Colonel E1, but also for the planning of the research and development of such equipment, through his Colonel E2, working through his Brigadier General Staff, formerly the Deputy Engineer-in-Chief. Actual responsibility for design, development and procurement of engineer equipment remained with the Director Royal Engineer Equipment, or DREE, a Brigadier on the staff of the Master General of the Ordnance, or MGO. During the war the MGO and his staff had been transferred to the new Ministry of Supply, set up in 1939, but with the demise of the Ministry in September 1959, the MGO, together with DREE and his staff, once more became part of the War Office.

In 1963 the decision was made to set up a unified Ministry of Defence. One recommendation of the Nye Committee (chaired by Lieutenant General Sir Archibald Nye), which in 1964 reduced the responsibilities of Arms Directors, was that responsibility for policy on Engineer equipment and sponsorship thereof should pass to the Sapper branch of a new Directorate of Army Equipment Policy, namely AEP7, within the new Army Department of the Ministry of Defence. This Directorate subsequently became a part of the General Staff, known as General Staff, Operational Requirements, the

Sapper branch being GSOR(7), and later GSOR(13). Since then the branch has come under the tri-service control of the Deputy Chief of the Defence Staff (Systems), where it is part of Land Systems, Operational Requirements, and the Sapper branch now became LSOR 5.

Another recommendation of the Nye Committee, implemented in September 1964, resulted in the replacement of DREE by a Director of Fighting Vehicles and Engineer Equipment, or DFVE, now responsible only for research and development, but obviously over a wider equipment field. At the same time responsibility for production became that of a Director of Procurement (Fighting Vehicles and Engineer Equipment), or DP(FVE). Thus the production branches of DREE (ie RE1 to RE6) became separated from the development branches (ie RE7 to RE9).

In 1972, as a result of the report of the Rayner Committee (chaired by Sir Derek Rayner, Chief Executive PE MOD 1971-72) into equipment procurement, a new branch of the Ministry of Defence was set up, namely the Procurement Executive (PE), which brought together procurement for all three services into one branch of the Ministry. Development and procurement of Engineer equipment then became the responsibility of the Director General Fighting Vehicles and Engineer Equipment, or DGFVE, at two-star level, working through a number of Directors of Projects, to Project Managers at Colonel level. The devolving of responsibility for the development and production of a complete project or group of projects to a Project Manager was, and indeed is still, common in industry and in a number of foreign armies, and has proved very successful. In the case of bridging equipment, the project manager concerned is currently the Project Manager General Engineer Equipment, or PM GEE.

One further recent policy change, resulting from the 1980 report by Lord Strathcona (Minister of State, MOD, 1979-81), was to take the development of equipments away from the Research and Development Establishments wherever possible and place such development competitively within industry. The role of the R and D Establishments thus became predominantly one of basic defence research, examining new materials, concepts and systems, the latter sometimes requiring full-size research Concept Demonstrators. The Establishments still retained a role to advise DGFVE staff on development matters when so requested, however, and worked closely with Project Managers. In the case of the Army, various R and D establishments were amalgamated on 1 April 1984 into a single establishment, the Royal Armament Research and Development Establishment, or RARDE, with a number of outstations, such as the one at Christchurch, which became known as RARDE(Cc).

With the reductions in the Services resulting from the end of the Cold War in the late 1980s, reorganization was taken one stage further with the introduction of the Defence Research Agency (DRA) on 1 April 1991. This new Agency took over the equipment research responsibility for all three services; a number of the existing R & D Establishments were absorbed into the Agency, whilst others ceased to exist, now that development was firmly placed with industry. With the creation of a customer/supplier relationship, the responsibility of determining the requirements and objectives of research undertaken thorough DRA now rested with LSOR 5. Further reorganization took place in April 1995 with the setting-up of the Defence Evaluation and Research Agency (DERA). The establishing of DERA brought together into one agency the core of the Ministry of Defence's non-nuclear scientific and technical assets, forming the largest single research organization of its kind in Western Europe. DRA became one of its three divisions.

Theoretically the introduction of the Project Manager system should have speeded up the introduction of new equipments, but in practice the development cycle was still long and protracted, involving a number of stages before equipment entered service. These stages initially involved an extensive examination of the need for the equipment, followed by the development of a detailed statement of the required capabilities of the new equipment, possibly backed up by operational analysis studies. Procurement from industry, upgrading of existing equipment or development of a new equipment were alternatives to be considered, taking account of operational and cost effectiveness of the alternatives. A firm Staff Requirement followed, including a clear statement of the equipment performance required, and once final approval was given to go ahead, a suitable equipment could be purchased 'off the shelf' or a development contractor would be appointed by competitive tender, under control of the Project Manager.

In due course prototype equipments would be produced for extensive testing, first by the contractor and subsequently for full-scale user trials by troops, and, after formal acceptance of the equipment, full-scale production could proceed. With such a lengthy procedure it is perhaps not surprising that it can take many years for equipments to reach the troops, many getting cancelled along the way because of changes in operational policy, the advent of better alternatives, or simply diversion of funding to more important projects. International co-operation in the development of an equipment can make the whole process even more lengthy, as will be seen with the Bridging for the 80s project considered in Appendix F. There may be some truth in Lord Mountbatten's comment that 'If it works it is obsolete.'

The re-equipment cycle has thus evolved over many years. Many of the important changes took place a number of years ago, but the fundamental decision of the Strathcona Report to take development of equipments away from the R & D establishments and place it in industry is a more recent change that affects, as far as bridging is concerned, only the next generation of equipments, dealt with in this chapter. Thus it must be stressed that development of bridging equipments such as the Airportable Bridge, the Medium Girder Bridge, the No 8 and No 9 Tank Bridges, the Pipe Fascine and indeed most engineer equipments up until the late 1980s was based firmly in the Establishment at Christchurch.

Looking to the Future

In the late 1960s the bridging equipment of the British Army, either in service or coming into service, was first class. The Medium Girder Bridge, with its pier and span junction set, had proved to be an outstanding fixed bridge, second to none and shortly to be adopted by many nations throughout the World; the Amphibious Bridge M2 enabled the large rivers and canals of Europe to be crossed with celerity; and the Chieftain Bridgelayer, with its No 8 and No 9 Tank Bridges, was proving to be an excellent equipment in the assault role. However, all equipments have a limit to their useful life, a limit set by advances in technology, revisions of operational requirements, and basic wear and tear, taking account of such factors as a limited fatigue life, stress corrosion and operational damage. It was therefore anticipated that by the late 1980s there would be a need for replacement of all of these excellent equipments. Since experience had shown that the peacetime development and introduction of any major military equipment took at least ten years, with some equipments taking very considerably longer, it was decided to initiate the replacement of the British bridging equipments in good time.

This anticipation on the part of the United Kingdom was matched by a similar interest in other nations. In the late l960s a Quadripartite Working Group on Bridging and Gap Crossing had been set up, embracing design experts and operational requirement staff from the ABCA countries, that is America, Britain, Canada and Australia. At the second meeting of the Group, in 1969, it was agreed that joint research studies should be set up to consider concepts for a new generation of bridging equipments. It was agreed that, ideally, such studies should be carried out collaboratively, in the hope that this would lead to joint development and production, eliminating the duplication of effort within the participating countries, reducing production costs by virtue of a much larger potential market and improving standardization within NATO. Exploratory discussions took place in 1970, involving the ABCA countries, the Federal Republic of Germany, and France, and, as a result, the United States, Germany and the United Kingdom set up a joint study team in 1971, known as the International Concept Study Team (ISCT).

The project came to be known as **Bridging for the 1980s** or simply **BR80**, and is worth considering in more detail, in Appendix F, not only because it was the first collaborative bridging project in which UK had been involved, but also because it was to engage a very considerable bridging design effort at Christchurch for many years to come. Although at the end of the day it did not lead to collaborative development of a new bridging system, the bridging equipment coming into service for the British Army in the 1990s evolved from the BR80 project and used the girder configuration originally proposed by the UK during the study.

400

The Operational Requirement

After the preliminary meetings held in June 1970, Operational Requirement staffs of the three participating countries met to agree an Operational Requirement Guidance Document for the study team, using for the first time the terms **Wet** and **Dry Support** to define previously described floating and fixed bridges. The outline requirement was for a bridging system that could be used in all three roles, with the following specific demands, some essential and some desirable:

Assault Role:	A 20m (66ft) span to be essential, with a 30m (98ft) span desirable; the bridge to be launched in less than 5 minutes with crew protection as for the main battle tank.
Dry Support:	A 40m (131ft) span to be essential, with the capability for use at shorter spans; the 40m bridge to be built in 15 minutes, by day or by night.
Wet Support:	A 120m (395ft) bridge to be constructed, crossed by a battle group of 150 vehicles, dismantled and dispersed to a distance of 4km (2½ miles) in one hour. Construction of ferries was essential.

The required load class was initially set in the Class 50/60 range, although this was subsequently amended to MLC 60 to achieve greater standardization within NATO. Further amendments to the requirement evolved as the project continued, and these, together with other details of the work that followed until the project was finally wound up in 1981, are detailed in Appendix F.

Mechanically Assisted Construction by Hand.

After the ICST had reported in 1974, studies proceeded nationally, during what was known as the Interim Phase. Mechanically Assisted Construction by Hand, or MACH, had been an essential UK requirement from the early days of the BR 80 project, the UK view being that MACH would be useful in airborne operations and in rear areas, and that, operationally, mechanical failure of a possible BR80 Wheeled Vehicle Launcher (WVL) should not preclude the launching and building of a bridge. During this next phase the BR80 UK study team therefore proposed a low-cost construction system as an alternative to the WVL, making use of a mobile launching platform. However, the US had only a desirable requirement for such a system and FRG, initially, no requirement at all.

BRAVE. Arising from their requirement, the UK Interim Phase programme included examination of a MACH system making use of logistic vehicles and a bridging crane. This led to a proposal by Mr T S Parramore for a concept for the carriage and launching of the BR80 bridge girders which UK

Figure 15.1. *The automotive mock-up of BRAVE during the 1977 road trials in UK.* (T S Parramore).

felt had considerable advantages over the proposed WVL. The concept, known as the Bridge Articulated Vehicle Equipment, or BRAVE, proposed use of a tractor with a fifth wheel coupling towing a semi-trailer on which 32m of BR80 flip ramp bridge would be carried, with the girders close-spaced to reduce the road width to 3m. On site the girders would first be moved apart to increase the bridge width to 4m. A telescopic launching nose, fitted with bipod legs to support its end on the far bank, would then be extended across the gap and the bridge launched by winching across a trolley from which would be suspended the front end of the bridge. Once the bridge was across the gap both ends would be lowered to the ground by use of simple hoists, and the launching rail retracted. An automotive mock-up of BRAVE was made, using a DJB 30ton dump truck chassis, a mock-up semi-trailer and a dummy load. (Figure 15.1). Road trials proved satisfactory, but the UK proposal put to the BR80 Steering Committee (SC) met with little interest from US and FRG, although eventually the concept was evaluated during the final stages of the project.

ABLE. Further consideration of the BRAVE concept by UK led to the concept for the Automotive Bridge Launching Equipment, or ABLE. This proposed use of a purpose-built vehicle that incorporated a building platform and a light crane mounted behind the driving cab. From the

402

Figure 15.2. Early trials of the ABLE concept at Christchurch. (T S Parramore).

vehicle a full-span modular launching rail was to be constructed and launched across the gap, adjustable bipod legs being attached to the leading end so that the rail could be supported and levelled once in position. Standard sections of BR80 bridge girder, brought alongside the base vehicle on logistic vehicles, would then be swung into position on to rollers mounted on the vehicle, making use of the lorry-mounted crane. The front end of the bridge would then be supported from a trolley mounted on the launching rail, and more sections of bridge added at the rear, on the building rollers, as the trolley was winched along the launching rail and across the gap. Once the bridge reached the far bank, the far end of bridge would be lowered into position from the trolley, and the rear end of bridge lowered from the vehicle; the launching rail would then be retrieved and dismantled. (Figure 15.2). The system had the distinct advantage that the width of the launch vehicle would be only 3m compared with 4m for the WVL, and would additionally be a lighter, more compact and more manoeuvrable vehicle. The UK ABLE proposal was also put to the full SC, in late 1979, but again met with little interest from US and FRG.

Carbon Fibre - a New Material

During the national programmes of the Interim Phase of the BR80 project, attention was given to experimental use of Carbon Fibre (CF) material. For their prototype girder the US experimented with graphite epoxy pultrusions sandwiched between aluminium face sheets for bottom-chord members, and with corrugated KEVLAR epoxy composite web members; both uses exhibited excellent strength/weight properties. They also used KEVLAR cables experimentally for their girder-reinforcing kit and considered it an ideal material to use for a launching nose or traversing beam for the bridge, showing a possible 66% reduction in weight when compared with the use of aluminium alone. In Germany Dornier System GMBH manufactured a complete 42m (138ft) span aluminium alloy bridge extensively Carbon Fibre Reinforced (CFR), demonstrating savings in weight that reflected throughout the whole concept and in particular increased the stiffness of the bridge girder. And UK carried out studies into the use of selective reinforcement of their girder design showing a good reduction in weight; UK also completed a design study for a CFR bridge module with an aluminium deck surface that showed a 50% saving in weight for no envisaged increase in production costs.

Prior to the Interim Phase studies, CF had been in use for a number of years in various small-scale applications, but very high production costs had prevented its use in a structural role to any great degree. However, as a

Figure 15.3 An approximate indication of the advances in material effectiveness in bridge design, taking account of improved strength, weight decrease and material utilisation. (D Webber).

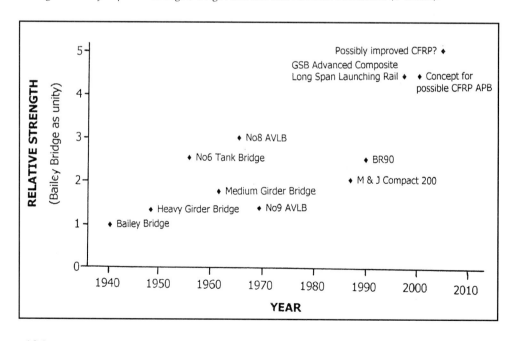

result of the BR80 Interim Phase work, the project's Final Concept Team (FCT) considered that the use of CF composites in bridge design offered the promise of a real breakthrough for the future, although its use in their concept recommendations was precluded by the limited extent of the experimental work carried out. Subsequent developments of the ABLE concept in the UK (which is discussed later) included the construction of a prototype launching rail for the new bridge, using Carbon Fibre Reinforced Plastic (CFRP); this could enable bridges up to 56m long to be launched, whereas the maximum bridge length achievable with an aluminium alloy launching rail was thought to be limited to 44m. Further use of composite materials has also been proposed for manufacture of the scissoring rods for the existing tank bridges. In this case the material suggested was an amarid fibre rope called Parafil, which shows a possible 60% saving in weight. Some details of these new materials are included in Appendix B and an approximate indication of the advances in material effectiveness in bridge design over the years is shown in Figure 15.3.

The Way Ahead for UK

After the collapse of the International BR80 project in the early 1980s, at the Assessment 2 stage, the UK had to decide on the best way ahead. Requirements were drawn up for what had now become Bridging for the 1990s, or BR90, and it was at this stage that the chance was taken to further amend the nomenclature used for bridging, in part to fall in line with NATO allies and in part for logical reasons. It was reasoned that the armoured vehicle mounted Assault Bridge was likely to be used in a variety of roles in support of troops and not merely in the assault role; it was therefore decreed that henceforth such a bridge would be known as a **Close Support Bridge** or **CSB**. Wet or Dry Support Bridges were to be known as **Deliberate Wet** or **Dry Support Bridges**, or **DWSB**s and **DDSB**s, although later this was changed yet again and these bridges became known as **General Support Bridges**.

After considerable discussion four GSRs associated with BR90 were approved, setting out the UK bridging requirements into the next century; these GSRs were:

> GSR 3983 - A Close Support Bridge System;
> GSR 3984 - A Deliberate Dry Support Bridge System;
> GSR 3985 - Long Span Equipment for a DDSB System;
> GSR 3986 - Two Span Equipment for a DDSB System.

A great deal of work on a Reference Concept for a new Christchurch Bridge was now carried out at the Christchurch Establishment. This included the design of a demonstrator model of ABLE, under the supervision of Mr Stuart Parramore, whose work on the project was later recognized by the MOD Committee for Awards to Inventors. The full-scale model was eventually

Figure 15.4. *The demonstrator model of ABLE produced by Fairey Engineering.* (Williams Fairey Engineering)

made by Fairey Engineering Ltd, using a Foden 8 x 4 chassis; the hydraulic equipment was supplied by Dowty. (Figure 15.4).

Industrial Participation

In line with the recently introduced equipment procurement policy, it was decided that the new CSB and DDSB would be developed by industry and not at Christchurch. Accordingly, in late 1984, RARDE(Christchurch) was charged with briefing a number of firms that were judged to have the necessary design and production capability to undertake the work. The firms were required to undertake full-scale development of the equipment to meet DGFVE Specification 535, which laid down full operational requirements. This would be followed by production and testing of prototypes, and, subject to final acceptance of the equipment and successful competitive tender action, full-scale production. Seven firms agreed to participate, including Fairey Engineering Ltd, a consortium of the Royal Ordnance Factories and Freeman Fox Consulting Engineers, and NEI Thompson (later Thompson Defence Projects Ltd, part of the Rolls Royce Industrial Power Group). The firms were required to submit fully costed proposals for development and production, designs for the DDSB being based upon ideas that evolved during the development of the Christchurch Reference Concept. However, the firms were given a free hand to improve upon the Reference Concept and also to include alternative proposals in their

406

submissions, and many useful ideas were submitted.

The detailed submissions required very careful examination to determine not only the soundest technical proposal but also the most cost-effective solution, and Consulting Engineers Gifford and Partners were retained by the Project Manager, General Engineer Equipment, to assist RARDE(Cc) in carrying out a review of the proposals. This review eventually resulted in NEI Thompson being awarded a £M30 fixed-price contract, in November 1987, for the design and development of the new bridge; various production options were included in the contract, with the possibility of raising the value of the contract to over £M100. NEI Thompson worked directly to the MOD Project Manager in London, with RARDE(Cc) providing engineering support to the PM when required. The firm was subsequently sold by Rolls Royce PLC to Vickers PLC in 1995, becoming integrated into the defence Division of Vickers as Vickers Bridging. In 1999 Rolls Royce acquired Vickers PLC, now as Vickers Defence Systems, and so Rolls Royce once again owned a military bridging business.

The Bridging for the 1990s Equipment..

After extensive trials, the BR90 Bridge System that evolved is an excellent equipment. It is a comprehensive MLC 70 bridging system that can be used to produce both a close support bridge and a general support bridge (as the deliberate support bridge is now known), capable of spanning gaps from 9 to 56 metres (29 to 184ft). All bridges can be built from seven modular panels manufactured from the aluminium/zinc/magnesium alloy DGFVE 232B. Panels are interchangeable throughout the system and are used to form two interconnected trackways, with an overall bridge width of 4m (13ft 1½ in) and a girder depth of 1m (3ft 3in). The basic panels are either 8m (26ft 3in), 4m (13ft 1½in), or 2m (6ft 6¾ in) long. There is also an 8m ramp panel, a 4m reinforced panel, a 2m articulating panel and a 2m hinge panel. (Figure 15.5).

Figure 15.5. The modular panels used for the Bridging for the 1990s bridges. (Thompson Defence Projects Ltd).

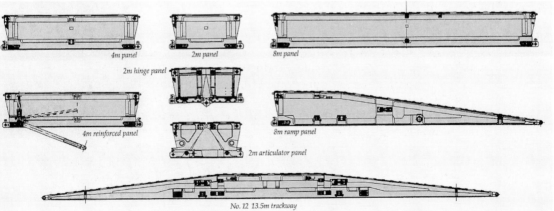

Figure 15.6. *A No 10 Tank Bridge carried on its Tank Bridge Transporter, travelling cross country in Bosnia.* (Vickers Defence Systems).

The Close Support Bridge System consists of three tank-launched bridges (known colloquially as Tank Bridges), which can be carried on a Tank Bridge Transporter or TBT (Figure 15.6) and are launched from a modified Chieftain Bridgelayer. The **No 10 Tank Bridge** is a 26m (85ft) scissor-launched bridge. (Figure 15.7). Each girder is constructed from 2 x

Figure 15.7. *A Chieftain Bridgelayer launching a second No 10 Tank Bridge in combination.* (Vickers Defence Systems).

Figure 15.8. Launching the lower of two No 12 Tank Bridges carried by the Chieftain Bridgelayer, from a No 10 Tank Bridge in Bosnia (Captain H Morehead, RMonRE(M)).

8m ramp panels, 2 x 4m standard panels and a 2m hinge panel; one 4m panel can be omitted from each girder to form a shorter bridge. The **No 11 Tank Bridge** is 16m (52ft 6in) long and is formed by connecting up 8m ramp sections of bridge; it is launched by the up-and-over method as used with the No 9 Tank Bridge. The **No 12 Tank Bridge** is 13.5m (44ft 3½in) long, and is also launched by the up-and-over method; the bridge is constructed from two special 13.5m trackways, 0.72m (2ft 4in) deep which are not interchangeable with the other bridge panels. The Chieftain Bridgelayer can carry two of the No 12 Tank Bridges, which can be launched one after the other. (Figure 15.8).

All of the tank bridges can be used for combination bridging, the far end of each bridge being supported on a trestle, a floating pier, or the riverbed. All can be launched in less than three minutes without exposure of the crew, and can be recovered from either end in less than five minutes.

The General Support Bridge System consists of the ABLE vehicle, two crane-mounted flatbed Bridging Vehicles, and a 32m (105ft) Bridge Set. ABLE has been developed on the lines of the original demonstrator model described earlier and has a similar chassis to the TBT and the Bridging Vehicle, with common cab and major automotive assemblies. Haulamatic (subsequently Unipower of Watford, a subsidiary of Alvis) undertook development of the vehicles. The bridge launching mechanisms, which include a 20 tonne-metre hydraulic crane, are hydraulically driven from the ABLE cab, and can accommodate launching gradients of plus or minus 10%. The launching rail is capable of launching bridges up to 44m long.

The 32m bridge set, carried on the two Bridging Vehicles, consists of 4 x 8m

409

ramps, 2 x 8m panels, 3 x 4m panels and 2 x 2m panels; this enables bridges to be constructed in 2m increments from 16m to 32m in length. The DGFVE Specification for a 30 minute construction time for a 32m bridge, employing no more than ten men, has easily been met during trials. Indeed, during a

Figure 15.9. *A timed building trial between a 32m General Support Bridge and a 30m Medium Girder Bridge.* (Vickers Defence Systems).

trial in the summer of 1993, a team of eight men from 7 Field Squadron RE built a 32m bridge in just 18 minutes.

The **Long Span Equipment** makes use of the 4m Reinforced Panel, (which is fitted with a reinforcing system king post) and high-strength launching rail units. This enables bridges with a clear span of up to 42m to be built and at this span the reinforced bridge can carry the 105 tonne loaded tank

Figure 15.10. An MLC 70, 56m long General Support Bridge, trafficked by a Chieftain Main Battle Tank. (Vickers Defence Systems).

transporter. Although the current system is limited by the launcher to the 44m long bridge, mid-life improvements making use of the CFRP launching rail previously mentioned, will enable already designed and fully proven MLC 70 bridges up to 56m in length to be deployed. (Figure 15.10)

The **Two Span Equipment** uses the 2m Articulating Panel and rocking roller assemblies to enable multiple-span bridges to be constructed over fixed or floating piers. This equipment, and the Long Span Equipment, were accepted into service in 1999/2000.

A **Tank Bridge Trestle** was developed at Christchurch during the Interim Phase of BR80, but was not included as part of the initial contract with NEI Thompson. An original design for the trestle intended it to be carried on the Chieftain Bridgelayer and launched with a No 8 Tank Bridge, from which the forward ramp section had been removed to compensate for the increase in launch weight. The shortened No 8 Bridge could then be used as a launch platform from which to launch a further bridge. The trestle was not developed further because of the complexity of its hydraulic system, but a simple steel trestle was designed, to be carried and launched in the same way. Two heights of trestle were investigated, 2.5m (8ft 2½in) and 3.1m (10ft 2in) high, and five of the 2.5m trestles were manufactured for use in BAOR. The concept proved very successful and

412

Figure 15.11. No 8 and 9 Tank Bridges used with a Tank Bridge Trestle by 26 Armoured Engineers Squadron at Sanski Most, Bosnia. (The Sapper - July 1996).

eventually seventeen pairs of the 3.1m trestles were produced for use with the No 8 Tank Bridge. (Figure 15.11).

Further Developments for BR90

In August 1994 a formal Acceptance Meeting for both the Close Support Bridges and the General Support Bridge was held, including the Long Span and the Two Span Equipments. This opened the way for full-scale production to proceed and the equipment started to come into service in 1996. Later that year it was suggested that the bridge should be known as the **Christchurch Bridge**. However, this name was never formally adopted and the equipment became known as the **BR90 Bridge**, Vickers Defence Systems marketing the bridge as the **Vickers Modular Bridge**.

Design and development of a **Close Support Trestle**, capable of use in a gap up to 5m deep, is under way by Vickers Bridging, with the target of fourteen production trestle sets coming into service in 2002. (Figure 15.12). Vickers Bridging has a further contract with the MOD to design and produce a two-span pontoon version BR90 Bridge, with an inservice date of 2004; the design would use three- or four-bay floating piers to support MLC70 and MLC110 bridge loads respectively. Vickers Bridging are also developing an alternative bridge reinforcement system, avoiding the use of 2m deep

413

Figure 15.12. *A Bridge Transporter crossing a three span Close Support Bridge using the new trestle, under trial at Bovington. The 60 m gap was crossed in 20minutes.* (Vickers Defence Systems).

kingposts needed for the longer span bridges. This system employs aramid fibre cables pretensioned as the bridge is launched so that the trackways are hogged prior to load application; subsequent application of live load deflects the bridge through, and a short distance below, the level plane. The family of MLC 70 axially tensioned long span bridges (ATLSBs) will comprise 38m, 44m, 48m and 52m bridge lengths, the two longest bridges requiring continued development of the carbon fibre launch rail previously mentioned.

The Amphibious Bridge M3

Initial replacement of the Amphibious Bridge M2 was planned for 1985 and would of course have been provided by a successful conclusion to the BR80 project. As has been seen, however, delays in that programme meant that, even before the FCT had assembled, UK had decided that a BR80 solution could not provide a replacement for M2 within the required time frame, despite slippage of the re-equipment date to 1986-8. Serious thought was therefore given to UK procurement of the US Ribbon Bridge. However, with a further postponement of the M2 replacement date, resulting from an extensive factory overhaul programme for the existing equipments, considerable interest was shown in the development of a new Amphibious Bridge, M3, being undertaken at Kaiserlautern, Germany, by EWK, the manufacturers of the M2 Amphibious Bridge. GSR 3987 - An Amphibious

414

Deliberate Wet Support Bridge was endorsed in February 1985, calling for 120m (394ft) of Class 70 bridge to be built, desirably, in less than 30 minutes by night and, essentially, in not more than 60 minutes. A requirement for a Class 70 ferry to be built, desirably, in 15 minutes and, essentially, in no more than 30 minutes, again by night, was also included.

The development became a collaborative project between the UK and FRG, with UK fully supporting the EWK programme. A number of prototype rigs were produced for evaluation by the German and British Armies, with a possible total requirement of 130 rigs for the West German Army and 70 rigs for the British Army. However, the end of the Cold War and the subsequent re-examination of commitments under the Army's 'Options for Change' policy drastically reduced this requirement in the 1992 Long Term Costing to thirty-eight rigs. After competitive tender a production contract for these rigs was placed with EWK in mid-1994, thus ensuring an amphibious capability for the Corps beyond 1998, the planned date for the M2 to become obsolete. (Figure 15.13). Technical differences between the M2 rigs and the M3 rigs are set out in Table 8.

Figure 15.13. *An outrigged M3 unit on trial in Germany.* (EWK GMBH).

TABLE 8 – COMPARISON OF TECHNICAL DETAILS FOR THE AMPHIBIOUS EQUIPMENTS

TECHNICAL DETAIL	M2D	M3
Vehicle length (m)	11.31	12.73
Vehicle width (m)	2.99	3.35
Vehicle height (m)	3.69	3.39
Vehicle weight (tonne)	22.0	26.0
Maximum road speed (km/hr)	60.0	75.0
Maximum ferry speed (km/hr)	14.0	14.0
Ramp length (m)	5.88	8.35
Bridge module (m)	8.70	11.50
Roadway width (m)	5.60	4.76
Military Load Class	70	70T/100W

Operationally the M3 equipment is much superior to the M2 and exhaustive trials with the Bundeswehr have proved highly successful. In essence twenty-four men can build a 100m (328ft) amphibious bridge in 20 minutes, using M3 equipment, whereas it would take forty-eight men 45 minutes to build a similar bridge using a greater number of M2 rigs.

Meanwhile, under 'Options for Change', 28 Amphibious Engineer Regiment reorganized as a Field Engineer Regiment on 1 April 1992, now with just one amphibious squadron, that is 23 Amphibious Engineer Squadron. Half of the Regiment's M2 Rigs were brought back to UK and were based at Hawley Lake, near Minley, for use by a newly formed 227 (Hampshire Yeomanry) Amphibious Engineer Squadron (V). This squadron formed part of the new 78 (Fortress) Engineer Regiment (Volunteers), based at Southampton.

The Infantry Bridge

One last bridging equipment completes this story of bridging in the British Army from the thirteenth century to the present time. This is the **Bridge Set, Infantry Assault**, or the **Infantry Bridge** as it is known. The need for such a bridge was highlighted in 1985, during a study of Infantry assault river-crossing capabilities, carried out by 1 (BR) Corps in Germany. As a result of the study, a design and manufacture contract was let, by competitive tender, to the German firm EWK, manufacturers of the Amphibious Bridges M2 and M3. After trials in UK and Germany the bridge was accepted for service in 1992 and first issues to troops were made the following year.

Figure 15.14. *A 44m span Infantry Bridge, using an intermediate float.* (EWK GMBH).

The Infantry Bridge set comprises seven 4.5m (14ft 9in) long aluminium modules, a cigar-shaped 'swimmer' and ancillary gear, which can be assembled and dismantled from either bank to form either a 16m (52½ft) single span bridge, constructed by eight men in less than five minutes across a wet or dry gap, or a 30m (98½ ft) single span bridge launched across a wet gap by using the swimmer and built in less than ten minutes by eight men. A 44m (144ft) double span bridge can be built by using components from two bridge sets, with two swimmers acting as an intermediate pier. (Figure 15.14 and Appendix B).

The bridge is intended for use by Infantry Assault Platoons, with whom it is very popular, but is held by RE Support Squadrons to facilitate storage, inspection and repair, and to concentrate the limited number of bridges for more efficient use. A complete bridge set is carried as a palletised load on either a 4 or 8 tonne vehicle, but once the load is broken down it can conveniently be carried as four loads, each by two men in fighting order, at distances up to 600m or more.

The use of advanced design techniques and material at optimum strength, achieving high performance at low weight, has placed some constraints on the use of the bridge. Thus, regardless of the span of bridge, the maximum

417

load must be restricted to three men, evenly spaced and weighing no more than 135kg, that is a 220 pound soldier in full battle order. The maximum single load permitted is 200kg, but a stretcher adapter kit permits a casualty to be pushed across the bridge by one man, with no other load on the bridge.

To the Future

Future possible developments outlined in earlier chapters include the Trojan and Titon armoured engineer vehicles, the new Air Portable Ferry Bridge, to replace the APB, and the adoption of the Mabey Compact 200 Bridge as the Logistic Support Bridge for the Army. Together with the latest bridging equipments, now in service and described in this last chapter, it is clear that the Sappers of this new millennium will be well served by their bridging equipments for many years to come.

Sadly, however, the establishment at Christchurch closed on 28 February 1994, exactly seventy-five years after the setting up of the Experimental Bridging Company RE, under Martel, in 1919. Dr Bulson had retired in July 1985, to be succeeded by Mr G K Booth, formerly a Sapper major. Unfortunately Mr Booth had to retire early due to ill health and in early 1990 Mr D I Knight, another retired regular Sapper officer, took over as Head of Establishment. In turn he was succeeded later that year by Mr G J Hambly, a Scientific Civil Servant, who then handed over to Mr M T Gillman in 1993. By this time the reorganization by the Ministry of Defence previously mentioned had taken place, resulting in the setting up, in April 1991, of the Defence Research Agency, or DRA.

With the closure of the Christchurch Establishment responsibility for research into engineer equipment for the Corps passed to the new Christchurch Building on the DRA Chertsey site. Only a small five-acre area was retained within the Christchurch Barrack Road site, to include the Bridge Test Rig and the Fatigue Test Rig. The rest of the 30-acre site was cleared for disposal, bringing to an end a seventy-five-year era devoted to the design and development of engineer equipment for the Corps of Royal Engineers.

A Chronological List of British Military Bridging Equipments

The development/in-service dates given below for the 170 or so equipments listed are quoted from a number of sources and are indicative only.

EQUIPMENT	DESIGN/IN SERVICE DATE	COMMENT
Edward I's Floating	1303	Three bridges were built at King's Lynn for the invasion of Scotland.
Tin Pontoons of various types	1692	Used at the Battle of Flanders, but probably in use earlier.
Wellesley's Pontoon	1803-04	A local improvisation used in India.
Congreve's Trough	early 1800s	Forerunner of the Track Bridges.
Colleton's Pontoon	1814	A cylindrical pontoon with conical ends; not introduced into service.
Pasley Pontoon	1817	The first use of a pontoon to form bipartite piers; widely used.
Blanshard Pontoon	1828	A cylindrical pontoon, still in use in the 1870s. A smaller version of the pontoon was known as the Blanshard Infantry Pontoon.
Blaydes' Pontoon	c 1830	A model only, but one of the first inflatables.
Forbes' Pontoon	c 1840	Not introduced into service.
Caffin Pontoon	c 1856	Basically a modified Blanshard Pontoon
Fowke's Pontoon	1858	Not introduced into service.
Berthon's Boat	1860	Various versions, one later adopted as the Light Infantry Bridge Equipment.
Blood Pontoon	1870	Replaced the Paisley and Blanshard Pontoons.

Light Bridging & Rafting Equipment	1885	Based upon Berthon's Boat; one version still in service in 1914.
Birago Trestle	c 1885	Developed from an Austrian design.
Clauson or Mark II Pontoon	1889	A bipartite pontoon with bow and stern sections; remained in service during the First World War.
Weldon Trestle	late 1890s	Later known as the Mark IV Trestle.
Air Raft Equipment	c 1900	An inflatable raft, in service in 1914.
Inglis Portable Military Bridge (Light Type)	1913	The first British equipment dry bridge; known also as the Pyramid Bridge.
Sankey Bridge	1913	Various types, based upon the Mark II Pontoon with a steel joist superstructure.
3ft Steel Cubes	c 1914	Used to form bridge piers and the forerunner of the Christchurch Crib.
Heavy Steel Pontoon	1914	Designed for a First World War Rhine crossing but not developed further.
Stock Spans, A Type and B Type	1914-15	A Type Bridges could carry a 17 ton and B Type Bridges a 13 ton axle load.
Canal Bridges	1915	Types used included the Davit Bridge, the Portal Bridge and the Pont Levis.
Barge Bridge	1915	A 60ft B Type Bridge mounted on a barge.
Inglis Heavy Type Bridge	1915	A heavy version of the Pyramid Bridge; designed to take lorries.
Inglis Bridge Mark I	1916	A more conventional rectangular cross section bridge with 12ft bays.
Pontoon Mark III	c 1916	Identical to the Mark II Pontoon except for the cladding (see Appendix B for details).
Bridging Fascine	1917	First used by British tanks at Cambrai to cross German trenches.
Stock Span, AA Type	1917	Redesigned A Type Bridge to carry tanks.
Hopkins Bridge	1917	Initially produced in a 120ft span version.
Lock Bridge	1917	A simple bridge carried at the front of a tank to cross canal locks.

Hopkins 75ft Span Bridge	1918	A lighter version of the 120ft span Hopkins Bridge, but only a few were manufactured.
Inglis Bridge Mark II	1918	A heavier version of the Mark I Bridge, with 15ft bays and designed to carry tanks.
Heavy Pontoon	1918	Manufactured for use with the Inglis Mark II Bridge for crossing major rivers.
Hopkins Lorry Bridge	1918	Experimental only.
Inglis Assault Bridge	1918	An Inglis Bridge mounted on twin idle tracks, tested at the end of the First World War.
Large Box Girder Bridge (LBG)	1920-21	Martel's bridge, adopted by the Army in 1925.
Infantry Assault Bridge	1920-23	The final version was the Kapok Assault Bridge.
Inglis Heavy Floating Bridge	c 1921	Prototype only built at Christchurch.
Mark IV Pontoon Equipment	1921-24	Came into service in 1927, replacing the Mark II/III Pontoons.
Trestle Mark V	1921-24	Developed as part of the Mark IV Pontoon Equipment.
Folding Boat Equipment (FBE)	mid 1920s	Adopted by the Army in 1928.
Bateman's Assault Bridge	1924-25	Prototype only tested.
Martel's Stepping Stones	1925-26	An improvised experimental river crossing device.
Mat Bridge	1926	The first of a number of similar types of experimental bridge.
Small Box Girder Bridge (SBG)	1926-30	Finally adopted by the Army in 1933.
Trestle Mark VI	1928	An improved trestle for use with the Mark IV Pontoon Equipment to carry heavier loads.
NW Railway Steel Road Bridge	1929	A design by W T Everall for use in India.
Roorkee Steel Crib	c 1930	Martel's version of the First World War bridging cube.

LBG Mark II	1931 et seq	Not finally adopted until 1938, because of the slow pace of rearmament.
Callender-Hamilton Bridge	1933-34	Adopted by the Army as the Unit Construction Bridge in the late 1930s.
Christchurch Crib	mid 1930s	A development of the First World War 3ft Bridging Cube.
FBE Mark II	mid 1930s	Minor redesign only.
SBG Mark II	1936	Slight modification only from the Mark I.
Dragon Assault Bridge	1936-38	Prototype only.
Mark V Pontoon Equipment	1936-38	Adopted and available for the Field Force in 1939.
Trestle Mark VII	1936-38	Developed with the new Mark V Pontoon and differing only slightly from the Mark VI Trestle.
SBG Mark III	1936-38	Replaced the Mark II version in 1939.
FBE Mark III	1938	Complete redesign of the Mark II superstructure for Class 9 loading; adopted in 1939.
Wild Assault Bridge	1938	Prototype only; developed by Messrs M B Wild & Co Ltd of Birmingham.
Scissor Assault Bridge	1938-40	Prototype only.
Callender-Hamilton Railway Bridge	1938-42	Hamilton's work progressed in India, where the bridge was manufactured.
Trackway Bridges	late 1930s	Various models were produced, details of which are given in Chapter 6.
Heavy Pontoon Bridge	1939-40	Prototype only with advent of Bailey Bridging.
Rolled Steel Joist Span Railway Bridge	1939-40	Span range rationalized in 1940 to give five spans up to 35ft.
Standard Unit Trestle	1939-40	Developed for rail use just before the war.
Inglis Bridge Mark III	1939-40	This design reverted to the 12ft bays used with the Mark I bridge.
Indian Mat Bridge	1939-44	An experimental development, initially in India, following earlier Mat Bridge trials.

Bailey Bridge (BB)	1940-41	The first Bailey design led to its adoption for a wide range of uses.
Scissors Bridge, 30ft, No 1 Tank Bridge	1940-41	Eventually mounted on the Valentine Tank chassis and widely used.
Sectional Welded Plate Girder Bridge	early 1940s	A railway bridge in the 34-40ft span range.
Standard Through Truss Railway Bridge	early 1940s	A substantial bridge used at spans up to 150ft.
Unit Construction Railway Bridge	early 1940s	The most widely used and adaptable of the railway bridges.
Bailey Pontoon Bridge (BPB)	1941	Used existing Mark V Pontoons with a new Bailey Centre Pontoon, and subsequently a new Mark VI Pontoon.
Track Bridge 12ft No 3	1941-42	A Class 9 version, replacing earlier models of Trackway Bridges.
Track Bridge 20ft	1941-42	Proved excessively heavy and soon obsolete.
Briggs Bridge	1941-42	One prototype produced in India but overtaken by the introduction of BB.
PN Boat	1942	Designed and produced in the Far East, and used to form bipartite piers.
Bailey Suspension Bridge (BSB)	1942-43	A 400ft span Class 9 bridge.
Tank Bridge No 2	1942-43	Mounted on the Churchill Tank chassis.
Inglis Mobile Bridge	1942-43	An update of the 1918 Inglis Assault Bridge using the Inglis Bridge Mark III.
ARK Mark I	1943	Developed by 79 Armoured Division.
Butterley Standard Unit Bridge	1943	Developed by Butterley Engineering Ltd but not adopted by the Army.
Elephant Bridges	1943	Timber improvised bridges constructed in Burma using elephants to lift and place heavy timbers.
Churchill Mk III and IV AVRE	1943-44	Used with fascines and SBG ramps in bridging role.
Bailey Retractable Bridge	1943-44	A design enabling the bridge to be rapidly withdrawn to allow passage of river traffic.

Canal Lock Bailey	1943-44	A short span lift bridge.
Bailey Railway Bridging	1943-44	For use when standard railway bridging was not available.
Bailey Mobile Bridge (BMB)	1943-44	Superseded the Inglis Mobile Bridge.
Class 50/60 Raft	1943-44	Developed for assault crossing of wide rivers.
Close Support Raft, Mark I (CSR)	1943-44	Class 9 and Class 12 version were used.
Tank Bridge, Small Box Girder, Mark 1	1944	SBG ramp sections, mounted on the Churchill AVRE.
AVRE Fascine	1944	Made from chespalings, 6-8ft in diameter and 12-16ft long.
Tank Bridge SBG Mark II	1944	As the Mark I but with improved launching mechanism.
Everall Sectional Truss Railway Bridge	1944	Designed for major bridges at spans up to 400ft.
Flambo Bridge	1944	A mild steel version of BB produced by Royal Engineers in Italy.
ARK Mark II	1944	Converted ARKs Mark I with longer front ramps.
Italian ARK	1944	An improvised version of the ARK used during the Italian Campaign.
Great Eastern Tank Ramp	1944	Only twelve were produced, too late for the Normandy invasion.
Plymouth Bridge	1944	A variation of the BMB, used in Italy.
Brown Bridge	1944	A development of the Plymouth Bridge.
Dalton Bridge	1944	An improved version of the Brown Bridge.
Skid Bailey	1944	Another variation of the BMB, developed by 79 Armoured Division.
CSR Mark II	late 1944	Deck panels and joists were of aluminium alloy, the first such use for a bridging equipment.
BURMARK	1944-45	A light ARK based upon a Valentine

		chassis for use in the Far East; not used in action or developed further.
Eastern Army Boat	1944-45	Timber pontoons developed in the Far East.
No 3 Tank Bridge	1945	Designed for tanks with wider tracks and launched from the Churchill AVRE or Bridgelayer.
No 4 Tank Bridge	1945	A light alloy replacement for the No 1 Tank Bridge; only one prototype was built.
Standard Widened Bailey Bridge (SWBB)	1945	Introduced to cope with the increased width of the new tanks.
Light Alloy Pontoon	1945	An experimental nesting and collapsible alloy pontoon, intended for use in the Far East; limited production only.
ARK Mark III	1945	Increased width and length of the trackways compared with the Mark II; pilot model only.
Class 18 Raft	late 1945	Prototype only; the first use of aluminium alloy bridge girders.
FV 203 ARK	1946-47	Progressed to full scale mock-up stage before cancellation of the FV 200 project.
No 5 Tank Bridge	1946-47	To be mounted on the FV 208 Bridgelayer, but did not get beyond mock-up trials.
Light Assault Floating Bridge (LAFB)	1947-54	Initially Class 24 and later Class 30; came into service in 1958. Later renamed Light Floating Bridge (LFB).
Heavy Ferry (HyF)	1947-55	Class 80 equipment to replace the 50/60 Raft; first off production not until 1957.
Heavy Girder Bridge (HGB)	1948-55	A Class 100 bridge similar to BB; in full production by 1955; an overbridge, a pier set and floating HGB evolved.
Extra Widened Bailey Bridge (EWBB)	1949	Widened roadway for the new range of tanks.

Churchill Mark VII AVRE	1950-54	Stop gap equipment pending introduction of the Centurion AVRE
No 6 Tank Bridge	1950-60	Carried on a Mark V Centurion chassis; did not finally come into service until 1963.
Heavy Assault Floating Bridge (HAFB)	early 1950s	Scaled up Class 80 version of LAFB; in service in 1962 and later renamed Heavy Floating Bridge (HFB).
Storey Bailey Bridge	1950s	A commercial development of BB involving a number of modifications and improvements.
Sectional Plate Girder Railway Bridge	1950s	Did not progress beyond accurate models and prototype component stage.
No 3 Tank Bridge Mark II	1953	An upgrade of the Mark I version to Class 80 to carry the Conqueror Tank.
Churchill Linked ARK	1954	Two Churchill chassis with wide trackways used side by side; acceptance in 1955.
Improvised Heavy Girder Railway Bridge	1955-57	Experimental construction at Longmoor; not proceeded with.
Storey Uniflote (subsequently the Mabey Uniflote)	1956	A unit construction flotation system, similar in many respects to the later Mexeflote.
Centurion Mark V AVRE	1957-63	Long needed replacement for the old Churchill AVREs.
Centurion ARK	1958-65	Double hinged ramps at each end produced an 80ft long bridge.
50 ton Bridging Crib	late 1950s	A development of the 1930s Christchurch Crib.
Infantry Assault Boat Raft	late 1950s	Various proposals using the Mark IV Infantry Assault Boat were tested, but the requirement was dropped in the early 1960s.
Far East Assault Boat Raft	early 1960s	A local expedient produced in Singapore during the Borneo emergency.

No 7 Tank Bridge	early 1960s	A 20ft span bridge to be carried on a new AEV; prototype tested in 1965 but project eventually abandoned in favour of the CET.
No 8 Tank Bridge	1961-69	80ft long bridge launched from a Chieftain Bridgelayer; into service in 1974.
EWK-Gillois	1961	A French amphibious bridge, tested and accepted for British service in 1961.
Airportable Bridge (APB)	1961-67	First production sets of the Class 16 equipment available in 1970.
Amphibious Bridging and Ferrying Equipment - M2	1962	A German equipment, tested in UK in 1962 and accepted, as the M2B, in preference to the Gillois.
Medium Girder Bridge (MGB)	1962-67	An excellent light alloy bridge, sold throughout the World. Troop trials in 1967 with a 1971 in-service date.
20ft Inflated Bridge	1964-65	Experimental only, not proceeded with.
Inflatable Fascine	mid 1960s	Two prototypes produced but not proceeded with.
Centurion ARK Mobile Pier (CAMP)	mid 1960s	A normal ARK with ramps removed so that it could form a pier for Tank Bridges.
Mexeflote	mid 1960s	A harbour pontoon equipment for use by the Royal Corps of Transport.
Mabey Super Bailey	1967	A commercial development and improvement of the BB.
Acrow Heavy Bridge	1968	A long span, wide roadway bridge, but not of military significance.
No 9 Tank Bridge	1968-73	A shorter span bridge forming part of the Chieftain Bridge Layer family; into service in 1978.
Bridging for the 1980s (BR80)	1969-81	A US-UK-FRG project for a family of bridges to be jointly developed.
Callender-Hamilton Bridging	post war	Continued development of the C-H wartime range of bridges.

Chieftain AVRE	1970-72	Two equipments made for full scale trials but project was cancelled in favour of the CET.
Acrow Panel Bridge	1971	A further commercial development of BB, with improved materials and details.
Floating MGB	1974	Trials with various pier systems led to the development of the MGB Pontoon.
Pipe Fascine	mid 1970s	Formed from high density polythene pipes and carried by the AVRE or CET.
Mabey Universal Bridge	1976	A scaled up version of BB, with panels larger even than HGB; intended for long spans and wide roadways.
Bridge Articulated Vehicle Equipment (BRAVE)	1978	A British proposal within the BR80 development programme.
Automotive Bridge Launching Equipment (ABLE)	1979-83	A logical development of BRAVE; a full scale demonstrator model was made using a Foden chassis.
Mabey Compact Bailey	1983	A greatly improved version of the Mabey Super Bailey.
Mabey Compact Pontoons	1980s	A 'flat pack' pontoon intended for rapid transport and assembly world wide.
Vickers Armoured Bridgelayer	1980s	A commercial development by Vickers using their Mark 3 Tank chassis as a bridgelayer.
Bridging for the 1990s (BR90)	1984 et seq	The British programme for a family of bridging equipments; contract for development by NEI Thompson let in 1987; acceptance meeting Aug 1994, in service from 1996 on.
Tank Bridge Trestle	mid 1980s	A simple steel trestle developed as part of the BR80/90 programme and manufactured for use with the AVLBs in BAOR.
Amphibious Bridge M2D	mid 1980s	A version of the M2B to carry Class 70 loads, upgraded by the use of buoyancy bags.

Amphibious Bridge M3	mid 1980s et seq	A new German bridge, intended as a replacement for the M2; contract for UK procurement let in mid 1994.
Willich Chieftain AVRE	1987	17 MBTs converted to AVREs at Willich at a great saving in cost.
Mabey Compact 200 Bridge	1987	An improved version of the earlier Compact Bridge System.
Acrow Panel Bridge, 500 and 700 Series.	1987-8	Developments of the Acrow Panel Bridge.
No 10, No 11 and No 12 Tank Bridges	1987 et seq	Three new tank bridges developed as part of the BR90 programme.
Axial Folding Bridge	late 1980s	Produced by Williams Fairey Engineering for the US Navy.
K1 AVLB	late 1980s	A Vickers designed and developed tank bridge and launch mechanism for the Korean K1 Tank.
Chieftain AVRE	early 1990s	48 Chieftain MBTs converted to AVREs to replace the Willich AVREs which had used older and less reliable chassis.
Infantry Bridge	early 1990s	A light weight foot bridge for use by InfantryAssault Platoons. German design and manufacture.
BR90 Bridges	mid 1990s	New bridges coming into service, with the No 10 and No 12 Tank Bridges in limited service in Bosnia.
BR90 developments	1999/2000	Two span and long span versions of the GSB accepted for service, with the Close Support Trestle under development (ISD 2002).
Titan Bridgelayer and Trojan AVRE	2000	Under development by Vickers (ISD 2006).
Air Portable Ferry Bridge	2000	Under development by Williams Fairey Engineering to replace the APB (ISD 2003).
Mabey Compact 200	2000	The bridge adopted as the Army's Logistic Support Bridge.

APPENDIX B

Brief Technical Notes on Equipments and Materials

These brief notes give some technical details not included in the main text and also indicate the predominant materials used for major components of some of the equipments. The equipments have been arranged in alphabetical order.

Since the majority of the equipments listed were designed before the metrication of the British Imperial system of weights and measures, the Imperial system had been used throughout. To convert inches to millimetres multiply by 25.4, feet to metres by 0.305, and tons per square inch to Newtons per square millimetre by 15.44.

Acrow Heavy Bridge. The bridge was manufactured from BS 4360 weldable structural steel, predominantly Grade 43A and 50B. Mechanical properties given below are for steels listed in the 1986 version of the Standard, rolled as plate, strip or wide flats; there are slight variations in the case of rolled sections. The ranges given arise from variations with thickness of metal and from sub-grouping within the basic groups, the sub-groupings being denoted by use of the grade suffixes A to E. Strengths are given in tons/in².

TABLE B1 – PROPERTIES OF BS4360 STEEL

GRADE OF STEEL	MINIMUM YIELD STRENGTH	TENSILE STRENGTH	ELONGATION
40	12 – 17	22 – 32	22 – 25%
43	16 – 18	30 – 38	20 – 23%
50	21 – 25	32 – 41	18 – 20%
55	26 - 29	36 - 45	17 – 19%

Acrow Panel Bridge. Main components are manufactured from Grade 55C BS 4360 steel (see Acrow Heavy Bridge above).

Air Portable Bridge. The APB made extensive use of the medium strength weldable aluminium alloy to DGFVE Specification 232A, a slightly modified version of DGFVE Specification 232. The alloy contained 4% zinc, 2% magnesium and 0.35% manganese and was used in the TF condition, that is solution treated and artificially aged. This modified version was originally used for manufacture of the MGB, but subsequently production is in the latest version of the alloy, that is DGFVE Specification 232B, containing 0.15% copper to enhance resistance to corrosion without detriment to welding properties; within 30 days of welding the heat affected zone recovers to

430

approximately 80% of the parent metal strength. For extrusions, bar sheet and forgings the alloy has a 0.2% proof stress of 21.5 tons/in^2 and a tensile strength of 25 tons/in^2, with an elongation of about 10%.

Bailey Bridge. A high strength structural steel developed from BS 968 weldable quality steel was used for the chord and web members of the panels and the transoms. The BS 968 specification was modified to improve weldability by adjusting the carbon content, and this had the effect of raising the yield point from 21 to 23 tons/in^2; the carbon content was specified as being between 0.20 and 0.26% and the manganese content was limited to 1.7%. A manganese - molybdenum alloy steel was used for the panel pins, with a yield of about 65 tons/in^2, whilst all other components such as the stringers and sway-brace, gussets, jaw blocks and small components were made from normal BS 15 mild steel.

Bailey Suspension Bridge. Six cables were used at each side of the bridge. Each cable was of 7/7 construction and manufactured from 2⅝ in circumference wires of 100-110ton/in^2 tensile strength. The 750ft long cables each weighed 1000lb and were supported by 50ft high portal towers, of double/single construction; twenty suspenders supported each of the single/single stiffening girders.

Birago Trestle. The trestle consisted of an 18ft long transom, fabricated from deal planks and hardwood blocks, and provided with cleats, as on the pontoon saddle, to receive the end of the baulks supporting the bridge superstructure. Two pairs of legs were provided with each trestle, respectively 8ft and 15ft long, legs of the selected length being splayed at 75° before being clamped to the transom by 1⅞ in screws. The ends of the transom were additionally supported by iron chains, shackled to the tops of the legs, and a hardwood shoe was secured to the bottom of each leg by an iron pin.

Blanshard Pontoon. The 24ft 6in long pontoon weighed about 560lb, and was formed upon a hollow tin cylinder, 1¾ in in diameter and running the whole length of the pontoon; this acted as an axis for a number of light weight wheels upon which sheet tin cladding, of the grade known as XXX, was fixed. Each pontoon was divide internally into nine water tight compartments; the four rows of sunken handles placed at intervals around the circumference were used not only to carry the pontoon but also to lash down saddles used to support the bridge superstructure.

Blood Pontoon. See Pontoon Mark I below.

Bridging Cribs. A number of metal bridging cribs have been developed over the years:

The 3ft Bridging Cube. The cube, developed in WWI, was made from mild steel flats and sections riveted together, and could carry a load of 40 tons.

The Roorkee Pattern Steel Crib. The crib, measuring 18in x 18in and either 3ft or 6ft long, was made from 2in x 2in x ³⁄₁₆ in mild steel angles, with 1¼in x ³⁄₁₆ in flats for diagonal bracing. The crib could support a load of 12 tons when loaded vertically or on its side.

The 20 ton Crib (or Christchurch Crib). The 2ft x 2ft x 6ft welded crib was manufactured from 2in x 2in x ¼in mild steel angles, and was internally braced with 1½in x ¼in mild steel flats. The crib could support a load of 20 tons when loaded vertically on end and 40 tons when loaded on its side.

The 50 ton Crib. The 4ft x 2ft x 2ft crib was manufactured from 2½in x 2½ in x ¼in high tensile steel angles, braced with 1in x ½in mild steel flats, and was hot dipped galvanized. When used with a special load spreader the crib could carry a load of 50 tons when loaded vertically or 100 tons when loaded on its side.

Bridging for the 80s. During the Interim Phase of the BR 80 programme the prototype bridge girders developed by the three participating nations (ie UK, US and FRG) were, in the main, manufactured using one of the medium strength weldable aluminium alloys, similar to that used for the Air Portable Bridge (see above).

Bridging for the 90s. The panels of the BR90 bridges were manufactured in DGFVE 232B alloy, slightly enhanced to further improve its strength, fracture toughness, and stress corrosion resistance. Panel jaws were manufactured in high strength steel to Defence Standard 95-14/1, but the DGFVE alloy was used to manufacture the jaws of the launching rail.

Bridging Trestles

TABLE B2 – DETAILS OF BAILEY BRIDGE AND RAILWAY BRIDGE TRESTLES

EQUIPMENT	INTENDED USAGE	HEIGHT RANGE	CONSTRUCTION	TOP HAMPER	BASE DETAIL	REMARKS
Tubular Trestle	Bailey bridging to Class 70 and also for landing bays & shore spans of BPB	20ft to 35ft in 5ft lifts	5ft long legs of 4½in D tubes; horizontal struts 3in D tubes; steel rod bracing	Steel joists and fittings to suit construction of pier	3ft 8in square base plate for each tubular leg	Complete pier could have 6, 8 or 12 legs spaced at 7½ft centres
Heavy Trestle	As for the Tubular Trestle	11ft 2in to 35ft in 4in lifts	Two 7in x 3½in channels with welded batten plates forming 6ft long legs	1 normal and 2 special half Bailey panels to form a 20ft cross girder to carry BB bearings. RSJs added for 4 legged trestle	3ft square steel baseplates for each leg on standard BB grillage units	Two or four leg trestle bents used, with bents at 11½ft centres for the latter
Light Standard Unit Trestle	UCRB spans and 20 BS unit rail loading	15ft to 85ft	Two 10in x 3in channels with welded batten plates forming 3, 4, 8, & 12ft leg units; 2½ in D tube horizontal struts and angle bracing	A grillage of joists	A grillage of joists with 3ft D camel's foot bases used on unprepared ground	Columns spaced at 5ft centres in both directions; 4in D raking struts used as CSA of pier reduced with height
Standard Unit Trestle	ESTB spans and 20 BS unit rail loading	20ft to 200ft	Two 12in x 3½ in channels forming four leg lengths from 2ft 8in to 14ft 8in long; 4in D horizontal struts	Similar to the LSUT	No camel foot available as substantial foundation usually required	A heavier version of the LSUT, with columns spaced at 6ft centres

Briggs Bridge. The 16ft sections were joined together using long pins which passed through the complete width of the section. The bottom chords and bracing were formed from angles but the 2ft 6in wide top chord was formed from thin plate with upstanding flanges at either edge and transverse stiffeners on the underside. Spacing of the two girders provided twin tracks for vehicles to cross, without the need for additional transoms or decking; bankseats were provided to support the bridge and maintain correct spacing of the girders. Apart from a launching nose and rollers, the components needed for a 64ft span bridge were eight girder sections, twelve connecting pins, and two end bankseats. For longer span bridges, 6ft x 6ft flat braced panels could be assembled to form a bridge pier, 12ft x 6ft in plan.

Butterley Bridge. The chords and diagonal members of this bridge were connected at their ends using 2in diameter pins and a circular connector or bobbin, enabling a two storey bridge to be built if required. For the road bridge 20ft steel joists were fixed at 10ft centres to support the decking panels, giving a clear roadway width of 10ft 6in. In appearance it looked very like an Inglis Bridge, but with a smaller module length.

Callender-Hamilton Bridges. The range of C-H bridges are currently manufactured in weldable structural steel to BS EN 10025, and all components are galvanized.

Clauson Pontoon. See Pontoon Mark II below.

Class 50/60 Raft. The pontoons were each 35ft long and 3ft 6in high, with a beam of 8ft; they were constructed with a steel and timber framework and ⅜ in plywood cladding; each carried its own superstructure of two hinged panels, folded down on to the deck and raised into position after the pontoon had been launched. The pontoons were coupled into raft by connecting together the top and bottom chords of adjacent panels with panel pins, using mild steel connecting links at top chord level to give necessary articulation to the raft. The 15½ ft long ramps were then constructed at either end of the raft deck, using hornbeam ramp girders, transoms and decking. The ramps were connected directly to the pontoon panels at bottom chord level and via an adjustable link at top chord level, to enable the ramps to be raised and lowered as required, using deck mounted winches, and then locked into position.

Carbon Fibre Reinforcement. During the BR80 programme all three nations experimented with Fibre Reinforced Plastics (FRP), essentially an assembly of fibres held together by a plastic media, which is present merely to hold the fibres in place and transfer the load between them; for structural purposes continuous fibres are used to give greater stiffness and strength than is obtainable with chopped fibres. In their experimental work the UK and FRG used carbon fibres (CF), which have better structural properties than some other fibres in use; the US also used carbon fibres but prefer to call the carbon 'graphite', which is in fact a soft form of carbon. The US also made use of Kevlar cables, Kevlar being an aromatic polyamide polymer fibre which can be used as an alternative to CF.

The BR80 studies demonstrated the potential of CFR in bridge design, and its possible use for the BR90 bridges have been mentioned in Chapter Fifteen, although extensive use would need to be accompanied by a reduction in cost. Further research is also necessary into such aspects as fatigue and environmental behaviour. Typical properties show, approximately, a 10% increase in proof stress, a 50% increase in Young's Modulus, and a 45% reduction in unit weight, when compared with aluminium alloy to DGFVE Specification 232B.

Close Support Raft, Mark II. The Mark II version of the raft used welded aluminium alloy road bearers and cast alloy deck panels. This was the first time that an aluminium alloy was used for a bridging equipment; that for the bearers cannot now be identified but that for the deck panels was almost certainly STA7/AC10, an aircraft alloy. The STA were a series of wartime standards drawn up by the MOS to rationalize production, AC standing for Aluminium Cast and AW for Aluminium Wrought; the subsequent alloy numbers were the same as those adopted after the war in *The British Standard for the Structural Use of Aluminium*. Typical strengths are given below, in tons/in², the two values given for AC10 being for sand casting & chill casting respectively.

TABLE B3 - PROPERTIES OF WARTIME ALUMINIUM ALLOYS

ALLOY	0.1% PROOF STRESS	ULTIMATE STRENGTH	ELONGATION	CONDITION
AC10	10 – 11	16 – 18	7 – 12%	Solution treated
AW10	15	18	10%	Fully heat treated
AW15	26	30	8%	Fully heat treated

Christchurch Crib. See Bridging Cribs above.

Everall Sectional Truss Railway Bridge. The Type 15 bridge had main girders 15ft deep, with a span range up to 180ft in 5ft increments; this type could be built either as a deck bridge or through bridge, and used fabricated plate girders as cross girders. The Type 30 bridge, with its 30ft deep main girders, was a through bridge and could span up to 330ft, whilst the Type 45 bridge could span up to 400ft. Flame cutting of end chords enabled span variations of 6in to be achieved, so that spans could be tailored to fit exactly the spacing of existing piers. Fairly short spans, that is up to 200ft for the ESTRB, were built by the conventional roller and launching nose method. Longer spans were built by cantilevering out across the gap, and made use of a counter-weight span, built either on the bridge approaches or as the first span of the bridge, to provide the necessary stability; two types of crane were used for this cantilever construction and obviously construction times were not inconsiderable.

Folding Boat Equipment - Mark I. The flat bottomed boat, with pointed bow and stern, was about 21½ ft long, with a beam of 6ft 7in and a depth of 2ft 9in. When raised, the sides of the boat were held in position by two pairs of hinged tubular struts, attached to the gunwales and sliding on a plate fixed to the bottom panel of the boat. The boat was a twelve man load weighing about 870lb and, since it was fitted with rowlocks and had a payload of about 3½ tons at 9in freeboard, was a very useful boat in its own right.

Gillois Amphibious Bridge. Each unit was 39ft long overall, 12ft 10in high, and 10ft wide, weighing some 26 tons. Units were capable of a road speed of about 37mph with the 225HP Kaelble M130 water-cooled engine (later versions had the 290HP Deutz F 12L 714 air-cooled engine). The welded steel hull was divided into a crew compartment, an engine/air compressor compartment, two wheel wells, and a bow compartment (the rear of the vehicle when road travelling). Buoyancy and stability in the water were enhanced by the fitting of pneumatic floats, 36ft long and 4ft 6in in diameter, to each side of the vehicle, the floats being strapped to saddles which first had to be attached to the ten mounting brackets on each side of the hull; the floats were then inflated using the vehicle air compressor.

Heavy Assault Floating Bridge. The light alloy centre pontoon was 23ft long, 7ft 9in wide and 3ft deep, with square ends; the two scow ended bow pontoons were of steel construction and 18ft 6in long, and thus each bridge pier had an overall length of 61ft.

The prototype design for the bridge panels used forgings for top and bottom chords. Each chord was forged in two halves, complete with jaw blocks, from high strength DTD 683 alloy. The two halves of each chord were then bolted together, side by side, and the web members were riveted to the gusset plates forming part of the forgings. However it was realized that the half chord forgings were at the limit of industrial forging capacity, and the final design for the panel used back-to-back channels for the chords in the alloy HE-15WP. (See Table B4). The chords were separated by spacer blocks and the jaw blocks, which were machined from large extrusions and riveted in place.

The landing bay cross girders and the deck units were made from H30-WP. The frames and runners of the centre pontoon also used H30-WP, but were clad with N6 ¼H plate. Mild steel to BS 15 was used for the bow pontoons. Strengths of the various aluminium alloys, in tons/in², are given below, and details of composition are given in the relevant British Standards.

TABLE B4 – PROPERTIES OF ALUMINIUM ALLOYS QUOTED IN BS CODE OF PRACTICE 118:1969

ALLOY	0.2% PROOF STRESS	TENSILE STRENGTH	ELONGATION	SOURCE
NS6-¼H	14.5	19	8%	BS 1470
HP15-WP	22	27	8%	BS 1477
HE15-WP	25 - 28	28 – 31	8%	BS 1476
HP30-WP	15.5	19	8%	BS 1477
HE30-WP	16.5 – 17.5	18 - 20	7 – 10%	BS 1476

Note: Details in the table relate to the British Standards in use at the time of manufacture. The first prefixes, N and H, indicate either non-heat treatable or heat treatable alloys and the prefixes S, P and E, before the alloy number, refer to sheet, plate and extrusions respectively. The suffix ¼H indicates the degree of cold working after annealing and WP indicates that the alloy has been solution and precipitation treated. A 1973 amendment to CP 118 replaced the alloy N6 with H17, indicated a degree of hardness from H2 to H8 instead of from ¼H to ¾H, and introduced new symbols for heat treatment.

Heavy Ferry. The equipment was of riveted construction, with no welding. Extensive use was made of aluminium alloys, and the pontoons and the ramps were all clad in H15-WP plate (see Heavy Assault Floating Bridge above). Extrusions were generally of H10, H15 or H30 alloy, all in the WP condition.

The Main Pontoon was 32ft long, 4ft in depth and 7ft 6in wide, with a 20ft long ramp hydraulically operated and folded over onto the pontoon deck for transport; the Buoyancy Pontoon was 16ft long and 6ft 9in wide; it was merely needed to provide additional buoyancy for the ferry, and its flush deck could only carry light stores; the Propulsion Pontoon was 18ft long and was also 6ft 9in wide. Three different methods of propulsion were considered, namely the Hotchkiss Cone system, a Multiple Jet Centrifugal Pump system and the Gill system. All were water jet propulsion systems and after comprehensive trials the Gill unit was finally adopted; this used an axial flow pump, which drew water through an inlet grating in the bottom of the pontoon into a U-tube, and then forced it out again through guide vanes as a composite jet, 15° to the horizontal. The axial flow pump was driven by a standard Rolls-Royce B80 Mark 5L engine, through a retractable shaft, a dog clutch, and reduction gear; the power unit was mounted on the pontoon deck and had a power take-off to operate the hydraulic gear of the ferry ramps.

Heavy Girder Bridge. The bridge panels and transoms were manufactured from a weldable high strength steel, either Colville's Ducol W27 or United Steel's Fortiweld, with tensile strengths in the 35-40 ton/in² range; heat treatment after rolling was necessary to improve the limit of proportionality. The 6ft x 3ft 10in deck panels and ramp panels were fabricated from H30-WP aluminium alloy extrusions, welded together, and the launching nose cross girders were also manufactured from H30-WP alloy (see Heavy Assault Floating Bridge above).

The standard trussed and welded transom was 26ft 3½ in long, with a hornbeam section at either end where it fitted into the main girders; the transoms were located at the bottom of the panel diamonds, unlike those in Bailey, which were located adjacent to the panel vertical members. The standard transom gave a road width of 18ft 10in, suitable for normal two way road traffic. Shorter 22ft 11½ in transoms were originally provided for narrower, single way construction, with a roadway width of 15ft 6in, but these were largely discarded at a later date, and retained only in a Narrow Bridge Conversion Set.

Heavy Pontoon. The Heavy Pontoon was 40ft long, 9ft wide and 3ft 7½ in deep; it weighed 4 tons and with a displacement of 30 tons, it had a nett buoyancy of about 26 tons. It was constructed of timber and canvas; completely decked, it was divided into six watertight compartments, so that it would remain afloat even when awash. Rollers were provided on the pontoon centre line, on which the transoms of the Inglis Bridge could rest. Long floating bridges could thus be formed, with landing bays up to 105ft on length, but in very long bridges the floating section of the bridge had to be hinged by introducing articulated joints to avoid undue stresses in the girders.

Infantry Assault Raft. This equipment did not proceed beyond the prototype stage and was fabricated using an experimental version of the then recently introduced weldable aluminium alloy. (see Air Portable Bridge above).

Infantry Bridge. The 4.5m (14.75ft) long bridge module consists of two lightweight girders spaced 660mm (26in) apart and connected by cross members which support a footwalk 350mm (13¾ in) wide; the top members of the girders are supported by internal rakers connected to the footwalk. Modules thus have a U shaped cross-section, and are transported as part of a palletized load in pairs, one inverted within another. The swimmers, which are reminiscent of the Nineteenth Century Blanshard Pontoon, are 3.5m (11ft 6in) long, with a maximum diameter of 450mm (17¾ in).

Large Box Girder Bridge. The basic unit of the bridge was a steel skeleton box, 2ft 6in wide, 4ft high and 8ft long. It was made from standard steel sections, riveted together, and in its final form weighed about 1,400lb, deemed to be a 16 man load. The boxes were joined together to form a girder of the required length, using special steel pins which passed through male and female lugs riveted to the box corners; the lugs were very prone to damage and had to be protected during transport of the bridge by steel distance pieces. Hornbeam or tapered sections, also 8ft long, were used at each end of the girders and when positioned on bank seats eliminated the need for ramps. The bridge was a deck bridge, the decking being formed by 11ft long 9in x 4in timber planks known as chesses laid on top of the girders. An important feature of the bridge was that two, three or four girders could be used alongside each other, depending on the span and load capacity required. Thus whereas four girders were required to carry a heavy tank over an 80ft gap, only three girders were needed for spans up to 48ft.

The riveted steel girder construction used for the Mark I version of the bridge was superseded by welded construction using high tensile steel in the Mark II version. The steel had a maximum working stress of 11.25 tons/in² and the dogs used a special chrome molybdenum steel with a working stress of 42 tons/in².

Light Alloy Pontoon. The framework of this experimental pontoon was made from extruded and rolled sections, with light alloy castings as required; the pontoon was clad in 16 gauge aluminium alloy sheet.

Light Assault Floating Bridge. The all welded bridge panels used high tensile steel for the chords and diagonals and mild steel for the vertical members. The riveted pontoons, each 17ft 6in long and 5ft 9½in wide, were constructed from H30-WP aluminium alloy and clad in N6-¼ H plate (see Heavy Assault Floating Bridge above), whilst the landing bay cross girders were manufactured from H30-WP extrusions in the form of 15in x 6in I-beams.

Light Suspension Bridge. The design for the 10ft wide bridge used 5 gauge 3in square mesh known as ARC; flat sheets of the mesh, 6ft x 10ft, were connected by double helix joints. A 14ft 6in wide version used 5 gauge 5in square mesh (known as BRC) and was constructed from two 7ft 3in wide rolls of mesh, again connected by a double helix joint, the wire helixes being easily made on site. Both types of bridge were stiffened by Bailey chesses or similar timbers spaced at 2ft centres and attached under the mesh. Standard ground anchorages were used at the ends of the bridge, which was launched across two 2½in SWR launching cables, removed after the bridge was in position.

M2 Amphibious Bridge. This German manufactured equipment made extensive use of the aluminium alloy Constructal, one of the Al-Zn-Mg alloys designated by the Aluminium Federation as a 70/20 alloy. The vehicle was 36ft in length, 9ft 10in wide and 12ft 10in high with the wheels in the normal position, although the wheels could be lowered to improve cross-country ground clearance and fully retracted once the vehicle was in the water. The welded hull was divided into engine, transmission and wheel wells, and the strengthened deck provided an 18ft 4in roadway across the vehicle. The bridge/ramp stringers used to connect the units in the water were approximately 18ft long and 4ft 6in wide.

In the final production version (ie the M2B) two 180HP Deutz F 8L 714a V8

438

multi-fuel, air cooled engines were installed in each rig; these were connected to a universal gearbox, so that either engine could be used for automotive travel, to give the vehicle a maximum road speed of about 38mph. For marine drive both engines were used; one to drive the central steering propeller through a Schottel unit housed in a tunnel in the hull, which provided 360° steering, and the other to drive the two side propellers, one housed in a tunnel at the stern end of each of the side pontoons; the three propellers ensured a ferry water speed of about 8 knots unladen and 6 knots laden. The installation of two engines guarded against possible failure of one of them; it also meant that marine propulsion was available as soon as the vehicle entered the water, and that propeller thrust was available during the critical stage of water exit.

The M2C version of the equipment was that supplied to the Singapore Government, and used Deutz F 8L 413 diesel engines, whilst the M2D version incorporated engine inflated air bags, to upgrade the equipment to Class 70.

Mabey Compact Bailey. Main components are manufactured from BS 4360 weldable structural Grade 55C steel (see Acrow Heavy Bridge above).

Medium Girder Bridge. The bridge is manufactured by Williams Fairey Engineering Ltd in a weldable aluminium alloy to DGFVE Specification 232B (see Airportable Bridge above). Details of dimensions etc are given in the main text.

Mexeflote. The three distinct units of this equipment were all 8ft wide and 4ft 9in deep, and were made from steel to BS 4360 (see Acrow Heavy Bridge above), with connecting jaws made from 9% nickel steel. The bow pontoon was 26ft long and the centre and stern pontoons, each divided into two watertight compartments, were both 20ft long. The centre pontoon was boxed shaped, and the stern pontoon generally similar but with a shaped stern to improve the underwater profile and to allow free flow of water to the propellers of outboard motors, when fitted. All pontoons had four slinging points at deck level and full depth connecting slots in the sides and ends into which 4ft 10½ in long pontoon connectors were fitted to connect up the units.

No 1 Tank Bridge. The bridge was of welded construction, and consisted of two 2ft 11in wide trackways, each 34ft long overall, linked together by cross diaphragms and cross bracing to give an overall bridge width of 9ft 6in. Each trackway consisted of two girders, connected together by a reinforced track plate and hinged at the centre of their length at bottom chord level. The two webs of each trackway were made from ⁹⁄₁₆ in thick mild steel plate whilst the chords were formed from 2¼ x 2¼ in high tensile steel angles. The inner girder web plate of each trackway was 5in deeper than the outer web plate, thus allowing the inner top chords, consisting of one angle only, to act as wheel guides.

No 2 Tank Bridge. The two trackways forming the bridge were of welded construction, 34ft in length overall, and each weighing about 2.4tons. The connecting diaphragms and a single tubular diagonal brace were removable, so that the trackways could be closed together for transportation. As with the No 1 Tank Bridge, the inner girder of each trackway projected about 5in above the level of the deck to act as a kerb. The trackways were of welded steel plate construction, and were each 2ft 11in wide, spaced to give an overall width of bridge of 9ft 6in.

No 3 Tank Bridge. The trackways were made from welded steel plate girders, the tracks being connected at each end by rigid welded steel bankseats. The deck panels were of the aircraft aluminium alloy STA7/AC10 (see Close Support Raft above)

No 4 Tank Bridge. The single prototype bridge was made from high strength aircraft aluminium alloys, using riveted construction. The deck extrusions were made from STA/AW10, fully heat treated and copper free, and other extrusions from STA/AW15, fully heat treated (see Close Support Raft above).

No 6 Tank Bridge. The trackways of the bridge were of riveted aluminium alloy construction, manufactured from H15-WP plate and H15 and H30-WP extrusions. Their depth at mid-span was 4ft 6in and they were connected by two inverted portal frames and diagonal bracing. Each trackway was made in two identical 26ft long sections, pin connected at bottom chord level and bolted at the top; this ensured that sections could be transported on a 3 ton truck. The bridgelayer was provided with a jib to lift sections off the trucks and facilitate their assembly into a bridge. Decking panels were provided to fill the gap between the trackways once the bridge had been launched; this was to permit the passage of the mono-wheel fuel trailers towed behind the Centurion gun tanks, although use of the trailer was later abandoned and the infill sections were thus rarely used.

The bridge was carried upside down on top of the bridgelayer, the rear supported on a simple framework at the very back of the chassis, and the front connected to the launching mechanism through lifting brackets which were fitted to both ends of the trackways, to enable the bridge to be launched and retrieved from either end. The lifting brackets engaged with a centrally placed launching arm, connected through an articulated framework and two aluminium alloy hydraulic cylinders to a triangular supporting frame fixed rigidly to the front of the bridgelayer chassis; the cylinders were manufactured from HE-15 alloy rather than from steel. The launch mechanism was operated by a hydraulic pump, driven by a Rolls Royce B40 petrol engine located in the fighting compartment of the bridgelayer. The Stage 1 (lower) cylinder first raised the bridge to the vertical position, after which an automatic limit switch transferred the oil flow to the Stage 2 (upper) cylinder, which then lowered the bridge to the ground. When the bridge reached the ground the launching arm continued to rotate, to disengage itself from the bridge lifting brackets, and the bridgelayer could then reverse clear of the bridge.

No 7 Tank Bridge. The prototype bridges were manufactured in the then recently developed weldable aluminium alloy (see Air Portable Bridge above).

No 8 Armoured Vehicle Launched Bridge (No 8 Tank Bridge). The bridge consists of two trackways, 80ft long and with an effective width of 5ft 4in. There is a 3ft gap between the trackways, which gives an overall bridge width of 13ft 8in. Each trackway comprises two tapered centre sections, 25ft long, and two ramp sections, 15ft long and tapering to a depth of 5in at the toe. Each section consists of two main girders, connected by cross girders and stiffeners, and the sections are pinned together through jaws at their bottom corners and have butting joints at the top corners. The top chord joints between the centre and ramp sections are secured by pins during the launch of the bridge, and remain so during normal usage. However circumstances may arise, on awkward sites or at shorter spans, when it is desirable to allow the ramp sections at one or both ends of the bridge to droop. If this is foreseen, the eight pins securing the top chord joints can be replaced with explosive blow-out type pins that can be fired electrically from within the vehicle. The two trackways are connected by bracing frames and bracing struts, and by two lifting beams, one spanning the gap between the outer ends of each pair of centre sections. These lifting beams provide the point of attachment for the launching mechanism of the bridge.

The main girders, lifting beams and scissoring rods for the bridge were manufactured from an 18% nickel-cobalt-molybdenum maraging alloy steel. The three main grades of this alloy steel available during the design period contained 18, 20 or 25% nickel respectively, but the first of these alloys was chosen because it was easier to work; the 18% nickel alloy was available in three sub-grades, depending upon slightly differing quantities of the other alloying metals added. The grade used has a 0.2% proof stress of 90 tons/in^2 and an ultimate tensile strength of 110 tons/in^2. The high strength of the alloy, coupled with its toughness and its good ductility, relies on adequate heat treatment to develop its full properties - that is heating to about 850°C and then cooling to the annealed state, followed by a simple maraging or hardening process at 450-500°C for about 3 to 4 hours; this of course causes problems with field repairs of the equipment. During manufacture complete sections of the bridge were welded and then placed in large ovens for the maraging process, in order to develop the full strength of the weld metal and restore the strength of the heat affected zones. The decking, bracing frames and bracing struts of the bridge are made from DGFVE Specification 232 aluminium alloy.

No 9 Armoured Vehicle Launched Bridge (No 9 Tank Bridge). The main structure of the bridge was manufactured in Grade 55E weldable structural steel to BS 4360 (see Acrow Heavy Bridge above). Each trackway of the bridge is formed from two 22ft long sections, pinned together at bottom

441

chord level and butting together and bolted at top chord level. The aluminium alloy decking is formed from the same extrusions used for the No 8 Tank Bridge, which are bolted to the top of the cross beams and diaphragms. The two 5ft 7in wide trackways are held together by two bracing frames and two lifting beams which facilitate the launching of the bridge, the overall width being 13ft 8in, the same as that of the No 8 Bridge. The bridge is launched by the up-and-over method, using the same launching mechanism on the bridgelayer that is used to launch the No 8 Tank Bridge. Stage One raises the bridge from the horizontal to about 45°, Stage Two raises it to the vertical position, and Stage Three lowers the bridge to the ground.

No 10, 11 and 12 Tank Bridges. See Bridging for the 90s above.

Pasley's Pontoon. The pontoon was constructed with a light wooden frame, clad with copper sheeting, and was decked with timber. Each pontoon was divided by a transverse partition to reduce the possibility of swamping should the pontoon be accidentally holed, and a pump was provided to pump the pontoons dry if necessary. Two of the sometimes named demi-pontoons could be lashed together, stern to stern, to form a single bridge supporting pier, 22ft long, 2ft 8in deep and with a maximum width of 2ft 8in.

Pipe Fascine. The 30 pipes forming the outer band of the Maxi Pipe Fascine have an outer diameter of just over 8½ in (220mm) and a wall thickness of about ⅜ in (10mm), whilst the 45 pipes of the inner core have the same outer diameter but a wall thickness of about ¼ in (7mm). Four pairs of lifting/recovery chains are positioned around the circumference of the fascine and these are connected to the construction chains.

Pontoon Mark I (The Blood Pontoon). The pontoon was 21ft 7in in overall length, and 5ft 3in wide at the extreme, weighing just over 1000lb. It was timber framed, with sides and bottom clad in thin planks of yellow pine; both sides of the cladding were covered with canvas, secured with India rubber, and the outer covering was then painted with two coats of marine glue. The 15ft 9in long baulks, which spanned between the saddle beam and pontoon saddle in bridge, were made of Canadian red or Kawrie pine. Ribands and long chesses, also of Kawrie pine, completed the superstructure, 15ft of superstructure being carried on each pontoon wagon.

Pontoon Mark II (The Clauson Pontoon). The bow section of the pontoon was 11ft 6in long and had a tapered bow and square stern; the stern section was 9ft 6in long but had two square ends. Both sections were 5ft 3in wide and 2ft 5in deep. The timber framed pontoons were clad in American white pine, with ⅜ in side and 7/16 in bottom planking; both sides of the cladding were covered with canvas, secured by five layers of India rubber solution, and the canvas was then coated with marine glue. The superstructure was basically identical to that used with the Blood Pontoon, being supported by pontoon saddles placed centrally in the pontoons.

Pontoon Mark III. The pontoon was identical to the Mark II Pontoon

442

except that lighter scantlings were used to compensate for the heavier cladding. The cladding used 4in x ³⁄₁₆ in planks of Honduras mahogany, in two skins which were copper riveted together with a layer of painted calico between them. The planks of the two skins were placed at right angles to each other, at 45° to the gunwales for the sides and transversely on the bottom and ends of the pontoon.

Pontoon Mark IV. Consuta Ply was a special type of plywood used for the manufacture of the Mark IV pontoon developed in the mid 1920s. The separate plies of Honduras mahogany were so arranged that the grain of one was at right angles to that of the next. The plies were stuck together using water-proof glue and were then sewn with pure flax thread, in lines 1¼ in apart and at 45° to the direction of the grain. The plywood was formed over mahogany cross frames to form a pontoon weighing some 1,350lb, 21ft long and 5ft 6in wide. It was flat bottomed and had a scow shaped bow developed after model and full scale towing trials; the stern end was square, enabling two pontoons to be coupled together as a bi-partite pier. The 22ft long road bearers were of nickel chromium steel, and ribands and Oregon pine chesses completed the decking.

Pontoon Mark V. The Mark V Pontoon did not differ greatly in appearance from its predecessor; once again the pontoon was decked, its length of 20ft and width of 5ft 9in were little changed, and it was timber framed and clad. It was again plywood covered, but was clad in the more easily manufactured and obtainable birch-gaboon-mahogany-birch ply. An important difference was that it was designed for gunwale loading, whereas the Mark IV Pontoon carried its load on the pontoon centre line, making use of a pontoon saddle. A steel framework was incorporated in the pontoon sides to take the load from the newly introduced raft connectors and to support the extra loading on the gunwales. The superstructure of the bridge again consisted of timber chesses supported by 21ft long steel road bearers; however the nickel chrome steel previously used for roadbearers was now required for more urgent armaments, and high tensile structural steel, with about half the tensile strength, had to be used instead.

Pontoon Mark VI. Of similar construction to the Mark V Pontoon but with additional steel reinforcement of the timber framework.

Small Box Girder Bridge. The girders of the bridge were made up of parallel sided box sections, 16ft long, and hornbeam sections, 17ft 3in long, pin linked together; both types of section weighed about 1100lb; 8ft long ramps were used at either end of bridge. The all welded high tensile steel bridge was developed at a time when arc welding was confined almost entirely to non-stressed structures and the application of welding to the 37-42 tons/in² (ultimate strength) structural steel did cause some problems. These were resolved by limiting the carbon content to 0.3% and restricting the manganese and chromium content. All test pieces were required to meet a yield stress limit of 21 tons/in².

Standard Plate Girder Railway Bridge. The 30ft span bridge was a deck bridge consisting of two welded plate girders, 34ft 6in overall and 2ft 8¾in deep, rigidly attached to each other with a system of diaphragms and diagonal angle braces. Each plate girder was in one piece so that the only field work required was the bolting on of the bracing members. The other three spans were of riveted construction. The 40 and 60ft span bridges were designed to be used either as a deck bridge or as a through bridge. The main girders were of similar construction, with a mid-span joint, the girder depth of the shorter bridge being 4ft 6in, and that of the longer bridge, 6ft. The girders consisted of a web plate and four flange angles, with no flange plates, so that sleepers could be laid directly on to the top of the flat flanges when used as a deck bridge. The same floor system was used for both through bridges, consisting of riveted steel stringers placed under each rail position and supported on cross girders spaced at 8ft 6in centres. The 80ft span bridge was a through bridge, the 6ft deep girders each weighing about 17½ tons; the girders were made in three sections, the heaviest being about 30ft long and weighing 5½ tons.

Standard Through Truss Railway Bridge. The trusses of the bridge were made up from shop riveted sections so that only simple joints had to be made in the field, using rivets or, in some cases, bolts and drift pins. The floor of the bridge was the same as that used for the 80ft span Plate Girder Bridge, the 2ft 6in deep riveted plate girder cross girders being similarly spaced at 10ft 3in centres.

Stock Spans. There were two categories of these First World War bridges, depending upon the load class to be carried.

A Type Bridges were designed to take a 17 ton axle load. The 16ft, 21ft 6in and 30ft spans consisted of rolled steel joist beams. The 60ft and 85ft spans consisted of two Warren girders with decking between, but the 85ft bridge was never popular, because of the excessive weight of one of its components, which exceeded 3 tons, and it was subsequently replaced by the Hopkins Bridge.

B Type Bridges were designed for a 13 ton axle loading. The 13ft span consisted of four 12in x 6in rolled steel joists, whilst the 30ft and 60ft bridges both consisted of two light Warren trusses with decking between. The earliest of these sent out to the BEF were deck bridges, but these were subsequently modified for use as either deck bridges or as through bridges, to allow their use where head room under the bridge might be restricted.

Storey Bailey Bridge. Main components were manufactured from Grade 55C weldable structural steel to BS 4360 (see Acrow Heavy Bridge above).

Tank Bridges. See No 1 Tank Bridge etc above.

Tin Pontoons. The large Tin Pontoon was 21ft 1in long overall, 4ft 10in wide, and 2ft 3½in deep, weighing just over 1,000lb, but towards the end of the Napoleonic Wars a smaller version was introduced, 16ft 10in long, 4ft wide and 2ft deep, weighing only about 750lb. The early Tin Pontoons were constructed with a framework of timber scantlings upon which a cladding of sheet tin was fixed. Tin was used in preference to copper because it was, at that time, very much cheaper, although it was much more subject to corrosion from the action of sea water. Copper was sometimes used but it was usually tinned so as to be more easily soldered; at a later date sheet iron, coated with tin and then with zinc, was used, being stronger and lighter than the copper cladding used for example for the Pasley Pontoon.

A Pontoon Train assembled before Waterloo included 18 large pontoons and 20 of the new smaller pontoons. Each pontoon was provided with its own wagon, drawn by six horses, and carried a proportion of the bridge superstructure, including six chesses, 11ft 6in long, oars, anchors, and of course the baulks, 22ft 8in long, needed to span between the pontoons in bridge.

Track Bridges. The 12ft and 20ft Track Bridges were of all welded construction, using thin walled chromium molybdenum steel tubes in order to obtain maximum lightness. Welding of the special steel required considerable experiment before satisfactory results could be obtained. Some versions of the 12ft No 3 Track Bridge were manufactured using standard rolled sections.

Trestle Mark II. The transom of the Mark II or Weldon Trestle was 13ft 2in long, and was supported at each end by a grip strap, which locked the transom to the trestle legs. The 16ft 3in legs were positioned vertically and if the trestle was used on a treacherous or muddy river bottom, a bottom ledger could be used to maintain them in the vertical position whilst the height of the transom was adjusted. The transom and legs were made from Oregon Pine. The Mark III and Mark IV Trestles were slightly modified versions of the Mark II.

Trestle Mark V. The trestle came into service in the 1920s. The 14ft 3in long trestle legs were made from 8in x 4in mild steel beams; the legs were fitted with pitch pine mud shoes and were drilled at 6in centres to enable the 13ft long nickel chrome transom to be adjusted to the correct height, using jacks fitted to the legs.

Trestle Mark VI. The 11ft 3in long welded box section trestle legs were manufactured from 40 ton steel, and had steel instead of timber mud shoes; a 40 ton steel welded box section was also used for the trestle transom, although experiments were initially carried out with a trussed transom. The stronger trestle meant that it could be used singly at each end of the Heavy Bridge, in place of the double trestle pier needed with the Mark V Trestles.

Trestle Mark VII. This trestle varied in minor detail only from the Mark VI Trestle, the trestle legs and the transom again being of 40 ton steel.

Unit Construction Railway Bridge. For a 16 BS Unit loading half-through bridge, two girders were used at 16ft 2in centres, using 18in x 7in cross girders at 5ft centres; later however the 20 BS Unit loading half-through bridge became standard, using two or four girders and a shorter and heavier 28in deep cross girder, with the inner girders at 12ft 6in centres; 10in steel beams were used between the cross beams as stringers to carry the rail tracks. All site connections were made using a prescribed combination of black bolts, drift pins and turned bolts.

Senior Appointments at Christchurch

OFFICERS COMMANDING
EXPERIMENTAL BRIDGING COMPANY ROYAL ENGINEERS

Bt Maj G Le Q Martel DSO MC RE	28 Feb 1919 - 11 Jan 1921
Bt Maj A V T Wakely MC RE	12 Jan 1921 - 9 Jan 1923
Bt Maj H H Bateman DSO MC RE	10 Jan 1923 - 6 Aug 1925

SUPERINTENDENTS
EXPERIMENTAL BRIDGING ESTABLISHMENT

Bt Maj H H Bateman DSO MC RE	7 Aug 1925 - 13 Nov 1926
Capt R D Davies RE	14 Nov 1926 - 13 Nov 1930
Maj J B H Doyle OBE RE	14 Nov 1930 - 13 Nov 1932
Capt S G Galpin RE	14 Nov 1932 - 13 Nov 1936
Capt S A Stewart RE	14 Nov 1936 - 24 Sep 1941
(Maj - 3 Sep 1939)	
Maj G H Hunt MC RE	25 Sep 1941 - 14 Jan 1944
(Lt Col - 19 May 1943)	

CHIEF SUPERINTENDENT
EXPERIMENTAL BRIDGING ESTABLISHMENT

Col G H Hunt MC	15 Jan 1944 - 21 Mar 1946

CHIEF SUPERINTENDENTS
MILITARY ENGINEERING EXPERIMENTAL ESTABLISHMENT

Brig G R McMeekan DSO OBE	22 Mar 1946 - 11 Apr 1950
Brig Sir Millis R Jefferis KBE MC ADC	12 Apr 1950 - 20 Jul 1953
Brig L R E Fayle DSO OBE	21 Jul 1953 - 4 Apr 1956

DIRECTORS
MILITARY ENGINEERING EXPERIMENTAL ESTABLISHMENT

Brig L R E Fayle DSO OBE	5 Apr 1956 - 31 Dec 1956
Sir Donald Bailey Kt OBE	1 Jan 1957 - 30 Sep 1962
Brig H A T Jarrett-Kerr CBE ADC	1 Oct 1962 - 5 Oct 1965
Mr R A Foulkes	6 Oct 1965 - 31 Mar 1970

DEPUTY DIRECTOR
MILITARY VEHICLES AND ENGINEERING ESTABLISHMENT

Brig R A Lindsell MC ADC	1 Apr 1970 - 7 Apr 1972

HEADS OF ENGINEER EQUIPMENT DIVISION
MILITARY VEHICLES AND ENGINEERING ESTABLISHMENT

Mr B T Boswell	8 Apr 1972 - 31 May 1974
Dr P S Bulson	1 Jun 1974 - 31 Mar 1984

HEAD OF ENGINEER EQUIPMENT GROUP
ROYAL ARMAMENT RESEARCH AND DEVELOPMENT
ESTABLISHMENT

Dr P S Bulson	1 Apr 1984 - 31 Jul 1985

SUPERINTENDENTS, TRIALS AND ENGINEERING DIVISION
ROYAL ARMAMENT RESEARCH AND DEVELOPMENT
ESTABLISHMENT

Mr G K Booth (TE3)	1 Aug 1985 - 17 Aug 1986
Mr A D Freed (TE4)	1 Aug 1985 - 17 Aug 1986

HEADS OF ROYAL ARMAMENT RESEARCH AND DEVELOPMENT
ESTABLISHMENT (CHRISTCHURCH) AND SUPERINTENDENT
ENGINEER EQUIPMENT

Mr G K Booth	18 Aug 1986 - 1 Jan 1990
Mr D I Knight	2 Jan 1990 - 12 Sep 1990
Mr G J Hambly	13 Sep 1990 - 31 Mar 1991

HEADS OF DEFENCE RESEARCH AGENCY (CHRISTCHURCH)
AND MANAGER ENGINEER SYSTEMS DEPARTMENT

Mr G J Hambly	1 Apr 1991 - 28 Feb 1993
Mr M T Gilman	1 Mar 1993 - 28 Feb 1994

At the end of February 1994 the Establishment at Christchurch closed for good, with the exception of a very small bridge test element, bringing to an end its seventy five year era devoted to the design and development of engineer equipment for the Royal Engineers.

APPENDIX D

The Pedigree of the Assault/Armoured Engineers

The Background

Engineer equipment was first used operationally in combination with armoured vehicles at the battle of Cambrai, in 1917, when fascines carried on tanks were used to cross enemy trenches. However, although it was planned to form three specialist Royal Engineer Tank Bridging Battalions in 1918, their formation was forestalled by the end of the War. Some experimental work on tank bridges was undertaken at the EBE, Christchurch in the 1920s and 1930s, but the first Royal Engineer units equipped with specialist armoured vehicles were not formed until the Second World War. These units were formed specifically for the final assault on Europe, and were known as Assault units, for example 26 Assault Squadron RE, and 1 Assault Brigade RE. During the campaign in North-West Europe the term **Armoured** was substituted for **Assault**, and 26 Squadron, for example, became 26 Armoured Engineer Squadron. Titles were changed yet again just after the war, when the term Assault Engineer was again adopted, the squadrons subsequently forming part of 32 Assault Engineer Regiment. The final change took place in 1957 when the title **Armoured Engineer** was adopted.

Throughout this period, tank mounted bridging was always referred to as **Assault Bridging**, as opposed to the more slowly built **Floating Bridging** and **Fixed (or Dry) Bridging**, such as the Heavy Floating Bridge and the Heavy Girder Bridge, normally built well behind our forward forces. In the early 1980s however it was decided to take account of the fact that assault bridging was just as likely to be used in a defensive role as in an attack and, in line with our NATO Allies, such bridging was renamed **Close Support Bridging**. At the same time Floating and Fixed Bridging was renamed **Deliberate Wet** and **Deliberate Dry Support Bridging**, and then subsequently, for BR90, **General Support Bridging**.

Date	Event
1942-1943	In August 1942, as part of the overall plan for the forthcoming invasion of mainland Europe, it was decided to set up a new armoured formation composed of specialist vehicles to be used in this final assault on Europe. 79 Armoured Division was selected as the most suitable unit on which to form the new formation, and adopted to its new role in April 1943. During the summer of 1943 the six

448

companies of 5 and 6 Chemical Warfare Groups Royal Engineers joined the division and became 5 and 6 Assault Regiments RE. By the end of October six more units had been converted to Assault Squadrons, to form 1 Assault Brigade RE, which now comprised a Headquarters, three assault regiments (42 Assault Regiment RE being the third) each of four squadrons, 149 Assault Park Squadron and the Brigade Signal Squadron.

There were very few specialist vehicles available with which to equip the new Division, and the Division therefore took a leading role in the development of suitable equipments up until the end of the war.

1944	Sapper units of the Division played a leading part in the D Day landings, with the establishment of the assault regiments each now reduced to three squadrons.
Late 1944	1 Armoured Regiment RAC/RE was established in Italy and in early 1945 the regiment was absorbed into the newly formed 25 Armoured Engineer Brigade. The Brigade comprised an RAC Regiment (armed with Flails and Crocodile Flame Throwers), 1 and 2 Armoured Engineer Regiments (each of three squadrons), and an Armoured Engineer Park Squadron; Sapper equipment included AVREs, ARKs, and Armoured Dozers.
May 1945	42 Assault Regiment RE, as it was now known, moved back to UK to prepare for service in the Far East.
August 1945	The end of the War in the Far East pre-empted the move of the Regiment, and it was subsequently reformed in Hameln, Germany.
January 1948	42 Assault Engineer Regiment was redesignated 32 Assault Engineer Regiment and later in the year returned to UK from Hameln, being reformed at full strength at Perham Down.
June 1951	The regiment took over responsibility for Flail Tanks from the RAC, and now consisted of 81 HQ Assault Squadron, 26 Assault Squadron (AVREs), 59 Assault Squadron (Flails), and 31 Assault Park Squadron.
1954	31 Assault Park Squadron was disbanded and 59 Assault Squadron was reorganised as 59 Airfield Construction Squadron, moving to Chatham and then Christmas Island.

July 1957	32 Assault Engineer Regiment was disbanded, and in September, 26 Assault Squadron, moved to Hohne in Germany, redesignated as 26 Armoured Engineer Squadron. It was equipped with Flail Tanks and AVREs, and the No 3 Tank Bridge on the Churchill Bridgelayer; later equipment included the Churchill Linked ARK.
1963	The No 6 Tank Bridge, mounted on the Centurion Bridgelayer, was first introduced into service with 26 Squadron; the Centurion AVRE also came into service.
March 1965	2 Field Squadron converted to 2 Armoured Engineer Squadron and moved to Hohne, to join 26 Squadron and form a new 32 Armoured Engineer Regiment. The Regiment's equipment included the No 6 Tank Bridge, Centurion AVREs and the Centurion ARK.
April 1969	A reorganization of the Royal Engineer units of 1 British Corps was put in hand, eventually leading to two smaller Engineer Regiments (each comprising just two squadrons), an Armoured Engineer Squadron and a Field Support Squadron in each Division, all commanded by a Divisional CRE at full colonel level. As part of this reorganization the role of 32 Armoured Engineer Regiment was changed and it became 32 Engineer Regiment. The regiment remained at Hohne, eventually consisting of 7 and 30 Field Squadrons. For a time 26 Armoured Engineer Squadron remained as part of the Regiment, although not under operational command, but 2 Armoured Engineer Squadron moved to Iserlohn, provisionally as part of 26 Engineer Regiment. In September 1969 31 Armoured Engineer Squadron was formed at Hohne, and moved to Osnabrück in March 1971. As a result of this reorganization the Sappers were once again without an Armoured Engineer Regiment as such.
1969	During the year 26 Armoured Engineer Squadron carried out trials with the prototype Chieftain Bridgelayer and the No 8 AVLB. The bridge eventually came into service in 1974.
April 1971	The three Armoured Engineer Squadrons finally became fully independent, each being placed under command of one of the BAOR Divisions. 2 Squadron was based at Iserlohn, under command of 4 Armoured Division, 26 Squadron remained at Hohne, under command of 1 Armoured Division, and 31 Squadron was based at Osnabrück, under command of 2 Division.

Late 1971	The Sappers took over the last of the No 6 Tank Bridges operated by the RAC.
April 1978	The BAOR Restructuring Plan resulted in the disbandment of 2 Armoured Engineer Squadron; 26 and 31 Armoured Engineer Squadrons amalgamated to become 26 Corps Armoured Engineer Squadron, based at Munsterlager, and under direct command of HQRE 1 British Corps. The squadron comprised an HQ and six tank troops, each with two sections; each section held one Centurion AVRE and two Chieftain Bridgelayers, with the No 8 and No 9 Tank Bridges.
January 1980	Since 26 Squadron had retained most of the equipment and armour previously held by the Regiment, its size was almost unmanageable. 31 Armoured Engineer Squadron was therefore reformed, at Munsterlager, and joined 26 Squadron, a Regimental HQ and a REME Workshop to form a newly constituted 32 Armoured Engineer Regiment.
April 1983	77 Armoured Engineer Squadron was formed, to complete the three squadron establishment of the Regiment at Munsterlager.
1984	A number of Centurion MBTs, previously used by the RA as forward observations posts, were converted to AVREs. They retained the 105mm L7 gun and were known as AVRE 105s to distinguish them from the original Centurion AVREs armed with the demolition gun, and now known as AVRE 165s.
1987	Seventeen Chieftain MBTs were converted to AVREs at Willich in Germany, each equipped with mine plough or dozer blade and a top hamper to carry fascines and other loads, but had no main armament. Only four of these new AVREs went to the Regiment, the others being used by 21 and 23 Engineer Regiments in connection with Close Support Squadron trials.
late 1980s	Close Support Squadron trials continued, culminating in use of the concept by 21 and 23 Engineer Regiments during the Gulf War of 1990/91.
January 1991	32 Armoured Engineer Regiment was deployed in the Gulf War.
early 1990s	Vickers undertook the conversion of 48 Chieftain MBTs to

AVREs, leading to the demise of the Centurion and the Willich Chieftain AVREs.

July 1991	The Ministry of Defence 'Options for Change' outlined the formation of five Close Support Regiments, by increasing the number of Armoured Engineer Squadrons to five, and allocating each to an Engineer Regiment on deployment.
January 1993	8 Field Squadron re-roled as 8 Armoured Engineer Squadron and remained co-located with 3 Field Squadron, similarly re-roled in August 1993, at Perham Down, Hampshire. The squadrons formed part of 22 Engineer Regiment but were earmarked for operatiuonal deployment to their Close Support Regiments ie 36 and 38 Engineer Regiment.
September 1993	26, 31 and 77 Armoured Engineer Squadrons moved from Munster-Lager to Hohne as part of what now became, once again, 32 Engineer Regiment; the Regiment retained its famous tactical sign - a black bull's head in a yellow triangle. The three squadrons were earmarked for wartime deployment to their Close Support Regiments ie 21, 32 and 35 Engineer Regiments.
August 1994	An Acceptance Meeting formally accepted the Thompson Defence Projects designs for the new range of Close Support and General Support Bridges, opening the way for full scale production, and eventual re-equipment of the Armoured Engineer Squadrons.
1996	The No 10, 11 and 12 Tank Bridges, manufactured by Vickers Defence Systems, came into service with limited use in Bosnia, and subsequently in Macedonia and Kosovo.
July 1998	The Strategic Defence Review heralded the re-birth of 26 Engineer Regiment to act as a Close Support Regiment in support of 1 Mechanized Brigade, thus forming the sixth CS Regiment in the Corps. Each Mechanized or Armoured Brigade in the British Army was thus supported by its own CS Regiment. Formation of 23 Engineer Regiment in a similar role, to support 16 Air Assault Brigade, was envisaged.
June 1999	26 Armoured Engineer Squadron deployed with 21 Engineer Regiment to Bosnia. Both AVREs and AVLBs were used extensively, with No 10 and No 12 Tank Bridges, to effectively aid mobility.

APPENDIX E

Victoria Crosses Won in Bridging Operations

Since the Victoria Cross was instituted in 1856, during the Crimean War, fifty VCs have been awarded to members of the Corps. And yet, strangely, only six have been awarded for supreme gallantry during bridging and rafting operations, and these all in connections with operation in France in the First World War. The official citations for the six awards are given below.

Captain Theodore Wright, Royal Engineers, late Adjutant, 3 Division Engineers.
Citation: Gallantry at Mons on 23rd August 1914, in attempting to connect up the lead to demolish a bridge under heavy fire; although wounded in the head he made a second attempt. At Vailly, on 14th September, he assisted the passage of 5th Cavalry Brigade over the pontoon bridge, and was mortally wounded whilst assisting wounded men into shelter. *(London Gazette 16 November 1914)*

Captain William Henry Johnston, Royal Engineers, 59 Field Company RE.
Citation: At Missy, on 14th September 1914, under a heavy fire all day until 7pm, worked with his own hand two rafts, bringing back wounded and returning with ammunition; thus enabling the advanced Brigade to maintain its position across the river. *(London Gazette. 25 November 1914)*

Corporal James McPhie, Royal Engineers, late 416 (Edinburgh) Field Company RE.
Citation: For most conspicuous bravery on 14th October 1918, when with a party of Sappers maintaining a cork float bridge across the Canal de la Senseé, near Aubenchuel au Bac. The farther end of the bridge was under close machine-gun fire and within reach of hand grenades. When infantry, just before dawn, were crossing it, closing up resulted and the bridge began to sink and break. Accompanied by a Sapper, he jumped onto the water and endeavoured to hold the cork and timber together, but this they failed to do. Corporal McPhie then swam back and, having reported the broken bridge, immediately started to collect material for its repair. It was now daylight. Fully aware that the bridge was under close fire and that the far bank was almost entirely in the hands of the enemy, with the inspiring words 'It is death or glory work that must be done for the sake of our patrol on the other side', he led the way, axe in hand, on to the bridge and was at once severely wounded, falling back partly into the water, and died after receiving several further wounds. It was due to the magnificent example set by Corporal

McPhie that touch was maintained with the patrol on the enemy bank at a most critical period. *(London Gazette 31 January 1919)*

Captain (A/major) George de Cardonnel Elmsall Findlay, MC*, Royal Engineers, 409 (Lowland) Field Company RE.

Citation: For most conspicuous bravery and devotion to duty during the forcing of the Sambre-Oise Canal at the Lock, two miles south of Catillon on 4th November 1918, when in charge of bridging operations at this crossing. Major Findlay was with the leading bridging and assault parties which came under heavy fire while trying to cross the dyke between the forming-up line and the lock. The casualties were severe, and the assault was stopped. Nevertheless, under heavy and incessant fire, he collected what men he could and repaired the bridges in spite of heavy casualties in officers and men. Although wounded, Major Findlay continued his task and after two unsuccessful efforts, owing to his men being swept down, he eventually placed the bridge in position across the lock and was the first man across, subsequently remaining at this post of danger till further work was completed. His cool and gallant behaviour inspired volunteers from different units at a critical time when men became casualties almost as soon as they joined him in the fire-swept zone, and it was due to Major Findlay's gallantry and devotion to duty that this most important crossing was effected. *(London Gazette 15 May 1919)*

Captain (T/Major) Arnold Horace Santo Waters, DSO, MC, Royal Engineers, 218 (Leith) Field Company RE.

Citation: For most conspicuous bravery and devotion to duty on 4th November 1918, near Ors, when bridging with his Field Company the Oise-Sambre Canal. From the outset the task was under artillery and machine-gun fire at close range, the bridge being damaged and the bridging party suffering severe casualties. Major Waters, hearing that all his officers had been killed or wounded, at once went forward and personally supervised the completion of the bridge, working on cork floats while under fire at point-blank range. So intense was the fire that it seemed impossible that he could escape being killed. The success of the operation was entirely due to his valour and example. *(London Gazette 13 February 1919)*

Sapper Adam Archibald, Royal Engineers, 218 (Leith) Field Company RE.

Citation: For most conspicuous bravery and self-sacrifice on 4th November 1918, near Ors, when with a party building a floating bridge across the canal. He was foremost in the work under a very heavy artillery barrage and machine-gun fire. The latter was directed at him from a few yards' distance while he was working on the cork floats; nevertheless he persevered in his task, and his example and efforts were such that the bridge, which was essential to the success of the operations, was completed quickly. The supreme devotion to duty of this gallant Sapper, who collapsed from gas poisoning on completion of his work, was beyond all praise. *(London Gazette 6 January 1919)*

The US/FRG/UK Bridging for the 1980s Project

The International Concept Study Team

The setting up of the US/FRG/UK project for the development of a new bridging system for the 1980s and beyond has been covered in Chapter 15. Details of the initial operational requirement that was agreed by the three countries after preliminary meetings in June 1970 are also included in that chapter. A Memorandum of Understanding (MOU) authorizing a two-year concept study programme with an initial budget of just under £M0.25 followed, but was not formally signed until June 1972. Meanwhile the International Concept Study Team for Bridge Systems for the 1980s, abbreviated to the ICST for BR80, had already assembled at the Military Vehicles and Engineering Establishment, Christchurch during the previous summer. The team was set up under the chairmanship of Major J N Barnikel, mentioned previously as the project officer for the Amphibious Bridge M2, and he was supported by two members from each of the participating countries.

The team was directed and monitored throughout its work by the International Technical Steering Committee (SC), which met at six monthly intervals under the chairmanship of Mr B T Boswell, a retired Sapper Major who had served at Christchurch during World War II, had stayed on as a Scientific Civil Servant, and eventually become Head of the Engineer Equipment Division of MVEE(C) in April 1972.

The Work of the ICST

In addition to their main task of recommending a concept for a new bridge, the ICST carried out a number of important studies as part of their overall programme. These included:

1. An analysis of probable obstacle statistics.
2. A review of possible structural materials.
3. An examination of design criteria within the three countries, which led to the setting up of an International Working Group of Military Bridge Designers and eventually to the writing of the Trilateral Design and Test code for Military Bridges.
4. The development of a method to assess the effectiveness and whole life costs of recommended concepts. This proved to be one of the more difficult problems facing the ICST, because of widely different

opinions on the relative importance to be attached to the various aspects involved.

The Concept

The team unanimously agreed the final concept, although there were differences of opinion with regard to design details that were to persist right through to the end of the BR80 programme. In developing this concept a major consideration that influenced the team was the tight limits placed on construction times and manpower, which indicated the use of long lengths of pre-assembled bridge, capable of being speedily launched from transporter/launcher vehicles in all roles. It was also clear that a commonality of components and launching systems between the various roles would lead to a reduction in unit production costs and to standardization of repair and maintenance procedures.

The Team therefore proposed a family of bridges using common panels, half panels and ramps, the panels and ramps both being 6-8m (20-26ft) long, 1.5m (5ft) wide and fabricated from weldable aluminium alloy. The double trackway bridge could span a 28-30m (92-98ft) gap at MLC 60 or a gap up to 60m (197ft) wide using a king post reinforcement system. It was proposed that the panel cross section should be rectangular, although the German members of the Team favoured a triangular cross section, considered less bulky and probably lighter, although involving a more complicated bridge launching mechanism.

In the Assault Role, 30m (98ft) of bridge would be carried on top of an armoured bridgelayer based upon current national main battle tanks. The ramps would be carried folded over on top of the bridge structure proper and would be flipped over into position prior to a sliding horizontal launch. Again the German Team members differed, favouring the launch method used for the German Biber AVLB, in which the two halves of bridge would be carried one on top of the other, the top half being slid forward and coupled up prior to the launch of the complete bridge.

A highly mobile transporter/launcher vehicle known as the Wheeled Vehicle Launcher, or WVL was proposed for the Support Roles, capable of carrying and launching up to 30m (98ft) of bridge by either of the two methods proposed for the assault bridge. A light launching nose would compensate for the lack of counterweight available with the armoured bridgelayer.

Two concepts were suggested for the Wet Support Role. The Discrete Flotation Concept would use large self-propelled pontoons, two of which would be carried and launched from standard WVLs. The bridge girder would then be launched directly on to the pontoons to form either a floating bridge or a ferry. The Continuous Flotation Concept was similar to that used for the US Army Ribbon Bridge, which had been developed from the Russian PMP Floating Bridge. In this system the bridge girders would be made

456

buoyant by the insertion of pneumatic floats inside the girders, and hinged bow pontoons, running the full length of the girders, would provide additional buoyancy. These pontoons would be folded over for transport and would unfold automatically as the 14-15m (46-49ft) length of floating bridge carried on each vehicle was launched.

The Interim Phase

The ICST Final Report in English and German was duly presented to the Steering Committee and subsequently to the National Authorities in early 1974. It was then agreed that further work on the ICST proposals should be carried out nationally, rather than trilaterally, during what was to be known as the Interim Phase. Chairmanship of the Steering Committee passed to Dr P S Bulson, who had taken over as Head of the Establishment at Christchurch on 1 April 1974, and the Committee set up four working parties, namely:

1. **The Operational Requirement Group**, charged with agreeing a trilateral operational requirement for the new bridging equipment.

2. **The Memorandum of Understanding Group**, charged with agreeing an MOU for the full scale development and production of the new equipment, including such matters as patent protection, manufacturers' rights and funding arrangements.

3. **The Assessment Group**, charged with the production of a procedure to compare and assess the Interim Phase work of the three nations.

4. **The Design and Analysis Group**, charged with the finalisation of the ICST's Trilateral Design and Test Code.

The Interim Phase Programmes

During the Interim Phase considerable progress was made on agreeing such matters as the split of future development work between the three countries (including the management and costing of the development phase), and details for prototype equipment production and trilateral user trials. At the same time considerable effort and expenditure went into the national Interim Phase programmes.

The UK Programme included:

1. The manufacture and test loading of two 32m (105ft) welded aluminium girders with rectangular cross section, intended for launching by the flip ramp and sliding method favoured by UK and US during the ICST studies.

2. Fabrication of a reinforcing kit for a 54.5m (179ft) bridge girder.

3. The production of a mock-up WVL, based upon a Foden chassis and fitted with a space frame representing the bridge as it would be carried on a vehicle, followed by extensive handling and road manoeuvrability trials in UK and Germany (Figure F1).

Figure F1. The UK mock up Wheeeled Vehicle Launcher, compared in size with an M2 rig and the Chieftain AVLB with its No 8 Tank Bridge. (MVEE slide)

4. A review of the Trilateral Design and Test Code, carried out by consulting engineers Flint & Neil.

The US Programme included:

1. Design of a 31m (102ft) trapezoidal cross section twin girder bridge at MERADCOM, Fort Belvoir and its construction by the Pacific Car and Foundry Co (PCF) at Seattle. Each girder web plate was formed by dimpling two plates and spot welding the dimples together. The bridge was designed for launching by the flip and slide method.

2. Manufacture of a reinforcement kit for a 52m (170ft) bridge.

3. Design and manufacture of a 10 x 10 WVL by PCF (Figure F2).

4. Manufacture of filler and bow pontoon sections to convert four 7m (23ft) bridge sections into units for continuous flotation, with the bows carried folded on top of the bridge girders and unfolded prior to the launching of 14m (46ft) sections of floating bridge from the WVL.

5. The mounting of both 24m (79ft) and 31m (102ft) bridges on an M60 battle tank chassis for mobility trials.

Figure F2. The US 31m BR80 Interim Phase twin girder bridge, mounted on their Wheeled Vehicle Launcher. (MERADCOM photo).

Figure F3. Different ramp sections used for the FRG BR80 Interim Phase bridge, mounted on the German Wheeled Vehicle Launcher. (German Defence photo)

The FRG Programme included:

1. Manufacture of a 42m (138ft) triangular cross section twin girder bridge. Some girder sections (designed and manufactured by F Krupp GMBH) were of fully welded construction and some (designed and manufactured by Linke-Hoffman-Busch GMBH) were constructed so that the webs and flange plates could be disassembled for ease of logistic carriage and storage.

2. Manufacture of two WVLs by Magirus-Deutz AG, each carrying 28m (92ft) of bridge, in two 14m sections, one on top of the other for launching by the slide method used for the Biber tank bridge (Figure F3).

3. Production of 18m (59ft) long catamaran type pontoons for discrete flotation of bridge girders. The pontoons, with in-built Shottel propulsion units (similar to those used in the M2), were joined together at deck level to straddle the launching beam on the WVL, which could thus carry two pontoons, one on top of the other.

The FRG programme demonstrated the extensive use of extramural design facilities, the design method currently used for the development of military equipments in the UK.

Revision of the Requirement

The Operational Requirement Group had considerable success in agreeing a joint requirement for the three countries, and by 1976 the only major difference was that of the FRG requirement for a 40m (131ft) Dry Support Bridge span compared with the now reduced 30m (98ft) requirement of UK and US, although even this difference was subsequently resolved.

All was not well however. Although the UK requirement had been finalized in GST 3693 - Bridging Equipment for the 1980/1990s, which was endorsed in 1976 and was based to a large extent on the original requirement agreed for the ICST, the UK OR representative announced in November 1978 that the UK now had an essential requirement for both Assault and Support Bridging to carry MLC70 tracked loads. This requirement arose from the anticipated advent of the new Challenger main battle tank, outlined in Chapter Thirteen. The UK amended its GST in early 1979 but the US and FRG were not prepared to amend their requirement at this stage, with less than a year to go before the projected issue of final Interim Phase reports. It was agreed, however, to examine the design implications of upgrading the load class of existing designs with a view to possible compromise during the Assessment Phase.

Collaboration Strained

In addition to the basic differences of opinion concerning load class, other signs of strain appeared at the November 1978 SC meeting at Fort Belvoir. At this time the development plan indicated a start of the trilateral development phase in late 1981, with a production phase starting in late 1987 and first off equipments available in 1989. UK now pointed out that it was clear that the proposed development programme would now not meet their 1986 essential in-service date for a new wet support bridge, and that they would therefore have to meet this requirement from other sources. FRG responded by stating that they would not be prepared to participate in a development programme for other than the full family of bridges originally envisaged, but hoped that compromise could be reached in due course.

A UK proposal to streamline the eventual Interim Phase assessment work of a Final Concept Team (FCT), which had been set up under UK chairmanship in early 1977, was now flatly rejected by the US and FRG. At this time the US were considering the production of approximately 1,350 WVLs, compared with FRG and UK productions of 400 and 100 WVLs respectively; comparable figures for lengths of bridge structure were 46,000m, 9,000m and 5,500m. The United States and German SC members therefore proposed that since they were likely to be the partners with the major interest in full development of the equipment, they should take over joint chairmanship of the FCT; this proposal was subsequently amended and chairmanship of the FCT by US was agreed.

Finally all OR Group members expressed user concern about the projected size and weight of the WVLs currently being examined. The US prototype vehicle had a laden weight of about 40 tons and the FRG vehicle loaded with two pontoons had a length of 18m (59ft), a width of 4m (13ft) and was about 4m high. The Group felt that vehicles of this size would be difficult to move and conceal on the battlefield, particularly on the approaches to crossing sites.

These difficulties were largely overcome at two 2 star (Major General or civil servant equivalent rank) meetings held in 1979. By then US tank development had persuaded them that an MLC70 bridge would be preferable to the MLC60 bridge originally proposed, whilst FRG agreed that by using a Class 70 bridge for Class 60 traffic they could achieve a span in excess of 30m (98ft), thus nearer to their own requirement of 40m (131ft). It was also agreed that the question of partial participation in the development programme by UK should be shelved pending completion of the FCT studies.

The Work of the Final Concept Team

By mid 1979 most of the national reports on the Interim Phase studies were ready or were in draft, and the FCT assembled at Fort Belvoir, USA, in early

September, a year later than had originally been envisaged to carry out their assessment (ie Assessment 1). Mr K K Harris, Chief of the Marine and Bridging Laboratory at MERADCOM, was Chairman of the Team and two members from each country supported him.

The Team faced a very difficult task, basically because each of the three nations was convinced that its proposals offered the best way to proceed. However the Team produced its report on time and reported to the SC in early September 1980. Its findings were not unanimous. The Majority Concept, recommended by US and UK, envisaged a bridge designed for Assault and Dry Support use and launched by the flip ramp/slide launch method, but needing added-on buoyancy units for use in the Wet Support Role. The FRG Minority Concept used the same bridge in all three roles, launched by the slide launch/cantilever method (as used with the Biber Tank Bridge) for the Assault and Dry Support Roles and making use of separate pontoons carried on logistic vehicles for the Wet Support Role. In addition the Minority Concept envisaged that in the Dry Support role, only one 12m bay of bridge would be carried by the WVL, a second ramp and further bays of bridge being carried by logistic vehicles.

Thus, after ten years, the three participating nations were still not agreed on a joint concept for collaborative development and still had some differences in national requirements. The Interim Phase alone had cost UK something like £M2.5 at 1978 prices, with a US expenditure of about £M8 and an FRG expenditure of about £M10.5, and after six years work the basic differences between the US/UK and FRG views, initially expressed by the ICST, were still unresolved. After lengthy discussion, and with all sides making concessions, the SC was able to bring the two concepts closer together and agreed a possible compromise for development. This was then presented to National Authorities, together with the FCT Report, at a number of joint presentations in late 1980.

Assessment Two

Detailed examination of the work completed during the Interim Phase and of the findings of the FCT now took place nationally, as what was known as Assessment Two. However by the following July, the US Combat Development Staff had radically revised their requirement, with the need for an 18m (60ft) span Class 30 air transportable Light Assault Bridge as top priority; they also required a Class 30 Light Assault Floating Bridge. Both of these equipments were defined as part of a 'System of Bridging for 1985 and Beyond', and were intended for use by their newly formed Rapid Deployment Force. Since in any case military bridging now had a low priority in the US Defence Budget, the BR80 project was at an end as far as the United States was concerned.

In October 1981 Germany formally withdrew from the trilateral collaborative project, noting the lack of an agreed concept between the three nations, and commenting that after consideration of the probable high development and procurement costs of a new equipment, they would proceed on the basis of improvements to existing equipments. The UK was thus the sole remaining member of the BR80 project, and in any case had already decided that the best way ahead was likely to be the development of the Automotive Bridge Launching Equipment, or ABLE, details of which were given in Chapter 15. Thus, after a ten year collaborative programme costing over £M21, the BR80 project finally came to an end in 1981.

Why did the BR80 Project Fail?

A great deal of very useful work was completed during the BR80 programme, not least of which was the production of the International Design and Test Code for Military Bridging. In the final analysis however, the object of the project had been to design and develop a family of bridges that could then be produced for use by the armies of the participating nations, and in this primary objective the project failed.

The main reason for this failure was probably the lack of agreement, at a very early stage, on a common operational requirement which could then be adopted by all three nations in entirety and without change during the design and development period. Admittedly one would not expect any nation to continue with the development of an equipment whilst ignoring a fundamental change that had occurred, for any reason, in their national requirement, but any such change would have to be internationally agreed if the project was to continue with any chance of success. The situation was not helped by the inevitable slowing down of a development programme that occurs once that programme becomes international; in this case the Steering Committee for BR80 had to answer to three sets of masters, in London, Washington and Bonn, obtaining approval for fundamental decisions in all three centres. In the event, the project took well over ten years to progress from the tentative statements of requirement of 1969 to the stage at which development proper could start; progress that does not compare favourably, for example, with that of the Medium Girder Bridge, which progressed from early design to operational use in Germany in less than ten years.

Another probable reason for the failure of the project was the initial acceptance of the two design alternatives proposed by the ICST in 1974. In retrospect the Team should have been charged with the re-examination of their proposals in order to produce a single acceptable concept for further examination during the Interim Phase. The FCT were of the view that national Interim Phase work programmes should have been co-ordinated as a single trilateral programme. If this had been done, after a single concept had been suggested by the ICST, much inevitable overlap of effort by the three nations would have been avoided, and time and money would have been saved. As it was, the financial involvement of the three nations during the Interim Phase made it difficult for any nation to accept a final solution not closely related to its own.

Bibliography

BOOKS

Military Bridges, by General Sir Howard Douglas (1832, T & W Boone)

One of Wellington's Staff Officers, Maj Gen Sir Louis Jackson

Military Bridges, by A M Hermann Haupt (1864, D Van Nostrand)

A Text Book on Fortifications etc, by Col G Philips (1884, Pardon & Sons)

The Work of the Royal Engineers in the European War, 1914-1919, Bridging (1921,The Institution of Royal Engineers)

In the Wake of the Tank, by Lt Col G Martel (1931, Sifton Praed & Co Ltd)

Four Score Years and Ten, by General Sir Bindon Blood (1933, G Bell & Sons)

AFVs of World War One, edited by D Crow (Profile Publications Ltd)

An Outspoken Soldier, by General Sir Giffard Martel (1949, Sifton Praed and Co)

British AFVs 1919-1940, edited by D Crow (Profile Publications Ltd)

British and Commonwealth AFVs 1940-1946, edited by D Crow (Profile Publications Ltd)

Tank - A History of the Armoured Fighting Vehicle, by K Macksay & J Batchelor (1950, Macdonald)

History of the Second World War - The Administration of War Production, by J D Scott & R Hughes (1955, HMSO)

The US Army in WWII – The Corps of Engineers – Transport and Equipment (1958, US Army)

British and American Tanks of WWII, by P Chamberlain & C Ellis (c1960, Arms & Armour Press)

The Churchill Tank, by P Chamberlain & C Ellis (1971, Arms & Armour Press)

British Military Vehicles, (1971, MOD and Society of Motor Manufacturers)

Valentine, Infantry Tank Mark III, by B T White

The Funnies, - 79 Armoured Division and its Specialist Equipment, by G W Futter (1974)

The Royal Engineers, by Derek Boyd (1975, Leo Cooper)

Centurion, by Simon Dunstan (1980, Ian Allan Ltd)

The Guinness Book of Tank Facts and Figures, edited by F Macksey (1980, Guinness Superlatives)

A New Excalibur - Tanks 1909 to 1939, by A J Smithers (1980 Leo Cooper)

Jane's Military Vehicles and Ground Support Equipment (1981)

The History of the Corps of Royal Engineers, Volumes I to XI, (The Institution of Royal Engineers)

Vehicles and Bridging, by I F B Tytler et al (1985, Brassey)

Vanguard to Victory, by D Fletcher (1984, HMSO)

Mediterranean Safari, by A P de T Daniell (1990, Buckland Publications)

ARE – The Story of 1st Assault Brigade RE 1943-45

Memoirs of Sir Henry Havelock, by J C Marsham

The British Tank – a Photographic History, 1916 – 1986, by Lt Col G Forty (Birlings (Kent) Ltd)

The Royal Engineers, by T J Gander (c 1980, Ian Allen Ltd)

Edward I, by Michael Prestwick (1988, Methuen)

The Chieftain Tank, by S Dunstan (1989, Arms & Armour Press)

History of the King's Works - The Middle Ages, edited by R A Brown et al

Builders and Fighters, US Army Engineers in WWII (1992, US Army Corps of Engineers)

Never a Shot in Anger, by Gerald Mortimer (1993, A Square One Publication)

Reflections from the Bridge, by Col K H Cima (1994, Baron)

The Vickers Tanks, by C F Foss and P Mckenzie (1995, Keepdate Publishing Ltd)

WAR OFFICE & MINISTRY OF DEFENCE PUBLICATIONS

Standing Orders for the Royal Engineer Department serving with the Army upon the Continent (Army Headquarters, Paris, 1815)

Aide Memoire to the Military Sciences, Volumes I and III (1842-52)

Textbook on Fortification and Works for use of RMC Students (1884)

Instructions in Military Engineering, Vol I, Part III (1887)

Manual of Military Engineering (Provisional) (1901)

Manual of Field Engineering (1911)

Pontoon Bridge (Consuta Wood and Steel Trestle) (1928)

Military Engineering Vol VIII – Railways (1929)

Manual of Field Engineering Vol II (Royal Engineers) (1936)

Notes on Military Railway Engineering – Part III Bridging (1940)

Notes on Military Railway Engineering – Supplement 1 – Unit Construction Railway Bridge (1942)

Notes on Military Railway Engineering – Supplement 3 – Single Truss Through Railway Bridge (1943)

Manual of Field Engineering - Part III Bridging and Watermanship (1943)

Military Training Pamphlet No 74 – Part III Assault Crossing Equipment (1944)

Royal Engineer Training Manuals (RETMs) (HQ E in C, WWII and subsequently)

AVRE Bridges – The SBG Tank Bridge (1944, RE7 Report 1005)

Engineers in the Italian Campaign, 1943-45 (1945, GHQ Central Mediterranean Forces)

Railway Reconstruction in Italy, 1943-1945 (HQ Tn (British) Central Mediterranean Force)

Bridging, Normandy to Berlin (1945, CE 21 Army Group)

Royal Engineers Battlefield Tour, Normandy to the Seine & The Seine to the Rhine (1947, CE HQ BAOR)

Field Engineering and Mine Warfare – Pamphlet 8 part II – Assault River Crossing (1951 & 1961)

Handbook on Armoured Engineer Equipment (1958)

Notes on the Centurion Bridgelayer (1959)

Chieftain Bridgelayer and the No 8 Tank Bridge – MVEE Notes (1969)

Various MEXE Open Day Brochures (1945 to 1971)

No 9 Tank Bridge – An R and D Report by MVEE (1975)

Royal Engineers in the Gulf, Op Granby 1990-91 (1991, Ministry of Defence)

PAPERS IN THE ROYAL ENGINEER JOURNAL

Tests on the Box Girder Bridge, the RE Board, October 1921

Mechanisation and Divisional Engineers, Part II – Bridging, Bt Lt Col N T Fitzpatrick RE, September 1931

Sir Charles Paisley – Development of the Pontoon, Maj I S O Playfair RE, September 1931

Replacement of Vauxhall Bridge, Monmouth, Capt A J Macdonald RE, December 1932

Military Bridging Equipment, Lt Col A P Sayer RE, September 1934

Modern Bridging Equipment – What of the Tank? Capt E V Daldy RE, September 1935

Modern Bridging Equipment – Part II, Capt E V Daldy RE, December 1935

The Conception of the Bailey Bridge, Lt Col S A Stewart RE, December 1944

Twenty Year in the Development of Military Road Bridging – 1925 to 1945, Col S A Stewart, March 1946

An Outline of Engineer Work in the Italian Campaign, Maj Gen N A Coxwell Rogers, September 1946

The Rhine Crossing at Rees, Col F C Nottingham, September 1946

Crossing the Rhine, Lt Col R N Foster RE, June 1947

Production of Engineer Stores in Italy, Col A H Glendenning, June 1947

ARKs in Italy, Major R L Frances RE, June 1948

'Clover' – The Indian Mat Bridge, Lt Col D W R Walker RE, June 1948

Sapper Bridge, Lt Col P A Easton RE, September 1951

The Battle for Cassino, May 1944, Lt Col A P de T Daniell RE, September 1951

Queens' Bridge, Major K M Robertson RE, September 1955

Armoured Engineers, Lt Col R L France RE, September 1957

The Gillois Assault Crossing Equipment, Major G H McCutcheon RE, June 1958

The Development of Engineer Equipment for the Army, Brig H A T Jarrett-Kerr, September 1961

Its not just Meccano, Lt Col J H Frankau RE, December 1962

Grant's Crossing of the River James, Col R A Lindsell, June 1963

Military Requirements and Employment of Engineer Equipment, Col T H Egan et al, December 1965

The Evolution of Equipment for the Royal Engineers, 1870-1970, Brig B G Rawlins, September 1970

Bridging Equipment for the 1980/90s, Maj J N Barnikel, December 1976

Wet Bridging in the 1940s; the New Pontoon Bridge of March 1936 – August 1939, The Editor, September 1977

The New Armoured Divisional Engineers, Col R Jukes-Hughes & Lt Col E G Willmott RE, September 1978

Operation Corporate – The Falkland Islands Campaign, Lt Col G W Field RE, December 1982

The Korean War Between June 1951 and August 1952, Brig E C W Myers, December 1983

One Engineer's War, Col A H Glendenning, December 1984

The 'Mowlem Army' Remembered, a Sapper Story, D G Carpenter Esq, September 1985

The First Welded Bridge in Japan, submitted by RARDE, June 1986

The Bailey Story, Col J H Joiner, December 1986 & March 1987 (also in Metal Construction, September 1986)

The Chieftain AVRE Project, Lt Col J F Johnson RE, September 1987

The Bailey Story, a letter from Brig S A Stewart, April 1988

Standard Military Railway Bridging, 1939-1945, Lt Col McMurdo, April 1990

Operation Granby, Preparation and Deployment for War, Col J D Moore-Bick, December 1991

Operation Granby, 23 Engineer Regiment, Lt Col D J Beaton RE, December 1991

The New M3 Amphibian UK User Trials by 28 Amph Engr Regt, Lt Col T H E Foulkes RE, April 1992

Disaster Relief in Central Nepal. Maj J R White RE, August 1994

Amazon Bridge, Col A P de T Daniell, August 1994

Bridging for the Nineties – A Bridge for the Future, Col T H E Foulkes, April 1995

Op Grapple 4 – The Tito Challenge, Capt R C Thomson RE, April 1995
One More River, Personal Reminiscences about Burma, Brig J Constant, April 1995
Armoured Engineers and Military Bridging, Some Operational Realities, Lieut R Thomson RE, December 1996

LECTURES AND PUBLISHED ARTICLES

Bridging in the Field, by Maj G Martel RE, lecture to the ICE, February 1921
The Progress of Mechanical Engineering in the Military Service, by Maj G Martel RE, lecture to the IMechE, January 1924
Military Field Bridging Equipment, by Col Galpin, lecture to the I Struct E, February 1944
Standard Military Railway Bridges, by F S Bond, articles in *The Railway Gazette*, 1945-46
Military Bridging, by Lt Col S A Stewart RE, lecture to the I Struct E, November 1946
The Bailey Bridge and its Development, by Sir Donald Bailey et al, symposium at the ICE, June 1947
The Bailey Suspension Bridge, by Sir Donald Bailey et al, symposium at the ICE, June 1947
The Erection of Military Road Bridges, by R Freeman (jun) et al, symposium at the ICE, June 1947
Military Railway Construction, by W T Everall et al, symposium at the ICE, June 1947
The Development of Military Floating Bridges, by Maj. L M Sebert RCE, an article in the Canadian Army Journal, January 1958
By Train to War in Abyssinia, by P A Vine, an article in the *Railway Magazine*, February 1973
The Short History of British Military Bridging, by Col J H Joiner, a lecture at Sheffield University and elsewhere, 1974 onward
Bridgelaying Tanks, translated by E L Applegate, an article in *Soldat und Technik*, July 1974
The Chieftain Bridgelayer, by M A Napier and T S Parramore, an article in *The Chartered Mechanical Engineer*. 1975 (also in the *RE Journal*, June 1978)
Armoured Bridging – Future Requirements, by J Bruge, an article in *The International Defence Review*, June 1981
Optimisation of Military Pontoon Bridges, by Beierlein and Konke, German symposium, 1990
The Design of the Bailey Bridge and its Subsequent Development, by Col J H Joiner, a lecture to The London Branch, IMechE, May 1999

REPORTS AND UNPUBLISHED PAPERS

A Record of Operations at the Establishment for Field Instruction, 1822-42
A History of RE Operations in South Africa, 1899-1902, by Col S Walker
Historical Records of 17 Field Company, 1926 – 1931
Report on a Tank Bridging Company, by Maj G Martell RE, 1927
Report on a Mechanised Field Company working with a Mechanised Force, by Maj G Martell, c 1927
Structural Engineering Committee Notes (Ministry of Supply), 1940s
Bridging Monogram on the Development of Armoured Bridge Laying Vehicles, by D M Delany, 1946
Box Girder Bridge award claim by General G Martell, 1955
Equipment extracts from Engineer-in-Chief liaison letters, 1947-58
MVEE Design Survey 1, Floating Bridges and their Buoyancy Systems, by Maj J N Barnikel, 1978

MVEE Design Survey 2, The Length of Girder Modules of Military Bridges, by Maj J N Barnikel, 1978
Some experiences of bridging in WWII, by Sir Ralph Freeman, 1980
MVEE Design Survey 3, Assault System Launching Systems, by Maj J N Barnikel, 1980
The Lead up to the Bailey Bridge, notes by Brig S A Stewart, 1982
Notes on the Briggs Bridge and service in Burma by Major M H Briggs, 1981

EDITIONS OF MILITARY ENGINEERING VOLUME III – BRIDGING

Military Bridging and the use of Spars - Part III – 1894
Military Bridging – Part IIIB – 1914
Bridging – Volume III (provisional) – 1921
Bridging – Volume III – 1928
Large Box Girder Bridge – Part II, Pam 1 – 1932
Folding Boat Equipment – Part II, Pam 2 – 1934
Pontoon Bridge – Part II, Pam 3 – 1934
Tubular Scaffolding – Part II, Pam 4 – 1935
Small Box Girder – Part II, Pam 5 – 1935
Small Box Girder, Mark II – Part II, Pam 5 – 1939
Small Box Girder, Mark III – Part II, Pam 5A – 1939
Large Box Girder, Mark II – Part II, Pam 6 – 1939
Unit Construction Bridge – Part II, Pam 7 – 1939
Folding Boat Equipment, Mark II – Part II, Pam 2 – 1939
Stock Spans – Part II, Pam 8 – 1940
Propulsion Unit Equipment - Part II, Pam 9 – 1940
Pontoon Bridge Mark V & Trestle Mark VII - Part II, Pam 3 – 1940
Motor Boats, Mark I, I*, II & III - Part II, Pam 10 – 1940
Bridging – Part I – 1941
Inglis Bridge Mark III - Part II, Pam 11 – 1942
Bailey Bridge - Part II, Pam 12 – 1942
Bailey Bridge - Part II, Supplement to Pam 12 – 1943
Bailey Bridge, Normal Uses – Part III – 1944
Bailey Bridge, Special Uses, Fixed Spans – Part IV, Chap 2 – 1944
Bailey Bridge, Special Uses, Wet Bridging– Part IV, Chap 3 – 1944
Folding Boat Equipment Mark III – Part II Pam 13 – 1945
Bailey Bridge, Special Uses, Fixed Spans – Part IV, Chap 2 – 1946
Close Support Raft Marks I & 2 – Part II, Pam 2 – 1946
Class 50/60 Raft – Part II Pam 1 – 1947
Bailey Bridge, Special Uses, Special Launch - Part IV, Chap 1 – 1949
Bailey Bridge, Special Uses, Fixed Spans - Part IV, Chap 2 – 1949
Bailey Bridge, Special Uses, Wet Bridging - Part IV, Chap 3 – 1950
Extra Widened Bailey Bridge, Normal Uses – Part V – 1955
Unit Construction Railway Bridge – Part XVI – 1955
Extra Widened Bailey Bridge, Special Constructions - Part VI – 1957
Bridging General – Part 1 – 1957
Light Floating Bridge – Part VII – 1964
Heavy Ferry – Part IX – 1964
Heavy Floating Bridge – Part VIII – 1967
Heavy Girder Bridge – Part IV – 1979
Medium Girder Bridge – Part III – 1980
Basic Bridging – Part I – 1981

PROVISIONAL WORKING INSTRUCTIONS (PWI), PROVISIONAL USER HANDBOOKS (PUH) AND USER HANDBOOKS (UH)

Inglis Portable Military Footbridge (UH) – 1915
Scissors Bridge, 30ft, No1 (PWI) – 1942
Bridge, Tank, 30ft, No 2 (PWI) – 1943
Bailey Suspension Bridge No 1 (PWI) – 1943
Bailey Bridge Adapted for Rail Traffic (UH) - 1944
Bridges Tank, SBG Mark II (PWI) – 1944
Tubular Trestle (PWI) – 1944
Heavy Trestle (PWI) – 1944
Bailey Suspension Bridge No 2 (PWI) – 1944
Bailey Mobile Bridge (PWI) – 1944
Bailey Retractable Bridge (PWI) – 1944
Widened Bailey Bridge (PWI) – 1944
Light Suspension Bridge made with Wire Mesh (PWI) - 1945
Bridges Tank 30ft, No 3 (PWI) - 1949
Standard Widened Bailey Bridge (PWI) - 1949
20 Ton and 50 Ton Bridging Cribs (UH) – 1950
Bridges Tank 30ft, No 3 Mark 2 (PUH) – 1953
Bridgelayer Centurion Mark 5 (UH) – 1962
Amphibious Bridge and Ferrying Equipment – M2 (UH) – 1969/71
AVRE Chieftain (Trials UH) – 1971
Chieftain AVLB (Launcher, No 8 and No 9 Tank Bridges) (UH) - 1974
Class 16 Airportable Bridge (UH) – 1974
LSL and Harbour Equipment (MEXE Flote) (UH) – 1974

PUBLICATIONS BY INDUSTRY

The Military use of Aluminium (Alcan Booth Sheet Ltd)
Callender-Hamilton Bridges (Balfour Beatty Power Construction Ltd)
Amphibious Bridging and Ferrying Vehicle (M2B) (Eisenwerke Kaiserslautern GmbH)
Fast Floating Bridge Amphibious Equipment M3 (Eisenwerke Kaiserslautern GmbH)
Infantry Bridge (Eisenwerke Kaiserslautern GmbH)
Class 16 Bridge (Laird (Anglesey) Ltd)
Mabey Super Bailey (Mabey & Johnson Ltd)
The Mabey Universal Bridge System (Mabey & Johnson Ltd)
Mabey Unit Construction Bridges (Mabey & Johnson Ltd)
The Mabey Compact Bridge System (Mabey & Johnson Ltd)
Mabey Compact Pontoons (Mabey & Johnson Ltd)
An Account of Mabey & Johnson Logistic Bridges in Bosnia (Mabey & Johnson Ltd)
Bailey Uniflote Handbook (Thos Storey (Engineers) Ltd)
Bailey Bridging (Thos Storey (Engineers) Ltd)
Acrow Heavy Bridge (Thos Storey (Engineers) Ltd)
Acrow Uniflote (Thos Storey (Engineers) Ltd)
Acrow Panel Bridging – 500 and 700 Series (Thos Storey (Engineers) Ltd)
Bridging for the 1990s (Thompson Defence Projects Ltd)
Vickers Main Battle Tank Mark 3 (Vickers Defence Systems)
This is the Medium Girder Bridge System (Williams Fairey Engineering Ltd)
Floating MGB (Williams Fairey Engineering Ltd)
The New Axial Folding Bridge. (Williams Fairey Engineering Ltd)

INDEX

1. In this index military units hve been listed as Field Companies/Squadrons, Divisional Engineers/Regiments, Military Engineer Units/Formations, or Military Engineer Units – non-British. In this connection the following abbreviations have been used: Amph for Amphibious, Armd for Armoured, Aslt for Assault, Bn for Battalion, Coy for Company, Div for Division, Engr for Engineer, Fd for Field, Pk for Park, Sp for Support, Sqn for Squadron, Tps for Troops and Wksp for Workshops.

2. For entries of officers I have used the rank first mentioned in the book, ignoring subsequent promotions.